The Cambridge History of British Foreign Policy, 1783-1919

THE CAMBRIDGE HISTORY
OF
BRITISH FOREIGN POLICY

IN THREE VOLUMES
VOLUME ONE

THE CAMBRIDGE HISTORY

OF

BRITISH FOREIGN POLICY

1783–1919

EDITED BY

SIR A. W. WARD, Litt.D., F.B.A.

AND

G. P. GOOCH, M.A., Litt.D.

VOLUME I

1783–1815

NEW YORK

THE MACMILLAN COMPANY

1922

(***, 31.2(1)),

✓

PREFACE

IN offering to our readers the First Volume of *The Cambridge History of British Foreign Policy*, from the beginning of Pitt's first Administration (1783) to the Peace of Versailles (1919), we have little to add to the announcement put forth by our University Press less than two years and a half ago. The work was designed as a connected narrative of the subject and a consecutive account of its bearing on the political history of this country and empire, and on that of the world at large. As such, it is intended to combine with a strict adherence to historical truth, wherever ascertainable, a national point of view—in other words, an avowed regard for the interests, and above all for the honour, of Great Britain; and the list of contributors to it has been confined to historical scholars who are British subjects by birth. Our work has accordingly not shrunk, and will not shrink as it progresses, from seeking to vindicate for British Foreign Policy that claim to consistency which in certain respects has been denied to it by some of its censors, and in others allowed to it only in the way of sarcasm. Its relations to political aims or ideals not confined to a single nation, or to particular groups of thinkers and their followers within it, have been neither overlooked nor, we believe, prejudged—whether or not these aims have in the past been submerged with efforts made to accomplish them, and whether or not on the fulfilment of these ideals depend the future peace and prosperity of the world.

Our readers will understand that, in the several chapters of this *History*, military and naval events, as well as the progress of parliamentary legislation and administrative changes at home or in other parts of the empire, due to the influence of the Crown, of parties and movements in Church and State, and to the voice of public opinion and the Press, have been kept in constant view, without being themselves discussed. The successive stages of Indian and (British) Colonial history have in no instance been regarded as detached from that of Great Britain and Ireland. The narrative is throughout based on documentary evidence and has, so far as possible, been arranged in chronological sequence, though without any attempt, more especially in certain summarising sections of the later Volumes, to maintain a synchronistic system of dates.

This *History* is divided into six Books, each consisting of a very small number of Chapters, which again are, in the large majority of cases, subdivided into sections of varying length, dealing with particular subjects, episodes or aspects of British Foreign Policy. The First of these Books is preceded by an *Introduction*, which attempts to summarise the course of English, or British, Foreign Policy, in the whole of the period to which these terms may be held applicable, and to indicate some of the threads lending coherence to its processes and tendencies. Though the narrative is continued till the Peace of 1919, our readers will be prepared to regard the sketch of the War of 1914–1918 and of the settlement in the character of an *Epilogue*. The narrative as a whole will be followed by a brief general survey, undertaken with the cognisance and approval of authoritative opinion, of the administrative system of the British Foreign Office, from 1793 (at which date an important change was introduced into it) to the present time.

Both narrative and *Introduction* are accompanied by brief notes, chiefly references or of the nature of such, or reproductions of extracts from important documents, treaties, Instructions, despatches, or speeches. In the *Appendices* to vols. I and II, particular documents of this kind, hitherto either unpublished or inaccessible without difficulty, are printed *in extenso* or in extract. To each Volume is appended a short *Bibliography*, which in no instance pretends to be exhaustive or to do more than supply titles of some of the books and papers not mentioned in the Bibliographies to corresponding portions of *The Cambridge Modern History*, or to similar works, with the addition of those of a few specially used by the writers of Chapters or shorter sections of the present History.

It has been thought well to find room for a brief general characterisation of the principles and achievements in Foreign Policy of the chief British statesmen and diplomatists engaged in it in the course of the period here surveyed. In the case of Castlereagh or Canning, Palmerston or Salisbury, whose foreign policy left its mark not only on its own age, and also in the case of Stratford Canning and a few other representatives of Great Britain at the contemporary centres of diplomatic activity, a summary estimate of the sort seems irresistibly called for. On the other hand, our narrative will abstain from attempting to influence a general judgment of the public services of the agents, at home or abroad, of our Foreign Policy by remarks or suggestions as to their personalities.

In issuing the First Volume of this work, the Editors desire, on behalf of the Syndics of the Press as well as on their own, to express their thanks for the countenance and goodwill shown to their project

by those to whom it was notified before being carried into execution.
The Most Hon. the Marquess Curzon of Kedleston, K.G., H.M.'s
Principal Secretary of State for Foreign Affairs, kindly permitted resort,
under proper conditions, to the Archives of the Foreign Office, and
Sir J. A. C. Tilley, K.C.M.G. (British Assistant Secretary for Foreign
Affairs, and now His Majesty's Envoy Extraordinary and Minister
Plenipotentiary in Brazil), and Mr S. Gaselee, C.B.E., Librarian,
have already facilitated our proceedings in this direction[1]. We owe
a similar debt to the Public Record Office, more especially to
Mr Hubert Hall, Litt.D., Assistant Keeper of the Records and
Literary Director of the Royal Historical Society, whose support is
never denied to any endeavour for securing or widening the foundations of historical knowledge. The Editors are, also, particularly
indebted to the advice and encouragement of the Right Hon. Lord
Sanderson, G.C.B., whose great experience as Permanent Under
Secretary of State for Foreign Affairs, and the Right Hon. Lord
Fitzmaurice whose public services as Under Secretary of State,
together with his eminence as a political historian, gave high value
to their counsel. They desire to add their thanks for similar suggestive
aid to the Right Hon. Viscount Bryce, O.M., who at an early period
in his public career (1886) held the office of Under Secretary of
State for Foreign Affairs, and was, as we all know and rejoice, our
Ambassador to the United States from 1907 to 1913; to the Right
Hon. Sir Ernest Satow, G.C.M.G., late His Majesty's Minister at
Tokyo and Pekin and author of the invaluable *Guide to Diplomatic
Practice*; to Sir G. W. Prothero, Litt.D., F.B.A., who knows how
gladly they would have welcomed him as a collaborator; to Professor
C. H. Firth, LL.D., Litt.D., F.B.A., and other friends. Special
instances of assistance will be duly acknowledged as the work progresses; but the Editors are anxious to take the first opportunity of
recording their deep sense of the generous confidence with which
the Rev. J. Wallace Kidston and the other Executors of the late Sir
Donald Mackenzie Wallace, K.C.I.E., K.C.V.O., have placed in their
hands a very large collection of MSS. designed by him as materials
for a History of European Policy. They consist mainly of classified
extracts and notes concerning the Foreign Policy of the chief European
States from the 16th century onwards—Russia of course occupying

---

[1] To the latter we owe the permission to print, at the head of the successive
Books of this *History*, the list of Secretaries and Under Secretaries of State for
Foreign Affairs from 1873, published in the Foreign Office List.

the most prominent place among them. This varied collection was carried on by Sir D. M. Wallace in connexion with his lifelong study of modern politics and history and his services from 1891 to 1898 as Director of the Foreign Department of *The Times*. It is obvious that, as the lines on which Sir D. M. Wallace's contemplated History would have been constructed differed from those followed by the present work, so our references to his MSS., could not but be, in the main, incidental. As such, should any particular use be made of his MSS., it will be duly acknowledged in the course of these volumes; but, in the meantime, the Editors are desirous on behalf of the Syndics and of themselves of acknowledging the obligation under which they have been generously laid by his Executors.

The Editors have to thank the officials and staff of the University Press for the care they have bestowed upon the production of the present volume, and Miss M. Pate for her indefatigable assistance in preparing its contents for the Press. They are also much obliged to Miss A. D. Greenwood for undertaking, at an inevitably short notice, to supply the *Index*.

A. W. W.
G. P. G.

December, 1921.

Since the above Preface was in print, Lord Bryce, whose interest in our scheme is noted there, has died—seemingly in the very midst of his long and unwearied labours. In him has passed away a scholar, who, just sixty years ago, by a University prize essay illuminated a path of historical enquiry hitherto rarely trodden among ourselves, and whose contributions to political history as a whole cover a uniquely wide range of observation, research and deduction in the fields successively surveyed by him. And there has also passed away a statesman whose services, especially in the sphere of foreign policy and diplomatic action, have found their consummation in helping, more directly than those of any of his contemporaries, to draw closer the bonds of friendship, based on mutual understanding, between a great kindred nation and our own. The relations thus established, largely through his insight and influence, will we believe constitute one of the firmest foundations of a world's union of peace, and will, in any event, transcend in their intrinsic strength any of the alliances, compacts and concerts discussed in these pages.

February, 1922.

CONTENTS

INTRODUCTION

By Sir A. W. WARD, Litt.D., F.B.A.
Master of Peterhouse

CHAPTER I

PITT'S FIRST DECADE

1783–1792

By J. H. CLAPHAM, Litt.D., C.B.E.
Fellow and Tutor of King's College

CHAPTER II

THE STRUGGLE WITH REVOLUTIONARY FRANCE
1792–1802

By J. HOLLAND ROSE, Litt.D.

Late Fellow of Christ's College
Vere Harmsworth Professor of Naval History

CHAPTER III

THE CONTEST WITH NAPOLEON
1802–1812

By Professor J. HOLLAND ROSE, Litt.D.

CHAPTER IV

THE PACIFICATION OF EUROPE
1813–1815

By C. K. WEBSTER, M.A.
Late Fellow of King's College; Professor of Modern History
in the University of Liverpool

CHAPTER V

THE AMERICAN WAR AND THE TREATY OF GHENT
1812–1814

By PROFESSOR C. K. WEBSTER, M.A.

APPENDICES TO CHAPTERS II—III

INTRODUCTION

I

THIS work proposes to treat, within definite chronological limits, the history of British Foreign Policy—in other words, to discuss the relations in that period of the British Empire to Foreign Powers, the conditions at home and abroad which governed the conduct of those relations, the principles more or less consistently followed in the conduct of them, and the personal influence of the principal British agents responsible for it. However interesting, it cannot be imperative, in setting forth upon such an undertaking, to go back at length into a past which, as a matter of course, contained in it innumerable germs of the future, but which differed essentially from the period marked out for present treatment in many of the conditions of its public as well as of its private life.

A brief sketch indicating some at least of the threads connecting earlier with later epochs of our Foreign Policy as a State and as an Empire is, therefore, all that can be attempted here by way of introduction to the narrative that is to follow.

Whether or not a people is only to be held happy when its rulers are without a foreign policy, none can assuredly afford to dispense with such unless it has no foreign affairs. In our own records, an era of the kind could hardly be found from the time onwards when, under Egbert, the English nation first achieved political unity, and the kingdom, as a polity moulded by its great monarchs Alfred and Edgar, after in turn resisting and accepting Danish sway, became the prize of what was no longer a dynastic, but a national struggle, to be apparently settled by the Norman Conquest in its own favour. But England still remained merely the extreme Western home of civilisation—an *ultima Thule*, it has been grandly said, as of old; and her insularity was a chief determining element in the early course of her historical life—making her exceptionally strong in unity—long before the seas engirdling her carried her into the world of modern life and assigned to her a controlling place in it.

Meanwhile, William the Conqueror had not only prepared, but throughout his reign maintained and developed, his great achievement by a system of foreign alliances, of which the most signally important was that with the Papacy—in the Hildebrandine age in particular. With his active and efficient diplomacy began that long chapter of medieval history which is concerned with the political and military relations to France of England and her ruling dynasty. Little more than a century after the Conquest, Henry II (the first conqueror of Ireland) might be described as a greater potentate in France than his French suzerain; but his power was feudal, and, even of this, most was lost in the reign of John. Yet this unhappy King, too, followed a foreign policy of his own. His quarrel with Pope Innocent III, though not especially of the King's making, rendered *Magna Carta* possible; but the victory of the Barons did not suffice to overthrow his Throne. Soon after his death, Lewis of France was driven from England; and, after John's successor had come of age, he and his dynasty, encouraged by a continuous growth of national consciousness, showed every desire to revive the aggressive foreign policy of their predecessors. Henry III accepted the Crown of Sicily for his son Edmund, and his brother Richard of Cornwall was elected German King. The interests of the Papacy, together with those of the dynasty, lay heavy upon all classes of the subjects of the Crown; and, while Pope Alexander IV duly declared the Provisions of Oxford void, their immediate sequel was the expulsion of foreigners from the realm. Notwithstanding the catastrophe of Simon de Montfort, England's first great Protector, a memorable constitutional change —borough representation—was finally established under Edward I, reflecting what, like all sound reforms, was already a historical fact —viz. the importance of the towns (from London downwards) in the public life of the nation. English foreign policy, moreover, had ceased to be absorbed in dynastic enterprises or designs, or satisfied with the advantages to be gained by the landed magnates, no longer isolated as these were by their nationality from the rest of the population. On the other hand, a different kind of foreign connexion had steadily advanced. Flemish and Low-German towns—not sea-ports only, but towns in the interior of the Empire also—had maintained trade relations with this country already before the Norman Conquest. Henry II had confirmed the privileges of the Cologne "factory" in London, before its parent association had been outrivalled by a body of Lower-Saxon towns, headed by Lübeck, which, in the course of the thirteenth century, appropriated to itself the once generic name of the Hansa. The progress of this intercourse, and of that with the Flemish towns, which reached its height at a later date, could not otherwise than directly affect the continental relations of England and her Government and shape the beginnings of a commercial, which became an integral element in her foreign, policy.

But as yet the sword was the determining factor. The great reign of Edward I, who came out of the midst of a crusade to enter upon the mighty task awaiting him nearer home, was one of widespread foreign conquest, though at the same time of the firm planting of domestic reforms. He mastered both Wales and Scotland, though the principality was not incorporated in the English State till the reign of the second Tudor King, while Scotland retained her recovered autonomy even after the personal union under our first Stewart. Edward I's relations with France had become embittered before he entered upon his first conquest of Scotland, and had led to his conclusion of a futile alliance with the German King Adolphus; on the other hand, the defensive alliance concluded with France by John Balliol before his deposition, established the tradition of a Scoto-French league, which beset English foreign policy almost continuously down to the days of Elizabeth. But, if it was Scotland herself which at Bannockburn undid the English Conquest, that Conquest itself and the whole of Edward I's overbearing policy could not have been carried out by the King without a nation at his back, or without the widespread resources of a singularly active commercial diplomacy[1]. When, under his grandson Edward III, after an unstable settlement with Scotland, the country resumed warlike action against France, which now remained, for a hundred years, its dominant passion, diplomatic transactions of a directly political kind were an inevitable necessity. The chain of foreign alliances concluded by Edward III with the German Princes along the Lower Rhine, and thence even with the potentates of the Palatinate, Württemberg and Savoy, forms an early example of the series of subsidy treaties which is, perhaps, the most long-lived feature of British foreign policy; and (in 1337) the "system" was extended so as to include the Emperor, Lewis the Bavarian, himself. But the Peace of Brétigny (1360), which, by a drastic partition, was to have at last ended the struggle for the throne of France, held good for less than nine years; and the renewed War speedily led to disastrous

[1] When his supply of money fell short in consequence of his banishment of the Jews, Parliament came temporarily to the rescue, and he was able, with advantage to the Crown, to fall back upon the banking guilds in the North Italian cities.

results for the English dominion in France. Thus, in the tragic reign
of Richard II, the efforts against France, following on that of
England's Flemish ally, broke down in their turn, as did the attempted
invasion of Scotland; and failure abroad, coupled with the effects of
the social catastrophe at home, brought the national life to the state
of despair which precedes dissolution. In the end, the unfortunate
King, lured back to England from an expedition to Ireland, lost his
English Crown. The kinsman who took it from him was a prince of
wide foreign experience acquired by travel, and would have willingly
entered into the inheritance of the foreign policy of Edward I. But
the insecurity of his tenure at home deprived him of the power of
action in France, though the distracted internal condition of that
kingdom offered so favourable an opportunity for intervention in
its affairs.

The renewal of the French policy of Edward III, and the assertion of claims at once wider and weaker, fell to Henry V, in whose
settlement, as after Agincourt it found expression in the Treaty of
Troyes, the Alliance with Burgundy was a necessary factor. But
it was not written in the book of fate that England should be permanently burdened by the inheritance of a great foreign dominion,
which, had she retained possession of it, must have strained beyond
bearing the powers of the nation in the satisfaction of an unnatural
ambition. The Wars of the Roses, while they went far towards destroying the ascendancy of the great Houses, left the economic condition of the people largely untouched; so that, at the close of the
struggle, the country stood face to face with the intelligent despotism
(a phrase to which the Eighteenth Century has no prerogative claim)
of the Tudors. At the same time (since foreign policy is a branch of
government to which public opinion, accustomed as it is to judge
mainly by results, is not wont to apply logical reasoning), there can
be no doubt that the dissatisfaction caused by the loss of France
sensibly contributed to the downfall of the rule of Henry VI; or
that his rival, after seating himself on the Throne, had actually to
seek a momentary refuge against French intrigue in the Netherlands.
With their master, Charles the Bold, Edward IV was on friendly
terms, though he could not depend on him as an ally against France,
and death overtook him on the eve of a struggle with an adversary
whose equal he had never proved himself.

This counterplay of foreign rivalry and domestic plot still continued, when, after the brief and bloody epilogue of the reign of

Richard III, the long dynastic and baronial conflict had come to an end with the accession of our first Tudor Sovereign. By far the most dangerous of the Pretenders who tried to oust Henry VII from the Throne of which he had, at the time of Buckingham's rebellion, sought to possess himself, was Perkin Warbeck, an adventurous Fleming whose first attempt was "financed" by the Roman King Maximilian. He was afterwards made welcome as the true heir to the English throne by King James IV of Scotland, whose goodwill King Henry VII more effectively secured by bestowing on him the hand of his daughter Margaret—a step which ultimately led to the Union of the two kingdoms.

The foreign policy of Henry VII—for, in this age marriages were coming to constitute a very notable feature in the foreign policy of the European dynasties—was a combination of circumspection, if not of foresight, with caution. Naturally enough, its beginnings display more of the latter, and its subsequent developments more of the former, characteristic; but they rarely fail to be blended with each other. The monarchical rule of the Tudors transmuted the land—which had been the battle-field of a turbulent Baronage—into a State peacefully united in itself and thus gradually grown fit to find its place in the group of rival European nations. And, so early as the beginning of the sixteenth century, England began, likewise, to pursue an economical policy of her own in lieu of one which merely suited itself, as best it might, to the interest of her customers. It took a century, more or less, to break the domination of the Hansa over English trade, and for English trade to assert itself in the Northern Seas; and the Tudor age was approaching its close, when England began to enter into the maritime life of the Atlantic, and thus at last to realise the true value of her insular position and to face the gradual unfolding of the possibilities of her imperial future.

But the process was both slow and full of interruptions, and refuses to be detailed even in a chronological sequence of reigns. Before mounting the English Throne, the future King Henry VII had found a refuge in Brittany; and, soon after his accession, he assisted its ducal House in its struggle against the French Crown, though he could not prevent the incorporation, in the end, of the duchy in the monarchy. But he went out of his way in safeguarding the position of England in the event of future troubles between France and the Spanish monarchy, as is shown by his extreme caution in the method of the successive marriages of his sons Arthur and Henry to the

Infanta Catharine. While it seems questionable whether Henry VII actually contemplated a decided resumption of the anti-French policy of the Plantagenets, he was certainly alive to the chances opening for a relatively weak country like England in the age of Discovery, and was, in different ways, interested in both Columbus and the Cabots, though unequal, afterwards, to the thought of disputing the Spanish-Portuguese control of the New World sanctioned by Papal Bulls. Before England could claim her place in the sun, the mercantile marine had to be fostered, and rendered capable of service to the royal navy, of which a beginning was once more made.

With Henry VIII, the foreign policy of the English Crown once more, but under new conditions, enters into the main current of European affairs, and thus contributes to the beginning of a new period—the Habsburg period, as it has been appropriately called, though this subdivides itself into several chapters of the international history of Europe. By acknowledging the Spanish Infanta as his legitimate consort, Henry seemed to have declared that he had definitively ranged himself on the side which had not yet come to be the "monstrous aggregate" of Spanish-Austrian power; and, in 1512–14, he took part in a war with France which brought him no profit. The vagueness of his own political ambitions is illustrated by his posing, on the death of Maxmilian I in 1519, as a candidate for the succession to the Imperial Throne. But, in the great contest which ensued between the Emperor Charles and King Francis, he again chose his side, and proposed to his victorious ally a further enterprise which should restore to himself the French Crown worn by his predecessors. He was disappointed in his designs, and in the Emperor; and, by the advice of Cardinal Wolsey, he thereupon brought to pass one of the most notable *renversements des alliances* recorded in European diplomatic history. In general English history, this political episode is above all noticeable as forming part of the transactions which ended in Henry's divorce from Catharine, followed though it was by a very different marriage from that originally contemplated by Wolsey. In the history of our foreign policy in particular, the significance of this episode lies in its having been the first application, in a critical connexion, of a conception which was afterwards to become, and to remain longer than is always allowed, the guiding principle of English, and subsequently, of British foreign policy. This principle was that of the Balance of Power.

The Balance of Power is, as has been well pointed out, an idea practically inseparable from all policy properly so called—nor in the domain of international relations or "foreign affairs" only. But, in this domain—to pass by whatever precedent Italy, the mother of modern diplomacy, may have to offer in her sixteenth century history—the action or conduct of the English Government after the first great self-assertion of the united Habsburg Power may be described as the beginning of a new "system." To this system the political world of Europe was not to cease to have recourse in the succession of crises undergone by it from the times in question onward to those of the Thirty Years' War, of the War of the Spanish Succession, of the Napoleonic rule, and of the German design of overwhelming the world. So far as England is concerned, the English archer's motto *Cui adhaereo praeest* might seem to denote sufficiently the way in which this country has, by prescribing its remedy, been wont to apply the doctrine of the Balance of Power; and, for our present purpose, it is needless to enquire in what measure the changes in the attitude of the Papacy towards King Henry's divorce proposal was a cause, and in what a consequence, of the change in his general foreign policy.

In any case, the English Reformation was long left by Charles V to proceed on its way, nor was it till after the critical dates of 1544 and 1547—Crépy and Mühlberg—that the head of the House of Habsburg brought the whole weight of his designs, political and religious, to bear on our national future. This was now that of a monarchy whose unity and independence seemed both to have been consolidated, like those of no other European kingdom, with the final aid of the Reformation. But the two reigns which followed brought with them the extreme of vicissitudes. Under Edward VI, Somerset planned the achievement of a union between England and Scotland —this design, also, taking the form of a marriage-scheme, between the young King Edward and the still younger Queen Mary Stewart, which was to result in the hegemony of the united realms over Protestant Europe (whose refugees had already found a welcome on English soil). The plan came to nothing; nor was it even possible to maintain the good understanding with France which was a necessary preliminary condition for such an enterprise. Mary Tudor's religious creed combined with the traditions of her descent in bringing about the return of England to the Spanish Alliance; though it may savour of the Castilian style to magnify as "the Habsburg invasion of England" her marriage to the master of Spain and the champion of Rome, followed by the persecution of heresy and the humiliation inflicted on Queen and country by the loss of its naval outpost of more than two hundred years' standing. Under Elizabeth, English foreign policy slowly shook itself free, and thus gradually recovered an influence upon the political relations of the European States which Henry VII had tentatively striven to acquire by means of foreign alliances, and Henry VIII had exercised in action within restricted limits. As the aggressive strength of Spain and Rome combined—we are now in the age of the so-called Counter-reformation—the goodwill of European Protestantism (from which in form, and largely in spirit, the ecclesiastical system of England remained aloof) was a sure support against them. A special advantage, which might almost be called adventitious, was derived by Elizabeth from her encouragement of the Reformation in Scotland. For, as the deeply rooted contention between herself and the Scottish Mary merged into the European religious conflict at large (so early as 1562, English aid was promised by Treaty to the French Huguenots, but the price demanded was not obtained), Elizabeth was at last driven by Spanish machinations and Roman arrogance into an attitude of consistent opposition, and the English Throne and its policy became identified with the resistance of Europe to the general undoing of her Peace.

The English goodwill, at first permissive only, towards the Revolt of the Netherlands, and the daring piracies of Drake, provoked the final despatch of the Armada—the combined effort of Spanish southern Europe, undertaken with no less a design than that of securing to Philip Mary Stewart's bequest of the English Throne. The effort was, necessarily, made by sea, and by sea it was scattered. This one great victory—comparable only to Salamis—had at the same time placed England in the position of a Great Power, and shown that, unapproachable herself by sea, it was by sea that her national destinies were to be accomplished. But, both before and after the critical years 1586–8, the safety of England and that of her Sovereign depended on a resolute vigilance which, alike in the observation of European (more especially Spanish) policy in all its windings and in the use of an incomparable spy-intelligence system, called for the single-minded devotion of diplomatic statesmanship. This was the period of the Cecils, of whom the elder (Burleigh) served the Crown as Secretary of State (with a five years' interval) and Lord Treasurer for nearly half a century of indefatigable and unflinching labours.

At the height of these, he had the assistance of Sir FrancisWalsingham as Secretary of State (less fortunate than Burleigh in the requital of his zeal), and, later, that of his second son. Sir Robert Cecil, afterwards Earl of Salisbury, was sworn Principal Secretary to the Queen in 1597, in which year he returned to England after a futile mission to Henry IV of France, in time to take his father's place in the conduct of foreign (and not a few other) affairs. He gave the most unequivocal proofs of his staunchness in the unhappy Essex episode, which followed soon after Burleigh's death in 1598, and remained in authority till his own decease. This took place in 1612, the year before the arrival in King James's Court of the most notable of Spanish diplomatists, Gondomar, under whose influence English policy once more swerved from its course, and began to lie low without really competent guidance.

To go back, for a moment, to the beginning of James I's reign. By land, the settlement of the English Crown and the consequent Personal Union with the northern kingdom, were effected without resistance. Great Britain was henceforth, as Lord Acton expresses it, politically as well as geographically an island, and no apprehensions of the designs of a warlike neighbour any longer entered into the foreign policy of its larger half. Moreover, the age into which King James was born was one of limitless conceptions of monarchical authority. These conceptions, as adopted by James I, included not only questions of religion (treated by him after a fashion which failed to commend itself to his subjects, Protestant or Catholic) but also questions, often mixed up with these, of foreign policy. He began as a peacemaker, proclaiming the blessedness of this task to the Spanish grandee who came over to conclude peace with him immediately after his accession[1]. And it was as a peacemaker that, though "on all hands he heard the call of battle," the younger of the Cecils, in the words of his descendant and biographer, carried on "the traditions of peace he had learnt from his father." But the forces at work against James I's persistent desire to remain on friendly terms with Spain were too strong for him; so that, before he died, the two countries were again to all intents and purposes at war with one another, and an immediate French marriage was arranged for his successor. As for the Dutch, it is worth noticing that what in much later times was

---

[1] *Beati Pacifici* (the phrase put into King James's mouth by Scott) was the inscription in the apartment in Somerset House occupied by the Constable of Castile, who negotiated the Peace with Spain of 1604.

to become an accepted maxim of British policy—a strong and, in a wider sense, United Netherlands, both Protestant and Catholic—only very slowly became even so much as a pious wish. While Salisbury, a true Conservative like his father before him, directed the foreign policy of James I, there was no fear of extravagances or paradoxes. After that (from 1612), the King reckoned altogether amiss when, though no longer guided by proved principle and matured experience, he credited himself with the power of adjusting the scales swinging in the political atmosphere around him. The marriage of his daughter to the leader of German Calvinism, in other words of the actual opposition to the Habsburg designs for the future of the Empire and Western Europe, brought him a strong breeze of popularity at home; but the match was incompatible with the repeated proofs given by him of his desire to cement his friendship with Spain, who was still planning a revival of the Habsburg monarchy of Charles V[1]. Meanwhile, the fierce disillusionment experienced by James early in his reign as to Catholic goodwill towards himself at home by no means remained without effect, but led to no decisive move in the game. He seized the opportunity of a quarrel between Pope Paul V and the Signory of Venice (which culminated in 1606) to instruct his willing Ambassador there (Sir Henry Wotton) to denounce Pope and Papacy as "the chief authors of all the mischiefs of Christendom." And after, ten years later, the great Religious War had already begun in Bohemia, the same diplomatist was chosen (though Lord Doncaster was ultimately appointed in his place) to conduct the negotiations as to the acceptance of the Bohemian Crown by the King's son-in-law, in which the King himself played a part which it would be a euphemism to describe as ambiguous. So early as 1619, Wotton had entered into negotiations with the heads of the Protestant Union, which turned a deaf ear to his inglorious proposals for an anti-Papal propaganda, and while the star of the Emperor Ferdinand soon rose triumphant over that of the unfortunate Winter-king, the foreign policy of his father-in-law had to concentrate itself upon the attempted recovery of the Palatinate for the Elector and his family, who had "lost it in Bohemia." But the efforts of English volunteers under Sir Horace Vere, Mansfeld and Christian of Brunswick were futile, and before, quite at the end of James's reign, Mansfeld's plan of

---

[1] Bourgeois (vol. I. p. 19) dwells on the successive attempts of Philip III to secure the Imperial Succession for himself or his son. The various Spanish marriage projects of King James for his children are well known.

settling the claim with an imposing English force had, in the midst
of Anglo-French misunderstandings, miserably collapsed (1625),
James had fallen back upon the last and most ill-starred of his futile
Spanish marriage schemes. But Charles, Prince of Wales, who, to
bring it to an issue, had travelled to Spain with Buckingham, had
come home free (1623); and, when he actually mounted his father's
Throne, England was once more, in conjunction with the Dutch
Republic, at war with Spain, and the alliance with France was confirmed by the marriage of Charles to Henrietta Maria, the daughter
of Henry IV.

Meanwhile, and largely in consequence of the altered conditions
of the relations between England and Spain under which Queen
Elizabeth's reign had drawn to its close, the island Kingdom had
definitively entered into the paths of overseas colonisation. The power
of Spain, the dreaded adversary of rival transatlantic adventure, was
shaken, though not annihilated; and her acquisition of Portugal (1580),
without adding to her political strength in Europe, had diverted enterprise to the Portuguese settlements in Brazil and the East Indies,
inevitably leading to angry jealousy between the English and the
Dutch. The English attempts, in Elizabeth's days, upon Spanish
possessions on land and sea, however conspicuously supported (on
occasions by the Queen herself), cannot properly be described as
measures of colonial policy, but are simply evidence of desire for
gain, stimulated by jealousy and hatred; just as the charge of a
broken promise to which Raleigh was (so late as 1617) sacrificed
was a signal demonstration of accumulated Spanish wrath. But the
early course of English Colonial history was consistently attended
by the rivalry of other Powers. The English East India Company
(more strictly, the East India Company of London) received its
original Charter in 1600, nearly two years before the Dutch, and
within the following decade the two were at open war. But the first
settlement directly controlled by the English Crown, and therefore
the actual beginning of our colonial system, dates from the grant to
"Virginia" of her earliest Royal Charter in 1606, followed by the
second in 1609, and later by the Charters secured by the several
new English Colonies. The early history of these shows their safety
in constant danger from Dutch, and more particularly from French,
enterprise or ambition; while, to the north, France, after a struggle
terminating, in 1632, with the Peace of St Germain, maintained her
power in her province of Acadia (Nova Scotia). Hence, too, the

earliest suggestions of a scheme of federation among the English
North American Colonies, which might very possibly have earlier
taken lasting shape, but for the Civil War at home. The action of the
Crown towards the beginnings of our Colonial system cannot safely
be criticised as closely connected with the turns and changes of our
foreign policy; but the time was not far off when the two currents
were effectively to unite.

Under Charles I, so long as his Government was able to carry
on any foreign policy at all, it may be regarded as having been chiefly
actuated by the motive of gaining for the King and Buckingham
some of the popularity which their method of government at home
was rapidly forfeiting. The French marriage of Charles I had seemed
likely to bring about friendly relations with the French Court and
Government, and to favour an anti-Habsburg Alliance, as to which
negotiations were in progress with both Sweden and Denmark so
early as August 1624. Apart from other friction, Buckingham's
failure at Cadiz (1625) promised ill for the Spanish War; and the
French Government would have nothing to say to the agreement
into which the English Government had actually entered with the
States-General for the recovery of the Palatinate by a force under
the command of Christian IV of Denmark, Mansfeld cooperating.
But the English supplies failed; and the defeat of Christian IV at
Lutter (1626) put an end to the whole design, as it did to England's
futile participation in the Great War. Before long (1627), the tension
between France and England had ended in the outbreak of hostilities;
and Buckingham, who two years earlier had been fain to lend English
ships to Richelieu for the suppression of the Huguenots of Rochelle,
now threw his French policy to the winds, taking command of the
expedition for their relief. The attempt, the success of which was to
have rejoiced the hearts of Protestant Englishmen, broke down; and,
like an unlucky gambler, its author at once entered upon a vaster
design against the adversaries of Protestantism, in which the relief
of Rochelle was to be but the initial step. The assassin's dagger,
however, settled his account with an angry Parliament; the last refuge of the Huguenots soon fell; and the failure in France had been
as complete as that in Germany (1628). The time was at hand when
the domestic strife in which the second Stewart reign had opened
was to end in the Civil War.

II

The eminent historian of European Foreign Policy[1] may seem to
go too far in saying that England, at the end of a half-century during
which hardly more weight had attached to her in European politics
than to Venice or Saxony, suddenly became the first Power of the
world. But it is true, that few, if any, later generations have witnessed a transformation at once so astonishing in itself, and one so
full of the promise of endurance. The period in question covered the
Thirty Years' War, the great European struggle in which England
interfered only after the fitful and insignificant fashion to which
reference has been made; while the late but decisive intervention of
France finally shaped the close of the War and the Pacification which
ended it, thus, as has been well said, preparing her hegemony in
Europe during the half-century that was to follow. In settling that
Pacification, neither England nor Poland, nor the Grand-duke of
Muscovy, had taken any part; but they were named in the Peace as
Allies of the Allies of the Emperor and Sweden (the Grand-duke,
of Sweden only), and thus became parties to the Peace, so that it
bore the character of a fundamental act and international procedure
of Christian Europe. And it is in this sense that the conditions of
the Peace of Westphalia, as a whole, served to recast the State-system
(*societas gentium*) of which England (or Great Britain) formed part,
and essentially affected or modified, in accordance with their respective circumstances and interests, the foreign policy of the several
States (England with the rest) included in it. In the first place, from
the Peace of Westphalia onwards, the Empire was no longer, as such,
an organic factor in the European State-system in question, notwithstanding its own formal endurance and the glamour of tradition
which still attached a lingering weight to its occasional self-assertion[2]. For the Estates of the Empire were now in possession of the
rights of sovereignty expressly recognised in the Peace as theirs.
Moreover, the Empire could now no longer lay claim to control, in
any way, the foreign relations of the United Provinces or of Switzerland. The independence of the former, which specially interests us
here, was recognised in the Peace by Spain herself, who retained her
direct or (since 1598) indirect control over the Belgic Provinces, till,
in the Peace of Rastatt (1714), they became the Austrian, instead of the

---

[1] M. Émile Bourgeois.
[2] More especially, as the leader of Christendom in its resistance to the Turks.

Spanish, Netherlands. Again, however absolutely the Vatican might, for this very reason, denounce the Westphalian Treaties, the religious affairs of the Empire were henceforth definitely regulated by a recognition of the rights of the three Confessions—for none besides these three were taken into account; and this provision took away (though, as it proved, not altogether) future occasions for religious conflicts within the Empire in which foreign Powers might seek to interfere[1].

Such were the chief general changes to which the European State-system was subjected by the Peace of Westphalia—changes of high importance, but not such as to mark any signal advance towards international relations favourable to an enduring Peace of the World. So far as England in particular was concerned, the War had brought about, and the Peace established, relations between the Continental Powers which she could not possibly ignore and which, in one way or another, must, for a time at all events, greatly affect her foreign policy. The long-sustained military enterprise of Sweden, and the well-timed intervention of France, had enabled them to obtain, in the Peace, compensations ("satisfactions") which gave to the former a strong footing in northern, and provided France with continuous opportunities for action in western, Germany; while Sweden had acquired the command of the mouths of Oder, Elbe and Weser, and was placed in antagonism to Brandenburg, whose Elector held Ducal (Western) Poland as a fief of the Polish Crown. France had, by acquiring Breisach and the right of garrisoning Philippsburg, secured direct access to the German South-west, had taken the place of Austria in Alsace, and had secured sure opportunities for future intervention in the affairs of the Empire and its Estates at large. The acquisition of the Belgic Provinces themselves remained an unachieved project of French political ambition, as it had under Richelieu, and the "natural frontiers" of France were proclaimed by him in his last will (now accepted as genuine) as a legitimate claim of the France of the future[2]. As for the sea, though at the close of the Great War (which did not include peace between France and Spain) Mazarin's

---

[1] It is true that, although the idea of a United Christendom was thus, in Church as well as in State, abandoned, an attempt was made at Münster to provide the settled system of States now adopted with a tentative guarantee, in the form of a "wish" that, in case of any dispute, three years would be allowed for securing a solution sanctioned by all the States not parties to that dispute. But the guarantee included no appeal to arms; and no instance seems to be on record of its having ever been called into operation.

[2] Cf. Hanotaux, *Mélanges Historiques*, vol. III. (1880), pp. 705 ff.

Italian policy had not achieved complete success, there was now every prospect that the Mediterranean would henceforth be under French rather than Spanish control. The command of the Baltic, on the other hand, ultimately a matter of far more importance to Great Britain than it was to the United Netherlands, the Suedo-French Alliance had assured to Sweden for the period immediately following on the conclusion of the Peace; whether it could be retained by her depended in the first instance on her relations with her neighbour and ancient rival, Denmark.

From the settlement or discussion of all these questions, the English Government and people, which, in the early stages of the Thirty Years' War, had shown so keen an interest in its progress, held aloof at its close. The country was on the very eve of the termination of the long struggle between Crown and Parliament, by the transfer of supreme authority to a section of the House of Commons. The foreign policy of the Commonwealth was at first out of touch with either of the belligerents still in arms against each other (France and Spain); nor was it even clear what line the new Government would pursue towards the Power which was at the time in command of the carrying-trade of Europe at large. Would mercantile jealousy prevail, in this latter day, over the religious sympathies which, in Elizabeth's time, had induced England to take the side of the now Free Netherlands in their long struggle with Spain?

Meanwhile, soon after Europe, as a whole, had accepted the Westphalian settlement designed to govern the future relations between her States, England signified, as it were once for all, what was the part she proposed to play among them. This she accomplished by the assertion of her sea-power; which not only made possible the great Victory (Dunbar), but put an end to such resistance as was offered by Continental Europe to her new Commonwealth. French piracy was suppressed, and Lisbon was blockaded (1650)—the capital of a nation which, a decade earlier, had secured its independence and had, without loss of time, concluded Treaties with France and the United Provinces, and another with the English Government (1642). The last of these was the precursor of the still more important Treaty with Portugal, negotiated in 1654 by the Rump and signed by Cromwell, and may thus be regarded as having laid the foundation of the most long-lived, as well as the oldest, of all European Alliances[1]. Its

[1] Cf. Guernsey Jones, *Beginnings of the Oldest European Alliance* (Washington, 1919).

beginnings were, however, interrupted by the catastrophe of the
Stewart Throne, of which, among contemporary Sovereigns, King
John IV of Portugal alone took note by acts of overt hostility, though
his Government was, also, the earliest to enter into diplomatic
relations with that of "the Parliament of the Commonwealth of
England." Before long, King John's cherished design of the marriage
of the Prince of Wales to a Portuguese Infanta was to be resumed,
and the Anglo-Portuguese Alliance to enter into a new stage of its
long-protracted course. But, for the present, Prince Rupert, the
stormy petrel of the Restoration, had fluttered away into Mediterranean waters, and English foreign policy had been revolutionised.

In order to achieve these results, Blake, one of the greatest of our
naval heroes, had found it necessary to complete the creation of a
permanent English navy of war and to secure its requisite bases of
action. When, therefore, an English fleet entered the Mediterranean
in 1651, it could not do so without the goodwill of some Power possessed of harbours where English vessels could be refitted or re-
victualled; and this Power could be no other than Spain (by means of
the Spanish ports in the Two Sicilies and Sardinia), so long the foe
of England and sure to become such again. For the moment, political
advantage had drawn the two nations nearer together; how could the
Government of Philip IV remain on unfriendly terms with a Power
which had swept the seas clear of French and Portuguese ships? Thus,
so early as May 1650, the Spanish Government had recognised that of
the Commonwealth; and a resident diplomatic agent had been sent
to Madrid. But the murder of that agent (Ascham), on the day after
his arrival, could not but lead to friction with Spain; and the effect
of this was a friendly turn in the relations between the Commonwealth and the French Government, more especially as the Huguenot interest for a time made head in France against the sway of
Mazarin. French commerce, however, continued to suffer from
English naval activity, and the Commonwealth was now strong
enough to pass an Act prohibiting trade with such of the American
and West India Colonies as adhered to the Royalist cause (1650).
By sea and land, the Commonwealth had resolved to be master
where the Crown had been.

As for the relations at this time between England and the Free
Netherlands, they passed with most notable suddenness from extreme
to extreme. At first, the States-General, under Orange influence,
refused to enter into other than commercial negotiations with the

Commonwealth. But the death (October, 1650) of the Stadholder William II (before the birth of his son, the future William III) led to a complete change in the conduct of the affairs of the Dutch Republic, which now, with the exception of the two Provinces acknowledging the Orange Stadholdership, fell under the control of the Province of Holland. This change caused the Government of the Commonwealth to form the design of concluding as close as possible an Alliance with the United Provinces, and even to entertain, as a possible result of negotiations to this end, the notion of converting the Alliance into a political union between the two countries. But the Commonwealth leaders and their envoys (Chief Justice St John and Strickland) insufficiently understood the political organisation of the body politic with which they had to deal, and they made no allowance for the violent Orange predilections of the populace. Thus, after a protracted negotiation, at an early stage of which the Dutch had proposed as the basis of a treaty the *Intercursus Magnus* (agreed upon in 1495, at the time of the Perkin Warbeck scare), this far-reaching design was allowed to drop—chiefly on the narrow ground that the English negotiators insisted on the strict exclusion of the English Royalists from the Netherlands. The immediate result of the attempt and its failure was a growth of illwill between the two communities—stimulated, on the part of England, by the consciousness that her sea-power was no longer inferior to the Dutch, and by the acceptance of the Commonwealth Government (notwithstanding Prince Rupert) in the greater part of the English New World.

Hereupon, the Parliament carried on, with increased determination, the restrictive policy on which it had fallen back after the collapse of the Dutch Alliance or "Union" project, and of which the main end was to advance English commerce at the expense of that of the Provinces. Their legislation and diplomacy had been long, and at times unscrupulously, directed to the maintenance of their commercial ascendancy, north and east as well as west, at a height dangerously near to monopoly; and the first *Navigation Act*, of October, 1651, which practically annihilated Dutch trade with the English West Indies, though not intended to provoke war with the United Provinces, was very intelligibly looked upon as conceived in the spirit of retaliation[1]. Thus, when, in 1652, the first of the Wars between

---

[1] It was, at the same time, in thorough agreement with the economic ideas of the age. Gardiner points out that this was the one legislative achievement of the Commonwealth which not only found favour in the eyes of the Convention Parliament, but was reenacted by it in a more stringent form (1660).

England and the Dutch Republic broke out, though not occasioned
by the Navigation Act, it was largely due to the commercial tension
which culminated in this memorable piece of legislation.

Meanwhile, the turn taken by domestic affairs in France had inevitably reacted upon the party in the Long Parliament by which
that Parliament was itself to be overthrown, and of which Cromwell
himself stood at the head. The rally round Condé of the Huguenot
nobles of the South, supported by Bordeaux and other southern
towns, had aroused Cromwell's interest. He had dreamt of a Protestant and republican France; but, of course, it was only a dream,
and the notion of persuading the French radical organisation called
the Ormée to construct a Constitution on the Fifth Monarchy model
(though the precursor of later political fancies) proved equally futile.
On the other hand, Condé had taken the paradoxical step of applying
for aid to both Spain and England; and, for a time, Cromwell and his
following, while desirous for the preservation, if possible, of peace,
hesitated between two possible alliances. They were drawn to Spain
by her recognition of the Commonwealth, which France had hitherto
persistently refused, and to France by the possibility of her transfer
of Dunkirk to England, as well as by the further possibility of her
being induced to put an end to the persecution of the Huguenots.
Early in 1652, Mazarin was once more at the helm, and though a
proclamation of the young King Lewis XIV confirmed the Edict of
Nantes and paid a tribute to the loyalty of his Huguenot subjects,
the French recognition of the Commonwealth was still distant, and
the transfer of Dunkirk quite out of the question. When, therefore,
in the same year (against Cromwell's wish), hostilities began between
the English and the Dutch, there was no little danger of a speedy
declaration of war by England against France, and Blake lost no time
in inflicting reprisals on French ships. But, the fall of Gravelines
and the surrender of Dunkirk into Spanish hands notwithstanding,
Mazarin was unwilling to hasten an open conflict with England; where
there was a corresponding wish not to break with France, unless an
understanding should have been reached with Spain. Neither Power
was, or could be, welcome as an ally to the Commonwealth, although,
near the end of 1652, it had been (at first with a doubtful grace) recognised by the King of France. The Dutch War, which opened in 1652,
at first, notwithstanding several well-contested battles, remained
unattended by any decisive result. A period of uncertainty seemed
to have befallen the foreign policy of England, and one which even

the most expert diplomacy would have found it difficult to bring to a satisfactory close. Meanwhile, it was not to any question of foreign affairs that the dissolution of the Long Parliament was due; and the day of the Lord-General was not yet quite at hand. When it came, the moving spirit in every branch of foreign as well as of home affairs was the same militant Protestantism that had, in turn, remodelled the army and succeeded in transforming the State, and that was, also, more and more potently impressing itself upon the beginnings of English Colonial life. Thus, far more distinctly than the tentative efforts of Elizabeth's later years, Oliver's conduct of our foreign policy in the middle of the seventeenth century, while advancing the material interests of England, put her in the van of the process of reconstituting Europe. The problem of effecting this by securing her the command of the sea, and, incidentally, depressing the Papacy to a thing, or at least a Power, of the past, was not one for which even the genius of Oliver Cromwell could find an enduring solution; but the attempt lit up the scene of the world for a brief and brilliant period of national action. After these years—fewer even than those which sufficed Bismarck for establishing the new Germany as a dominating European Power—English foreign policy soon sank back into a restricted sphere, but not without retaining the consciousness of impulses and traditions which it could not easily resist or lightly abandon.

But Oliver's was a political genius, and as such dealt with political realities. The consummation was, therefore, not achieved suddenly or at once. In 1653, while the control of English government had been committed to a *doctrinaire* assembly, but when the public mind was already looking to the Lord-General for the direction of its foreign affairs, he continued for some time to lean towards the paradoxical combination which would have allied England with Spain and the French Dissidents. Although, in July, 1653, the city of Bordeaux surrendered to the King, and the Huguenot outlook darkened, Cromwell continued in this mood even beyond the beginning of the Protectorate, irritated by the plots hatched in France against the English Government, and notwithstanding the overtures of Mazarin early in 1654.

He had, in fact, made up his mind that, before choosing between France and Spain, England must be at peace with the United Netherlands. In carrying out this resolution he showed his greatness as a politician; but in the several stages of the process he displayed that other

2—2

quality of his mind—its imaginative impetus—which was in a different way, an essential element in his greatness. The Dutch War, after a series of grandly contested naval battles, had, by Tromp's defeat off Portland in February, 1653, left the command of the Channel in English hands, and the battle of the Gabbard (June) had proved the inability of the Dutch to recover it. The peace negotiations hitherto carried on between the belligerents had broken down through the severity of the terms demanded by the English Council of State, and the new negotiation proposed by the States-General at the instance of de Witt (before he was named Pensionary of Holland) had been rejected by the new Council. But now, de Witt's insistence upon the necessities of the case, and the despair of the Dutch population, led to the appointment of four Dutch Peace Commissioners to England (June), and the moment had arrived for Cromwell's intervention. Whether or not (and it seems more than doubtful) he had been in favour of the War, he was now certainly in favour of peace, and the advantages of an intimate alliance in his mind outbalanced those of the abasement of England's chief mercantile naval and mercantile rival. As for the United Provinces, they must make their choice between a territorial sacrifice to France, and joining hands with England—though not precisely falling into her arms. Peace must be made, but on a generous basis—not of jealousy, but of amity, between two great Protestant nations. Thus, Cromwell first informally proposed, as the security of peace, the appointment of a small number of Dutchmen and Englishmen respectively to the English and Dutch Councils of State (or States-General). And, when the Dutch Commissioners were unable to see their way to this, or to a fresh suggestion by Cromwell of a religious and commercial union only, to which the Council of State had added the demand of a complete political blending of political power and policy under one Supreme Head, Cromwell made one more effort—the most astonishing, as it was the most characteristic, of all. There was no longer—and with Cromwell there cannot be said to have been during the whole of this crisis—any thought of a revival of St John's grandiose but impracticable idea of a political union between the two peoples, which had broken down on a previous occasion. What was now informally asked for was at once less and more than this. Instead of political amalgamation a Perpetual Alliance was to be established between the two nations. This Alliance was, together with them, to include Denmark, Sweden, the Protestant Princes of the Empire and France—but the last-named on condition that her Government should grant full liberty to the Huguenots. It was to be directed against all Princes and States who employed the services of the Inquisition and acknowledged the authority of the Pope. To this sufficiently vast scheme was added a particular plan for the partition of the New World—England to be assigned America, with the exception of Brazil, and to be assisted by the United Provinces in accomplishing the necessary conquest. Each of the two Allies was to establish a Commission consisting of four representatives of each. Finally, the Christian purpose of this strange League of Nations was to be attested by the sending of missionaries to any people willing to receive them.

Cromwell's design—for, though not of his drafting, it seems certainly to have commended itself to him as a basis for future action—is invaluable as indicating the present state of his mind and the bent of his future policy. It is possible that the bitter hostility to Spain which marks the document may have been partly due to the refusal of the Spanish Government (at the dictation of the Inquisition) to entertain any proposal for the toleration of Protestants in its dominions, and by its natural efforts to obstruct the Anglo-Dutch Peace which Cromwell and his followers had at heart. In any case, the States-General deferred consideration of it, either in its first (both wider and cruder) or in a subsequently modified (narrower and less aggressive) form. Hereupon, after his installation as Protector, Cromwell suggested to the Dutch Commissioners, once more in London, a far less comprehensive scheme as a basis of peace. A Defensive League was to be concluded between the two Powers, binding each side alike to enter into no treaty without the consent of the other, and proclaiming freedom of trade between them, but leaving their existing laws (the Navigation Act, of course, included) untouched. After not a few hitches, the Treaty of Peace was signed and ratified in April, 1654, and the Act of Exclusion which barred the admission of any member of the House of Orange to civil or military office was, thanks to the management of de Witt, passed by the States-General in the same month.

What Cromwell had obtained could hardly be considered as a diplomatic victory; but the success of the War had not been used by him in vain; for the eyes of France were once more bent on Flanders. As for the Protector's wider views, nothing might seem left of them but words; yet his ideas were not dead, and inspired fresh efforts on behalf of the combined interests which he had at heart.

Whitelocke, on leaving for his Swedish embassy (at the end of 1653), had been charged by Oliver himself to "bring us back a Protestant Alliance." This he was not likely to obtain from Queen Christina; but he brought back with him a Commercial Treaty, which, together with one concluded with Denmark (now at peace with Sweden), placed English commerce on the same footing as Dutch in the Baltic. While thus at least a good understanding was effected with the Protestant Powers of the North, the Protectorate had entered into similar relations with certain Protestant Princes and Cities of the Empire, and with the Swiss Protestant Cantons, aided no doubt by the negotiations of John Dury throughout Europe on behalf of Christian unity. And it may be added, in the same twofold connexion, that, about the same time (1657), a Treaty with Portugal secured to English trade with that country and its dependencies the intimate commercial relations which were to be consummated by the Treaty of 1661 between the two monarchies. The free intercourse, and the immunity from interference by the Inquisition, were the very concessions which it had been sought in vain to secure from Spain.

In the meantime, the great changes effected by the Thirty Years' War in the general condition of European politics, together with the continuance of the contest between France and Spain in particular, favoured the realisation of, at least, part of the Protector's plans. Though his vision of a new European conflict on a religious basis seemed unlikely to take shape, yet England was rapidly assuming a position of decisive influence among the States of Europe. For different reasons, neither France nor, even more manifestly, Spain was strong enough to assert an undisputed predominance; while they were alike anxious to add to their respective weight in the scales by securing the alliance of England. For a time, as has been seen, Oliver inclined to a Spanish combination, and asked for Dunkirk as an eventual pledge for Calais. But secret preparations were, meanwhile, made for assailing the Spanish Power in the remote, but attractive quarter of the West Indies; and, moved as he always was, in the last resort, by religious convictions, Oliver, as he settled down firmly in the seat of supreme authority at home, proceeded to find his bearings in the sea of foreign policy. Thus, once more, the ship of State consciously and decisively pursued the course which it had followed in Elizabeth's unforgotten days.

To weaken, if not to put an end to, Spain's hold upon the New

World was, now as then, but under conditions already different from those obtaining when Drake singed King Philip's beard, a fundamental part of the Protestant policy which England found herself carrying out. But the Protector had rated too low the difficulty of a West Indian conquest, when he deluded himself into the belief that he could make war upon Spain in America while remaining at peace with her in Europe. The attack on Hispaniola (San Domingo) was abandoned; but Jamaica, little esteemed in comparison by its first conquerors, was occupied (1655). Spanish pride, however, took fire; and Philip IV, who had more than countenanced the damage inflicted by Blake upon French Mediterranean commerce, now laid an embargo upon all English vessels and goods in his dominions. By the end of October, 1655, the breach was complete; and Oliver was left to defend in high-sounding words, which may have convinced himself, a course of action irreconcilable with good faith, but seeming to be imposed on him by resistless forces.

The effect of England's breach with Spain upon France was impeded by the indignation aroused in the Protector, and assiduously spread by him through the country at large, at the news of the Duke of Savoy's persecution of the Vaudois Protestants. Neither in the remonstrance to the Duke (composed by Milton) nor in the appeal to the good offices of the King of France (erroneously rumoured to have taken part in the outrage) was there anything in the nature of a threat. But so far were these efforts from being mere demonstrations of sympathy, that the other Protestant Powers of Europe were called upon to join in seeking redress. The tone of Mazarin's reply reveals his anxiety that the incident should not thwart the conclusion of the expected Anglo-French Alliance; and, before the memorable agitation in England on the subject had subsided, Duke Charles had promised an amnesty to his insurgent subjects, as a concession to England. The concession was mainly due to the policy of Mazarin, and to some fear of Swiss armed intervention; but the main credit of the whole transaction rested with "the World's Protector."

The Treaty hereupon concluded with France was, as yet, only concerned with the establishment of friendly relations: the question of an Alliance could not be treated while England was ostensibly at peace with Spain. In the final negotiations preceding the conclusion of the compact, the prohibition of the assistance of "rebels" to either party was limited to the case of rebels "now declared"; but a secret agreement was added banishing the Stewarts and their adherents from France and excluding Condé and his House from England. On October 21, 1655, the Treaty was at last signed. The mixture of motives which impelled Cromwell to conclude it lay at the root of a foreign policy in which a personal element cannot for a moment be ignored. Nevertheless, together with the actual Treaty of Alliance which followed a year later, it marks the beginning of an epoch of the utmost significance in the history of English foreign policy—the epoch of a cooperation between English and French interests, which, though with certain interruptions, may be said to have lasted for the better part of a quarter of a century—till the European Coalition of 1674 and the change in English policy consequent upon it.

Now that Cromwell had declared for a policy which meant war with Spain—whom he was soon to denounce (to his second Parliament) as England's "natural enemy"—he found himself involved in foreign complications hardly less difficult to meet than the designs of Royalists and Levellers at home. A war with Spain, as a naval war on many coasts, necessitated the constant use of the right of search against the Dutch, with whom it was most desirable to avoid a renewal of hostilities. Fortunately for England, the Dutch navy was at this time actively employed in the Baltic. When, in this year 1655, the new King Charles Gustavus had taken up arms against Poland, he was, in accordance with the political canon now obtaining at Whitehall, regarded as a militant champion of Protestantism against Popery. (He was, in truth, anxious to add to the territorial gains of Sweden in the Peace of Westphalia, and to lower the ascendancy of the Dutch trade in the Baltic, where it then quadrupled that of the rest of the world.)

In the face of Sweden's designs, and of the Counter-alliance of the Powers threatened by her advance, Oliver hesitated about responding to the overtures made to him on either the one or the other side. He would have rejoiced to see Charles X's war against Poland extended into a general Protestant League against the supposed designs of the Emperor Ferdinand III and their supposed originator, Pope Alexander VII; yet he could not but perceive that the ambition of the Swedish King constituted a serious menace to English as well as to Dutch trade in the Baltic. Thus (partly in consequence of the financial embarrassments of the Protectorate Government, and partly because, with the unprofitable war with Spain and the effort to hold Jamaica, it already had enough on its hands and must have left operations against the House of Austria mainly in those of its Allies) the sole result of the negotiations between the English and Swedish Governments amounted not even to a political alliance. The Treaty between them (July, 1656) merely permitted Charles X to levy a certain number of volunteers in England and placed this country on the footing of the most favoured nation with regard to Baltic ports actually in Swedish hands. Much the same terms as to duties were shortly afterwards secured for themselves and other nations by the Dutch, though at the cost of a naval demonstration, which England's good understanding with Sweden had saved her. But, if so far satisfactory, this was a tame ending of the whole of this episode in the foreign policy of the Protector; and the design of a League against Pope and Emperor had once more vanished into thin air.

But the War with Spain and the definitive Alliance with France had to be pressed on. Mazarin had again wavered in the direction of peace, and there were rumours of a Papal mediation between the belligerents. Oliver's manifesto justifying the breach with Spain was published on the day after the earlier agreement with France, and Spain was (in accordance with diplomatic precedent) declared to have begun the War. In April, 1656, Charles II made his contribution to the conflict by concluding a compact with Spain; and the War now ran its course, at first indecisive. In November, the Treaty of Alliance between France and England against Spain was concluded, though not put into its final form till five months later (March, 1657). Mazarin had succeeded in preventing the extension of the Treaty into a general league of the Powers adverse to the House of Austria; and Cromwell had obtained the substantial pledge of a transfer to England of Dunkirk, after it should have been jointly re-taken by the French and English forces. Then, at the time when the Protector seemed to have reached the height of his power at home, there came the news of Blake's great victory over the Spanish fleet at Vera Cruz (April, 1657) which crippled the resources of Spain, put a stop to her invasion of Portugal and seriously shook her general position. The fall of Dunkirk, however, did not take place till more than a year later (June, 1658); and before Cromwell could thus feel assured of the pledge he had exacted from France, his foreign policy had to face new difficulties.

Though he could not call into being the Protestant League to which from religious motives he aspired, he persistently clung to the supreme necessity of maintaining peace between the Protestant Powers. Notwithstanding the seductive efforts of Sweden, which actually made him an offer of the duchy of Bremen as the price of his cooperation (November, 1657), he declined to join her in crushing Denmark, with whom she was now at war, into utter inferiority; but neither could he see his way to the demand for a settlement by a Congress brought forward by Denmark under Dutch instigation. The process of Cromwell's attempted mediation between the Scandinavian Powers thus depended, with much else, upon the relations between England and the United Provinces. These relations were growing more and more strained—mainly in consequence of the long-standing contention as to the right of search, heightened by the many occasions for friction offered by the Anglo-Spanish War, in whose aspect as a Protestant crusade the Dutch showed scant interest. (Moreover, they had picked a quarrel with England's ally Portugal about Brazil.) But, when Dutch goodwill to the Danes seemed not unlikely to take the form of actual naval aid against the Swedes, the Protector held to the way of peace. He determined to utilise the French alliance in this direction, and suggested to Mazarin joint diplomatic action on the part of England and France for the settlement of the Suedo-Danish, as well as the Portuguese-Spanish question. The Cardinal (without paying any formal attention to the accompanying, as it were indispensable, proposal of an offensive and defensive alliance against the House of Austria) entered into the suggestion, and the result was that the Danes found themselves able to accept the terms imposed by the victorious Charles X in the Peace of Roeskilde (February, 1658). The Treaty, by which each of the two Northern Powers renounced any alliance hostile to the other and closed the Sound to any fleet hostile to both, was a diplomatic victory for Cromwell and his agent Meadowe, though followed neither by a Suedo-English treaty of alliance nor by any other approach to the idea of a Protestant League. The Dutch, who could not but regard it in the light of a discomfiture, and notwithstanding the efforts of de Witt, drew back from the conclusion of a defensive alliance with England and France (though they nominally accepted English mediation with Portugal about Brazil).

When at last (June, 1658) after the brilliant victory on the Dunes, in which Cromwell's soldiery took part, Dunkirk capitulated and was placed by Mazarin in English hands, his policy was seen to have, at last, with England's aid prevailed over Spain. This was made manifest by the Elective Capitulation signed by the Head of the German Habsburgs before he assumed the Imperial Crown as Leopold I—a Capitulation which marked the isolation of Spain. It was followed by the League of the Rhine (August, 1658), which, though, in the end, redounding to the advantage of France (against whom nearly all national feeling had died out), closed any prospect of a participation of the German Princes in a Protestant league against the House of Austria.

Before the success of Mazarin's designs thus encouraged France and her King to look forward hopefully to the developments of the future, Oliver Cromwell died (September 2nd, 1658), with the high hopes and aspirations unfulfilled, of which his foreign policy at no time lost sight—sometimes almost suddenly recurring to them. With the Dutch he had, largely owing to de Witt's single-minded efforts, kept the peace; but his patience was sorely tried, not only from first to last by the old trade grievances, but in the end also by the violent action of Charles X of Sweden, who had broken through the Treaty of Roeskilde and was manifestly intent on incorporating the Danish dominions into one great Scandinavian monarchy. The Dutch, here-upon, determined on the relief of Copenhagen; and it was widely believed in Europe that Cromwell was an accomplice in the present designs of "the King of the North" in expectancy. What is certain is that Cromwell's design of a twofold Northern Alliance was in ruins, and that the danger of a breach with the United Provinces, to avoid which was a more difficult, as well as a more important part of the same general policy, was greater than ever. The chief balance to this twofold political failure—apart from the acquisition of Jamaica, and its maintenance in the teeth of the efforts of Spain and her ad-joining possessions—was the success of the Anglo-French Alliance in Flanders, and the actual tenure of Dunkirk. Yet no survey of the Protector's foreign policy and its results could rest satisfied with a reference to its material gains; the power of the country was now acknowledged by friend and foe alike, and known, at home as well as abroad, in Colonies and in Motherland, to be largely the product of the religious zeal which, resting in the last resort upon his army, he had inspired in the Government personified in him.

No change of principle or method in this foreign policy could be in question during the months of domestic faction and civil strife which ensued after the great Protector's death and brought the Puritan Revolution to a close. With the Restoration, the foreign policy of

England, although no longer animated by the religious convictions and aspirations that held possession of Oliver's soul, underwent no such complete revulsion as might have *a priori* been supposed. In 1659, the Peace of the Pyrenees was at last concluded between France and Spain; and, while any possibility of a future union between the Spanish and the French Crowns[1] was at present ignored by Spain, Spain was left so weak that her efforts to recover Portugal proved in vain. Nor could the Empire, under its new Habsburg Chief, revive any of its former pretensions to direct the course of European politics, wholly dependent as he was (except in his Turkish Wars) upon the resources of his own hereditary dominions. But, though the gains of France and the losses of Spain had been great, the policy of Lewis XIV, professedly conducted after Mazarin's death (1661) by the King himself, with the aid of Mazarin's pupil and successor, de Lionne, called for unremitting vigilance. On the death (in 1665) of Philip IV of Spain, Lewis XIV, on behalf of the Infanta his consort, pressed her claim to the Spanish Netherlands by "right of Devolution," thus laying bare his desire for the acquisition of, at least, part of the Spanish inheritance. The attempt might be prevented by a combination of the other Powers against France, such as was advocated with extraordinary persistence and resource by the eminent Austrian diplomatist Lisola. But for the execution of this the time had not yet arrived; and, of the two Powers most directly concerned, the United Provinces and England, the former, though well aware of the French appetite for the Flemish coastline, remained under the guidance of de Witt in favour of a pacific attitude, and in 1662 had concluded a defensive alliance with France.

It may be that the fact of this Alliance was unknown to, as well as left unnoticed by, Charles II and Clarendon, still his Chief Minister, and himself generally well inclined to France. They were, at the time, much perturbed by the state of the British finances, and all the more ready to gratify French national feeling by the sale of Dunkirk (1662)—a transaction which afterwards contributed to Clarendon's downfall. For the present, the acquiescence of England in the aggressive schemes of France might thus seem assured. The

---

[1] It can hardly be an error to regard the conditions under which King Philip IV accepted Lewis XIV's suit for the hand of the Infanta Maria Teresa—her renunciation of her rights to the whole Spanish Succession—as illusory, and intended to be such. The contention that, in consequence of the local laws of Brabant, this renunciation did not apply to the greater part of the Spanish Netherlands, was thus, actually or virtually, an afterthought.

growth of political intimacy between the two Governments had been marked by the ominous marriage of King Charles II's sister Henrietta to Philip Duke of Orleans. Soon afterwards (May, 1662), Charles II's own marriage with the Infanta Catharine of Portugal, as placing England in direct antagonism to Spanish interests, and therefore in accord with those of France, amounted to a resumption, in its most important issue, of the foreign policy of Cromwell. The policy of Charles was in accordance with that of the Protector in conciliating the mercantile interest by showing hostility to Spain, with a view to keeping hold of Jamaica, while at the same time securing access to the East Indies by the proposed cession of Bombay as part of the Infanta's dowry. Thus, after some vacillation on the part of Charles II, the marriage was concluded which, in the end, brought to Portugal, with England's aid, the recognition of her independence by Spain and to England the beginnings of her Indian Empire.

The adherence of England to the policy of France might now seem a working *entente*, while amicable relations had continued between the dominant party in the United Provinces and the French Government. But material interests and popular feeling combined, as of old, to keep asunder the two Maritime Powers, with both of whom France desired to remain on friendly terms. There had been acts of aggression on both sides, in America and in Africa; and in 1664, notwithstanding the unwillingness of King Charles II, England and the United Provinces were again at war. For a time, it seemed as if the continuance of hostilities might be transitory; for the course of the War was favourable to England; and in Holland the republican party continued to desire peace. But, before long, the catastrophic events of the years 1665–6, and the continuance of the contest at sea, made the situation one of greater danger and difficulty; and, at the same time, the problem of the impending action of France overshadowed the Anglo-Dutch War. The death of Philip IV of Spain (1665) had decided Lewis XIV to put forward the claims of the Infanta his consort to the Spanish Netherlands by "right of Devolution"; and with this end in view, he, early in 1666, as bound by his defensive alliance with the States-General to take their side, declared war against England (January, 1666). But he had no intention of preventing either of the combatants, alike reduced in naval strength, from concluding a peace which would suit his own policy. In this sense, he entered into an agreement with Charles II (March, 1667), binding him to abstain from any interference with the action of France in the matter of the Spanish Netherlands, in return for an undertaking that France would abstain from further assistance to the Dutch. Safe as he thought himself against England and sure of her adversary, his way now seemed clear; and shortly afterwards, he invaded the Spanish Netherlands, and the "War of Devolution" began.

But, though Charles II wrote to the Queen-mother in France that he would not for a year enter into any contention against that country, de Witt had already perceived whither the situation was tending, and that the future of the United Provinces lay with the designs of Lisola. Thus a Peace, though not such a peace as Lewis XIV had had in view, was rapidly concluded between the English and the Dutch Governments at Breda (July, 1667), which, so far as their colonial rivalry was concerned, might perhaps be regarded as a fair compromise. Its European significance consisted in the curb which it put upon French aggression, before a more comprehensive effort was made in the same direction.

In January, 1668, when the hand of France lay heavy on the Spanish Netherlands, and her King was negotiating in grand style with the pacific Emperor (Leopold I) as to the future partition of the Spanish inheritance at large, the Treaty called *par excellence* the Triple Alliance was concluded at the Hague. De Witt had, a few years earlier, pointed out to Sir Willam Temple, the clear-sighted English Ambassador there, that the choice for the United Provinces lay between two alternatives—a corrupt bargain with France, and a fair but effective pressure upon her, which would be impossible without the cooperation of England. Very unwillingly, but unable to resist the flow of home opinion, to which his policy always remained sensitive, Charles II instructed Temple to offer a defensive alliance between England and the United Provinces, which should insist upon peace between France and Spain, on terms allowing France to retain what she had conquered in her campaign in the Spanish Netherlands, or an equivalent; with a secret proviso that the contracting Powers might in the pursuit of their object have resort to arms. The Triple Alliance, of which Sweden had become a member on the day after its conclusion (subsidies being promised her as a condition of her accession), was not, in any sense, a final settlement of the French design. It was a rebuff, and an exposure of the policy of France before the eyes of Europe; but, even within these limits and with many reservations as to its effect upon the aggressor, it justifies the opinion of Lord Acton, that it was "the earliest of that series of coalitions which ended by getting the better of the power of Lewis XIV, and is therefore a landmark in History." But, as he continues, its extension into a wider European alliance was out of the question, and the jealousy between the two mercantile Powers concluding it was not one to be removed by politicians. Thus, the advance of the French Power (which was fain to outrival both on their own ground) was checked, not ended. For the rest, Charles II never ceased to remain in touch with Lewis XIV, and took care to minimise to him the significance of the Alliance jubilantly received in England. Thus, after some hesitation, Lewis decided to give way, and play before Europe the game of moderation (the actual terms of the Treaty consisting, indeed, of conditions previously offered by himself), which for himself meant a willingness to wait.

The Peace of Aix-la-Chapelle which followed (May, 1668), and which ended the first stage of the advance of France under Lewis XIV, may, therefore, be said to begin the second, which had for its primary purpose the isolation, and for its ultimate goal the absorption, of the United Provinces. To effect this, an intimate connexion and cooperation between France and England became imperatively necessary; and to subserving the policy of which this was the cardinal principle, Charles, primarily intent on the interests of his monarchical power and of his purse, now wholly lent himself.

The Secret Treaty of Dover, successfully negotiated by Henrietta Duchess of Orleans in 1670, was, therefore, merely a successful manoeuvre for binding down Charles to a line of action after his own heart, in the prosecution of which he had sought to engage from the very day of the conclusion of the Triple Alliance. The new feature added to it—the promised conversion, *at his own time*, of King Charles himself to Rome—was, on the above condition, most attractive to him, but hardly of supreme consequence to Lewis XIV, who, like his predecessors, had shown little repugnance to Protestant Alliances. It was not mentioned or reckoned as an item on either side of the money bargain in the version of the Treaty brought home from Paris by Buckingham, which alone was signed by the Protestant members of the Cabal (*le Traité simulé*). For the rest, the Treaty, in both its versions, bound Charles to the policy of his Ally both in the immediate and in the remoter future—*i.e.* Lewis was to have the assistance of England both in making war upon the Dutch, and, eventually, in securing the whole of the Spanish inheritance. The partners in the Treaty were to endeavour to obtain the adherence to it of Sweden and Denmark, or of at least one of these States, and of the Elector of Brandenburg and other Princes.

In the meantime, the Triple Alliance having, as a matter of course, fallen to pieces, though not till after its members had resolved on an agreement guaranteeing the subsequent Peace of Aix-la-Chapelle, de Witt and Lisola drafted the hoped-for expansion of the Alliance into a wide European league. The proposal was inevitably rejected by Charles II, whose immediate efforts against the republican *régime* in the United Netherlands had been met by the nomination of Prince William III of Orange to the stadholderate of five of the Provinces, with the expectancy of that of Holland and Zeeland on the day of his coming of age. Before, however, that day arrived, the Secret Agreement with France had come into operation: the Declaration of Indulgence, into which the King's religious undertakings had for the present shrunk, had been proclaimed; and, a few days later (March, 1672), the English Declaration of War against the United Provinces appeared, outrunning, like a jackal, that of France. The foreign policy of Charles II, at once timid and treacherous, had at last come into the open. This and his home policy were not so much detached from each other as antithetically mixed. For he was anxious, above all things, for the retention of the Throne which, after so long an exile, he had secured; and yet he was secretly averse from what was at bottom, though by no means consistently, the national policy towards foreign Powers whose motives he, unlike Cromwell, perfectly understood and whose action he was often personally disposed to support.

Thus, in the War which from 1672 to 1674 they had to sustain against England as well as against France, the United Provinces were left without an Ally (except the Elector of Brandenburg, who soon found it necessary to secure himself by a separate Peace). Sweden, under its youthful King Charles XI, had been early detached from the Triple Alliance, and in April, 1673, when the French had already invaded the Free Netherlands, had concluded an Alliance with France, and another with England, promising her (in this strangely inverted triple compact) Swedish help in the case of any attack "for the sake of France."

The French invasion of the United Provinces in 1672 had seemed to justify the self-confidence of Lewis XIV, till after the murder of the brothers de Witt, and the committal of the fortunes of the Provinces to the guidance of their young Stadholder William III of

Orange, the Dutch people had made a heroic stand behind their wall of waters. The bellicose English feeling against them, stimulated by factious invective such as Shaftesbury's, was dying out. Our share in the War had brought no laurels, and no East India fleet spoils, to our navy; and public feeling was becoming strongly agitated against France. Meanwhile, the desire of the other European Powers to bring about the restoration of peace in Europe had led to the assembling of a Peace Congress at Cologne, from which England necessarily held aloof, and which came to nothing (1673). But diplomatic activity continued; and, while France and England severally carried on their secret negotiations with the Dutch for a peace satisfactory to themselves, the Imperial agents were busily employed on the project of a wider combination against the aggression of France, whom it was hoped King Charles would, notwithstanding the influences surrounding him and his own inclinations, be obliged to abandon.

On the action of the English Government, hard pressed more especially by the Spanish (December, 1673), much depended; and Charles gave way so far as to indicate that he was prepared to treat as to peace with the Dutch on his own account, and without consulting his Ally. He threw himself on Parliament for the decision of a question which, by virtue of his prerogative, it really appertained to him to settle, and sought to conciliate parliamentary and popular feeling by denying the existence of any Treaty with France beyond the "simulated" one. (This suppression had seemed all the more desirable after the Test Act agitation and the Catholic marriage of the Duke of York, in the same year 1673.) Thus, he allowed himself to be detached from the obnoxious Alliance, and the result was the conclusion of the Peace of Westminster (February, 1674) between England and the United Provinces.

The conditions of this Treaty were honourable to England as well as in other ways satisfactory, so far as her claims on the United Provinces were concerned; but the Secret Article which prohibited either Power from allying itself with an adversary of the other bore ominously upon the events that were to follow. In the following August, the Coalition against France was formed, which included with the United Provinces, the Emperor, the King of Spain and the Duke of Lorraine, in the confident belief that, besides other Princes, England would soon come over to their side—and a new era in the history of Europe actually began. In this, England at first took only a tentative and, indeed, uncertain part. The Emperor Leopold now declared war upon Lewis; and France (left with no support but that of Sweden, whose neighbour Brandenburg had joined the Coalition) resolved on evacuating the Low Countries and turning against Franche-Comté and the Palatinate. There, her arms were on the whole successful, and Charles II might feel that it was not the losing side from which he had been so strongly pressed to turn away. As a matter of fact, he had left auxiliary troops with the French army, who, by a strange irony of fate, took part in the devastation of the Palatinate; but neither this circumstance nor his known personal inclinations could incline the Emperor to accept the mediation proffered by Charles in the War against France. On the other hand, William of Orange, now Hereditary Stadholder and Captain-General of the United Provinces, would willingly have accepted such a mediation, and suggested Nymegen for requisite negotiations. But, after a series of both parliamentary and diplomatic manoeuvres, the design failed and with it, for the present, the attempt to establish a dynastic connexion between the English Throne and the Stadholder-ate by means of a marriage between William and the Princess Mary. But he could bide his time, and firmly stood out against Lewis XIV's endeavour to draw him over to the policy of a separate peace between France and the United Provinces. Meanwhile, in the same year (1676) Charles signed another Secret Treaty with Lewis, binding him by a yearly subsidy to adherence to the French alliance.

Thus what has been well called the period of two foreign policies —marked by an impotence due to this duality more than to any one other cause—continued into the eventful year 1677 and the beginning of the following year. In spite—or partly in consequence—of the French successes in the field, the feeling against the Court and its inclination towards France was stronger than ever; in the spring of 1677, notwithstanding the corruption of the members of the Opposition by Lewis XIV, the House of Commons unanimously voted an address explicitly hostile to France, Lord-Treasurer Danby being in favour of the policy urged by the House. It then refused to grant supplies for the defence of the country, unless the King concluded an offensive and defensive alliance with the States-General against France and for the preservation of the Spanish Netherlands. While Charles now began to haggle with his Ally, public feeling rose higher and higher; in the end, Parliament was adjourned, and an addition was made by

Lewis to the price he had agreed to pay for the English adhesion to his Alliance.

Charles II, in the pursuit of the policy on which he was bent, had many resources; but they did not include those of an inflexible will and of a deeply meditated statesmanship. William of Orange, by whom the great change in the foreign policy of England was to be brought about, and who was in possession of both these qualities, was, in the first instance, called upon to use all the tact and circumspection at his command. The proposal was unpopular in the United Provinces and suspected in England; but, with some difficulty, he gained over, first the King, and then his brother the Duke, to consent to his marriage with Princess Mary—a step which, as Charles calculated, would at least reassure the English people as to his own relations with France, without in any way subjecting him to the influence of the Prince.

But the effect of the transaction was not long in showing itself. Lewis XIV had refused the terms of peace with the Coalition offered by Charles II as mediator and proffering the return of part of his conquests in the War, including Lorraine. Now, after the Orange marriage (November, 1677) the policy of Charles II took a turn— which, if carried to its logical consequences, would imply that the last link in the European Coalition against Lewis XIV was to be supplied by the accession of England. The English auxiliary contingent in the French army was now actually recalled, and (in January, 1678) a Treaty was concluded with the United Provinces, defining the French retrocessions on which the Powers must insist. But, when Parliament assembled, it went even further in the conditions to be imposed on France, demanding that the Peace of the Pyrenees should be made the basis of the intended settlement, and that, in the meantime, all trade with France should cease. King Charles, though called upon by Parliament to inform it of the state of his Alliances, this time held to his view of his prerogative, and ventured to enter into a private negotiation with Lewis XIV, offering in return for yet another subsidy to modify in his favour the peace terms demanded. They were accordingly presented to the Powers at Nymegen (April, 1678), but rejected by them; and England found herself in the unfortunate position of standing definitely on neither side in the contest.

She had before her, on the other hand, the prospect of a new conflict as to her foreign policy between Crown and Parliament, in which the latter went so far as to bid the King disband his army or break with France. He determined to settle the matter by promising Lewis XIV, in return for the consolidated subsidy, to preserve neutrality in case of the rejection by the Coalition of the French terms of peace.

On August 10th, 1678, Lewis XIV having at last signified his unconditional assent to the territorial arrangements demanded of him, the Peace of Nymegen was signed between France, Spain and the United Provinces. But Charles II, who was, through Temple, acting as Mediator at the Conference, declined to append his signature, or to enter into any further understanding with the Emperor and Spain. Thus, largely by the inaction (or double-faced action) of the English policy, Lewis had in the Peace obtained Franche-Comté and sixteen fortified places in the Spanish Netherlands, and (since no compromise could be mooted on this head) kept Lorraine in his hands for the present. So far as English foreign policy was concerned, Lewis XIV replied to the congratulations of Sunderland on behalf of his master, and to his claim of a share in the result as due to the action of England, that he regarded himself no longer under any treaty obligation towards her. The great advance of France towards a complete predominance in the affairs of Europe, in which consists the real significance of the Treaties of Nymegen, had thus been effected neither against England nor through her aid. The ratification of the Treaties by the States-General and other Powers was long delayed, and (so strong was public feeling in England) Temple joined William of Orange in impeding it. But, in the end, the work of pacification was accomplished (1679); and, by a series of agreements with which no one concerned in them was content, Europe had secured a breathing-time. It was within this breathing-time that English foreign policy at last freed itself from the duplicity which had beset it through the personal designs—hesitating in the case of Charles II, but persistent in both him and his brother. A statesman had come to the front who viewed the course of European politics from an international as well as from a national point of view, yet who stood too near the Throne of England for his political future to admit of being dissociated from hers.

The ink was hardly dry on the Nymegen Treaties when Lewis XIV's operations against the Empire began; and, in 1686, the Emperor Leopold I, on behalf of the Empire, concluded with Spain and Sweden the League of Augsburg, countenanced by Pope Innocent XI.

This League forms another landmark in this age of coalitions. But England, notwithstanding the Orange marriage (November, 1677) was still out of the reckoning. Charles II, after being harassed by the exploitation of the Popish Plot, was even more nearly touched by the Exclusion Bill agitation (1679–81). His increased estrangement from Lewis XIV, after an attempt at an understanding on the old lines, actually led to an Anglo-Spanish Alliance (1680). While the tortuous diplomacy of the French King aimed at rendering the breach between Charles and his subjects impassable, the States-General (without the interference of William of Orange), urged him to relinquish his opposition to the Exclusion Bill. But he was encouraged by the conservative reaction in Church and State of his last years to go his own way, trusting, in the last instance, to the support of Lewis XIV. As the Continental policy of Lewis grew more and more aggressive, Charles gave repeated proofs of his resolution to persist in his non-intervention in European affairs, and turned a deaf ear to the appeal made to him to take part in the defence of Vienna against the Turk (1682). Thus, Charles II quitted the scene, without having changed the "system" of foreign policy —ultimate dependence upon France and refusal to enter into a European combination against her—to which, with the occasional semblance of divergences, he had adhered throughout his inglorious reign.

Near its close (in February, 1684) Charles II supported new proposals for peace made by Lewis XIV to the States-General, which were denounced by William of Orange and rejected by a majority in favour of continuing to aid Spain in the defence of the Spanish Netherlands. When, in the following August, the Truce of Ratisbon left France in possession for twenty years of her acquisitions (the so-called *reunions*) made up to 1681, and of Strassburg, as well as of Luxemburg, more recently captured, Charles II, in his desire for peace, promised the Imperial Ambassador to guarantee the agreement; though Lewis XIV's intention of ultimately keeping what he had gained could be no secret to him. The importance of this double-faced course both for him and his successor is manifest. His own end, however, was close at hand (he died on February 16th, 1685). By receiving, at the last, the Sacraments of the Church of Rome, he had kept at least part of his bond with France. For the rest, he had, during the last ten years of his reign, preserved the peace of England, at the cost of refusing to throw such weight as she still possessed into the scale of the only policy by which tranquillity could be permanently restored to Europe. If his policy is viewed as a whole, it must be said to have found no other way of deferring the catastrophe of his dynasty, than that of depressing the English monarchy to the position of a vassal State.

The event to which Lewis XIV had looked forward so hopefully —the accession of the Catholic James II to the English Throne—was to prove the final cause of the French ascendancy in Europe. At first, King James seemed not unwilling to come to an understanding with the Prince of Orange, and through him with the States-General. But the Revocation of the Edict of Nantes, which was judged very differently in different parts of the Catholic world, certainly had the effect of constituting the Prince, in the public eye, the representative of Protestant feeling against the King's Catholic sympathies and policy. Thus, though neither King James nor the nation paid much attention to the course of foreign affairs, the suspicions of an understanding between him and the King of France soon spread, and William of Orange continued, to the best of his ability, to cement the defensive league of the other Powers. James II's home policy— blind from the point of view of the preservation of his Throne— was, like his foreign policy, shortsighted, except on the supposition that he had made up his mind to follow France in any event. In April, 1687, he issued the fatal Declaration of Indulgence, and, in August of the same year, he declined the Emperor's request that he should guarantee the Truce of August, 1684. Yet, to make his isolation more complete, he incensed the States-General by attempting to recall his regiments in their service, while seeking to form a body of disbanded Catholic officers with the approval of Lewis XIV. The Dutch saw through the intrigue; and William of Orange could thus lay before the States-General a plan for offensive operations against his father-in-law's Throne.

Yet, while he was engaged in these manoeuvres, he had still disbelieved in war being made upon him by the United Provinces; and had continued his course of government at home. The birth of the Prince of Wales (June 10th, 1688) had only served to heighten the public distrust in the King. On the day of the acquittal of the Seven Bishops (June 29th), the invitation to the Prince of Orange was issued, and the last stage in the catastrophe of the Stewart Throne began. From this moment till the assumption of the royal power by William and Mary, it is idle to speak of an English foreign policy. But though by his declaration to the States-General, on September 9th, 1688, the French Ambassador formally identified his Sovereign with the preservation of the Throne of James II, the latter declined King Lewis' proposal of a joint war on the part of England and France against the United Provinces; nor is there any reference to it in the Prince of Orange's famous Declaration.

III

William of Orange, one of the most far-sighted of great statesmen, had, so far back as 1686, taken counsel with a contemporary Prince who, in this respect, most resembled him, the Elector Frederick William of Brandenburg (already the leading State of Protestant Germany), as to an invasion of England. In 1688, William had sent word to the Great Elector that the moment had come; but Frederick William died in 1688, before the sailing of the expedition. His successor (afterwards King Frederick I in Prussia) undertook to cover the United Provinces on its departure; his brother-in-law, Landgrave Charles of Hesse-Cassel, followed suit; and, soon afterwards, the Lüneburg Dukes (Duke Ernest Augustus only indirectly) took part in the enterprise. Prince George Frederick of Waldeck, whose masterly diplomacy had been invaluable to William of Orange in preparing the great stroke, was named by him his vicegerent in the Stadholderate during his absence.

The object of William's invasion was the object of his life—the preservation of the independence of the United Provinces, which, as their Stadholder only, and in uncertain relations with England, it had been beyond his power to guard effectively, but which, when in assured control of both countries, he felt confident of securing. The final warrant of success in the accomplishment of his life's task would be the formation of the Grand Alliance against France, at which William had long been aiming, and which was now consummated in fact (though in name not till near the close of his reign). The Declaration of War by England against France was the work of William; for Lewis XIV, even after James II and his consort had found a refuge with him, preferred to avoid open war; and William's opportunity was the landing of James, with French support, in Ireland (April, 1689). The Treaty of Offensive and Defensive Alliance between the Emperor and the Dutch Republic was concluded (May), after King William had announced to the Emperor his accession to the English

Throne, and had declared his readiness to adhere to all the Treaties
of Alliance in existence between the United Provinces and the Empire. Its object was stated to be the reestablishment of the Pacifications of Westphalia and of the Pyrenees—*i.e.* the retrocession by
France of all her subsequent territorial acquisitions. In a Secret
Article, the Contracting Powers eventually promised their armed
support of the Imperial claims for the whole of the Spanish inheritance. The Treaty, also, provided for the adhesion to it of England.
Though Spain, Duke Victor Amadeus of Savoy, and the Princes of
the Empire afterwards joined the Alliance, they neither signed the
Treaty nor, so far as we know, were aware of this Secret Article. Inasmuch, however, as it provided for the mutual support of those who
joined in it against the Crown of France and its adherents, it implied
a guarantee of the existing tenure of the English Throne. In a word,
the Alliance of 1689 amounted to an anticipation of the Grand Alliance of 1701–2, and was by no means a mere repetition of the League
of Augsburg of 1686. The critical importance of the 1689 Alliance in
the history of European politics can, therefore, hardly be exaggerated[1].
When (on September 9th) King William, without submitting the
Treaty of Alliance of May 12th to Parliament, without even requiring the signature of it by any Minister of State, signed his own
Act of Adhesion to it, he, in effect, guaranteed the restoration and
the preservation of the Peace of Europe, and once more placed England
in the forefront of those who barred the way to the assailant Power.

Although, in the ensuing conflicts, Lewis XIV kept no ally stedfast
to the end but the Ottoman Turk, and although the only member of
the League whom, quite at the last (1696), he succeeded in buying off
was Savoy, the Peace of Ryswyk (1697) could not be regarded with
satisfaction by his leagued adversaries. Yet, although, by this Peace,
he lost nothing that he had held at the time of the commencement
of the struggle organised against him by William, the French advance
had at that point been decisively arrested, and the recognition by
Lewis XIV at Ryswyk of William's tenure of the English Throne
proved which Power had taken the lead among those opposed to the
' Grand Monarch's' aggression.

In the actual Ryswyk negotiations, no reference had been made
to any secret undertaking as to the eventual treatment of the Spanish

---

[1] Nor must the fact, though incidental only, be overlooked, that it finally
abandoned the recognition of difference of religious confession as a determining
element in international agreements; albeit appeal continued, from time to time, to
be made on the one side or the other to confessional sympathies and antipathies.

inheritance. But Lewis XIV—though historians differ as to whether he then had any serious design of adhering to the compact—had, so far back as January, 1668, concluded an actual Treaty of Partition of the Spanish monarchy with the Emperor. Thus, the idea of a Partition was no novelty; it could hardly fail to come to the front in a period of European politics during which neither side was prepared to contemplate the appropriation of the whole inheritance by a single claimant; and it became a question of practical politics, so soon as King William's statesmanship addressed itself to this solution. He had to use great caution, for he knew how slow English politicians are in "taking up" questions of the future, more especially in the field of foreign policy; and he was, also, aware that public opinion in his English kingdom was far less interested in the employment of its forces in foreign offensive warfare than in the reduction of the standing army at home. To William III, the idea of a partition of the Spanish monarchy, *i.e.* of an arrangement whereby, on the extinction of the Spanish Habsburgs in the male line, the distribution of their inheritance should not unsettle the Balance of Power in Europe, and above all not unsettle it in favour of France, was of the essence of the result to be aimed at. To Lewis XIV, it was nothing but a *pis aller* solution, when he found it impossible, at an earlier or later date, to secure the whole inheritance for France. The logical position, in view of the result contemplated by Lewis, was that of William; but the policy which reckoned with arguments coming home to national feeling, and which, considering the possibility of unexpected incidents, had time on its side, was that of his adversary. This judgment seems borne out by the actual sequence of events, here only noticed in so far as they concern the history of English foreign policy in particular.

What is usually called the First Partition Treaty—the first, *i.e.* of which William III shared the responsibility—was concluded by him with Lewis XIV in 1698. By it, the bulk of the Spanish inheritance—viz. Spain, the Spanish Netherlands, and the West Indies—was, on the death of Charles II, to fall to his great-grand-nephew, the Electoral Prince Joseph Ferdinand of Bavaria; but the Two Sicilies, with Guipuscoa, were to pass to the Dauphin Lewis of France, and the Milanese to the Archduke Charles, son of the Emperor Leopold by his third wife. This arrangement, though seeming to go some way towards meeting the principle of the Balance of Power, was, as a matter of fact, more in the French than in the Austrian

interest, and would hardly have been favoured by William III, but
for the critical condition of his own affairs at home. It was, however, frustrated by the death of the Electoral Prince in January, 1699;
and, about a year later, a second scheme was devised by Lewis and
William, in which the Austrian claims were necessarily treated after
a different fashion, but still so as to indicate the desire of Lewis to
show regard for the principle of European policy upheld by William
III. The Archduke Charles was now to receive Spain, while the
Netherlands and all the Spanish Colonies, together with the Two
Sicilies and the Milanese (to be ultimately exchanged for Lorraine)
were to be the share of France—not perhaps the lion's share, but
something not altogether unlike it. The scheme was rejected by the
Emperor—from what motives, it is not quite easy to decide—and
was profoundly unpopular in Spain, where the indivisibility of the
monarchy had become an article of popular faith. The ambition of
Lewis XIV, hereupon, throwing over any further consideration of
schemes of partition, exercised all possible pressure in the French
interest on the Spanish Sovereign, now near the close of his days.
He died (in November, 1700), shortly after signing a will, in which,
in accordance with Spanish sentiment and with the approval of Rome,
he left the whole Spanish monarchy to Philip Duke of Anjou, the
second grandson of Lewis XIV. As such, he would not, in the
ordinary course of events, succeed to the Throne of France; should
he, however, come to stand next in the French Succession, and accept
that position, the Spanish monarchy was to pass to his younger
brother, the Duke of Berry. To this testamentary disposition the
King of France agreed in the teeth of the certain opposition of the
House of Austria; and there could be no doubt as to the action with
regard to it of England and of the United Provinces—so long as
they were under the joint guidance of William III.

Although religious motives cooperated, it had been the commercial interests of his country which had induced Oliver Cromwell
to challenge the still unrelinquished claims of Spain to oceanic rule.
Still more definite was the conviction of the King-Stadholder that
England and the United Netherlands were alike menaced in the very
foundations of their future prosperity by the prospect of the Power of
Spain falling under the control of that of France. The fact that French
aggressive ambition was now rising to its height had led William III
to adopt irrevocably the policy carried on by him consistently since
the Alliance of 1689. It had entered into no new phase when the

Spanish Succession question came to the front. Public opinion in England had cared little for the Partition schemes, and might, as time went on, have rested content with a provision for the perpetual separation of the French and Spanish Crowns; and in Amsterdam the funds rose on Philip of Anjou's acceptance of Charles II's inheritance. But William's statesmanship was not to be checkmated in the midst of the game; and the action of Lewis XIV speedily justified the attitude maintained by him and Grand-pensionary Heinsius. While formally reserving the French rights of the Duke of Anjou, Lewis XIV ordered his troops to lay hands on the Barrier Towns and (1701) promised to the dying James II to recognise his son as his successor.

The Emperor Leopold I, after at once protesting against the Will, entered into negotiations with William III, and began war in Italy on his own account in the summer of 1701. Early in the same year, an Alliance was contracted with Denmark. And, though the Empire did not formally declare war until a year later, the Coalition of 1689, of the direction of whose operations the lead was from the first assumed by England and the United Provinces, was renewed on September 7th, 1701. The limits to which the stipulations of this Treaty, the Grand Alliance Treaty proper, were restricted should be carefully noticed, if the policy of William III is to be rightly judged. It did not, like the Secret Article of the Treaty of 1689, insist on the right of the Austrian claimant to the whole Spanish inheritance; it merely demanded for him, as a due satisfaction, the Spanish possessions in Italy. On the other hand, while France was in no circumstances to acquire any Spanish Colonies in America, the question of the addition of any of these to the English or Dutch Colonies was left to depend on the course of the War. No express reference was made to the future occupancy of the Spanish Throne; except that France and Spain were never to be under the same Sovereign. A clause was added to the effect that no peace should be concluded by the parties to the Alliance, till England had received satisfaction for the insulting recognition of the Stewart Pretender by the King of France. These conditions, to a large extent, coincide with those afterwards—at the end of the great War of the Spanish Succession—secured at the Peace of Utrecht. Thus, the statesmanship responsible for engaging England and the United Provinces in the great struggle was essentially of a piece with that of the Ministers who brought it to a conclusion. The "War of the Spanish Succession" was fought by the Maritime Powers, and by England in particular, for ends with which the actual satisfaction of the claims to that Succession was only in so far concerned, that France was to be prevented from succeeding to the Spanish dominions in the Netherlands, and becoming the leading Mediterranean, and a great Colonial, Power. These latter were the interests ultimately at stake, and through its care for them the policy of William III itself takes its place within the general course of British foreign policy.

The accession of Queen Anne was, in itself, favourable to the prospects of a War on the issues of which the whole foreign policy of her reign concentrated itself. The national support indispensable for its victorious prosecution was assured by her having inherited an ancestral Throne, and being both an Englishwoman by birth and (as now required by law) a Protestant. On the Act of Settlement (1701) rested, also, the nation's assurance against being involved without the consent of Parliament in any war on behalf of its sovereign's foreign possessions from which it desired to keep aloof. Thus, the conservatism of the nation rallied round her, and made legislation possible under her which her predecessor had in vain sought to bring about. It included the Act of Union with Scotland (1707), which, though it did not put an end to Jacobitism, was essential to the future of Great Britain as a European Power. And, at the very time when our national political life was definitively adopting the system of party government, a practical conjunction between the more moderate men of both the parties in the State enabled the Queen's Government, for a number of years, to carry on with extraordinary success the War actually in progress.

A great war, extending over several years, almost inevitably becomes an evolutionary process, testing, at each successive stage of it, the statesmanship which directs its course. The primary purpose of England and the United Provinces when, in 1701, setting on foot the Alliance, in which they had been successively joined by Denmark (1701), the Emperor (1701), the Empire (1702), Portugal (1703) and Savoy (1703), had been, as was seen, to prevent the union at any time of the French and Spanish monarchies, or the transfer of the kingdom of Spain itself, to the reigning House of France, without providing any suitable compensation for the House of Austria. In other words, the maintenance of Balance of Power had been the primary object of the last great achievement of William III's foreign policy. But, so early as 1703, the Emperor Leopold I renounced

with great solemnity his claims, and those of his elder son Joseph, to
the Spanish inheritance, declaring that they scrupled to unite it with
the hereditary dominions of their own line. The attempt, however,
of the English Government, about the same time, to supplement the
Grand Alliance Treaty by a declaration that no part of the Spanish
monarchy should at any time come under the rule of any member of
the House of Bourbon, failed, because of a difference on another point.
Soon afterwards (1704), the Austrian claimant himself appeared on
the scene, where he called himself Charles III; but his progress was
slow, though Gibraltar was soon taken by an English fleet. On the
other hand, Marlborough's great victory of Blenheim, in the same
year, ended a long period of unbroken French military ascendancy;
and in 1705, though the English Government, on good terms with
Marlborough and Godolphin, was vigorously prosecuting the War,
the idea of Peace was mooted. In August, 1706, Lewis XIV made his
first serious overtures to the States-General, offering them a good
Barrier and suggesting the recognition of Archduke Charles' tenure
of Spain proper, if he would agree to Philip's sovereignty over all her
Italian dominions. But Heinsius ascertained from Marlborough that
the English Government would not now listen to the thought of a
Partition, and that, if desirous of a satisfactory Barrier, the Dutch
must act with the rest of the Allies. On the other hand, the party
now in entire control of British foreign policy, in December, 1707,
passed in the House of Lords an (amended) resolution, that no Peace
would be honourable or safe that allowed the House of Bourbon to
retain possession of any part of the Spanish monarchy[1]. Thus in 1709
after Oudenarde (1708), Lewis felt forced to assent to the peace
terms of the Allies, so far as the surrender of the entire Spanish
monarchy; but he could not bring himself to give the required promise of joining hands with the Allies, should it prove necessary, in
enforcing their demand upon his grandson. It is, assuredly, to the
credit of Marlborough's good sense, that he regarded this condition
as unreasonable; but he allowed himself to be overruled by Heinsius

---

[1] Though they form a curious chapter in the history of our foreign policy in
this period, it must suffice merely to refer to two among the diplomatic efforts
made on both sides to extend the range of the War, so as to include Northern
Europe in its complications. Marlborough was not successful in moving King
Frederick I in Prussia out of his neutrality; but (at Altranstädt, in 1708) he persuaded Charles XII of Sweden to abandon the idea of entering, with the aid of
France, on the task of liberator of Protestant Germany, which had of old been
taken upon himself by Gustavus Adolphus. (The Pretender's attempt, in the
same year, at invading Scotland with a French force broke down.)

and Prince Eugene; and, in the absence of any other guarantee of the Peace satisfactory to the Allies, the negotiations broke down. After Malplaquet (fought in September, 1709), they recommenced (March, 1710), at Gertruydenberg, between the States-General and France, Great Britain and the Emperor alike at first taking no part in them. But, when he did so, it was as adhering to the refusal of any cession to France (that of Sicily was, also, opposed by Savoy). Thus, though Lewis XIV actually declared himself ready to pay a subsidy towards the execution of coercive measures against his grandson, the Conferences of Gertruydenberg ended, under French protest, in July, 1710. Inasmuch as there can be little doubt that Marlborough and Townshend (our Ambassador at the Hague), shared the wish of the Dutch to go back to the policy of a Partition of the Spanish inheritance—to the policy, in other words, with which the War had been begun by this country—the failure of the Conferences casts a shadow on the part played in these transactions by Great Britain. With the aid of the Dutch, with whom it had concluded the First Barrier Treaty (1709), thereby securing them the protected frontier they desired, the British Government could probably have succeeded in moderating the policy of the Allies, and of the Emperor in particular. The chief responsibility for the failure, therefore, must lie with Marlborough and Godolphin. Aware of their imminent political downfall, they shrank from ·the responsibility of bringing about a peace unacceptable to their party at home, and to the Allies abroad, with whom they had so successfully cooperated in the prosecution of the War.

Be this as it may, before the end of 1710, Archduke Charles (Charles III) had lost his hold over any part of Spain except Catalonia; and, even before the news reached England, Harley and St John, without communicating with any of the Allies, opened secret negotiations with Lewis XIV, on the lines of the retention of Spain by King Philip V. On the main theatre of the War, no important change had taken place; but the prospect of its continued vigorous conduct had been gravely affected by the change of Ministry in England, when a new element was introduced into the European situation at large by the death of the Emperor Joseph I (April 17th, 1711). The titular King Charles III of Spain had now become ruler of the whole of the dominions of the House of Austria. Should the entire Spanish monarchy be secured to him, the Balance of Power would be permanently unsettled by the union of all the possessions of the

Emperor Charles V in the hands of his descendant and namesake. It is the great merit of the English Tory Government, of Harley (Oxford) and St John (Bolingbroke) the Lord Treasurer and the Secretary of State—and of the latter in particular—to have perceived at once, that the future of Europe must be protected against the new danger, as it had been from that of the union of France and Spain. Thus, Bolingbroke's name is, more than that of any other man, identified with the policy resulting in the Treaties which we call by the collective name of the Peace of Utrecht, and of which, whatever exceptions he may afterwards have taken to some of their provisions, he is known to have prided himself on being the real author. On this international settlement the Peace of Europe, for more than a generation—shall we say from 1714 to 1746?—virtually hinged; and, though within this period there are to be noted several Wars and several Congresses or Conferences by which they were successively brought to a conclusion—these led to no important unsettlement or resettlement of the Utrecht Treaties[1]. Thus, the Utrecht pacification, more especially, sufficed to put a stop to the aggressive policy favoured by France during nearly the whole of the reign of Lewis XIV and not resumed by her, at least with any measure of consistency, till the Revolutionary War. It will hardly be asserted, *per contra*, that the Peace of Europe would have been more effectually secured by a Treaty or Treaties securing to the House of Austria the full fruits expected from the victories of Eugene and Marlborough, and that, in this case, the "gratitude" of that House would have been itself more notable in the long run than was its wont. And a candid review of the processes for preventing a possible future union between the French and the Spanish Crowns which, in the eyes of the British Government at all events, formed the *nodus pacis*, will hardly condemn the conclusion reached as lame and impotent. Philip of Anjou solemnly renounced his eventual rights to the French Throne (November, 1712); and this renunciation was supplemented by those of the Dukes of Berry and Orleans of their contingent rights to the Spanish, which were confirmed by the Cortes and assented to by Lewis XIV (in the form of an Amendment of the Reservation of December, 1700). No doubt, it was the unexpected survival of the Prince afterwards crowned as Lewis XV which actually prevented the agreement from coming into operation; and no doubt, at one

---

[1] The most notable exception, with which we have no direct concern here, was the complicated (so-called Third) Treaty of Vienna (1738).

time, Lewis XIV had himself regarded such an event as undesirable in the interests of France, so that Bolingbroke had accordingly been induced to revive an alternative plan (in favour of Savoy). But, in itself, the policy ultimately approved and accepted by Great Britain was, in the circumstances, definite and moderate, as well as consistent with the principles to vindicate which she had entered into the War.

We must, however, pass from the special question of the Spanish Succession to the general results of the War to which it gave its historic name, as affecting the political future of the world, and of Great Britain in particular. France came forth from the struggle, no longer the arbitress of the destinies of Europe—exhausted, though (as in later periods of seeming decline in her national life) not beyond recovery; but more closely connected than before with Spain, though not by a personal or institutional union. Spain herself was sinking into a European Power of the secondary order, though by no means without hopes of a partial recovery of her former external (Italian) possessions, as well as of a beneficial change in her administrative system. To the Empire, France would have to yield up some, but not all, of her spoils when the Emperor concluded his own Peace, which he preferred to postpone, and by which he would be left in possession of the now "Austrian" Netherlands—the least-desired by him of his reextended dominions (Sicily falling to Savoy). The United Provinces, who had played their game with characteristic persistency, by the so-called Third Barrier Treaty in 1715 negotiated with the Imperial Government, and guaranteed by Great Britain, finally entered into possession of the full military security which had been their primary object in declaring and carrying on the War. Necessarily, their influence in the counsels of the Allies had sunk, in consequence of the change of Sovereign in England, and afterwards through the collapse of the Whig Government; but though they, afterwards, to some extent, recovered this influence, the time had passed for them to play a leading part in European politics; for, while their merchantmen still outnumbered those of any other country, they were certainly falling behind as a Naval Power.

The inheritance of Charles II of Spain had included a Colonial dominion far more extensive than that which had, before the date of his decease, been acquired by the Dutch in India and by the English in the New World. Had France, unlimited as her aspirations were in this period, been allowed to annex this domain with the rest of the

Spanish possessions, and to consolidate it with her own Colonial settlements, she might have laid the foundations of an empire far exceeding, in extent, that afterwards under the sway of Napoleon. In this regard, the Treaty of the Grand Alliance (1702) had provided that France should never be allowed to take possession of the West Indies, or to enjoy any rights of commerce and navigation not granted in precisely the same measure to Great Britain and the United Provinces. In the Utrecht Treaty with Great Britain, the King of France undertook, in even more comprehensive terms, never to accept, in favour of his own subjects, any advantage in the way of trade or navigation with regard to Spain or her American Colonies which should not also be conceded to subjects of other Powers.

As for specifically British questions, we remember how, before the outbreak of the War of the Spanish Succession, British popular feeling had indignantly resented the French autocrat's arrogant interference in the matter of the Succession to the Throne of these Islands. Thus it was significant as well as appropriate that the earliest article in the Anglo-French Treaty concluded at Utrecht should concern the difficult and delicate subject of this Succession. Much intrigue, more or less secret, in which "persons near the Queen" may or may not have had a hand, and of which the object no doubt was to diminish the responsibility of Lewis XIV for the observance of the undertaking which he was about to accept, had preceded its inclusion in the Treaty. France recognised the order of Succession established by the Act of Settlement (1701) in favour of the issue of Queen Anne, or, in default of such, of the House of Hanover. At the same time, King Lewis XIV promised that the son of King James II ("the Old Pretender") should not at any time return within the realm of France, whence he had "voluntarily" taken his departure.

Among the territorial acquisitions accruing to Great Britain from the Peace of Utrecht a significance of its own attached to the so-called "Dunkirk Clause"; for the control of the Narrow Seas had long been treated as a cardinal principle of English foreign policy. After Dunkirk had been taken from Spain in 1658 by France and England, and placed in the hands of the latter Power, the sale of it to France in 1662 had aroused great resentment against Charles II's Government and more especially against Clarendon; and additions to the fortifications had, beyond doubt, made it a serious menace to the English command of the Narrow Seas. In the Treaty of Utrecht, it was stipulated that the King of France should, at his own cost, *in perpetuum*, rase the fortifications of Dunkirk, and fill up its harbour within six months. Lewis XIV subsequently showed a palpable want of good faith in his manipulation of this clause, and great agitation was provoked in England by the construction at Mardyke of a harbour connected with Dunkirk by a canal and intended to be of greater depth than the previous Dunkirk harbour. The Mardyke works had to be suspended, and finally when, under the Regency, amicable relations obtained between the two Governments, the dimensions of the scheme were so reduced as to render it harmless (1717). The "Dunkirk Clause" continued to be regarded by British Governments as a security in need of careful watching, and the question of its observance caused trouble both in 1719 and later[1]. The clause reappears in the chief European Treaties till the Peace of Paris in 1783, when its abolition was, at last, obtained by France.

Of far greater importance were the British acquisitions from France secured at Utrecht, although, from the nature of the case, this fact could only gradually come to be understood, more especially by the very Power about to enter on a half century's struggle for the preservation of her overseas dominion. After the temporary overthrow of French sovereignty in North America, the whole of the former province of Acadia was, in the Peace of St Germain (1632), restored to the French Crown, and the long contest between English and French enterprise (in Newfoundland and elsewhere) seemed to have come to an end. In the latter half of the seventeenth century, the Colonial ambition of France took a wider flight than it had previously pursued, and she claimed, as her Colonial empire, the whole region from the mouth of the Mississippi to the Great Lakes and the St Lawrence. To this vast dominion was attached the familiar name of New France, though it was administered in full accordance with the political and ecclesiastical principles of the old country.

It was, therefore, a notable step towards a transformation of the Colonial relations between the two Powers, when, in the Peace of Utrecht, Acadia (once more renamed Nova Scotia) was again transferred to Great Britain. In a separate article of the Peace, France added the cession of Newfoundland and the adjacent islands (except Cape Breton and one or two others, which remained French and were

---

[1] See W. Michael, vol. II. pp. 236-9. In 1720, an English engineer was residing at Dunkirk to invigilate.

left in possession of certain rights of fishery[1]). At the same time, Great Britain's possession was recognised of the whole island of St Christopher's (St Kitt's), where the Peace of Ryswyk had restored a bipartite occupation with France.

On the same day as the Utrecht Treaty of Peace between Great Britain and France was signed a Treaty of Navigation and Commerce between the two Powers which (besides placing them eventually on the footing of the most favoured nation) seemed to promise a more momentous change than actually ensued in a most important sphere of international maritime law[2]. Inasmuch as a Treaty of the same purport was signed a few weeks later, between France and the States-General, these agreements would have greatly benefitted maritime (neutral) commerce, had they but been duly observed. Such, however, in spirit, at least, was not the case, certainly not on the part of Great Britain, who concluded no similar compact at Utrecht with any Power besides France, and the principle of the Anglo-French agreement had to await revival, half a century later, when the aspect of things had altogether changed.

The Peace between Great Britain and Spain, though not concluded till July 13th, 1713, formed an integral part of the resettlement of the relations between the Western Powers of Europe. Hence it is in this, quasi-supplementary, Treaty that is to be found the earliest mention of the fundamental provisions for the prevention of a future union on the same head of the Spanish and the French Crowns; while, in further Articles, the King of Spain agrees to the prohibition of the transfer to France or any other Power by Spain of any land or

[1] By the exercise of these rights, the French fishermen were enabled to carry on their trade on a large scale, so much so that, at the time of the Peace of Aix-la-Chapelle, it greatly exceeded the British. Hence the long-lived fishery disputes, which continued to be a source of mutual vexation, until the Peace of 1763 excluded the French altogether from the Gulf of St Lawrence and the Newfoundland waters; and even this proved no permanent settlement.

[2] In 1681, when the French navy had risen to a condition of unprecedented strength, and the pride of Lewis XIV as its head to a corresponding height of arrogance, a royal ordinance had declared any vessel a fair prize in which should be found goods belonging to enemies of France. This ordinance directly controverted the principle of "free ship, free goods," which was so prized by the Dutch, and which had been acknowledged by this country in several Treaties—including that with France of 1655, as well as by France herself in her Treaty with the Dutch of 1646. To the practice which, accordingly, prevailed during the following period (including that of the War of the Spanish Succession), the Utrecht Treaty opposed, so far as Great Britain and France were concerned, the provision that all goods (except contraband of war) should be held, even in the case of a vessel proceeding to a port belonging to a belligerent, to be covered by the flag of the (neutral) State to which such vessels belonged.

lordship owned by her in America. (He, also, expressly approves the Succession in Great Britain as settled by Act of Parliament.)

Among the remaining articles in the Anglo-Spanish Treaty stands forth that which confirmed the cession by Spain to Great Britain of the town, citadel and port of Gibraltar. Of this famous possession the retention or abandonment was at different times in the history of our foreign policy differently viewed by successive Governments, but never in more than one way by public opinion in this country. In Spain, the loss and humiliation suffered by the capture (almost accidental) of the Lion's Rock in 1704, led to the investment of Gibraltar, in the following winter, by a strong Spanish force, and then by a French under Marshal de Tessé. But the resistance was successful, and the British hold on the fortress was confirmed by the Peace of Utrecht, on condition that, should the British Government ever propose to sell or otherwise alienate Gibraltar, the Spanish should always have the first refusal of it. By another article of the same Treaty, Spain ceded Minorca, which had been taken from her by British arms in 1708. But this island, though at first more highly prized, from a naval point of view, than Gibraltar, was not destined to hold the same continuous place among British conquests. In the meantime, while the simultaneous possession of Minorca and Gibraltar satisfactorily secured the future of British trade with the Levant, where the French were by far the most dangerous competitors, to Spain, in the words of Philip V, a British Gibraltar was "a thorn in the flesh"; and the question of its removal could not be a transient one[1].

[1] See, for an account of the attempts made in this direction, Michael, vol. II. part 1. pp. 257–82. As the peaceable return of Gibraltar to Spain was not likely to be made without a *quid pro quo* (besides the saving of expense), it seems explicable why (apart from any personal reason) the thought for a time commended itself to the statesmanship of Stanhope—if it did not originate with George I himself. Leaving aside the questionable story of Louville's secret mission, we cannot doubt that in 1717, when Stanhope was seeking to obtain the adhesion of Spain to this European Alliance, he secretly communicated the idea to Dubois, and that he returned to it in 1719–20, before he had definitively convinced himself of the reception with which it would meet in Parliament. He then resolved to identify himself with what he had recognised to be an irresistible current of public opinion, and made the position clear to the Regent Orléans (who was still inclined to harp on the idea of the cession), through the new French Ambassador Senneterre, and was encouraged, naturally enough, by the Imperial Resident Hoffmann in his new attitude of *non possumus*. There was no question of the suggestion being discussed at the expected Congress; and as for public opinion in England, any return to the policy of a cession would have been utterly scouted. No reference need be made here to Richard Cumberland's futile secret mission to Spain in 1780, when he was instructed to abstain from any mention of the idea of a cession, though the question was, notwithstanding, the real *crux* in the endeavour to bring about a separate Peace between Great Britain and Spain. After the failure of the great siege,

No further provisions or omissions in the Anglo-Spanish Treaty need be dwelt upon in the present connexion. The Article securing to Great Britain (through the South Sea Company) the *Asiento* monopoly formerly enjoyed by France, and henceforth by her chief rival till she and Spain were once more at war, belongs to a happily transient phase of international trade relations; the British abandonment of the Catalans, whom under cover of an amnesty by King Philip the Utrecht settlement left to their fate, was a breach of good faith over which a veil must be cast.

Manifestly, the chief shortcoming of the Utrecht Treaties as securities of the Peace of Europe lay in the fact that they had been concluded without the Emperor Charles VI, on behalf and in conjunction with whose House the great War had been waged. Perhaps, had the campaign of Prince Eugene in 1712, continued by him after the Franco-British Armistice, not proved a failure, the Emperor might have, from the outset, refused to take any part in the Conferences. As it was, they duly opened in the presence of an Imperial Plenipotentiary (Count Sinzendorf); but the capture of Denain further increased the confidence of the French negotiators; and the interests of the Empire, notwithstanding the visit of Prince Eugene to London, became (as in some measure did the claims of the United Provinces) a matter of relative indifference to British statesmanship. On the evening of the very day of the signature of the Peace between France and Great Britain, the British Plenipotentiaries, the Earl of Strafford and the Bishop of Bristol (Robinson) handed to their Imperial colleagues the final offer of Lewis XIV, which proposed the Peace of Ryswyk as the basis of the present Treaty, and the Rhine as the frontier-line between France and the Germanic Empire. These terms differed widely from what France might have proposed a very short time earlier; but, though British diplomacy contrived to bring about a few further conferences between the Imperial and the French Plenipotentiaries, by May, 1713, Sinzendorf and his colleague had quitted Utrecht. The bitterness of feeling which ensued might be illustrated from the party pamphlets published on both sides; but the Imperialist invective against the servile submissiveness of British public opinion

the Peace of Versailles (1783), otherwise not unfavourable to the latter Power, left her face to face with an apparently unredeemable loss. Later proposals for making it good have been hardly more than speculation. Minorca was recaptured by the French in 1756, but restored to Great Britain in the Peace of Paris (1763). The island was again subjected to recapture and recovery, before, at Amiens (1802), it was definitively given up by Great Britain, to whom, in view of her continued occupation of Malta, it had come to be of secondary importance.

to the wishes of the Crown missed fire. Continental statesmanship had been taught a lesson which it might, to its own advantage, have more readily remembered—that British foreign policy was not, as a matter of course, under the imperative control either of established historical tradition or of supposed commercial interests.

When, however, before long, the Emperor Charles VI, finding himself hemmed in by successive calamities, began to go back upon his unwillingness to fall in with the British policy, British diplomacy brought about the communications between the French and Imperial Commanders-in-Chief which led to the opening of Peace Conferences at Rastatt (November, 1713). The Peace of Baden (September, 1714), which finally wound up these negotiations, was concluded without the mediation of either Great Britain or Spain being accepted by France or the Emperor, whose frontiers were settled on a plan of mutual compromise, while the Spanish Netherlands were now definitively acknowledged to be a possession of the House of Austria. British interests had no direct concern with this Peace. On the other hand, they were not unaffected by the Supplementary Pacifications concluded at Utrecht, in February, 1715, between Portugal and Spain. This Treaty had been long delayed by the unextinguishable hatred between the two neighbouring peoples, and, also, by the hopes of the Portuguese for better terms than Spain was willing to allow to them in requital of their faithful adherence to the Grand Alliance throughout the War (which the diplomatic skill of Sir Paul Methuen had induced them to join so early as 1703). Portugal, whose Alliance with England was but an extension of relations which had now lasted for half a century, had, apart from the subsidies paid to her during the War, owed much to this Alliance; in return, she had incurred considerable losses in its course, including the French capture of Rio, with much booty. Yet, as a matter of fact, she was in the Peace negotiations left very much to her own efforts, till, at a later stage of the negotiations, Great Britain's leverage was with some effect applied on behalf of her faithful Ally.

Finally, some reference must be made to the "Barrier Treaties," concluded in this period by the Power our Alliance with whom may be described as a fundamental part of our whole policy in the War and the Peace. Nature had done less than nothing for the Low Countries in the way of Barrier; and the French invasion of 1672, which, but for the opening of the dykes, might have swept over Holland itself, was only stayed by the patriotic efforts of William of Orange, assisted in the following year by Spanish and Imperial troops. The clause in the Grand Alliance Treaty giving the United Provinces assurance of a Barrier against France, without naming the places which should constitute it, had, therefore, led to protracted discussions between the States-General and the Court of Vienna; and, when the latter became aware of the possibility of offers of a separate peace being made by France to the States, Sinzendorf was sent to the Hague (1706) to open negotiations, under the mediation of Marlborough, on the subject of a Barrier Treaty. The Austrian point of view was that, if the Spanish Netherlands were definitively secured to the Austrian claimant, there was no necessity for a Barrier at all; while the Dutch had prepared a list of towns that were to form it, including Ostend, and at first even Antwerp. At this point, British interests came into play. A war between Great Britain and the United Netherlands could, as recent history showed, not be regarded as absolutely impossible; how then, with such an event in view, could these places be permanently committed to Dutch custody? When, however, the peace negotiations of 1709 broke down, and cordial cooperation between the British and Dutch Governments became once more imperative, negotiations on the Barrier question were renewed between the two Powers. In these Austria, though one of the Powers primarily interested, took no part; and the result was the First Barrier Treaty (1709), signed by Townshend. The British Government undertook to secure for the Dutch the right of garrisoning, at their own cost, nine strong places in the Spanish Netherlands, with two others if retaken from the enemy. This Barrier Treaty amounted, in point of fact, to a renewal, on conditions more favourable to the United Provinces, of the Offensive and Defensive Alliance between them and Great Britain. It was, accordingly, decried with much vehemence by the Tory party, soon to return to political power in England, where much jealousy and animosity against the Dutch still survived and were augmented by what seemed an undue morigeration to Dutch interests, so that, in the agitated period of British public life that followed, the First Barrier Treaty acted as a constant irritant. The Dutch, on their side, had little gratitude to spare for British promises; and when, in 1711, Marlborough was dismissed from his offices, the States-General, instead of entrusting the command of their troops to his successor, the Duke of Ormond, made it over to the Commander-in-Chief of the Imperial forces, Prince Eugene.

Hereupon, in the course of the peace negotiations of 1711 and

1712, in accordance with the general course of the relations between the Powers, the British Government was found prepared to revise its previous Barrier Treaty, after such a fashion as considerably to reduce its value for the States-General. Several of the Barrier-places enumerated in the First Treaty had now been marked out for cession to France; and it became necessary for Great Britain to conclude a Second Barrier Treaty with the States-General, which finally revoked the First. By this Second Treaty (January 30th, 1713) the United Provinces acquired the right of garrisoning eight places, four of those included in the First (Lille was one of them) being omitted in the Second. Military and naval contingents were promised on both sides for the maintenance of the Treaty; but the United Provinces lost Upper Gelders, which had now been disposed of to Prussia.

At Utrecht, as well as afterwards at Rastatt and Baden, the House of Austria's possession of the once "Spanish" Netherlands was consistently treated as part of the settlement effected. Yet, in all these agreements, provision had been made that, until the States-General should have arrived at a satisfactory understanding with the Emperor in the matter of their Barrier, they should retain their hold over the Austrian Netherlands. To bring about such an understanding, an Austro-Dutch Conference was held at Antwerp, once more under British mediation. The task was no easy one, especially after the Dutch, whose influence among the Allies had been much depressed during the last four years of Queen Anne, found their position improved by her death (August 1st) and the consequent Governmental changes in England. The death of Lewis XIV (September 1st, 1715), and the accession to power of the Regent Orléans, who was consistently desirous of maintaining a good understanding with the United Provinces, likewise redounded to their advantage.

The Third Barrier Treaty, concluded November 15th, 1715, proved a settlement with which, when it had been with great difficulty brought to paper, the Dutch had every reason to be satisfied. British policy, genuinely interested in the security of the Belgic Provinces, in view of the always possible contingency of hostilities with France, was naturally inclined to meet the wishes of the Dutch, if only because of their guarantee of the now imperilled Protestant Succession. But it had been a very far from easy task for British statesmanship to seek to reconcile the claims of the United Provinces with those of the House of Austria, which had never welcomed with any warmth the acquisition of the Catholic Netherlands, though, of course, unable to countenance the idea, soon afterwards started by France, of forming them into a neutral State. In November, 1714, Stanhope (whose personal influence already counted for much) had paid a visit to Vienna, but found no disposition there to yield; General (afterwards Earl) Cadogan, however, who followed, proved more successful, and, in the end, an arrangement was agreed upon to which the Emperor reluctantly gave his assent. The Barrier-places were now to number seven, including Namur, Tournay and Ypres (with a joint garrison at Dendermonde); and Venloo, with a small further addition of Flemish territory, was to be transferred to the United Provinces. Great Britain (while obtaining for herself certain commercial advantages) undertook as Guarantor of the Treaty in all its parts to provide a considerable force for the defence of the Barrier by both land and sea, and if necessary to declare war against any aggressor. Thus, the Dutch had succeeded in securing a well-protected frontier against France; while at the same time a relation, which was in a measure one of dependence upon them, had been established with the "Austrian" Provinces. It is therefore not difficult to understand that the ratifications of the Treaty had to undergo considerable delays, on the particular causes of which we need not dwell. The Dutch declined, as will be seen, to join the Quadruple Alliance till the Third Barrier Treaty should be complete, and, as a matter of fact, till their joining had ceased to matter. Moreover, as was asserted by their neighbours, they had at the same time acquired a practical control of the Belgic waterways and (since the Scheldt could at any time be closed) of every port in the country, except Ostend. The delimitation of the Netherlands was finally accomplished by a Supplementary Convention signed at the Hague (December, 1718). As for the House of Austria, it had, for the sake (as will be seen) of British goodwill, consented that the fortresses of the territory acquired by it should be left, partly at its own cost, in the hands of another Power; so that, in course of time, it anxiously sought to exchange this for a less remote acquisition.

The Treaties of Utrecht (to use the term, once more, in its widest sense) had thus, taken as a whole, carried out the policy of William III, as representing the interests of Great Britain, on the one hand, and those of the Netherlands on the other; but had not carried it out in full. France had acquired for a member of her royal House, though he was no longer included in the Succession to it, part only of the inheritance of Charles II; but this part included what William

III had sought to withhold from the French candidate, viz. Spain herself. Furthermore, France was deprived of the new vantage-ground which she had seized in the Spanish, as against the United Netherlands, and which was now, though not without certain inconvenient liens, in Austrian hands. Finally, France had formally renounced any pretension to interfere with the stability of the British Constitutional settlement. So much for the results of the Treaties which ended the War of the Spanish Succession.

What may be called the moral results of that War were due, above all, to its actual course, and to its effect on the material resources of the Powers engaged in it and upon the relations between them and the political system of which they formed part. For the attainment of these results, the policy which had originated the War and that which directed the Peace were primarily and jointly responsible. And more than this: the Peace of Utrecht, though negotiated and concluded by a statesmanship in most important respects out of harmony with that of the author of the Grand Alliance, was, not less than the War itself, in the main Great Britain's work; and, if it failed to gather in fully what the War seemed to have laid at her and her Allies' feet, to her credit was to be placed what, within limits deliberately chosen by herself, it achieved for Europe and her dependencies. In this, as in all but the rarest instances of similar magnitude, history is called upon to judge by other standards than those of person or party.

IV

George I, wise in his generation with a wisdom recalling, in its degree, that of the great politician in whose school he had been bred, had fully learnt a modern ruler's primary obligation of moving with his times and acting in accordance with their exigencies. Yet, although, in his kingdom, he discreetly forbore from interfering with the existing system of government, the influence exercised by him on British foreign policy was unmistakable. To a considerable extent, it subserved Hanoverian interests, and was guided by Hanoverian advice, though these, in their turn, in a large measure, coincided with the traditions that had come down from the age of the Grand Alliance. Thus, while his reign as a whole justified the national preference—at first far from assured—of the continued acceptance of the Revolutionary settlement to a "Restoration" of the Stewart

Pretender, the doubts and jealousies of foreign Governments were successfully met by a policy blending national (British) and dynastic (Hanoverian) purposes; and, although George I was neither an Englishman nor a popular King, it was, on the whole, fortunate for Great Britain that he should have come from his well-beloved Hanover to ascend the Stewarts' uneasy Throne.

It may be worth pointing out that the "Personal Union" brought about under George I is not quite correctly described as a union between a powerful monarchy and a small secondary State. The relations between England and the United Netherlands in the reign of William III, even after the death of his devoted Queen, furnished no sort of precedent, and had never come near to what had once been Cromwell's ideal; and the course of the War of the Spanish Succession, and of the negotiations at its close, had shown how unintermittently each of the two Maritime Powers kept its own particular ends in view. Moreover, at the beginning of the Hanoverian period, the foundations of the British Empire were, after all, still in the laying; and the Elector of Hanover, although hardly even among the foremost of the Princes of Germany, was entirely, in the words of a modern historian[1], "a leading personage in Europe." The politics of the Brunswick-Wolfenbüttel branch of the Guelfs had been Imperialist before the days of the Thirty Years' War; and the Lüneburg-Celle branch had, six years before the conclusion of the Peace of Westphalia, signed with the Emperor a separate pacification favourable to themselves. Thenceforward, the Brunswick-Lüneburgers had remained on the best of terms with the Court of Vienna. The Elector George Lewis, in especial, had borne an active part in several campaigns against the Turks, including the rescue of Vienna —a fact not forgotten when, at Carlowitz, in 1699, English mediation had secured to the Emperor Leopold the fruits of Austrian prowess against the Crescent, as, in substance, it again did, nineteen years later, at Passarowitz. In the West the Lüneburg-Celle Princes had, in the main (though in the case of those ruling at Hanover, not from the first), supported the policy of William III and of the Grand Alliance, and had been rewarded by the Electoral investiture (1792) of the father of George Lewis, under whom the whole Lüneburg-Celle dominions were reunited (1705).

---

[1] Mr J. F. Chance, in his most valuable monograph, *George I and the Northern War* (1909). As Mr Chance notes, "that George I might have succeeded Charles VI, on the Imperial Throne, was in 1714, a possibility not disregarded."

The reign of George I, regarded from the point of view of its foreign policy, divides itself most conveniently into three periods, coinciding, more or less, with those of the ascendancy in this respect of Townshend (1714–7), of Stanhope (1717–21), and of Townshend and Walpole (not yet "Walpole and Townshend") (1721–7), respectively. In the earliest of these periods, the two statesmen chiefly concerned with the conduct of foreign affairs served side by side as First and Second Secretaries of State—Townshend, who held the former post, being regarded as Head of the Government, but the disposal of business between them being left to their own discretion. The arrangement proved itself inconvenient, especially since both these Ministers were high-minded as well as able men. Stanhope's views were, to a far greater extent than his colleague's, in accordance with their Sovereign's; and, on the split in the Whig party declaring itself and Townshend giving up the Seals, Sunderland was associated with Stanhope. Among the Secretaries of State in this reign were the excellent Addison (a steady party-man) and the younger Craggs (Pope's Pollio, of whose capacity in or out of Parliament there is abundant evidence)[1].

While the chief operations of British foreign policy during the larger half of George I's reign had the approval and were due to the suggestion of the King's Hanoverian advisers, it by no means follows that they should be held responsible for the conception, any more than for the execution, of that policy as a whole. Apart from the fact that few British Sovereigns have exercised so close and continuous a personal interest over the country's foreign affairs as George I, it should be remembered that the British statesmen entrusted with the management of these affairs in the earlier part of the reign and the Hanoverian advisers of the King were, from the nature of the case,

---

[1] The force and lucidity of Craggs' despatches might be illustrated without difficulty. Of Addison's, that to Count Gallas (the Imperial Ambassador at Rome) asking for his mediation with Pope Clement XI, who is required, in a conciliatory tone, to redress a series of British grievances of which the arrest of Peterborough at Bologna was the foremost (October, 1717), is notable as showing the absence of direct diplomatic relations between the Holy See and the Court of St James. Cf. W. Michael, *u. s.* vol. II. part I. pp. 309 ff. Lord Stanhope (*History of England*, etc., 5th ed., 1858, vol. I. p. 202), notices that the House of Commons remained without its due share in appointments to high administrative offices, and therefore in the direction of the administration of the country itself, till after the passing of the Septennial Act (1716). The real change in the relative importance of the two Houses of Parliament in the public eye dates of course from the age of Walpole; but the part taken by members of the House of Lords in the conduct of foreign affairs continued, for obvious reasons, to preponderate up to the days of the younger Pitt.

in substantial agreement. Townshend had been chosen as Principal Secretary of State with the approval, if not at the direct instance, of Bothmer (whose confidence, with that of the leading Dutch statesmen, he had gained during his residence at the Hague); while the entire Whig Government with which George I began his reign had been recommended to him by Bernstorff (who accompanied him from Hanover to England on his journey for taking seisin). The approval of Bernstorff implied the assent of Robethon, the inevitable (and indispensable) Huguenot refugee, whose connexion with English affairs dated from the days of his secretaryship to William III, at the end of his reign[1]. For the rest, we need say nothing further here as to Hanoverian influence on British political action, except in the instances adverted to below of the Bremen and Verden, and the Mecklenburg episodes. It may, however, be worth observing that the leading members of the "Junta" were by no means always at one with each other. Bothmer's star seems to have waned as Bernstorff's rose to its height, which it reached while Stanhope's Government could still be, with any reason, popularly called the German Ministry. Of course, the Hanoverian influence was far more fully asserted in the affairs of Northern than in those of Southern Europe; and Bernstorff's political principles (as well as his personal interests) long obstructed these negotiations with Prussia, the success of which were, in 1720, followed by his downfall, the end of the Hanoverian era proper, and the reunion of the Whigs.

At the time of the accession of George I to the British Throne, the Peace recently concluded was still virtually Great Britain's peace. The Emperor would have none of it, even after he had, a few weeks later, concluded his own at Baden. The Dutch had only assented conditionally on a satisfactory Barrier being granted them by the Emperor. In France, the Peace was regarded with a sense of mingled relief and distrust. At home, it was loudly condemned by the great body of the Whigs; and, both here and across the water, the resumption of the War seemed for a time on the cards, even before King Lewis XIV's end had come (September 1st, 1715). To Great Britain the old Alliances were of more value than ever; and, so early as November,

---

[1] He had then entered the Celle service and had (if one may so say) become the *âme damnée* of Bernstorff, having been appointed "Privy Councillor of Embassy" at Hanover, and continued to exercise the undefined functions of this office in England till his patron's fall. The personalities and history of the members of the "Hanoverian Junta" are briefly noticed in the Appendix to Lecture II of my *Great Britain and Hanover* (1899).

1714, Stanhope, when, at Vienna, he sought to bring about the acceptance of a Barrier Treaty which would satisfy the United Provinces, confidentially propounded, in the first instance, to Prince Eugene the conclusion of a defensive alliance, to be afterwards joined by the United Provinces—the germ of the later Triple Alliance. But nothing came of the project so long as the Third Barrier Treaty remained unsigned. As has been seen, the jealousy between the Imperial and the Dutch Governments continued even after this; but, in the meantime, although the death of Lewis XIV had brought France under the rule of a Government favourable to Great Britain, the British Throne itself had been, though as it proved only transitorily, placed in a position of danger. Thus, while through the efforts of British diplomacy the Third Barrier Treaty had been brought to its conclusion under British guarantee (November, 1715), there remained behind the urgent expediency of securing to Great Britain the old Allies—more closely tied to her by their own interests, and, it may be said without prejudice, more trustworthy than the existing French Government.

The relations between these Allies—the United Provinces and the Emperor—were, however, even after the signature of the Barrier Treaty, the reverse of easy, and their dissensions about the time of the years 1715–6, owing to incidents connected with territorial transfers, rose to such a pitch that a joint alliance including both of them was for the present out of the question. The new Austrian Ambassador in London (no official of his rank had been accredited here since 1712), was a most unfortunate choice; and thus it came to pass that the first Treaty of Alliance signed by the British Government (February, 1716) was with the States-General, and that a Treaty, of mutual territorial guarantee, with the Emperor was not formally signed at Westminster till the following May. To this second Treaty, though declared by the Emperor to be defensive only, the Dutch Government never formally signified their adhesion, though they gradually reconciled themselves to it, the more readily when it proved not to be incompatible with the Anglo-French undertaking that was, above all others, of value to their most important interests. It was concluded by George I, as King of Great Britain only, and therefore contained no guarantee of Hanoverian territories; moreover, though his Hanoverian Ministers had taken part in the negotiations, their signatures were not added to the Treaty. But, though a joint alliance with both the Emperor and the United Provinces seemed for the moment impossible, there was no doubt of the friendly intentions of both her old Allies towards Great Britain. Of the two storm-points which, in the early years of the reign, seemed to threaten a continued disturbance of the Peace of Europe and a consequent interference with the Hanoverian Succession included among its conditions at Utrecht, one had even now not yet reached its final stage. A considerable change had gradually come over Great Britain's relations with the Powers engaged in the still unfinished great Northern War, and in particular with the militant Baltic Power to which she had long been drawn by strong religious sympathies as well as by important commercial interests.

So early in the reign of Charles XII as 1700, Sweden had concluded a Treaty of mutual defence with England for eighteen years; and another immediately followed, in which the United Provinces of the Netherlands joined, and which, in a secret article, bound the Contracting Powers to use their best endeavours for preserving the endangered Peace of the North. By virtue of this compact, Sweden, in the same year, 1700, obliged Denmark to sign the Peace of Travendal, which detached that Power from the league of the adversaries of the young Swedish King. During the eventful years of his victorious advance that followed, Great Britain kept her hands free from engagements on either side, successfully foiling the efforts of Lewis XIV to gain over the Northern hero to the side of France in her own War. British trade with Sweden continued brisk, although its volume was probably not more than half that of the Dutch, the Swedish exports being, practically, confined to materials for shipbuilding. During the Northern War, Sweden treated neutral commerce with a high hand, so that, on the plea that they had carried contraband of war into Russian ports—of which Sweden had declared a blockade—many British merchantmen were seized by Swedish men-of-war and privateers. On the other hand, it is noticeable as bearing upon the future, that the relations between Charles XII and the Elector George Lewis of Hanover had always been excellent, and had stood the Swedish King in good stead in the earlier part of his course.

Accordingly, even after "Pultawa's day," when the counter-current of *revanche* gradually overflowed half Europe, Great Britain held her hand, and, in course of time, non-intervention in the North became part of her general policy of peace. Moreover, so long as the Spanish Succession War was still afoot, it was contrary to the interest of all the Allies, though of course to that of the Emperor and Empire in particular, to allow Germany to be set in a blaze with the aid of large forces still indispensable at the actual theatre of war. Accordingly, a Convention was signed at the Hague (March 31st, 1710) declaring the neutrality of the German Provinces of Sweden, so as to protect them, if necessary, against attack, and at the same time to prevent their serving as bases of counter-attack.

One of the most wholehearted supporters of this Convention was the Elector of Hanover, whose dominions were bordered in part by Swedish annexations which, in the day of Sweden's dire distress, were certain to become so many coveted prizes. Among these were the "duchies" of Bremen and Verden. Apart from the fact that, when succeeding to the insecure grandeur of the British Throne, George I had excellent reason for "cultivating" what he left behind him, the ownership of these lands was a matter of considerable consequence, as well as historic interest, to the Elector of Hanover. The duchy, formerly belonging to the archbishopric, of Bremen had, after the Reformation, been held by cadets of neighbouring princely Houses, including that of Brunswick-Lüneburg, but in the Peace of Westphalia had passed as a secular duchy into the possession of the Swedish Crown. The bishopric of Verden, of old part of the dominions of Henry the Lion, had likewise been assigned to the Swedish Crown as a secular principality. The duchy of Bremen and the principality of Verden, respectively, commanded the course of the Weser from Bremen to its mouth and that of the Elbe to the sea from the vicinity of Hamburg, Holstein lying to the north-west of the river; above Harburg, the Elbe formed the north-eastern boundary of the Brunswick-Lüneburg territories. In the days of William III and Anne, the vigilance of the Elector of Hanover had been directed less against Sweden, the actual mistress of Bremen and Verden, than against her inveterate foe Denmark, who, should she possess herself of these territories, might, because of their immediate vicinity to Holstein, prove far more unwilling at any time to relinquish them.

Thus, before the question of the future of the Swedish monarchy and of its provinces had to be faced by Great Britain as a European Power, a very direct Hanoverian interest had become mixed up with it. Tsar Peter I, against whom about this time (end of 1709) Charles XII was seeking to induce the Sultan to declare war—while he was, also, believed to be in communication with the French Government— was intent upon ousting Sweden from her control of the Baltic and from the territories still belonging to her in Germany. He was annoyed by Prussia's hesitation about asserting her dynasty's claims on Stettin and its district; and assiduously worked upon the Elector of Hanover, through his able representative there, Prince Boris Kurakin, to press his interest in Bremen and Verden. But the first actual step towards the acquisition of the "duchies" was not taken by George Lewis till the year before his accession to the British Throne. When Frederick IV of Denmark, notwithstanding his rout in Scania (1710), made another attempt to carry out his part in the anti-Swedish league formed after Pultawa, and to this end, in 1713, after a severe struggle, occupied the duchy of Bremen, the fit conjuncture seemed to present itself for carrying out the long-harboured design. In the same year, George Lewis occupied Verden, with Ottersburg, just across the Bremen boundary and, though still at peace with the Swedish Government, announced his intention of continuing to hold the lesser territory, so long as the Danes held the larger. Though, even after the accession of George I and the arrival of Charles XII at Stralsund (November, 1714), cordial messages were exchanged between them, there was no longer any mutual confidence; and, though the British ships sent in 1715 took no actual part in the Dano-Prussian siege of Stralsund, the continuance of eight of them in the Baltic implied the approval by Great Britain of the Treaty between Denmark and Hanover, finally ratified in July of this year. By this compact, the duchy of Bremen was (in return for a payment variously reckoned, but over 600,000 dollars) to be given up to the Elector. The transfer was accomplished by October, and the Elector's declaration of war against Sweden immediately followed. On the other hand, Sir John Norris, while carrying out a demonstration on behalf of trade wrongs at the head of a fleet composed of British, Prussian and Danish ships, carefully kept out of the way of the transaction concerning the "duchies," and contributed only indirectly to the fall of Stralsund (December). As for the duchies, their Estates had at once done homage to their new ruler. The Danes, fearing that Charles XII might seek to purchase the friendship of the King of Great Britain by a voluntary cession of the duchies to the Elector of Hanover, had, without loss of time, safeguarded the transfer by means of Treaties with Hanover and Prussia; but the Hanoverian possession of them was not formally recognised by Sweden till 1719 (in the Peace of Stockholm) when this complicated, and not altogether ingenuous, transaction was at last wound up. When the Hanoverian annexation of Bremen and Verden had actually been perpetrated, there could, of course, no longer be any thought of friendly relations between George I and Charles XII. But this was not the time for the latter to think of a raid on any part of the British dominions on his own account, and the Jacobite insurrection of 1715-6 collapsed without a serious hope or fear of any such incident[1].

Meanwhile, a great design (if this historic term should be applied to a vast, but largely shadowy, web of intrigues such as "Görtz's Plot") was in preparation, which, while imperilling the continuance of the existing British Government and dynasty, had in view a complete change in the relations between Sweden and her most formidable enemy, Russia. The ultimate object of Görtz, now in the service of Sweden and loyally devoted to her interests, was a peace between the two Baltic Powers, which would have extinguished the anti-Swedish league, now, as has been seen, virtually including Great Britain. The political relations between George I and the Tsar Peter had, indeed, become friendly, as British grievances and Hanoverian cupidity jointly increased the tension with Sweden; and, in October, 1715, a Treaty had been agreed upon between the Tsar and the Elector of Hanover at Greifswald mutually guaranteeing Bremen and Verden to the Elector of Hanover: and Esthonia, with Reval, to the Tsar. But to this Treaty the King of Great Britain could not give effect without the assent of his Parliament, and, since the British Ministers were not prepared for joint armed action against Sweden, Bernstorff informed Kurakin that the full purpose of the Treaty must be kept secret and only the commercial clauses made known at present. Meanwhile, Peter ruthlessly excited the violent wrath of George I by his high-handed interference in German affairs, and more especially by taking advantage of the marriage of his niece Catharine to Duke Charles Leopold of Mecklenburg Schwerin, to quarter among the nobility there, traditionally impatient of their Sovereign's rule, a large body of Russian troops intended to take part in the Danish invasion of Scania agreed upon between Peter and Frederick IV at Altona. Prussia (who had just expelled the Swedes from Wismar) held her hand; but Russia could depend on her good-will, while Hanover and Prussia were as a matter of course at odds. The invasion was postponed, though Sir John Norris was in the

---

[1] It is, by the way, illustrative of the entire relations between England and Scotland after the Union, that, there being at the time no Treaty of Alliance between Great Britain and Hanover, while a subsidiary treaty would no doubt have been deemed inadvisable, Stair's suggestion of shipping some Hanoverian battalions to Scotland at the time of the Insurrection was not carried out.

Baltic, prepared to take part in it; and King George was with difficulty prevented from sending the Admiral orders to seize on the
person of the Tsar in requital of his arbitrary ways. But although
the British Ministry shared the desire to keep Peter and his designs
in check, his violation of German territory could not be held to warrant a *coup de main* by the British fleet against a Sovereign who was,
virtually, an Ally[1].

Meanwhile, "Görtz's Plot," of which neither the genesis nor the
ramifications can be traced here, had become known to British statesmen, and at the end of January, 1717, was discussed in Council. In
setting it in motion, the arch-intriguer Görtz had had the assistance
of the Swedish envoys, Gyllenborg in London and Sparre at Paris,
and had depended on the connivance of the scheming Alberoni at
Madrid and of the Chevalier, still *à disposition* at Avignon. Nor was
he altogether out of touch either with the Regent of France (in the
earlier stages of the affair), or with the Tsar. The discovery, though it
rendered the plot as such hopeless, with the arrests, and the intern-
ment of Görtz in Holland, caused a sensation almost unparalleled in
modern diplomatic annals, but exercised no decisive influence upon
British policy. Charles XII kept silence, and the Regent Orléans'
disclaimer of any aggressive intentions against Great Britain found
willing credence. As for George I and the more resolute among his
Ministers, they had already made up their minds to a more vigorous and
far-reaching "system" of action, which would place Great Britain in
a firm position of her own among the European Powers, unassailable
by machinations such as those of either Görtz or Alberoni.

In the summer of 1716, Stanhope had accompanied King George
on the pathetic occasion of his first visit home. *En route*, the Minister
contrived to manage the earliest of his celebrated "unbuttoned"
conversations with the Abbé Dubois, the trusted intimate of the
Regent Orléans, who was anxious to safeguard his personal future
against the Spanish Bourbons and their (never wholly impossible)
speculations as to the French Succession. With these speculations
the designs of Alberoni, inspired, in the first instance, by the ambition of Queen Elizabeth (Farnese) of Spain, were interwoven, and
these naturally came to a head after the death of Lewis XIV. Their

---

[1] The Mecklenburg quarrel had an interesting sequel, which, however, had no
direct connexion with British policy, though George I as Elector of Hanover was
one of the Princes of the Empire charged with its execution against Duke Charles
Leopold in 1717, and though its results led to complications which engaged the
attention of George II to so late a date as 1735.

aim was, should it prove impossible to secure the French Throne for the Spanish Bourbons, at all events to revive in Elizabeth's line the Spanish dominion in Italy. While the resistance of the Emperor would of course be the obstacle-in-chief, Great Britain's attention must be distracted by the overthrow of her new dynasty. For the moment, however, since the working out of such a scheme required time, Alberoni was in no hurry to break with Great Britain, and was, indeed, desirous of cultivating her goodwill, especially since that of the French Government was no longer at the service of the Spanish. Hence the Anglo-Spanish Commercial Treaty of December, 1715, highly favourable to British interests, negotiated by George Bubb (afterwards Lord Melcombe who, before entering on the later un-edifying part of his career had been Sir Paul Methuen's successor at Madrid) and Alberoni, though, on his part, neither sincere in conception nor effective in its results. Meanwhile, the British negotiations with France had been all but brought to a satisfactory conclusion. Instead of being conducted through the Earl of Stair at Paris (whose addiction to the pomps of diplomacy by no means rendered him averse from the use of its byeways), the business was, in August, 1716, transferred to the management of Stanhope and the ambitious and intriguing Sunderland, with the cooperation of Bernstorff, in the still surroundings of Hanover. Here it was brought to a successful issue by the signing of an agreement between France and Great Britain confirmatory of those portions of the Peace of Utrecht which concerned their respective interests, more especially the order of Succession in the two monarchies, and guaranteeing their territorial possessions in a form including the new acquisitions of the House of Hanover. The Pretender was excluded from France, and the Mardyke question was, with some difficulty, satisfactorily settled. The complementary assent of the Dutch Government had been assumed, to the righteous indignation of the British Minister at the Hague, Horace Walpole (the elder); but it arrived on January 4th following, and the "Triple Alliance" was now complete. It was the work of Bernstorff and Stanhope (to write their names in the order of sequence proposed by the same critic at the Hague). Townshend, the absence of whose countersignature had been suspiciously noted by Dubois, had sent it in time; but there could be no doubt that he had looked askance upon the Alliance and the policy of warlike operations in the North to which it seemed to him to point. The King, moved in his turn by angry jealousy of

Russia, was wholly against Townshend. Hence, a split among the Whigs, and a reconstruction of the British Ministry, which was completed when, in April, 1717, Stanhope became First Lord of the Treasury and Sunderland Secretary of State (1717), Townshend having accepted the Lord-Lieutenancy of Ireland, but being subsequently dismissed from this office also. (Stanhope and Sunderland exchanged offices in the following year, 1718.) Finally, whether or not the treatment of the Pretender in the Triple Alliance offended the chivalrous spirit of the Swedish King, the British Government more directly defied him, in the following March, by prohibiting all trade with Sweden, and, in the same year (1718), sent another fleet into the Baltic.

In the period of Stanhope's Ministerial ascendancy which ensued, the "Quadruple Alliance" (August, 1718) forms his most momentous achievement. It might, possibly, not have been carried through the difficulties besetting it, but for the active part played in the negotiations of the years 1717 and 1718 by Bernstorff and Bothmer[1], whose main purpose was to strengthen the authority of the Emperor in Germany and to promote the intimate relations between him and the House of Hanover. Yet, however sorely these efforts vexed the souls of Sir Robert Walpole and the section of the Whigs with which he acted, the plan courageously and circumspectly formed by Stanhope for settling the affairs of Europe was successful, in the face of reckless ambition abroad as well as of intelligible distrust at home. The Triple Alliance, well-omened as had been the fact of its conclusion, stood on no firm footing, and could not prove an enduring safeguard of the Peace of Europe, should Spanish policy, urged on by dynastic and Ministerial ambition, venture to revive the quarrel with the House of Austria, and should that House seize the opportunity of renewing its pretensions to the Spanish Throne. Cardinal Alberoni, the embodiment of the new Spanish aspirations, was, accordingly, the second stormpoint on the European horizon, which, even before the Northern War had become extinct, threatened to overwhelm the European order of things established by the Utrecht and supplementary Treaties, and including the settlement in Great Britain.

The storm broke, in this quarter, before the plan of action devised by Stanhope and Dubois could be applied as a prophylactic.

---

[1] Of the importance attached to their counsels, more especially by the able Austrian negotiator Penterriedter, we have ample evidence from Bothmer's own hand, in his *Mémoire* on the Quadruple Alliance.

The Emperor was harassed by his Turkish War; and, influenced perhaps by this circumstance, Alberoni, though aware that the time was hardly ripe, yielded to his Sovereign's resentment of an accidental insult offered to Spain by Imperial officials, and seized Sardinia by a *coup de main* (August, 1717). Emboldened by his rapid success, he was preparing to seize Sicily (now under Savoy rule) when Stanhope intervened. In March, 1718, his kinsman Colonel William Stanhope (afterwards Earl of Harrington) appeared at Madrid to offer a protest, which was (not very strenuously) supported by France and the United Provinces. The British and the Spanish Governments were still on amicable terms, though Alberoni had already begun to disregard the recent Commercial Treaty with Great Britain, besides rejecting her offer of good offices with the Emperor. By July, however, a British fleet was sent into the Mediterranean, to deal with Spanish naval operations which might conceivably have been followed up by a demonstration or a raid on the British shores. About this time, too, the Emperor's Turkish War was brought to a close, on terms satisfactory, so far as his interests in this quarter were concerned, by the Peace of Passarowitz (July, 1718)—a Treaty to be placed mainly to the credit of British diplomacy, whose twofold object seems to have been to bring about an immediate close of hostilities between the Porte and the Emperor (so as to enable the latter to take part if necessary in the Western conflicts) and to make trouble between the Porte and the Tsar[1].

Thus, in the midst of this medley of East and West, the Anglo-French Convention, signed in July, 1718, received the adhesion of the Emperor, and in the following month the Quadruple Alliance was concluded with him in London. Its name—to some extent a misnomer—was due to the adhesion of the United Provinces, which was, after some delay, unwillingly given (February, 1719). That of Savoy had preceded it, though, as will be surmised from the bargain proposed to her, it had not been much more readily accorded. Victor

---

[1] The policy of the Peace of Passarowitz, as noted above, repeated under equally critical circumstances, that of Carlowitz (1699), concluded under the mediation of Great Britain at a time when William III was anxious to put an end to a War diverting the military forces of the Empire from the Western theatre of action. In the midst of the Passarowitz negotiations, Prince Eugene took Belgrade; and the Peace marks an epoch in the history of the Eastern question and especially of Austria's Eastern policy, besides showing the interest taken in these matters by Great Britain at this time, largely under Hanoverian inspiration. The fruits of the Peace of Passarowitz were largely sacrificed by Austria in that of Belgrade (1739), which Russia (then her Ally), though victorious, had to follow up by a pacification of her own.

Amadeus II was suspected of playing a double game; but the traditional friendship of Great Britain for the House of Savoy (which, however, failed to show the steadfastness of that of Braganza) prevailed over the wiles of the Cardinal at Madrid. The negotiations for the Alliance had been difficult and protracted; for both the French and the British-Hanoverian counsels lacked unity of purpose; but, thanks to the energy of Stanhope, and the skill of his subordinates[1], the scheme of which he was the primary author reached its consummation.

The essential object of the Quadruple Alliance, which made a direct appeal to the principles of the Peace of Utrecht and the Grand Alliance, was to establish these agreements on an enduring basis, or, if the expression be preferred, to give to them their logical development. While the Emperor was to renounce definitively all pretensions to Spain and the Indies, Spain, in her turn, was to relinquish for the future any claim to any former Spanish province now under the rule of the Emperor. Sicily was to pass into his possession out of that of the House of Savoy, which was to receive, instead, the island of Sardinia, with the title of King. Finally, the Emperor was eventually to invest Don Carlos (or another son of the Queen Elizabeth of Spain) with the duchies of Parma, Piacenza and the greater part of Tuscany, but on condition that none of these should in any case become part of the Spanish monarchy.

Would Spain, under a guidance which wooed Fortune by temerity, now that her armada was at sea and the drift of her audacious designs becoming manifest to the world, dare to proceed, and to reject the compromise imposed upon her? Or would these designs, with the more or less vague hopes of support with which they were buoyed up, collapse in face of a mandate from the Powers united in the Quadruple Alliance? To decide this issue, Stanhope himself, immediately after the signature of that agreement, betook himself to Madrid, accompanied by Schaub. In one hand, he brought the offer of peace, with certain concessions, including (though with what accompanying conditions, seems to remain unknown) a secret proposal for the cession of Gibraltar[2]—in the other, war. Alberoni refused to give way, even when (after Stanhope's departure) the startling

---

[1] One of these was St Saphorin, who had passed from the Hanoverian into the British service and was British Minister-resident at Vienna. He was by birth a Swiss, like Sir Luke Schaub, who, after varied services, became Ambassador at Paris in 1721. The British diplomatic body, never more notably than in this period, recruited itself by the admission of natives of other countries.

[2] See Lord Stanhope, vol. I. p. 310.

news had arrived of the destruction of all the Spanish ships by the British fleet off Cape Passaro on the Sicilian coast (August, 1718). But the die had been cast. Alberoni, *more suo*, now that his scheme of anticipating the Italian stipulations of the Quadruple Alliance had failed, and that it had been joined by Savoy, resorted to fresh offensive plans. In France, however, the discovery of the Cellamare plot against the Regent put an end to any elements of hesitation; and when, in December, 1718, the Government of Great Britain, of which Alberoni was planning both a Spanish and Swedish invasion, declared war against Spain, the French Government speedily followed suit (January, 1719). As will be seen, the Cardinal had also in mind a joint attack upon Hanover by Sweden and Russia, whose Governments were then discussing conditions of peace in the Åland Islands. The Spanish War—or the War against Alberoni—was unpopular in England, except for the losses in it of the Spanish navy; for no immediate British interests were involved in the Emperor's desire to make himself master of Sicily.

Before, however, it began its course, the news had arrived of the death of Charles XII (December 11th, 1718); and, though his intentions had remained uncertain to the last, a sudden end had come to the designs of Görtz, and a severe blow had been dealt to those of Alberoni. In April, 1719, the Spanish expedition under Ormond was scattered off the Irish coast, and, in the same month, the French began their invasion of Northern Spain, seconded by a British raid by sea. On the other hand, the Cardinal was encouraged by a gleam of success which had attended the Spanish arms at Franca Villa against the Austrian reinforcements sent to Naples (June), to hold out a little longer. The persistency of the British and French Governments, however, prevailed. In December, with the aid of a series of intrigues, in which the self-proffered diplomacy of Peterborough made itself conspicuous, the Spanish Prime-minister's career as such, at last came to an end. Yet, even so, the tenacity of Philip V—or, rather, that of his Consort—once more necessitated the personal intervention of Stanhope. In January, 1720, he, at Paris, joined in a declaration on behalf of Great Britain, France and the Emperor, firmly upholding the "system" of the Quadruple Alliance. A week later, King Philip accepted that agreement, subject (secretly) to certain points left over for the decision of a Congress, to be held at Cambray in 1722. The Spanish adhesion to the Quadruple Alliance was followed by two Treaties, between Spain and Great Britain, and between those Powers and France respectively (1721), intended, with a view to this Congress, as a sort of reinsurance against the understanding by which France and Spain, distrustful of the intentions of the Emperor, had thought to safeguard themselves. But these Treaties were alike concluded after Stanhope's death. The political structure which he had raised into being cannot, in itself, be described as built on a rock; but his courage and resolution, brought home alike to foe and friend, had successfully trodden down the embers which the efforts of Spain and the daring enterprise of her master-politician had begun to rekindle into flame in Western and Southern Europe.

About the same time, the Northern War, which, as a matter of course, had considerably affected British trade, but with which Hanoverian political interests had latterly become inextricably mixed up, had, at last, been ended by the Peace of Nystad (1721). Before the death of Charles XII (December 11th, 1718), while the effects of Görtz's now patent designs had not yet quite died out, and the Swedish negotiations with Russia in the Åland Islands were, under the influence of these projects, still pursuing their tortuous course, the relations between Sweden and Great Britain were more strained than ever, involving most of the discomfort, with much of the cost, of regular warfare. In the spring of this year, Norris had again sailed into the Baltic, ostensibly in order to redress the continued grievances of British trade and navigation, in conjunction with the Danes (still at war with Sweden), and with the less certain support of the Dutch. He had instructions to present himself at Petrograd, where he might still be able to thwart the proposed combination between Russia and Sweden. The Tsar Peter had never swerved from his purpose of extending his dominions along the Baltic. To this end, he had first joined the League against Charles XII, and there now seemed an opportunity of compassing it by treaty. But the Mecklenburg trouble was not yet over; and there was nothing really satisfactory in the assurances of the Russian Court. Thus, a reconciliation might, not without some French encouragement[1], have, after all, taken place between Sweden and Russia, which would have furthered neither

---

[1] The Treaty of Amsterdam of the previous year (1717) was the work of the Regent's Government, anxious to play the part of Mediator; Great Britain had no share in the Treaty, but Russia's proposed Concert against Sweden was counteracted by the effects of Prince Eugene's victory at Belgrade and Stanhope's success in bringing about the Quadruple Alliance; and Prussia, whose policy was more suspect than before to Great Britain, had, for the moment, to fall back on a waiting game.

British nor Hanoverian-Imperial interests—but for the catastrophe which happened near the end of the year.

The death of Charles XII before Frederikshald (December 11th, 1718) was one of those catastrophes which bring with them a sense of relief to half the world. The Swedish Crown descended to Charles's sister, Ulrica Eleanora, to the disappointment of his nephew, Duke Charles Frederick of Holstein-Gottorp (afterwards son-in-law to the Tsar Peter); but its diminished authority was soon made over to her husband, King Frederick I (Prince Frederick of Hesse-Cassel), with whom George I was on the most friendly terms. After the death of Charles XII, Sweden had no policy left but one of peace. Among the many claims which that peace would have to meet, Hanover's were of the latest, Denmark's of the earliest, date; Prussia (intent on the acquisition of Stettin) stood firmly by her Russian ally.

The Emperor Charles VI, whose Congress of neutral German Princes had sat long and uselessly at Brunswick, still continued as friendly to Hanover as he was adverse to Prussia. In this sense he had, not long before the death of Charles XII became known, concluded with Augustus II of Poland (Frederick Augustus I of Saxony) and the Elector of Hanover (King George I) an agreement for the defence of their German territories. The Hanoverian counsellors of King George were anxious to secure the support of the British fleet in the execution of this Treaty; and this was secured by a diplomatic *ruse*, which, as the Treaty never came to be carried out, only threw discredit upon them and him[1]. Since the French Government was likewise inclined to favour Swedish rights and disregard Prussian claims in Germany, a general combination adverse to Russia and Prussia might have been formed, which would have prevented the Tsar from acquiring the supreme control of the Baltic, in return for Sweden's cession of all German territories belonging to her by Treaty. But George I and Bernstorff, with whose policy Stanhope's was in partial agreement, were not to carry through their scheme. British relations with Prussia became friendlier, and the policy of the Tsar in the end prevailed.

Meanwhile, the efforts of British diplomacy at Stockholm had

---

[1] The story of these transactions has, for the first time, been clearly told by W. Michael (vol. II. part I. pp. 461 ff.). It turns on the omission, in the copy of the Treaty of January 5th, 1719, sent for ratification to London, of the declaration binding King George to send a British fleet to protect Danzig and Elbing in case of a Prussian attack. The daring policy was the King's; the peccant diplomatist was St Saphorin.

not been wanting in vigour. A leading part in them was taken by Lord Carteret in June, 1719, at Stockholm, where he was actively assisted in the Hanoverian interest by the Mecklenburger Adolphus Frederick von Bassewitz. Carteret (afterwards Earl Granville and Secretary of State) was a statesman of extraordinary ability and personal charm, and had, moreover, gained the personal confidence of his Sovereign by his knowledge of the German tongue—an accomplishment then unique among British Ministers. He was, also, supposed to exercise a potent influence over the counsels of the Abbé Dubois in France. But at the root of his successes lay his self-trust; for the opinion of others he had a contempt (by no means only inspired by burgundy) which easily consoled him for his occasional failures.

At Stockholm, Carteret, with Norris's squadron in the background, lost no time in bringing about, with the assistance of his Hanoverian colleague, an understanding with the Swedish Government, which, in the form of a Preliminary Convention (July, 1719), settled the matters at issue, including the cession of Bremen and Verden, in return for the payment of a million crowns. By the time when the ratifications of the Treaty which carried out this agreement in a modified form, and provided for a renewal of the old friendship and Alliance, were exchanged (February, 1720), Carteret at Stockholm and Sir Charles (afterwards Lord) Whitworth, a diplomatist of notable insight, at Berlin had succeeded in bringing about a Treaty between Sweden and Prussia, by which on payment of a large sum Stettin, with the Pomeranian region between Oder and Peene, was relinquished by Sweden to Prussia. The network of Treaties was now nearly complete and the anti-Swedish League had been all but transformed into a protective combination against Russia. Of the former, there now only remained its earliest member—Denmark. In this quarter, the efforts of British-Hanoverian and French diplomacy at last (in July, 1720) prevailed upon King Frederick IV (afraid lest the claims of the Duke of Holstein-Gottorp on parts of Schleswig should obtain the support of the Tsar) to agree on terms with Sweden, under a British and French guarantee of that duchy[1]. When, in this year, Sir John Norris arrived with instructions to notify to the Russian Government and its naval and military commanders Great Britain's

---

[1] In connexion with the Schleswig-Holstein question of later times, it is worth noting that this (Frederiksborg) guarantee in no wise affected the question of the Succession to the whole of Schleswig.

willingness to initiate a peace with Sweden, but in any case to concert operations with the Swedish fleet, he found nothing in readiness at Stockholm. And, though there was a strong wish that Great Britain should exert her influence with the other Powers to bring about a Concert in opposition to Russia's Baltic policy, it proved impossible in face of the Emperor's *non possumus*, Prussia's caution, the religious difficulties in Germany which placed the Lutheran Elector of Hanover in a most unwelcome position between the two chief German Powers, and the uncertainty of the policy of France. Probably, the decisive element in the resolution ultimately taken —to abandon the naval offensive (August, 1719)—is to be found in considerations which could only be usefully discussed in a Naval History. But a great political opportunity had been missed.

Norris sailed home again, and the British design of an active intervention in the settlement of the North had come to naught. This barren result of a long episode of British foreign policy was not, however, wholly due either to the European complexities of the time, or to the naval difficulties of the situation. With the moment, the spirit needed for using it was not to return. The end of 1720, in May of which year Norris had reappeared in the Baltic, dates the Bursting of the South Sea Bubble, which, in more ways than one, shook the stability of the British Cabinet. In the midst of these troubles, Stanhope died (February, 1721), and, in April, Walpole, who had rescued the country from the consequences of the crisis, succeeded him as Head of the Government. Townshend, from whom no continuation of Stanhope's actively anti-Russian policy was to be expected, had, on his death, been appointed to his Secretaryship of State.

But Sweden had, before this, ceased to reckon any longer on the direct support of Great Britain. The idea of a British League with Prussia, Denmark and Hesse-Cassel on behalf of Sweden speedily collapsed, and the Russian ships devastated the Swedish coasts. But, when Norris appeared for the last time in the familiar waters, in April, 1721, it soon came to be understood that no aid, even in the form of further subsidies, was to be expected from his Government —at all events for the present. The advice of Great Britain to Sweden was now simply *cedere malis*. In the following month, the Nystad Peace Conference opened, and the Tsar's Plenipotentiary, Rumyantseff, made it clear that if his Sovereign's conditions were accepted, he would leave the Duke of Holstein-Gottorp's pretensions to the Swedish Throne to take care of themselves. In the Peace of

Nystad (May), the Tsar Peter was triumphant. Livonia, whose possession implied the virtual command of the Baltic trade[1], was, with Esthonia and part of Carelia, yielded up by Sweden, on payment of a wholly inadequate money compensation. Finland was left to her, and a promise given that Russia would not interfere in her home (dynastic) affairs. Great Britain was not mentioned in the Treaty as mediator, guarantor or otherwise, except indirectly as an Ally of Sweden. The attempt to insert a clause for the protection of the Lower-Saxon Circle (of which Bremen and Verden formed part) had broken down; and the relations between the British and Austrian Courts and Governments had become so uneasy, that Bernstorff, who persistently adhered to the Emperor, lost his credit with his own Sovereign. The attempt to break the force of the Peace by a quadruple alliance or concert between the Contracting Powers (Russia and Sweden) and those who had not been accepted as Mediators (Great Britain and France), of course, remained a phantasm. The Tsar Peter, or as he now called himself, the Emperor of all the Russias, was master of a dominion comprising some of the fairest provinces of Sweden and clasping Poland in its deadly embrace; and British policy, after coming into conflict with Russian, for the first time in the hitherto almost wholly secluded action of the latter, had undergone a most signal rebuff, which estranged the two Powers politically for the better part of a generation[2].

This signal discomfiture can, at least, not be imputed to want either of prescience or of activity. One of its causes was, no doubt, the coldness between the British and the Imperial Courts, due in part to the delays in the investiture of the Elector with Bremen and Verden, caused in its turn by the Emperor's jealous hesitation as to the parallel investiture of the King of Prussia with Stettin, and in part to the religious disputes in the Empire mentioned above. So strangely were political and religious difficulties still intertwined, that the blindness to its own future interests was in this instance on the side of the Empire. As for Great Britain, the Northern policy of

<hr>

[1] Of this Riga, more and more distinctly, became the centre; and it was Livonia which supplied the bulk of the war material exported from the Baltic to Great Britain.

[2] In 1742, during the Russo-Swedish War which ended with the Peace of Abo and the humiliation of Sweden, Great Britain concluded with Russia the Treaty of Moscow. This was the period of the ascendancy of Carteret and the so-called "Drunken Administration." Commercially, it may be noticed, the Baltic had become of less importance to Great Britain in the matter of naval materials, after these had begun to be imported in increasing quantities from America.

George I and Stanhope, as it may be described without injustice being done to either, had failed, though not more conspicuously so than that of France. It would be futile to conjecture what use Cromwell, with the support of English Protestant feeling, would have made of the situation, the commercial aspects of which can hardly be said to be quite free from obscurity. In any case, the Emperor had not been induced by the authors of the Quadruple Alliance to play an effective part in it; but, though the Alliance had in so far proved a failure, the cause of its breakdown is not, in this case, to be sought in Hanoverian motives, which no longer dominated, though they had not ceased to influence, British foreign policy.

After Stanhope's death, the conduct of British affairs inevitably passed into the hands of Walpole and Townshend, the former having, as was seen, been appointed First Lord of the Treasury and Chancellor of the Exchequer, and the latter one of the Secretaries of State. Walpole, whose thoughts were as entirely English as his ways, and who made no secret either of his personal dislike of the King's Hanoverian counsellors, or of his distrust of the House of Austria, could not pretend to any diplomatic training and at first affected an indifference to foreign policy, in the narrower sense of the word. Townshend's experience was therefore indispensable to him, and they were at one in resisting the self-assertion of Carteret, who was appointed to the other (Southern) Secretaryship, on the death, hastened no doubt by his being implicated in the South Sea disaster, of the younger Craggs. For a time, the influence of Carteret over the King seemed paramount; but, before long (April, 1724), a dispute between him and Townshend (at Hanover[1]) brought about the transfer of the Southern Secretary to the Lord Lieutenancy of Ireland. Carteret's successor, the Duke of Newcastle, was an adherent of the policy of Walpole, or at least preferred to support him as the leader of the most powerful party in Parliament.

Walpole had, however, not yet taken to himself the chief direction of the foreign policy of Great Britain, when his Government was called upon to intervene in European affairs, which seemed to be experiencing a strange metamorphosis. Early in 1720, on acceding to the Quadruple Alliance, Philip V of Spain had left over some of the perplexities

---

[1] The intrigue to which it had reference, and which involved both the French Court and the Hanoverian clique, led to the substitution at Paris of Horace Walpole the elder for Sir Luke Schaub.

confronting him (including the perennial question of Gibraltar) to be
settled by the Congress of Cambray, which however did not actually
meet till four years later, and, largely because of the matters here
noted, broke up without result. Marriage contracts had been arranged between the heir to the Spanish Throne and his brother
Charles and two daughters of the Duke of Orleans, and the Infanta
Maria Anna had, at a very early age, been betrothed to the young
King Lewis XV of France. But the ex-Regent had died, and had been
succeeded in the control of French affairs by the Duke of Bourbon-
Condé, his deadly enemy. A few months later (March, 1725) the
Duke of Bourbon, by sending back the Infanta, offered an unpardonable insult to Spanish pride. When it was found that the British
Government would not abandon the French Alliance, the Congress of
Cambray was broken up by the Spanish Court, and Ripperdá, the chief
instrument of its policy, set to work for the conclusion of a league
with the Emperor against the original members of the Triple Alliance,
while waiving all the points that had remained in dispute between
the Spanish and Imperial Governments.

Not only had the Emperor Charles VI been with great difficulty
induced by Great Britain to join in the Quadruple Alliance, seeming
thus to shut the door against any future revision of the Utrecht
Settlement; but he had come very near to a quarrel with Great
Britain herself and the United Provinces, on account of his project
for the development of the commerce of the Austrian Netherlands
by the establishment of an East India Company at Ostend. Moreover—and this was doubtless the main motive of his present line of
action—he was most anxious to take advantage of the present isolation of Spain by obtaining from her a guarantee of the Pragmatic
Sanction of his daughter Maria Theresa's succession in all his
dominions. The ambition of the Spanish Prime-minister, the newly
created Duke of Ripperdá—an Alberoni of a very inferior type—
met the Emperor's cherished desire halfway; and, by April, 1725,
the two Governments had come to an understanding which found
expression in an open and a secret Treaty signed at Vienna. In the
former, which, while accepting the conditions of the Quadruple
Alliance and a Spanish guarantee of the Pragmatic Sanction, also
contained an Imperial promise of good offices for the recovery of
Gibraltar and Minorca by Spain, there was nothing directly provocative to Great Britain; but the secret Treaty was, besides promising armed assistance for their recovery and continued action on

behalf of the Stewart Pretender, understood to provide for the cementing of what was thus converted into an offensive Alliance, by arranging for the marriage of the Infante Don Carlos and his brother with two Austrian Archduchesses. It was further hoped that the Tsarina Catharine, who had in this year succeeded Peter I, and who had inherited his hatred of the British Government, would join in the Alliance. Alberoni's network was being patched up again, though by a far less able hand; and once more England was filled with alarm. Again, British interests, political and commercial, co-incided with the security of the Hanoverian dynasty, and prompt intervention seemed imperative.

Thus the Alliance of Hanover, signed in September at Herren-hausen, though negotiated at the Hague, was a necessary and essentially defensive reply to the Alliance of Vienna; nor, though Parliament was not sitting at the time, could it be asserted, except by party spite, that this important transaction was under the control of Hanoverian influence; indeed, the King looked upon it as dangerous. The main credit of it was due to the courage of Townshend; France and Prussia were partners in the Treaty, though the accession of the latter (who in the same year concluded the wellknown Treaty of Wusterhausen) was secured with some difficulty and contained a reservation of Prussia's relations with Russia, who, in her turn, soon joined the Austro-Spanish Alliance. The United Provinces, after vainly attempting to secure by negotiation a stoppage of the Ostend Company, also acceded to the Austrian Alliance.

A European war seemed, in the circumstances, inevitable; and, in accordance with the obligations undertaken in the event of a declaration of war by the Emperor against France, the British Government concluded a Subsidy Treaty with Hesse-Cassel. The Spanish Government began preparations for the siege of Gibraltar; but, in the meantime, there had been signs of a change in the general aspect of things in Europe. In 1726 Ripperdá had been dismissed in disgrace, and in the same year Cardinal Fleury became Prime-minister in France, whose ascendancy in conjunction with that of Walpole brought peace in its train. The death of Catharine I, who had so faithfully adhered to her great Consort's principles of rule, followed in 1727.

Thus it is not surprising that the Emperor Charles should have given way to the new current, and have agreed to the signing of Preliminaries of Peace with Great Britain, France and the United

Provinces at Paris (May 31st, 1727). While all Treaties concluded before 1725 were confirmed, any particular questions for discussion were referred to a General Congress; but—and the exception shows, so far as Great Britain is concerned, what lay at the root of the so-called Alliance of Hanover—the charter of the Ostend East India Company was suspended for seven years. Spain still held aloof, but her acceptance of the Preliminaries must sooner or later follow. Little more than a week after the signing of these Preliminaries, King George I died on his return journey from Hanover. The foreign policy of his reign was, at the moment, in a critical phase, but not in one foreboding the collapse of the principles it had followed, and the interests it had served with, on the whole, indisputable consistency. After the conclusion of the War of the Spanish Succession, Great Britain could not renounce the leading part she was called upon to play in general European politics. The Triple and the Quadruple Alliance made the Peace of Utrecht a reality, and the ambition of Spain, not once but twice, both when opposed to and when temporarily reconciled with the dynastic purposes of the House of Austria, broke down in face of the Alliance between Great Britain and France. The Alliance had not sunk very deeply into the soil; but it seemed more likely than before to hold out, as, in its general tendency, the conduct of affairs in both countries, united in resistance to a disturbance of the existing settlement, became more clearly pacific. In the North, new relations between the Baltic Powers, of which Great Britain had in vain resisted the establishment, had taken the place of the old; but towards the problems certain to arise from these and other more nearly imminent changes, the attitude of Great Britain could not yet be determined.

The first decade, roughly speaking, of the reign of George II (1727–37) is the period in which Walpole, the friend of peace, remained, virtually, undisturbed in his Ministerial sway. While the country at large saw in him its ablest financier, who had rescued it from the South Sea *débâcle*, his action in the Spanish-Austrian crisis of 1726–7, although he was inclined to blame Townshend for precipitancy, had materially contributed to check the policy of Spain, which had already begun to lay siege to Gibraltar. For, without Walpole, Parliament, when it met in January, 1727, would not have shown, by voting supplies, that the nation was prepared. Peace had been thus preserved, though the eleventh hour might seem to have passed; the Emperor had drawn back; and the Spanish question had been reduced to that of the time needed for soothing Spain's ruffled pride, and reconciling her to the Concert.

The European position of Great Britain in these years was greatly strengthened by the cordial relations between her own and the French Government. Walpole's brother, the elder Horace, at that time British Ambassador in France, had, in ready deference to Fleury's wish, crossed the Channel to second Queen Caroline in impressing upon George II the necessity of keeping the Minister in power. This was done, though no serious danger would probably have, at least for the present, threatened the security of the Hanoverian dynasty, or that of the British interests bound up with it, had the King followed his first inclinations. The Jacobites were, as usual, quite alive to the chances of the situation, but really unprepared to take advantage of them, should an opportunity present itself. The Pretender hurried from Bologna to Nancy, whence he was formally expelled by the French Government, and had to take refuge at Avignon, and then at Rome. The Jacobite faction in the new Parliament (1728) was impotent for action, and, when the arch-intriguer Bolingbroke appeared on the scene, it was in the character of an independent supporter of the Hanoverian Throne, merely desirous that it should change its counsellors.

Meanwhile, the pacification of Europe which had seemed so near at the time of the death of George I had been, though but slowly, accomplished. The mock siege of Gibraltar was reluctantly given up; nor was the conduct of the Emperor, bound as he was by his Treaty with Prussia, altogether loyal. It was only by very vigorous proceedings on the part of the British Government (which by means of the subsidy Treaty of Wolfenbüttel with Brunswick kept that duchy open for occupation by British troops) that he was made to understand the seriousness of the situation, and that Spain was obliged to relinquish her hope of a resumption of the Austro-Spanish Alliance. Philip V signified his acceptance of the Preliminaries of Paris in the Act of the Pardo (March, 1728), in which an ulterior settlement was referred to a Congress of the Powers.

In this Congress, originally summoned to Aix-la-Chapelle, and thence transferred in the following June to Soissons, where it sat for several months, Great Britain's first Plenipotentiary was Colonel William Stanhope (subsequently Earl of Harrington, and after the dissolution of the Congress one of the Secretaries of State). The main question for settlement here was the satisfaction of Spain; for the Emperor, intent upon using the opportunity for as general as possible a recognition of the Pragmatic Sanction, had given up both his resistance to the establishment of a Spanish Prince in the North-Italian duchies, and the maintenance of the Ostend Company. But it was the Pragmatic Sanction which Fleury, in accordance with the traditions of French policy, steadily declined to recognise, and which the Congress left where it found it. The Spanish Government, hereupon, after in vain seeking to exact the cession of Gibraltar which British public opinion showed itself determined to resist, passed over to the other side, and concluded, with Great Britain and France, the Treaty of Seville, the United Provinces, as was their custom, acceding later. This Treaty (November, 1730) which patched up the trade relations in America between Spain and Great Britain, but passed over the subject of Gibraltar in silence, was Townshend's last achievement. It was much approved in the City, whose interests had been jeopardised by the previous attempt of the Spanish Government to transfer to Austria the concessions enjoyed (since Utrecht) by British trade; and gratified the Court, annoyed by the recent Austrian *rapprochement* to Prussia (for securing whose friendship Queen Caroline had already formed projects of her own). While, however, the Emperor seemed the loser, he contrived to possess himself of the Italian duchies which the Treaty had intended to secure to Spain; whereupon it was denounced by the Spanish Government itself. The British now once more returned to the Imperial alliance, and, in the so-called Second Treaty of Vienna (March, 1731) guaranteed the Pragmatic Sanction, the Emperor in return abolishing the Ostend Company. When he further agreed to the succession of Don Carlos in the Italian duchies, Philip V of Spain, for his part, also acceded to the Treaty (July, 1731). Since it, also, received the adhesion of the Estates of the Empire and finally of the States-General (1732) a general Concert seemed to have been reached. In promoting this settlement, the conciliatory diplomacy of Earl Waldegrave, now British Ambassador at Paris, fully carried out Walpole's pacific policy. At the same time, Droysen, not without reason, regards the transaction as illustrating the "parliamentary" style of foreign policy characteristic of Walpole—a policy which provides for the day and the morrow, and leaves the day after to take care of itself. While by this Treaty the real gainer was the Emperor (as his concessions in return suffice to show), it was concluded without the assent of France; and, at a time when the relations between her and her Ally were by no

means altogether as easy as Fleury desired them to be, Great Britain
had, in order that Europe should obtain peace for the present, yielded
to the wishes of the House of Austria in a matter of vital importance
for the European Balance in the future. France had taken no part in
the Treaty. On the other side, it must be added that Great Britain
, and the United Provinces were afterwards accused of having failed
to carry out the commercial concessions they had made to the Austrian
Netherlands in return for the abandonment of the Ostend Company.
With regard to the future, France, though under the genuinely pacific
and conciliatory guidance of Fleury, had always been impatient of
pacific Ministers, and to a generation not yet oblivious of the glories
of Lewis XIV—even to Fleury himself—a realisation of the Pragmatic
Sanction was intolerable. Thus, the disagreement on this head
between France and Great Britain inevitably tended to bring about
closer relations between the former Power and Spain, and to promote the signing, so early as November, 1733, of the First Bourbon
"Family Compact." On the other hand, the renewed good understanding between Great Britain and the Emperor could, in the end,
hardly fail to involve this country in the conflict between Austria
and Prussia, which, although they had in 1729 concluded a Perpetual
Alliance, could no longer be far distant. But, for the present, all
seemed to promise well; and Walpole's method of advancing national
prosperity by assuring the continuance of peace, and leaving over
remoter difficulties, commended itself to public opinion. Great
Britain required peace after the long strain of the active foreign policy
of the first Hanoverian reign; nor is it easy to see how, without the
material resources accumulated by her during the Walpolean age, she
could have taken upon her the mighty responsibilities awaiting her.

Thus, we have reached a chapter of modern history marked by
a European War in which Great Britain took no part. Notwithstanding the efforts of the Emperor to draw her (and the United
Provinces) into the War of the Polish Succession (1733-8), she had
contented herself with offering her mediation, after (in November,
1733) the Government of Lewis XV had agreed to a Convention at
the Hague, by which it undertook to refrain from invading the
Austrian Netherlands. The War and the so-called Third Treaty of
Vienna, which in 1738 definitively terminated it, exhibit the most
turbid depths of eighteenth century diplomacy; and it was only with
the utmost difficulty that Walpole had succeeded in restraining King
George II's dynastic and military aspirations from casting a line into

waters so troubled. Nor is it astonishing that the Courts of France and Spain which—the latter on acknowledging the Pragmatic Sanction—had been the territorial gainers in the issue, should have cherished the thought, developed in them by the course of the War, of turning their united strength against the Power whose neutrality had favoured an unprecedented growth of its commercial prosperity. They could not do so in secrecy; for, as Seeley has pointed out, the Bourbon Family Compact of November, 1733, which showed that France was weary of a policy of peace, was known from the first to Walpole, whose own policy had seemed to be an element in its prospects of success. There can be no doubt that the purpose of this Compact, besides aiding in securing the position of Don Carlos in Italy, was to resist the advances of Great Britain by sea, and, while making joint war upon the Emperor, to keep Great Britain in check by naval armaments. At all events, the promise of French aid in the efforts of Spain to recover Gibraltar was included in the agreement. For the rest, the encroachments of British maritime trade offered a constant opportunity for Spanish grievances; though it might better suit Walpole's parliamentary adversaries to find effective opportunities of attacking him in the Spanish treatment of British traders—opportunities of which, in 1738, they availed themselves with relentless factiousness. If Walpole has been justly charged with moulding his foreign policy too closely upon the necessity of satisfying Parliament, it must be remembered that a bitter personal hostility to himself was the guiding motive of the whole Opposition against which he had long stood at bay. Carteret, after he had been replaced in his Secretaryship by Newcastle, had returned to the Parliamentary arena in 1730, and, an attempt at reconciliation with Walpole having failed, he, with the often invaluable aid of Chesterfield in the House of Lords, and that of Pulteney in the Commons, divided the conduct of the Opposition between them. The Jacobites under Wyndham, and the Boy Patriots clustered round Bolingbroke (William Pitt, from 1735, among them), treated foreign affairs as they treated domestic, from the same point of view—the baiting of Walpole. In the face of such an Opposition, no harder task ever fell to the lot of a British Minister. To his honour, Walpole was animated by a sincere desire for peace; though the spirit of the nation had been effectually roused against Spain, while the Spanish Court, with the Family Compact to fall back upon, was never indisposed to war. In the negotiations which occupied the autumn and winter of 1738, Spain showed herself willing to give satisfaction for past transgressions, but not prepared to relinquish the right of search; "No Search" had become the demand of the British mercantile interest, and, owing to the persistence of the Opposition, the cry of British public opinion[1].

Quite early in 1739, a Convention was signed at the Pardo by the Spanish Minister de la Quadra and Sir Benjamin Keene, a diplomatist who represented Great Britain at Madrid with much ability both before and after the War[2] which broke out later in this year. This preliminary agreement stipulated that, before the execution of the final Treaty, Spain should pay to Great Britain the amount by which the British claims exceeded the Spanish counter-claims. Into the accompanying reservations and protests it is the less requisite to enter here, since public opinion in England, led by the Opposition, would in no case have been satisfied with the Convention, which Walpole, in one of his Pyrrhic victories, only carried by small majorities (March, 1739). The Opposition hereupon seceded, thus enabling the Government to carry a Danish Subsidy Bill. Whether the object of this measure was to patch up a Hanoverian quarrel or to prevent a Danish alliance with Sweden and France and thus leave Great Britain without an ally in the imminent War, the incident at all events illustrated the inconvenience of mingling questions of foreign policy with party manœuvres. Before long, it became evident that, though the Opposition was unable to oust Walpole from office by their onslaughts, they had created a situation involving the country in the War to the avoidance of which his policy had, above all, been directed. When the Spanish Government declared that negotiations could proceed on no other basis than one repudiated by British public opinion, and that, till a particular Spanish demand (the claim on the South Sea Company) had been satisfied, Spain would suspend the *Asiento*, the chances of peace had been reduced to nothing. The usual votes followed in Supply; but Carteret's advice to conclude an alliance with Prussia was not followed. Keene's *ultimatum* was declined by Spain, and war was declared (November, 1739). France protested her pacific intentions, but began to arm.

The outbreak of the War found Great Britain without an ally (except Denmark). The Emperor Charles VI was sick to death. He had consented to the humiliating Peace of Belgrade, and was not to

---

[1] Pitt was, in course of time, to come to see the Spanish side of the argument.
[2] He was also commissioned at Madrid as South Sea Agent. It was Keene, who, in 1757, reluctantly obeyed Pitt's instructions to offer Spain the restoration of Gibraltar, if she would join Great Britain against France.

be tempted by British suggestions as to the recovery of Naples and
Sicily; the United Provinces, this time, stood altogether aloof;
Frederick William I (whose death, like the Emperor's, followed in
1740) would give no encouragement to British overtures, being,
above all, anxious to preserve the goodwill of France. As for France,
she would no doubt join Spain in the War at the moment most convenient to herself; and, though it began with Admiral Vernon's naval
exploit (celebrated at home as a party triumph), this was not successfully followed up, and Anson's brilliant circuit had no influence on
the course of the War: the conflict between two European Great
Powers could not be decided in the Pacific. Thus the spirit of the
Opposition was by no means quelled. In 1741, what Lord Stanhope
hardly exaggerates in calling the "cry for the blood of Walpole"
went up louder than ever. He successfully resisted a drastic censure
on his entire foreign policy moved in the Lords by Carteret and in
the Commons by Samuel (afterwards Lord) Sandys; but, immediately
before the dissolution of Parliament, he had felt obliged to follow
public opinion, with which part of the Opposition identified itself,
in carrying the grant of a subsidy to the Queen of Hungary (April).

By this grant, Great Britain became a participant in the War of
the Austrian Succession, for which Frederick II's invasion of Silesia
in December, 1740, gave the signal, and which was destined to
dominate the next epoch of European politics. Although Carteret,
a consistent friend of the House of Austria, hoped from the first that
Maria Theresa would come to terms with her determined assailant,
the subsidy granted sufficed to make her believe that Great Britain
would support her to the end; and Walpole's plans for the preservation of peace fell to the ground. Thus, the battle of Chotusitz (1742),
which ended the First Silesian War, lost two provinces to her, and,
while the Alliance of Great Britain had only helped her to conclude
a humiliating peace, the result had still further increased the
unpopularity of Walpole at home. Upon him too fell a share of the
indignation aroused by the Treaty by which, in September, 1741,
the Elector of Hanover agreed to remain neutral in the War, and even
to abstain from voting for Maria Theresa's Consort in the approaching election to the Imperial Throne. The Prime-minister's position
had become untenable[1], as was shown by Newcastle's averted

---

[1] His desperate, or at least paradoxical, notions of recovering popularity by
a separation of Hanover from Great Britain on the King's death, and of obtaining
Jacobite support by overtures to the Pretender, had, practically, no connexion with
his foreign policy.

attitude; and though his was not the last instance of a peace Minister
drifting into war, Walpole's sagacity failed him more signally in
1741 if less ignobly, than it had in 1739. Carteret, as Secretary of
State, guided the foreign policy of the new Administration; but it
was only at sea (by forcing Don Carlos at Naples to remain neutral)
that Great Britain interfered effectively in the European conflict.

   The Peace of Breslau (June, 1742), in which both Russia and
Great Britain were included (the former continuing for the present
to hold aloof from the struggle), was "mediated" by Lord Hyndford,
as representing Great Britain. Although in truth there was little to
effect by mediation, the friendly spirit of Carteret's policy had found
occasion for manifesting itself; and, in the same year, an enlarged
subsidy and a large vote in Supply testified to the nation's warlike
enthusiasm, though as yet Great Britain and France, a direct contest
between whom could not be far distant, were only in arms against
each other on behalf, respectively, of the Queen of Hungary and of
the Nymphenburg Alliance against her. At the beginning of 1743,
a brighter prospect seemed opening for the Queen and her British
sympathisers; and Carteret's spirited foreign policy steadily (the
adverb is perhaps ill-chosen) advanced in its course. Prussia was
satisfied, so long as she was left in possession of Silesia. The Tsarina
Elizabeth had entered into an Alliance with Great Britain, though
this was not to extend to any Russian action against Turkey, or to
any British intervention against Spain in Italy, where the House of
Savoy had come to an understanding with that of Austria. Thus, the
time seemed to have arrived at last when the British nation, weary
of a condition of things which was neither peace nor war, might take a
leading part in a struggle which was now a far from hopeless one,
and when King George II might satisfy both his political wishes and
his military impulses by leading into battle a "Pragmatic" army, composed of both Englishmen and Germans, in British as well as (to do
him justice) in Hanoverian pay. In the face of vehement opposition
the vote was carried (December, 1742). The battle of Dettingen was
fought (June, 1743), and, while the Nymphenburg Alliance was
virtually dissolved, the Treaty of Worms (September) united, as the
Allies of Maria Theresa, Great Britain, the United Provinces, Sardinia and Saxony, and promised an annual British subsidy "so long
as the necessity of her affairs should require." But the Treaty was
never ratified, and, though kept secret, confirmed the decision at
which, though against his own wish, George II had arrived, to pass

over Carteret in the choice of a new Prime-minister (August); for
the unpopularity of the Crown and of the Hanoverian interest had
reached its height, and Pitt's thunder already filled the sky. A term
was thus set to a line of policy which was easily held up to scorn as
subservient to Hanoverian ends or motives, but in truth signified a
resumption of the Whig policy in Queen Anne's reign as opposed to
the vague peace policy of Walpole, and exhibited, curiously enough,
points of resemblance to the ideas of Bolingbroke. Yet, as a matter
of fact, Carteret's "system" would not fit in with the existing relations between the European Powers chiefly concerned. On the one
hand, the two principal German Powers were too much absorbed in
their own quarrels to care for a close cooperation with Great Britain;
and her political action was more and more concentrating itself upon
the protection of her own trade, whether lawful or illicit. She was,
in fact, a Maritime Power before everything else, and, as such,
unable to combine with any one other Power in an alliance like the
Family Compact, which France and Spain were (still quite secretly)
renewing on terms of the closest intimacy.

The outbreak of the Second Silesian War (1744–5), in which
George II encouraged Maria Theresa to engage ("*ce qui est bon à
prendre est bon à rendre*"), found Great Britain firm in her support.
Though Henry Pelham, the younger brother of the Duke of Newcastle,
and himself a more timid statesman of Walpole's school, was now at
the Head of the Government, Carteret continued to conduct foreign
affairs till the King was obliged to dismiss him (November, 1744),
when the Earl of Harrington was appointed in his place[1]. Before
this, France, no longer ruled by Fleury, had declared war against
Great Britain, though not till after a vain attempt had been made to
throw an army on her shores, promptly answered by a British blockade of the French and Spanish ships at Toulon. There was no longer
any pacifist opposition in England, while the open outbreak of war
between Great Britain and France seemed once more, as in the greater
days of the past, to promise that the consent of all loyal parties would
enable the Crown to carry out its policy to the full. But the case was
altered. Perhaps, had Maria Theresa's only Ally encouraged her to
persevere, instead of concluding the Peace of Dresden (December,
1745) she might have successfully prolonged her struggle; but public
opinion in England, because it was now less under the influence
of sentiment, had taken a turn less favourable to her cause and was

[1] Carteret (Granville)'s return to office in 1746 lasted only four days.

certainly much preoccupied with the course of events nearer home.

Maria Theresa's prospect of recovering Silesia depended, as a matter of fact, on the continuance of British subsidies; and in the end, she had, therefore, to content herself with the advice of George II —if it was actually proffered—to wait for a better day. In Italy, Austria was, notwithstanding the assistance of a British fleet, unable to establish her claims. But, for Great Britain, the significance of the War, into which a generous impulse had mainly caused her to enter, soon concentrated itself upon what came to be more and more clearly recognised as the beginning of a struggle with France for maritime, Colonial and East Indian supremacy. The ultimate break-down of the last and most formidable Jacobite Insurrection (1745–6) reacted but slightly on the conduct of the War (only in so far as British troops had to be transferred from Flanders). On the other hand, the British capture of Cape Breton, the "Dunkirk of the West" (1745), was a serious blow to France; and found no compensation in the surrender, in the following year, of Madras and its British settlement, which after a long and gallant contest was recovered by the Peace of Aix-la-Chapelle. In 1747, two great British victories—off Cape Finisterre and near the Isle of Aix—placed the superiority of the British navy to the French beyond all doubt; and, in the following winter, peace negotiations began. The previous French attempt, in the Breda Conferences (1746), to cow the United Provinces, who had little stomach for joining in the aggressive policy of Great Britain, had failed; but the consequent French invasion having (notwithstanding the French victory of Lauffeldt) led to no decisive result, the British and Dutch Governments now entered jointly into these negotiations.

In June, 1747, Great Britain had concluded a subsidy Treaty with Russia (who in the previous year had concluded a defensive Treaty with Austria, and whose troops were already on their march), and to this the United Provinces had acceded. With the view, no doubt, of putting a final pressure on France, the two Maritime Powers, at the beginning of 1748, signed a Convention at the Hague, in which Sardinia was included, declaring their alliance with Austria. Yet, by now negotiating for peace, in spite of the martial ardour of George II and the Duke of Cumberland, the British Ministry attested the fact, to which they could no longer shut their eyes, of the uselessness of the War, as undertaken in support of Maria Theresa. The essential condition of the Preliminaries insisted on by Great Britain and the United Provinces was the *status quo ante bellum*—the restitution, in other words, of the conquests made during the War, including the Barrier Towns recently taken by the French, and Madras.

The Peace Conferences of Aix-la-Chapelle began in April, 1748, and, Maestricht having been taken early in their course, were prolonged during the summer. On October 18th, the Peace was signed, its terms being virtually those of the Preliminaries and not more favourable either to Maria Theresa or to her Ally Great Britain than they would have been, had the winding-up of the peace negotiations with France, Spain and their Allies not been delayed, in deference to the personal wishes of George II, till public opinion in England had rendered it imperative. While the House of Austria was now assured of the European recognition of the Pragmatic Sanction, and Prussia (which had kept out of the Treaty, leaving the care of her interests to France) of the guaranteed possession of Silesia, Maria Theresa had, besides losing that Province, made definite cessions in Italy, and had been grievously disappointed by the War in which Great Britain had chivalrously undertaken to support her. Great Britain herself issued forth from the War with little clear gain. But she had well sustained her military repute, and stood before the world as the all but undisputed mistress of the seas. Thus, she had proved equal to staying the revived ambition of France, even when that Power commanded the allegiance of Spain—and had in so far justified the fears of Fleury.

The foreign policy of the Pelham Administration (1744–54) had, up to the conclusion of the Peace of Aix-la-Chapelle, lacked the strength of which the true foundations lie in definite political principle, and not in a "broad bottom" of caution and craft, such as respectively marked the Prime-minister and his brother, the Duke of Newcastle. Neither of them had proved high-spirited enough to withstand the King's tenacious adherence to a policy of war, which Walpole had so long succeeded in restraining; and Chesterfield, the only member of the Government possessed of the required courage, had, in 1745, after the retirement in the previous year of Granville, to whom he was bitterly opposed, been, after a successful diplomatic mission to the Hague, transferred to Ireland.

The Peace concluded at Aix-la-Chapelle had nearly been broken in the following year by the refusal of Spain to carry out a compensation clause for war losses contained in it, and to renew the

Asiento; but Great Britain proved conciliatory, and the trade between the two countries was restored to the conditions which had prevailed in the reign of Charles II of Spain. In other respects, the Peace of Aix-la-Chapelle, far from glorious as it was, had not been concluded too soon for British interests, considering the incompetence of either the Government[1] or the utterly factious Opposition to rise to a policy alike definite and reasonable. The German question seemed to slumber; though Hanoverian influence was at the bottom of the protracted manoeuvres for gaining the votes of the Electors for Archduke Joseph as Roman King[2], and for obtaining grants of subsidies to them with that object from the British Parliament. French diplomacy, on the other hand, was still hampered by the reserve maintained by King Frederick II of Prussia in his relations with France.

The Peace of Europe had now been restored; but the question of its endurance was full of uncertainty. However much the soul of Maria Theresa had been vexed by the behaviour of Great Britain in the Aix-la-Chapelle negotiations, she found it necessary to follow the advice of the majority of her counsellors, and to adhere to the British (and Dutch) Alliance, with the additional security (such as it was) of the Defensive Treaty with Russia of 1746. But, already before the Treaty of Aix-la-Chapelle was actually signed, Kaunitz, the Austrian Plenipotentiary there, had, at a Secret Council held by the Empress, declared his view that the King of Prussia was her most dangerous foe; but that, since the Maritime Powers would no longer come to her aid against him, the only policy left open to her was to invoke the assistance of France. In this counsel we have the germ of the Seven Years' War; but though, so early as 1750, Kaunitz went as Ambassador to Paris, it was not till three years later that he was actually called to the conduct of Austria's foreign policy; and even then no change was as yet made in its system. Thus, the idea of seeking to recover Silesia was not resumed as a practical political purpose till complications between Great Britain and France obliged the former Power to consider her attitude towards what might still be called the German question[3].

Although the most important issues decided at Aix-la-Chapelle

---

[1] Granville, after his return to office as President of the Council in 1751, no longer influenced the course of affairs, foreign or domestic.

[2] The election, however, did not actually take place till after the close of the Seven Years' War.

[3] Cf. A. von Arneth, *Geschichte Maria Theresia's*, vol. IV. (Vienna, 1870).

had been those bearing upon the contention between France and Great Britain for the mastery of a great part of the known world, the settlement on this head reached in the Treaty could not possibly be regarded as definitive. Great Britain had deemed it so important to remove the French garrisons from the Dutch Barrier-fortresses that, by way of compensation, she had allowed the French to recover their possessions in North America—a withdrawal which seemed intolerable to the British Colonists. In the East Indies, the warfare between the Companies continued; while, on the West Coast of Africa and in the Levant, British trade was outstripped by that of its rival. In Russia, while the Baltic trade was chiefly in British hands, in the Black Sea region France consistently kept up intimate relations with her old friend the Turk, and her rivalry was, again, dangerous. In both directions, French diplomacy—never more imaginatively active than at this season of internal decline—sought to provide for the possibilities of the future, keeping the Porte in hand as a check upon European operations of the Eastern Powers, and intriguing with the dominant party in Sweden (the ' Caps ') for a defensive alliance against Great Britain[1]. In Poland, British and French influence were at issue on the burning question of the next Succession to the Throne. In Denmark, French, in Portugal, British influence predominated, and even in the United Provinces, where, after the death of the Stadholder William IV (1751) his widow, the British Princess Anne, carried on the functions of his office on behalf of her son, a French faction asserted itself, which here, of course, was in favour of peace. On the other hand—as if to meet paradox by paradox—in Spain, where internal prosperity was the chief care of King Ferdinand VI and his Minister Carvajal, there was now evident friendliness to Great Britain, partly due to a dispute as to the succession in the Two Sicilies between the Bourbon lines, which had in its turn led to a combination between Spain and Austria.

It was thus inevitable that the conflict of interests between the two Powers which thus divided between them the good- and the ill-will of the rest of Europe should declare itself with peculiar strength in the affairs of the Germanic Empire, where the Sovereign of Great Britain had a legitimate standing as Elector of Hanover, while the intervention of France in them had—for a century past at all events—

---

[1] The British relations with the opposite party, the 'Hats,' were so close that a rumour actually attributed to George II the intention of bringing about the elevation to the Swedish Throne of the Duke of Cumberland.

been a regular element in her political action. Great Britain's subsidies had, as noted, continued, so late as 1752, to flow into the Austrian exchequer, and into the pockets of the Electors to the Roman Kingship, and, though disliked by Pelham, were defended in Parliament by his brother, who, at the close of the previous year, had succeeded in ousting from the other Secretaryship of State the Duke of Bedford and putting in his place the Earl of Holderness, a diplomatist not possessed of the Duke's parliamentary influence.

But it was not in Europe, or in connexion with European disputes, that the rivalry which constitutes the chief political interest of the years following on the Peace of Aix-la-Chapelle most signally declared itself. That Peace had failed sufficiently to define the boundaries between the Colonial dominions of France and Great Britain; more especially, the limits of the Colony of Nova Scotia (Acadia) were disputed, and the frontier between Canada and New England. On the peninsula connecting Nova Scotia with the mainland, both Powers had constructed forts against one another, while Virginia was up in arms to recover a fort on the Ohio captured by the French (1754). The War between the two Governments did not actually break out on this occasion; for neither side was eager for a precipitate rupture. But there were other Colonial quarrels, and it was felt throughout the British dominions that the unbroken maintenance of them along the whole line must be very soon definitively settled. At such seasons, the most competent diplomacy may find itself incapable of doing more than delay for a time or hasten, according as it may suit the purpose of its Government, the first unretraceable step. But Great Britain seems at this time to have been singularly ill-served in the most important quarter. The British Ambassador at Paris, as Lord Stanhope reminds us, was the Earl of Albemarle, whom Chesterfield held up to his son as an encouraging example of how to succeed without a single recommendation except good manners; and his political secrets were carried from his embassy to the French Government. In 1754, the year in which this diplomatist was removed by death, Newcastle succeeded his brother as Prime-minister, and entered upon the last decade of nearly half a century of public service. On his personality satire has, not always quite fairly, exhausted itself; though a consistent time-server, he was also loyal to the dynasty on the Throne, and, while he corrupted others, he, at least, took no thought of personal gains.

In choosing a Leader of the House of Commons, Newcastle had

been virtually reduced to the choice between Henry Fox and William
Pitt, of whom the latter had entered that House in 1735. Since,
however, neither of these politicians would submit to give up that
side of the conduct of affairs which he most prized, Newcastle offered
the Leadership, together with a Secretaryship of State, to Sir Thomas
Robinson, who possessed diplomatic experience without parliamentary ability, and who was welcome to the King because of his familiarity
with German politics. For a time, Pitt (whom the King detested)
and Fox hereupon joined hands against the new Leader and his
master; Robinson retired to the Mastership of the Great Wardrobe,
and Henry Fox, without Pitt, allied himself with Newcastle[1]. But
even this makeshift was not to hold out for long. Already the storms
were lowering, and the nation was looking towards its destined pilot.
When Parliament met at the close of 1754, the King's wishes were
met by an Address from the Commons undertaking to support him
in defending his rights and dominions against all encroachments; a
credit of a million was at once granted; and, had he not, with his
customary want of tact, hereupon immediately set out for Hanover,
this might have proved the season of his greatest popularity since he
had ascended the Throne. On the following day, Admiral Boscawen
sailed for Newfoundland, and soon afterwards came the news of
General Braddock's catastrophe on the Ohio, which was speedily
avenged. The brink of war had been reached[2].

Few wars, as statesmanship knows to its cost, are easily localised;
but the difficulties besetting the process were nothing short of insuperable in the case of the present struggle between Great Britain
and France. Apart from all questions of Treaties and Alliances, the
Netherlands could not but be involved in a struggle with which they
must be brought into contact by both sea and land; and, if so,
Germany could not remain outside it. But there were of course now,
as there have so often been, special considerations which would
implicate severally or collectively the German States in a conflict
between the Western Powers; and who, at the close of the year 1754
could have reckoned otherwise than that in the War now imminent
Prussia would take the side of France, and Austria that of Great
Britain?

And yet, as indicated above, the Austro-British Alliance was,

[1] For these transactions cf. Earl of Ilchester, *Henry Fox* (2 vols. 1920) and the
Earl of Rosebery, *Chatham: His Early Life and Correspondence*, 1910.
[2] As to what follows, cf. Ranke, *Der Ursprung des Siebenjährigen Krieges* (Leipzig,
1871).

notwithstanding, on the eve of dissolution. Apart from lesser grounds
of complaint, which British diplomacy was certainly not disposed to
minimise, a difference of great historical significance seriously disturbed the relations between the United and the Austrian Netherlands. Much importance attached to the view taken of these relations
by Austria, which had grown weary of the conditions on which she
held the Provinces now called by her name, while the British conception of the proper function of the Low Countries in the political
system of Europe necessitated as close as possible a connexion between the Austrian and the United Provinces. Although the British,
which was necessarily also the Dutch, view had prevailed at Aix-la-
Chapelle, the Vienna Government had administered the Austrian
Netherlands as possessing interests of their own and free from the
control of their neighbours, who occupied the Barrier fortresses, and
had actively promoted Belgic prosperity on these lines. When, in
August, 1754, a provisional Treaty was proposed for the adjustment
of these differences, it was rejected through the influence of Kaunitz
against the strenuous efforts of the British Ambassador, Keith. A
grievance of a different description is interesting, inasmuch as it illustrates the part still occasionally played by the old religious disputes in
the philosophical "eighteenth century," and the importance attached
to them by the Hanoverian dynasty, whose tenure of the Throne, after
all, depended primarily upon its Protestantism. In the complicated
quarrel at the Germanic Diet in 1754 as to the guarantee demanded
on behalf of the Hereditary Prince Frederick of Hesse-Cassel (whose
Consort was the British Princess Mary), George II and the King of
Prussia were alike opposed to the House of Austria. But these and
other lesser quarrels apart, Austria would certainly not adhere to
Great Britain, unless the latter would aid in the recovery of Silesia
and could, even as an Ally, be of no assistance to her except by making
war on Prussia, from whom Great Britain, in her turn, had nothing,
and even Hanover, at this time, had not very much, to fear. In other
words, the interests of the two Allied Powers were quite divergent,
and while certainly much British treasure had been spent and not a
little English blood spilt, purely for Austria's sake, Kaunitz might,
on the other hand, speciously argue that the Alliance had only been
carried on by Great Britain so long as it served her own purpose.

Undeniably, the motives for maintaining the Austro-British Alliance had long prevailed, and Great Britain's differences with France
continued to be regarded as the beginnings of a quarrel in which

Austria's own part was marked out for her beforehand; while, should France attack Great Britain by way of Hanover, Austria was doubly bound to contribute to the defence of the Electorate. No exception was taken in England, so late as 1755, either to the Subsidy Treaty with Hesse-Cassel (where there was an easy market for soldiers) or to a Russian Subsidy Treaty, in which the Austrian Government had interested itself. If Austria and Russia remained friendly, there seemed no reason why the present situation should not be prolonged, provided always that, as in the last year of the War of the Austrian Succession, Prussia remained neutral. Great Britain would not suffer, and, so far as the game of Alliances went, France would have gained nothing.

But this calculation was absolutely intolerable to Kaunitz and to his Mistress, who had made up their minds that, after despoiling her monarchy, Prussia must not be suffered to hold by its side the position which she had acquired among the European Powers. Thus, the more surely that the outbreak of war between France and Great Britain announced itself, the more resolute was Kaunitz, in the first instance, to turn the force of the Austro-British Alliance against the "new Power," as he called Prussia, as well as against France.

V

The British Government, for its part, had no intention of reversing the general policy it had pursued up to Aix-la-Chapelle, or, on the other hand, of abandoning the guarantee of the tenure of Silesia by Prussia, in which it had joined. According to the view duly placed before the Austrian Government, the present task of Great Britain was to aid in the defence of the United Provinces and the Hanoverian Electorate; and Kaunitz promised to augment the Austrian forces in the Netherlands and to assume the offensive against Prussia, should her troops march against Hanover. But Great Britain had no reason for apprehending any Prussian attack of the kind upon the Electoral frontier. And, as the words of Holderness (whose intelligence has perhaps been underrated) show, the British Government was beginning to understand, that Kaunitz and the Empress meant to utilise for the recovery of Silesia the Alliance desired by the British Government for the purpose of its contest with France. When it became clear that Great Britain was not disposed to fall in with an extension of her plan of action, and that

Austria would therefore not find her account in joining in such a war, there remained for her only the choice between neutrality (hardly possible, in view of the situation of the Austrian Netherlands) and the radical change of policy long and explicitly recommended by Kaunitz[1]. An alliance with France would be the foundation of the new policy; the cooperation of Russia, and probably of Sweden, Saxony and the Palatinate, might be secured; and the division of the spoils after the overthrow of Prussia was already prospectively planned. France might have to be attracted to the projected alliance by a territorial cession either in Italy or in Flanders (the complicated details of which illustrate the imaginative force of the projector's diplomacy) and by the promise of Austrian support of the candidature of Prince Conti for the Polish Throne[2]. Such was (of course in barest outline) the great design of Kaunitz; and the first move in the game was the audience vouchsafed to the Austrian Ambassador in Paris, Count Starhemberg, with Mme de Pompadour (September, 1755). At the present moment, when France was on the point of entering into an all-important war with Great Britain, there could be no question of the simple rejection, by Lewis XV's Government, of such a proposal on the part of Great Britain's historic Ally—the House of Austria. The only difficulty in the way of its acceptance by the French Government—but this, at first, seemed insuperable—was the improbability of the renunciation, by Frederick II, of the French in favour of a British Alliance; for Austria could not carry on negotiations with France on any basis but that of the severance of her Alliance with Prussia.

It was about this time (summer of 1755) that the American news already referred to arrived in France, where the remainder of the year was mainly consumed in armaments and taxation. An invasion of England was at least talked of; the hopes of the Jacobites simmered up, and the French Government resolved to fight out the struggle against Great Britain by every means in its power. True, it had other support in view; but it continued to think, as it had thought in 1741, friendly relations with Prussia, to whom, in her turn, the French Alliance must be indispensable, the basis of its system. Frederick II, on the contrary, even apart from any secret evidence he might possess on the subject, felt his position insecure, so long as Austria had the support

---

[1] See, for what follows, R. Waddington, *Louis XV, et le Renversement des Alliances* (Paris, 1896).
[2] On this head, the wishes of Lewis XV soon began to cool.

of her present Continental Allies, and so long as France was weakened by the maritime and colonial rivalry of Great Britain, as well as by the unsoundness of her own condition at home. Thus, for Frederick II of Prussia there was during these busy years (1748 to middle of 1755) but one way of staving off war—namely, that of holding himself prepared for it. There seems, however, no reason for concluding that, at any time in this period, he intended either to renew the War with Austria, or to become implicated in that imminent between Great Britain and France. But, as we know, and as the French Government was not slow to point out to Frederick II, this latter War might bring with it a French attack upon Hanover, in which the cooperation of Prussia would be of very direct value to the French. Frederick II, though he kept his own counsel, could not close his eyes to the part, at once difficult and inglorious, which he might thus find himself called upon to play.

British statesmanship, while loth to accept Kaunitz's view that a real concert with Austria required Great Britain to join in an attack upon Prussia, also perceived that Prussia could have no wish, for the sake of her friendship with France, to cooperate in an attack upon Hanover. The situation was critical; and George II's visit to his electoral dominions in the summer of 1755, with Holderness in attendance, accordingly proved the first step towards a change in the relations between Great Britain and Prussia of the utmost importance in its bearing on the impending European War. Taking advantage of the friendly relations between the Prussian Court and Duke Charles of Brunswick-Wolfenbüttel, Holderness contrived to elicit from Frederick II, in reply to the question whether he would refuse to prevent the defence of Hanover against a French invasion, the reply that he saw no objection to treaties concluded by Hanover with her neighbours for this purpose, but that the time had not yet arrived for a declaration on the subject. For some time Frederick II (whose present Defensive Alliance with France would naturally terminate in 1756) would go no further; but he finally made up his mind that, while he had not guaranteed to France her overseas possessions, the relative smallness of his own military forces would not justify him in going to war against an Alliance which might bring the Russians into Germany. Hence, the only course open to him seemed to be to enter into the Treaty of Neutrality as to Hanover suggested to him by Great Britain, without on that account breaking with France.

Thus it came to pass that, in the Treaty of Neutrality concluded between Great Britain and Prussia in January, 1756, and sometimes called the Treaty of Westminster, Frederick II and the British Government, directly instigated this time by the Hanoverian interests of King George II, met halfway. Henry Fox devised the expedient of adding this Prussian Treaty to a Russian (and a Hessian) Subsidy Treaty, which he carried in one of the most famous debates of the age; Pitt, who had accepted the Paymastership of the Forces in the Government, being foremost among the opponents of the proposal. One object of the Anglo-Prussian Treaty was declared to be the preservation of the Peace of the Continent, and that of Germany in especial. Holderness introduced into it a concise guarantee of the Prussian tenure of Silesia; and the Prime-minister, Newcastle, proclaimed King George II's personal anxiety to place himself on an amicable footing with King Frederick II. Henry Fox was, on the following day (November 25th, 1755), appointed Secretary of State, while Pitt was dismissed from office with other opponents of the Russian Subsidy Treaty, which the Prussian Neutrality deprived of its force.

For the "Treaty of Westminster," drafted as proposed by Frederick II, went further than George II, and his Ministers could have at first anticipated. By it, Great Britain agreed not to permit the entry of a Russian army, or Prussia that of a French, into Germany[1]. Even so, the Treaty appears to have been generally approved in England, where it was regarded as preventive of any fear of trouble ensuing on account of Hanover, and the funds are stated to have risen on its conclusion. Whatever the history of its origin, its effect on the Court of Vienna was to leave no doubt that British aid in any attempt to recover Silesia was now altogether out of the question. But could Prussia, after arriving at this friendly understanding with Great Britain, remain on good terms with France? The Duc de Nivernais, sent to Berlin to find out whether French interests were in any way prejudiced by the guarantees contained in the Anglo-Prussian Treaty (from which Gibraltar and Minorca were expressly excepted), made it clear to King Frederick, who had actually thought of patching up the quarrel between France and Great Britain, that this was now impossible. And, in fact, the French Government, while seeking (by way of justification or pretext) to multiply causes

---

[1] This term was substituted by Frederick II for 'The Germanic Empire,' after Podewils had pointed out that the wider term might have been interpreted by Great Britain to comprise the Austrian Netherlands, which the King of Prussia had certainly no wish to see included in it.

of quarrel with Great Britain, declared itself unable to assent to the
principle of a permanent neutrality for Hanover. Thus, at the beginning of 1756, it had, so far as Frederick II's relations with France
and Great Britain were concerned, become more than doubtful
whether he could adhere to the policy, hitherto followed by him, of
remaining on a friendly footing with both Powers. At Vienna, the
Anglo-Prussian Treaty was at first received with tranquillity; for an
Imperial attack in conjunction with France upon Hanover seemed
wholly out of the question, and Russia's only complaint against Great
Britain was that she should have entered into such an agreement without informing her Allies. But so rooted were the jealousy of Prussia
and the suspicion of the advantageous position secured by her, as
between France and Great Britain, entertained by Kaunitz and his
Sovereign, that they resolved on an effective counter-move to the
Neutrality Treaty; and their overtures fell on receptive and well-
prepared ground. France was unwilling, while carrying on a Naval
War with Great Britain, to lay aside what had long been a primary
part of her policy—intervention in the internal affairs of Germany.
The negotiations between the Austrian and French Governments
(represented by Starhemberg and Bernis) at Versailles now (February, 1756) treated the Prusso-French Alliance of 1741 as at an end,
and passed on to the question whether, if France allowed her
Alliance with Prussia to drop altogether, Austria would in turn
consent to drop hers with Great Britain.

Thus the advisers of Lewis XV, Bernis in particular, may be said
to have inspired in him the idea of avenging upon George II his
Treaty of Neutrality with Prussia; while to the arguments by which
Kaunitz persuaded Maria Theresa to put an end to the long-lived
Alliance with Great Britain, was added the hope that the example of
Austria would be followed by Russia. Austria, the Power so long
identified with the guardianship of the Empire, allowed Prussia, of
whose aggressiveness it stood in dread, to assume this time-honoured
function, while, at this very time, itself entering into an Alliance with
France. The Franco-Prussian Alliance was at an end; the relations
between Austria and Russia had, on the other hand, become friendlier,
and though on Bestucheff's advice, the Tsarina Elizabeth had reluctantly agreed to the British Subsidy Treaty of September, 1755, they
were, by April, 1756, shaping towards a closer Alliance. But the effects
of such an Alliance, more especially for Great Britain, must depend on
the decision of France as to her own action. One by one, the obstacles

in the way of the actual conclusion of an Alliance between France, on the one hand, and Austria, with Russia, on the other, disappeared. The French negotiators would have been ready to conclude the business, on the twofold basis that Austria might make war upon Prussia, and France upon Great Britain, as they chose, without calling upon each other for offensive cooperation. But the Austrian Government wanted more than this—viz., the offensive cooperation itself (more especially when there would be no more British subsidies forthcoming), and, in the event of success, a territorial repartition which would avenge the shameless league which, on the death of Maria Theresa's father, had proposed to divide among its members her inheritance.

The Austro-French negotiations were resumed in April, 1756; and, after a Ministerial Council had been held at Versailles, and on the ground chiefly that the Austrian Alliance was the only way by which the King of France could use his right of attacking Great Britain through the Hanoverian Electorate, the Ministry approved the conclusion of that Alliance. The Two Treaties, known as that of Versailles, were hereupon signed, on May 1st, 1756. The first of these consisted of a Convention of Neutrality, whereby the Court of Vienna bound itself to take no part in the War with Great Britain; i.e., the Imperial Power would not be used against a Sovereign who was Prince of the Empire; while France promised not to attack either the Austrian Netherlands or any other part of the Austrian dominions. This, then, was the Austro-French answer to the Anglo-Prussian Treaty of Westminster, which had been the motive cause of the Austro-French negotiations. Its effect would be to let the French into Germany, from which the Westminster Treaty had excluded them, without any resistance on the part of the Head of the Empire. But the first of these Versailles Treaties was not in itself a Treaty of Alliance, and even the second, which purported to be a Treaty of Mutual Defence between the Contracting Powers, declared that it was not directed against any other Power; and the number of troops to be furnished on both sides, if the *casus foederis* should arise, was very moderate accordingly. This second Treaty contained, however, in addition, Secret Articles corresponding more closely to the motives with which the compact had been concluded. If, during the Anglo-French War, France or Austria was attacked by any other Power, the Contracting Power so attacked should be entitled to the support of the other Contracting Power. And, further, a revision of the Treaty of Aix-la-Chapelle was taken into contemplation; so that, though the Treaties by no means amounted to an offensive alliance for the recovery of Silesia or any other purpose, they contained this ominous reference to the more remote future. The Treaties, more especially since Russia would assuredly be invited to adhere to them, could not but be looked upon without apprehension in England, though they by no means implied an offensive alliance against this country; and there can be no doubt but that the religious, or confessional, aspect of the combination exercised its effect now, as it did when Great Britain had made her choice, and when a large part of her population regarded Frederick the Great as "the Protestant Hero."

It was not till May, 1756, that Maria Theresa, in giving audience to Sir Robert Keith, the British Minister at Vienna, who had been instructed to demand explanations of the Versailles Treaty or Treaties, threw the blame of her Alliance with France upon the combination between Great Britain and Prussia—her only enemy in the world, as the Empress afterwards confidentially told him, besides the Turk. Undoubtedly, this attitude on the part of the Empress Maria Theresa, formerly the subject of so much admiring sympathy in England, taken together with the ratification which speedily followed of the Versailles Treaties (the drift of whose Secret Clauses was sufficiently suspected), roused deep indignation against a Power, now the Ally, under whatever conditions, of our mortal foe—after, for the sake of that Power, we had shown so much forbearance at Aix-la-Chapelle, and when it had been the recipient of a long series of our Subsidies. Popular feeling in England had, throughout the winter 1755-6, been in so excited a state as to take the almost inevitable form of a conviction that we had been betrayed. Apprehensions had actually arisen of a French invasion; and when, at last, in the spring of 1756, the immediate designs of France had declared themselves, Newcastle's Government had been found ill-informed. Byng had failed to protect Minorca, and, though Newcastle, after sailing with the blast of popular fury against the Admiral was by a change of Ministry to escape from the responsibility of carrying out the sentence against him, this very change had shown that a vigorous foreign policy was now imperatively demanded. On May 18th, 1756, Great Britain declared War against France. Before the end of June, Port Mahon surrendered, a few weeks before Frederick II began his War against Austria by crossing the Saxon frontier (August).

Thus, Great Britain had been driven into open hostilities with France at a time when her ancient Ally, Austria, had entered into relations of mutual amity with that Power, and when an estrangement of her from Great Britain inevitably followed. There remained the question whether this estrangement necessarily implied a corresponding change of relations between Great Britain and Russia. Such had not been the design of the Tsarina Elizabeth. The negotiations concerning the still-born Russian Subsidy Treaty had not been allowed to drop; and the brilliant British Ambassador at Petrograd, Sir Charles Hanbury Williams, who had consistently promoted (in every way) the Russian Subsidy Treaty and the Austrian Alliance, and of whose diplomatic career this humiliating episode was to be the end, had been kept in the dark as to the transactions in progress between Austria, Russia and France. The Russian intentions at this time are surrounded by some obscurity; but it must be remembered that the Franco-Austrian negotiations had not come to an end with the Versailles Treaties. While Kaunitz and Starhemberg hoped for the support of France in the reconquest of Silesia, it was to be recompensed by the transfer to France of the Austrian Netherlands, or the main part of them, including, in view of the struggle between France and Great Britain, at least the temporary occupation of Ostend and Nieuport. The Naval War between the two Powers was already in progress, and at no time could an opportunity of establishing her ascendancy in Flanders have been more welcome to France than at present. The French "ideas" for a "new Europe" suggested in 1756 did not stop short with this. As for the North, Bremen and Verden might be cut out of Hanover for the benefit of Denmark; and, as for the Mediterranean, Gibraltar might be taken from Great Britain, as Minorca had been; and she might be confined to the possessions of her own chalk-cliffs, just as Prussia would again be reduced to the dimensions of a meagre Brandenburg Electorate.

But it was not till May, 1757, that the spirit of these notions was compressed within the limits of a Secret Treaty; and, on the part of Russia, upon whose military cooperation the execution of much of the airy design depended, the Tsarina Elizabeth and Bestucheff were at this time unprepared with the armaments which their share in the process would have required. At Potsdam, on the other hand, Frederick II reckoned with realities; and he had by his side the British Envoy, Sir Andrew Mitchell, a Scotsman so full of commonsense as to be without any trace of Jacobitism, and yet endowed with a power of sympathy which on occasion induced the King to reveal his inmost feelings to him[1]. Frederick II had, from the first, suspected that at the bottom of the Versailles Treaties lay the thought of an attack on Hanover; but of this, he considered, neither Great Britain nor Prussia need be afraid if they were united and prepared. For this end he was ready to make any sacrifice. But when reports reached him of a triple alliance between France, Austria and Russia, when they were corroborated by further intelligence derived by him partly from stolen papers in the Austrian and Saxon Chanceries[2], partly from other communications to himself and Mitchell, and when Austrian troops began to be massed in Bohemia and Moravia, he began to recognise that he was sure of no Alliance but the British, whether or not the British Government still succeeded in avoiding a quarrel with Russia[3]. He, therefore, resolved to explode the combination against him before it was ripe for action, arguing to himself that, besides France and Austria, Russia might, in a year's time, be prepared to draw the sword. Sir Andrew Mitchell, anxious that Frederick II should do nothing to affront British public opinion, professed himself contented with Maria Theresa's assurance that the interests of the other Power—Great Britain being of course the only Power in question—would not suffer from the measures which she had commanded. Frederick II, on the other hand, after his question, whether Austria would promise not to attack him in the current or following year, had remained without a reply from Vienna, started at the head of his troops (August 28th) from Potsdam for the Saxon frontier.

The Seven Years' War (1756–63) which had now opened in Old World and New, was essentially a double war, the two parts or sides of which had each a different origin and were fought (as the combatants recognised) with distinct objects. Yet the successes of their Ally, in the face of difficulties altogether unprecedented, came home so closely to the British nation, that to popular feeling here this War seemed throughout a single War, and that, while our own flag waved victorious over every sea, and our arms prospered in Asia as well as in America, the glory of the conflict seemed a glory earned in common. On whomsoever may rest the responsibility of its actual opening, the

---

[1] Cf. Carlyle's *Frederick the Great*, Bk XVIII. c. 5.

[2] These are the so-called "Menzel Documents" which began so far back as 1753.

[3] Saxony-Poland, it seems necessary to add, had so far, notwithstanding French overtures, adhered to its neutral attitude.

Seven Years' War as a whole may be regarded as an endeavour, on
the part of France, to arrest, and if possible put an end to, the growing maritime and colonial ascendancy of Great Britain, and, on the
part of Austria, to deprive Frederick II of the prize which, at the end
of the previous two Silesian Wars, she had been obliged to leave in
his hands. The diplomacy of Kaunitz had succeeded in blending
these two purposes into one. This purpose was compassed before
long; but the interests for which France contended beyond the seas
were not thereby rendered identical with those for which her armies
fought in Germany. Thus it came to pass, that the year (1759), which
may be regarded as the climax of Austria's attempt to lay low the
power and the ambition of Frederick II, was also that in which
Great Britain gained her most momentous success over the French
in Canada. And, when the Seven Years' War came to an end—in
Great Britain's case by a Peace thoroughly unpopular at home and,
in that of her solitary Ally, as a gift of good fortune as well as the
reward of heroic perseverance—the cup of national glory was full in
each case, and the names of Frederick the Great and the elder Pitt
were linked together for ever as emblematic of victory.

We are here only concerned with the policy which directed the
action of Great Britain in the successive stages of the conflict. The
gradual unfolding of the prospect of a great European War, and the
general want of confidence, deepened by the course of the miserable
Byng episode, in the competence of the Newcastle Government
proved fatal to it. Newcastle's success in securing Henry Fox as
Secretary of State was as ineffectual as it was transitory, and a
series of overtures and manoeuvres ended in his being left without
a supporter fit to cope with the opposition of Pitt, while the Duke
still retained power—or a share of power—himself. The ensuing
attempt at a combination between Fox and Pitt, having, thereupon,
broken down, the Duke of Devonshire formed his Administration
(December, 1756 to April, 1757), of which Pitt, at the King's personal request, formed part as one of the Secretaries of State[1]. Newcastle's influence being still predominant, and the King dissatisfied
at having had to include Pitt, whose personal following was limited to
the Grenvilles, the Ministry was not so strong as it might have been.

But a new spirit had begun to reign and to animate the foreign
and colonial policy, which under Pitt were from the first blended.

---

[1] Pitt's tenure of the Southern, and Holderness's of the Northern Department,
were reversed in June, 1757.

And after the King, who had in vain negotiated on his own account for the assistance of other German Princes in maintaining the neutrality of his Electorate, had spent all his Hanoverian income on behalf of its defence, a bolder course was taken. While, with the aid of Mitchell, Frederick concluded a Treaty with Brunswick and other smaller States for the defence of northern Germany, Pitt proposed a substantial Parliamentary grant for the defence of Hanover, and early in 1757 the Duke of Cumberland was appointed to the command of the British troops sent out to take part in the operations. Thus the defence of Hanover had by a strange fortune become the corner-stone of Pitt's policy in the European part of the War. Yet, even at the last, it was not without great difficulty that George II had been persuaded by Frederick II's Envoy Schmettau to abandon the neutrality of Hanover. Before Pitt's hand was laid on the helm, there had been some hesitation and some ill-success—the latter in the operations to prevent the French seizure of Corsica and in the fighting in Canada in the region of the Great Lakes; while the dismal tidings from India (the massacre of the Black Hole) were soon overtaken by the news of Clive's great victory of Plassey (June, 1757).

By the beginning of this year the cards were at last all on the table. The French Government was so much impressed by the determined action of the British Government as to signify, by way of the Hague, its willingness to conclude peace on terms proposed. The answer (February 8th), made at a time when affairs in Canada were in a doubtful position, was worthy of Great Britain, and sufficiently verified Frederick's saying that she had at last found a man. Great Britain, the King was assured, would never assent to terms of peace in which he was not included. The overture was evanescent, and the war proceeded, on the British side with unprecedented vigour, after the personal intrigue directed by Newcastle against the control of foreign affairs by Pitt had brought about an interregnum which was almost an anarchy, and after, early in July, 1757, Pitt had formed what is rightly called his First Ministry. It was, in a word, the most powerful Administration the country had, or has, ever known. Parliamentary opposition was at a standstill; and when, little more than four years later, Pitt went out of office it was as if the glory of Great Britain, of which he had consummated the reestablishment, departed with him.

The unexampled popularity enjoyed by Pitt from the time onwards in which the conduct of the country's affairs, foreign, colonial and commercial, blended together, at last came under his immediate control, cannot be analysed in a few sentences. That popularity itself was the cause as well as a consequence of the consummation not prepared in a day. So far back as 1736, *The Craftsman* had commented on his close study of foreign affairs; and though he had to cast to the winds much on which he had insisted during his long years of Opposition, partly (as he afterwards confessed) for Opposition's sake, partly from ignorance, he had come into power with a mind made up, an initial plan formed, and a knowledge of British as well as foreign commercial conditions accumulated and well arranged in his mind. His wonderful power, not only of influencing others as an orator, but inspiring the agents of his policy to end in action, did the rest, in the days of his personal supremacy—for no word short of this would be appropriate. He had at his command the devoted services on which his conduct of British foreign policy depended—the Foreign Office and its agents, diplomatic and consular, who suddenly found their instructions clear and precise, instead of being left like servants in doubt as to the intention of their masters, the Admiralty and the Board of Trade. The City was devoted to him throughout almost the whole of his career. The American Colonists regarded him as one of the few British statesmen who understood colonial affairs[1], although it is only just to the memory of the Duke of Bedford, whose qualities as a statesman deserve higher recognition than they have always received, to remember that a memorial of his to Newcastle, a decade before Pitt fully described his American policy, foreshadowed it in its comprehensiveness.

During the Ministerial interregnum which, in the spring of 1757, had preceded Pitt's assumption of full power, Frederick II had sent to him assurances of his unchanged regard; but the British Government had not ventured to press on George II, who had still hoped to

---

[1] See the admirable summary in Miss Kate Hotblack's *Chatham's Colonial Policy* (Routledge and Sons, 1917) which treats the several parts of the subject with a rare combination of fulness and point. Of particular value in the present connexion is her demonstration of the economic implications of Pitt's foreign policy—and of his efforts, from this point of view, to frustrate the union of France and Spain, to strengthen the Portuguese Alliance, to stir up Italian distrust of France, and even to induce the Porte to embarrass Austria by an attack upon Hungary. His continuous purpose was that of enabling Great Britain, without self-exhaustion, to outlast France; his conquests beyond sea were designed to pay for the War; and the union of the great variety of measures which he crowded into action—from the Senegal expedition of 1757 onwards—was essential to the total of success. His carefully managed dealings with the Barbary States (from 1757) were of high importance for the British Mediterranean trade as well as for his Spanish policy.

play a mediating part between the two chief German Powers, the plan of Frederick II, against whom Imperial Execution had been declared by the Diet, for uniting the dissenting Estates in resistance against it. Of much greater importance for the progress of the War was the question of an active Alliance between Russia and Austria, which after some delay (owing to differences of opinion at Petrograd and the suggestion, rejected as insufficient, of the exclusion of British trade from Russian ports) was actually concluded (January, 1757). By it, the two Empresses bound themselves not to lay down arms till Silesia and Glatz should have been restored to Maria Theresa. In March, a Franco-Swedish Alliance against Prussia followed, and in the same month the French troops crossed the German frontier. The British Government, under the influence of the wishes of King George II, was still haggling about Hanoverian neutrality with the Austrian, when, in May, the Secret Treaty of Alliance between France and Austria—the Partition Treaty of Versailles—was signed, the final hesitation of King Lewis XV having been overcome by his being shown a forged Treaty of Alliance between Great Britain and Prussia. The Franco-Austrian compact, while providing for Austria's recovery of Silesia and for the transfer to Duke Philip of Parma of the whole of the Austrian Netherlands, except Ostend, Nieuport and Mons, ceded to France, further promised the Empress's cooperation in securing Minorca to that Power[1]. The accession to the Treaty of Russia and other Powers was to be asked in due course.

The House of Austria, which in this Treaty had in fact gained all it desired, had by it completely detached itself from the time-honoured Alliance of Great Britain, but had neither undertaken to enter into any active operations against her, nor precluded a reconciliation with her at some future date. The contents of this Secret Compact remained for some time unknown. But, inasmuch as its designs, when they came to light, showed that they affected the future of nearly the whole of Europe (it is noteworthy that the Treaty itself contained no mention of the Ottoman Power), and inasmuch as there existed between the Contracting Powers no international bond of union unless the Roman Catholic religion be regarded as such, the War which it converted into a European War was surrounded with that general uncertainty which challenges the use of all the resources of statesmanship. And it was in the face of a Europe engaged or involved in such a War as this

[1] As already noted, the Utrecht stipulations as to Dunkirk now came to an end.

that Great Britain and France carried on, through its most momentous stage, their own struggle for empire beyond seas.

Two months before the formation of Pitt's first Ministry Frederick the Great's dearly bought victory at Prague had not failed to exercise its effects in England, and George II had met the attempts of the Austrian Ambassador still resident at his Court (Colloredo) with contemptuous rudeness. The Austrian victory of Kolin (June 8th, 1757) had been followed by a French invasion of Germany and a successful conflict with a British army; Russia and Sweden had followed suit. But, by this time, all hesitation was at an end in the counsels of Great Britain, though the season had advanced too far for any material effect to be exercised by British intervention on the progress of the Continental War. Great Britain had no ships to spare for the protection of the Prussian coasts against Russia and Sweden; and the States-General had, after the shedding of some tears by the Regent, the British Princess Anne, allowed the transit by way of Maestricht of French troops, who, besides garrisoning Ostend and Nieuport, occupied the chief towns of Westphalia. The Duke of Cumberland arrived in time to be defeated, though not decisively, at Hastenbeck and to sign the notorious Convention of Kloster-Zeven (September) which was, in reality, a capitulation. Even now, George II would have gladly concluded a Treaty of Neutrality for Hanover with France and Austria, and confidence was rising at Vienna and Versailles; but Pitt, who had his own plans for British cooperation in the Continental War, would not hear of the acceptance of the Convention. The ultimate refusal of George II to ratify it, accordingly, signified the final and complete adoption by the British Government of the policy of active cooperation with Prussia, instead of attempting to carry out a Hanoverian, side by side with its own (British), policy. Before the year 1757 was over, the most brilliant of Frederick's victories, Rossbach (November), sealed the compact of mutual confidence and relegated into political oblivion the Capitulation of Kloster-Zeven. The Duke of Cumberland was superseded in his military command by Prince Ferdinand of Brunswick; the Hanoverian army was taken into British pay; and success crowned the recasting, as it might almost be called, of the lines of the Personal Union[1].

---

[1] Not, however, so as to cause this aspect of it to be recognised in the Peace which ended Great Britain's participation in the War, and which, while abandoning Frederick II, ignored Hanover.

In December, 1757, there followed Frederick II's second great victory gained in this wonderful year of military history—the battle of Leuthen. The moral, as well as the financial, support of Great Britain had been of high value to the victor, and the question now became: in what measure was his Ally prepared to help him to carry the Continental War to the successful end which his military genius had made possible. For the British enterprises of the latter part of the year had by no means proved successful; the Rochefort expedition had been a costly failure; and in America and elsewhere the British Navy had not asserted its superiority over the French. But the great battles won by Frederick, with the news of our victorious progress in India, enabled the high spirit of Pitt to carry Parliament with him in his forward policy, and he was sanguine enough to conceive, and to embody in a famous despatch composed at this time (end of 1757), the idea of an alliance with Spain, which should subsequently be extended to Naples and Sardinia. Gibraltar was once more to be the price paid. But the scheme was as inopportune as it was unsound, and the goodwill towards it of the Spanish Minister, Wall, proved a broken reed.

Yet, when Parliament met in the last month of 1757, the German news had, together with the Indian, raised popular enthusiasm to the highest pitch in favour of the War and Pitt, though neither of the early policy of Clive, nor of the victory which crowned it in Bengal, can the credit be claimed for the British statesman. In 1758-9, however, his plans against France were in organic cooperation with the action of the East India Company, though his design upon Mauritius was diverted. (The capture of Manilla was not carried out till after his resignation.) Nor should it be overlooked that the material prosperity of Great Britain had not suffered from her warlike exertions and preparations; her credit stood high, and British trade, the interests of which were from the first at the bottom of Pitt's foreign policy, prospered under his care. The British fleet were masters of the Mediterranean, French trade with the Levant was checked, and Dutch trade in the West Indies, at the risk of a serious collision with the States-General, was subjected to a strict application of the right of search[1]. Pitt's vigilance was unsleeping; nor could any notion be

[1] The difficulties as to the Dutch trade with the French West Indies by way of the Dutch West Indian Islands gave rise to a prolonged dispute, which really defied settlement, so long as there was no agreement as to the principles of international maritime law. There were similar disputes with the Danish Government, which, however, was less pertinacious. (Sweden's attitude towards Great Britain was hostile.)

more futile than that of his eloquence having been his main contribution to the progress of the War.

For the campaign of 1758 Pitt was ready to furnish Frederick II with the promised subsidies; and the demand for military and naval support, pressed by him after the Russians had occupied Königsberg, was (after acrimonious discussion with Fox) met by the Subsidy Treaty and the accompanying Declaration (April), which made the aid of troops and ships conditional upon the requirements of British action in America. This carefully drawn 'Declaration of London' is of the highest importance as marking the progress of the Anglo-Prussian Alliance from its first to its second stage; but it shows, at the same time, beyond what length Pitt was unprepared to go, well aware as he was of the outcry to be eventually expected against the employment of men and ships needed for home and colonial defence on the expulsion of the French from Hanover and the sweeping the Baltic clear of Russian vessels. This latter service, therefore, except in the interests of both the Allies, the Declaration expressly declined on the part of Great Britain.

The year 1758, marked by British successes beyond the seas (the reduction of Cape Breton and the capture of Duquesne, now renamed Pittsburg), brought no decisive results to Frederick II; for the occupation of Prussian provinces by his adversaries was, in a manner, balanced by his continued tenure of Saxony. The presence and successes of the Hanoverian army under Ferdinand of Brunswick, however, freed him from the obligation of keeping watch and ward against the French and their German mercenaries, and materially contributed to strengthen the Alliance. The Austrian Netherlands were in serious danger; and, if the British Government had chosen to support Prince Ferdinand by a naval descent upon the Belgian coast, a momentous effect might have been exercised upon the progress of the War. But the resources at hand were expended upon two of those lesser expeditions (St Malo and Cherbourg), which must be reckoned among the mistakes in Pitt's conduct of the War. On the other hand—for his sway was absolute in all directions, both before and after he and Holderness exchanged Departments—his Russian policy at this time aimed at inducing the Tsarina Elizabeth, whose forces had occupied the Prussian North-East, to conclude peace with Frederick II; and the instructions of Sir Robert Keith (who remained British Ambassador at Petrograd till the crisis of 1762) were so intended. But, though he had consulted King Frederick, he found the political situation unmanageable. He had, therefore, to turn to the secondary purpose of his mission, the conclusion of a Commercial Treaty with Russia, whose trade had suffered grievously from British privateers, and who in her turn was suspected of designs in which she would command the support of Sweden and Denmark (with both of whom France had signed Subsidy Treaties) and might thus ultimately acquire the control of the navigation of the Baltic. It was not till after much manoeuvring, nor until after the accession of Catharine II, that the Commercial Treaty was signed. But between Sweden and Great Britain a rupture of diplomatic relations had taken place in 1758 (March), and it was only the prudence of Pitt which, in this instance, avoided serious complications for British policy.

Thus, in 1758, while on the whole the British arms had made progress both in Canada and in Bengal, the course of the campaigns in Germany had (notwithstanding Hochkirch) been such as to afford a kind of negative encouragement to Frederick II, and to raise serious doubts in influential quarters in France—even in Cardinal de Bernis, formerly one of the chief promoters of the Austrian Alliance—as to the expediency of seeking peace. But the hesitation was overcome; the Tsarina Elizabeth stood firm by the Partition Treaty; after making some pacific overtures to Great Britain through Denmark, Bernis was banished (December), and in the last days of the year a new Treaty was concluded between Austria and France. This compact upheld the promise of France as to the recovery of Silesia, and made the conclusion of a French Peace with Great Britain conditional on regard for Austrian interests; but it otherwise considerably diminished her obligations under the Partition Treaty of 1757, to which a Secret Agreement now put an end. This "diplomatic masterpiece" of Choiseul—for he was now in entire control of the foreign policy of France—amounted to no very considerable improvement of the position to which that Power had been reduced by Madame de Pompadour's friends; and it left unchanged the essence of the situation. In other words, the Austro-French Alliance continued, while, so long as Pitt was in power, there was no fear of the bond between Great Britain and Prussia being broken. On the contrary: though Frederick II could not but long for as early as possible a peace through victory, Pitt, as the triumph of British arms by land and sea assumed wider dimensions, perceived that fullest advantage must be taken of the opportunity for utterly overthrowing the naval and colonial power of France; and George II was, after his wont, speculating on an enlargement of his Electorate in the direction of Westphalia. But, for the present, a new Subsidy Treaty passed the House of Commons (December), Pitt taking occasion to defy the Austrians, as if they were treacherous conspirators against the honour of the British nation.

The year which followed (1759) splendidly vindicated his confidence. For it was the year of the capture of Quebec—a heroic memory—though it was not till the following year (1760) that, by the capitulation of Montreal, the whole of Canada fell into British hands, and the possessions of France in America were reduced to Louisiana alone. The fall of Quebec was only one of a long series of British victories at a stage in the War intended by Choiseul to have been marked by the invasion of England—in lieu of which the French coasts were subjected to a complete blockade. Later in the year (November), Hawke's great exploit at Quiberon Bay followed; and, after this victory, Pitt's foresight in ignoring the hopes placed by France on the cooperation of the Italian States was justified, and the gallant Thurot's invasion of Ireland ended in death and disaster (February, 1760). So far as Great Britain was concerned, the main result of the War, the establishment of her naval supremacy, had been already achieved, though part of Pitt's American design was in his eyes still unaccomplished, so long as the fishing monopoly which he wished to establish for Great Britain in the Gulf of Newfoundland was not in her possession.

Meanwhile, the year 1759 had seemed to bring Great Britain's Ally to the verge of ruin; his resources were all but reduced to his requisitions in Saxony and some petty Saxon States, and to the British subsidies. The moral advantage of Great Britain's maritime and American successes contributed to sustain him in resisting what seemed his doom; and Prince Ferdinand of Brunswick, though the effects of his victory of Minden (August) fell short of what they should have been, much more than held his own against the Western foe. It is not surprising that the vicissitudes of the German campaigns in this year should have overshadowed other aspects in the history of the Alliance; but the projects, independently conceived by both Frederick II and Pitt, directed to the permanent exclusion of Austrian dominion and influence from Italy, should not be overlooked. The death of Ferdinand VI had brought to the Spanish Throne his brother Charles III, whose goodwill was of so much importance that France and Austria were alike willing to promote a drastic revision in his favour (or in that of his third son, Ferdinand) of the settlement of Italy agreed upon at Aix-la-Chapelle. The House of Savoy (with its wonted vigilance) declined to fall in with the arrangement; and this suggested to Pitt a scheme which should at the same time satisfy that House and the Spanish dynasty, and involve Austria in a war on behalf of her Italian interests. While the Spanish infante Don Philip of Parma was to be indemnified by Tuscany, Charles Emmanuel of Sardinia was to acquire Milan, and the North-Italian duchies, with the title of King of Lombardy[1]. But Charles III, who (not inexplicably) hated Great Britain in his heart, had no intention of allying himself with her and entering into a war, of which the chief Italian gain would accrue to his Sardinian rival, whose desire for territory equalled his own. He was secretly longing for the day when, by the side of Great Britain's present chief adversary, he might take revenge upon her and her dictatorial policy towards his monarchy and himself. The British proposals were refused at Naples, where, according to the Treaty of Aix-la-Chapelle, Philip of Parma was to have succeeded Charles III on his mounting the Spanish Throne; and, when subsequently repeated by Frederick II, they met with a similar rebuff. But the new King of Spain thought it well at present to conceal his enmity to Great Britain, although he made no secret of it to the French Government, whose plans of an invasion of England in this year (1759) he warmly approved. He was, indeed, intending to proceed to his new Throne at Madrid by way of France, in response to an invitation from Lewis XV, and with a view to confirming or renewing the Bourbon Family Compact[2], when he was restrained, partly by the fear of offending Spanish pride, partly by the tidings of recent brilliant successes. At Madrid, he found feeling very strong against Great Britain, more especially on account of offences against Spanish neutrality imputed to British vessels. The Spanish Government, which, at the close of 1759, had offered its mediation between Great Britain and France, in the following year sent a memorial to London reciting all the Spanish grievances. Pitt received it with surprise, as he had the offer made by Don Ricardo Wall with indignation—for he was well aware of the real aim of Spanish policy. He had, before this, judiciously declined the suggestion of Frederick II, that the former Jacobite Earl Marischal, now Prussian Ambassador at Madrid, should proffer his mediatory services.

On the other hand, Great Britain and Prussia had agreed, towards

---

[1] See R. Waddington, *La Guerre de Sept Ans*, vol. III. p. 451.

[2] This was effected in August, 1761, when the most important of the three agreements known under the name of the Family Compact was signed at Paris.

the end of 1759, on the expediency of proposing to the Powers at war with them the assembling, in regular form, of a Peace Congress. This they did by handing to the Envoy of these Powers at the Hague through Duke Lewis Ernest of Brunswick-Bevern (guardian of the Hereditary Stadholder William V), the so-called Declaration of Ryswyk (November). But it remained ineffective, and was in truth designed to conciliate public opinion in England by taking advantage of the popular craving for peace in France, which Choiseul, like Bernis before him, could no longer gainsay, and which (March, 1760) actually induced him to carry on at the Hague secret negotiations with the British Government for a separate peace. But, while France was negotiating without her Allies—Austria having declared it necessary to arrive, in the first instance, at an understanding with Russia, and the Tsarina Elizabeth having sent a point-blank refusal to discuss the subject—Great Britain, from the first, loyally declared that her Ally should be apprised of every step in the negotiation. And Pitt held to his promise, while Frederick II, also, kept himself informed through a secret channel—no other than his friend Voltaire—and then directly through a Prussian agent, and, in the stress under which he was placed, showed himself not averse from the proposal of a separate peace between France and Great Britain. But Pitt judged more correctly (as his Ally was afterwards fain to acknowledge) and insisted on the inclusion of Prussia in the peace as indispensable. The negotiations, hereupon, broke down, and (April, 1760) the three Allies, once more united, presented to the Regent of the United Provinces the "Counter-declaration of Ryswyk," which, while stating that the King of France was prepared to negotiate with the King of Great Britain through the King of Spain, accepted a Congress on Peace with Prussia only on condition of the admission of the representatives of the other Powers at war with her (Poland and Sweden). All hopes of peace were now at an end; and the proverbial tenacity of the House of Habsburg had succeeded in keeping its Allies under arms together.

But, though Austria had thus been enabled to resume the design, with which she had entered into the War, of crushing her archfoe, and though bankrupt France had to continue her twofold struggle, Russia's adhesion to her Allies, albeit assured, for the period of her reign, by the Tsarina's determination, was not accorded without promises of future gains in the event of common victory. In March, 1760, these were secured to her by the so-called Schouvaloff Treaties with Austria (ratified in July), which, while signifying Russia's accession to the Versailles Treaty between Austria and France of December, 1758, in a Secret Article laid down the obligations undertaken by the two Powers for their respective satisfaction at the end of the War. In the event of Austria's recovery of Silesia—but not otherwise—Austria bound herself to secure the acquisition by Russia of "Prussia," *i.e.* Ducal Prussia, with the addition of Danzig; Poland, helpless as usual, notwithstanding the friendship of France, being compensated by some lesser cessions. When it is remembered that in the previous year (March, 1759) Russia had concluded a Treaty with Sweden for the effective maintenance, for trade purposes, of Baltic neutrality, and that Denmark was obliged to adhere to this agreement in the following year, it will be seen how, in the event of a victorious issue of the War, the power of Russia would have been rendered irresistible in the Baltic.

It was against an Alliance thus extended in its aims as well as strengthened in its cohesion·that Pitt and Great Britain prepared to take part in the progress of the struggle, when it reopened in the spring of 1760. Pitt's Government, in order not to interfere with the British trade in the Baltic, declined to send a fleet into those waters, where it would have been welcomed by the Danes; so that the Russians and Swedes had their hands free for operating there against Prussia, while her Allied enemies could, with the exception of France, address themselves with renewed energy to the German War. Maria Theresa had made up her mind to carry it to a decisive issue. But there were differences of plan between Austria and Russia; and in the end Laudon had to raise the siege of Breslau (August) though the Russians for a few days (October) occupied Berlin. The confidence of Maria Theresa was severely shaken by the Austrian defeat (at first reported a victory) at Torgau (November); and, while Frederick II remained in his headquarters at Dresden, no important result had been reached by his adversaries' campaign against him in eastern and central Germany. In the west, Prince Ferdinand had, partly in consequence of the numerical inferiority of his forces, been unable to deal any effective blow; but, at least from the British point of view, he had not carried on the fight in vain, having kept the French forces out of Hanover and done his best to exhaust the resources of the enemy. Thus, Great Britain was the better able to continue her efforts against the same foe beyond sea, where the French siege of Quebec was raised and Montreal capitulated.

The indecisive character of the German campaigns of 1760, and the extensive losses of the French Power in the East Indies and the New World, rendered Choiseul anxious to bring about negotiations in the direction of peace with the Prussian and British Governments. But, afraid of challenging Austrian (and Jesuit) influences at Court, he once more had resort to King Charles III of Spain. The latter at this time gave much of his confidence to Marquis Grimaldi, who had convinced himself that, instead of continuing to mix herself up in the German War, France ought, in close alliance with Spain, to apply all her energies to the War with Great Britain. Spain, of whose grievances mention has been already made, actually began to arm, and a diplomatic contention followed between the Spanish Ambassador at the Court of St James' and Pitt. Though France still hesitated about changing her policy and concluding peace with Prussia, it seemed as if the year 1760 was not to end without the outbreak of hostilities between Spain and Great Britain. But the death of the bellicose Spanish Queen (Maria Amalia) and, far more signally, a month afterwards, that of King George II of Great Britain, led to a change—the latter event to an all-important one—in the situation.

King George II died—on October 27th, 1760—as the Ally of a Prince whom he detested almost more than any other, and counselled by a Minister from whom he shrank with unconquerable aversion. But it was the nation which had sustained Walpole so long as its mind was bent on peace; and the nation, not King George II, had brought Pitt into favour and kept him there, so long as its mind was set on war. The change in the system of government which began with the accession of George III was, in the first instance, fatal to the complete ascendancy of Pitt, and could not but become so to the continuation of the foreign policy with which he was identified. At the very time when the War was extending itself towards the participation in it of Spain, Pitt was on the eve of having to resign power into the hands of a royal favourite, who was prepared to conclude a peace short of the measure of aggrandisement which Great Britain had actually achieved, and which would have satisfied the nation. On the very first day of his reign, George III proposed to appoint Bute one of the Secretaries of State, though it was not till six months afterwards that, Holderness having made way for the favourite, the offer was reluctantly accepted by him. (Bute had been at once admitted by the new Sovereign into the Privy Council.) On opening his first Parliament (November 2nd) George III announced his intention of steadily pressing on the victorious War, and Frederick II was so sure of the *bona fides* of the British Government, so long as Pitt was at its head, that he even declared his readiness to acquiesce in a separate peace between Great Britain and France, provided that limits were set to French assistance to Austria. Moreover, he remained in control of the greater part of the army of Prince Ferdinand. Thus, the proposed revision of the Anglo-Prussian Treaty of Alliance came to nothing, and the old Subsidy Treaty was renewed. But some of Pitt's followers, as well as "the King's Friends," were inclining to the view that the War had accomplished enough; and Bute's acceptance of the Secretary-ship, with certain other Governmental changes, no doubt weakened Pitt's position. He was ready to make peace with France, though he still pressed on British conquests in order to command what were, in his judgment, reasonable terms, and, being aware of the intimate relations between France and Spain, he was anxious to take advantage of Choiseul's increased anxiety to conclude a tolerable peace. Influenced, among other pacific symptoms, by the Swedish popular dislike of the War, Choiseul pressed his views in favour of peace on Maria Theresa, who for the first time in the course of the War, showed signs of discouragement; but Kaunitz and Russian influence prevailed, and his notion of a Congress was in the end accepted by Choiseul, in lieu of the plan of a separate negotiation between France and Great Britain. Thus, the campaigns of 1761 began without any actual movement in favour of peace, and, though Pitt's willingness to entertain the notion of concluding it with France on his terms had been in vain, his alternative of pressing on the War till these terms should have become possible remained and justified itself.

For, while, in 1761, the struggle of Prussia against Austria and Russia remained undecided, want of money, though not of men, having delayed an agreement between the Allies on a joint plan of action, and Laudon's brilliant surprise of Schweidnitz (October) having then reduced Frederick II to the defensive in Lower Silesia, things had gone badly for the French in the west. Here the French armies had been unable either to drive Prince Ferdinand out of Westphalia or to encroach further on Hanoverian territory. These failures had increased the longing for peace in France, and, though the ill-judged Belle-Isle expedition, a lesser effort of the sort on which Pitt at times set his heart, and intended to secure an eventual equivalent for Minorca, was allowed by him to delay the assembling of the proposed Peace Congress at Augsburg, he saw no objection to secret communications with France in the same direction in Paris (through Hans Stanley) and in London (through de Bussy). In these negotiations, Pitt let it be known that no separate peace with France would be allowed by Great Britain to prevent her from continuing effective aid to her Prussian Ally. But the Austrian Government succeeded in stiffening Choiseul's attitude, and even in insisting on a guarantee to Spain being attached to any Treaty with Great Britain. Thus, through the efforts of Grimaldi, Choiseul, in his Memorial of July 15th, formulated the Spanish claims against Great Britain and implicitly adopted them. Pitt's Government on the other hand, declared their inclusion in any Peace Treaty with France wholly inadmissible. The temper of the nation, encouraged by the news from the Indies both East and West, was still high; and peace with France was still out of the question, so long at least as Pitt was at the helm.

On July 25th the British Government forwarded its own conditions to the French; they proposed that Great Britain should be allowed to assist her Prussian Ally in accordance with her Treaty obligations; but the real difficulty lay in Choiseul's mind being now obsessed by the idea of the Spanish Alliance. The Third Family Compact between France and Spain, in whose mutual guarantee the Bourbon Princes in Italy took part, was signed on August 15th. It contained a Secret Article, of even greater moment than the public agreement, binding Spain to declare war against Great Britain on May 1st, 1762, should that Power then still be at war with France, and, in this event, promising the restoration of Minorca to Spain. The point of the Compact was obviously directed against Great Britain; but by concluding it France violated the Versailles Treaty of May 1st, 1756 with Austria, who had been left without so much as cognisance of it. As for the British peace negotiations with France, they were broken off, though not till October, and the Congress of Augsburg, for which the Plenipotentiaries had already been named, collapsed in its birth.

But, on finding the preservation of peace with Spain impossible, Pitt, as if desirous of taking a leaf out of the book of his Ally, and (if it may be so put) anticipating the inevitable, gained an advantage over the now accomplished Alliance at the outset. Reckoning that the seizure of Spanish ships could, if rapidly effected, be carried out without any augmentation of the British navy, and at the same time lead to the seizure of Spanish Colonies, he, so early as September 18th, 1761, proposed to the Cabinet to declare war against Spain.

But the proposal appalled the whole Ministry, except Temple, and was resisted by Bute, who thought that the opportunity had at last arrived for overthrowing the Ministry's master. The question was debated in three Cabinet meetings, and on October 2nd was finally decided against Pitt. On December 5th, he resigned, Temple following him out of office.

Bute had now the leading voice in the Government, though Newcastle remained its nominal head till 1762. Lord Egremont, who had been designated as Plenipotentiary at Augsburg, and who was regarded as wholly under Bute's influence, took Pitt's place as Secretary of State. He perceived at once that, popular as the great war Minister had been, there was no other way of ending that popularity than the conclusion of that Peace which Pitt had declined to seek to bring about prematurely, but which was favoured by the majority of the new Parliament (November), whether through the influence of the Court or through the manipulation of Newcastle, or both. The Speech from the Throne made no mention of Spain; but the Spanish Government vindicated the insight of Pitt by throwing off the mask. Its military preparations were hurried on, and Wall now propounded a long series of grievances against Great Britain, accompanied by an indignant message of sympathy with France. The request for information of the Earl of Bristol, the British Ambassador at Madrid, as to the Family Compact was received with cynical boldness, and, when a formal reply was made five weeks later, its tone was unaltered. Immediately afterwards, the Spanish reply to the British ultimatum, enquiring whether or not King Charles III designed to ally himself with the foes of Great Britain, arrived in London; and on January 4th, 1762, there followed the British Declaration of War against Spain. In March, a peremptory joint Spanish and French Note was despatched to the King of Portugal, desiring him to put an end to all correspondence and commerce with Great Britain, and, on the demand being refused, a Spanish army entered Portugal (April).

But while, in this quarter, the British Government had done what seemed indispensable, it had taken the momentous negative step of leaving the Subsidy Treaty with Prussia unrenewed. This, indeed, did not amount to her abandoning Prussia to her foes, and was not so regarded by Frederick II, who at this late stage was formulating proposals as to the terms on which, as he hoped, Great Britain would insist on his behalf in the event of her concluding a separate Treaty with France. Nothing, however, came of this negotiation; and there can be little doubt that Frederick's recent ill-success had, about the turn of the years 1761–2, inclined Bute and those who thought with him, or who, like Bedford, went even further in their desire for peace than he, to place very little store on the continuation of the Prussian Alliance, or to favour its abandonment. At the beginning of 1762, Frederick II was, though with a much reduced army, still holding out, and his best chance of recovering himself lay in the growing French weariness of the burden of the Austrian Alliance. But, of a sudden, the whole situation changed by the death of the Tsarina Elizabeth (January 5th, 1762) which abruptly transferred Russia's support of the Austrian Alliance to Frederick II. In the next month (February), the new Tsar Peter III issued a formal Declaration in favour of peace throughout Europe (February). To Bute and the friends of peace in England this utter change in Russian policy came at a most inopportune moment; and he revealed his ulterior intention of leaving Prussia out of account in the impending peace negotiations by proposing to her that an annual grant should take the place of the renewal of the Subsidy Treaty. Before Frederick's answer arrived, the changed attitude of the British Government had been made clear to him by the resignation of Newcastle (May), who had objected to the insufficiency of the grant asked for the expenses of the War (including that to Prussia), while Bute insisted that the perilous position of Portugal, which in this month declared war against France and Spain, was now the matter of chief moment to Great Britain. In vain, Pitt had protested that even Portugal could be best protected by upholding the Prussian Alliance. The "King's Friends" now had the ball under their feet, and prospectively, there was no doubt of Prussia being left by Great Britain to her new friendship. About the same time, Russia entered into an Alliance with Prussia, and Sweden concluded Peace with her. The complications which ensued with Denmark need not occupy us. On the deposition and assassination of Tsar Peter III (July), his Consort and successor, Catharine II, did not renew the alliance with Prussia. But, in substance, the relations between the two Powers remained unchanged till the close of the War, when, in circumstances of altered significance for Great Britain, they were reformulated as an actual Alliance (1764)[1].

---

[1] Treaty of St Petersburg, April, 1764. With this Treaty, accompanied by a Secret Convention concerning Poland, the British Government had no concern.

The Prussian campaigns of the year 1762 had ended successfully for Frederick II at Schweidnitz and Freiberg (October), and in the west Prince Ferdinand had by the capture of Cassel (November) victoriously closed his brilliant military career. But, who lacked courage rather than insight, had not as yet dared to interfere openly with the prosecution of the War; but, while Prince Ferdinand was still about to push his advance, the news arrived that, as will be seen immediately, the British negotiations with France and Spain had resulted in the conclusion of Preliminaries of Peace. Choiseul's policy of prolonging the War in Germany, in order, at the last moment, to carry on effectively the War against Great Britain with the aid of Spain had rapidly broken down, even after this joint effort had been practically restricted to an attack on Portugal—a failure in the end, thanks partly to British supplementation of the national resources. The British supremacy by sea had in this year been everywhere maintained. In the West Indies, where, with the solitary exception of the capture of San Domingo (1761), warlike operations had for some time been suspended, in order to spare Spanish susceptibilities, there was, of course, no reason for showing consideration for an open enemy. Martinique was taken (February, 1762), and in accordance with a design of Pitt's, the whole of the Windward Islands were now under British rule. Havana was captured (August), and before long (October) the Philippines in the Eastern Seas were added to the Western gains—or rather, would have been added, had not the British Government already placed both these acquisitions on the list of those of which it was prepared to make a present to Spain.

The War was virtually over, so far as Great Britain was concerned. She had been victorious in almost every quarter of the globe; but her Sovereign and his Minister had made up their minds for peace with France and Spain, and almost dreaded successes which might seem to oblige them to raise their terms as towards these Powers. About April (1762), diplomatic correspondence on the subject had been resumed with France, Spain being taken into confidence. The negotiation was kept carefully secret from Prussia, though Shelburne, who had boldly demanded the withdrawal of our troops from Germany[1], was informed that the Government had no intention of further carrying on the German, in addition to the Spanish War. But, as the business proceeded, Choiseul thought it desirable (May) confidentially to apprise the Austrian Government, which was pressing

---

[1] Cf. Lord Fitzmaurice's *Life of Shelburne*, vol. 1 (1875), p. 124.

Great Britain for aid, of the design of a separate Peace between the
Western Powers; when it was found that, though the assembling of
a Congress might have seemed more favourable to her interests, Maria
Theresa and her counsellors were prepared to transact directly, and
to seek to obtain fair conditions for herself (the retention of Glatz)
and her Saxo-Polish ally. The persistence of her foe, the desertion of
her by Russia, and the coolness of France, had at last overcome her
resistance. It now only remained to inform Frederick II of the conditions under which she was prepared to make peace with him, if
the Army of the West were withdrawn from Germany during the present War. Frederick II, still professing his disbelief in the willingness of his Ally Great Britain to safeguard his interests, asked for a
direct communication from the Austrian Government as to its intentions. The opening of official negotiations between France and
Great Britain, hereupon, followed (September), Frederick's old
acquaintance the Duc de Nivernais being sent to London, and the
Duke of Bedford, a firm friend of peace, to Paris.

The Cabinet, on which the final settlement of one of the most
momentous questions that a British Ministry has ever been called
upon to determine, had recently undergone certain changes. Bute,
who, on the resignation of Newcastle, had, as a matter of course,
become First Lord of the Treasury, had appointed George Grenville,
in whose valuable support he placed great trust, one of the Secretaries of State in his place; and it now appeared that both he and his
fellow Secretary, the Earl of Egremont, insisted that, before signing
the Preliminaries, Bedford, who had a strong will of his own, should
submit them to the Cabinet. The news of the British success at
Martinique added to the arguments in favour of this view, and Bute
had to bow to it, though he took his revenge by transferring the
seals from Egremont to Halifax and shifting Grenville to the Admiralty. The transaction of the Preliminaries was accordingly pushed
on, and, on November 3rd, the Preliminaries of Peace between Great
Britain, France and Spain were signed at Fontainebleau. Six days
later they were approved by Parliament, after Pitt had liberated his
soul in a speech of three hours and a half, a majority of 319 to 65
supporting an address of thanks to the Crown. On February 10th,
1763, the Peace of Paris, based on these Preliminaries, was signed.

This Peace replaced Great Britain in possession of Minorca, and
left in British hands the whole of Canada, with Cape Breton and
the other islands (except two) in the Gulf of St Lawrence; certain

religious rights were reserved for the Roman Catholics of Canada, and certain rights of fishery in the Bay of Newfoundland (the nursery, as it has been called, of the French navy) were left to the French. On the Gulf of Mexico, Florida and Louisiana, except New Orleans and its district, became British—partly as an equivalent for Havana. In the West Indies there was a partition, and in Africa, Great Britain obtained Senegal, but gave up Goree. In the East Indies, France recovered possession of certain factories and settlements in Bengal, but only on the undertaking to keep no troops and raise no fortifications there. In general, it was agreed that all conquests "not yet known" should be restored without compensation, so that Havana and the Philippines were alike surrendered. On the other hand, Spain waived all the claims on which her participation in the War had been founded.

Notwithstanding the signal moderation shown by the British Government in agreeing to these terms, King George III must be allowed to have had, in more ways than one, reason for declaring that Great Britain had never before concluded such a peace, and that perhaps no other European Power had ever concluded another like it. It established British maritime supremacy in both hemispheres; it placed Great Britain in the position of the foremost Colonial Power in the world; and it opened for British commerce an incomparable prospect of expansion. But this Peace, at the same time, wore a more dubious aspect, with regard to its provisions connected with Great Britain's participation in the recent European War. Whether, even so, it contained in it the germs of national animosities for whose outbreak the course of time could not fail to provide opportunities, was a question which history would be called upon to solve; but, most assuredly, an insistence upon the policy of Pitt—the policy of absolute commercial monopoly—would not have been accepted by France except at a stage which the late War had not reached—that of her absolute prostration.

It is impossible, from this point of view, not to compare the Peace of Paris with the Peace of Utrecht, or to gainsay that, in both instances, the motives impelling the British Government to press a pacific conclusion were those of political partisanship, and jealousy on the part of the Crown and its followers of one great man preeminently fitted to carry on the War and associated by public opinion with its continuance[1]. Nevertheless, Great Britain cannot justly be

[1] In a powerful passage in Lecky's *History of England in the Eighteenth Century*, vol. III. (ed. of 1882), pp. 44 ff.

said to have at Paris, as she had at Utrecht, purchased for herself whatever advantages accrued to her from the Peace at the cost of her Allies. Portugal recovered all that she had lost by the War, and —which is, of course, the main question at issue—Great Britain's conduct to Prussia, though inevitably resented by Frederick II (in whatever measure he may have expected it) cannot fairly be described as desertion. By a strange coincidence, the Article of the Treaty providing for the restoration by France of the territory and strong places in her occupation omitted to specify the Powers to whom they were to be given up; and, but for Frederick's vigilance, Austria might have taken advantage of this lapse. But the real defence of Great Britain's action towards Prussia consists neither in this omission, nor even in the fact that Great Britain was under no formal obligation (as Frederick had been made aware) to continue indefinitely her Annual Subsidy to him. It lay in the complete change of the circumstances from those in which her Alliance with him had been concluded. Austria and Saxony apart, he was now on the friendliest of terms with Russia; Sweden was following suit, the great league against him was dissolved, and France alone, from whom he had little or nothing to fear, and who in the Peace undertook to give no fresh assistance to her Allies still involved in the German War, remained unreconciled[1].

We leave aside the disentanglement of the relations between France and her Allies in Germany. The British Government had devised a scheme of its own for solving the difficulties which attended the process by proclaiming—with a resolution savouring of Pitt rather than his successor—the neutrality of the Prussian Rhinelands during the remainder of the War, when the news of the conclusion of the Peace of Hubertusburg rendered the acceptance of the scheme superfluous (February 15th, 1763). The Prussian and Austrian Governments had rapidly reached the conclusion that the time had come for them to settle their differences directly, while keeping in good humour the new Tsarina in her own right, who was anxious to assume the part of Mediatrix. The Peace of Hubertusburg, which left the Austrian, Prussian and Saxon dominions precisely the same in extent as they had been before the War, while Prussia made certain concessions of no primary significance to the Houses of Austria and

---

[1] Frederick put faith in the report that Bute had held out hopes of British support of demands from Prussia of territorial compensation for Austria; but this gravamen rests on the uncorroborated evidence of Prince Galitzin, Russian Ambassador in London, and need hardly be taken into account.

Saxony, was regarded by Frederick II's contemporaries as a masterly close to a masterly War, and he and Kaunitz were at one in their satisfaction at its having been reached without actual foreign (*i.e.* Russian) intervention. George III was included in it among the Allies of Prussia both as King of Great Britain and as Elector of Hanover. No warmer congratulations on this Peace attended Frederick II than those of Mitchell, who during the most critical part of the War had adhered to him and upheld his action with unflagging energy; and when, after nightfall on March 30th, the great King entered Berlin, there rode by his side Prince Ferdinand, whose prowess had lifted from his shoulders a great part of the burden. And though there was truth in his boast, "I made the War"—for in his self-reliance at the supreme crises of his course lay the final cause of his victory—there were also on his side the forces by which history works, and of which the greatest of warriors and statesmen are but the agents.

In England, if the Peace of Paris had been carried through in a different spirit, and by other statesmen, it might have been welcomed with acclamations. As it was, the hopes of the Court party that the assurance implied in the Peace of the young King's having, in the conclusion of it, been moved by no German sympathies would cover him with popularity were to be speedily disappointed As for his chosen Minister, though the charge of having been induced to make the Peace by a French bribe was momentarily bruited abroad, he was severely handled in the Lords, and, with an insight into the situation creditable to his loyalty as well as to his good sense, unexpectedly resigned his office as early as April. It is significant that, in the most notorious effort of the demagogues who virulently attacked him and his *régime*—in No. 45 of Wilkes's *North Briton*, published a few days after Bute's resignation—the abandonment of Frederick II and the inadequate conditions of the Peace are among the charges urged against the fallen, but even now by no means powerless, Minister.

VI

The intrigues which followed scarcely concern us here. Bute was succeeded by George Grenville, the conduct of foreign affairs being left to Egremont (whose influence among the Tories was considerable) and to Halifax, personally popular, but not a statesman of high mark. After Egremont's death, the King was forced to have recourse to the counsel of Pitt, who, while advocating the exclusion from office of all who had taken part in the Peace negotiations, dwelt on the necessity of giving the great Whig families their share in the administration of public affairs. The illogical result was the inclusion in the Ministry of the Duke of Bedford (September), and, after further difficulties, which the King had made yet another effort to overcome with Pitt's aid, Grenville and Bedford were superseded in office by the Marquis of Rockingham, the leader, respectable according to any use of the word, of the main body of the Whigs (1765).

Within the closing months of Grenville's Government falls the event—the passing of the Stamp Act—with which a new period begins in the history of British foreign policy. For, as was soon to become manifest, it was henceforth constantly affected, and for many a long day dominated, by the relations between the Colonies and the mother-country. Hitherto, the North American Colonies, which are primarily in question, had in times of peace been virtually left to themselves; and Grenville's Stamp Act, by which half North America was lost to Great Britain, was an almost incidental result of his endeavour to utilise discreetly for the defence of Great Britain what he looked upon as her resources beyond seas. In the process legalised by this Act there is nothing altogether new; but the application of its principles—which of old Walpole had said he would "leave to a braver man"—proved the supreme test of Pitt's colonial statesmanship[1]. During the earlier stages of the Anglo-French warfare in North America, the British Colonists had fought bravely with little help from home. The formation of a central authority to direct their efforts had, accordingly, been felt so strongly that, on the eve of the Seven Years' War, a Congress had been summoned to Albany (1754) by the Colonial Governor, to discuss a common organisation of defence and a central fund for supplying the necessary means. But the War, while it preserved the Colonies from French dominion, almost ruined them by putting an end to their unlawful trade with their French and other foreign neighbours, as well as by the exhaustion of their own resources; and Grenville's proposal to raise by parliamentary taxation of them part at least of the money necessary for the permanent establishment of a force in North America was as inopportune as it was offensive, while it might very possibly prove inadequate to its purpose.

The history of the Stamp Act, which, while passing with very little notice in England, at once aroused the most violent opposition

---

[1] See Miss Hotblack, *u.s.*, in the chapter "Stamp Act."

in the Colonies, and that of its Repeal, supported by Burke and opposed by Pitt (February, 1766), must not detain us. The Repeal was accompanied by a Declaratory Act, asserting that the taxing power of the British Parliament extended to the Colonies. Pitt, though seeking to maintain a distinction between legislation and taxing powers, declined to bind the Colonies by an absolute declaration of right. The Repeal, however, was accepted in America as a binding measure, though the wound still smarted. On every ground, the remembrance of it should have been left to die out as speedily as possible.

In the following July (1766), the King dismissed Rockingham and recalled Pitt, now created Earl of Chatham, into office as Lord Privy Seal. The Duke of Grafton, who had resigned the Secretaryship of State under Rockingham, had been persuaded to accept the nominal headship of the Government, while Shelburne and Conway, both strong adversaries of the Stamp Act, were appointed Secretaries[1]. But, though Chatham remained a member of the Government till 1768, he was such in name only; and his life had already lapsed into that of an invalid in retirement, with fitful emergings into the light of public day—its normal condition in his later years. His Colonial policy, which he clearly expounded to the House of Commons on the eve of the War of Independence (February, 1775), underwent no fundamental change; and he held fast to the principle that the legislative authority of Great Britain must remain supreme, with the rider that no tax should be imposed on a Colony without the assent of an assembly duly convened there to vote supply for imperial uses. Grafton's Government, to which Chatham had for a time given the support of his name, had, in the meantime, carried out the policy of the (repealed) Stamp Act through Charles Townshend's imposition on the Colonies of a port duty on tea—the occasion, as it proved, of the outbreak which led to the War of Independence. After Townshend's death, his successor as Chancellor of the Exchequer, Lord North, who in 1770 became First Lord and virtual Prime-Minister, continued the same policy, of which the primary inspiration was the will of the King.

[1] It is worth noticing, as showing the increased importance attached to British North America, that, in 1768, the Earl of Hillsborough (afterwards Marquis of Downshire), who had served under Grenville as President of the Board of Trade, but whose sympathies were Tory, was appointed Secretary of State for the Colonies. But the office was abolished in 1782—a proof of the difficulty, in this period, of distinguishing Colonial from Foreign Affairs.

It would serve no purpose to touch here on the personal incidents and influences more or less affecting British Colonial and foreign policy in this period of rampant faction, and of the prostration of the powers of guidance to which Parliament and nation had, during four glorious years, accustomed themselves to look. "The late frequent changes in England," wrote, about the end of 1767, Sir Andrew Mitchell, whom experience had taught what his country could achieve under a great leader, "have created a degree of diffidence in foreign Powers which renders all negotiation with them difficult and disagreeable." While in America discontent and disaffection were becoming more and more formidable, and while at home the attention of the public was concentrated upon domestic agitation, the regard paid to Great Britain by the European Powers was rapidly sinking[1]. Significant of this decline, though, of course, its importance was much exaggerated by Burke when he represented it as changing the Balance of Power in the Mediterranean, was the ignoring by France of the protest of the British Government against her purchase of Corsica and enforcement of it, after the heroic struggle of the islanders under Paoli against their Genoese oppressors[2]. Much about the same time, an essentially Colonial question, that of the Falkland Islands, brought Great Britain to the verge of war with Spain. The first British design of a settlement on these barren islands (valuable because of their nearness to Chili) had been formed in 1748, but abandoned in consequence of a protest by Wall. In 1766, a formal attempt was made to take possession of one of them (now called Port Egmont)[3] for Great Britain; but, in 1770, a strong Spanish expedition captured the British garrison, detained a British frigate, and for a moment assumed the mastery of the South Seas. Since Spain, also, refused to pay the money due for Manilla, war seemed unavoidable, but was averted by the skilful diplomacy at Madrid of the British Chargé d'affaires, James Harris (afterwards Earl of Malmesbury) and the apprehension of Grimaldi that war with Great Britain, on which Choiseul had determined, could not be carried to a successful issue. But it was an untoward incident for the British Government, and seems to have led to the resignation

[1] The only step of importance taken at this time by Great Britain with regard to India was the enquiry into the affairs of the East India Company, instituted before Chatham was wholly disabled by illness.

[2] Corsica was actually annexed to France in 1769.

[3] France had effected a settlement on another (Port Louis). For a full account of the Falkland Islands affair, see Winstanley, *Lord Chatham and the Whig Ministry* (Cambridge, 1912).

of Lord Weymouth (who had succeeded Conway as one of the Secretaries of State). On the other hand, it likewise led to the dismissal
by Lewis XV of Choiseul. Chatham's laments over the decadence
of Great Britain, when he found strength to make them, resounded
in vain, and with the recovery of his bodily powers he had only
partially recovered his personal authority; so that, although he could
help for a time to weaken Lord North's Ministry, he was unable
either to prevent the American War or to agree with Burke as to the
conditions of maintaining the union with the American Colonies,
which they were both unprepared to sacrifice.

In 1775, without any wish on the American side for separation
from Great Britain, and with very little belief in the British of the
power of the Colonists to carry through the resistance on which they
had determined, the War of Independence broke out. There existed,
at the time, no kind of understanding between the Americans, or the
majority of them resolved on resistance, and any of the European
Powers; but there was a cooperation, unseen and unnoticed, between
the historic forces at work in very different regions of the world. As
has been well said, Europe was strewn with the wrecks of the liberties
of the past, and all the great or leading States were under the sway
of despotisms, benevolent or other. In the United Provinces, where
the House of Orange had recovered a quasi-royal position, corruption
and decadence were visible on all sides. Poland was already in the
throes of anarchy, and in 1772 underwent her First Partition[1], of
which the Powers that had perpetrated it obtained a formal recognition from the Republic itself. The prospects of Constitutional liberty
were almost universally enshrouded in gloom; and during the American War not a few Whig politicians were haunted by the belief—
though this fear acted in different ways on different minds—that
the defeat of the American Colonists would be followed by a subversion of the foundations of the British Constitution.

It was after the British Government had resolved to bargain with
certain German Princes, in order to raise the King's forces to what
seemed the requisite *minimum*, but before, in July, 1776, the Declaration
of Independence had been voted by Congress, that the advanced party
among the leaders of American opinion took into serious consideration the question of foreign assistance. In the first instance, at all
events, this could be no other than that of France[2]. Hitherto, France

---

[1] " England," Frederick II, had in the previous year written to his Envoy in
London, " need not worry herself about Poland."

[2] See for a full exposition of the situation, in this respect, Lecky, IV.

had been regarded as the natural enemy in the American Colonies even more distinctly than in England itself; but the early course of the War, and the manifest fact that the Colonists were far from united in their resistance, or, outside New England, had made so much as an approach to unanimity, soon placed it beyond doubt that the action of France must determine the result of the struggle. That intervention was by no means a mere question of *revanche*; for it was the evident interest of France to obtain for herself a share of the commerce from which she had been excluded since the time of the Navigation Act, to recover the losses which she had suffered through the deliberate policy of Pitt, and to gain comparative security for her West India Islands. French political opinion, which had of late become very active, anxiously noted the alteration in the conditions of the European equilibrium—more especially the augmentation of Russian, and of Prussian, power and influence by such a process as the First Partition of Poland. So early as 1776, Vergennes in his Memorial on American affairs, while affecting to deprecate war with Great Britain, urged the adoption by both France and Spain of a policy which would secretly encourage and assist the Americans in their struggle; and, though Turgot, when called upon to report on this Memorial, insisted on the maintenance of peace as the immediate and pressing necessity for France, the more active policy prevailed, and the Government of Lewis XVI, while duping the British Ministry, subsidised the American Revolt.

Spain, partly under the influence of France, partly on her own account—for she could not have entertained any real desire to foster Colonial independence—supplied the American Colonies with money and gunpowder, and allowed their ships ampler trade privileges than she granted to those of any other country. Grand-duke Leopold II of Tuscany secretly did away with all duties impeding American commerce with his dominions, besides giving open expression of his goodwill to the American cause. And a still more 'intelligent' despot, Frederick the Great, who had never forgotten Great Britain's conduct towards him at the close of the Seven Years' War, without committing himself publicly, or even consenting to receive an American diplomatic representative, threw every obstacle in the way of British enlistments in Germany, and took pains to assure France that, if she went to war with Great Britain, he proposed to remain neutral. The Emperor Joseph II (Co-regent with his mother since 1765), hostile to Frederick II on all other points, agreed with him as to discouraging the British enlistment of German recruits for the American War. Finally, the United Provinces found a single-minded satisfaction in obtaining a new market in America, and organising the little Dutch West Indian island of St Eustatius as a station for supplying the needs of the insurgents. Thus, French sympathies were the reverse of isolated in their varied manifestations on behalf of the War—one of them being a flow of French officers into the American army. For a time, the resolution of the French Government wavered, and the counsels of Spain (who was engaged in a brief War with Portugal) were against opening hostilities with Great Britain. But, at the close of the year 1777, after the British disaster at Saratoga, the American Commissioners at Paris were informed that France was prepared to enter into a Commercial Treaty with the American Government, and to acknowledge and support its Independence, on the sole condition that the Americans would conclude no peace with Great Britain, which did not include the actual recognition of that Independence. No advantage was asked for France in the Treaties formally signed at Paris in February, 1778; France was to have her place in the sun—her due share in American commerce—and Great Britain's monopoly of it was to be ended by the severance of the political tie between her and the Colonies now in revolt.

The recognition of their independence was precisely the basis on which George III had made up his mind not to treat with the Americans. In deference to a unanimous vote of the Cabinet, he at last consented that new proposals should be made to the American Commissioners, and in February, 1778, North moved and passed Bills of Conciliation, which yielded all the points originally in dispute, but maintained the political union between the Colonies and the mother-country. The final oratorical effort of Chatham, true to his point of view, and true to his policy of resistance to France, was in support of this principle[1]. But when the British Commissioners, recently appointed[2], reached America in May, they found all doors closed against them, and, after they had appealed to the nation from Congress, returned home. For, in the same month, the French Treaties of Commerce and Alliance, signed in February at Paris, but kept secret

---

[1] April 7th, 1778, against the Duke of Richmond's notice of an Address. See, as to the extreme probability that had he survived, he must have been called to office, Stanhope's *History of England*, chap. LVII, where the historian defends Chatham's policy against Croker and Macaulay.

[2] The Earl of Carlisle, William Eden (afterwards Lord Auckland), George Johnstone.

for some time, had become known in America; and, by June, France and Great Britain were at war. Great Britain had entered into the last phase of the struggle without an ally; but it can neither be denied that the challenge of France for a time strengthened the Government by arousing the national indignation, nor that Chatham's death gave unity to the Opposition led by Rockingham, who were now unanimous in advocating the concession of complete American Independence.

At first, the clouds seemed to gather more and more darkly, and the foreign policy of Great Britain to be reduced to an anxious defensive, though in America the fortunes of war were in her favour. French naval enterprise appeared to be reviving: in 1779, a French squadron seized the British possessions in Senegal, and in the same year a combined French and Spanish fleet sailed up the Channel, as the Dutch had, rather more than a century before. For the Bourbon Family Compact, and the irritation, old and new, provoked by British self-assertion at sea, with the hope of recovering losses of which that of Gibraltar transcended all others, had once more prevailed   A proposal made by the Government of Charles III, who, with his Minister Florida Blanca, had shown pacific tendencies, to mediate between Great Britain and France having fallen through, a Convention between France and Spain, in which each Power stated the objects it desired to secure, and the Spanish Government stipulated that no peace should be signed till Gibraltar had been restored, was signed in April, 1779; and, in June, Spain declared war against Great Britain. The combined fleets, as noted, appeared in the Channel; but, ere the day of peace had dawned once more, Rodney had brilliantly reasserted British naval supremacy in both hemispheres, and, before his final victory over de Grasse in the West Indies (April, 1782), the last assault upon Gibraltar had, after being prolonged for three years, hopelessly broken down.

While North's Ministry still held out, British diplomacy had been much occupied with the relations between Great Britain and the Powers not involved in the momentous conflict into which she had been drawn. It was not unnatural that, in the earlier days of the American War, the great Continental monarchies and Russia in particular, should have leant to Great Britain; but that at the same time jealousy should have been provoked, in northern as well as in western Europe, by the continuous growth of her naval ascendancy. The ambition of Catharine II, accordingly, might be depended upon to lend a willing ear to grievances on this head. So early as 1778, both the vigilant Vergennes and several of the minor Maritime Powers of Europe had invited the Tsarina to place herself at the head of a combined movement towards restricting the British pretensions to interfere in times of war with the commerce of neutral nations—but without much success. At her Court, Panin's party carried on the recent tradition of serving the interests of Frederick II of Prussia, and was consequently, in view more especially of his bitterness towards Great Britain, ill-disposed towards that Power. Her imperious favourite, Potemkin, on the other hand, leaned towards a British alliance, though his aims were essentially selfish. Catharine, who was not at heart hostile to Great Britain, and who distinguished the British Ambassador Harris by her special favour, was prepared, in these matters, to pursue a line of policy highly inconvenient to Great Britain. The British Government had given orders that Russian ships should be left unmolested; but the Spaniards searched and made prizes of two which they erroneously thought to be trading with Great Britain. The Tsarina, henceforth, angrily gave instructions that a number of Russian vessels should be equipped for the protection of Russian commerce, evidently with the intention of at least making an effective naval demonstration against Spain. Frederick II's counsel, however, induced her to restore the ships, and Panin took advantage of the occasion to persuade the Tsarina to summon a Congress under her presidency for defining the rights of neutrals by sea, so as to prevent a recurrence of the incident. In March, 1780, she issued a Declaration to the effect that in times of war neutral vessels may navigate freely along the coasts of belligerents, carrying any such goods of belligerents as are not contraband; that contraband articles are such only when expressly enumerated in a Treaty concluded between the British and Russian Governments, and that blockade must be really effective. This Declaration, amounting to acceptance by Russia of principles first put forward by the Prussian Government in 1752, laid claim to an almost universal authority. The British Government, without directly disputing the doctrine set forth by this "Armed Neutrality" Declaration, contented itself with answering it in general terms. But it was extremely unfavourable to the interests of Great Britain, as arraying the greater part of northern Europe in diplomatic hostility against her, while increasing the probability of an extended War, in which she would have no chance of assistance from Russia. Catharine II, however, had no wish to engage in hostilities, and promulgated the 'Declaration of Armed Neutrality,' which, as she told Harris, ought rather to be called an Armed Nullity, chiefly to satisfy her self-consciousness.

A further difficulty connected with the commercial relations of Great Britain, about the same time, led to actual warfare. This was primarily due to the use made of their island of Eustatius, mentioned above, by the Dutch during the War between Great Britain and France. The latter Power permitted the City of Amsterdam, and finally the whole Province of Holland, to trade with her Colonies duty-free through this channel, and came to depend most largely on Dutch supply for materials needed in the equipment of her ships. The consequent animosity gradually deepened between Great Britain and the United Provinces, where the party of Amsterdam and the Pensionary van Berkel had, from the first, strongly opposed that of the Stadholder and the British interest; and where the ambition of ultimately securing a large share of the American trade had never before risen so high. The Dutch traders, with contraband and other articles on board, swarmed in the Western seas, and American privateers freely ran their prizes into Dutch harbours. In return, British ships freely applied the right of search and captured Dutch vessels which refused to allow it. In September, 1780, a secret Treaty between Amsterdam and the "United States of America" (drafted for approval by the States-General) was brought to light by a daring capture, and, when it was only met by a dilatory and evasive disavowal, Great Britain declared war against the United Provinces.

Thus, at the close of 1780, Great Britain's isolation was complete. She was confronted by the united hostility of the American Colonies, France, Spain—against which she was defending Gibraltar—and the United Provinces, while Northern Europe was threatening her with the loss of her best weapon of offence. Meanwhile, in Hindustan, Hyder Ali was desolating the Carnatic and menacing Madras. In Ireland and at home in England—in the capital itself—the foundations of the monarchy seemed to be trembling. The recovery in America (1779-80) had temporarily strengthened North's Government and the national resolution of resistance; but with the surrender of Yorktown (October, 1781), followed by the Spanish capture of Minorca, and the complete establishment of French naval supremacy in the West Indian seas, that resistance came to an end, and the Ministry resigned (March, 1782). Its place was, after attempts at reconstruction by Lord Shelburne and Lord Gower, taken by the (second) Rockingham Ministry, in which Shelburne (who represented the followers of Chatham) and Charles Fox held the Secretaryships of State. After the death of Lord Rockingham, and the succession of Shelburne to the headship of the Ministry (July, 1782), the Secretaryship of State for Foreign Affairs held by Fox was transferred to Lord Grantham[1].

When, just before the resignation of North, and before King George III had reluctantly committed the conduct of affairs to the Whigs, with the avowed task of terminating the War and recognising the Independence of America, the question of Peace had virtually become only a question of time, Benjamin Franklin, American Commissioner in Paris, had transmitted to Shelburne certain conditions of Peace, privately suggested by Vergennes to a Scottish intermediary named Oswald. They included the cession, by way of reparation, to France of Canada and Nova Scotia. In April, 1782, the British Cabinet decided to suggest, through the same channel, peace conditions of which the essence was the grant of Independence to the Americans and the restoration of Great Britain to the position in which she had been left by the Peace of 1763. In May, Fox commissioned Thomas Grenville (son of George Grenville) to write a similar communication to Vergennes; and the Cabinet authorised him (after Rodney's great victory) to propose, in the first instance, the recognition of the Independence of America by Great Britain. A most untoward difference of opinion, hereupon, arose between Fox and Shelburne as to the meaning of this offer—whether or not it was, as the latter contended, to be conditional on the conclusion of a general peace, instead of preceding it? Fox's motion that Independence should be unconditional was lost by a narrow majority; and, on Shelburne's appointment as successor to Rockingham, Fox, as stated, resigned, with certain other members of the Cabinet.

The result was a hitch in the informal peace negotiations at Paris; but, inasmuch as the American War—largely because of want of money—languished, though the Dutch as well as the French Govern-

---

[1] In 1782, the system of three Secretaries of State had ceased (the third or American Secretaryship being abolished); and there was instituted for it that of two Secretaries, one for Foreign and the other for Home and Colonial Affairs. But this arrangement did not prevent an anomalous state of things under Rockingham, when the two Secretaries of State, Fox and Shelburne, were at daggers drawn; so that, in Lord Rosebery's words (*Pitt* (1892), p. 22) it "is not matter for surprise that, within a month of their assuming office, Shelburne and Fox, the two Secretaries of State, had each their separate plenipotentiary at Paris negotiating for peace."

ment had now recognised American Independence, it was felt on all sides that the advent of peace could no longer be delayed. King George III's resistance had now been overcome, and France and Spain before long perceived the futility of the hope that Rodney might still be crushed and Gibraltar and Jamaica captured, or that, though their united navies, even without Dutch aid, still outnumbered the British, this condition of things would outlast America's remaining in the conflict, and their own solvency would continue. The negotiations for the Preliminaries of Peace were, accordingly, carried on at Paris with renewed assiduity in the later months of 1782; Vergennes, of course, representing France, d'Aranda Spain, and Franklin, John Adams and Jay America, while the British Government had commissioned, together with Oswald, its original agent in the proceedings, Alleyne Fitzherbert (afterwards Lord St Helens). The Preliminary Articles with the United States were signed on November 30th, and those with France and Spain on January 20th following. (The notion of giving up Gibraltar for an equivalent had approved itself to the King and Shelburne, but had been successfully resisted—among others by Pitt.) The definitive Treaties were signed, at Paris and Versailles respectively, on September 3rd, 1783; the Duke of Manchester and David Hartley having taken the place of the negotiators of the Preliminaries, and the Tsarina and the Emperor Joseph II being, by way of compliment, named as Mediators in the Treaties with the two European Powers. The Pacification with the United Provinces was characteristically delayed till 1784, when freedom of commerce was secured to Great Britain in the Indian Seas.

Compared with the Peace of Paris of 1763, which France and Spain had resolved to undo, the new Peace wears a depressing aspect on any British page of history, and reflects the balance of losses experienced by her in the War. Yet it should not be overlooked that almost everything now relinquished by her to her European adversaries had been taken from them by her in previous Wars, and that a great part of her acquisitions in the Peace of 1763 was still retained by her. The gains of France were, in substance, restricted to those in Africa and India; to the abrogation of the Utrecht Clause providing for the demolition of the fortified port of Dunkirk, and to the acknowledgment of the French right of fishery on the Newfoundland coast. Spain recovered Minorca and Eastern Florida, while agreeing to the British rights in Honduras and restoring the Bahamas.

The American settlement turned on that recognition of Independence with which the negotiation virtually began—the promise of a compensation to the Loyalists, in lieu of the restoration of their estates, was a matter of secondary, though of considerable moral, consequence. On the whole, the American negotiations had been the most successful part of the entire transaction; and it should be noted that there had been considerable differences, at the end, between French and American diplomacy as to how far the latter had fulfilled its pledge of communicating, before signing, all preliminary agreements. Nor was Vergennes free from doubts whether, if Fox came into power in the place of Shelburne, he might not be disposed to conclude a separate peace with the United States. Yet there was no rupture, and the new loan which France had promised to the Americans was not refused to them. Spain detested the notion of American Independence, and cherished to the last the hope of an exchange with Great Britain of Guadaloupe for Gibraltar.

It will not be necessary, in the ensuing survey of British Foreign Policy from the Peace of 1783, to advert, except incidentally, to the Ministerial changes which occurred in the interval between the downfall of Shelburne's shortlived Administration, and the advent of the younger Pitt, who had held office in it as Chancellor of the Exchequer, to full power as Prime-Minister. Until the right solution was found in the appointment of the Minister who enjoyed the confidence of the nation in the first instance, and that of the Sovereign in the next, these changes turned on men rather than on measures; though of Shelburne, whose public conduct it is perhaps more difficult to judge with fairness than that of any contemporary British political leader, it was said, with some point, by his colleague, Lord Grantham, that he always trusted too much to measures rather than to men[1].

Indeed, his chief defect in his public career was, perhaps, his neglect of the Machiavellian maxim, that in politics everything depends on making and keeping friends—our enemies will take care of themselves. Yet it should not be forgotten that it was Shelburne[2] who, after his own resignation, suggested Pitt as the new Prime-Minister to the King, who was more than ready to act on the suggestion, in order to escape the hateful alternative—to which he after all had to submit— of the Fox and North Coalition. It lasted for little beyond eight months, under what is not very happily described as the "ornamental" headship of the Duke of Portland, the two reconciled adversaries

[1] See Lord Fitzmaurice's *Life of William Earl Shelburne*, III, p. 410 (1876).
[2] See J. Holland Rose, *William Pitt and National Revival* (1911), p. 125.

holding, Fox the Foreign, and North the Home and Colonial, Secretaryship of State. This was the Ministry—mistrusted by the nation,
and looked upon with bitter resentment by the King—during whose
tenure of office the Peace Treaties with the United States, and with
France and Spain, were definitively signed, without any modification
being introduced into them by the Whigs, who in Opposition had taken
exception to them so strongly.

When, through the unconstitutional action of King George III,
encouraged by the unscrupulous violence of Lord Thurlow and aided
by the selfish ambition of Earl Temple, the Coalition had been, in
December 1783, brought to a fall over Fox's East India Bill, Pitt was
appointed Prime-Minister by the Sovereign, in the face of a hostile
majority in the House of Commons. From Pitt's Cabinet, the Earl of
Shelburne, long the leader of the party—or fraction—to which
the new Prime-Minister had belonged, was left out, and William
(afterwards Lord) Grenville, though a member of the Government,
was admitted into the Cabinet till 1791; the Marquis of Carmarthen
(eldest son of the Duke of Leeds) being, however, included in it as
Secretary for Foreign Affairs. Defeated again and again in the
Commons, but rendered confident by the gradual dwindling of the
Opposition members, Pitt resolved—in the full sense of the phrase—
to appeal to the nation. Early in March, 1784, Parliament was dissolved, and in May he met the new House of Commons at the head
of an overwhelming majority. It was thus that he became the most
powerful Minister ever known in our history. The foreign policy
of the younger Pitt presents almost as many points of contrast with
that of his father as could have coexisted with the personal qualities
characteristic of both. But the task of the one was conditioned
by the achievements of the other, and, though their rates of resolution
differed, they alike proved equal to the unexampled responsibilities
laid upon them by a nation whose self-trust they inspired and shared.

BOOK I

FROM THE PEACE OF VERSAILLES
TO THE SECOND PEACE OF PARIS
1783–1815

SECRETARIES OF STATE FOR FOREIGN AFFAIRS,
1783 TO 1815.

December, 1783 : Marquis of Carmarthen (Duke of Leeds).
June,   1791 : Lord Grenville.
February, 1801 : Lord Hawkesbury (Earl of Liverpool).
May,   1804 : Lord (Earl of) Harrowby.
January, 1805 : Lord (Earl of) Mulgrave.
February, 1806 : Charles James Fox.
September, — : Lord Howick (Earl Grey).
March,   1807 : George Canning.
October, 1809 : Earl Bathurst.
December, — : Marquis Wellesley.
March,   1812 : Viscount Castlereagh (Marquis of Londonderry).

UNDER-SECRETARIES OF STATE FOR FOREIGN AFFAIRS,
1783 TO 1815.

         1783 : George Aust (*Permanent*).
August,   1789 : James Bland Burges (Sir J. B. Burges Lamb).
—   — : Hon. Dudley Ryder (Earl of Harrowby).
February, 1790 : George Aust (*Permanent*).
October, 1795 : George Hammond (*Permanent*).
January, 1796 : George Canning.
April,   1799 : John Hookham Frere.
September, 1800 : Edward Fisher.
February, 1801 : Lord Hervey (Marquis of Bristol).
November, 1803 : Charles Arbuthnot.
June,   1804 : Hon. William Eliot (Earl of St Germans).
January, 1805 : Robert Ward.
February, 1806 : Hon. George Walpole.
March,   1807 : George Hammond (*Permanent*).
March,   1807 : Viscount FitzHarris (Earl of Malmesbury).
August,   — : Hon. Charles Bagot.
October, 1809 : William Richard Hamilton (*Permanent*).
December, — : Culling Charles Smith.
February, 1812 : Edward Cooke.

(Later titles in brackets.)

CHAPTER I

PITT'S FIRST DECADE.
1783-1792

ELEVEN months before he died, that is to say in September, 1785, Frederick the Great of Prussia, with the Duke of Brunswick in attendance, gave to a Special Envoy from Great Britain[1] a survey of the state of Europe as he saw it, or affected to see it, and of England's position among the Powers since the Peace of 1783. Frederick was gloomy—gloomy with intent, as Englishmen thought; but his view was a possible one and no statesman in Europe had better opportunities for gaining information than "old Fritz who knew everything that he wanted to know." The Balance of Power in Europe, he said, was lost. France, Spain, Austria and Russia "were in alliance," and Holland was dragged in their wake. England and Prussia were isolated. Even united, they would hardly be a match for "that mass which he had described." A struggle between such unequal forces might be attempted; but it "was not a game to play often." He very much doubted whether England could tackle the combined fleets of France, Spain, the United Provinces and Russia. The position of the United Provinces, he said, was particularly unfortunate. The power of the Stadholderate and of the House of Orange which held it was undermined: France wanted to destroy it and to govern the Provinces through her Ambassador. How could he—although the wife of William V of Orange was his niece—how could he prevent the Franco-Dutch alliance, which was at that moment in the making? Did England suggest an Anglo-Prussian alliance?—There had been talk of this. Well: he did not care to alarm the opposing "mass" by a treaty, but he would always be well disposed towards England. He had no doubt, he concluded with malicious courtesy, that Pitt would restore her "to the importance which she had formerly held in the scale of Europe," and render her "as great and respectable as his father had done[2]." It is likely that he had grave doubts. A few years earlier he had written to Brunswick, who stood at his elbow while he spoke to Lord Corn-

[1] Lord Cornwallis, the Special Envoy, to Carmarthen, September 20th, 1785.
[2] Salomon (*Pitt*, p. 316) takes this to be a considered judgment of Frederick on Pitt. To me it reads differently.

wallis, that "wealth,...luxury, the spirit of corruption, had all helped to rot that formerly so respectable Government." He was probably too cautious, in his sceptical old age, to hold, with Joseph II of Habsburg, that England had fallen "for ever," or that she had "gone down to the rank of a second rate Power like Sweden and Denmark[1];" but combined with an old grudge against her for deserting him in 1763, which made him unable altogether to conceal his *Schadenfreude*, was a real doubt as to her present efficiency, a doubt which he shared with all the chanceries of Europe. That British statesmen felt the need to silence this doubt is shown by the pains which Cornwallis took to convince him that we had not suffered in pocket by our recent disasters more than our rivals had suffered in defeating us, and that we were in a position "to support our weight and dignity with the other Powers of Europe[2]."

Lord Cornwallis had not been sent to Berlin on this occasion precisely to seek Frederick's alliance, though he was instructed to make it clear that England would prefer Prussia "to all possible allies." He went at Frederick's request, or rather at the request of Frederick's Ambassador in London. He had been warned to put no trust in the King and to be infinitely circumspect[3]. But his mission falls in a period during which the British Cabinet, conscious of its isolation, had put out feelers among the Northern Courts and at Vienna. These feelers had all been cautious; for, as Pitt wrote to Carmarthen in June, 1784, it was necessary "to lay the foundation of such connections, keeping clear at the same time of being too soon involved in the quarrels of any Continental Power[4]." If England could secure the support of Catharine of Russia, Frederick told Cornwallis, he would enter into a triple alliance "as soon as she pleased." He knew that Catharine disliked and despised the British Government more than he did himself; that advances had been made to her from London: and that these advances had been very coldly entertained. Having no intention of committing himself, and being anxious not to risk an open breach, either with France, who for the moment dominated western, or with Catharine, who seemed to rule eastern Europe, he could afford to speak warmly of his own readiness to enter this unlikely combination.

[1] Sorel, *L'Europe et la révolution française*, I. 346.
[2] Joseph Ewart to Carmarthen, September 10th, 1785 reporting an earlier interview of Cornwallis with Frederick.
[3] Draft of instructions for Cornwallis, September 2nd, 1785.
[4] Salomon, *Pitt*, p. 300 n. Salomon gives a full account of the feelers of 1784.

His reference to "an alliance" between Spain, France, Austria and Russia was, strictly speaking, incorrect, and he knew very well that these Powers did not form a compact "mass." But they were linked together; and it was at least conceivable that, should the loose and selfish Alliances of Europe be consolidated by the threat of war, should the "General War," whose chances of outbreak the eighteenth century statesmen were always calculating, begin again, they would be found operating together. The Family Compact between France and Spain was a reality. It had worked already and would probably work again. The Alliance between France and Austria, the second link in the loose chain, seemed to have been tightened since an Austrian Princess had shared the Throne of France. Frederick knew how strong the anti-Austrian party in France was. The Alliance of 1756 had, from the first, been regarded as unnatural by the best Frenchmen. It was believed to have been unprofitable in a high degree. French politicians were always anticipating that Austria would again exploit it to their disadvantage. If France became engaged in "a complicated unsuccessful war," wrote a member of the French Council of State in 1785, who could promise that the Emperor[1] "would not claim Alsace and perhaps other provinces?" On the other side, also, the Alliance was not popular. At the end of 1784, the coolest head in the House of Habsburg, Leopold of Tuscany, Joseph's brother, called the French "our natural enemies, disguised as allies, who do us more harm than if they were open enemies[2]." Yet, uneasy as the Alliance was, the directors of policy on both sides found it for the present worth maintaining. Frederick told Viscount Dalrymple in December, 1785, that he knew there was no love lost between France and Austria; but that an Anglo-Prussian alliance would drive them together, and then he would have to face the nightmare risks of the Seven Years' War. So, he concluded, he must humour France[3]. It was a reasonable calculation.

The link in the chain of understandings most dangerous to Prussia was the recent agreement between Joseph and Catharine of Russia. At their first meeting, in Mohilev on June 4th, 1780, Joseph had replied to the Tsarina's mocking and calculated enquiry, why it was that he, a Roman Emperor, did not fix his capital at Rome, that there were difficulties in the way which he could not at present overcome, but

---

[1] *Mémoires lus au Conseil du Roi en 1784 et 1785*: quoted by Sorel, I. 295 n.
[2] Sorel, I. 441 n.
[3] Dalrymple to Carmarthen, December 3rd, 1785.

that there would be no great difficulty in her case. Her Rome was
not out of reach. By thus flattering her dearest ambition, he had won
her favour once for all[1]. Frederick's agents lost ground at Petrograd;
and the world knew, during the next five years, that the Imperial
Courts were revolving schemes for the partition of the Ottoman
Empire and the establishment of Russian rule at Constantinople.

In 1785 Catharine was not "in alliance" with France, as Frederick
asserted to Cornwallis. But there was a very good understanding
between Petrograd and Versailles. Catharine appreciated and admired
the conduct of French policy under Vergennes. Relations were so
confidential that, in 1784, she had received from one of Vergennes'
subordinates a detailed account of the inner organisation of that
French Foreign Office which had accomplished so much[2]. The
traditional friendship between France and Sweden was a permanent
obstacle to a Franco-Russian alliance. Yet it was not insuperable.
Frederick's insight into the realities of European diplomacy was
proved, rather more than a year after his death, when England and
Prussia had actually drawn together; for, in the autumn of 1787,
Ségur, the very popular and accomplished French Ambassador to
Catharine's Court, an old friend of England's enemies, transmitted
to his Government a Russian project for precisely that Quadruple
Alliance of France, Spain, the Tsarina and the Holy Roman Emperor
which Frederick had feared[3]. The proposal came to nothing; but it
was actually made.

Pitt's desire not to be "too soon involved in the quarrels of any
Continental Power" was most natural. He was nursing British finance
and the British navy, which depended on finance. This he was doing
with no definite intention of revenge either on France or on America.
He had probably less natural animosity against France than any of
his colleagues; and certainly less than any of the leading British
diplomatists of his day. When, in 1786, he protested in a famous
apostrophe that "to suppose that any nation can be unalterably the
enemy of another is weak and childish," he was expressing a conviction, not making a point in debate. But if he did not desire for his
country revenge, he desired honour, weight in the counsels of Europe,

---

[1] Heigel, *Deutsche Geschichte*, I. 37.
[2] Doniol, *Le Comte de Vergennes et P. M. Hennin*, p. 47. Hennin was the subordinate who drafted the report. M. Doniol shows that it was Vergennes who "*or-
ganisa ce qui paraît ne l'avoir guère été jusqu'à lui: le ministère des affaires étrangères,*"
p. 44.
[3] Sorel, I. 522, 532.

"respectability," as the word was understood in the eighteenth century. These were things which money, well used, could buy. Hence, in part, those great financial measures which filled the early years of his Ministry.

When Cornwallis assured Frederick that Great Britain had not suffered in power more than her foes, he made an understatement, either discreet or unconscious. Much as Englishmen groaned about the cost of the late War, many as were the prophecies of national collapse under the burden of the Funded Debt, the British finances, even before Pitt's reforms, were in a far better condition than the French; and the British financial system was probably the best in Europe. In a few years, Pitt made it incomparably the best. He was aided by the beginnings of those economic changes which were to fashion modern England. Canal building was now in full swing. The roads had become good enough to permit Palmer to start his swift mail coaches in 1784. Steam was first used to drive the air through a blast furnace in 1790. Between 1788 and 1796, the output of pig iron in Great Britain doubled. Those who directed European foreign policy were either completely ignorant of these things or did not reckon them at their full value. British statesmen had better opportunities of knowing the truth; and the least economic among them could see and appreciate the amazing expansion of the public revenue which set in, when a competent and upright financier handled freely the expanding resources of the nation.

From the first, Pitt had seen to it that a full share of his takings should go to the Navy. He maintained a larger *personnel* than had ever been maintained in time of peace. He insisted on receiving at regular intervals reports on the state and progress of the Fleet. In 1784 he set aside £2,400,000, a sum about equal to the total income of Frederick of Prussia, to build ships of war. By 1790, twenty-four new line-of-battle ships had been turned out from the private ship-yards. By 1787, he was prepared to risk war. In 1790, when, for a time, war seemed certain, he had ninety-three sail of the line ready[1]. At sea he would not have feared to meet France, Spain, Russia and the Habsburg Empire. By that time, he had not to face the possibility of meeting the Dutch also.

Some critical aspects of Great Britain's international position not referred to in Frederick's survey were very present to the minds of Pitt's Cabinet and of Continental diplomatists. And, first, the Irish

[1] Rose, *Pitt*, I. 210-1.

aspect. The establishment of Ireland's legislative independence in 1782 had seemed, to outside observers, a final proof of British decadence. Clearly perceiving the dangers of a semi-independent Ireland, Pitt put forward, in 1785, his generous scheme for Anglo-Irish Free Trade, to bind the two countries together; but English political and commercial prejudice ruined it[1]. So natural did it seem to our Ministers to find the enemies of England fishing in the troubled Irish waters, that they were always on the look out for French intrigues. A careful watch was kept on the letter-post; and among the papers of the Duke of Rutland, Lord Lieutenant, for the year 1784, is a copy of a private letter from Sir Edward Newenham of Belcamp, Co. Dublin, to Lafayette, inviting him to a friendly visit, and promising him a warm welcome[2]. The French knew well that Ireland was a source of weakness to England; but, as a matter of fact, French Ministers were not at this time, nor for several years later, engaged in intrigues there[3].

If Ireland was a source of weakness, India was on the way to become a source of strength, though also of sustained anxiety, to British Ministers. British influence there had been steadily extended throughout the century. The Peace of 1783 had secured Negapatam from the Dutch. The need for some regular Constitutional link between the growing Eastern empire and the British Crown had led to Pitt's India Bill of 1784. When Cornwallis went to Berlin, he was already, in the mind of the Prime-Minister, the first parliamentary Governor-general designate. At first, Cornwallis had demurred, raising objections to the scope of his powers. These powers were extended by the Amending Act of 1786. The Governor-general could now override the views of his Council at Calcutta, and thus was in no danger of factious opposition from colleagues such as Warren Hastings had been obliged to face. Under Cornwallis (1786-93) what might be called the nineteenth century era of British rule in India began, with the power in the hands of a series of men of high ability, who enjoyed the full confidence of the Home Government.

Consolidation of British power in India had two main consequences in the sphere of international politics. First, France was forced to

---

[1] For the Irish propositions see, *inter alia*, Murray, *Commercial relations between England and Ireland*; O'Brien, *The economic history of Ireland in the eighteenth century*; Rose, *Pitt*, I.

[2] H.M.C. Rutland MSS. III. 119. Newenham happens to mention "my agent for my landed estates," Napper Tandy.

[3] The evidence is in Lecky, VI. 369 *sqq.*

grope about, at times in India itself, at times elsewhere in the nearer or further East, for some equivalent—as the statesmen of the eighteenth century put it—in trade or dominion. Secondly, there began to emerge out of Asia the first true conflict of interests between Russia and Great Britain. Catharine was mastering the northern coasts of the Black Sea. Her orders were executed on the shores of the Caspian and on the banks of the Oxus. Her designs in the nearer East were frankly advertised. Henceforward, Russian policy became a matter of concern to every Asiatic Power—and Great Britain was now such. Moreover —though how far this was understood in England is doubtful—that policy might conceivably work in with France's gropings for an equivalent. In 1782, Joseph II had suggested to Catharine that perhaps France, a traditional ally of the Turk, might be induced to acquiesce in his destruction by the offer of Egypt. The case was debated at the French Council of State, with special reference to the effect of a French occupation of Egypt on Indian trade and politics[1]. France had no wish to see Turkey dismembered; but she had to prepare for all the chances of a shifting world. The world did not shift so far at that time; so the hypothetical situations never arose. But the first of those clashes of British, French and Russian interests in the East which the occasion foreshadowed was not long postponed; nor was their termination to be the matter of a day.

Contrary to the expectations of the average diplomatist, apt to identify prestige and power, dominion and wealth, and not holding with Adam Smith that Britain's American empire had been "not a gold mine, but the project of a gold mine," the loss of the Thirteen Colonies had made singularly little difference to British prosperity. Independent, they traded with the United Kingdom very much as they had traded when dependent. Had it been possible to make a clean and satisfactory settlement in 1783, it is probable that the empire might have seemed to gain greatly by disruption; and it is certain that such a settlement would have contributed enormously to the world's peace during the succeeding century. But such a settlement was not made. Throughout the ten years 1784–94, the Treaty of Versailles remained imperfectly executed, and Anglo-American relations in the unwholesome condition of standing water. Since America had no part in the ever shifting "systems" of Continental Europe, to which Great Britain had to adjust her policy from year to year, their mutual relations in those ten years may be described here without reference to any of

[1] Sorel, I. 328–9.

these. Not until the French Declaration of War in 1793 were they really affected by the course of European affairs.

The final Treaty with the United States had been signed at Versailles three months and a half before Pitt took office; but, owing to distance and the inevitably slow working of the new American Constitution, the ratifications were not exchanged until May, 1784. After the exchange, David Hartley, the British representative, reported the anxiety of Adams, Franklin and Jay to proceed at once to the negotiation of an Anglo-American Commercial Treaty[1]. The project was not new. It had been put forward at the time of the Preliminary Treaty, and had been pressed on Hartley by his American colleagues during his whole negotiation, from April to September, 1783. They wanted, as he reported to Fox, reciprocity "upon any terms whatsoever, from the narrowest limits to the utmost extent of mutual intercourse and participation." For himself, he had dreams of perfectly free intercourse, leading to a "family compact between our two nations[2]." But the letter in which he expressed this hope crossed his final instructions from Fox, to complete the political arrangements separately from the commercial. The British Cabinet was not ready to open the whole question of commercial policy and commercial law, and to define its attitude by treaty; though it was ready to make important concessions to the United States by Order in Council[3]. In any case, it was not prepared to show its hand at Paris. The Anglo-French and Anglo-American Treaties were to be signed simultaneously; and Fox held that commercial arrangements "ought not to come under the eye of the French Minister, much less to make part of a Treaty the completion of which he insists upon previous to the signing of his own, and which consequently he may be said in some degree to take under his protection[4]." This point of diplomatic procedure was a good one; but the unreadiness of London was the deciding factor.

David Hartley, a friend of Benjamin Franklin and of America, no ordinary diplomatist, an advanced Whig, a fellow of Merton College and, like Franklin, something of an inventor, was recalled

[1] Hartley to Carmarthen, May 13th, 1784.
[2] Hartley to Fox, May 20th and August 2nd, 1783.
[3] Fox to Hartley, June 10th, 1783. He expresses his wish to put off "for a time the decision of that important question which you think at last must come to an issue, i.e., how far the principles of our Navigation Act ought to be sacrificed to commercial considerations drawn from the peculiar circumstances of the present crisis."
[4] Fox to Hartley, August 4th, 1783.

by Carmarthen without thanks or compliments on May 25th, 1784. He refused to understand a perfectly clear phrase of this letter—that commercial matters would "require a considerable degree of deliberation"—and lingered in Paris until September, in spite of further recall orders. At last he was brought back by the cutting off of his appointments at a week's notice[1]. In June, Franklin was still hopeful that a commercial negotiation might be started; but by the end of July he had "begun to suspect that no instructions were intended[2]." Hartley should have perceived this earlier. Pitt's Cabinet was no more ready to begin negotiations than Fox's had been.

As, however, the American deputation remained in Europe, negotiating on economic questions with other Powers; and as a subordinate diplomatic agent reported them to be "very inquisitive" about the prospects of an Anglo-American treaty[3], they were encouraged to come to London at the end of the year. "Your people are ready to listen to us," wrote Franklin to Hartley, who was at Bath, occupied in drafting the final report of his mission for the unsympathetic Carmarthen; "but they thought it more for the honour of both that the treaty should not be in a third place[4]." There is no evidence that the British Minister had written so definitely of "the treaty."

John Adams, the first American accredited to the Court of St James', was presented to King George on the afternoon of June 1st, 1785. Two months later he transmitted to Carmarthen a draft treaty, hinting in his covering letter that the results of inaction would be most serious for Anglo-American commercial and political relations[5]. The draft was not merely commercial; there were included in its twenty-six clauses important proposals of a political kind. Relations between the two countries were to be based on "the most perfect equality and reciprocity." Subjects of either were to reside and pay duties in the other as if they had been citizens of it. They were to be free to send any kind of goods, wherever produced or manufactured, in ships of any description, with any class of crew, to all points in one another's territory or elsewhere, subject to the right of either Power to prohibit,

---

[1] Carmarthen to Hartley, May 25th; August 20th; September 5th; September 17th.

[2] To B. Vaughan, July 26th. *Memoirs of Franklin*, III. 154.

[3] Ed. Bancroft to Carmarthen, Paris, December 8th, 1784.

[4] Franklin to Hartley, January 3rd, 1785. *Memoirs*, IV. 423. Hartley's report to Carmarthen, dated from Bath, is of January 9th.

[5] Adams to Carmarthen, July 29th, 1785. *The Diplomatic Correspondence of the United States*, 1783–1789, IV. 257 *sqq.*

for reasons of State, particular imports and exports. This clause (No. 4) was a direct challenge to the sections of the British Navigation Code which reserved inter-imperial trade to ships built and owned in the British empire, and manned by crews predominantly British, while excluding foreign ships from most of the carrying trade between British ports and ports outside their own territory. By subsequent clauses, each country was to guarantee the other most favoured nation treatment in the matter of customs, and to give every facility for the establishment of consular offices.

So much for pure commerce. In time of war between either country and a third Power, the legal principles of "free ships, free goods" and "enemy ships, enemy goods" were to be recognised: contraband, if found on the vessels of one of the Contracting Parties, was not to be confiscated, but deposited in a port of the capturing country and paid for; no embargo was to be placed on the shipping of the Party not engaged in the war "for any military expedition" or similar purpose; the subjects of neither Party should take from any third Power letters of marque for preying on the commerce of the other. In case of war between the Contracting Parties themselves, merchants were to have nine months' grace in which to wind up their affairs, and prisoners were not to be sent into distant and inclement countries, but to be housed in barracks such as were used for the captor's own troops.

Such were the main points of this remarkable draft. Apparently it fell dead. There survives a record of a conversation between Carmarthen and Adams in October, at which Carmarthen confined himself to generalities about Great Britain's desire for reciprocity[1]. Four months later, an explanation of his reserve is suggested by a very stiff note to Adams, complaining of the failure of the United States to carry out the Treaty of 1783[2]. Then, on April 4th, 1786, Adams, now in conjunction with Jefferson, sends him, "as requested in conversation," another draft treaty. It contains the commercial clauses of the previous draft, almost verbatim, but nothing else. Probably, Adams had pressed the matter and Carmarthen had responded *pro forma*. A month later again (May 8th) a confidential agent reports Adams as being "highly dissatisfied with his situation and the supposed dispositions of H.M. Minister towards the United States," and his correspondence as being "calculated to excite them" to commercial

---

[1] Minute of a conversation with Adams, October 20th.
[2] Carmarthen to Adams, February 28th, 1786.

and political hostility. At this point, the negotiation, if so it may be called, was broken off, and no more is heard of it in Great Britain for another four years.

There is no reason to think that, at any time between 1783 and 1793, Pitt's Cabinet was ready to throw overboard the Navigation Code; though Pitt acquiesced in those administrative relaxations which alone rendered Anglo-American trade possible. American produce, coming to the United Kingdom in American or in British ships, was treated just as if America were still a colony. Facilities were given, as in the old days, for the reexport of American tobacco and rice; and so on. But the strong American wish to trade freely with the Canadian and West Indian Colonies, and to carry between those Colonies and the Mother-country, was never frankly gratified. In 1783, Fox had explained to Hartley that the notion of admitting West Indian produce in United States bottoms must be ruled out: "the prejudice (if that be the name these opinions deserve)" was, he said[1], far too strong. So it remained. But this and other prohibitions were freely evaded. The West Indies, in particular, required food and lumber from the United States; and their merchants had pressed for a commercial treaty in 1783[2]. Failing the treaty, they had to help themselves. A common device, as our early Consuls reported, was for a ship to be owned jointly by British and American traders and to utilise its double nationality[3]. Such evasion, though it might help traders, did nothing to promote an Anglo-American "family compact."

There is no need to assume, as Franklin did in 1784, that Great Britain had "still at times some flattering hopes of recovering"..."the loss of its dominion" over the United States[4]. The difficulties as to the Treaty of 1783 are sufficient to explain a great measure of reluctance to enter into further obligations. "By the fourth, fifth and sixth articles of the Treaty no impediments were to be put in the way of the recovery of debts [by British subjects]; the States were to be recommended to repeal their Confiscation Acts [directed against Loyalists]; and there were to be no future confiscations nor prosecutions of any sort against any person because of the part taken by him in the late war. But the States gave no heed whatever to these articles. The Confiscation Acts were not repealed; impediments were placed in the way of the recovery of debts; and thousands of Loyalists

[1] Fox to Hartley, June 10th, 1783.
[2] Resolutions of the West Indian Merchants, November 26th, 1783.
[3] *E.g.*, Bond (Consul at Philadelphia) to Carmarthen, May 14th, 1787.
[4] *Memoirs*, III. 154.

were driven from the country[1]." By way of retaliation, the United Kingdom refused to evacuate an important line of frontier posts on United States territory, from Lake Michigan to Lake Champlain. The diplomatic and consular correspondence of the years 1783-94 is full of the resulting difficulties and mutual grievances. Franklin had recognised in 1783 that the ill-treatment of the "Tories," which he deplored, gravely impeded the commercial negotiation[2]: the question remained an impediment for years. In view of this unfortunate experience, the British Government might well doubt to what extent a commercial treaty, assuming it to be desirable, would become operative. True, under the Articles of Confederation of 1781, no single State might enter into treaties or levy import duties in conflict with the stipulations of treaties entered into by the United States; but, if particular States defied one Treaty, they might defy another, and it was wellknown that Congress could not collect its own taxes. Meanwhile, several States were passing Navigation Acts and levying extra duties on goods imported in British bottoms.

John Adams returned home in 1788. Before the arrival of his successor, Morris, early in 1790, the Foreign Office had learnt that, under the new Constitution of the United States, Congress alone could levy duties affecting foreigners; that Congress had not adopted any commercial policy discriminating against Great Britain; and that everything contrary to the definitive Treaty of 1783 was repealed. It was now the law of the land[3]. This settlement paved the way for easier relations between the United States representative and the British Foreign Secretary. Morris had to explain the absolute inability of his Government to carry out the Treaty to the letter, at this late date. The debts were in many cases irrecoverable; the Loyalists had suffered persecution and had long since fled. Leeds replied that His Britannic Majesty could not evacuate the frontier posts until the position was regularised. He suggested some "fair and just compensation" for the parties who had suffered. As to the treaty of commerce, of which Morris had spoken, he was profuse in expressions of goodwill, but made no definite proposal[4].

In the course of the year, however, Pitt's new Committee of Council on Trade was instructed to report on the question of com-

---

[1] Professor McMaster, of Pennsylvania University, in *The Cambridge Modern History*, VII. 307.
[2] Report of Franklin's article in *The Salem Gazette*, F.O. November, 1783.
[3] Consul-general Sir John Temple to the Duke of Leeds, September 23rd, 1789.
[4] Leeds to Morris, April 28th, 1790.

mercial negotiations with America. The report, transmitted to Leeds on March 3rd, 1791, was generally favourable to the opening of negotiations "especially as Congress appears inclined to this measure; but," it went on to say, "it will be right, in an early stage...explicitly to declare that Great Britain can never submit even to treat on what appears to be the favourite object of the people of the United States, that is, the admission of the ships of the United States into the Ports of Your Majesty's Colonies and Islands[1]." The Committee inclined to the view that America stood to lose more than Great Britain in a trade war and suggested measures of retaliation, should Congress make "further Distinctions to the detriment of our trade."

In the autumn of 1791, Grenville now being in charge of the Foreign Office (see p. 207, below), George Hammond, who had been Hartley's secretary at Paris in 1783, was sent as the first British Minister Plenipotentiary to the United States[2]. His main business was the settlement of the question of the frontier posts and the British claims for compensation. There were also American counterclaims arising out of the carrying off of American property, in the shape of negroes, at the evacuation of New York by the British forces in 1783. If the American Government was anxious to proceed to commercial negotiations, Hammond was instructed to aim at securing most favoured nation treatment for British goods and, if possible, a promise that the existing duties on them would not be raised. Similar treatment for American goods was to be offered in exchange. For his guidance on the wider questions of navigation policy, he was given the report of the Committee of Council, with its clearly expressed intention to retain the British monopoly of imperial trade. But he found at an early date that what the United States, speaking through Alexander Hamilton, most wanted was the right of trade with the West Indies, if only in small craft[3]. A regular commercial negotiation was, however, never started during 1792, Hammond's time being entirely occupied with the interminable questions of debts and compensations, alleged failures of individual States to accept the Treaty of 1783 as the law of the land, and the British garrisons in the frontier posts. Then came the French Declaration of War against the United Kingdom. The outstanding legacies from the Treaty of 1783 remained unliquidated. No treaty of commerce existed, and all the

[1] The report is a very elaborate one, extending to about 150 MS. pp.
[2] His special instructions are of September 1st, 1791.
[3] Hammond to Grenville, January, 1792.

problems of neutrality, contraband, and the exercise of sea power, which John Adams's draft had attempted to provide against in advance, were revived in aggravated forms.

American sympathy was overwhelmingly on the French side, and Washington's Declaration of Neutrality, of April 22nd, 1793, was received with a storm of abuse[1]. Great Britain's refusal to admit the right of American shipping to enjoy the trade of the French West Indies, now thrown open to it as a war measure; an Order to British cruisers to bring into port neutral cargoes of corn and flour destined for France; and the beginnings of the search of American ships for British seamen —all played into the hands of the Anglophobe party in America. These events, and those that followed, lie outside the chronological scope of the present chapter; but their outline, in their relation to the abortive negotiations of the ten years of peace, may be most conveniently sketched here. Pitt's Government had been sincerely anxious for a settlement when Hammond was despatched. The dangers of war stung it into decisive action. The initiative, however, came from Washington. With the approval of the Senate, he sent John Jay to England to arrange a treaty. His task was eased by an Order in Council of January, 1794, instructing naval commanders and privateers to stop only such neutral ships as were engaged in the direct trade between the French West Indies and France. By October 7th, 1794, Jay had signed with Grenville the Treaty which is usually called by his name. It was approved by President and Senate nine months later. "Jay was burned in effigy, guillotined in effigy, hanged in effigy, from Maine to Georgia[2]"; but ratifications were exchanged next year.

The Treaty reflects very imperfectly some of the principles of international intercourse which American negotiators had put forward in the previous decade; but it was in the main concerned with specific cases and grievances. The United Kingdom agreed to withdraw all troops from United States territory on or before June 1st, 1796. Intercourse across the continental frontier was not to be impeded by either Power. The navigation of American rivers in the territory of either was to be free up to the highest point to which seagoing vessels could proceed. A Commission was to be set up in America to provide "full and complete compensation" for the British creditors, who had waited nearly a dozen years. Per contra, Great Britain offered com-

---

[1] On the American situation see McMaster in *The Cambridge Modern History*, VII. 318 *seq.*
[2] *The Cambridge Modern History*, VII. 320.

pensation for damage done to American shipping under the harsh
Orders in Council of 1793. United States vessels were authorised
to carry on direct trade with British ports in the East Indies (they had
done so to a considerable extent already without authorisation) and
with British possessions in Europe. The trade between the United
States and the West Indies was opened, as Hamilton had urged on
Hammond, to small vessels, up to 70 tons burden. The most favoured
nation principle was mutually adopted in matters of customs, tonnage
and harbour dues. Neither Contracting Party was to entertain in its
ports pirates or privateers with letters of marque from an enemy of the
other, or to allow its subjects to accept from foreign Princes in time of
war letters of marque which might authorise them to prey on the
commerce of the other Party. Contraband was more closely defined.
It was agreed that enemy property, but enemy property only, might
be taken from neutral ships in time of war; the United States hereby
abandoning the principle of "free ships, free goods." There were
other more detailed clauses dealing with the problems of neutrality,
capture, and the exercise of sea power. Finally, in the event of war
between the Contracting Parties, the property of individuals was not
to be confiscated—a reminiscence of the American Confiscation Acts;
merchants might remain and carry on trade in spite of the existence
of a state of war; and no reprisals for alleged illegal acts were to be
initiated by either Party without notice. It should be added that all
the clauses of a general character dealing with the problems of warfare
were accepted for twelve years only, except the clause which forbade
the confiscation of private property. It may, also, be noted, in the
words of an American historian and in anticipation of the war of 1812,
that "nothing was said about search, or impressment, or paper
blockades, or indemnity for the negroes whom Carleton took away
in 1783[1]." The British Navigation Code was rendered less water-
tight by the clauses relating to the West Indies and India; but it was
not wrecked. The Treaty, in short, was a *pièce de circonstance*, and
as such something of a triumph for British foreign policy: it had few
of the elements of a "family compact" broad-based on principle.

Had it been possible for the United Kingdom to have, from the
first, an Ambassador to the United States in touch with Washington
and his colleagues, as the Ambassadors to the Great Powers were with
the Courts to which they were accredited, Anglo-American relations
in this critical decade might have worked out differently. For the

[1] *The Cambridge Modern History*, VII. 320.

Ambassadors and other diplomatic agents played a great part in the development of British policy. In the last resort the policy was Pitt's. Early in Carmarthen's tenure of the Foreign Secretaryship (1783-91), Pitt gave advice on all delicate matters; and later, as Great Britain became more closely involved in the politics of Europe, he assumed the control at every crisis, often preparing the drafts of decisive despatches himself[1]. When Grenville succeeded Carmarthen (Leeds), these personal incursions become less frequent, but only because of the complete identity of views between the Prime-Minister and the Foreign Secretary. Owing to Grenville's great industry—a trait less conspicuous in the character of the Duke of Leeds—Pitt could be certain that their common policy would receive prompt expression and execution. But, in contributing to form his own opinion, in preparing the diplomatic situation for his decision, and in determining the attitude of foreign Courts towards Great Britain, the greater diplomatic agents were all-important. In quiet times, they were little interfered with and rarely instructed. This was specially so while Carmarthen was at the Foreign Office. At an out-of-the-way Court a Minister might receive no despatches at all: none went to Warsaw in 1782-4. Sir Robert Keith, Ambassador at Vienna from 1772 to 1792, said that on the average he received one answer to every forty official letters. Once, in times far from quiet, he received no line of instructions for five months[2]. The ablest and most independent of all the Ambassadors, Sir James Harris (Malmesbury), did not regret this neglect, because, as he once said, he "never received an instruction which was worth reading[3]." He served at Madrid, Berlin, Petrograd (1777-82) and the Hague. He knew how to play a lone hand, and preferred it. He could impress an Empress, plan a revolution, or bribe a royal valet to deny the presence to an anti-British Minister[4]. Centrally placed at the Hague from 1784 to 1788, he saw most of the northern correspondence, which passed through the Hague under flying seal; he was within easy reach of Paris news; and through Messrs Hope, the Scotch-Dutch bankers of Amsterdam, he knew how the world's gold was moving. No one could write more brilliant or more persuasive despatches. His career helps to explain Burke's opinion, expressed in 1791, that "those in power here, instead of governing their Ministers

---

[1] For the evidence, see Rose, *Pitt*, I. and Salomon, *Pitt*, *passim*. It is summarised in Rose, I. 618.
[2] *Memoirs of Sir R. M. Keith*, II. 219, 221, 224.
[3] To Joseph Ewart, *Malmesbury Diaries*, II. 112.
[4] He did this at Loo (see p. 180, *post*). Harris to Carmarthen, June 15th, 1788.

in foreign Courts, are entirely swayed by them[1]." This was not true; but there was truth in it.

Permanent "combinations" were even more foreign to English than to Continental diplomacy in the eighteenth century. But there were traditions of friendship and of hostility which affected, in varying degrees, the atmosphere of diplomatic life. That France was suspected, and that French and British diplomatists worked, steadily and courteously, against one another with mine and countermine, goes without saying. They had done so for a century. A tradition, now rather remote, of friendship with the House of Habsburg had not been completely effaced by nearly thirty years of Austro-French alliance. So long as Austria remained the Ally of France, Prussia was obviously a possible friend. But friendship with her had been intermittent, and as a first-class Power she was very young; so that there was no weight of tradition behind this relation. Her Protestantism still had some little weight at home; but the word does not occur in the diplomatic correspondence. Russia, until recently, had seemed a natural friend, by virtue of old commercial connexions and the apparent impossibility of any real conflict of interests. But, of all friendships, the most natural and obvious was that with the Dutch. Nothing seemed more shocking to British diplomatic opinion than the decline of British influence at Amsterdam and the Hague during the War of American Independence. For four years (1783-7), the struggle to recover that influence is the master-thread of British policy in Europe. For rather less than four years more (1787-91), the recovery of it is the keystone in the rather ill-cemented structure of the Triple Alliance of Great Britain, Holland and Prussia. Two years later, Britain had accepted without hesitation a war with France, which she had not sought, in order to retain that influence and to uphold threatened Dutch interests.

The United Provinces had not lightly gone to war against the United Kingdom in 1780. There were material reasons why they should not, apart from all considerations of friendship: "England is I believe the only Power that can ever literally annihilate Holland," Carmarthen wrote a few years later[2]; and the point of this remark was always appreciated at Amsterdam. Three out of the seven Provinces had opposed the War with Great Britain. The influence of the Stadholder, William V of Orange, the unworthy bearer of a great name, was always

---

[1] Ed. Burke to Rd. Burke, August 16, 1791, *Correspondence*, III. 268.
[2] To Harris, November 8th, 1785.

used on the British side—so much so that he was accused of treachery, whereby the old aristocratic Opposition, with its headquarters in the States of Holland, was greatly strengthened. Under the cumbrous and intricate federal system of the Provinces, the main utility of the office of Stadholder was in time of war. If it did not serve as a rallying point for the people then, there was some presumption that it was of no use. Certainly, it had not so served in 1780-3. William V was dilatory in business. He was neither able nor courageous. He was known to be much influenced by his Prussian wife. He was supposed to have acquired alien sympathies from his English mother. All those who disliked Great Britain or favoured France, and the still larger number who valued above all things the pure Dutch traditions of their Province or their town, were turning against him.

Great Britain was on her guard, even before Peace was signed with the Dutch. "His Majesty," wrote Fox to Sir John Stepney, Ambassador at Berlin, on September 19th, 1783, "is much alarmed at the accounts we receive every day of the state of affairs in Holland. The remaining authority of the House of Orange seems to be in the most dangerous state." In a manner hardly worthy of his position, Fox had asked the advice of Frederick as to "what steps, if any, could with propriety be taken by this Court in the present juncture." Frederick replied that this was a matter on which he could not pretend to give advice. "No notice whatever was taken of the two Courts acting in concert[1]." It was a palpable snub. However, in April, 1784, Count Finkenstein, speaking as was assumed for his master, suggested that England should send to the Hague a Minister "who would employ quiet and conciliatory measures[2]." This was, certainly, not a close description of Harris, whom Pitt sent over seven months later. But Harris was not sent merely to please Berlin.

The situation in the United Provinces required skilled handling. While the "Patriots" were working against the Orange interest, the whole country became engaged in a quarrel with the Emperor Joseph, about treaty rights to which Great Britain was a party. Joseph's passion for what was rational and absolute was stirred by the irrational checks and balances of Low Country politics. "His" Netherlands had been protected against France, his Ally, by Dutch garrisons in the Barrier fortresses. Of these he had got rid during the late War, Great Britain not being in a position to uphold the Barrier Treaty. Now (1784), he

[1] Stepney to Fox, October 11th, 1753.
[2] Stepney to Carmarthen, April 6th, 1784.

repudiated the "unnatural" arrangement by which the Scheldt was shut, and Antwerp's trade ruined, for the benefit of the Dutch. Also, he revived an old claim to an outlying bit of Dutch territory about Maastricht, which lay conveniently adjacent to lands of his in Limburg. He seized some Dutch forts and set an army in motion late in the year.

It could not be supposed that any Dutch party, least of all the "Patriots," the commercial aristocracy of Holland, would yield to such demands without a fight. As this party was in close relation with France, Carmarthen hoped to see France involved, to her disadvantage, in the quarrel between her friends and her Ally[1]. The strain increased throughout the early months of 1785; but in the summer it began to appear that the prospect for France was promising. She would mediate, bring the disputants to terms, and thereby increase both her own prestige and, if the terms were satisfactory to the Dutch, that of the "Patriots" also. That France should stand as protector of Dutch interests in the Scheldt was intolerable to Harris; but this was what he saw coming. Carmarthen's attempts to provoke Austria against France proved futile. Frederick of Prussia could not be induced to come forward as an open supporter of the Dutch, even though he might have been expected to welcome a chance of checkmating Austria. He was waiting on France[2]. Carmarthen tried in vain to move Berlin, as he saw France and Austria coming together again during 1785. "Interested as Great Britain and Prussia must be to watch every move of their respective rivals, so formidably connected," he wrote to Ewart on May 14th, why should they not cooperate "to emancipate the Republic from the shackles of her slavish dependency on France"? Frederick was absorbed in the contemplation of another Habsburg scheme, the proposed exchange of the Austrian Netherlands for Bavaria. When this finally collapsed (June, 1785), he was busy building up his German League of Princes to hold the Imperial Court in check. He was on the whole in favour of the British policy towards the United Provinces; but he was circumspect, timid, rather malicious, and, as has been seen, doubtful of England's resolution and competence. In return for active support in the Dutch matter, not necessarily military, he might have won British assistance for his League of Princes. King George joined it in

[1] See Salomon, *Pitt*, p. 304.
[2] Joseph Ewart (Chargé d'affaires at Berlin) to Carmarthen, September 18th; November 9th, 1784; April 2nd, 1785.

his Hanoverian capacity, but, as usual with him in such cases, without consulting or informing his British Ministers. Harris and Ewart were anxious to use the League as a steppingstone to an Anglo-Prussian alliance. The Cabinet was less eager. Both the desire not to commit Great Britain too far prematurely, and a justifiable suspicion of Frederick's interest and sincerity, held them back, as the September Instructions for Cornwallis show. But had Frederick responded, something might have been accomplished. He contented himself with his discouraging survey of Europe and his double-edged compliments to Pitt.

Harris worked desperately. He interviewed the Stadholder—and would have felt happier if he "would act one half as well as he spoke" —as well as the Princess—and got the impression of his having warned Berlin that open intervention might hurt the Orange cause; and he interviewed every accessible person of importance. The Prince lacked all "firmness and conduct." Some months before, he had talked of selling his estates and retiring to Germany—"a resolution," said Harris, "which, if ever he carries it into execution, will compleat his character." As with other nervous Princes, King Charles's head entered into his conversation. Harris thought that "the more temperate members of the aristocratical party," though hostile to Orange, disliked dependence on France. So he had long discussions with the Directors of the Dutch East India Company, as a result of which he suggested that Great Britain might guarantee all their Eastern possessions, and so prevent them from becoming centres of French influence[1]. But to no purpose. Preliminaries of an agreement between the United Provinces, France and the Emperor were signed in September. They showed, said Harris, "the low and abject situation to which this Republic is reduced." He worked on, nevertheless, to block the completion of the Treaty, through friends in Zealand, the most Anglophil of the Provinces. Correspondence with Ewart convinced him that "the King of Prussia was acting a hollow and insidious part," but that his heir, Frederick William Prince of Prussia, took a more lively interest in his sister's fate[2]. Yet nothing but words came from Berlin. The States-General rated them at their true value, and proceeded to consider proposals for removing the arms of the House of Orange from regimental colours, postwaggons and public proclamations.

[1] Harris to Carmarthen, August 2nd, 9th, 16th; September 2nd, 9th, 13th, 1785. Also, a private letter of March 11th, quoted in Rose, *Pitt*, I. 309.
[2] To Carmarthen, September 27th (two despatches of the same date).

On November 8th and 10th, 1785, two Treaties signed at Fontainebleau registered Harris's failure. Joseph withdrew. He recognised the absolute rights of the United Provinces over the lower Scheldt, which was all that mattered, and agreed to abandon his claims on Maastricht in return for a money payment. To win the Dutch, France undertook to pay almost half the sum herself. In return, the Dutch Envoys signed the second Treaty, a political and commercial Alliance with France. The two Powers were to aid one another, if either were attacked, by land and sea; neither was to carry on negotiations to the detriment of the other; and in matters of trade a "most favoured nation" system was established between them.

On the day on which the first Treaty was signed, Carmarthen wrote to Harris the threatening despatch already quoted. The Dutch were, he said, running a fearful risk, Britain "could destroy their credit or annihilate their very soil. Desperate and distasteful as such a step would be, it sure would be justifiable and I trust be effected (and the attempt I think could scarcely fail) without remorse or hesitation[1]." He approved a proposal of Harris's for the presentation of a memorial of protest by the British Ambassador to the States-General, a most unusual proceeding as between independent Powers. And he authorised Harris to do what that active Minister had done already—impress the risks they were running on the Dutch traders, who "would be the first to suffer and the last to be recompensed" in case of war[2]. Nevertheless, the Treaty of Alliance with France was ratified at Christmas, 1785.

The months from January to August, 1786, were the blackest of Harris's mission to the Hague. "It is not on the cards at this moment to reclaim this country. Everything...concurs to throw it into the arms of France" (March 31st). Yet hope must not be abandoned. At all costs, by combinations somehow to be devised, England must manage "to disentangle the Republic from her present connexion with France and to restore her to her former treaties with England" (June 13th). From Prussia there was no hope. "His Prussian Majesty is only a friend to the Stadtholder by affinity—and not politically so —and...providing his Niece enjoy the honours usually attached to the Office, he is very indifferent as to the preservation of its privileges" (August 1st). This was so. The King had told Viscount Dalrymple, British Ambassador at Berlin, in the previous December, that he

---

[1] Carmarthen to Harris, November 8th.
[2] To Harris, November 17th.

hoped to see the title of Stadholder secured to his Niece's husband, "but not a shadow of power, nor did he expect it." It could not be helped, he said. France must not be provoked[1].

Harris was troubled, also, by the silences and apparent indifference of Pitt. He wished him to write and encourage the rump of the "English" party among the merchants of the United Provinces. "Is it impossible to move him who speaks so well, to write one poor line to these sound shillings and pence men?" Such was his postscript to a letter for Carmarthen in July[2]. Pitt's silence and apparent indifference were due, in part, to preoccupation and overwork; in part, to a certain insularity, natural to a very young man with no first-hand knowledge of Continental problems; in part, to his lack of Harris's flaming hatred of France; and in part, it may confidently be assumed, to his wish at that moment to avoid any appearance of hostility towards her. If Carmarthen ever asked him to write a "poor line," there was an excellent reason for refusal. The French secret service was well organised. A letter to be communicated even to reputed friends was unlikely to remain hidden. And Pitt was just concluding with France a Commercial Treaty most advantageous to British interests. The signatures were attached to it by William Eden, whose name it generally bears, and Gerard de Rayneval on September 26th, 1786.

In the eighteenth article of the Treaty of 1783, France and England had agreed to nominate, without delay, Commissioners to draw up a commercial treaty, "on the basis of reciprocity and mutual convenience," this treaty to be completed not later than January 1st, 1786. The initiative had come from Vergennes. Vergennes, it has been said, had no trace of genius[3]. He had, however, immense diplomatic experience and an enlightened commonsense. He had served for nearly ten years in Portugal; for five in Germany; for nearly fifteen at Constantinople. He had created the modern French Foreign Office[4]. All his experience had failed to assimilate him fully to the ordinary diplomatic type of his day. True, he could play the diplomatic game with any man. He had led France into the American War, and had won back for her from Great Britain, by a timely use of force, the position among the Powers—but not the territory, which in the Seven Years' War Great Britain had by force taken from her. He had advised Lewis XVI against a policy of mere spatial aggrandise-

---

[1] Dalrymple to Carmarthen, December 3rd, 1785.
[2] B.M. Add. MSS. 28061. Quoted in Rose, *Pitt*, I. 275.
[3] Sorel, I. 297: "*Turgot avait du génie, Vergennes n'en avait point.*"
[4] Above, p. 146 n. 2.

ment. In memoirs presented to his master, he had protested with passion against the partitions, exchanges and mechanical roundings-off of territory, which occupied most of the time of the German chanceries. France, he said, had "in herself everything that constitutes real power (*la puissance réelle*)[1]." Of course, he desired that she should influence—his enemies would have said dominate—her lesser neighbours; but the notion of annexing them was abhorrent to him. Between France and Great Britain, he desired mutual respect and free intercourse, not the alternations of actual with commercial war which had marked the last century. He once told a colleague that, if he could annihilate England, he would not do it. But there was nothing that he would not do "to bring about a change in her jealous policy, which damages both us and her, and which, if well examined, proves to be folly." And he added, with a wonderful insight: "for a century and a half we have been ruining one another to enrich Europe, to strengthen Powers from whom we have nothing to fear or to create brandnew Powers. As a consequence, we lose weight in proportion as the others grow, and we shall end by making them our equals[2]." In 1783, he had been determined to begin an era of more neighbourly relations; and he had been delighted to find in Shelburne a statesman who needed no compulsion[3]. Each had a strain of the cosmopolitan idealism of the century and a contempt for some of the idols of the marketplace.

Vergennes was far too good a diplomatist to miss such opportunities for extending the moral dominion of France as Dutch and other affairs offered him. His agents throughout the world played the game for influence as Harris played it, each side calling the play of the other "intrigue." In 1785 he approved the recreation of a French East India Company. British statesmen suspected that this Company would exploit the new connexion with Holland, and possibly amalgamate with the Dutch Company[4]. Therefore, Harris paid special attention to the Dutch Directors. These intrigues, suspicions and counter-intrigues did not improve the prospects of the commercial treaty. Further, Pitt was no doubt anxious that fiscal union between

[1] Sorel, I. 313–5. This was in 1777.
[2] These sayings were credited to him by Hennin after his death. (Doniol, *Le Comte de Vergennes et P.M.Hennin*, pp. 103–4.) They may not be verbally correct, but they are in accordance with his conduct.
[3] Pitt was Shelburne's Chancellor of the Exchequer; but Rose (*Pitt*, I. 325) has "found no sign of his opinions on the subject" of Vergennes' proposals and Shelburne's reception of them.
[4] Harris's correspondence contains many references to this suspicion.

England and Ireland should precede changes in Great Britain's external economic relations[1]. His Irish attempt and failure were not complete until June, 1785. By that time, Vergennes was putting pressure on Great Britain to carry out Article 18. Early in 1784, a British Commissioner had been sent to Paris; but he had been kept waiting months for Instructions. In March, 1785, he was still without a reply to letters written in the previous September and November. But he had been advised to reject the French proposal for negotiations on the basis of mutual most favoured nation treatment, since the British Government was not prepared to abandon the specially favoured treatment of Portuguese wines stipulated for in the Methuen Treaty of 1703. Vergennes retaliated by arguing that if the new treaty was not completed, as agreed, by January 1st, 1786, the existing commercial arrangements between the two countries arising out of the Treaty of Utrecht must lapse. He next instigated a series of edicts interfering with British exports to France, of which the most serious was one of July 10th, 1785, forbidding the import of foreign linens, cottons and muslins. This was suspended, in consequence of a protest from London; but it showed what England might expect if her delays continued. Vergennes was well within his rights; for French silks had been prohibited in England since 1765. With considerable forbearance, however, he agreed to waive the claim to negotiate on a basis of complete reciprocity and most favoured nation treatment, on condition that negotiations were really opened. This was in October, 1785[2]. Two days before, he had prohibited the import of iron, steel and cutlery.

Pitt was already preparing to send over a highly qualified agent to treat with France; but he showed himself strangely dilatory in the whole business. While he delayed, Vergennes secured his Treaty, and most favoured nation terms, from the United Provinces. At Pitt's request, he now agreed to extend the "period of grace" for the British Treaty by six months, and eventually by twelve. Having gained time for consideration, Pitt instituted elaborate enquiries, partly by his new Committee of Council on Trade, partly by the agent whom he selected: William Eden, the future Lord Auckland. Eden, now in his forty-second year, had a varied political experience, no excessive tenacity of political friendship or principle, but great

[1] This is Rose's suggestion (*Pitt*, 1. 328). It lacks documentary evidence, but is inherently probable.
[2] Vergennes to Barthélemy (the French representative in London), October 13th. Salomon, *Pitt*, p. 212.

knowledge of economic affairs. Since 1772, he had been, in succession, Under-secretary of State, First Lord of the old Board of Trade, and Vice-treasurer of Ireland. In Ireland, he had helped to establish the National Bank. His economic horizon had been widened by intercourse with Adam Smith; but his conduct of the negotiation shows little trace of that desire to introduce a freer trade between nations, with a view to the future and in defiance of accompanying drawbacks, which can be discerned among the French negotiators. He was sent to make the best bargain possible, and excellently he succeeded. It is not suggested that concern for the far future was the deciding motive with the French. Their statesmen wished British goods to be imported, in order that Frenchmen might learn to imitate them; they wished them to be imported legally, in order that the King's revenue might benefit by the cessation of smuggling; they desired a freer market for French wines, for obvious reasons; and they wished to draw the teeth of England's jealous commercial system, both because it did France harm and because so difficult an operation would add to her prestige. But Vergennes' final despatch to Barthélemy, when all was over, seems sincere and takes higher ground. "It is not," he wrote, "a question as to which nation gains most in the early years, or of whether the balance of gain will ever be exact. We desire to give trade and industry a great stimulus, to procure an outlet for our wines, and still more to establish a permanent community of interests between many individuals of both nations, which in time of need may serve as a corrective to the warlike passions of our neighbours[1]."

Not till late in March, 1786, did Eden cross to France. He had worked hard in England since December. His appointment was popular among English manufacturers, whose right to protection against the competition of Ireland he had championed against Pitt in the previous May. Josiah Wedgwood, who had organised the manufacturers' opposition to the Irish proposals, wrote to congratulate him and placed his extensive knowledge at his service. Daily interviews with the interested parties had given Eden exact information, with regard to every important trade, as to whether reciprocity with France was desired; what level of duties would be most suitable; what was the highest level at which the trade could still manage to export to France; whether it was greatly in need of new markets;

[1] To Barthélemy, November 26th, 1786. (Paraphrased from the German version of the French MS. original in Salomon, *Pitt*, p. 235.)

whether it could bear French competition at all; and so on[1]. The representatives of most British industries were confident in their own competitive efficiency, Wedgwood in particular; but the silk manufacturers, although they boasted of giving employment to nearly 200,000 people, maintained that, for them, the choice was merely between continued prohibition of French silks and ruin. Arrived in Paris with all his material, Eden was surprised to find that the French Ministers were not equally well prepared. He suspected that, in consequence, they would aim at a vague sweeping kind of treaty, avoiding, so far as possible, the dangers which might result from pitting their relative ignorance against his carefully acquired knowledge. He intended to make that knowledge tell; and no doubt he succeeded. Vergennes' final disclaimer of all interest in the exact amount of immediate gain or loss from the Treaty seems sincere; but, in view of its unpopularity among French manufacturers and its unquestionably painful operation on French industry, the disclaimer might be interpreted as a veiled admission of failure, a half-apology for his agents' inability to beat Eden on his own ground. There had been no elaborate enquiry among experts. A single official, the Inspector-general of Manufacturers, appears to have furnished all the technical information on the industrial side.

This apparent neglect was, however, mainly the result, not of oversight, but of principle. Vergennes, with no parliamentary criticism to fear, could take risks and incur unpopularities such as Pitt became every year more reluctant to face. His right-hand man, G. de Rayneval, strongly influenced by physiocratic thought, stated dogmatically that the most useful and solid trade was that in agricultural produce; that the interests of industry were secondary; that it was an economic blunder for a nation to aim at complete industrial self-sufficiency; that an industry which could not maintain itself without high tariffs was not worth maintaining; and that prohibition was in all circumstances vicious. If he could widen the market for French agricultural produce—that is, for French wines—he was relatively indifferent as to Eden's successful bargaining about woollens and porcelain and silk and hardware and Birmingham "toys" He was aware that the years immediately following the Treaty upon which he was engaged might be difficult years for French industry. He was planning means for obviating these difficulties, including the intro-

---

[1] "Evidence for commercial treaty with France," B.M., Add. MSS. 34462 (Auckland Papers).

duction of English methods. He had hopes at this time that no less
a firm than Boulton and Watt might be induced to transfer their
business across the Channel.

The French negotiators were, also, fully conscious of the shattered
state of the French finances. This was what Vergennes had in mind
when he spoke of commercial relations "serving as a corrective to
the warlike passions of our neighbours." He believed that England
desired revenge for Yorktown and the Treaty of 1783. He wished to
divert her interests from war to commerce, because he thought that
France could not afford another war for some considerable time. In
the last War he had saved her honour, and at its conclusion had shown
moderation. To postpone or avert a fresh war, he was again prepared
to give something away. If the English valued above all things what
his physiocratic advisers considered relatively worthless, he naturally
made no objection.

Before the end of April, Eden was reporting that, in his opinion,
France would gain nothing essential through the Treaty beyond a reduced duty on her wines, whereas Great Britain would get rid of all old
and new prohibitions and other obstacles to her export trade. He had
still difficulties to surmount; and at times he found the very exacting
Instructions from home, inspired by Jenkinson at the Council of
Trade, difficult of execution. In August, he became nervous because,
the French manufacturers having had wind of the course of the
negotiations, letters of protest against their ruinous character were
pouring in to Calonne, now Controller-general of Finance. Eden
saw risk of a fall at the last fence and regretted that it had not been
possible to make the pace hotter. Having avoided the fall, he wrote
home on the day before signature (September 25th), that he hoped the
English manufacturers would, for a time at any rate, moderate their
expressions of joy. Fortunately for him, when the news arrived,
although the King had "never been seen in such spirits," "the principal merchants in the City did not choose to give an opinion about it,"
because—so Dorset, Eden's correspondent, held—"anything, if
novel, is apt to stupify merchants[1]." And as no such agreement ever
completely satisfies commercial men, there were some complaints
and talk of a sacrificing of British interests. It was Pitt who, in
defending the Treaty in the House during February, 1787, against the
usual factious Whig opposition, was indiscreet enough to argue that,
while advantageous to France, it was still more so to Great Britain.

[1] Dorset to Eden, *Auckland Journals*, I. 392.

Eden's anticipation of the provisions of his Treaty had been substantially accurate. Its earlier clauses provided for general freedom
of intercourse and free exercise of religion in time of peace, and for
civilised treatment of domiciled enemy subjects in the event of war[1].
Its later clauses dealt at length with privateering, contraband, piracy
and the legal relations of shipmasters of either nation to the local
authorities of the other when in its seaports. The chief central clauses,
first, reduced the duty on French wines to the level of that on the
wines of Portugal, and adjusted, favourably to France, duties on
vinegar, brandy and oil; secondly, fixed a maximum duty of 10 per cent.
ad valorem, in either country, on hardware, cutlery, and miscellaneous
metal wares; thirdly, fixed a similar maximum duty of 12 per cent.
on cottons, woollens, porcelain, earthenware and glass. Silk and all
goods mixed with silk remained mutually prohibited. This was
regarded as Eden's great coup; for England had small hope of export-
ing silks to France.

Although, during the debates on the Commercial Treaty, Pitt
denounced the belief in unalterable hostility between any two nations
as "weak and childish," during the negotiations he had told Eden
that, while counting the French sincere on the economic side, he was
suspicious of their assurances of political friendship[2]. Thorough-
going haters of France, like Carmarthen and Harris, were convinced
that there was no sincerity anywhere: economic compliance was a
mere political subterfuge. The success of France in the United Provinces during 1785, followed by an energetic development of her
defensive and naval works at Cherbourg, and by an Eastern policy
which kept England constantly on the alert, served to nourish Pitt's
suspicions and Harris's conviction. While Eden was working in Paris
during the summer of 1786, Harris—as has been seen—was as near
despair as was possible with his vigorous and sanguine temper. Two
deaths and a crisis in French internal affairs happened opportunely
for his policy. On August 17th, 1786, Frederick of Prussia died. Six
months later (February 13th, 1787), Vergennes died. Within a fortnight of Vergennes' death, Calonne was explaining to the First
Assembly of Notables the desperate condition of the French finances.

The British representatives at Berlin had long hoped that the new
King, Frederick William, brother of the Princess of Orange, might

---

[1] In case of war, Englishmen domiciled in France, and *vice versa*, might stay
and trade; if their conduct made it necessary to remove them, they were to have
twelve months in which to wind up their affairs (Art. II).
[2] To Eden, June 10th, 1786. *Auckland Correspondence*, I. 127.

introduce into Prussia's Dutch policy a change favourable to British interests. Frederick the Great was hardly buried, before the Princess told Harris that "the only means of saving" the House of Orange was "a united support in its behalf from England and Prussia." She read to him letters from her brother expressing determination[1]. She (naturally) did not explain, if indeed she knew, that her brother's determination was intermittent, liable to be suspended at almost any moment by the influence of what an English Ambassador once called the "female appendices[2]" of Potsdam. A fortnight later, a Prussian Envoy, Görtz, was explaining to Harris that, though his master would prefer above all things to "conciliate matters" in the United Provinces through France, yet there were lengths of conciliation to which he would not go, and that, in certain contingencies, he would break with France, unless, indeed, he were faced by the superior might of "Austria and Russia siding avowedly with France on this occasion." Since France would have carried Spain with her, it is clear that opinion in Berlin was still much influenced by fear of that quadruple *entente*. As a protection against such a combination, Görtz urged "the necessity of a Continental System being formed between England and Prussia." Harris listened; but he had no instructions to take the matter up[3].

"So long as M. le Comte de Vergennes lived," wrote the French Foreign Office official who was responsible for correspondence with the United Provinces, "all the measures adopted by England to regain preeminence in Holland were fruitless[4]." During the last months of Vergennes' life it seemed probable that Dutch affairs would be "conciliated" by way of Paris. Late in the year, definite proposals, drafted by Rayneval, for a settlement between the Stadholder and the Patriots—proposals which Prussia was believed to favour— were brought by Rayneval himself from Paris. Harris was, no doubt, glad to be able to report that both the Prince, whom Rayneval described as "a complete fool[5]," and the Princess regarded them as "absolutely inadmissible[6]." He added that the English party was growing, led by van de Spiegel, Pensionary of Zealand. Early in 1787, he could report that the Prince was still firm and that, since France, he

---

[1] Harris to Carmarthen, September 1st, 1786.

[2] Morton Eden to Lord Auckland, November 23rd, 1792. *Dropmore* (Grenville) *Papers*, II. 347.

[3] Harris to Carmarthen, September 19th, 1786.

[4] Doniol, *Vergennes et Hennin*, p. 95. Hennin was the official in question.

[5] In a despatch of January 3rd, 1787. P. de Witt, *Une invasion Prussienne en 1787*, p. 142; quoted in Heigel, *Deutsche Geschichte*, I. 136.

[6] To Carmarthen, December 12th, 1786.

assumed, would try to force her solution, "civil war...might be a very near event[1]." In February, Vergennes was succeeded by Montmorin, a much inferior statesman, and the mess of the French treasury was disclosed by Calonne. Harris continued to work hard at propaganda, organising meetings, subsidising journals and pamphleteers, and evidently making progress[2].

By May, civil war in Holland had practically begun. The "Patriotic" party, by its origin that of the commercial aristocracy, was acquiring a revolutionary and democratic tinge by intercourse with France. Hitherto, the permanent limitation of the powers of the Stadholderate, and perhaps the removal of the undeniably incompetent and universally unpopular Stadholder in favour of his son, had been the measures contemplated. Now, the total abolition of the office was certainly being discussed. This enabled the English party to appeal to old deep-rooted popular sentiment in favour of the House of Orange. Even in the Province of Holland itself, the stronghold of the Patriots, there were Orange elements. The dockers of Amsterdam, for instance, preferred a remote Prince to the local *Mynheers*—capitalistic Patriots—and were accessible to Harris's propaganda. The French Ambassador Vérac was working, also with success, on the other side. Such external interference in domestic affairs was singularly easy in a state "built up in the most amazing fashion out of Federation, Republic, Monarchy, Crown Property and heritable Privileges," as Clausewitz described the United Provinces at this time[3].

The crisis came in June. Both sides had armed. The Prince had about 4000 men; the Patriots a larger, but less compact, body of Free Companies (militia). Some months earlier, the Prince and Princess had left the Hague and the Province of Holland for a safer residence at Nymwegen. But recent changes of opinion encouraged Princess Wilhelmina to think that, by a personal appeal at the Hague, she might yet win a majority of the States-General for the Orange cause. She set out, with a very small following, early on June 28th— spent the night in a peasant's house, a prisoner of the Free Companies of the province of Holland, and returned next day to Nymwegen.

Thereupon, her brother, who had heard an exaggerated report of the insults offered her, sent a threatening despatch to the States of Holland

---

[1] To Carmarthen, January 2nd, 1787.
[2] See his correspondence, February-April, *passim*.
[3] *Der Feldzug des Herzogs von Braunschweig von* 1787, p. 259; quoted in Heigel, I. 133.

and ordered his nearest troops to hold themselves in readiness. He
was careful to treat the issue as personal, not political, and to explain
that he was far from contemplating war. "She wants to drag me into
a war," he told one of her confidential servants, "but I will soon show
her that I am not to be led by her[1]." Yet war might come; and, if
it came, he knew he must look to England. For some years, Hertzberg had been advocating an Anglo-Prussian-Dutch "system" at
Berlin. The growth of the English party in the Provinces, and the
fear of a Dutch democratic republic subservient to France, had roused
Pitt and the Cabinet, hitherto not very responsive to Harris's despatches. Harris had been in consultation with Ministers at Whitehall
in May. The Cabinet, most certainly, did not want war; but in view
of the financial embarrassments of France it was prepared to adopt
a course which might conceivably lead to war. Harris went back
with a promise of £20,000 for the Orange cause[2]. Next month, he
obtained £70,000 more. In July, Carmarthen assumed, almost as
a matter of course, the armed intervention of the King of Prussia[3];
and Pitt sent for the Prussian Ambassador, with whom hitherto he
had had few dealings, to tell him that the insult to Princess Wilhelmina
concerned her brother only and that France had no right to intervene
in any way. It is evident that, if he could get the famous Prussian
army in motion, he was prepared to risk war. On August 2nd, he wrote
instructing Cornwallis to seize Trincomalee from the Dutch, so soon
as hostilities began, in order that the French might not use it as a base,
and that the English might—possibly for an attack on the Cape of
Good Hope[4].

Rather better diplomacy on the part of France, a diplomacy such
as Vergennes could, almost certainly, have commanded, or a different
course of events in Eastern Europe, might have shattered Carmarthen's
assumption; for in July Frederick William was trimming. He wanted
a settlement without war; and it should have been easy for France
to make the Patriots offer satisfactory, but not to them humiliating,
terms. This she failed to do, thus giving the impression that she meant
to support them through thick and thin; yet, at the end of August,
Vérac, her Ambassador at the Hague, their party's patron and *faiseur*,
was recalled and succeeded by St Priest, a representative who was not

[1] Luckwaldt, *Die englisch-preussische Allianz von* 1788, p. 67.
[2] *Malmesbury Correspondence*, II. 306. Pitt himself was not in favour of a policy
which might lead to war: but he agreed to the financial assistance. Rose, I. 360.
[3] *Malmesbury Correspondence*, II. 329, July 3rd.
[4] *Cornwallis Correspondence*, I. 321.

committed. Meanwhile, Frederick William was relieved of anxiety towards the east, by the growing internal difficulties of the Habsburg dominions, where Joseph's reforms were bearing their fruit of disaffection, and still more, in August, by the sudden decision of the Porte, weary of Catharine's insolence, to declare war on Russia. Sir Robert Ainslie, our Ambassador at Constantinople, had warned the Foreign Office of the impending Declaration. It was issued so opportunely as an embarrassment to the Imperial Courts, that contemporaries credited it to Ainslie or his Prussian colleague. The suggestion is unproved and, in view of the dates of the various relevant decisions, unlikely. Certainly, Ainslie had no Instructions in this sense.

News of Turkey's decision reached Berlin in the first days of September. Vérac's recall from the Hague had taken place at the end of a month during which French diplomacy had seemed definitely provocative. The recall suggested a weakening of purpose. Great Britain had already sent a General to Germany to hire Hessians, and had put ammunition at the disposal of the Orange party. The King of Prussia had failed to secure any apology or satisfaction from the States of Holland. He had just decided to send an ultimatum to the Hague and to close with English offers of cooperation. The news that his imperial neighbours would now probably have their hands full greatly eased his mind[1].

On September 13th, Ferdinand of Brunswick, all his plans having been mathematically drawn out and the risks of cutting the dykes carefully weighed[2], crossed the Dutch frontier with 20,000 men, to attack the Province of Holland only. Brunswick's preparations were superfluous. The Hollanders, unsupported by France, collapsed. Opinion swung round at the Hague. By the 20th, the mob was tearing a Patriots' flag in pieces in front of the British Embassy, with cries of *Oranje boven*; and Harris's eyes were moistening as he met again the Prince of Orange, of whom he had so exceedingly low an opinion. Next day, he induced the States of Holland to rescind a decision, which they had taken on the 9th, appealing to France for aid. Amsterdam showed fight, but capitulated on October 10th. In Berlin, Hertzberg quoted *veni, vidi, vici*; and in Europe the conviction was confirmed that Prussian troops, led by Ferdinand of Brunswick, were invincible.

[1] It was not until November that Austria's participation in the Russo-Turkish War was definitively known.

[2] He started at the new moon, so as to secure the minimum variation of the tides. Clausewitz, who was with him, thought the campaign reckless and its success due almost entirely to Dutch incompetence, Heigel, 1. 143-4.

Montmorin was bewildered at the speed of events. Before the States of Holland had rescinded their appeal, he had issued a declaration that France could not reject it (September 16th). Two days earlier, Pitt had written to William Eden, who was still clearing up the aftermath of the commercial negotiation in Paris, that, if France wished to maintain predominance in Holland she would have to fight[1]. Carmarthen had already told Harris that France was not ready and, in his opinion, was unlikely to fight[2]. Harris, who heard no news of French military action down to September 22nd, concurred[3].

On September 21st, a despatch, drawn up by Pitt himself, went to all British Embassies, notifying them that, since France had declared her intention of assisting that party in the Province of Holland which resisted the King of Prussia's just demands, and since her intervention had not been called for by a majority in the States-General, and thus there was no *casus foederis*, His Britannic Majesty was arming a fleet and augmenting his land forces. Very soon, forty ships of the line, from the fleet which Pitt had been nursing, were ready for sea. Once more, events moved too quickly for Montmorin. Late in September, Amsterdam was still holding out in the expectation that he would act; but he was already telling Eden in confidence that, if the French party in the Provinces proved utterly weak, action would be folly[4]. Before the end of the month, he was interviewing William Grenville, sent over as a Special Envoy to smooth matters down if possible, but was protesting that he could discuss nothing until the Prussian troops were withdrawn, and meanwhile was proceeding with belated military preparations[5]. The fall of Amsterdam, apart from all other circumstances, made French intervention hopeless; and on October 27th Montmorin exchanged with Eden and Dorset, the ornamental British Ambassador to the Court of Versailles, a Declaration and Counter-Declaration of Disarmament, the French Declaration stating that France had never intended to intervene in Holland and retained no hostile views towards any party involved in the affair—that is to say, towards Prussia. After the signature, Dorset reported

[1] *Auckland Correspondence*, I. 192.
[2] Carmarthen to Harris, September 8th.
[3] To Carmarthen, September 22nd. Harris's despatch of September 18th, written in the full rush of events, is a most brilliant document. At 11.30 p.m. he wrote "and I think I can now venture to congratulate your Lordships that the revolution in this country is as complete as it was in 1747."
[4] Eden to Carmarthen, September 25th.
[5] Grenville to Carmarthen, September 28th.

that "there did not seem to remain any degree of ill-humour, tho'
there was visible a little awkwardness on occasion of the humiliating
terms to which this Court had been obliged to subscribe[1]."

But Montmorin told Eden that war had been nearer than might
have been supposed. For "exclusive of all objects of internal interest,
there had been some opinion of weight that a war was the best mode
of finishing the internal troubles which had prevailed at the time of
the King of Prussia's march[2]." The suggestion recurred again and
again in France during the next five years; for foreign war, it has
been said, was the classical cure for internal troubles[3].

Even before Amsterdam had fallen, Harris was pressing the Dutch
for an alliance. But with so complex a polity as the United Provinces
negotiations were exceptionally slow. In November, while the
Prussian troops were beginning to withdraw, the Orange party was
consolidating its power by the dismissal of "Patriotic" functionaries.
In December, Harris's friend van de Spiegel became Grand Pensionary of the United Provinces. Though a friend, he did not wish
to sell his friendship too cheap; and, since in any Anglo-Dutch discussion colonial questions at once came to the front, the Dutch statesman suggested that Great Britain should give back Negapatam[4]. Harris
managed to put this suggestion aside. By the end of March, 1788,
his draft had passed the States of Holland, and on April 15th, the
Defensive Alliance between His Britannic Majesty and Their High
Mightinesses the States-General of the United Provinces was signed[5].
A Prusso-Dutch Treaty was signed the same day.

Great Britain and the Provinces promised one another friendship
and armed assistance if involved in war, specifying the amount of
that assistance. A clause, to which England attached great importance,
provided for military and naval cooperation in such an event between
the Dutch and British authorities in the East. In case of war with
a common enemy, neither was to disarm or make peace without the
consent of the other. Great Britain guaranteed to the Prince of Orange
the Hereditary Stadholderate of the United Provinces, and the office
of Hereditary Governor in every Province, "engaging to maintain
that form of Government against all attacks and enterprises, direct
or indirect, of whatsoever nature they might be." The contracting

[1] To Carmarthen, November 1st.
[2] Eden to Carmarthen, November 1st.
[3] The point is repeatedly referred to by Sorel.
[4] Harris's despatches, December and January, *passim*.
[5] Harris to Carmarthen, April 15th, 1788, enclosing the treaty.

parties agreed to negotiate further about Negapatam. On May 8th, 1788, the Treaty was ratified, and the Dutch skiff appeared to be once more in tow behind the British ship of the line. This, however, was the year in which Mirabeau, in his pamphlet *Aux Bataves sur le Stathouderat*, told the Dutch that England was working through the House of Orange "to turn them into European Indians." In the long run, the reimposition of a personally unpopular and incompetent Stadholder by foreign arms worked as Mirabeau hoped it might—to increase the existing dislike of the office and of the Powers who propped it. It did so the more surely, because Great Britain in fact never opened the promised negotiations about Negapatam.

Brunswick's military promenade to Amsterdam and its brilliant results proved a curse to Prussia. They set her statesmen planning other and greater *coups*, to be brought about by an opportune waving of the Prussian sword, and confirmed her King in his natural inclinations. "When once prevailed upon to exert himself," wrote Joseph Ewart from Berlin about this time[1], "he is by no means deficient in judgement and penetration; but he requires to be roused from his dissipation and inactivity." It might well seem to him, now, that an occasional rousing was enough. Frederick William emerged from the Dutch crisis pledged to Great Britain, by a secret agreement of October 20th, 1787, to maintain the Dutch Constitution. Beyond that point he was not committed; nor was Great Britain. Throughout the winter, both Governments worked at the Dutch Treaties, which in themselves constituted a political *consortium* of the three Powers, if not exactly a Triple Alliance.

For a time, Great Britain had not been anxious to go further. There were once more rumours of a Quadruple Alliance of the Imperial and Bourbon Courts, and Pitt wished to learn what they were worth. The scheme came from Catharine, who during 1787 had partly shown her hand by refusing to renew her Commercial Treaty with Great Britain, while including one with France. She now (late in 1787) sounded Montmorin through Ségur, the French Ambassador at Petrograd. But an alliance with Russia meant for France the sacrifice of three of her oldest diplomatic friendships—those with Sweden, Poland, and the Porte. Montmorin could not bring himself to make such sacrifices: the Quadruple Alliance remained a scheme[2], and Pitt was for the moment free of that risk.

Intimate relations between Great Britain and Prussia were first post-

---

[1] To Carmarthen, January 9th, 1785.   [2] Sorel, I. 322, 323.

poned and always imperilled by the working of the anti-British party
at Berlin and by the fantastic programmes of European rearrangement
which, at this time, were being put forward by Hertzberg. Hertzberg,
as a Prussian, was not greatly interested in the United Provinces, where
Prussian interests were dynastic rather than territorial, except in so
far as Dutch affairs might promote that closer cooperation with Great
Britain which he had always favoured, in opposition to his colleague,
Fink von Finkenstein, who inclined to a French connexion. While Pitt
regarded Anglo-Prussian cooperation *via* the Netherlands as a safeguard for the peace of Europe, and for those colonial and maritime
interests which the Dutch Alliance was especially intended to promote,
Hertzberg saw in it a means of promoting the territorial consolidation
and expansion of Prussia in the east, for which the state of affairs in
Austria, Russia and Turkey seemed to present opportunities. Before
the end of the year 1787, he had outlined a gigantic system of rearrangements and "compensations," which Joseph Ewart, the British
Secretary of Legation at Berlin, described in January, 1788, as "equally
extravagant and impracticable in the present circumstances[1]."

In Prussia, no Ministerial plan had the weight and influence
belonging to plans agreed on by a British Cabinet, since it was always
uncertain to the last moment whether any such plan would receive
the royal sanction. So, British diplomatic representatives at Berlin
had to keep in constant and unwelcome touch with what Morton
Eden, in 1791, called "the wretched and dirty intrigues that pervade
this Court." Eden, in a fit of disgust, actually went so far as to say,
in a very private letter, that the Prussian Ministers "knew about as
much and had as much influence in public affairs as his boy"—an
overstatement, but significant[2].

Hertzberg's plans during 1787 and the early part of 1788 were
based on the assumption that Russia and Austria would profit by
the Turkish War. Russia was known to covet the Black Sea port of
Oczakoff and the province of Bessarabia, Austria the provinces of
Moldavia and Wallachia. Assuming that they secured these or other
important territories, Prussia must put forward a claim for compensation backed by force and British influence. The compensation was
to be secured by a reshuffle of Polish territory. In the First Partition,
Prussia had linked her detached province of East Prussia to the mass

---

[1] To Carmarthen, January 9th, 1788.
[2] Eden to Grenville, December 31st, 1791; Morton Eden to Lord Auckland,
November 23rd, 1792. *Dropmore Papers*, II. 245 and 347.

of her territory by securing West Prussia from the Poles; but she had not acquired Danzig. The core of the schemes was that she should obtain Danzig and the palatinates of Posen and Kalisch (Great Poland), the Poles being in their turn compensated by the retrocession of Galicia, Austria's acquisition in the First Partition. Ewart was "informed, in private confidence," at the beginning of 1788, "that the King of Prussia would have no objection to Russia's obtaining Oczakoff and Bessarabia, but that he was more averse than ever to the Emperor's making any acquisitions, without his having the equivalent, on the side of Poland[1]." Thus, in broad outline, the King and his Minister were in agreement.

Great Britain can hardly be said to have had any Polish policy at that time. Her Embassy at Warsaw was regarded mainly as an outpost for securing information about the plans of Poland's neighbours—a function which it fulfilled imperfectly, owing to "the extreme dearth of news at this place," as Charles Whitworth wrote in 1786. His Instructions, when sent there in January of that year, had been simply to watch all designs for the dismemberment of Turkey or Poland, and to safeguard British commercial interests[2]. It was not the habit of the British Foreign Office to embody political "systems" or hypothetical policies in the initial Instructions for Ambassadors. The British Instructions would make a very meagre collection, if placed side by side with the great French series of ambassadorial Instructions; but the almost complete absence of subsequent despatches from London to Whitworth shows that the bald Instructions in this case correctly outlined the Polish interests of his Government.

Although schemes for rearrangements of Polish territory, certainly, did not greatly concern the Cabinet of St James', it was necessary, when drawing closer to Prussia, to weigh the resulting commitments. It was therefore important to keep abreast of Hertzberg's plans and his master's impulses, and to move with some caution. The history of the Triple Alliance, which dominated British foreign policy from 1788 to 1791, proves that, in his desire to terminate a period of isolation and secure continental support for his general policy, Pitt showed too little rather than too much caution when dealing with his principal

---

[1] To Carmarthen, January 15th, 1788.

[2] Whitworth to Carmarthen, April 8th, 1786 and his Instructions, January, 1786. The Foreign Office only showed interest in Warsaw when it instructed Whitworth to attend, on some pretext, the meeting of Catharine and the King of Poland at Kieff, in April, 1787. He was sent to collect news, but failed to make Catharine talk politics. To Carmarthen, April 24th and May 7th, 1787. Whitworth was promoted to Petrograd in October, 1788.

Ally. Not because Prussia was abnormally lacking in scruple, if judged by the diplomatic standards of the day; but because her real interests and those of Great Britain lay in such different fields, sustained and active cooperation between the two Powers was always difficult.

Just before the Treaties with the United Provinces were signed, *i.e.* early in April, 1788, Pitt had written down his notion of the form which an Anglo-Prussian alliance might take[1]. Putting on one side a definite proposal which had come through Ewart from Hertzberg for joint action in the east, he suggested that a treaty guaranteeing the Dutch settlement should include also a general defensive alliance and guarantee of territories between the two Powers, which might be kept secret so long as the Quadruple Alliance of the Imperial and Bourbon Courts remained incomplete. The Cabinet was more cautious, and decided against the suggested mutual guarantee of territory. It fully agreed that Great Britain ought not to be in any way committed to Hertzberg's territorial speculations. Hertzberg tried again. Again, the British Cabinet raised difficulties and refused to commit itself too deeply[2], unless Prussia would make very general promises of military assistance. This angered King Frederick William. He told his Minister that he was determined not to employ his troops outside Germany and the Netherlands, and thanked God that he had no need to snatch at alliances[3]. Within a fortnight he had accepted the Alliance, though not quite on the terms which had provoked this outburst.

His acceptance was the work of Sir James Harris. The Prussian King had an appointment to visit his sister, the Princess of Orange, at her château of the Loo, in the second week of June. Just before he started, Ewart at Berlin was not very confident. The French party in Prussia was active, and Ewart could only express the hope that the King would be "undeceived at Loo[4]." To accomplish this, the full apparatus of diplomacy was brought to bear. King George wrote an appropriate autograph letter to the Princess, which Harris delivered[5]. During the critical day (June 12th), Harris concentrated the whole strength of his trained and impressive personality on the King —and bribed the King's valet to block the access of a hostile personality.

---

[1] April 2nd, 1788. Pitt MSS. In Salomon, p. 342.
[2] Carmarthen to Ewart, May 14th, 1788. Hertzberg's proposal to Ewart was dated April 19th. Luckwaldt, pp. 105-6.
[3] In a note of May 30th. Salomon, p. 345.
[4] To Carmarthen, May 31st.
[5] *Malmesbury Correspondence*, II. 420.

Matters were settled between King and Ambassador after midnight during a walk in the gardens, away from the music of the State ball. The King returned to the music, while Harris, with the Minister Alvensleben, spent the small hours of the morning drawing up the Treaty on the basis of one of Hertzberg's drafts. The King looked through the draft at 9 a.m., and signed the Treaty at 2 p.m. on the 13th. Harris despatched his courier to Helvoetsluys, and spent the afternoon going over the European situation with England's new Ally. On the 14th, he must have begun the series of despatches in which he told his Cabinet how it had all been done[1]. His rewards were a peerage and the right to bear the Prussian Eagle in his coat of Arms. Meanwhile, from Berlin, Ewart was able to report that "the French emissaries were discarded" and that the Countess Ingelheim—the reigning Mistress—"warmly applauded" the King's conduct[2].

The Treaty was officially described as provisional. The definitive Treaty was signed by Hertzberg and Ewart, exactly four months later; but not many changes were made in Harris's work. The final Treaty was a Defensive Alliance, the United Kingdom and Prussia pledging themselves to support one another, if attacked, with a force of at least 20,000 men or an equivalent in cash, and to uphold the Dutch Settlement of 1787. As a concession to Frederick William's known prejudice, Prussian auxiliaries were not to be used by Great Britain outside Europe or be shipped to Gibraltar. Secret articles stipulated that the promised contingents should not be furnished, unless the Party attacked had set 44,000 men of its own in motion; and that Prussia might count on the help of a British fleet, should she require it.

Hertzberg acted on the principle that Prussia's policy was to have no policy—she ought to be always adjusting her programmes to a changing world, in order to extract from it the maximum of land and of power. He held to the main objects of his great scheme; but he was prepared to put in operation any lesser, or greater, scheme which circumstances might favour. Now the early course of the War of Russia and Austria against Turkey suggested that the vast conquests of the Imperial Courts, in return for which Prussia was to press for compensations equally vast, might never be achieved. Wars got under way slowly in eastern Europe, and nothing considerable was attempted during 1787. In 1788 disease ravaged the ill-organised Russian armies and the Act of God at sea crippled the fleet of

---

[1] They are dated June 15th and have been fully utilised by Salomon and Rose.
[2] To Carmarthen, June 28th.

Sebastopol. It was only at the very end of the year (December 17th) that Oczakoff was carried in a last desperate assault and its population massacred. Austria, by an immense effort, had put 180,000 men into the field, but in scattered and ill-coordinated armies. Disease broke out in them. Their Generals were incompetent, but so, too, was the Emperor, who insisted on retaining the supreme command. So unsuccessful were the early months of the War that in August, when news of the Anglo-Prussian Treaty came, Joseph was writing to Kaunitz that, if Prussia and England joined in, "then the monarchy was lost," and there was nothing to prevent the King of Prussia from "occupying all Bohemia and Moravia and marching on Vienna[1]." By September, the Austrians were retreating, leaving the Banat of Temesvar to be ravaged by the Turks and in fear for Transylvania. The Emperor's letters were more despairing than ever. Very naturally, the thought arose in Berlin that Prussia by an opportune show of force—she had already troops massed on the Austrian frontier— might get compensation, though Austria got nothing from her Turkish war but disgrace. Hertzberg began to see the most brilliant prospects opening out for Prussian policy[2].

For a time, in the summer, Catharine had seemed in even greater danger than Joseph. The chivalrous, autocratic and inconsequent Gustavus III of Sweden had suddenly declared war, come to an understanding with the Turks, and marched on Petrograd through Finland. In the north, Catharine had only a small force and her Cronstadt fleet. The fleet fought an indecisive action and the Empress had horses ready for the journey to Moscow. Then, partly as a result of Russian manipulation, the powerful party among the Swedish nobility and gentry which detested Gustavus, on account of his autocratic home policy, connived at revolts among the troops and desertions of officers. At the same time, the Danes, secretly bound to Russia in case of a Russo-Swedish war, prepared to invade Sweden from Norway and beset Gothenburg. On September 2nd, Carmarthen wrote to Joseph Ewart: "The last accounts which we have received of the situation of the King of Sweden represent his difficulties as much increased, and state the probability of his applying to this Court and that of Berlin, as well as to France, for good offices and mediation." It was most desirable, he added, that England and Prussia should "prevent France having a share in the event," and hinder Russia

---

[1] August 26th. Quoted in Sorel, I. 526.
[2] Krauel, *Hertzberg*, p. 43; quoted in Salomon, p. 488.

from becoming supreme in the Baltic[1]. Pitt and his colleagues began to see their new Triple Alliance not only preserving for Great Britain that peace which they sincerely prized, but also acting as the great and honoured European peace-maker, the preventer of France, the curb of Russia, the saviour of Sweden and, should she need saving, of Turkey. At Constantinople, Sir Robert Ainslie and his Prussian colleague Dietz were influencing Turkish policy and preparing the way for mediation by the Triple Alliance, when the time for peacemaking should come. In the struggle for prestige among the Great Powers mediations had long played an important part. Could Great Britain mediate, so as to save two old dependants of France, Sweden and the Porte, nothing would more clearly demonstrate that to her was already passing that moral leadership of Europe which in 1783 the French seemed to have recovered.

That the Alliance should strike in upon the weakness of its neighbours and thus upset existing territorial arrangements, did not enter into the British conception. The British point of view was expressed clearly, if not concisely, a year later by Leeds (Carmarthen), when Hertzberg's scheme, in a fresh form, had again been put forward. The scheme, he said, went much beyond "the spirit of our Treaty of Alliance, which is purely of a defensive nature and by which, of course, we cannot be considered as in any degree bound to support a system of an offensive nature, the great end of which appears to be aggrandisement rather than security, and which, from its very nature, is liable to provoke fresh hostilities, instead of contributing to the restoration of general tranquillity[2]."

In the autumn of 1788, Catharine was not in a mood to accept British or any other mediation. She supposed, wrongly[3], that Great Britain and Prussia had some hand in the King of Sweden's adventure, and wished to punish him and them. She had saved herself by her own energy and did not intend to be beholden to that "*grandissime politique fr. Ge.*" (*frère George*), as she called Pitt's master in her private correspondence[4]. But, if Catharine was inaccessible, the Court of Copenhagen was not; and there Great Britain was strongly represented, by Hugh Elliot. He was instructed to call off the Danes.

---

[1] See also Pitt to Grenville, September 1st, 1788: "Our intervention may prevent his (Gustavus') becoming totally insignificant, a dependent upon Russia, and it seems to me an essential point." *Dropmore Papers*, I. 353.

[2] Leeds to Ewart, June 24th, 1789.

[3] The evidence is in Rose, *Pitt*, I. 494–5.

[4] To Grimm, quoted in Sorel, I. 528.

Mediation between Denmark and Sweden had been offered in a despatch from Carmarthen to Elliot, dated August 15th. The great Minister Bernstorff had seemed well disposed; but the young Prince Royal repeated what Elliot had been told before, that Denmark was bound by treaty to Russia and must stand to her word. This brought Pitt forward in person. A despatch to Elliot drafted by him left this country on September 9th. It criticised Danish policy on the ground that it was certain "to extend the mischiefs of the present war in a manner which cannot fail to excite the most serious attention, and to have a great effect on the conduct, of all those Courts who are interested in the relative situation of the different Powers of the Baltic." Before he received this rather obscurely veiled threat, learning from Ewart that Prussia was in agreement with Great Britain and was contemplating an invasion of Holstein, also that there was imminent risk of Gustavus' accepting French mediation, Elliot crossed to Sweden, to come into personal contact with the King, who, in spite of his high spirit, was almost overwhelmed by external danger and domestic treachery. Abandoning his natural inclination to trust in Sweden's ancient ally France, Gustavus, who knew that time was short, accepted Elliot's magniloquently worded offer without reserve: "Sire, give me your Crown; I will return it to you with added lustre."

The return of the Crown was not entirely Elliot's work. He went at once to the Danish camp, for the Danes were now advancing on Gothenburg; but, at first, he failed to impose mediation upon the Prince Royal. The siege of Gothenburg was prepared; but so was the defence—by Gustavus himself, with the assistance of English sailors from ships then in the port. As the prospect of carrying the town by a *coup de main* seemed over, the Danes accepted a short Armistice, on October 9th. During the period of the Armistice, news of Prussia's threat to Holstein arrived. This strengthened Elliot's hand. In the middle of November, the Armistice was extended for six months and the immediate danger to Sweden was over[1]. There was no peace: the state of war continued between Sweden and Russia: Denmark's good faith was doubted; yet, at the close of the year, the Triple Alliance was looking forward with confidence to a general pacification and a satisfactory settlement during 1789. But its members were not agreed as to what constituted a satisfactory settlement. The fall of Oczakoff, following on Sweden's breakdown, closed the year not unsatisfactorily, if not brilliantly, for Catharine. She had the

[1] This account is based on Rose, *Pitt*, I. 495.

patience and the long views of her adopted country. If not Constantinople or Bessarabia in this War, then in the next or in some yet remote war. Only for a moment, during Gustavus' Finland raid, had she ever feared attack—and even then not for Russia proper. Without bitterness or any recrimination, she acquiesced in the change of plan which circumstances seemed to force on her Ally. She wrote to him just before Christmas, and before she can have had the news from Oczakoff, that she would raise no objection at all to his making peace with the Porte, if he so desired. But she would have nothing to do with mediation from any quarter. The view now prevalent at Vienna was put by Kaunitz thus: "so long as Prussia's power has not been curtailed, all the intentions, plans and enterprises of the two Imperial Courts will always be hindered and destroyed by her[1]." It was therefore necessary, if in any way possible, to settle accounts with Prussia. On New Year's Day 1789, the chances of doing so in the near future would have appeared, to any cool observer, scanty.

The relations between Berlin and the Imperial Courts had just been complicated by events in Poland. For years diplomatists had anticipated dissolution for this country, "precluded from every exterior commerce by its neighbours and deprived of every interior improvement by its Constitution[2]." Now, the Poles, hoping to be relieved of Russian pressure by the withdrawal of Catharine's armies for use elsewhere, initiated a constitutional reform. The Diet met on October 6th, 1788, and prepared for action by "confederating" itself. By "confederation" it acquired the power to make decisions by an ordinary majority vote, instead of by that unanimity, the need for which, under the old Polish Constitution, had done more than anything else to ruin the country[3]. Catharine, who was in fact compelled to remove her troops from Polish soil, called to Poland over her shoulder, so to speak, that she would regard the least change in the Constitution as a breach of treaty (November, 1788). Prussia egged the Poles on to defy her, and the work of the Diet went forward. Early in December, the Diet decided to enter into negotiations with a view to a Prussian alliance, and to send missions to the European Courts to explain the contemplated reforms in the Polish Constitution. Thereupon, the Prussian representative at Warsaw, Lucchesini, let it be known, about Christmastime, that his master would guarantee

---

[1] Martens, *Traités de la Russie avec l'Autriche*, II. 188–9, quoted in Sorel, I. 528.
[2] Viscount Dalrymple (from Warsaw), October 1st, 1782.
[3] There is an excellent series of despatches on the work of the Great Diet from David Hailes who took over the embassy from Whitworth in November, 1788.

the independence of the Republic without interfering in its internal affairs. Prussia at once became popular among the patriots of Warsaw. They began, also, to approach the British representative and ask whether, if they made an alliance with Prussia, England would accede. The British representative was civil; but, not seeing what commercial advantage England could derive from a Polish alliance, with Prussia astride the trade route down the Vistula, and inclining to the view that Great Britain could only get any such advantage by working through Berlin, he advised his Polish friends to lean on Prussia, or else "they would never be able to effect any purpose, either commercial or political[1]." Approached again, rather later (March, 1789), he advised his Government that to step into Polish affairs might endanger relations with Prussia; that it would mean for England "taking the Republic under her protection"; that this was "undoubtedly the wish of the Poles and their chief design in proposing their commerce to us"; but that he was very doubtful how far we ought, "to engage for their independence" or incur "the danger arising from the protection of a sort of new Colonies[2]." The despatch, though not that of a Cabinet Minister, reflects perfectly the Polish problem, as seen from London[3].

In these opening months of the great year of Revolution, Prussia was encouraging revolutions wherever she could in the Habsburg dominions, which contained hardly one contented province, while blessing officially what Catharine called revolution in Poland. Prussian agents in Hungary were working on the pride and dissatisfaction of the Magyar leaders. In Galicia, they were explaining the benefits of reunion with a reformed Poland. In the Austrian Netherlands, they were blowing the fires of that revolution of Brabant which preceded the revolution of France, and gave half its title to Camille Desmoulins' first revolutionary journal[4]. Hertzberg, so a French agent reported from Berlin, wanted to push his master into action and glory, but was opposed by the courtiers and favourites: "all that lot are most anxious that the King of Prussia should not escape them, which would happen inevitably if that monarch went to lead his armies. So these people and the mistress are all for the maintenance of peace— and England still more so[5]." To Great Britain, at least, he did justice.

Among all the revolutions, actual or projected, that which touched

---

[1] Hailes to Carmarthen, February 8th, 1789.
[2] Hailes to Carmarthen, March 27th, 1789. The English Alliance was a favourite scheme of the Prince Sapieha of those days. Hailes to Carmarthen, July 13th, 1789.
[3] See below, p. 188.   [4] *Les Révolutions de France et de Brabant.*
[5] Report of the Comte d'Esterno, April 21st, 1789, in Sorel, I. 531.

Great Britain most nearly was the revolution of Brabant. Brabant, like all the other duchies and counties which formed the Austrian Netherlands, had inherited its own customs and constitution; and, until Joseph's day, the Habsburgs had respected this inheritance. No new taxes could be levied without the consent of the Provincial Estates, and the established taxes were voted from year to year. The country, as a whole, was passionately Catholic, though French philosophy had made headway in educated circles. The combination of autocratic tendencies, a striving after governmental uniformity, and a definitely anti-clerical strain in the Josephine system, had provoked all sections of Belgian society. The crisis began when Joseph attempted, by edicts dated January 1st, 1787, to introduce a centralised bureaucratic system for the whole country. Within four months, the Estates of Brabant had declined to vote the taxes, and the Council of Brabant had refused to accept dissolution. A lawyer demagogue, Henri van der Noot, called the men of Brussels to arms. On May 30th, the ancient militia of the gilds, swollen by peasants from the neighbouring villages, overawed the Regent and her husband—Marie Christine, Joseph's sister, and Duke Albert of Saxe-Teschen. The Government on the spot gave way; but, in the autumn, Joseph sent a soldier to enforce discipline. In January, 1788, the first blood was shed by the troops, while dispersing a mob in the streets of Brussels.

Joseph supposed that he had won and went forward with his reforms, especially the educational and ecclesiastical. In the course of 1788, opposition and refusals to vote taxes came from the Estates of Flanders and Hainault also. This opposition Joseph once more set himself to crush. By June, 1789, just before the fall of the Bastille, he supposed that he had succeeded. "At last we have won our game in Brabant," he wrote to his sister on the 26th[1]. In truth, the losing game for the Habsburg rule in the Low Countries had just entered on its final stage.

The English view of the Belgian situation was stated very clearly by King George, in a letter to the Duke of Leeds, later in the year. It would never, he said, be in the interests of Great Britain, "either that the Emperor should become absolute, or that a Democracy should be established there, as either must probably unite that country more with France[2]." During August, Pitt had drawn up a remarkable

---

[1] Heigel, *Deutsche Geschichte*, I. 199.
[2] George III to Leeds, December 1st, 1789. *Leeds Papers*, quoted in Salomon, p. 461.

memoir on the whole position, as a basis for replies to suggestions
from Prussia that Great Britain should encourage revolution in
Belgium and Galicia, with a view to their ultimate separation from
Austria[1]. Galicia, as it touched English interests, he put on one side
in few and significant words. "The object of increasing Poland with
a view to the extension of our commerce" he wrote, was "too remote
and contingent to be relied upon." But the Belgian question was of
another order. The prevention of a union of Belgium with France
was an object "worth the risk, or even the certainty," of a war. But
the mere creation of an independent Belgian State—one of the
possible results of supporting the Belgian patriots—was not a British
interest. Our sole direct interest was to keep Belgium in dependence
on Holland and ourselves. The *status quo ante*, a half-independent
Belgium, not too docile under Austrian rule, suited us perfectly; but
he recognised the difficulties in the way of its maintenance, and so
came to a rather lame conclusion. He might have mentioned that
the main cause why Great Britain, a few years earlier, had not looked
favourably on Joseph's scheme for exchanging the Low Countries
against Bavaria was the reasonable belief that a small independent
Belgian State was far more likely to fall permanently under French
influence than a group of Belgian Provinces, laxly ruled by a remote
but powerful Prince, who could make his voice heard in the counsels
of Europe. An alternative to independence or the maintenance of
the *status quo* was the union of Belgium with Holland. This suggestion
came from the Belgian leader van der Noot. Noot was not a democrat
of the '89 type—the leader of the growing democratic party was his
rival, Vonck—but a clerical and an upholder of the old Provincial
privileges. Driven from home by Joseph's temporary success in 1789,
he visited van de Spiegel, the Pensionary of the United Provinces, went
later to Berlin, and sent an agent to London. How sincere his proposal was, or what weight should be assigned to such schemings of
a party leader in exile, may be left undecided. He undoubtedly
made the suggestion to van de Spiegel that a son of the Prince of
Orange should be nominated Regent of Belgium[2]. The proposal was

---

[1] It is in the *Leeds Papers*, B.M. Add. MSS. 28068, and is dated August 27th.
A German translation is in Salomon, p. 453 *sqq.*

[2] *Résumé des Négociations qui accompagnèrent la révolution des Pays-Bas Autrichiens*, by L. B. J. van de Spiegel, 1841, quoted in Heigel, *op. cit.* I. 199. Van der
Noot's agent in England was a certain van Roode. Van de Spiegel mentioned the
scheme for Belgian independence, but apparently not the Regency scheme, to the
British Minister, Alleyne Fitzherbert. Fitzherbert was "not a little surprised that...
he could condescend to listen for a single instant, to a scheme which to my mind

weighed in London and known in Paris. A French agent in England reported it, in what seems a distorted form, in the course of September. England, he said, had for a time played with the idea of uniting the two countries and attaching the new composite State to the German Empire, as an additional electorate[1]. In his August memorandum, Pitt had in fact considered the scheme, and had dismissed it. It appeared to him, he wrote, that "the difference of religion and the clashing interests of commerce, particularly with respect to the navigation of the Scheldt, seemed to make that project difficult, if not impracticable." Nothing more was heard of it for years.

Discussing the possibility of an ultimate war with France on some Low Countries' issue, Pitt stated that he would rather become involved in such a war, "having the Emperor and Holland with us, and Prussia not against us," than run the risk of forcing it on now, and so driving France and Austria into a joint war with England, the United Provinces and Prussia. He had not yet come to understand the new France, nor foreseen that henceforward Franco-Austrian cooperation would be an impossibility. His conclusion of the whole matter was to wait, but to assure the Belgian insurgents that Great Britain would not allow the Emperor to destroy their Constitution.

Pitt did not anticipate any immediate complications with the French over the Belgian question; but he thought that, if "either the rashness of their councils, or the enthusiasm of the present spirit which prevails among them should lead them to measures of this nature, a war would be in any case inevitable." The sentence contains one of the earliest hints by a European statesman of a possible French war of democratic propaganda. That France might be plunged into war by the partisans of the Old Order, with a view to distracting attention from internal trouble, was a commonplace of diplomatic speculation[2]. Pitt's representatives and agents in the Belgian Provinces kept the Foreign Office well informed as to every move of the French and democratic parties there[3]; but so late as August, 1789, at least, and, in the minds of most statesmen, down to a much later date, the

appears wild and chimerical in the extreme" (to Leeds, July 10th, 1789). Nor does van der Noot appear to have broached the Regency scheme at Berlin (see Ewart to Carmarthen, September 5th, 1789, reporting his proposals there). Pitt's serious discussions of it suggest that his agent pressed it in London.

[1] Report of La Luzerne, September 29th, 1789, quoted in Sorel, II. 60.

[2] There are many such suggestions: for example, the discussion between the British representative and the Spanish Minister Florida Blanca reported by the former. Wm. Eden to Carmarthen, March 30th, 1789.

[3] See the F.O. Correspondence, Flanders, 1789, passim.

possibility of French democratic propaganda being conducted by the sword seemed remote and in no way dangerous. What might be called the correct diplomatic opinion during 1789 undoubtedly was that for years France, whatever she might do, would involve no real danger to anyone. William Eden, for example, writing to his brother on September 29th, said it was "beyond any speculation that in our time France should again make the same appearance among nations that she has made...I fairly and sincerely wish to see order restored:—she is no longer an object of alarm; and her prosperity would now be very compatible with ours, which certainly is at this hour far beyond what the nation has ever experienced." He added, a month later: "The troubles of France have increased, so as to render that unhappy country very interesting as to its interior, but probably for a long period of little importance with regard to its external, politics[1]." Eden was a representative observer, cool, experienced and intimately acquainted with French affairs[2]. Other cool heads were of the same opinion. "The situation of France," Ewart reported from Berlin[3], "seems to have made the Empress of Russia fairly sensible that no reliance whatever can be placed on the power or influence of that country at least for many years." The Court of Berlin, also, was persuaded that—"the great popular revolution in France will prevent that country effectually from interfering in any shape in favour of the Imperial Courts[4]."

Hertzberg no longer felt any fear of that Quadruple Alliance which had haunted his first and great master. He could go forward, if Great Britain would. Throughout the latter part of 1788 and the whole of 1789, Anglo-Prussian diplomacy is one long struggle between Prussia's forward policy and the British conception of the Triple Alliance. Hertzberg's plans evolve and shift. His master's military enthusiasm flares up, and dies down, and flares up again. The British Foreign Office reiterates that "it is impossible to pledge this country beforehand to the consequences of measures which go beyond the limits of a Defensive Alliance[5]." By May, 1789, Frederick William

[1] Wm. Eden to Morton Eden, September 29th and October 20th, 1789, Auckland MSS., B.M. Add. 34429.

[2] By April, 1790, however, Eden had become alarmed at what he called the French "enthusiasm of giving what they called liberty to all nations." To Sir R. M. Keith, printed in *Memoir of Sir R. M. Keith*, II. 270.

[3] To Leeds, October 20th, 1789.

[4] Ewart to Leeds, July 28th, 1789.

[5] Leeds to Ewart, September 14th, 1789, following the lines of Pitt's August Memorandum.

was writing to his Ambassador in London that he was losing all
patience and did not know what to think of this indifference of the
British Cabinet, which he had not deserved. "There was no such
delay and indifference shown on my side, when the Dutch affairs
were under consideration[1]." When the Bastille had fallen, Prussia
tried to scare England into activity; not by suggesting that France
might begin a war of democratic propaganda, but by suggesting
a Franco-Prussian alliance—the French, free from autocracy, might
cast off the Austrian connexion, and return to their true interests
and to their old relations with Prussia[2]. England was not fright-
ened. Her Minister had just stated once more that "she could not
be considered as in any degree bound to support a system of an
offensive nature[3]."

Prussia then tried the argument that she need not support it very
actively. The King himself told Ewart, in October, that in "case of
his being committed with Austria, either separately or in conjunction
with Russia, relative to the affairs either of Poland or of Turkey, he
did not pretend that England should become a party in the War;
mais qu'elle voulut seulement lui tenir le dos libre, du côté de la France,
and continue to cooperate in maintaining the neutrality of Denmark[4]."

At this time, Frederick William was desirous of war, Hertzberg
eager for a diplomatic triumph, but apparently not for war. The
King was in high spirits at the successes of the Belgian insurgents,
successes which culminated in the return of van der Noot with
triumph to Brussels, a joint repudiation of the Habsburgs by the
Estates of Flanders and Brabant, and the junction of the other
Provinces with them at the end of the year. "He is so over-elated
that he thinks of nothing less than depriving the House of Austria
both of the Netherlands and Galicia," Ewart wrote on November 28th.
His Minister at Constantinople was working for a Turkish Treaty,
a Treaty which was signed hurriedly and, as Hertzberg thought, with
an amazing lack of foresight in the drafting, on January 31st, 1790.
During December the Polish Diet approved the preliminary arrangements with Prussia which ripened next year into the *traité d'amitié
et d'union* of March, 1790. These two negotiations explain Frederick
William's reference to "the affairs of Poland and of Turkey." The
Polish Treaty was the starting-point for the series of events which

[1] To Alvensleben, May 4th. Salomon, p. 450.
[2] To Alvensleben, July 31st. Salomon, p. 450.
[3] Leeds to Ewart, June 24th. The despatch quoted above, p. 183.
[4] Ewart to Leeds, October 17th.

led up to the Second Partition; but, at the time of its signature, Prussia was not planning partition. All her statesmen were determined to secure, by any means, at least the key-towns of Thorn and Danzig; but the ruling design in 1789–90 was that for compensating Poland at Austria's expense by the gift of Galicia. In gratitude, Poland was to pass from the Russian sphere of influence into that of Prussia. This plan did not allow sufficiently for the strength and resource of Catharine, or for the storms which were blowing up from the west.

At the close of 1788 Catharine had hoped that George III's insanity and the Regency of the Prince of Wales might bring Fox back to power. She approached Fox through Woronzow, her Ambassador in London, and expressed the conviction that he and the Prince would not allow themselves to be dragged at the heels of Prussia[1]. But King George's recovery (February) left Pitt stronger than ever; so that door was closed. However, the succession of a weak Sultan, Selim II, in April, 1789, raised hopes in Petrograd for the campaigns of that year. They proved, in fact, most successful. Joseph's armies recovered. The Danubian Provinces—Bessarabia, Moldavia and Wallachia—were invaded, and by the end of 1789 the original postulate for Hertzberg's compensation schemes, that the Imperial Courts would be in a position to claim much Turkish territory at the end of the War, seemed to have become valid. Hence, Frederick William's desire to utilise the Belgian revolt to the utmost, and to blood his fine army on Austria while the mass of Joseph's troops were on the Danube. British troops he neither needed nor expected, but he required the British fleet, for Denmark was not to be trusted. She had not yet made peace and, thanks to her passive assistance, Russia was in control of the Baltic. Prussia, therefore, hoped that Great Britain's firm wish to reestablish the *status quo* in the Baltic, and to keep France in check, would suffice to ensure her cooperation at least long enough for the Prussian sword, or the threat of the Prussian sword, to do its work.

Great Britain was exceedingly cautious, but correct. At the end of 1789, she was given an opportunity by the Imperial Courts of throwing over Prussia altogether. They sounded her as to the terms on which she would agree to an eastern peace[2]. This offer she put aside: she must act with her Allies, she said. But as the offer indicated a desire for peace, it confirmed the British Cabinet in its policy of using the Triple Alliance as a peace-making and conservative combination. All that Frederick William, to his annoyance, was able

---

[1] Rose, *Pitt*, I. 509.   [2] Details in Salomon, p. 463.

to secure in relation to the Netherlands was a Convention, signed at Berlin on January 9th, 1790, by which the three Powers declared their joint interest in the Belgian Provinces; their resolve to uphold Belgian liberties; and their willingness to recognise Independence, should Independence become quite evident[1]. In spite of its annoyance, the Court of Berlin made a swift calculation and fell into line. This was the calculation: that the Triple Alliance, taking its cue from Great Britain would come forward with a proposal for a general peace on *status quo ante* terms: that the Imperial Courts would be too proud to accept: and that Prussia would thus secure her war, her compensations, and her Ally[2].

Early in the morning of February 20th, 1790, Joseph II died at Vienna. He had worked to the end at the task of government which had now broken him—signing documents that same night. His wiser, cooler, more diplomatic brother Leopold, the liberal-minded Grandduke of Tuscany, was his heir. Two days after the news of Joseph's death reached Florence, Leopold summoned the British Resident, Hervey, to a private interview in the evening. He told his visitor that he wanted peace, and that Hervey was to state this emphatically to his own Court. He referred to the unhappy Alliance with Russia and the sacrifice of the natural Austrian friendship with England. Let England mediate and save him from a breach with Prussia. He would dearly like a defensive alliance with England. He praised her correct and reserved handling of the Belgian revolution, and said—with seeming sincerity—that no nation in Europe was now so highly esteemed. France, he added, was laid aside for years. For himself, he cared for no conquests. He would make peace tomorrow. Russia and the Porte were war-weary, and would no doubt concur. To the Belgians he had made offers which they could not refuse: if desired, he would accept England and Prussia as guarantors of the Belgian liberties. To the Magyars, also, he would restore their ancient customs and liberties. As for Poland—he would give back his share of it tomorrow, if the other Partitioning Powers would do the same. Hervey left the presence late at night, with Leopold's parting protestations of friendship in his ears[3].

[1] Ewart to Leeds, January 9th, 1790. For the King's annoyance, Ewart to Leeds, February 22nd.

[2] *Minute au Roi*, March 5th, 1790, and the King's reply (Salomon, p. 465). Compare the unexpectedly cordial reception given to a despatch from Leeds of February 26th, as reported by Ewart to Leeds, March 8th.

[3] The report is in the Leeds MSS., dated February 28th. A full summary in Salomon, pp. 467-9.

Nothing could have been more welcome to the English Cabinet than ·Hervey's report. "It seems highly expedient," Leeds wrote at once to Ewart, "to communicate to his Prussian Majesty in the strictest confidence some very interesting information we have received respecting the general views of the King of Hungary[1]." The information followed, with hopeful estimates of the new Sovereign, and of his sincerity. These estimates were shortly confirmed by the shrewd and humorous British Ambassador at Vienna, Sir Robert Murray Keith. "I have every reason to be persuaded of the sincerity of his pacific professions, and it appears to me that he uses his best endeavours to restore the general tranquillity." But as a Scotsman and a soldier, Keith added: "It may not however be amiss to remark that with a brave army of·above three hundred thousand effective men...and with a population as well as money sufficient to keep it up to that strength, he may be supposed to be able to maintain...a vigorous war against Prussia...particularly if that war shall be made (as every appearance seems to prognosticate) on a plan merely defensive[2]."

Campaigning had now begun, and what Keith anticipated is clear. Leeds had followed up his letter to Berlin of March 16th by another, in which he stated categorically that "it would be impossible for this country to give any expectation of supporting Prussia in a contest" waged to tear Galicia from Austria[3]. The Prussian Court was for a moment dismayed. Should Leopold act as reasonably as he spoke, and accept the *status quo*, there would be neither war nor compensations[4]. There was talk of British treachery at Berlin. But having secured his Turkish and Polish treaties, considering that Russia was far away, the King, after much vacillation, decided to risk Great Britain's defection and stand by Hertzberg's Galician plans, on the ground that either he would get something by them, or they would provoke Austria to war. He arranged "to have his whole army on the war establishment about the middle of next month," as Ewart wrote in April. "This has been judged necessary on every account and particularly as very considerable corps of Austrian troops are already assembled in Bohemia and Moravia and are daily receiving reinforcements[5]."

---

[1] Leeds to Ewart, March 16th, 1790.
[2] Keith to Leeds, April 5th, 1790. Prince Henry of Prussia, a constant enemy of Hertzberg, also thought that Austria would fight a successful defensive war. Heigel, *op. cit.* p. 255.   [3] Leeds to Ewart, March 30th.
[4] For details of Prussian opinion see Salomon, pp. 470–1. See also Lecky, VI. 127 *sqq.*   [5] Ewart to Leeds, April 19th, 1790.

Leopold wanted peace; but, as Keith had hinted, he was not prepared for humiliation. Perhaps his resolution was stiffened by the maritime quarrel about Nootka Sound which had suddenly broken out between Great Britain and Spain. It might give the former occupation. But, as he already knew that she would not support Prussia in a war for Galicia, this must have been a secondary consideration. He continued warlike preparations; but he wrote most reasonable letters to Berlin[1]. In June, Frederick William moved to Schönwalde on the Silesian frontier, whither Ewart followed him, so as to keep in touch[2]. The King was growing impatient. "It is ridiculous to lose so much time, when you have an army like mine," he wrote to Hertzberg: matters must be settled within three weeks, or he would fight[3].

From Vienna, the British Ambassador did not vary his estimate of Leopold's good intentions and sincerity. But conflicts of royal with Ministerial policy, very typical of the State systems of the day, puzzled Keith. It is possible that Leopold utilised them to throw dust in his eyes. The old Chancellor Kaunitz, with his "haughty inflexibility," became so impracticable that another Minister, Count Philip Cobenzl, was authorised by Leopold to explain away the Chancellor's communications. Keith was asked to show them to Cobenzl, who would bring back his master's glosses. "It is at best (rejoined I) but an awkward method of doing business, and the sooner an end is put to it the better. But I subscribe to it for the present.... Here, My Lord," Keith concluded, "ends the history of Prince Kaunitz's political career: Heaven forbid that I should ever hereafter insult his ashes[4]." Kaunitz was not so easily buried; but, by June, the King of Hungary—Leopold was not yet Emperor—was in effective control of his own policy, and seemed ready to accept British mediation of a peace on the basis of the *status quo*[5].

Pitt and his Cabinet, fully occupied at that time with the Spanish problem, could not bring their full weight to bear either on Leopold or on Prussia. Leeds had written, on May 21st, that Great Britain would acquiesce in minor territorial rearrangements, should an

---

[1] Copies were regularly sent by Ewart to Leeds.
[2] He writes from Breslau on June 16th. On June 21st, he moved to Reichenbach.
[3] June 11th. Heigel, *op. cit.* p. 257. Hertzberg must have told Ewart, who wrote to Leeds on the 16th in these very words.
[4] To Leeds, April 24th, 1790.
[5] Keith's June despatches, *passim*. It may be worth noting that the Dutch Ambassador in Vienna reported at this time that there were three policies there—Kaunitz's, Cobenzl's, and Leopold's, "often totally distinct and separate from them both." Auckland [from the Hague] to Leeds, July 16th, 1790.

armistice and, eventually, peace be attainable on no other terms. A few weeks later, Leopold, in one of his friendly letters to Frederick William, had made it clear that he could not go beyond some such minor adjustments without sacrifice of honour[1]. At the same time he sent Envoys, Baron Spielmann and Prince Reuss, to treat with Hertzberg, who was now established within twenty-five miles of the Bohemian frontier, at Reichenbach.

Here, the formal Conference opened on June 27th. On the first day, Prussians and Austrians discussed compensations, exchanges and the *status quo*. On the 29th, Ewart and his Dutch colleague van Rheede were invited to attend. Ewart found that the negotiators were contemplating much more extensive "arrangements" than England could possibly approve. The Austrians were standing out for heavy compensation at the cost of the Porte—which looked ugly after their master's professions. Leopold, in fact, was far less radically friendly towards Great Britain and British schemes than he led her agents to suppose. He criticised her bitterly in letters to his sister, and he would almost certainly have risked the rejection of the *status quo*, for his armies were doing well on the Danube, had Catharine promised more powerful support[2]. On both sides, Great Britain's influence was limited—far more limited than a first reading of Ewart's despatches suggests. Ewart threw every ounce of it into the scale; but the deciding weights were in other hands, as can be read between the lines of his despatches[3].

For a month the discussions continued. Private agents came and went between Reichenbach and Vienna. All the personal forces at work in the Prussian Court made themselves felt. Varying news from the seat of war, and as to whether the Sultan would accept territorial sacrifices, supposing such were suggested by his new Ally Prussia—who left the Treaty of January still unratified—affected the course of the negotiations. The British and Dutch representatives laboured for peace. In the back-ground stood Russia, refusing to participate in a conference which implied mediation from outside, but influencing its course by a policy shifting and hard to interpret[4]. About July 21st, war seemed certain; and Frederick William sent Hertzberg "repeated orders to prepare the manifesto[5]." By this time, the Prussian King

---

[1] Copy in Ewart to Leeds, June 17th.
[2] Wolf, *Leopold und Marie Christine*, pp. 163 *sqq.* Salomon, p. 585.
[3] A long series, July 1st, 8th, 16th, 18th, 22nd, 25th, 28th, August 4th. I overrated the importance of Ewart's influence in my *Causes of the War of 1792*, pp. 61-2.
[4] See Rose, I. 527.   [5] Ewart to Leeds, July 25th.

had anchored his tossing mind to the alternative of the strict *status quo* or war. He hoped to pin Austria on one horn of this dilemma. Hertzberg's view was that Leopold could not accept the strict *status quo* without dishonour[1]. Thus, he expected, and now desired, war. At Vienna, Kaunitz shared Hertzberg's view. But on July 23rd came news that Austria would not fight for her compensation; and on the 27th Déclarations and Counter-declarations were exchanged.

Austria declared herself ready to conclude an armistice with the Porte, with a view to a *status quo* peace, though a hope was expressed that the Sultan might accept a few frontier adjustments. She would not participate in the Russo-Turkish War, should it continue. Prussia stipulated that, if the Sultan freely gave Austria anything, Austria must give Prussia something. Prussia and the Sea Powers were to guarantee Belgium to Austria, but also Belgium's ancient Constitutions. The Sea Powers promised to support the whole settlement —which was exactly what the British Cabinet had always desired— and to continue their mediation at the ensuing Peace Congress[2]. At the last, both Hertzberg and Kaunitz had to be forced to sign, by personal notes from their respective masters[3].

And now, wrote Frederick William to Hertzberg, we must work through Ewart to get English support in forcing the *status quo* on Russia. He had already used an opportunity of binding England to him by gratitude for services rendered. Two months earlier, Hertzberg had told Ewart that, if England's quarrel with Spain led to war, she might count on Prussia.

On January 7th, 1790, Consul-general Merry had written to the Duke of Leeds from Madrid: "Accounts have just been received here from Mexico that one of the small ships of war on the American establishment...has captured an English vessel in the port of Nootka (called by the Spaniards San Lorenzo) in Lat. 50 North of the coast of California. There are different relations of this event." A month later[4], the Spanish Ambassador in London claimed for his country the sovereignty of those parts, *i.e.* the modern Vancouver Island and British Columbia. Leeds replied stiffly that, until the ship was restored and the violence atoned for, the question of principle must wait[5], though, as his despatches show, the British Cabinet had no

---

[1] Salomon, p. 485.   [2] Ewart to Leeds, July 28th.
[3] Heigel, I. 267.
[4] February 11th, Rose, I. 565. As to the very complicated question of what actually happened in Nootka Sound, see Rose, *passim*.
[5] February 16th. A rather bullying despatch, drafted by Pitt.

intention of conceding the principle. In Spain, Count Florida Blanca was distressed, so he said, at the British tone: in these times especially, such matters ought to be discussed without heat[1]. In April, there were preparations both in English and Spanish dockyards; and at the end of the month the heat in this country was not lowered by the reception of a memorial from the aggrieved party, Meares, an ex-lieutenant of the Navy, who had bought land from the Indians at Nootka and was carrying on the fur-trade there. He made strong charges of cruelty and bad faith against the Spaniards.

War was already in sight. "I can see only one circumstance," Merry wrote on April 12th[2], "which may incline the King of Spain and his Ministry to war—it is the idea that it might be the means to re-establish the royal authority in France, as that Kingdom would naturally take a part." The whole tone of Florida Blanca's communications with Eden in 1789 justifies the assumption that the motive indicated may have been at work[3]. But, when Merry wrote, he did not think it would prevail to overcome the Spanish Minister's desire for peace. However, after Great Britain had officially intimated that she was arming, and had sent out the pressgangs, opinion at the Spanish Court became more warlike. This was in the first week of May[4]. Merry's explanation was "that the national vanity of Spain had so much increased of late, as well by the situation of France, as by the manner in which she has been flattered by the Imperial Courts"—in connexion, that is, with the schemes for a Quadruple Alliance[5]. It is true that Florida Blanca had been losing his hold on affairs, since the death of Charles III in 1788; persons vain in every sense of the word were acquiring influence at Court. Indeed, the British agent had suggested that the Count might conceivably be contemplating war, in order to secure his position against them[6].

Meanwhile, Pitt, who had not forgotten how the Family Compact had helped Washington, took a hand in the game of revolution-making in a rival's discontented provinces, as played by Hertzberg,

[1] Merry to Leeds, March 22nd.
[2] To Leeds.
[3] See, especially, Eden to Leeds July 27th; August 10th. It may be noted that Eden had "never...seen reason to doubt either the veracity or the candour of Count Florida Blanca." To Leeds, February 23rd, 1789.
[4] Leeds to Merry, May 3rd, notifying armament, and the May despatches from Madrid. The pressgangs were out on the 5th. A French agent in England wrote: "Si l'on juge des projets du gouvernement anglais par les preparatifs, on doit croire à une guerre la plus longue et la plus sévère possible." Sorel, II. 85.
[5] To Leeds, May 20th.
[6] In his letter of April 12th.

by entering into personal relation with Miranda, Brissot's friend, the exiled advocate of South-American independence[1]. Pitt, with the full support of his King, was now challenging Spain on the question of principle[2]—the claim to sovereignty over the Pacific coast up to 60° N. Not wishing to exclude a peaceful solution, he sent Alleyne Fitzherbert on a special mission to Madrid, at the end of May. But it would appear that in no case did he mean to withdraw. His ready, almost brutal, acceptance of this challenge to a struggle in which maritime prestige and the freedom of colonisation were at stake is in notable contrast with his laboured approach to any Continental problem. The reaction is instinctive: there are to be no abstract rights over blocks of parallels of latitude: the beard of the King of Spain is to be singed.

Fitzherbert went by Paris, to test the strength of the Family Compact; for no one supposed that Spain would fight, if the Compact now proved too weak to hold France to her. He was "inclined to believe that M. de Montmorin is perfectly sincere in the desire that he professes to see our difference with Spain terminated amicably," but could "plainly perceive that many of the other members of the aristocratical faction are anxious to bring on a war." "However, their opponents begin to be aware of their drift and...have chosen the present time for carrying into execution their plan of transferring the power of making war and peace from the Crown to the National Assembly[3]." It was the King's intimation, given on May 14th, that he proposed to arm forty ships of the line as a precautionary measure, which had roused the Assembly. Montmorin hoped that the threat from the old enemy, risen from her humiliation of seven years ago, might rally the representatives of the people to the Throne. On the contrary, it crippled French diplomatic and military action by rendering the seat of authority uncertain. Robespierre was up on the 15th of May, proposing that France should renounce all wars of conquest; Pétion followed on the 17th, Volney on the 18th, Barnave on the 21st. Mirabeau stood for the King and was called a traitor. By the 22nd it had been decided that the King might propose war to the Assembly, but might not declare it without their concurrence. "England has nothing more to fear from France and can lay hands on the hegemony of the two worlds, without scruple and without

[1] Details in Rose, 1. 569.
[2] Despatch of May 4th.
[3] Fitzherbert to Leeds, May 20th.

fear," bitterly wrote a French agent from London[1]. Fitzherbert went on to Madrid with some confidence.

He found the Spaniards unexpectedly, and as he thought stupidly, warlike—from a feeling of jealousy, he supposed. They seemed, he said, not to count much on France, but had hopes of the United States[2]. However, before the end of July he had signed an agreement with Florida Blanca as to the actual episode of Nootka Sound. Spain promised satisfaction[3]. "Their present object," he now reported, "is to preserve peace on almost any terms."

No doubt, one reason was that they had asked France for armed assistance in the middle of June and had hitherto received no reply. Montmorin only laid the matter before the Assembly on August 2nd. It was referred to the Diplomatic Committee, presided over by Mirabeau. Not knowing what the outcome might be, Pitt kept his fleets ready. On August 25th, at Mirabeau's suggestion, the Assembly decided to arm forty-five capital ships and begin a negotiation with Spain for the transformation of the Family Compact into a National Compact. A little earlier, Florida Blanca had told Fitzherbert that his appeal to France had been merely *pro forma* and occasioned by England's similar, and earlier, appeal to her Ally the United Provinces. He did not expect help from the National Assembly, "nor in truth did he desire to receive any, at the immediate risk of introducing by that means into this kingdom those democratic principles now so universally prevalent...in France[4]." He would, however, welcome support from Russia and Austria, but—this of course he did not say —he had received no encouragement from either. When the proposal for a new sort of Compact was ready, in September, he explained that his King loathed it, but would have to accept, "if the Court of London pressed too hardly upon him in the present juncture[5]." But, since the proposal was accompanied by the suggestion that Spain should restore Louisiana to France, and since Spain neither wished to do this, nor desired an alliance with the democrats, nor yet believed in the fighting value of such an alliance, Florida Blanca yielded to relentless pressure from London[6], and signed, on October 28th. The claim to

---

[1] Sorel, 11. 91.
[2] To Leeds, June 16th.
[3] Fitzherbert to Leeds, July 25th.
[4] Fitzherbert to Leeds, August 19th.
[5] Fitzherbert to Leeds, September 16th.
[6] On October 2nd Leeds is writing of "one further effort" and "our final and unalterable decisions," which if not accepted negotiations are to be broken off. To Fitzherbert.

Pacific dominion north of the actual Spanish settlements was withdrawn: the Pacific, though not these settlements, was declared open to
British commerce and fishery: and full restitution and compensation
were guaranteed to the parties aggrieved at Nootka Sound[1].

In Continental history, the most famous aspect of the Nootka
Sound affair is its relation to the career of Mirabeau. What was
his policy? Why did he suggest armament yet go no further? What
were his exact relations with Pitt's two semi-official agents, his own
friend Hugh Elliot and W. A. Miles? Did either of them use the
legendary "gold of Pitt"? The probability is that they did[2]. But
these are, in truth, all secondary problems in the history of British
Foreign Policy. Nothing suggests that, had France vigorously supported Spain, Pitt's policy would have been altered. From the
French side, it is most doubtful whether such vigorous support could
have been given, whatever course Mirabeau had followed. And Spain
never really wanted alliance on the only terms considered in France.
"His Catholic Majesty could not reconcile it to His Feelings to
contribute, at a critical moment like the present, to the extinguishing
the reviving hopes of the partisans of the French monarchy by...a
renunciation on his part of the Family Compact[3]."

But the correspondence relating to the negotiations with Mirabeau
raises a wider issue. When consenting to Elliot's mission, King George
stipulated that there should be no interference whatever in French
internal affairs, no taking sides among the French parties. "We have
honourably not meddled with the internal dissensions of France,"
he wrote, "and no object ought to drive us from that honourable
ground[4]." Pitt's relations with Miranda show that such interference
was not beneath the dignity of the British Cabinet; but the King's
statement was nevertheless true. The British inaction had surprised
Continental observers. Even in 1789, the diplomatic gossips in Berlin
could not understand Pitt's conduct; they thought he could not be
such a fool as not to declare war[5]. And a German scholar wrote:
"What do you think of the French Revolution? That England has

---

[1] For the final stages see Fitzherbert's despatches of October 14th, 18th, 24th,
28th. On October 14th, on receipt of Leed's of October 2nd, he feared rupture.

[2] Rose, *Pitt*, I. 577 *sqq.*—a discussion which goes nearer to providing satisfactory
answers to these questions than any other.

[3] Fitzherbert to Leeds, November 28th, 1790.

[4] To Pitt, October 26th, 1790. P. V. Smith MSS. p. 368 in H.M.C. Duke of
Beaufort MSS. and others. The collection was made by Pitt's secretary, Joseph
Smith.

[5] Report of the Comte d'Esterno from Berlin, September 9th, 1789. Sorel,
II. 29*n.*

allowed it is a tribute to her heart, but not to her head[1]." No doubt, the heart had its influence. An English statesman could scarcely have interfered, had he wished it, in the early days of sympathy for a people struggling for freedom. And the King's honourable horror of such interference as that from which he had himself suffered during the American War was always a restraining force. But a main reason for abstention was a calculation of the head, which proved to be wrong—that France was no longer dangerous. That "the rival of Great Britain was, at least for the present annihilated," was still an axiom in the Foreign Office at the end of 1790[2]. Great Britain did not at once realise, as the German scholar did, that "the republic of twenty-four millions would give her more trouble than the autocracy." In 1789–90, she did not foresee a republic.

In one of his despatches to Fitzherbert, Leeds had explained that Great Britain could not reduce her naval establishment until France did the same. He had added that it would not be wise to do so, with the Russian matter still pending[3]. At that time, the representatives of Great Britain, Austria, Prussia, Holland and Turkey were preparing to move to the dirty little oriental town of Sistova on the Danube[4], to arrange an eastern peace on the basis of the *status quo*. Sir Robert Keith arrived there on December 20th[5]. No Russian came. On December 22nd, Suvoroff, Bessarabia now behind him, stormed Ismail, far down the river, and was in a position to organise an invasion of the Sultan's home provinces, by way of the Dobrudja. Earlier in the month (December 2nd), Leopold's armies, set in motion against his rebellious subjects in Belgium, had entered Brussels without difficulty. The Belgians had been ruined by their divisions. All through 1790, the democratic party, headed by Vonck, had been working against the Catholic and Constitutional party of van der Noot. These "Red Patriots," as an English agent called them[6], had been encouraged by the visits of two French agents, first La Fayette's confidant Sémonville, then Dumouriez, who had reported very unfavourably on the military prospects of any Belgian Government[7]. By

[1] Georg Forster. Cf. Gooch, *Germany and the French Revolution*, p. 304.
[2] From a long unsigned and undated memoir *On a Defensive Alliance with Spain*, a subject under discussion after the Nootka settlement.
[3] Leeds to Fitzherbert, October 2nd, 1790.
[4] Now in Bulgaria.
[5] *Memoirs of Sir R. M. Keith*, II. 324.
[6] Colonel Gardiner to Leeds, February 2nd, 1790.
[7] Gardiner's reports of July 12th and 26th and August 2nd contain a full account of this mission and an excellent appreciation of Dumouriez.

the beginning of 1791, not only had Belgian opposition to Leopold collapsed; his tact and discretion had calmed the rest of his dominions.

It is not therefore surprising, nor really very discreditable, that the Austrian representatives at Sistova should have wasted time and attempted to escape from their promise about the *status quo*[1]. The promise had been extracted by pressure. Suvoroff was now exerting great, if indirect, counter-pressure. That the Triple Alliance would be able to force Catharine to renounce her conquests seemed unlikely. If Turkey collapsed, were the Habsburgs, who had suffered much in contributing to that collapse, to go away empty handed?

Catharine's position had been strengthened during 1790 by the action of Gustavus III of Sweden. Saved from what looked like a risk of destruction in 1788, he had managed to carry through a *coup d'état* against the aristocratic party, in 1789. But his political successes at home had not improved his financial position. He always tried to drive hard bargains with the Triple Alliance; and, at any time, the prospects of active Swedish campaigning depended on the success of such bargains[2]. In 1790, he could only secure a small part of his demands—from Great Britain and Prussia, the Dutch being unwilling to assist. Catharine made him attractive offers after Reichenbach. Moreover, ever since October, 1789, he had been passionately interested in the fate of his ancient Ally the King of France, and he wished to be free to champion the cause of monarchy. His solicitude for that cause, if romantic and impracticable, was disinterested. Suddenly, in July, 1790, although a British fleet was ready to sail to the Baltic, and although he had promised not to conclude a separate peace with Russia, he sent Baron Armfelt to conclude such a peace. The way was made easy for Armfelt, and Peace was signed on August 14th, 1790[3].

This defection had increased the desire, which had long existed in London, to widen the Triple Alliance. Gustavus himself had been an ally designate. Among other possible allies were Denmark—but she was unlikely—and the reformed Republic of Poland, which would have been glad of this admission to the circle of Great Powers. As the chief British promoters of this extended system of alliances were

---

[1] See Keith's *Memoirs*, II. 369 *sqq*. Letters of February to June, 1791.
[2] "The Swede is not much to be depended on even when highly paid." Auckland to Grenville, April 20th, 1791. *Dropmore Papers*, II. 49.
[3] See Geffroy, *Gustave III et la cour de France*, II. 102 *sqq*. and Rose, *Pitt*, I. 530–2. In January, 1791, Gustavus wrote to Catharine to suggest a joint refusal to recognise the tricolour flag. Geffroy, II. 111.

Ewart at Berlin and Hailes at Warsaw, the chances of Poland's admission to what these Ambassadors, in their despatches, referred to as "the great federal chain[1]" at one time seemed good. The final detachment of Poland from her Russian connexion was specially attractive at a time when Catharine appeared the chief obstacle to "the restoration of general tranquillity." But Prussia looked on Poland as her own preserve and suspected any proposal for a commercial treaty, the form into which the projected Anglo-Polish *rapprochement* was first thrown. "It is contrary to my interests and insidious and must be set aside," King Frederick William wrote in October[2]. He was conscious that any strengthening of Poland would make her less likely to cede the necessary minimum after all these years of effort, that is, Thorn and Danzig. At the end of the year the Poles had a representative in London, Count Oginski, who had a series of interviews with Pitt[3]. Poland was, also, in treaty with the Porte for a commercial outlet down the Dniester, to evade a Prussian throttling of the Vistula trade. She was most reluctant to cede anything, and was furious with Prussia who had not won for her any part of Galicia, yet still talked of compensation. Pitt gave Oginski good economic advice, and suggested the cession of Danzig alone, in return for a commercial treaty with Prussia providing for outlets in that direction. The suggestion was acceptable neither to Poland nor to Prussia. Thus, when, in January, 1791, actual proposals for the admission of Poland to the Triple Alliance were sent to Berlin and Warsaw, the business languished until the break up of the Alliance in April; and it was never revived[4]. At this very time, Hertzberg was preparing the way for the Second Partition by secret personal dealings with Russia[5].

Catharine was known to demand Oczakoff and its district. It was supposed, but not certainly known, that this was meant to cover all the land to the Dniester, including Odessa—at that time a village never mentioned in the despatches. Frederick William was committed to the support of Turkey, and was at this time resolute for the *status quo*. If he could force it on Russia, Austria could not evade it, and, at least, no rival would gain territory and "souls"—the currency of Princely bargains—when he as yet had acquired none. But he did not want war. In England, his most valuable advocates were Whitworth,

---

[1] Hailes to Leeds, June 18th, 1790. He has heard with delight from Ewart of the prospect of Poland, Sweden and the Porte entering our "great federal chain."
[2] October 21st. Salomon, p. 500.
[3] See Rose, I. 594 *sqq.* and Salomon, pp. 506–7.
[4] Rose, I. 595, 599.   [5] See Rose, I. 597.

whose despatches from Petrograd led Pitt to suppose that Russia must yield to a threat of force[1], and Joseph Ewart, on leave from Berlin in the winter of 1790-1. Ewart had laid before Pitt a series of *Considerations on the expediency of combining Poland, Turkey and one of the inferior Baltic Powers in the defensive System of the Allies*[2]. He insisted on the enormous importance of Oczakoff and the risk to British prestige which its acquisition by Catharine would involve. There was also the certainty of losing our chief Ally, who had stood by us in the Nootka business, and, with him, all control over Leopold and the course of events. Ewart's argument was traversed by Auckland, now Ambassador at the Hague. Writing to Pitt personally he urged "the importance of peace to your whole system of government," suggested that "we overrated the object in question," as Oczakoff was not really vital, and explained that he had good reason to believe that the King of Prussia had no wish for a Russian war[3]. The Pensionary van de Spiegel supported Auckland.

Ewart won. By the beginning of February Great Britain was committed in principle to the enforcement of the *status quo* on Russia by a threat of force, though a final decision was postponed. Reluctance to risk the break up of an Alliance which had done much for the peace of Europe and our own prestige; a measure of gratitude to the King of Prussia; fear lest the Austro-Turkish Peace, for whose character Great Britain stood pledged, should miscarry; forebodings of an ultimate clash of interest between Russia and ourselves in the Near East; and perhaps some desire to school a particularly arrogant woman—all contributed to the decision. Ewart was arguing his case, but also stating the main issue as he induced Ministers to see it, when he wrote to Auckland on January 5th: "I am sure your Lordship will agree with me...that Oczakoff and its district are very secondary considerations in comparison of the great influence which the decision of the present question must have on the strength and permanency of the system of the Allies on which the preservation of peace likewise depends[4]."

Auckland did his duty at the Hague with reluctance. "If that Russian business could happily be settled we might sit still and look

[1] Rose, I. 598.
[2] Pitt MSS. Salomon, p. 502. There are also two able Memoirs by Ewart on Anglo-Russian relations, dated April, 1791, in the *Dropmore Papers*, II. 44 *sqq.*
[3] To Pitt, January 29th, 1791. *Dropmore Papers*, II. 22.
[4] Auckland MSS., B.M. Add. 34435. J. B. Burges, the Under-secretary for Foreign Affairs, wrote more and more in this same strain to Auckland—*e.g.* March 1st, 1791, showing that Ewart's doctrine had become official orthodoxy.

at the French story like spectators in a theatre," he wrote to his brother in January. And, in March, he wrote to Grenville: "This phantom of Oczakoff has appeared to me for some time to beckon us towards an abyss of new debts and endless difficulties at a moment ...when it may be essential perhaps to the very existence of our government and of many other civilised states, that we should maintain our own internal peace...[1]." Auckland had now comprehended the possible dangers from "a republic of twenty-four millions," which Georg Forster foresaw in 1789.

Pitt took no risks and worked at all the Courts, beginning with his Allies, before reaching his final decision. Plans were communicated to the Hague and Berlin. At the Hague, information was sought from the Dutch Admiral Kingsbergen, who had recently visited Oczakoff. Frederick William was told that London saw no possible counter-alliance which might prevent the humbling of Russia in the spring[2]. At Madrid, Fitzherbert was to solicit Spanish help or, failing that, a promise of neutrality. He secured the latter—a promise of "the strictest neutrality[3]." Copenhagen made the same promise. At Stockholm, Liston failed to catch "the Swede" with offers of money. Lord Elgin, who had been sent on a special mission to Leopold II in November, 1790, to congratulate him on his accession and facilitate a Belgian settlement by direct negotiation, was, if he could, to secure Austrian cooperation in a general settlement, and to speed up the Congress of Sistova; or at least, to keep Leopold from helping the Tsarina[4]. Paris was not neglected. Hugh Elliot and Miles were to let it be known privately that Pitt was not making preparations against France[5].

By the end of February, Frederick William had learnt, as he supposed, that Austria might be kept quiet—possibly by concessions at Sistova—in the event of a Prusso-Russian war. He had learnt it, in a way characteristic of his methods, by the despatch to Vienna of his personal favourite and confidant Colonel Bischoffswerder. Pitt, meanwhile, was testing the information about Oczakoff supplied from Holland, which, coming through Auckland, insisted on the un-

[1] To Morton Eden, January 11th; to Grenville, March 5th. B.M. Add. 34435-6.
[2] Leeds to Jackson (Ewart's deputy), January 8th.
[3] Leeds to Fitzherbert, January 3rd; Fitzherbert to Leeds January 29th.
[4] Elgin's special mission, *F.O. Austria*, vol. 23. Despatches of January to February.
[5] *Miles Correspondence*, I. 43, 280. All these various negotiations are referred to by Salomon, pp. 504-6.

important aspects of the place[1]. Leeds was talking of how to avoid war without sacrificing honour. He feared we were too far committed[2]. In Berlin, at the same time, Hertzberg was thinking of the same things, though from another angle. Hertzberg, however, was not Prussia. The King did not desire war, but wrote, on March 11th, a personal letter to his Ambassador in London explaining the reputedly favourable attitude of Leopold, and suggesting the coercion of Russia by a "display of force[3]." This letter decided the British Cabinet. On March 27th, the ultimatum went to Russia, and plans for naval and military preparations to Berlin[4]. Catharine was to resign all the conquests of this war, but might retain the Crimea, absorbed in 1783. It was to recover the Crimea that Turkey had declared war in 1788.

· There remained Parliament, which was apprised next day of the need for naval preparations. The Lords were critical, but yielded a substantial majority. In the Commons, Pitt seems to have opened badly; the Whigs had excellent opportunities; but the majority was again considerable. Yet there was no enthusiasm for the policy of Ministers, which is in no way surprising, in view of the remoteness of the object and the hesitation they had themselves shown in adopting it. Further, on the day they despatched their ultimatum, news came, first, from Auckland—who controlled a better *cabinet noir* than any other British diplomatist—that "he had happened to see" a ciphered Prussian despatch which showed clearly that, in spite of the King's letter, the Emperor was not to be trusted, and, secondly, from Drake at Copenhagen, that Catharine was likely to prove reasonable in negotiation[5]. The Cabinet met often and discussed long, early in April. Some change of front was suggested, but opposed by Leeds, who did not see how it could be managed with honour[6]. By April 10th Pitt was confessing to Ewart, that he had failed to make the House understand the matter and could never carry the vote of credit, and was "repeating, even with tears in his eyes, that it was the greatest mortification he had ever experienced[7]." Within a few days, Leeds had refused to sign despatches suggesting a modification of the ultimatum, and had made way for William Grenville. Before the

---

[1] Rose, I. 604.
[2] To Auckland, March 11th. Quoted in Rose, I. 605, from B.M. Add. 34436.
[3] Rose, I. 607-8, where the King's letter is quoted from the F. O. records. Salomon (p. 514) failed to find the original at Berlin.
[4] Leeds to Jackson and Leeds to Whitworth, March 27th.
[5] Rose, I. 614-5.
[6] See Browning, *Political Memoranda of Francis, Fifth Duke of Leeds*, 150-73.
[7] Major-General Sir Spencer Ewart's MSS., first used by Rose, I. 617.

end of the month, Ewart, returning to Berlin from a sense of loyalty towards Pitt, in order to undo his own policy, had seen the King, who said repeatedly that, "as he was convinced the intentions were good, however mortified he might be at the change, he would concur in doing everything in his power to prevent bad consequences[1]." In July, Auckland was explaining to his brother how much he preferred Grenville to Leeds, and how "from the hour of his taking the seals we have laboured hard to get not quite disgracefully out of a very bad scrape, and I begin to hope that it will end tolerably well[2]." This was after the flight to Varennes—the hinge on which European history in 1791 swings. "All political speculation will now turn to France," Auckland wrote in August. Russian affairs, he said, were not working out so ill after all[3]. Catharine would obtain her Dniester boundary, but no more. His desire to see these affairs out of the way, that the English might "look at the French story like spectators in a theatre," seemed near fulfilment.

Spectators they became for a year and more. From every Court, when once the débris of Russian policy and the Sistova Congress have been cleared up, the reports of the British Ambassadors are those of a profoundly interested audience at the great Continental play. The Triple Alliance faded into nominal life, a "conviction of good intentions" being a poor foundation even for a political friendship. "I know now," Ewart wrote in August, "that though the King and Colonel Bischoffswerder professed to be satisfied with the explanation I gave them, they immediately lost confidence in the resources both of the Alliance and of this country[4]." So, Great Britain lost her diplomatic *point d'appui*. The Congress of Sistova was speeded up, not so much because Elgin demanded it, as because Leopold became absorbed in French affairs, anxious to put others aside, and thus accessible to Colonel Bischoffswerder, the leading Prussian advocate of interference in France. In May and June, Elgin was following Leopold up and down Italy, trying to detach him from Russia, according to instructions. While Elgin was talking in terms of the previous year's diplomacy, Leopold—aware of his sister's projected flight—was debating whether the friendship which Great Britain offered might not be used to establish a European Concert for the settlement of France. Elgin came to think that Leopold was mainly

[1] Ewart to Grenville, April 30th.
[2] July 10th. B.M. Add. 34438.
[3] To Morton Eden, August 12th. B.M. Add. 34439.
[4] To Grenville, August 21st.

concerned to check the "progress of democratical principles." "Nay, his Imperial Majesty went so far as to suggest the expediency of guaranteeing not only the possessions, but also the Constitutions of the different States of Europe[1]."

A month later, Bischoffswerder came to Italy from Berlin to offer an alliance, and was well received. Before the news of Varennes arrived, Leopold had promised to finish at Sistova and had issued the necessary orders. He had agreed to a defensive alliance with Prussia, and to a personal interview with Frederick William. Elgin, though kept on the fringe of affairs, knew the outline of all this[2]. After the Varennes catastrophe, Leopold issued his Padua Circular to the Powers, with its suggestion of joint action to "vindicate the liberty and honour of the Most Christian King and his family, and to limit the dangerous extremes of the French Revolution."

Great Britain did not commit herself over this Circular, until she was sure that Leopold meant to finish at Sistova. Such was now his intention. By August 13th the Sistova Treaty was ratified at Vienna. After the lapse of a year, the Reichenbach agreement had been strictly carried out and British policy endorsed. Attached to the main Treaty was a separate Convention specifying "the small and voluntary concessions which the Turks were disposed to grant[3]"; but this had been allowed for at Reichenbach. Three days earlier, Catharine's negotiators had agreed to preliminaries of peace with Turkey. No mediating Powers were there: Catharine had never intended otherwise. She secured her Dniester boundary. In consequence of Great Britain's *volte-face* in the matter of Oczakoff, the event forms no part of the history of British Foreign Policy, though, perhaps, but for that policy and its reactions on Austria, Catharine might not have renounced Bessarabia.

After that, Great Britain hardly made a pretence of remaining in the Triple Alliance or of continuing to figure on the Continental stage. Witness Grenville's private letter to Auckland of August 23rd: "The conclusion of the Sistova business has removed every difficulty which there was in the way of our speaking out, and avowing our determination of the most scrupulous neutrality in the French business—and I now hold this language to all the foreign ministers, in order that it may be clearly understood that we are no parties to any step the

---

[1] To Grenville, May 9th, 1791.
[2] His despatches June 13th, 14th, 18th contain fairly full accounts, derived apparently from Bischoffswerder.
[3] Keith to Grenville, August 2nd, 1791.

King of Prussia may take on this subject[1]." Or see Grenville's Instructions to Keith a month later, after Leopold and Frederick William
had issued the Declaration of Pillnitz (August 27th), and the Emigrant
Princes their insolent address to King Lewis, in which they told him
he had no right to sign the new Constitution: "With respect to the
concert which has been proposed to His Majesty and to other Powers
by the Emperor, or to the measures of active intervention which
appear to have been in contemplation for the restoration of the French
monarchy...the King has determined not to take any part either in
supporting or in opposing them. This resolution he has already explained to his allies and also to other powers, and...he commanded
me to instruct you to use a similar language at Vienna[2]."

Six months later, March 20th, 1792, Auckland, now in retirement
at Beckenham, yet "every day seeing well-informed men of all
descriptions," wrote to a friend that he had heard recently from
Mr Burges, the Under-Secretary at the Foreign Office; but that "the
remarks which he makes are general and chiefly calculated...to explain
that England has little concern now in what is going forward on the
Continent"—the Revolutionary Wars began a month later—"except
perhaps with regard to Poland, to which the Empress seems to turn
her attention in a manner that may eventually interest other powers
though it will not implicate us." Catharine was moving up her
armies to destroy the reformed Polish Constitution, completed in
May, 1791, after the Triple Alliance and with it Great Britain's Polish
policy had cracked. She was also inciting Prussia and Austria to
attack France, in order to obtain "elbow room" in Poland[3]. "His
remark," Auckland continued, "that we have no concern in foreign
politics is true in another sense to a degree that I cannot describe to
you...and this indifference as to foreign affairs is general thro' the
kingdom; you may trace it even in your newspapers; perhaps it may
justly be attributed to the great prosperity of the country, which
confines all attention to interior and insular details. I have lately
much wished to pass a day or two at the Hague for the sake of a little
rational conversation[4]." Auckland instanced, as the kind of topic in
which no interest whatever was taken by representative Englishmen,
the death of the Emperor Leopold (March 1st, 1792). It was a well-

---

[1] B.M. Add. 34439.
[2] Grenville to Keith, September 19th, 1791.
[3] Sorel, II. 216-7. See also Kaunitz' analysis of her motives in Vivenot, *Quellen
zur Geschichte der...Kaiserpolitik Oesterreichs*, I. 358.
[4] B.M. Add. 34441.

chosen illustration; for, although it is most unlikely that Leopold
would have averted the clash between Old Europe and revolutionary
France in 1792—both he and the French were too deeply committed
to war before he died—yet it is certain that the loss of his skilful
and mediating personality and the substitution for it of a young and
ignorant Prince, dominated by a mixed group of advisers, were a
disaster for Europe.

Auckland wrote as a diplomatist, with a high standard of interest
in foreign affairs. There was in England no lack of vague interest;
Burke's *Reflections* sold well; but, from Pitt downwards, the country
was in a mood to wash its hands of Continental matters. Even Pitt's
interest in them had been intermittent. Now, the old enemy was
believed to be crippled. She must be watched, but need not be
countered. Hardly anyone had begun to think regularly of Russian
power as a danger to English interests. In 1790, some attention had
been given to a pamphlet which made much of the Russian threat to
the Balance of Power in Europe; but Oczakoff revealed the fundamental indifference. Only a handful of experts had ever understood
the working of the Triple Alliance. It was an affair of Cabinets and
Courts and favourites, of intercepted despatches and Congresses in
inaccessible places. No single event in its history, since the initial
strokes in the Low Countries, was of the least interest to the average
educated Englishman. With Nootka Sound it had been different. The
place was more remote than Sistova or Oczakoff; but, even down to
the No-Popery mobs of London, Englishmen could understand a
maritime quarrel with Spain.

"The English," we find Albert Sorel writing, towards the end of
the nineteenth century, "only make up their minds to fight when
their interests seem absolutely threatened. But then, plunging into
the struggle because they feel themselves bound to do so, they apply
to it a serious and concentrated passion, an animosity the more
tenacious because its motive is so self-regarding. Their history is
full of alternations between an indifference which makes people think
them decadent, and a rage which baffles their foes. They are seen, in
turn, abandoning and dominating Europe, neglecting the greatest
Continental matters and claiming to control even the smallest, turning
from peace at any price to war to the death[1]." During the early years
of Pitt's Ministry, they had been in one of these phases of apparent
indifference. From 1787 to 1791, they seemed to be preparing for

[1] *L'Europe et la Révolution Française*, 1. 240. (First published in 1885.)

the alternative phase. Had Oczakoff led to a general war—but for the change of front, a very probable contingency—then the phase of rage might have set in; for a general war would soon have threatened England's nearer interests. As it was, the phase of indifference never seemed more complete than in the eighteen months which preceded the longest of her modern Wars.

After the rebuff to the Padua Circular, the Powers of Europe made no attempt to influence her. The Emigrant Princes tried, now and again; but their cause was so hopeless, in view of England's deliberately adopted attitude, that the details have no place in the history of her foreign policy. "Repeated applications have been made to His Majesty," Grenville wrote at the end of August, 1791, "on the part of the Emperor, of the King of Sweden, and of the French Princes, to concert in the plans which are in agitation for restoring the French monarchy. But His Majesty has determined not to depart from... strict neutrality[1]." From that policy there was not the slightest deviation during the following year. It was the same when England was approached from another section of French opinion—the Constitutional revolutionary party. The approaches were made, first, informally before the outbreak of war in Europe in 1792, and then, formally, after the outbreak. On both occasions Talleyrand was the agent. The object was to ensure English neutrality and feel towards an Anglo-French entente[2].

Talleyrand came first, in the middle of January, 1792. The visit and its results were summarised, from the English side, by Grenville, writing to Lord Gower at Paris, early in March[3]. "Since I wrote to Your Excellency on the subject of M. de Talleyrand I have seen that gentleman twice. The first time he explained to me very much at large the disposition of the French Government...to enter into the strictest connection with Great Britain, and proposed that this should be done by a Treaty of mutual guaranty, or in such other manner as the Government of this country should prefer." Grenville told him that he did not expect to be able to enter into any kind of negotiation with an agent not officially accredited. At the second interview, he confirmed this, but had no difficulty in saying to Talleyrand, as an individual, "that it was very far from being the disposition of this Government to

---

[1] To Lord St Helens (Fitzherbert), August 26th, 1791. See W. Grenville to George Aust (of the Foreign Office), September 20th, 1791, with Instructions for a reply to the Emigrants. The critical passage is quoted in Lecky, v. 558.

[2] See Pallain, *La Mission de Talleyrand à Londres en* 1792.

[3] Grenville to Gower, March 9th.

endeavour to foment or prolong the disturbances there, with a view to any profit to be derived from them to this country." This last declaration was perfectly sincere. The day after Grenville wrote, Talleyrand returned to Paris.

He came back at the end of April, nominally second in command to Chauvelin, War against the Emperor having just been declared. The scheme which he was to advocate ran thus. For the moment, England's benevolent neutrality was to save France from complications with the United Provinces or Spain. She was to be made to understand that the coming French attack on Belgium was a military necessity, not a prelude to annexation. And then—then, when this war was over, the Constitutional monarchies of the west, the old and the new, were to rule Europe and the seas. There was to be a new commercial treaty. The Spanish Colonies in South America were to be liberated and thrown open to trade. Hand in hand, France and England were to share in that trade and in the maintenance of Constitutional liberties throughout the world[1].

Nothing was accomplished. The English Court was frigid, the people almost offensive—so reported Dumont, who was a member of the Embassy. Only the Whig houses were thrown open. Talleyrand said that the English Ministry was "the most secret in all Europe." It kept them waiting for a month; then moved King George to write a short, friendly, empty note to Lewis XVI (May 18th), and to issue a public Declaration of Neutrality (May 25th). England regretted the War; she intended to respect all Treaties; she wished to live at peace with France, and trusted that France would contribute to peace by showing respect for the rights of His Majesty and His Allies. There were no real negotiations, and Talleyrand spent his generous leisure in composing his *Lettres sur les Anglais*. He left this country early in July; the indiscreet Chauvelin remaining[2].

The rising tone of the French propaganda, and the attack on Belgium, explain the suspicious reticence of the British Ministry. It is indeed, at first sight, surprising that Pitt did not take an even stronger line as to Belgium. But, at this time, he was not faced, as he supposed, with that risk of absorption of the Belgian Provinces into France which he had so clearly stated, in 1789, to be at all times a *casus belli* for Great Britain. The first French attack northwards, at the

---

[1] *Réflexions pour la Négociation d'Angleterre en cas de Guerre*, March 30th. Pallain, pp. 172 *sqq.*

[2] Sorel, II. 440 *sqq.*

end of April, proved a pitiable failure. All through May and June, full accounts of the mismanagement and insubordination of the French armies in Flanders were arriving at the Foreign Office, from a most capable British representative on the spot[1]. By the beginning of July, it was reported that the French had "entirely evacuated" those frontier districts into which they had penetrated. A month later, the news came that the garrison towns and camps on the French side of the frontier were in good order, the fortifications "in the most perfect repair, and even considerably added to, since the probability of a war with the Emperor." But there was no discipline. The Emigration had ruined the corps of officers; "nor is there a remedy against this evil." So, although Dumouriez was said to be confident and "the soldiery (by which is meant only the private men) and the peasantry universally revolutionists," it seemed impossible that France should "frustrate, or even derange, the plans of the combined army" of Prussia and Austria[2]. Pitt might well conclude that the Belgian Provinces were in no danger.

Throughout the summer, the best-informed men in England discussed Continental affairs on the assumption that the military plans of the Allies would not be "even deranged." "As soon as the German troops arrive in Paris," Grenville wrote to Auckland on June 19th, "whatever is the ruling party in Paris must apply to us to mediate for them. Such at least is my speculation. Even in that case, it would, I think, be right to hold back, and to show no anxiety for that sort of interference....But if the opportunity presents itself, I know no end of this troubled scene so advantageous as the bringing about by our assistance, an agreement which, I am convinced, all the parties will equally wish[3]."

On the day on which Colonel Gardiner sent his sanguine military report to Grenville, the French monarchy fell. Great Britain recalled her Ambassador, accredited to a King, not to a revolutionary Assembly; but her calculations as to the near future remained unchanged. A circular was sent round the Courts of Europe, explaining that the withdrawal of the Minister made no difference to her neutrality. Grenville had still no reason to doubt the early arrival of the Germans in Paris. Presumably, he continued his speculations as to the most advantageous thing that could happen next. On September 3rd—the

[1] Colonel Gardiner to Grenville, May and June despatches, *passim* (F.O. Flanders).
[2] Gardiner to Grenville, August 10th, 1792.
[3] *Dropmore Papers*, II. 281.

day after that on which the massacres had begun—he heard from his Foreign Office subordinate the latest news from France. It announced that the successful march on Paris was sure[1]. From every source came the same confident news.

Before the month of October was out, Valmy had been fought and lost; Ferdinand of Brunswick had recrossed the French frontier; and Custine with his army of the Vosges had dashed into Germany, to occupy Mainz and Frankfort. On November 6th, Dumouriez, taking up in person the Belgian plan of campaign, broke the Austrians at Jemappes by Mons; and two days later the Austrian Government fled from Brussels. The postulates of British Foreign Policy had become uncertain.

[1] J. B. Burges to Grenville, September 3rd. *Dropmore Papers*, II, 308.

CHAPTER II

THE STRUGGLE WITH REVOLUTIONARY FRANCE

I

THE overthrow of the French monarchy on August 10th, 1792, established the supremacy of men who owed their power chiefly to the populace of Paris; and the ensuing September massacres, carried out by the Revolutionary Commune of that city, helped still further to cow the moderates, disgust the provincials, and establish the domination of the capital. Thenceforth, it was the misfortune of the French democratic movement, which had claimed to be universal, that the driving force was mainly Parisian—a fact which goes far to explain the course of French politics during the next two years. The Girondin chiefs, now installed in office, possessed little power; it rested with the men of the streets and of the clubs; and the nominal leaders always followed the spasmodic impulses of a populace agitated by Marat and infuriated by the threats of vengeance that came from *Émigrés* serving with Brunswick's army.

The psychology of Revolution renders difficult the maintenance of peace with neighbouring States of the old type. Suspicion and aversion naturally set in; and these are the parents of war. Nevertheless, proofs abound that, from August to October, 1792, Pitt and Grenville sought to continue the policy of strict neutrality which they had laid down as their guiding principle. True, they decided to recall Earl Gower from Paris, an act which seemed to betoken illwill. But Grenville at once informed him, and through him the Revolutionary Government, that his recall followed as a matter of course on the lapse of the authority of Lewis XVI, to whom he had been accredited, and was "conformable to the principles of neutrality which His Majesty has hitherto observed." Lebrun, the new Minister for Foreign Affairs, welcomed this announcement and expressed a hope for the continuance of friendly relations, especially in commercial matters. The credentials of Chauvelin, French Envoy at London, having been signed by the deposed monarch, he was informed that he could no longer be officially recognised[1]; but he was

---

[1] O. Browning, *Despatches of Earl Gower* (1790–2), p. 209; *Ann. Reg.* 1792, pp. 327–8.

received unofficially. For some time, he offered no objection to this arrangement; but later, whether from injured vanity or from a desire (as an ex-noble) to show his democratic ardour, he represented it as a slight to the French Republic. His frequent association with Opposition clubs in London tended to annoy Ministers, but assured his popularity in Paris. Unfortunately, during the autumn his appointed adviser, Talleyrand, fell under the suspicions of the French Convention, which decreed his arrest. He, therefore, remained in London, and his sage warnings conveyed to Paris against the aggressive tendencies of French policy remained unheeded[1].

The characters of the French Ministers were calculated to inspire distrust and dislike in George III and his advisers. Danton's appointment as Minister of Justice seemed a hideous farce; Roland for Home Affairs was a respectable nonentity; Clavière, originator of the *assignats*, became responsible for Finance; and Foreign Affairs fell to Lebrun, an adventurous journalist, well versed in the Belgian disputes, but otherwise displaying the half-knowledge and consequent conceit which marked his patrons, Brissot and Dumouriez[2]. With such Ministers, ever impelled by Robespierre and the all-powerful Commune of Paris, there was reason to expect the extension of Jacobin propaganda and the widening of the circle of hostilities. Yet Pitt and Grenville showed no sign of joining the party that called for intervention on behalf of the cause of monarchy. They differed even more sharply from Burke, on grounds not only of sentiment but of policy. They believed royalists of the old school to be a less potent force in home politics than radical reformers, whose influence would be enhanced if the cause of peace were associated with them. The great Irishman scouted these calculations as both timid and false. He dreaded revolutionary principles as a pest which, if not stamped out, would in its rank growth desolate all nations. Pitt, and to a less extent Grenville, trusted in the inherent strength of British institutions and their consequent immunity from Gallic ailments, formidable only to weakly organisms. Stripped of its literary adornments, Burke's crusading policy was one of pessimism and panic. Their policy, on the other hand, however briefly and baldly set forth, was nevertheless one of trust in the good sense of the two nations and in the principle of non-intervention. So late as November 6th, 1792, Grenville wrote that

---

[1] For his Mémoire of November 25th, 1792, see Pallain, *Le Ministère de Talleyrand sous le Directoire* (App.), and a summary in Sorel, III. 221-3.
[2] A. W. Miles, *Corresp. on the French Rev.* I. 24, 144-6.

he had, throughout, disapproved of the invasion of France by the Austrian and Prussian armies as tending to consolidate the power of the Jacobins and delay the reestablishment of order. He now expressed some apprehension lest Republican principles should spread into England, but deemed the danger minimised by the maintenance of a policy of non-intervention[1].

The comparative passivity of George III during this crisis in the fortunes of monarchy is not a little curious; but it may be explained by his dislike of a policy of costly adventure, his desire, owing to the growing claims of his family, to reduce national expenditure, his trust in Pitt and Grenville, and his inveterate dislike of Burke. He also utterly distrusted the quixotic proposals of Gustavus III of Sweden for the rescue of Marie-Antoinette by armed force[2]. On September 22nd, while at Weymouth, he approved the somewhat bold proceeding of Grenville in discouraging similar appeals from Vienna and Naples on her behalf, and added these words: "Undoubtedly there is no step that I should not willingly take for the personal safety of the French king and his family that does not draw this country into meddling with the internal disturbances of that ill-fated kingdom[3]." He viewed the Revolution as a series of disturbances judicially inflicted by Providence on France as a penalty for her intervention on behalf of the American rebels against divinely constituted authority, and therefore discountenanced any attempt to shorten the period of retribution. Thus it came about that, even after the September massacres at Paris, Burke's fervid appeals for action remained mere echoes in the void.

Alike in temperament and conviction, the men who guided British foreign policy were averse from a policy of warlike adventure. A decade of unremitting efforts in the direction of retrenchment and reconstruction attested the devotion of Pitt to the cause of peace. From this, as the sequel will show, he was with great reluctance drawn aside by the course of events; and to it he sought to return at the earliest opportunity compatible with prudence. Had he possessed

---

[1] *Dropmore Papers*, III. 463–7; Burke's Works (Bohn edit.) v. 231–3; *Auckland Journals*, II. 464–6; J. H. Rose, *Pitt*, part II. ch. II.

[2] Klinckowström, *Fersen et la Cour de France*, I. p. 173.

[3] *Dropmore Papers*, II. 317. Even on November 25th, George wished for a general peace, if it could be made "to the *real* satisfaction of the parties concerned" (*Ibid.* II. 339). This corrects the statement of E. D. Adams (*The Influence of Grenville on Pitt's Foreign Policy*, p. 21) that after September, 1792, George III was hostile to France. It was her Decrees of November 16th and 19th, 1792, which changed his attitude.

more imagination, greater foresight, and a readier power of expression, he might perhaps have succeeded in appealing to the heart of France during the negotiations of 1795–7, and have stood forth as the pacificator of Europe. But in his nature there was too much of the Grenville stiffness for him to understand, still less to placate, Gallic susceptibilities. In truth, he had no knowledge either of Continental peoples or their politics. But as to his longing for peace there can be no doubt[1]. Equally certain is it that his mistakes during the period 1793–1805 arose largely from inability to grasp the stern exigencies of war and the calculating selfishness which it often engenders in the conduct of Allies towards one another. Virtuous, high-souled, patriotic and intensely hopeful, he lacked the critical faculties, especially those of distrust and detachment, which are needed for the unravelling of intrigues, the detection of rogues, or a due appreciation of the chances of success and failure in complex enterprises. He understood mankind in the abstract, but he did not understand men. Therefore, while excelling in the more familiar spheres of British statecraft, he fell short of full success at a world-crisis. His nature was far better suited to the decade of reconstruction than to that of revolution.

Similar limitations marked even more strongly the character of his cousin. Lord Grenville's accession to the Foreign Office in the spring of 1791 marked the definite triumph of a pacific policy; but a certain austerity of manner and narrowness of outlook hampered his usefulness at all times. Uninspiring, prolix and somewhat tactless, both as a speaker and writer, he chilled his friends and irritated his enemies; so that, in 1794, we find him expressing to Pitt a wish at the termination of the War, to retire from his uncongenial duties[2]. We shall not be far wrong in connecting this desire with his later confession: "I am not competent to the management of men. I never was so naturally, and toil and anxiety more and more unfit me for it." A phrase of Windham's explains this failure: "He [Grenville] knows nobody and is known by nobody." Yet that acute observer pronounced him well-informed, high-minded, and more imbued than Pitt with ideas of national dignity. In Windham's view, the Prime-Minister was, also, unacquainted with mankind and too disposed to live on by making concessions and "tiding it over[3]." In these respects, Grenville

---

[1] *Malmesbury Diaries*, II. 101, III. 96, 516; Sorel, II. 383. R. Guyot, *Le Directoire et la Paix de l'Europe*, p. 303.

[2] *Dropmore Papers*, II. p. 513. See, too, *Malmesbury Diaries*, II. 441, for Grenville's predilection for non-intervention on the Continent.

[3] Stanhope, *Pitt*, II. 122; Malmesbury, III. 590.

supplied backbone to the more pliant and pacific nature of Pitt; but in knowledge of men and management of Parliament they both so far yielded the palm to that versatile *bonvivant*, Henry Dundas, that the Administration was dubbed Scottish. To Dundas, however, and his impulsive and acquisitive ways Grenville felt an instinctive aversion, which was to become more marked as he gained in experience of his own. His career is remarkable for the growth of confidence in the great qualities of the British people; and it is hardly an exaggeration to say that his will-power, patriotic pride and indomitable persistence provided the mainspring of the first two Coalitions against France. Grenville, however, lacked the wide sympathies, imaginative outlook and inspiring influence that mark a leader of men. To him, still more than to Pitt, the French Revolution was incomprehensible. He sought to combat it with the old weapons in the traditional ways. Therefore, despite his constancy, honesty of purpose and unflinching courage, he figures merely as an able Minister of George III, but unequal (like most of his colleagues) to the novel demands of the Revolutionary era.

Henry Dundas, Secretary of State for Home Affairs, supervised far more than the business of that Department and, in fact, claimed participation in all affairs of moment. To him Pitt entrusted the chief oversight of executive war policy; and in this sphere his unbounded energy and assurance not seldom led him to impulsive and diffuse designs. Indian affairs interested him intensely, and, from 1792 onwards, the development of British influence in the Mediterranean was his special care. For the present, he opposed all interference with France. So late as November 25th, 1792, he wrote: "I think the strength of our cause consists in maintaining that we have nothing to do with the internal politics of foreign nations[1]."

The Under-Secretary of Foreign Affairs up to the year 1795 was James Bland Burges, 1751–1814, who was unremitting in his warnings as to French aggressiveness and the danger of democracy. He, probably, inclined Grenville to the stiffer attitude adopted from November to December, 1792. On December 18th, he wrote to Auckland that a war with France was inevitable, and the sooner it came, the better; for public opinion in England was excellent, and there was "an earnest desire to go to war with the French[2]." Bland Burges was

---

[1] Veitch, *The Genesis of Parliamentary Reform*, p. 235. For mordant attacks on Dundas, see Fortescue, *British Statesmen of the Great War*, and *Hist. of the British Army*, vol. IV. parts I. and II.

[2] Brit. Mus. Add. MSS. 34446.

probably the only one of our leading officials or diplomats who had as yet come to this conclusion. We may note here that, in 1794, he received a hint from Grenville that his services would be better appreciated abroad; and, on ignoring it, he was superseded by a friend of his chief. George Hammond, who became his successor in October, 1795, had been British Envoy at Washington.

The influence of our Ambassadors has rarely counted for more in the shaping of Foreign Policy than in this period; for, as the ablest of them noted in 1785, Ministers at home were too engrossed in parliamentary affairs to attend to events on the continent. "I never yet received an Instruction that was worth reading[1]." This irreverent assertion (less applicable after Grenville's acceptance of the Foreign Office) was made by Sir James Harris [1746-1820], who in 1788 became Baron, and afterwards first Earl of, Malmesbury. After the retirement of Sir Murray Keith from the embassy at Vienna, Malmesbury was the most distinguished, though not the most important, personage in the British Diplomatic Service[2]. In 1792-3, his predilections were hostile to France, and his severance from the Foxites in 1793 paved the way for diplomatic missions of the first importance. The doyen of the diplomatic circle was then William Eden, first Baron Auckland (1744-1814). As Ambassador Extraordinary at the Hague in 1790-3, he displayed exceptional activity in the acquisition of news, for which his position gave him unequalled facilities; and his intimacy with both Pitt and Grenville contributed to the enriching of a correspondence which is of prime importance. Auckland advocated strict neutrality in regard to French affairs: "Our general wishes on the one hand" (he wrote on September 18th, 1792) "are that France may never again resume the same restless and troublesome system which has so often been fatal to the peace of nations; and, on the other, that an executive government may exist there so as to restrain the present lawless and atrocious spirit." He, also, agreed with Grenville in thinking that the armed intervention of Austria and Prussia only emphasised the disorders in France which it was designed to crush[3]. On November 9th, he suggested tentatively to Grenville the advisability of recognising the French Republic (in order to ensure Lewis XVI and Marie-Antoinette against violence) and

[1] Malmesbury, *Diaries*, II. 112.
[2] Cf. *ante*, pp. 160 ff., as to the personality and early achievements of *le rusé et audacieux Harris* (as Mirabeau termed him).
[3] *Journal and Corresp. of Lord Auckland*, II. 443, 465.

of making secret overtures to Austria and Prussia with a view to ending their contest with France[1].

The secondary figures in the diplomatic circle were Auckland's younger brother, Sir Morton Eden, Ambassador first at Berlin and then at Vienna, where his mediocre abilities failed to make head against the masterful personality of the Chancellor, Thugut; also, Sir Charles Whitworth, Ambassador at Petrograd in the years 1788–1800, a man of soldierly bearing and firmness of character which withstood alike the craft of Catharine and the whimsical impulses of Paul I. At Madrid, Lord St Helens and his successor, Francis Jackson, worked tactfully, and for a time successfully, in conciliating that Court, always touchy and exacting as an ally; and scarcely less difficult were the tasks of John Hampden Trevor at Turin and Colonel Gardiner at Warsaw, the latter being instructed by Grenville to avoid entanglement in the Polish imbroglio[2]. The Hamiltons at Naples belong rather to the spheres of art and romance, until the crisis of the autumn of 1798 involved them in events from which they emerged with discredit. Ainslie and his successors at Constantinople helped to avert the danger of a Franco-Turkish Alliance, which seemed probable in the winter of 1792–3; but, with this partial exception, British Ambassadors strictly upheld the policy of non-intervention enjoined by Grenville.

The general diplomatic situation furnished adequate reasons for a policy of strict neutrality. The Triple Alliance of 1788 with Prussia and the United Netherlands had virtually lapsed, so far as the Hohenzollern Power was concerned[3]. Frederick William II now sought to withdraw as speedily as possible from his adventure beyond the Rhine, in order to procure more profitable spoil on the Vistula. With our former Ally, Austria, we were, also, on cool terms, both the German Powers maintaining that they had fought our battles for us in Champagne, while, as has already appeared, we disapproved of that enterprise and somewhat distrusted Francis II and his advisers[4].

---

[1] *Dropmore Papers*, II. 329. Many more of his letters are in the Brit. Mus. (Add. MSS. 34446 *et seq.*).

[2] Gardiner's predecessor, David Hailes, in his last despatch, of July 25th, 1792, warned Grenville of the fragility of the Polish Constitution of May 3rd, 1791, and the discredit attaching to its authors. On August 4th, Grenville instructed Gardiner that Great Britain would not intervene in favour of Poland and charged him to discover the intentions of the three neighbouring Powers "on whom the fate of Poland seems now entirely to depend" (F.O. Poland, 6).

[3] *Dropmore Papers*, II. 194, 241, 257, 262, 279.

[4] Stratton, our *Chargé d'affaires* at Vienna, thought the Emperor's ability and steadfastness unequal to his moral rectitude; he had no mental vigour or decision

Spain, too, was still smarting under the grievance of the Nootka Sound affair, which the now all-powerful Minister, Godoy, Duke of l'Alcudia, kept open by all the arts of chicanery. It soon transpired that Spanish officials at Nootka refused to give up Nootka to Captain Vancouver, who had been despatched to take it over[1]. Further, the odd complaisance of Spain to the new French Republic betokened a desire for friendly relations with Paris, which, in fact, were only to be severed by the execution of Lewis XVI. Even at the close of 1792, Great Britain had to reckon Spain among her possible enemies.

Moreover, the attitude of Catharine II of Russia was ambiguous. The unscrupulous ambitions of the Tsarina, far from sated by recent triumphs over the Turks, now turned in the direction of Poland. Her many incitements to the Monarchs of Sweden, Austria and Prussia to champion the cause of Lewis XVI and Marie-Antoinette were accompanied by no tangible proof of crusading zeal; and, on November 9th, 1792, Whitworth reported that she would "continue to look on at the conflagration with the utmost composure"; and again, that she had throughout sought "to engage all Europe in the quarrel [with France] and to remain herself a spectator of the desolation." The knowledge of her Machiavellian designs on Poland not only weakened the efforts of the German Sovereigns against France, but imposed caution on the one Power which had maintained its neutrality (as Whitworth put it) "with so much dignity and sound policy." A slight ruffle of anxiety overspread the serenity of the Tsarina when she learnt that the French Republic was vigorously striving to set the Turks against her; for the incursion of a Franco-Turkish fleet into the Black Sea might involve the destruction of the new and almost unprotected fleet at Sevastopol. By the end of the year, therefore, a feeling of relief pervaded the Russian Court at the news of the Anglo-French complications, as tending to restrain the Republic from oriental adventures and thereby to leave Catharine free for her long meditated move against Poland[2]. It was now discovered that French principles were making alarming progress among the Poles—a source of infection which neither she nor Frederick William II could allow on the borders of their dominions.

of character. On Grenville pressing for a declaration of Austria's war aims, the Acting Chancellor, Count Philip Cobenzl, on December 22nd stated that she would insist on the complete liberty of Lewis XVI, and on applying to France the essentials of a monarchical Constitution (F.O. Austria, 32).

[1] F.O. Spain, 25. F. J. Jackson to Grenville, December 29th, 1792.

[2] F.O. Russia, 23. Whitworth to Grenville, November 9th, 23, December 11th; Sorel, *La Question d'Orient*, p. 770.

The atmosphere being charged with electricity in both the east and the west of Europe, the only wise course for the British Government was to maintain a watchful aloofness. But an unkindly fate began to extend the storm area over these islands. The persistent rains, which hindered Brunswick's operations in Champagne, also ruined the harvests of Great Britain and the north of France, thereby causing widespread dearth and an eager competition for foreign corn. Hence arose not only commercial tension between the two nations, but internal discontent, resulting, on both sides, in a notable increase of democratic and levelling ardour. These sentiments, again, were accentuated by the astounding triumphs of the French arms. September saw the Austro-Prussian forces retreat from Champagne and the Sardinians driven from the capital of Savoy; in October, the Allies recrossed the Rhine in disorder; early in November, the French occupied Frankfort and utterly defeated the Imperialists at Jemappes— a victory which laid at their feet the Austrian Netherlands and brought the victorious tricolour to the borders of the Dutch Republic[1].

In the nervous and irritable state of public opinion, these events wrought a magical change. The French were filled with boundless confidence in the complete triumph of democracy over all the old Governments; and cognate aspirations spread among their many sympathisers in the British Isles. The sharp rise in prices favoured the growth of discontent, which found expression in numerous "Constitutional clubs," where the principles of the new French Constitution were vehemently acclaimed. The next development was destined to have far-reaching results. Delegates from the most important of these clubs, especially those of London, Newington, Manchester, Derby and Norwich, proceeded to Paris, and read to the Convention addresses of congratulation and fraternity at the sittings of October 31st, November 7th, 10th and 28th. The address bearing the signatures of Thomas Hardy and Maurice Margarot declared that the Elector of Hanover was uniting his troops to those of traitors and robbers; but that England was not Hanover.—"A Triple Alliance, not of crowned heads, but of the people of America, France and Great Britain, will give liberty to Europe and peace to the world[2]." These addresses, which were circulated throughout France, created the

---

[1] Jomini, *Guerres de la Révolution*, Bk II. chs. IX. X.
[2] "A Collection of Addresses...to the Nat. Convention of France," London, Debrett, 1793; *Ann. Reg.* (1793), pp. 344–352. Veitch. *op cit.* pp. 221–230, 363–6; *Moniteur*, November 8th and 12th, 1792.

impression there that the British people would support France in any effort made by her on behalf of democratic movements in other lands.

The French Convention, hereupon, conceived aggressive designs. Already, it had ostentatiously favoured addresses from Dutch "Patriots"; and, elated by the occupation of Brussels and by promises of support from British and Dutch democrats, it passed the Decrees of November 16th and 19th. By the former, the navigation of the Scheldt and the Meuse was declared open to and from the sea, though the Dutch Republic, by the terms of the Treaty of Westphalia (1648), absolutely controlled that navigation within its borders. On the same day, the French Executive Council resolved that Dumouriez should pursue the enemy even on Dutch territory, if he took refuge there. On the 19th, the Deputies of France decided to grant fraternity and assistance to all peoples desirous of recovering their liberty. Lebrun laid great stress on the Scheldt Decree, and, on November 30th, communicated a dissertation on the subject to Chauvelin, in which he spoke of it as an affair decided by the imprescriptible laws of universal justice, which France must have the courage to apply[1]. By that time, he must have known of the British Declaration to support the United Provinces at all points; but his language implied a resolve to go to war rather than compromise on this head. The importance of the Scheldt question has often been denied. Now, it may freely be granted that the right of the Dutch to close the navigation of that estuary to all other vessels was *per se* unjust[2]. But they had enjoyed it since 1648. So late as 1785, France had formally recognised it; and to abrogate it without consultation was an unheard-of proceeding. Moreover, most Dutchmen clung to the privilege in question. In 1784, the Grand Pensionary declared that the Netherlands ought to expend their last florin in maintaining it[3].

Meanwhile, the conditions which induced the French Convention to pass these decrees, also led the British Ministers stiffly to oppose the first signs of aggression. In mid-October, they prepared to reassure the King of Sardinia by a Declaration stating, *inter alia*, that the retention of Savoy by France would create a new order of things which Great Britain could not accept[4]. But far more significant was

---

[1] Sorel, III. 233.   [2] Cf. *ante*, ch. I, pp. 161 ff.
[3] Malmesbury, *Diaries*, II. 89: see, too, Marsh, *Politics of Great Britain and France*, chs. X, XI, XIII.
[4] *Dropmore Papers*, II. 322. On November 27th, the French Convention annexed Savoy to France (Sorel, III. 203).

their action on receipt of the news that the French forces were before Brussels. Antwerp would be the next stage; and the siege of that stronghold must bring up the vexed question of the navigation of the Scheldt estuary. Moreover, on its banks, France would impinge on territory which for naval and commercial reasons England has never, since the days of Edward III, allowed to pass into the hands of a great rival Power. From the time of the battle of Sluys to that of the battle of Jutland, her action has been consistent on this head; and her resolve now to warn the French off the Scheldt estuary and neighbouring coasts opened the struggle which ended in 1815 with the expulsion of Napoleon from Belgium.

On the receipt at Whitehall of the news of the evacuation of Brussels by the Austrians, the Dutch Ambassador, Nagel, took alarm and came to Pitt to request advice and help. Pitt suggested the despatch of notes to the two German Powers offering mediation, with a view to ending the War with France. Grenville met the crisis more stiffly. He at once informed Auckland at the Hague that the danger to the Dutch must be encountered firmly—"for, much as H.M. desires to maintain peace, he does not hesitate to aid the Dutch Republic against any attempt to invade it or disturb its Government[1]." Accordingly, he forwarded a Declaration to that effect, which was at once to be delivered publicly to the States General of the United Provinces. It assured them of H.M.'s "determination to execute at all times with the utmost good faith all the different stipulations of the treaty of alliance so happily concluded in 1788," but added that the correct conduct of the two nations ought to remove all grounds of apprehension. Auckland delivered it to the States General on November 16th—the very day on which the National Convention passed the Decree abrogating the rights of the Dutch over the estuary of the Scheldt and the Meuse. The States General thanked the British Government for its assurances of support, but expressed the hope that it might not be needed. The Stadholder, Prince William V of Orange, in a letter dated November 16th, thanked King George III for the Declaration, and suggested that British warships should be moored in the Downs, in readiness to proceed to the Scheldt if occasion demanded. It soon arrived. On November 22nd, the senior

---

[1] F.O. Holland, 41, Grenville to Auckland, "most secret," November 13th, 1792. Pitt also believed that "the explicit declaration of our sentiments is the most likely to prevent the case occurring." See, too, Pitt to the Marquis of Stafford, November 13th, 1792 (*Diaries*, etc. of the Hon. G. Rose, I. 115); also my article in the *Eng. Hist. Rev.* (January, 1912).

officer of two French gunboats at Rammekens demanded, in the name of Dumouriez, the right to pass up the Scheldt "*pour faire prospérer les armes de la République Française*"—obviously, in order to assist their land forces in reducing the Austrian garrison of the citadel of Antwerp. The Dutch authorities refused permission, but secretly instructed the commander of their guardship not to use force if the gunboats persisted in forcing a passage. They did so, and were soon reinforced by more powerful craft. Auckland explained to Grenville, that the Dutch intended "to temporise as far as may be practicable without essential disgrace or detriment"; but Nagel made a strong appeal to the British Government for succour to a faithful Ally in view of the imminence of a French invasion[1]. In fact, the Dutch were utterly unprepared for war, and saw with alarm a large French force on their borders, having all but open communications with the malcontent "Patriots" who sought to overthrow the Dutch Constitution. The chief difficulty of the situation lay in the Dutch Government not daring to plead openly for British succour, lest the French should burst in, with the aid of the Patriots. To temporise and quietly prepare for defence was therefore the only prudent course. Grenville understood their difficulties, and hoped by maintaining a firm attitude to conjure the danger.

The occurrence of riots in parts of Great Britain, also, alarmed him; and he concluded that there was a close connexion between the aggressive policy of the National Convention towards the Netherlands and the republican propaganda in these islands. On hearing of the Scheldt Decree (on or just before November 27th), he wrote to Auckland: "There is, I am afraid, little doubt that the whole is a concerted plan to drive us to extremities with a view of producing an impression in the interior of the country, which I trust and hope will fail." These statements (repeated even more strongly in his letter of December 4th) differ entirely from those of November 25th, when he heard from Auckland of a possible opportunity of setting on foot an informal negotiation for a general peace, through the medium of a French agent in Holland. Grenville then commended the scheme and secured a guarded expression of approval from George III[2]. Two days later, after hearing of the Scheldt Decree, he completely changed his language; and thenceforth he never swerved

[1] F.O. Holland, 41. Nagel to Grenville, November 29th; Auckland to Grenville, November 27th, 30th.
[2] *Dropmore Papers*, II. 339, 341, 344. His letter of November 14th to the Marquis of Buckingham makes light of the supposed sedition. (*Mems. of C. J. Fox*, III. 29.)

in his resolve to oppose the novel pretensions of France. On November 30th he informed Auckland that a small squadron of observation would be sent to the Downs. On December 7th, owing to the outbreak of sporadic disorders, the Government issued a Proclamation ordering the embodying of the militia in certain counties, in consequence of the conduct of evil-disposed persons "acting in concert with persons in foreign parts"—a statement repeated in the King's Speech of December 13th. Fox denied the existence of seditious practices, and denounced Ministers for creating and utilising a panic. The charge has been repeated; but the utmost that can fairly be urged is that they exaggerated the connexion between British democrats and French aggressions. Such a connexion undoubtedly existed; but it was unfair to charge our democrats with consciously provoking French action. All the addresses to the National Convention were drawn up, and half of them presented, before that body passed the aggressive Decrees which occasioned the *volte-face* of November 27th in British policy.

War was certain to result from the decisions of the British and the French Governments, publicly announced on November 16th, unless one side gave way. But to give way was difficult; for principles, considerations of honour and material interests were alike at stake. Great Britain took her stand on the sanctity of treaties; France, on the imprescriptible laws of nature as to the navigation of rivers in general and the rights of Antwerp in particular. Great Britain was resolved to stand by her Dutch Ally; France, to support the Dutch Patriots in the attempt to reverse the events of 1787. Moreover, neither side could retreat without loss both of prestige and material advantages. For the French Republic, to secure control of the Dutch Netherlands involved a gain of power such as Lewis XIV had never achieved; for Great Britain, it meant the establishment of her rival in estuaries that threatened the mouth of the Thames and her long and exposed east coast. At bottom, the issue was naval, therefore vital.

Events now tended towards war. Dumouriez' occupation of Liége and his demand to enter Maestricht (over which the deposed Prince-Bishop had joint control with the Dutch) threw new light on the French Decree freeing the navigation of the lower Meuse[1].

---

[1] Nagel in a *note verbale* of November 29th to Grenville stated that French vessels were assembling at Dunkirk and Ostend to ascend the Meuse and Scheldt into the heart of the United Provinces. He begged for British support. (F.O. Holland, 41.)

Nevertheless, Pitt and Grenville endeavoured to come to a friendly agreement with the French Republic by means of informal discussions with a private French agent. On December 2nd and 14th, Maret (the future Duc de Bassano) had interviews with Pitt, the earlier of which promised a good understanding; but, in the later, Maret had to announce the resolve of his Government to adhere both to the November Decrees and to its demands for the recognition of the French Republic and of Chauvelin as a fully accredited Envoy. To the recognition of the Republic Pitt and Grenville might possibly have acceded at an earlier date; but that of Chauvelin (now a *persona ingrata* at Whitehall) was out of the question[1]. With Maret in his place much more might have been accomplished, though probably, in any case, George III would have vetoed the recognition of the Republic. Fox's motion in Parliament on December 15th for sending a Minister to Paris to treat with the French Government was negatived. The occasion was rendered memorable by Burke, Windham and other Whigs taking their seats on the Ministerial side.

The French Convention now took a highly provocative step. In a Decree of December 15th, it declared for the suppression of the existing authorities in all districts occupied by the French troops, whose Generals were ordered to place under the protection of the French Republic the whole property of the deposed Government and of its adherents. Further, it invited the liberated people to accept the principles of liberty and equality, and to form a Provisional Government on those bases. Wide powers were, also, given to French Commissioners to provide means for the maintenance of the troops. Finally, it denounced as hostile any people which desired to preserve its Prince and privileged castes. This Decree, offering limitless opportunities of extortion, plunder and malversation, was an added threat to neighbouring nations[2].

To Grenville's practical mind, this profession of a desire to extend the bounds of liberty meant merely spreading the control of France over all lands which she coveted. Such is the dominant note of his reply of December 29th to a recent proposal of Catharine II for joint action of the Powers in setting bounds to the expansion of French power and influence. He stated that King George III saw with great

---

[1] For details of these interviews and those of Auckland with a French agent in the Netherlands, see Rose, *Life of Pitt*, II. chs. III. IV.; W. A. Miles, *Correspondence*, I. 61–72.

[2] Fox privately expressed horror at the Decree of December 15th and "thought war likely" (Malmesbury, *Diaries*, II. 482).

satisfaction the similarity of their views and, while abstaining from all interference in French domestic affairs, he would oppose the efforts of the National Convention to abrogate treaties and overturn all institutions in neighbouring countries. He, therefore, agreed with the Empress in desiring to form a League of the Powers, not for the purpose of imposing on France by force any form of government or Constitution, but in order to assure their own safety and curb French aggrandisement. In a covering letter of the same date to Whitworth at Petrograd, Grenville emphasised the distinction, already drawn in the Russian note, between the policy of imposing a particular form of government on France, and that of providing for the security of the other Powers. He then suggested tentatively that the Powers not at war should consult together as to the conditions which they might offer to the French—viz., "the withdrawal of their arms within the limits of the French territory, the abandonment of their conquests, the rescinding any acts injurious to the sovereignty or rights of any other nations, and the giving in some public and unequivocal manner a pledge of their intention no longer to foment troubles or to excite disturbances against other Governments." If France assented to these terms, they would forego all thought of hostility to her and live in amity with her Government. If not, they would take active steps to secure those ends, and possibly require some indemnity for their exertions. For Great Britain and Russia, the War with France, if it ensued, would be mainly maritime and would assure supremacy at sea, especially if Spain did not join the French. Russia should induce Denmark and Sweden to stop all supplies going to France; and she might possibly send a force to be landed on the French coast under cover of the British fleet[1].

These pronouncements mark out clearly the line of policy which British statecraft was to follow down to 1815. They differ entirely from the original plans of Prussia and Austria, which aimed at the restoration of monarchy in France (together with considerable gains of territory at her expense) and very extensive acquisitions in Central and Eastern Europe. Great Britain desired little more than the *status quo ante bellum*, and was prepared to recognise the existing Government in France, in case it made peace and ceased all subversive propaganda. Catharine assented to these proposals, except that which referred to a negotiation with the French Government; for she refused to take any step which seemed to imply an acknowledgment of the

[1] F.O. Russia, 23; also in B.M. Add. MSS. 34446.

Republic. Whitworth toned down Grenville's expressions on this head, but without avail; the Tsarina scouted the thought of recognising any country in revolt from its lawful sovereign, and had, for this reason, refused to recognise the United States of America. In vain Whitworth pointed out "how difficult it would be for His Majesty to make the establishment of any form of government in France the pretext of a war with that country[1]."

With a royalism so flaming as Catharine's the cool and cautious Grenville could with difficulty frame a concert. Her political creed corresponded very nearly to those of the Habsburgs and Hohenzollerns. But under this display of zeal there was cunning. Whitworth found reason for believing that her recent overture was prompted by a desire to stiffen the attitude of the British Government towards France, and thereby to increase the chances of a rupture between the Western Powers. Her scheme of partitioning Poland was maturing apace; and, on the 27th, he reported the general desire in Russian official circles that it should remain unknown in London until the Anglo-French rupture occurred. That wish was to be gratified; for on March 1st, the day on which the Partition Treaty was ratified, he stated that there was great satisfaction at our being forced into hostilities "without any further negotiation, from which it was always feared some pacific system might ultimately have resulted[2]." It soon appeared, then, that between the United Kingdom and the Great Powers there existed a deep contrariety. We could count on frank and complete union with only one State—the United Netherlands.

We may pass rapidly over the ensuing negotiations with France. They were complicated by the suspicion that Chauvelin was intriguing with British malcontents, and desired to bring about the overthrow of the Pitt Administration. Certainly, he was jealous of the preference shown by our Ministers to Maret; and, perhaps because Maret's tone was conciliatory, his was haughty. He associated ostentatiously with the Opposition, and announced the resolve of Lebrun not to retract the Scheldt Decree, but to insist upon the acknowledgment of the French Republic in the person of Chauvelin. He also boasted that, if he were not received as Ambassador, the height of his ambition was to leave England with a Declaration of War[3]. These assertions harmonised with the Report of the French

---

[1] F.O. Russia, 23. Whitworth to Grenville, January 22nd, 1793.
[2] *Ibid.* Whitworth to Granville, January 22nd, 25th, 27th, March 1st, 1793.
[3] W. A. Miles, *Authentic Corresp. with Lebrun* (1792), p. 84; *id. Corresp. on the French Revolution*, 1. 369.

Diplomatic Committee, of which that mischievous busybody, Brissot, was chairman. In presenting it to the Convention on January 1st, 1793, Kersaint pointed out the vulnerable character of the British Empire, which could be revolutionised in Ireland and attacked with deadly effect in Canada and the East and West Indies. War, should it take place, ought to be considered as Pitt's War, not that of the British nation[1].

Chauvelin echoed these statements in his next notes, which elicited vigorous retorts from Whitehall. His reiterated claim to be considered the official representative of the French Republic met with a cold refusal. He also attacked the Aliens Bill for subjecting all foreigners, including himself, to official supervision (December 31st, 1792), alleging that that measure infringed the Commercial Treaty of 1786, which stipulated freedom of intercourse and sojourn for the inhabitants of both countries. But this Aliens Bill was less rigid than a similar measure adopted at Paris in May, 1792, which consequently had already infringed that Treaty. Equally unfounded was Chauvelin's assertion that the refusal to recognise him officially implied a rupture of relations with the French Republic. Grenville retorted that he (Chauvelin) could not be officially acknowledged except as the Envoy of Lewis XVI, though unofficial explanations might still pass between them. In answer to Chauvelin's assurances that the Decree of November 16th was not intended to impugn Dutch rights, save in a matter of minor importance (the Scheldt), and that the Decree of November 19th applied to a community desirous of assuring its new-found liberty—not to a few seditious persons in that community—Grenville pointed out that a French flotilla had forced an entrance up the Scheldt in spite of Dutch protests, and that the whole affair showed a resolve to set at naught treaties and the rights of neutral nations; also, that the later Decree was accompanied "by the public reception given to the promoters of sedition in this country and by the speeches made to them precisely at the time of this Decree." He further denied the imputation of harbouring illwill towards France, but enjoined her, if she desired to maintain friendship, "to renounce her views of aggression and aggrandisement and to confine herself within her own territory, without insulting other Governments, without disturbing their tranquillity, without disturbing their rights." The whole despatch, though needlessly stern in form, proves that Pitt and Grenville did not object to the French Republic *per se*, but

[1] *Hist. parl.* XXII. 365–378; O. Browning, p. 278.

to its aggressive claims and subversive propaganda. Lebrun's answer of January 7th, was temperate in tone; but he refused to give way on the main point at issue, the Scheldt Decree. On the same day, Chauvelin wrote an acrid note respecting the Aliens Bill; indeed, on this and other topics his tone embittered the discussions. The points at issue were far from irreconcilable; and a tactful negotiator like Maret would perhaps have found means to effect a reconciliation.

The whole affair, however, was complicated by the deepening conviction of Grenville (perhaps also of Pitt[1]) that the French were working hard to undermine the British and Dutch Constitutions, and that Dumouriez' forces were preparing to invade the United Provinces. Such was the news derived from a French agent at the Hague, who was on a confidential footing with the Grand Pensionary, and informed him secretly, but with absolute certainty, that the French would invade his country by January 25th. Grenville received this news on December 29th, and thereafter disregarded the pacific assurances of Lebrun and Chauvelin[2]. His despatch of January 10th to Trevor at Turin implied that hostilities were imminent—an inference rendered the more probable by the shifty character of Dumouriez[3]. So far back as November 20th, that General wrote to Maulde, French Envoy at the Hague, that he intended to carry liberty to the Dutch as he had to the Belgians[4]. During his visit to Paris at the end of 1792, he seems to have convinced the French Ministers of the feasibility of that enterprise and of the immense results certain to accrue from it; for, on January 10th, the Executive Council sent secret orders to his second in command, General Miranda, to prepare to invade Dutch Flanders and Zealand within twelve days[5]. Probably, he would have done so, but for lack of food and transport. Grenville did not know of these orders; but the evidence coming from the Hague pointed to the imminence of a French invasion. Thus, when most of the British warships were about to be withdrawn from off Flushing in

---

[1] On December 13th, Noel, a French agent in London wrote to Lebrun describing Miles's informal efforts for peace and his assurances that Pitt was entirely for peace—more so than Grenville. Miles added: "*Ne craignez rien de notre armement*" (referring to the embodying of part of the militia and the sending of a small squadron to the Downs). Miles, *Corresp. on the French Revolution*, 1. 68.

[2] *Dropmore Papers*, II. 360. For his reply of December 29th to Auckland, see *Appendix A*.

[3] See W. Eliot's despatch of February 23rd, 1793 from Berlin to Grenville in *Appendix B*.

[4] F.O. Holland, 41. Enclosure in Auckland's despatch of November 23rd, 1792.

[5] "*Corresp. de Miranda avec Dumouriez...*" (Paris, 1793), pp. 3–8.

order that their crews might help the press-gang, the Prince of Orange begged that they might not depart, as their presence greatly encouraged his Government. On January 20th Grenville enclosed for Auckland's use a copy of the French plan of campaign, which had been secretly procured at Paris, and urged greater expedition in the Dutch defensive preparations. He also stated that the transactions with Chauvelin, and the manifestos recently issued by the Convention, left little doubt as to the resolve of that body to bring about a rupture. If the Dutch were attacked, a British force would be sent to aid in their defence. By that date, even Pitt deemed a war with France inevitable[1].

In all these discussions, the fate of Lewis XVI, which was then trembling in the balance, was scarcely mentioned. Obviously, the rupture would have occurred, even if his execution had not taken place. But, on the news of that event reaching London on January 24th, the Privy Council at once met and ordered the withdrawal of Chauvelin from the realm within eight days. Technically, this measure was correct, as that Envoy had been accredited by Lewis XVI and was received solely in that capacity. On his arrival at Paris, Brissot and the Diplomatic Committee drew up a report declaring that George III had not ceased, especially since August 10th, 1792, to give proofs of his malevolence to France and his attachment to the Coalition of the Kings; that he had violated the Anglo-French Treaty of 1786 and ordered armaments clearly intended against France; that he had just concluded a Secret Treaty of Alliance with the Emperor, and had drawn the Stadholder of the United Provinces into the same Coalition. These falsehoods found ready acceptance; and an inflammatory speech by Brissot decided the Convention to pass unanimously a Declaration of War against the King of Great Britain and the Stadholder (February 1st)[2]. The inclusion of the latter in this Decree proved the aggressive designs of the French Government; for, whatever might be thought of the action of the British Government, that of the United Provinces had given no cause of offence. The acquisitive spirit of the Convention further appeared in the Decree of January 31st, annexing Nice, and in that of a few days later, annexing the Belgic Provinces, to France. It is also noteworthy that, among the charges drawn up in October, 1793, by the Jacobins against the Girondins as a party and against Brissot in particular, he and they were accused of brusquely

---

[1] Malmesbury, *Diaries*, II. 501.
[2] *Hist. Parl.* XXIV. 194–207.

proclaiming war against the British and Dutch peoples and other Powers which had not yet declared themselves[1].

It has often been stated that a conflict between Great Britain and the French Republic was inevitable because the one represented the old order, the other the new, so that between them there was a fixed antagonism. The statement is overstrained. There was no irreconcilable opposition between British statesmen and the French leaders, until the latter, amidst the exaltation produced by the conquest of Belgium, adopted an aggressive policy which was at variance with the best traditions of their predecessors. The French conquest of Belgium and the ensuing trial of Lewis XVI produced an artificial excitement, a flamboyant patriotism, an eager competition between Jacobins and Girondins each to outdo the other, which infused a dash of the old Chauvinism into the fanaticism of the new age. The heady mixture was not the true wine of the Revolution. It was nauseous to Talleyrand, the inheritor of the Mirabeau tradition; and, in his obscure lodgings in London, he had to look on helplessly while the fate of France and of Europe was decided by the coxcomb Chauvelin, the journalist-adventurer Lebrun and the charlatan Brissot. To assert that these men represented either France or the Revolution is to insult her and degrade her progeny.

Furthermore, the statement errs in assuming that George III, Pitt and Grenville desired to make war on the Revolution. The reverse is the case. Until near the close of 1792, the King wished to remain at peace. Pitt and Grenville disapproved of the two German Powers embarking on a monarchical crusade, because they foresaw its effect in identifying Jacobinism with France and, up to the end of November 1792, they hoped by an understanding with all the Powers to mediate with a view to a general pacification. They were, also, prepared to recognise such *de facto* rulers of France as should conclude peace—that is, to recognise the French Republic if it proved to be pacific and non-interfering. True, in Parliament, in December, 1792, they opposed the motion for sending a Minister to Paris; but, at the same time, they were quietly taking steps which might lead to the resumption of friendly relations, if France renounced her aggressive designs. For they were aggressive. The Scheldt Decree was a violation of a recent French Treaty with

---

[1] *Hist. Parl.* xxix. 435. For proofs that the so-called mission of Maret to London at the end of January was unauthorised, and that the pacific proposals of Dumouriez were unimportant and doubtful, see Rose, *Life of Pitt*, ii. 109–111; W. A. Miles, *Correspondence on the French Revolution*, ii. 62; Lecky (vi. 126) over-rates their importance.

the United Provinces and infringed the Anglo-Dutch Treaty of 1788. The British Government has been blamed for laying too much stress on the Decrees of November 16th and 19th; but, viewed collectively, they constituted a claim to the right to abrogate treaties and interfere in the internal affairs of neighbouring lands. Moreover, the French authorities followed up the Scheldt Decree by action which revealed their design of making Antwerp a French naval port. Their whole conduct with regard to the Austrian Netherlands was such as to warrant the belief that annexation was intended. The Decrees of November, therefore, became, not only a test question with respect to the maintenance of treaties, but a matter of vital importance to Great Britain and the United Provinces.

On the other hand, the procedure of Pitt and Grenville must be pronounced stiff and ineffective. Without divulging too much of the sacrosanct treasures of the Foreign Office, they might surely have made it clear, not only to diplomats but to the two nations concerned, that British policy was essentially peaceful and aimed at achieving a just settlement of the War, with a view to the eventual recognition of any truly pacific Government established at Paris. A declaration of this kind would have at the same time allayed resentments in France and discontents at home. But Ministers allowed their good intentions to be shrouded by old-world reserve; and Grenville met the pert insistence of Chauvelin with an aristocratic *hauteur* which irritated that Envoy and played into the hands of the aggressive party at Paris. Pedantic insistence, there, on the imprescriptible laws of nature, and rigid adherence, here, to the text of treaties complicated a question which, with goodwill and tactfulness on both sides, might have been settled in a month. As it was, the two great nations of the West drifted into a conflict which stirred the dying embers of Continental strife into a mighty conflagration, destined to rage over the whole of Europe and finally to bring back the exhausted principals to the original point in dispute—Antwerp.

II

The divergence between the policy of Great Britain and that of the chief potentates of the Continent appeared very clearly so soon as they deemed her entangled in the dispute with France. The conduct of Catharine has already been described, and that of Austria and Prussia now claims attention. In the first days of 1793, Sir Morton Eden reported that Prussia was about to send her best troops against

Poland, and that his request to spare some for the defence of the United Provinces was disregarded. The reason became clear in the course of an interview which Grenville had at Whitehall, on January 12th, with the Austrian and Prussian Ambassadors, Count Stadion and Baron Jacobi. They stated the decisions of their Courts: that Prussia should obtain in Poland an indemnification for her expenses in the French War, and should, in return, withdraw her opposition to the long-cherished Habsburg plan of acquiring Bavaria in exchange for the Belgic Provinces. Grenville protested against this cynical scheme and pointed out "the mischief which must result to the common cause from such an evident act of injustice[1]." But the transaction was irrevocably settled between Vienna and Berlin; for on January 19th Eden reported that the King of Prussia would no longer act as a principal in the French War, if these indemnifications were not forthcoming; also, that Russia had her plans for aggrandisement at the expense of Poland, those of Austria in that quarter being doubtful[2]. On February 5th, when the French Declaration of War was known, Grenville informed the German Powers that Great Britain, while protesting against the Partition of Poland, would not oppose it by force; also, that, if France continued the War, the Great Powers must exact from her the renunciation of all her conquests and of "all policy of interference in the affairs of other States."

As this programme involved the abandonment by France of the Belgic Provinces, part of the Rhineland, Savoy and Nice (not to speak of Avignon), it opened the way to an understanding with the German Powers and the Empire, as also with Sardinia and the Pope; and this prospect undoubtedly encouraged the Empire to declare war on France, as it did on March 23rd, 1793. The Court of Turin also resolved to persevere in a contest which, without Britain's financial and naval assistance, must have been hopeless. On this territorial basis, then, the foundations of the First Coalition could be laid; but in the sphere of moral, as distinct from material, interests there was slight hope of an understanding, save with the smaller States threatened by France. Our attention may now be concentrated, first, on the formation of the Treaties which built up the First Coalition, secondly, on British efforts to secure the active cooperation of Prussia and to lessen the friction with Spain.

<hr>

[1] F.O. Prussia, 27. Draft of January 12th, 1793, in Grenville's writing.
[2] *Ibid.* Eden to Grenville, January 19th. On February 5th, Eden was appointed to succeed Sir Murray Keith at Vienna. He arrived there at the end of the month.

Before the entry of Great Britain into the War, no attempt (apart from the rather doubtful proposal of Catharine) had been made to frame a general concert of the Powers; and in that sphere British policy was to effect results no less important than in the naval and military operations. From Catharine, little was to be expected except skilfully baited incitements to the continuation of the War. They took the form of two companion Treaties, signed by Grenville with Vorontzoff at London on March 25th, 1793, viz., a Commercial Treaty renewing that of 1766, with a few variations favourable to British trade, and a Treaty of Alliance containing vague offers of mutual assistance in the War, but binding each of the two Powers to prohibit all exports to France and to hinder neutrals from sending them, or from granting any protection to French property or commerce, whether in their ports or at sea. This last proviso, besides rendering impossible a renewal of the League of Armed Neutrality of 1780, implied an embargo on French ships and property in the ports or in the territory of neutrals. Moreover, it prevented the revival of the old French practice which, in time of war, opened up to neutrals commerce with French Colonies forbidden in time of peace.

On April 25th, Grenville signed with the Sardinian Ambassador, the Comte de Front, a Treaty granting to that kingdom during the War a subsidy of £200,000 a year, conditional on the maintenance of a Sardinian army of 50,000 men. Great Britain engaged to send a fleet into the Mediterranean, and to secure the restoration to Sardinia of her lost provinces of Savoy and Nice. A month later, the Treaty of Aranjuez with Spain established a close concert for the purpose of opposing French views of aggrandisement, and binding the two Powers to prevent neutrals from according protection to French commerce. With Naples no treaty was signed, until that Power knew that Lord Hood with a powerful fleet was in the Mediterranean. Then, on July 12th, 1793, Sir William Hamilton and General Acton, Prime-Minister at that Court, signed a compact of a more intimate nature than the preceding. The King of the Two Sicilies, thereby, agreed to supply for service with the British forces in the Mediterranean 6000 troops, 4 sail of the line, and 8 smaller warships; while Great Britain engaged to maintain in that sea "*une flotte respectable*" and to protect Neapolitan commerce. With Prussia, owing to the exertions of Sir James Murray and Lord Beauchamp, a Treaty was signed on July 14th, 1793, at the headquarters of Frederick William II at Mainz. It established a perfect concert with her, and assigned a subsidy for her military support, while obtaining from her assurances as to neutral commerce similar to those secured from Russia and Spain. These assurances, also, reappeared in the otherwise rather vague compacts concluded on August 30th and September 26th with the Emperor and the King of Portugal respectively. Subsidy Treaties with Baden and the two Hesses also promised to swell the totals of the Allied armies.

The Treaty of 1788 still subsisted with the United Provinces; and the first naval and military efforts were put forth by Great Britain in February, 1793, resulting in the blocking, at the Hollandsdiep, of Dumouriez' scheme of invasion of Holland. Foiled there, he was utterly beaten on March 17th by the Austrians at Neerwinden, with the result that the Belgic Provinces once more came under their control. When Dumouriez, after planning the overthrow of the regicides at Paris, was constrained to fly for refuge to the Austrians, the Allies seemed to have the game in their hands[1]. The opportunity was lost, largely because the Austrian commander, Prince Frederick Josias of Coburg, in the course of a conference on military affairs held at Antwerp early in April, issued a proclamation which implied that the Allies would demand territorial indemnities from France. Nothing could have tended more certainly to unite all Frenchmen together in defence of *la patrie*.

For this blunder Prussia's action in Poland was largely responsible. By the end of March, it was clear that Prussia and Russia would share between them the spoils of the Second Partition, to the exclusion of Austria. In consequence, Francis II honourably removed the Vice- and Acting-Chancellor, Count Philip Cobenzl, who had been duped by those two Powers, and in 1794 appointed to the general control of Foreign Affairs Thugut, a diplomat remarkable alike for his versatility in the choice of means and for his persistent pursuit of fundamental aims. Thugut resolved that Austria, while opposing the Partition, should make use of Prussia and Great Britain to secure acquisitions of territory proportionate to those of Prussia and Russia in Poland. He declined to specify where those acquisitions should be found[2]. The most obvious were the recovery of the Belgic Provinces (together with Liége) and the addition of territory to be conquered from France. He therefore pressed a close understanding with Great Britain; and Grenville now held out to the Court of Vienna the prospect of acquiring Lille, Valenciennes and other

---

[1] So urgent was the crisis that Lebrun wrote to Grenville, on April 2nd, to propose discussions for peace. For Grenville's reception of the proposal see his letter of May 18th, 1793 (*Appendix B*).

[2] F.O. Austria, 32. Eden to Grenville. April 15th, 1793.

strong and populous cities of north-eastern France as a barrier against
that Power. This revived Barrier-scheme offered some temporary
advantages. It would root Austria more firmly in her Belgic lands, and
thereby tend to efface her desire for the Belgic-Bavarian exchange, a
project always strongly opposed at Whitehall. When the Allied arms
prospered in May-July, the Court of Vienna viewed these proposals
with favour, and, in deference to British representations, seemed to
abandon finally the proposals for the exchange. This decision pleased
the Hohenzollern Court; but, dissembling its satisfaction, it now
proceeded to mark time in the west, to the exasperation of Great
Britain and Austria. The motives of Prussia were clear enough. Having
secured her booty in the east, she now desired to see her southern rival
go empty away from the territorial scramble planned between them
early in 1792; and, at the close of August 1793, Lucchesini, the Prussian
Envoy at Vienna, declared that his Government would object to any
serious diminution of the power of France as detrimental to the balance
of Europe[1].

These facts explain the course of the campaign in France. The slow
and methodical reduction of the French Barrier fortresses in the north-
east (most faulty as a military measure, when France had no good army
in the field) was due mainly to the Anglo-Austrian understanding as to
the eventual acquisition of those fortresses by the Habsburgs; and the
efforts of Coburg and the Duke of York, which, on the reduction of
Valenciennes (July 28th), came very near to success, were wasted
by the calculating selfishness of Prussia. The remonstrances of British,
Austrian and Dutch statesmen at her feeble and belated operations
in the west had no effect. Finally, on September 23rd, Lucchesini
handed to Lord Yarmouth, our special Envoy at Prussian headquarters (where Frederick William still was) a note bewailing the
expenses of the campaign, the troubles in Prussian Poland, and so
forth, and requiring, not only our guarantee for the possession of that
land, but also a subsidy by the Allies towards the expenses of the War.
These demands being declined, Frederick William quitted his army,
ordering it not to engage in serious undertakings; whereupon
George III commented: "The sudden retreat of the King of Prussia
completes the very ill-advised line of conduct that has attended every
step he has taken for these four or five years[2]."

The results of Prussia's apathy were severely felt in another sphere

[1] F.O. Austria, 34. Eden to Grenville, August 31st, 1793.
[2] *Dropmore Papers*, II. 441. See too, pp. 446, 451, 470.

of war, Toulon. On August 28th, the French Royalists, dominant in that city, handed it over, with its dockyard and fleet, in trust to the British Vice-Admiral, Lord Hood. The Spanish fleet under Admiral Langara sailed in immediately after. The plan of the British Government, who on September 13th heard of this unexpected success, was to collect as large a force as possible of Austrians, Spaniards, Sardinians and Neapolitans for the succour of the Royalist cause in the South of France, and to press the Republic hard on that side. The unwarlike character of the Spanish and Neapolitan contingents (those of Sardinia were highly efficient) rendered very necessary the despatch of at least 5000 seasoned Austrian troops from her Milanese province. On September 24th, Thugut reluctantly assented to Eden's requests to this effect; but, on various pretexts (chiefly the inactivity of Prussia in the Rhenish campaign), the Imperial Government delayed the fulfilment of its promise until too late. Toulon fell on December 19th, before the Austrian troops began their march seawards.

This disaster also strained severely the relations between Great Britain and Spain. The Court of Madrid had claimed the right to appoint the Commander-in-chief on shore, even though Toulon was surrendered to Hood, and though most of the seamen and troops present by the end of September were British or subsidised by Great Britain. Much friction ensued, but Pitt and Grenville ordered the retention of the command by a British General. Spain, also, harboured resentment at the overtures made by Paoli on behalf of Corsican Royalists to Lord Hood for placing their island under the protection of George III. Another faction, headed by Buttafoco, treated with Langara for calling in the Spanish forces[1]. Neither move had any effect until after the evacuation of Toulon by the Allies on December 19th; but Hood thereafter resumed his relations with the Paolists; and in the spring of 1794 British forces set about the reduction of the remaining French garrisons. The Spanish Government resented this conduct as unfriendly on the part of an Ally, and declared it one of the causes of the rupture of 1796. Grenville sought to divert the thoughts of Spain to acquisitions in Roussillon and Béarn; but his motive of promoting hostility between her and France was too obvious to draw away her attention from the leading preoccupations of her statesmen, viz., the extension of British power in the West Indies and the Mediterranean[2].

[1] F.O. Genoa. F. Drake to Grenville, December 22nd, 1793.
[2] F.O. Spain, 27. Grenville to St Helens, July 19th, 1793. (See *Appendix B*.)

Another relation which the Toulon affair brought to a crisis was that of the British Government to the French Princes and the Royalist party. Up to the month of August, 1793, the British Government declared its resolve not to intervene in favour of any party or form of Constitution. But the informal alliance with the Royalists of Toulon—perhaps, also, disgust at the deepening atrocities of the Reign of Terror—somewhat modified its attitude. It continued to discountenance the *Émigrés*. In common with all who had experienced their intolerable arrogance and old-world bigotry, British statesmen and commanders were determined to keep them at arm's length[1]. But a very delicate situation arose in October, when it appeared that the Comte de Provence (afterwards King Lewis XVIII) who had assumed the title of Regent of France, proposed to proceed to Toulon; also, that the Spanish Court favoured the scheme as a means of increasing Spanish influence there. At once, British Ministers took alarm; for it was certain that Monsieur would dictate military and political measures, and would prevent the Allies from holding any territorial conquests as gages for the indemnities on which they were still hopefully counting. On October 22nd, Grenville fired off despatches to St Helens at Madrid and Drake at Genoa, bidding the former oppose the scheme and the latter, in the last resort, even prevent the embarkation of the Prince[2]. His slow progress and the rapid success of the Republican arms prevented that harlequinade from taking place; but the whole affair strained our relations both with Spain and with the Royalists of Toulon.

While discouraging the "pure" Royalists, George III and his Ministers avowed their preference for a limited monarchy. In the Instructions, drawn up almost entirely by Pitt and signed on October 19th, for the three British Commissioners appointed to administer Toulon, there occurs this passage: "You will be particularly careful on all occasions in stating H.M.'s conviction that the acknowledgment of an hereditary monarchy and of Lewis XVII as lawful sovereign, affords the only probable ground for restoring regular government in France." A less distinctly monarchist Declaration, drafted by Grenville and issued from London on October 29th, stipulated merely that " some legitimate and stable government should be established, founded on the acknowledged principles of universal justice, and capable of maintaining with other Powers the accustomed

[1] F.O. Sardinia, 13. Mulgrave to Trevor, October 19th, 1793.
[2] Cottin, pp. 425, 428.

relations of union and peace." On this head, Grenville's policy was more flexible than that of Pitt and left the Administration free to treat with any French Government that did not pursue aggressive and subversive aims. Of this wider definition Pitt was glad to avail himself in the negotiations of 1796 and 1797; though by that time, as will duly appear, Grenville's predilections had become less pacific and rather more monarchical than those of Pitt[1]. The British Declarations were less royalist in tone than those of our German Allies and far less so than the vehement professions of Catharine. Thus, by the autumn of 1793, the four Allies had taken up a standing not unlike that of the year 1814. For the present, their pronouncements placed them signally at variance with French Republicans, and tended to rally all of them round any Government which could drive out the invaders. Thus, the Toulon episode, which bred discord among the Allies, solidified Jacobin rule in France. By the end of the year, her soil was almost freed from the Allied armies—a result due no less to the fatuities of their Generals than to the blunders and selfishness of their Cabinets.

The signal failures of the Allies in the campaign of 1793 emphasised the need of securing substantial help from Prussia for that of 1794. That Court, however, seemed resolved to continue marking time on the Rhine, while acting energetically beyond the Vistula. Its guiding spirit was Lucchesini, formerly reader to Frederick II. Having espoused the sister-in-law of Bischoffswerder, the still powerful favourite, he had secret means of influencing the highly susceptible Monarch; and, by dint of cajolery or bullying, generally had his way. Though his policy was persistently anti-British and anti-Austrian, he had gained too great an influence over our Envoy, the Earl of Yarmouth. Pitt, therefore, advised the despatch of Lord Malmesbury on a special mission to Berlin to clear matters up. At Whitehall Ministers differed as to the value of Prussia's Alliance. Grenville was so convinced of her falseness as to advise the refusal of all further subsidies. Pitt was more hopeful; but, on October 9th, the Cabinet decided on the withdrawal of the subsidy and the transmission of remonstrances (toned down at Pitt's suggestion) to the Court of Berlin. It was well not to insist overmuch; for the Prussian Ministers could claim that they had as much right to crush the so-called Polish revolt as we had to extend British sway in the East and West Indies; and, later, the Anglophil Duke of Brunswick mildly reproved our exigence at Berlin. Frederick

[1] *Dropmore Papers*, II. 433, 438, 443; *Parl. Hist.* xxx. 1060; Cottin, p. 423; E. D. Adams, pp. 22–24.

William II, with all his defects, was not devoid of chivalry, and a personal appeal of George III to him would probably have cleared the air. As it was, the British remonstrance produced an angry counterblast, which Yarmouth explained as due to annoyance at our refusal to meet Prussia's lofty demands for payment of actions required by her treaty obligations[1].

The Prussian problem being insoluble except by consummate skill and tact, Yarmouth was superseded by Lord Malmesbury. On his way to Berlin, he stayed at the Hague, Brussels and Frankfort, in order to probe the situation. He found it unpromising. At Brussels, he met the Austrian Ambassador, Mercy d'Argenteau, formerly the Anglophobe counsellor of Marie-Antoinette, who now, under the chastening stroke of her execution, confessed that everything depended on the union of England and Austria. He extolled the exertions of the Duke of York's army, but declared that Austria had no further troops available except 10,000 in the Milanese. In his view, the conduct of the Prussians, both Ministers and Generals, was equally reprehensible and foolish; but Frederick William must understand that abandonment of this contest spelt ruin. At Alost, Malmesbury found the Duke of York indignant at the mismanagement of the campaign, and his officers discontented or even insubordinate. At Frankfort, he gleaned useful hints from the Dutch Envoy, Vice-admiral Kinckel, as to the influences, male and female, which played upon the Prussian monarch, and as to the success of that arch-intriguer Lucchesini, in removing from the royal councils all friends of Austria and Great Britain. Austria's representative, Count Lehrbach, was unpopular, owing to his rough overbearing ways. The Prussian Court, therefore, oscillated between hatred of French principle and fear of Russia, the dominating motive being to incorporate thoroughly its late gains in Poland and to leave Austria beggared by her Rhenish campaigns. An imperious necessity, however, controlled these oscillations. The treasury at Berlin was nearly empty. Frederick William having squandered money on mistresses and official embezzlers, four-fifths of the treasure inherited from Frederick the Great had vanished; and Prussia possessed no system of finance capable of meeting the huge yearly deficits[2].

Herein lay the secret of Frederick William's complaisance to

---

[1] *Dropmore Papers*, II. 442, 446, 470.
[2] Malmesbury, *Diaries*, III. 14–23; Vivenot, *Quellen zur Geschichte der Politik Oesterreichs*, IV. 11 *et seq.*; F.O. Prussia, 28. G. Rose to Grenville, November 3rd, 1793.

Malmesbury. When our Envoy saw him at Berlin on December 25th, he proffered almost indignant assurances of his fidelity to the Treaty of 1788, though recent notes from Berlin had left it doubtful; but he added that, in the exhausted state of his exchequer, he could not undertake another campaign, and that, a loan being out of the question, he must recall nearly all his troops from the Rhine unless his Allies granted pecuniary support. Such a step he would regret, for he abhorred the French Jacobins; and he trusted that Great Britain would not leave him "degraded and sunk," but would enable him to proceed with the French War. These earnest professions, added to the assurances of George Rose (*Chargé d'affaires* at Berlin) as to Prussia's poverty, produced a great impression, especially when the King stated his keen desire to increase his Rhenish army to 100,000 men. Malmesbury hoped that, if the honest old Field-marshal Möllendorff commanded such a force, the results would be decisive. Despite warnings from Lehrbach, that Prussia meant to desert her Allies and join France, our Envoy hoped for the best; and his influence turned the scale in Downing Street[1]. Grenville cast off his scepticism, and, while grumbling that the Germans thought England a pretty good milch-cow, looked about anxiously for the necessary subsidy of £2,000,000. On January 28th, 1794, he wrote to Malmesbury, promising this sum—Great Britain to contribute two-fifths, Austria and Holland each one-fifth, the last fifth remaining as a charge either on a beaten France or on the conscience of Catharine[2].

The reception accorded to these offers at the Allied capitals threw light on the loose texture of the First Coalition. Frederick William at once computed that such a sum would not enable him to act up to the limit of his desires for the great cause. To the Dutch their quota seemed excessive. The appeal to the conscience of Catharine found it numb; and Thugut saw in the British subsidy to the Hohenzollerns a means whereby they could arm a great force, maintain it in a central position and possibly even launch it against Vienna[3]. The Austrian General, while less nervous than the Minister, protested against the advent of the great Prussian subsidised force near Liége, and pointed out West Flanders as its proper sphere of operations. As the spring approached, much ink was spilt in drafting plans for the defence of

[1] After January 24th, 1794, the F.O. despatches were dated from Downing Street. [2] *Dropmore Papers*, II. 491–7.
[3] F.O. Austria, 36. Eden to Grenville, February 15th, 27th, 1794. Malmesbury, *Diaries*, III. 53–68. The best survey of Thugut's policy is in H. Hüffer's *Quellen*, edited by F. Luckwaldt (1907), Pt II, vol. I.

Ypres and the lines of the Lys and Sambre; but the Imperialists now pointed out that the British and Dutch contingents were 30,000 below strength[1]. Worst of all, a revolt of the Poles strengthened the Francophil party at Berlin, which always received powerful support from the King's uncle, Prince Henry. Finally, the British Envoy induced the chief Prussian Minister, Count Haugwitz, to suggest the transference of the negotiation to the Hague. There, on the scene of Malmesbury's former triumphs in 1787-8, they concluded a Treaty (April 19th, 1794), whereby Prussia was to supply an army of 62,400 men, under a Prussian Commander-in-chief, for service against France, Great Britain and the United Provinces paying her £50,000 a month and £300,000 for initial expenses, also her costs in bread and forage, calculated at the rate of 32 shillings a month per head. The movements of this army and the conquests made by it were to be at the decision and disposal of the Maritime Powers. Of the yearly subsidy Great Britian was chargeable for £1,600,000 and the United Provinces £400,000 a year; also, for the other expenses in similar proportion. The Treaty was framed ostensibly for the year 1794, but a separate article stipulated its renewal and for the duration of the War[2].

Malmesbury had somewhat exceeded Grenville's instructions; but he could plead that only by liberal payments to Prussia could she be induced to act with vigour. As the compact aided her finances, spared those of Russia, and promised to fulfil the aims of the Allies, it should have formed the basis of a stable Coalition. Various circumstances, however, militated against it. *Inter alia*, Pitt and Grenville recalled Malmesbury to London for further information, but, on his arrival, were so absorbed in the suppression of sedition as not to see him or provide for the payment of the first subsidy during nearly three weeks. The delay was disastrous. It gave a handle to the Francophils at Berlin, and they seem to have won over to their side Haugwitz, whose constancy had always depended on the influence of Malmesbury. Thereafter, the Count always shunned meeting him[3]. Lucchesini now had his way at Berlin, the result being that Möllendorff, commanding the subsidised Prussian army, was induced to raise various difficulties as to the method of its employment beyond the Lower Rhine. Seeing that the Austro-British force under Clerfait and the Duke of York, on May 18th, suffered a heavy defeat at

[1] Vivenot, IV. 367.
[2] Martens, V. 283; Garden, V. 233; Malmesbury, *Diaries*, III. 91-3.
[3] Malmesbury, *Diaries*, III. 91-6.

Turcoing-Roubaix, the arrival of the Prussians for the defence of the United Provinces was urgently necessary[1]. The British and Dutch Envoys, General Cornwallis and Kinckel, added their arguments to those of Malmesbury during lively interviews with the Marshal near Mainz, but failed to overcome his objections to so lengthy a march. Malmesbury discovered that the Anglophobes of the Prussian Court had been influencing him; and, in the absence of Haugwitz, Baron Hardenberg seemed to be the only official at Prussian headquarters, anxious for the fulfilment of the Treaty. Hardenberg consented to represent to Möllendorff the disgrace and isolation which must befall Prussia, if, after receiving the British and Dutch subsidies, she failed to perform her bounden duty to those hard pressed Allies. It was in vain. Not without some show of reason, the septuagenarian Marshal represented the immense difficulty of a march northwards, and kept his army in cantonments with the maximum of economy, British and Dutch money being therefore available for the other requirements of Berlin[2].

Meanwhile, events had occurred which began to awaken jealousy of British maritime power. The occupation of the French colony of Hayti and the conquest of Tobago and Pondicherry in 1793 were followed up, early in 1794, by the capture of Martinique and St Lucia, the keys to the West Indies. On June 1st, 1794, Lord Howe gained a decisive victory over the Brest fleet, thus confirming British naval supremacy. On the other hand the Anglo-Austrian forces sustained a serious reverse at Fleurus (June 25th). Thereupon, in pursuance of Thugut's policy, Coburg tamely evacuated the Belgic Provinces, abandoning the garrisons of Valenciennes and three neighbouring fortresses. Probably Thugut now cherished the hope that, if Belgium were to be recovered at all, it would be at the cost of Colonial sacrifices made by Great Britain for the sake of maintaining the Flemish Barrier system. Thenceforth, he took little interest in the recovery of Belgium. The entry of Austria's troops into southern Poland, early in July, manifested her intention to claim her share of the now imminent Partition[3].

This event should have convinced British Ministers that Thugut's policy of finding an indemnity there for the loss of Belgium had definitely triumphed. Even in June, Whitworth reported from

[1] Fortescue, *Hist. of the Brit. Army*, IV. (Pt I), ch. x. Möllendorff always opposed the compact with England. See Hardenberg, *Denkwürdigkeiten*, I. 186.
[2] *Cornwallis Mems.* II. 248–256; *Dropmore Papers*, II. 577.
[3] F.O. Austria, 37. Stratton to Grenville, July 9th, 1794.

Petrograd that the King of Prussia pressed the Empress Catharine to undertake a Third Partition. For a time, she seemed to disapprove, probably from a surmise that the scheme would palsy his efforts beyond the Rhine, and thereby leave Austria weak for the acquisition of her promised indemnities in that quarter. In July, however, her scruples seemed to vanish, and her only difference with Frederick William was as to Austria sharing in the proposed Partition[1]. The Empress favoured it; he opposed it; but, after the Prussian troops had suffered sharp reverses at the hands of the Poles, his opposition relaxed. She, also, read him some severe lectures as to the evil influence of the former Partitions (primarily due to Berlin) on the struggle against France, and reminded him that she had shared in them only on condition of his waging war vigorously beyond the Rhine. There is no sign that these reproofs were received any more seriously than the original advice. But Whitworth continued to assure Grenville of Catharine's enthusiasm for the French War, in which, however, she reluctantly declined to participate until after the settlement of the Polish question[2].

The almost complete silence of Grenville on this question betokens a feeling of despair. Indeed, it is difficult to see how Great Britain, when immersed in the Revolutionary War, could have averted the Partitions. Certainly, neither Pitt nor Grenville assigned sufficient importance to these events. Pitt's knowledge of Continental politics, especially of those of eastern Europe, was scanty; and, looking at the European situation from a somewhat insular standpoint, both he and Grenville underestimated the drag of the eastern undertow. A signal proof of Pitt's hopeful half-knowledge appears in his Memorandum of July, 1794. While the Imperialists were evacuating Belgium, and Möllendorff refused to move northwards, the Prime-Minister insisted on the necessity of bringing up the total of the former to 100,000 men, with a view to the rescue of the besieged garrisons and the recovery of that land; he also demanded "the immediate march to Flanders of the army under Marshal Möllendorff." The hoped-for result of these combinations was to be the muster, by the spring of 1795[3], of 238,000 Allied troops in Belgium.

[1] F.O. Russia, 27. Whitworth to Grenville, June 27th, July 18th, 1794.
[2] *Ibid.* Whitworth to Grenville, September 26th, October 14th, November 4th, 1794.
[3] *Dropmore Papers*, II. 599–600. Grenville's note of July 19th to Spencer and T. Grenville gives an estimated total of 230,000—a proof of the close relations between him and Pitt. (F.O. Austria, 38.)

Pitt was, at this time, elated by the accession of the Portland Whigs, which left the Foxite or anti-War party a mere handful. One of the Old Whigs, Thomas Grenville, brother of the Minister, was now selected, together with Earl Spencer, to proceed on a special mission to Vienna for the purpose of stimulating Austria to further efforts by the prospect of her acquiring the French Barrier fortresses from Lille to Sedan[1]. A further attempt to galvanise Möllendorff into activity was made by a Supplementary Convention with Prussia on July 27th, 1794, which renewed and extended the stipulations of the recent Treaty.

It was a characteristic of British policy, in this period, to make these convulsive efforts, after the misfortunes which prompted them had become irreparable. Spencer and Grenville, on their arrival at Vienna, found a very general disposition to give up the struggle. The Emperor had just dissolved his Government of the Belgic Netherlands[2], thus fulfilling the wishes of Thugut to be rid of that encumbrance. The Chancellor now founded his chief hopes on Catharine's intervening to keep Prussia in the right path. To the British Envoys he laid stress on the financial plight of Austria, and, insisting that she could not continue her efforts without a liberal subsidy, claimed for Vienna that which was wasted on Berlin. On August 12th, Thomas Grenville thus summed up the situation: "They (the Austrians) will, I fear, again play with us by giving orders to move when they get money only, and they will probably get none till the places are lost which they ought to recover[3]." In comparison with this dominant fact, the difficulty of Lord Grenville having omitted to specify how extensive a barrier the Emperor was to acquire from France seemed trivial. In truth, the Allies were about to lose all the French strongholds acquired in 1793; and, whatever promises were forthcoming at Vienna, performance was lacking. To keep up appearances, Coburg was replaced by Clerfait; but the retirement continued[4]. When the French advance threatened Maestricht, Clerfait called on the Duke of York with his scanty British and Dutch forces to rescue it, but himself remained inactive, in spite of vigorous protests from Downing Street. Early in October, he retired behind the Rhine[5]. The Dutch troops, dismayed

---

[1] F.O. Austria, 38. Despatch of July 19th.
[2] Vivenot, IV. 375.
[3] *Dropmore Papers*, II. 614.
[4] Pitt and Grenville wished the Archduke Charles to take over the command, with Mack as adviser. (F.O. Austria, 38. Grenville to Spencer and T. Grenville.)
[5] Fortescue, IV. Pt I, ch. II; Vivenot, IV. 365–8.

at their abandonment by both Prussia and Austria, had already shown signs of collapse, the stronghold of Bois-le-Duc being surrendered in disgraceful fashion (September 28th).

This display of ineptitude and cowardice at the front was accompanied by chicanery both at Berlin and Vienna. Malmesbury had noticed a semblance of activity in Möllendorff's army, whenever the British subsidies fell due, and a rapid relapse after their payment[1]. At Berlin, also, the politicians showed alarm at the mere report that the British subsidy was to be transferred from them to the Habsburg Court. The hope of such a transfer (with substantial additions), kept up a show of energy at Vienna; but Thugut more than once hinted that Great Britain, having virtually destroyed the navy and commerce of France and captured several of her colonies, could well afford to "buy back" the Belgic Provinces for Austria at the general peace[2].

He thus gave expression to a notion always popular among Great Britain's Allies. It amounted to this: that her triumphs at sea were to atone for their failures on land, the sacrosanct principle of the Balance of Power being also invoked to justify her colonial renunciations and their territorial recoveries. The classic instance of this procedure had been the Treaty of Aix-la-Chapelle (1748), when George II sacrificed an important conquest overseas in order to re-establish Austria in the Flemish Barrier fortresses. Thugut, however, knew little of the British people, or even of George III, if he believed that a similar bartering away of colonial gains, made or likely to be made, would take place after the Flemish campaigns had aroused general disgust with the Austrian Alliance[3]. Mercy d'Argenteau, who was sent as Austrian Special Envoy to London, seems not to have urged any such argument. Thugut hoped that Mercy's action would avail at least to procure a loan; but he died at London on August 25th, after accomplishing there nothing worthy of note. The Ambassador, Starhemberg, continued to press for a considerable loan[4]. The more flagrant the incapacity of Habsburg officers and officials, the more urgent became their demands for money. Thugut now insisted on a

---

[1] F.O. Prussia, 35. Malmesbury to Grenville, September 26th, 1794. On September 30th he threatened to stop the subsidy unless Möllendorff moved to cover Clerfait.

[2] *Dropmore Papers*, II. 627.

[3] Those feelings were increased by the cowardice of the Austrian commander of Valenciennes, who, on surrendering that fortress, tamely handed over a large number of *Émigrés* to be butchered. (Vivenot, IV. 447.)

[4] Vivenot, IV. 389–407. See *ibid*. p. 441 for Austria's hopes of a new Barrier. It included Lille.

loan of £6,000,000, which both Spencer and Thomas Grenville declared to be an impossibly large sum. They returned to London late in October, *re infectâ*.

Early in that month, Pitt's indignation against Prussia boiled over in an interview with her Ambassador, Jacobi; and thereupon he stopped the subsidies. Grenville promptly intervened and resumed the payments; but the mischief could not be undone. Berlin clamoured at the breach of the Treaty; and Frederick William threatened to recall his Rhenish army, unless the full arrears were paid up[1]. Pitt's intervention in the affairs of the Foreign Office was the more unfortunate, because, as the autumn wore on, the rot spread alarmingly in the Grand Alliance. On October 24th, the Elector of Mainz proposed to the Diet of the Empire a motion in favour of peace, begging the Emperor and the King of Prussia to concert measures for an armistice, with a view to a pacification[2], provided that the integrity of the Imperial frontiers were maintained. Disgust at the War also pervaded the Allied armies, and to this cause, rather than to any special prowess of the French arms, must be assigned the discreditable collapse in the campaign of 1794. Not a sign appeared of the ancient determination of the Dutch in the defence of their land; and the powerful faction of the Patriots assisted the French invaders and paralysed the military preparations. In vain, the Prince of Orange added his entreaties to those of the British Government for help from Prussia. Frederick William replied that he was engaged in a war with Poland; and that, as the Dutch could not supply him with succours for that struggle, their demands on him were consequently cancelled. Another ominous symptom was the discontent of the Germans. Malmesbury found the Rhinelanders clamorous for peace, and prejudiced against Great Britain because of her "views of ambition and conquest." They were proof against his arguments that she was the chief bulwark against French ambition and conquest[3].

In a last attempt to stay the flood of French invasion over Holland, the British Government decided to despatch Malmesbury to Brunswick with a formal request to the Duke to command an Allied army assembled behind the Waal for the defence of the United Provinces. The Duke

---

[1] F.O. Prussia, 35. Grenville to Malmesbury, November 13th, 1794; *Paget Papers*, I. 50, 63.

[2] Malmesbury's despatch of October 21st to Grenville ascribes this proposal to Barthélemy, French Envoy at Berne, though Barthélemy said France would probably demand the Rhine boundary down to Coblentz or Cologne. (F.O. Prussia, 35.)

[3] Malmesbury, *Diaries*, III. 143; *Paget Papers*, I. 57.

himself had made proposals as to the operations of such a force[1], and the recent engagement of his daughter Caroline to the Prince of Wales furnished another reason for his consent. Malmesbury, therefore, undertook the mission with some degree of hope, but he met with a refusal. The Duke made it clear that His Prussian Majesty vetoed the project[2]. The Envoy passed judgment on Prussian policy as embodying "as many bad political qualities as can possibly exist at the same time in the same Power, weakness, perfidy, insolence, avarice and folly[3]."

The contempt felt by the Russians for their Prussian fellow-conspirators against the independence of Poland appeared in an incident at Warsaw. Scarcely had the King of Poland abandoned that city than the victorious Russians tore down the insignia from the Prussian embassy with every sign of contumely. Francis II so far demeaned himself as to congratulate the victor, Suvóroff, by declaring in a letter to him that his success would be the means of changing the system of all the Cabinets of Europe[4]. The fact was largely true, though the admission of it was needlessly humiliating. The fierce jealousies of the Central Powers subordinated them to Catharine; she virtually dictated the terms of the Third Partition now imminent, though it was not completed until October, 1795[5]. Great Britain, of course, was helpless to prevent this catastrophe. Thus, in the winter of 1794-5, as two years before, the scramble for Polish lands distracted the policy of Berlin and Vienna, nullifying all the efforts of Great Britain to construct a solid barrier against French aggressions in the West. When those efforts appeared to be futile, Pitt and Grenville turned to Russia, and concluded a Defensive Alliance, signed at Petrograd on February 18th, 1795, for granting mutual armed assistance in case either party was attacked, Russia furnishing 12,000 troops and Great Britain 12 sail of the line[6].

Meanwhile, the Dutch in despair of defending their land, proposed to the British Government to enter into negotiations for a general peace. With this plan our Government did not comply, but signified that, if the United Provinces chose to seek their safety in a separate peace,

---

[1] *Paget Papers*, I. 79.
[2] F.O. Prussia, 35. Malmesbury to Grenville, November 25th, 1794; *Paget Papers*, I. 98.
[3] *Dropmore Papers*, II. 653.
[4] F.O. Poland, 8. Gardiner to Grenville, January 7th, 10th, 1795.
[5] Sorel, IV. 447.
[6] Garden, V. 297. Probably the treaty contained a secret article specifying Russia's naval help; for in June, 1795, she sent 12 sail of the line to reinforce Duncan in the North Sea.

we would not oppose such a step[1]. The overtures were abruptly ended by the French, so soon as weather conditions favoured a renewal of their advance. Before the utter collapse of the Allied defence on the Waal, Pitt and Grenville induced the King to recall the Duke of York[2]. The leadership of that prince had been meritorious; but he was clearly unequal to the ever increasing difficulties ahead, not the least of them being the almost open insubordination of the British army and the active illwill of the Dutch. The Duke reported at Windsor that he was in every instance thwarted by the people whom he was trying to save[3]. Pitt further showed his zeal for the public service by substituting Lord Spencer at the Admiralty for the too leisurely Lord Chatham.

But no changes of men could as yet avail to turn the tide of events. What was needed was a change in the spirit of the nations concerned; and this came about only under the pressure of overwhelming calamities. The French Revolution, under the subtle alchemy of militarism, was to become by turns conquering, rapacious and tyrannical to its neighbours, until finally it was personified in the most awe-inspiring ruler of the modern world. Under his vigorous but oppressive sway, peoples previously torpid acquired new strength and a passion for independence unknown before. Rulers, too, were compelled to rely wholly on their subjects; and the national consciousness thus aroused on all sides served to endow peasants with patriotism, Generals with determination, officials with honesty and Governments with efficiency. That transformation, however, was to come only with a radical change in the methods of waging war and with the overthrow of the old governmental systems. So long as the Allies could jog along with hired troops and British subsidies, no reform was possible. The payment of such subsidies was irritating to the donor and humiliating to the receiver. It promoted exacting captiousness on the one side and slack performance on the other. Not until both parties could unite frankly and enthusiastically under the stimulus of a great cause could great deeds be accomplished. The story of the year 1794 is the story of the wreck of an imposing Coalition, partly through divergences of aim, but also through a demoralising reliance upon the cash-nexus[4].

---

[1] *Dropmore Papers*, II. 646. Minute of Cabinet of November 18th, 1794. This corrects the misstatement of Garden (*Traités*, v. 249), that we opposed the Dutch proposal.
[2] For the correspondence on this topic see Rose, *Pitt and Napoleon: Essays and Letters*. [3] *Dropmore Papers*, II. 644, 659.
[4] Thus, a delay (due to bankers) in the payment of the July subsidy led Frederick William at once to order Möllendorff to halt, until the sum due was paid. (F.O. Prussia, 35, Paget to Grenville, July 26th, 1794.)

As always happens, perseverance in a bad system led to increasingly evil results. The year 1795 completed what 1794 had begun. Illwill between London and Berlin strengthened the Francophils at the Prussian Court; and overtures made by the French Republic through the Prussian legation at Bâle were warmly welcomed on the ground of the inner community of interests between the two Powers. Haugwitz and others assured Sir Arthur Paget (now Secretary of Legation at Berlin), that Frederick William entered on this discussion only in order to sound the intentions of France, and to discover whether a general pacification were possible[1]. It soon appeared that the reverse was the case. Despite an urgent remonstrance from Catharine against his negotiations with France, the Prussian monarch persevered with them. The Tsarina, thereupon, more decidedly favoured Austria's territorial claims in the Partition of Poland[2]. The Prussian politicians, attributing her conduct to a resolve to humiliate their country, were, all the more, bent on making peace with France. Thus, as at all stages of the Revolutionary War, the efforts of Great Britain in the west were thwarted by the intriguers of the east, over whom (as Grenville now perceived) she had no sure hold. Indeed, her subsidies to them, which were intended for the protection of Flanders, were often used to effect the subjection of Poland. Earl Spencer, during a mission to Berlin, found the impressionable monarch occasionally intent on renewing the struggle against France; but, with very few exceptions, all his advisers counselled peace. Seeing that Grenville now differed from his colleagues as to the advisability of making further advances to Prussia, Spencer long remained without instructions, and could only observe helplessly Prussia's policy of drift. Instructions from Dundas reached him on April 20th, fifteen days after Prussia and France had concluded peace at Bâle.

That Treaty (due largely to the tact of Barthélemy, and the conciliatory ways of Hardenberg) empowered the French troops to occupy Prussia's lands west of the Rhine, prevented the Allies from passing across any of her territories, and brought about a truce with all the northern States of Germany. In pursuance of this last clause, a line of demarcation was agreed on, including the Circles of Saxony, West-

[1] F.O. Prussia, 37. Spencer to Grenville, January 6th, 10th, 1795. See, too, *Appendix B*. Sir Arthur Paget (1771–1840) had been in the Berlin Embassy under Ewart, then at Petrograd. After 1794, he was Minister at Mainz, Ratisbon, Naples and Vienna.

[2] F.O. Russia, 29. Whitworth to Grenville, February 16th, March 3rd, 19th, 27th, 1794.

phalia, Franconia, and part of those of the Rhine, in order to separate the territories no longer at war with France from those which remained true to the Emperor and therefore at war. Prussia, also, invited the Diet of the Empire to make peace under her mediation—an open bid for the substitution of Hohenzollern control for that of the Habsburgs.

As a retort to this move, the Emperor on May 19th, 1795, invited the Diet to take the first steps towards assuring a general pacification. On July 3rd, it requested him to summon a Congress for this purpose[1]. His position had been strengthened by a Treaty with Russia of January 3rd, 1795, which favoured his claims in the Third Partition of Poland and held out to the Habsburgs tempting prospects of acquisitions at the expense of France, Turkey or Venice[2]. Further, on May 4th, Thugut signed with Morton Eden at Vienna a compact whereby Great Britain agreed to be responsible for the payment of interest on a loan for £4,600,000 raised for the Emperor, he agreeing to maintain during 1795 an army of 200,000 men. And, on May 20th, they signed another Treaty, whereby the two Powers mutually agreed to guarantee their possessions and to invite Catharine to form a Triple Alliance for the maintenance of the European System. It was concluded on September 28th, 1795, when Catharine engaged to furnish to the two Powers either 30,000 troops or an equivalent in money. These compacts signified the retort of the Allies to the defection of Prussia and of two other States, whom Great Britain vainly sought to keep true to the Coalition, viz., the United Provinces and Spain.

Among the Allies of 1793, none underwent a harder fate than the United Provinces. In the winter of 1794-5, they were overrun and pillaged by the hungry and ragged troops of France, having already suffered from the disorderly elements in the British army. On January 19th, 1795, the tricolour was borne in triumph into Amsterdam. The Prince of Orange and his chief partisans fled to England; and, on February 24th, the Patriots, now dominant in the States General, declared for the abolition of the Stadholderate and for alliance with France. Early in the same month, the Dutch East India Company issued orders to all Dutch vessels to leave British ports, and requested the French to abstain from attacks on their merchantmen. The detention of British vessels in Dutch ports led the British Government to adopt, on March 19th, a similar measure and to order the capture,

[1] Garden, *Traités*, v. 284-290. For the negotiations at Bâle, see Hardenberg, *op. cit.* vol. v. chs. XI-XVI; *Papiers de Barthélemy...en Suisse*, vol. v. pp. 1-168; H. Stroehlin, *La Mission de Barthélemy en Suisse* (Geneva, 1900).

[2] Sorel, IV. pp. 193-5.

when necessary, of Dutch warships[1]. The Patriots now opened
negotiations with France, which resulted in an Alliance both defensive
and offensive, directed especially against Great Britain (May 16th).
France required from her new Ally the services of 12 sail of the line
and 18 frigates, also of half of the troops at the disposal of the Dutch
Government; she restored the conquered districts except the southern
parts and the Maestricht territory, and secured the right to garrison
Flushing. The United Provinces further agreed to pay 100,000,000
Dutch florins as an indemnity—a crushing fine, which the Committee
of Public Safety deemed essential for the avoidance of bankruptcy[2].
In return, the Dutch received a recognition of their Independence,
which can scarcely have deceived even the most credulous of the
Patriots. The rigorous conditions now imposed on the Dutch were of
world-wide importance; for they extended the War more than ever
over seas, and imparted to it, more and more, the character of a
Colonial struggle. Foreseeing that the French would use the Dutch
settlement at the Cape of Good Hope as a means of attacking India, the
British Government prepared to strike at that strategic point, which
was occupied, in September following, by Rear-Admiral Sir Keith
Elphinstone and General Sir James Craig.

As has been shown in this Chapter, the War between France and
Great Britain was not, for us at least, mainly a war of principle. The
material issues at stake always outweighed those arising from a clash
of political ideals. But now, the defection of Prussia and the Alliance
of the Dutch with France transformed the struggle increasingly into
one for Colonial and commercial supremacy. The change was to be
rendered more complete by the most striking events of the year 1796,
viz., the Anglo-Spanish rupture and the rise of Bonaparte.

The friction between the Courts of St James's and of Madrid
never ceased during the period of uneasy alliance, (1793-5). To that
old sore, Nootka Sound, there were now added the irritants often
arising from seizures at sea, disputes during the joint occupation of
Toulon and afterwards from the British occupation of Corsica. Despite
the offer of Paoli to place that island solely under the protection of
Great Britain, the Spaniards conceived a violent jealousy, when, after
the reduction of the French garrisons by British seamen and troops,
the assembly of chieftains at Corti proclaimed George III King of
Corsica. Possibly, jealousy played some part in the unceasing in-

---

[1] F.O. Holland, 57; *Cape Records*, I. 98; *Dropmore Papers*, III. 35.
[2] R. Guyot, *Le Directoire et la Paix d'Europe*, p. 106.

trigues which perplexed the British Viceroy, Sir Gilbert Elliot (afterwards Earl of Minto), and clogged his administration. The French quickly took advantage of this marked divergence between Great Britain and Spain.

But, already, a more serious cause of dispute had arisen, when the French planters of Hayti, in despair at the anarchy devastating that once wealthy colony, offered to place it in the hands of George III. In April, 1793, the King consented, and an expedition was subsequently prepared to occupy the chief port of Hayti (San Domingo). Grenville, foreseeing annoyance on the part of Spain, who owned the central and eastern parts of the island, sought to turn her attention towards acquisitions in the south of France[1]; but, after the servile revolt in the French part of Hayti, she revived her ancient claim to the whole of that island, and saw with disgust the occupation of the most fertile parts by the British. Among other influences hostile to the Alliance was that of the Spanish Ambassador at London, the Marquis del Campo, who exacerbated every dispute[2]. The Minister of Marine, Don Valdez, also openly declared the weakening of the French navy to be a misfortune for that of Spain; and the all-powerful Duke of Alcudia finally used his unbounded influence over the Queen against the British connexion. Early in February, 1795, during an interview with the King and Alcudia, Valdez hotly declaimed against Great Britain for her ambitious proceedings in Hayti and Corsica. Alcudia repeated these charges to Francis Jackson, our Minister at Madrid, and warned him of the results that might ensue, adding: "If His Catholic Majesty finds another road less dangerous than that which he now follows, he will take it with the dignity becoming his rank." The French incursion into Catalonia and the utter failure of all British military efforts in Europe, added emphasis to this statement, and the Spanish Ministers hereupon adopted a hostile attitude. In vain did Grenville point out the advantages to Spain accruing from British naval successes, and hold out prospects of help from Russia in 1796. It soon appeared that Spain would make peace with France in 1795[3].

In the hope of averting this disaster, Grenville despatched the Earl of Bute as Ambassador, with Instructions to placate the Court of

---

[1] See Grenville's despatch of July 19th, 1793 in *Appendix B*.
[2] *Dropmore Papers*, II. 383, 386, 398, 406; III. 10. The condemnation of the *San Iago*, a Spanish prize obtained by a French privateer, and rescued by a British warship, greatly annoyed the Spaniards.
[3] F.O. Spain, 36. F. Jackson to Grenville, February 11th; March 18th, 1795. Grenville to Jackson, March 20th, 1795.

Madrid, and incite it to further efforts for the acquisition of territory north of the Pyrenees[1]. The Instructions show that Grenville's tenacity clouded his imagination. For of what use was it to hold out such hopes to Spain, when Catalonia was in danger and French arms everywhere triumphed? But a phrase at the end of the despatch is highly significant. Bute is warned to observe closely the condition of the Spanish Colonies, and, if discontent exists, to ascertain where an attack may be delivered. From May to June, 1795, the accession of more moderate men to power at Paris and the reviving activity of the French Royalists induced Grenville to plead for help from Spain in a contemplated attempt to aid them in Brittany; but, by that time, Alcudia was deeply committed to negotiations with France. In April, 1795, he despatched an Envoy, Yriarte, to Bâle with instructions vague enough to leave him free to conclude peace. Yriarte, a friend of the French Ambassador Barthélemy, showed his bias by drafting proposals, early in June, for assuring a Franco-Spanish control of the Mediterranean and the complete exclusion of British trade[2]. Such, doubtless, were the aims of Alcudia and Valdez. On June 23rd, Alcudia informed Bute that England and Spain would soon be left alone in the War, and that financial distress, added to the troubles in the Spanish Colonies occasioned by emissaries from the United States and France, compelled the Court of Madrid to accede to French invitations for a "composition"; but "composition" did not imply peace. Spain had begun the War in order to suppress French principles; but the conduct of the Allies had united the French people. "Somehow or other" (added Alcudia), "England always got the better of Spain." Bute's comment was that the only way to keep Spain true to the Alliance was to bribe Alcudia[3].

But matters had gone too far even for this. The French negotiators, in view of the enormous advantages to be derived from the Spanish navy and commerce, gave way on certain points, and signed the Treaty of Peace at Bâle on July 11th, 1795. France thereby restored her conquests in the north of Spain, but acquired the Spanish portion of Hayti, and promised to acknowledge the mediation of the King of Spain for accommodations with Portugal and the Italian Princes at war with the Republic[4]. Considering the irritation caused by British

[1] F.O. Spain, 37. Grenville to Earl of Bute, April 13th, 1795.
[2] Tausserat-Radel, *Papiers de Barthélemy...en Suisse*, VI. 14.
[3] F.O. Spain, 37, 38. Bute to Grenville, June 23rd; July 11th, 19th, 1795.
[4] *Papiers de Barthélemy*, VI. 68 *et seq.*; Garden, V. 305–7; Sorel, IV. 368–70.

intervention in the west of Hayti, it is not easy to account for the joy manifested at Madrid at the news of a pacification which involved the abandonment of the whole of that island. The humiliation of the King was completed a few weeks later, when he conferred on his chief Minister, the Queen's paramour, the title of Prince of the Peace.

Grenville at once pointed out that the cession of San Domingo to France was a violation of the Treaty of Utrecht, which forbade Spain to cede to the French any of her American possessions; and he charged Bute to find out the strength of her forces in the West Indies. That Envoy, also, saw whither the recent compact tended, and foretold that it would soon be followed by war with England. He, therefore, warned Admiral Hotham, commanding the Mediterranean fleet, to be on his guard, and even hinted at a dash upon Cadiz[1]. Grenville's despatches to Bute at Madrid prove that the British Government desired to keep at peace with Spain. The attack on San Domingo was postponed, because Godoy asserted that it was not yet a French possession; and in other ways deference was shown to Spanish susceptibilities. But all was in vain. In the year 1796, the prospect darkened, and Ministers at home, as well as Bute, expected a rupture whenever it should suit Spain to attack us. Godoy's private appeal in July, that we should not consider his recent Offensive Treaty with the French as a *casus belli*, was clearly a ruse to postpone hostilities to a more convenient time[2]. On October 5th, Godoy handed to Bute the Declaration of War, the chief complaints of which referred to the conduct of Lord Hood at Toulon, the British conquest of Demerara, the occupation of Corsica and the west of Domingo, various naval incidents, and the establishment of British Commercial Companies along the river Missouri for the evident purpose of penetrating to the "South Sea." The rupture marked yet another stage in the transformation of the War into a commercial and colonial struggle. Its more immediate effect was the evacuation of Corsica, Elba, and the Mediterranean by the British forces, with the view of effecting a concentration in the Atlantic and in home waters. Its later results were the ruin of the Spanish navy, the capture of Trinidad and other Colonies, and the increase in the number of securities held by Great Britain as a set-off to the losses of her Allies on the Continent.

We have looked ahead, in order to survey connectedly Anglo-

---

[1] F.O. Spain, 38. Grenville to Bute, August 7th; Bute to Grenville, August 10th, 1795.
[2] See Despatches in *Appendix C*, also *Dropmore Papers*, III. 148, 214, 233, 246.

Spanish relations to the date of their rupture. But it is time to return to the autumn of 1795, which witnessed the first efforts of Great Britain for a general peace. By that time, the Coalition had sustained successive shocks in the defection of Tuscany, Prussia, Holland, and Spain; while the attitude of the Imperial Diet was doubtful and the prospects of Sardinia were gloomy. On the other hand, Great Britain had concluded Treaties of Alliance with Russia and Austria; her fleets had swept from the seas both the warships and the merchantmen of her enemies; she had captured, or was about to capture, their chief Colonies; her finances, though strained, were vigorous; and her spirit, in spite of sporadic riots, was undaunted. Accordingly, Parliament, at the opening of the autumn session, heard with some surprise the following sentence in the King's Speech (October 29th): "Should this crisis at Paris terminate in any order of things compatible with the tranquillity of other countries, and affording a reasonable expectation of security and permanence in any treaty which might be concluded, the appearance of a disposition to negotiate for a general peace on just and equitable terms will not fail to be met, on my part, with an earnest desire to give it the fullest and speediest effect." "Meanwhile" (the speech continued), "we must carry on the war with a vigour which would conduce to this desirable end." Ministers seem to have imposed their pacific views on George III; for, two days previously, he had written to Grenville that no attempt at negotiation ought to be encouraged, as it would tell against an active prosecution of the War[1]. Further, it appears that the Duke of Portland, Windham and their Whig followers who had coalesced with the Pitt Administration regarded with apprehension or active dislike a policy which implied recognition of the Republic and the abandonment of the monarchical cause[2].

It may be well here to recall Pitt's pronouncements on the subject of negotiation with France. On January 26th, 1795, he deprecated them as tending to encourage the enemy and "to bury the remains of opposition in France." On March 24th, in combating a motion by Fox, he disclaimed all notion of fighting in order to impose monarchy on the French people; but he added that "we shall gain all possible aid from the French Royalists": and he defined our leading object as "security." On May 27th he resisted Wilberforce's motion in favour of early negotiations for peace on the ground that "perseverance in the contest is more wise and prudent, and more likely in the end to

[1] *Dropmore Papers*, III. 143.   [2] *Ibid.* III. 135.

effect a safe, lasting and honourable peace than any attempt at negotiation." Admitting the reverses of the Allies, he yet claimed that France was nearly exhausted, her *assignats* being worth less than 5 per cent. of their face value; and, viewing her Government as regicide, he declared: "I will not acknowledge such a Republic."

How, then, are we to explain the proffer of the olive branch on October 29th? Probably, it was due to recent events in France. The new French Constitution had not the ultra-democratic character of its predecessors; and, though the Royalist or malcontent risings at Paris and elsewhere had been crushed, the prospect had arisen of a return to ordinary methods of government. In Pitt's words, if the new deputies could "speak on behalf of the people of France, I then have no difficulty in saying, from that time all objections to the form of that Government, and to the principles of that Government, all objections to them as obstacles to negotiation will be at an end." He still hoped for success in the War, bade the country show a firm front, and reproved the Opposition for dwelling on the reverses of the Coalition.

The present suggestion, then, was little more than an appeal to the French people for reasonableness in their foreign relations. It resembled somewhat that suggested by the Austrian Chancellor early in April. Thugut had then proposed the issue of a proclamation to the French people, declaring that they had been the aggressors and urging them to adopt "a Government such as may enable foreign Powers to treat with them with security[1]." British Ministers seem at the time to have passed by the suggestion, perhaps because Grenville harboured hopes of a Royalist reaction in France, which William Wickham was to further from the embassy at Berne. If we may judge by the number and length of his letters to Wickham, the usually cautious Grenville continued long to believe in this chimera[2]. Evidently, he had not learnt the lesson, writ large on the Toulon episode, that foreign help during an internal dispute tends to the discredit and undoing of the party thus supported[3]. The lesson was once more to be illustrated, in ghastly guise, in the British-Royalist expedition to Quiberon. The failure, also, of all Wickham's emissaries to Lyons and other centres of anti-Jacobin activity proved that the Royalists distrusted outside assistance[4], and that the French people wanted peace,

---

[1] F.O. Austria, 40. Eden to Grenville, April 8th, 1795.
[2] *Corresp. of W. Wickham*, I. pp. 9–86.
[3] *Ibid.* I. 93.   [4] Sorel IV. 350.

order, and the retention of the chief social conquests of the Revolution. The unpopularity of Lewis XVIII, his decision to stand by the principles of Henry IV, above all, the utter failure of the rising of the Royalists of Paris on October 5th, seem to have dispelled the hopes of Grenville. The baffling uncertainty as to obtaining military help, or even any definite decision, from the Court of Vienna, further disgusted him; and, though hitherto more favourable than Pitt to the Austrian connexion, he now decided to send Francis Jackson on a special mission, to press urgently for a decision, seeing that "we might possibly not find it very difficult to make either war or peace with advantage, if Austria will set her shoulders to the work in earnest[1]." Grenville, then, though of late less pacific in tone than his cousin, was apparently not averse from a negotiation with France.

On December 8th, the King sent a message to Parliament, stating that the crisis in France had led to an order of things which would induce him to meet any disposition to negotiation on the part of the enemy. Sheridan and Grey challenged Ministers to say wherein the order of things in France differed from that of 1793–4; but Pitt declared that her Constitution and her conduct need no longer prevent an accommodation. The distinction which he drew was overstrained; but it is clear that he objected to the French Republic only because it had been a mighty agency for the propagation of levelling principles. This it had now ceased to be. At home its democratic fervour had died down; and, on all sides, the liberated peoples were crying out against their Jacobin liberators. As a conquering and acquisitive organism, the Republic aroused none of the enthusiasm inspired by the appeals of Vergniaud and the challenges of Danton. Pitt, therefore, viewed with no grave concern the recent Declaration at Paris, which in effect pronounced "the natural boundaries," to be an essential part of the new Constitution[2]. Frenchmen have generally applauded that resolve. They forget that it has always involved a war with Europe. For the present, the helplessness of the Empire, the inertia of Austria, the short-sighted selfishness of Prussia, and the calculated aloofness of Catharine, postponed the struggle; but it lay in the nature of things; and British Ministers were not afraid of the prospect of a negotiation

---

[1] *Dropmore Papers*, III. 137; E. D. Adams, p. 37.
[2] Decree of October 1st, 1795 (Sorel, IV. 428–31, V. 2: Sybel, IV. 444 Eng. edit.). Soon after decreeing the natural boundaries, the French Government sent proposals to Vienna, offering Bavaria to Austria, if she would acknowledge the French annexation of the Belgic Provinces and not oppose that of the left bank of the Rhine —a bribe to her to desert England.

with France, which, if successful, would bring temporary relief, and, if unsuccessful, would exhibit the French Directors as the political heirs of Lewis XIV.

The sincerity of Pitt and Grenville in this overture for peace has been sharply questioned by Sybel, Sorel, and other historians; but the foregoing considerations both explain and justify the conduct of Ministers. Pitt, also—though perhaps not Grenville—assigned some weight to the news brought from Paris by Baron de Beaufort, to the effect that the Directory would gladly receive a pacific proposal[1]. Doubtless, the French Government hoped to separate England from Austria. If so, it failed; for, from the outset, the Foreign Office declared that no separate negotiation would be undertaken. Further, its good faith appears in the elaborate measures at once adopted to assure the collaboration of the Allies. On December 22nd, Grenville wrote a "most secret" despatch to Eden at Vienna, setting forth the desirability of the two Courts at once exchanging views so that they and, if possible, all the Allies should arrive at an agreement before a negotiation began. A recent statement by the Directory set forth terms of peace which Grenville regarded as "extravagant and insulting"; but the internal difficulties of France seemed to promise a more reasonable programme. On her side, Great Britain now abandoned the fantastic notion of annexing the north-eastern fortresses of France to the Belgic Provinces. She proposed the restitution to Austria of those territories (with the addition of Liége and the southern parts of the United Provinces recently acquired by France); also, the recovery of Savoy by Sardinia (Nice was not mentioned), and the restoration of the Stadholderate. From the outset, the British Government utterly disclaimed the plan, which busybodies in Vienna had fathered on it, of making a separate peace.

Circumstances appearing to favour this project, Ministers, on January 30th, 1796, approved the draft of a despatch to Eden inviting the issue of a joint Declaration by the two Powers as to their readiness to discuss terms of peace. George III disapproved it, but informed Grenville that he would not offer "any obstinate resistance," and hoped that the proposal would be rejected by France[2]. Grenville was, also, doubtful as to its success; but he instructed Wickham to open the matter to Barthélemy at Berne, with a view to the assembling of a Congress. The overture was made in Switzerland, mainly in order to

[1] Guyot, pp. 146–9.
[2] *Dropmore Papers*, III. 169, 170.

allow of Austria and Sardinia readily cooperating if they desired. Pitt was more sanguine; and, considering the hopefulness of his nature, there is no reason to doubt his sincerity in the matter. Grenville wrote to Eden that the Declaration should be issued "for the double purpose either of securing advantageous terms of peace or of laying the foundation of a vigorous prosecution of the war[1]."

Unfortunately, the British Government now held back the subsidies due to Vienna. Apparently, it deemed the defensive Austrian tactics, lately pursued with such fatal results, not worth the stipulated financial support, or else it believed in the speedy advent of peace. Nothing could have been more unfortunate. Austria was left without the sinews of war, just before the opening of Bonaparte's Italian campaign. On April 9th, Eden reported the utter inability of Austria "to provide even for the common expenses of the war"; and discontent on this head must have hindered cordial cooperation with regard to the peace proposals. Already, Thugut had thrown cold water on them, declaring that the Emperor, while declining to join in the Declaration, would, in due course, issue one of similar import. On March 5th, he harked back to the recently discarded notion of the Belgic-Bavarian Exchange—a proof that he was toying with that scheme which France had dangled before him. Eden expressed deep regret at the revival of this proposal, as to which the two Governments had so often been at variance[2].

Affairs at Turin were not more promising. Since the disasters of the year 1794, that Court had been a prey to constant fears, which found expression in tentative overtures for peace. Such at least was the first belief of Thugut and Grenville, the latter even for a time withholding the subsidy due to Sardinia, and thereby weakening her before the blows of Bonaparte fell upon her discouraged troops. The proposal of a joint Declaration of the Allies completed the dismay of the King and his advisers, who believed that the French Directory was bent on a ruthless prosecution of the War.

They were right. Aggressive aims were now uppermost at Paris, doubtless because the Directory detected further signs of collapse in the Coalition and felt confident of victory. In the month of January, 1796, when the British Government set on foot its scheme for a general pacification, Carnot accepted the plan of Bonaparte for the conquest of Italy. The final British note to Barthélemy, perhaps, erred

---

[1] *Wickham Corresp.* I. 271–3. See too my article in *Eng. Hist. Rev.* April, 1903.
[2] F.O. Austria, 45. Eden to Grenville, March 2nd, 5th; April 9th, 1796.

on the side of firmness, and it omitted all reference to the French Republic[1]. But the counterblast from Paris ended all hope of peace. As handed in at Berne on March 26th, it implied the retention by France of the "natural frontiers" (Rhine, Alps, Pyrenees and Ocean). The Belgic Provinces were not named among her acquisitions, because, by the Decree of October 1st, 1795, she had incorporated them[2]. The French answer, moreover, involved the restitution of all the Colonial conquests of Great Britain during the War. These conditions put an end to the negotiation. They were announced in the days when Bonaparte was preparing to drive the Allies from the passes leading from Savona into the plain of North Italy. His conquest of that land was destined to postpone for eighteen years a favourable opportunity of effecting a durable peace.

III

Criticisms on Pitt's proposals for peace were twofold. The most fundamental were those of Burke, Windham and other Old Whigs who rallied to his side. Their devotion to the Royal cause led them to censure the whole conduct of the War as having been waged for material securities, when in reality it was—to use Burke's trenchant phrase— a war against "an armed opinion." Stamp out that pest, or it will infect, enfeeble and finally destroy you! Wage the war not for self-interest but for a principle! Distrust Prussia, Austria and other acquisitive States! Ally yourselves with the French Royalists against the murderous despotism now enthroned at Paris! Spurn all thought of compromise and peace as a cowardly betrayal of a sacred trust! Such is the burden of Burke's *Letters on a Regicide Peace* (1796-7). It formed the fighting creed of Windham, and ultimately had great influence on Grenville, while it echoed, in philosophic tones, the primitive predilections of George III.

Over against this clear-cut theory stood the contentions of Pitt— that, for Great Britain, the War did not arise out of a Royalist crusade (which was undeniably true), but from a resolve to gain "security" against French encroachments on a land fronting our exposed east coast; that treaty obligations and expediency alike bade us expel her from that land; that we had entered into a Coalition already virtually formed, and, from the weakness of our army, could only play a second-ary part in military operations; that, therefore, we were inevitably drawn

[1] Guyot, pp. 153-5.   [2] Wickham (*Corresp.* I. 321), forgot that fact.

into the orbit of the Germanic Powers for land warfare and had to rely mainly on naval pressure to compel France to a peace. This implied the seizure of her Colonies, especially when the best of them, Hayti, was offered to us by the French inhabitants. Cooperation with the roving bands of Chouans or the Royalists of Provence, had been tried without success.

In the main, these statements were undeniable. Wholly unprepared, Great Britain was engaged in a struggle of unexpected magnitude and duration. Her methods were therefore empirical, her warfare tentative, her blunders colossal. Trusting inevitably to her Allies, she saw them falter or fall away, a prey to the jealousies necessarily aroused by her policy of limited largesse on land and unlimited acquisitions at sea. Critics from among his own supporters could, therefore, claim that his war policy was a failure, when judged by his own standard.

In a sense, both Burke and Pitt were right. The one Ally certain never to fail us was French Royalism. But how utilise it, when its champions were errant bands of Breton peasants and waspish cliques of intractable *Émigrés?* Burke's theory was as inspiring as its practice was impossible. He and Windham could demonstrate very forcibly the mistakes in Pitt's war policy. But, in the peculiar circumstances of 1793–4, how could they have conducted the War on purely Royalist lines? That was the question which Pitt, if he had had time for literary embroidering, might have pressed home in *Letters on a suggested Royalist Crusade.*

The all-important fact, however, was that by the year 1796 both of these methods of warfare had utterly failed. Royalism, after being half stifled by the scheming monarchs of Berlin and Petrograd, was now buried under the Old World trappings of "Lewis XVIII." On the other hand, Pitt's policy of winning security had ended in the loss of the whole of the Netherlands and the all but complete collapse of the First Coalition. Therefore, Royalist theorists and political pragmatists should have joined in discovering a way out of the impasse. Instead, the theorists held aloof and added to the difficulties of the men of affairs in seeking to retrace their steps.

Despite the fact that Pitt's peace overtures of the winter of 1795–6 had played into the hands of Bonaparte, the Prime-Minister prepared to renew them. His second proposal, however, was prefaced by schemes almost comparable to those of our Allies. As French victories in Italy and Rhineland portended disaster to the First Coalition, Grenville (now a partisan of the connexion with Prussia) sought to ensure her active support by suggesting her acquisition either of the Belgic Provinces or of extensive domains in Germany. George III returned the proposal with the cutting comment: "Italian politics are too complicated for my understanding[1]." Nevertheless, in its desperation, the British Cabinet prepared to act on the degrading principle of gaining the help of a powerful State by conniving at its annexation of a weak neighbour; and, at the close of July, 1796, George Hammond, Under-Secretary of State for Foreign Affairs, received instructions to proceed to Berlin to tempt Frederick William by the offer above noted. George III again demurred, but did not actively oppose. Grenville sought to gild the pill for Austria by pointing out the urgent necessity of bringing in Prussia; and he even held out the prospect of the acquisition of Bavaria by the Habsburgs. No palliative could reconcile Thugut. He received the suggestion very coldly, declaring that either alternative would break up the Empire[2]. Hammond's mission to Berlin, also, failed owing to the absence of Frederick William, during which no important business could be transacted; and the Envoy seems not to have considered it worth while definitely to offer the bait[3]. Useful assistance was offered by Gouverneur Morris, an American citizen who, after actual experience of the French Revolution, decided to support Great Britain by all the means in his power[4]. But neither the address of Morris nor the vaguely alluring suggestions of Hammond could elicit a definite reply from Haugwitz. He betrayed unusual embarrassment, which was not unnatural, seeing that he had just signed a Secret Treaty with the French Ambassador binding Prussia to a system of neutrality, and accordingly missed the advantages, both public and private, which would have accrued from Anglo-French competition for favours at Berlin. The Franco-Prussian Treaty marked out the line of neutrality for northern Germany along the course of the Fulda, Ruhr and Lower Rhine, and promised to Prussia the eventual acquisition of the Bishopric of Münster[5]. Another Treaty, also signed on August 5th, will be noticed later.

The British invitation for the support of Prussia having merely caused annoyance at Vienna, and the War in Italy going from bad to worse, Pitt recurred to his proposals for a pacification. In August,

---

[1] *Dropmore Papers*, III. 172–4.
[2] F.O. Austria, 45. Eden to Grenville, August 15th, 1796.
[3] *Dropmore Papers*, III. 225, 235.
[4] The unsigned letters to Grenville in *Dropmore Papers*, III. 222, 224, 230, 258 are almost certainly from Morris. See, too, III. 563, Sparks, *Life of G. Morris*, III. 93.
[5] Garden, v. 359; Guyot, 219, 265–7.

1796, he saw a politician named M. Nettement, who claimed to know that the Moderates in the French Directory secretly desired peace, which was certainly longed for by the great mass of the nation. If, therefore, so he assured Pitt's private secretary, Joseph Smith, an affable and tactful envoy were sent to Paris, who would interview the Directors privately and use his influence with the chiefs of parties, a reconciliation might well be reached; otherwise, the peace would be one of exhaustion[1]. So dark was the outlook, especially in regard to finance, that Pitt resolved to seize this opportunity, and for a time induced Grenville to make the effort. By September 2nd, Ministers had drawn up a Minute embodying the terms to be offered to France through the medium of Denmark. These were: the cession to France of Savoy and Nice (she had acquired them by her recent Treaty with Sardinia); also, of "all the conquered countries on the Rhine not belonging to Austria"; she would regain her Colonies lost in the War, while Great Britain restored to Holland the conquered Dutch Colonies, except the Cape, Ceylon and Cochin. Austria was to recover the Belgic Provinces and other territories conquered by the French; but, in case they refused to give back the Belgic Provinces to Austria, and the latter insisted on the Belgic-Bavarian Exchange, we would not oppose it, provided that those Provinces were placed' "in a situation of as little dependence as possible on France[2].'

Here were the outlines of a possible settlement. The chief objections to them were the considerable renunciations asked from France in the heyday of triumph, and the heavy losses to be imposed on the Dutch, in order that Austria might regain her pre-war position. The British Government, receding from its decision, of September 14th, 1794, not to sacrifice any of its colonial gains for the securing of better terms to Austria, now proposed to restore to the French our conquests overseas at their expense, also two or three small Colonies to the Dutch, in order to induce the French to evacuate Belgium, Lombardy and most of the Rhineland; but we retained the best of our acquisitions from the Dutch, who consequently would be the chief losers by the War. This shabby proposal was actually carried out, in part, at the Peace of Amiens, Spain, also, then figuring as a forced contributor to the expenses of the contest.

The proposals of September 2nd displeased George III, who deemed them undignified and untimely; but, in view of their almost

[1] *Beaufort MSS.* (Hist. MSS. Commission), pp. 369–71; Guyot, 273–6.
[2] *Dropmore Papers,* III. 239–42. As the Directory rejected the offer of the good offices of Denmark, the overtures were made direct to Paris.

certain rejection at Paris, he did not withhold his consent. Grenville also expected the Directory to find "a frivolous pretext for refusing a peace contrary to its interests"—so he wrote to Eden on September 7th —and he hoped the affair would merely serve to show who was guilty of the continuation of the War. He proceeded with the negotiation, but in a spirit different from that of Pitt. His despatch to Eden diverged somewhat from the proposals mentioned above. He (lately so insistent on an alliance with Prussia) now laid stress on maintaining the power of Austria, for which cause Great Britain would sacrifice many of her maritime gains, and he also insisted on the entire independence of the Belgic lands. Before sending Lord Malmesbury to Paris for the purpose of opening the negotiation, he reminded him that "the King is bound not to make peace without the consent of Austria, except on the terms of procuring for that Power the restitution of all it may have lost in the war[1]." Thus Grenville stiffened the original proposals, which bore the mark of Pitt's more pacific nature.

Even so, their reception at Vienna was very cool. Fortune then favoured the Imperialists. In October they threw back the French to the Rhine and confidently expected to drive Bonaparte from Mantua. Further, Catharine, true to her policy of prolonging war in the west, offered 60,000 Russians for the next campaign on consideration of receiving a British subsidy, which she finally fixed at nearly £8,000,000. Thugut, before he was aware of this exorbitant demand, had conceived great hopes of Russia's help and disapproved the pacific overtures as likely to arouse her distrust[2]. Thus Habsburg pride, reliance on Catharine, and the gleams of success in Germany disinclined that Court to thoughts of peace, even on the liberal terms outlined by Grenville. So stiff was Austria's attitude that, as will soon appear, he warned her of the fatal results likely to ensue.

The general situation in October, 1796, also offered but slight hopes of a settlement. True, the fortunes of France were for a time overcast. Nevertheless her diplomatic position was favourable, owing to the conclusion recently of Treaties with some secondary German States and Naples[3]. On the other hand, the Triple Alliance of September,

---

[1] *Dropmore Papers*, III. 260.

[2] F.O. Austria, 46. Grenville to Eden, September 20th; October 7th: Eden to Grenville, October 16th, 18th, 1796. For Thugut's confidence up to November 12th of military success see Vivenot, *Thugut, Clerfait und Wurmser*, pp. 511–518.

[3] Naples gave up no territory and was not compelled to exclude British ships. The Directory hoped probably to facilitate a separate peace with Austria, since the Empress Maria Theresa was a daughter of Queen Maria Carolina, of the Two Sicilies. Guyot, pp. 205–7.

1795, had also reconstructed the First Coalition, and now the prospect of the active participation of Catharine in the War seemed no longer a chimera. With the aim of averting a Franco-Spanish domination of the Mediterranean, which appeared imminent after the Anglo-Spanish rupture, the British Cabinet decided to offer to the Tsarina Corsica, the object of her ardent desire. So confident were Ministers of bringing in the Russian fleet as a makeweight, that on October 19th they decided to suspend the evacuation of that sea by Jervis's fleet, a change of plan heartily approved by George III[1]. So well balanced seemed the combatants that the French Foreign Minister, Delacroix, at his first conference with Malmesbury on October 23rd, adopted a tone far less truculent than that of his earlier despatches. He even affirmed the desire of France for peace—a statement confirmed by the deep weariness, the almost unbroken silence, which hung over the land. The issue, however, rested, not with the disillusioned populace, but with the masterful faction which still overawed it. Yet, the need of humouring public opinion being urgent, the British overtures could not be declined forthwith. Indeed, on both sides of the Channel they were regarded, at least by those who disliked them or doubted their success, as a means of influencing public opinion. In London it had to be stimulated, at Paris calmed.

These considerations explain the somewhat artificial character of the ensuing negotiations. The Directory tried to induce Great Britain to treat for peace separately, alleging the greater simplicity and speed of this procedure. She, of course, refused to separate from Austria. Thence ensued sharp differences, which were increased by the harsh tone of the French reply and by Grenville's stiff rejoinder on November 7th. It has been claimed that, by this time, Grenville had resolved on a rupture, and that Pitt resigned himself to that ending of his hopes[2]. But their letters of that date and Grenville's Memorial to the Directory do not warrant so extreme a statement. The French effort to separate the two Allies was calculated to increase the distrust of Grenville and overcloud the hopefulness of Pitt[3]. There is, however, nothing to show that even Grenville then desired a rupture of the negotiation. He instructed George Canning, now Under-Secretary at the Foreign Office, to commend Malmesbury's tact in passing over certain annoyances and irregularities at Paris. Further, his two im-

[1] *Dropmore Papers*, III. 261.
[2] Adams, p. 49. Guyot, p. 293.
[3] Malmesbury, *Diaries*, III. 295–303.

portant despatches of November 7th imply a desire for peace. In the former of them, he charged Eden to inform Thugut that, if Austria declined to share in the negotiation for peace, Great Britain might find herself compelled to open one separately, assuring to her Ally the best terms possible. In the latter despatch, he sent a warning calculated to dispel the last hopes of the Chancellor for the Belgic-Bavarian Exchange. No Power but Austria or Prussia (he said) could hold the Belgian Provinces against the French. If the Habsburgs declined, then Prussia should be invited, to do so. In either case, the success of any general settlement depended on her consent, and Austria must formulate her policy without delay[1].

These are not the words of a man who desires a rupture at Paris, but rather of one who seeks to avoid it by inducing Austria to act promptly and reasonably. By all the claims of honour he was bound not to make peace with the French without putting forth all possible efforts to include her in the settlement; and, in view of her precarious financial situation, his remonstrance of November 7th, together with his constant refusal to satisfy her exorbitant pecuniary demands, ought to have induced a desire to treat for peace. But the eyes of the Emperor and his counsellors were holden. Even the news of Bonaparte's victory at Arcola on November 18th, failed to open them. On Eden reporting Grenville's warning as to a possible reversion of the Belgic lands to Prussia, Thugut hotly exclaimed that his master would oppose it by force of arms. Not until December 13th, when the news of the sudden decease of Catharine reached Vienna, was that Court able to perceive its imminent danger; and then it was too late for participation in the negotiation at Paris.

There, the British decision to act along with Austria had aroused some annoyance, which was increased by our Foreign Office instructing Malmesbury not to disclose the essentials of his Instructions. This prudent reserve (fully consonant with diplomatic usage) resulted chiefly from the above-mentioned decision, which involved waiting on the ever-deferred declaration from Vienna. Thus, affairs gyrated in a vicious circle, from which there was no escape until the course of events declared decisively for one of the disputants. It favoured France and told against the Allies. Arcola confirmed her conquest of Italy. The death of Catharine shattered the new Triple Alliance; for it soon appeared that her successor, Paul I, would reverse her policy. Further, the Directory hoped much from Hoche's great expedition for the invasion

[1] See *Appendix D* for these despatches.

of Ireland; and it is significant that the date of his sailing from Brest (December 17th) coincided with the drawing up of a warlike note by Delacroix, in which he advised the rejection of the British proposals. Those proposals drawn up by Grenville on December 11th, were delivered to Delacroix after the news of the death of the Tsarina reached Paris. Since they included the retrocession of the Belgic Provinces to Austria and the evacuation of Italy by the French armies, with comparatively small colonial retrocessions by Great Britain, the Directory naturally termed them *ces conditions déshonorantes*, and, on December 19th, bade Malmesbury leave Paris within 48 hours. He believed this haughty conduct to result largely from the news of the death of the Empress[1].

Grenville's final proposals were, probably, designed to lead to a rupture. If so, he succeeded; for it came about in a manner calculated to throw the odium upon the Directory. But that Government could now afford to disregard the moderate or peace party in France. Its successes bade fair to overturn old Europe and extend French control to the Tiber and the Upper Danube. Moreover, the British Opposition hotly denied the good faith of Ministers in the late negotiation; but, in spite of a brilliant attack by Fox, Ministers carried the day against his amendment by 212 votes to 37 (December 30th, 1796)[2].

Thus ended this gloomy year. In European waters, the British Navy had achieved little of note; for the failure of Hoche's expedition to Ireland was due rather to a faulty start and bad weather than to the dispositions of Admirals Bridport and Colpoys. Nevertheless, in distant waters British seamen won several triumphs, securing from France St Lucia, Grenada and St Vincent; from the United Provinces Amboyna, Demerara, Berbice, together with Colombo and other Dutch settlements in Ceylon. On the other hand, our forces serving in Hayti suffered terrible losses from disease, which almost warranted the scathing censures of Windham on our West India policy.

In view of the growth of discouragement at home and of anti-British feelings in Austria, it is surprising that Grenville did not publicly explain the motives underlying British policy. Gouverneur Morris, a good friend to England, urged this course of action in a

[1] Malmesbury, *Diaries*, III. 339–65; C. Ballot, *Les Négociations de Lille* (1910), pp. 38–40.

[2] I doubt the story of the Prussian Ambassador, Sandoz-Rollin (in Bailleu, *Preussen und Frankreich*, I. 106), that Malmesbury went to him on December 20th and accused Grenville of bad faith—a breach of confidence of which (to say the least) Malmesbury would surely not have been guilty—and to the envoy of Prussia! E. D. Adams (p. 50), seems to accept the story.

letter of October 5th, 1796, from Vienna, stating that Anglophobes were accusing her of protracting the miseries of Europe in order to complete the conquest of the two Indies. He admitted that Grenville had to appease home opinion by dilating on the value of our Colonial acquisitions; but such statements were utilised by hostile pressmen. until they embarrassed even the autocrats of Vienna. He, therefore, suggested that Grenville should issue a reasoned defence of his policy, to the effect that the security of the British possessions required the capture of the French and Dutch Colonies; but that this, though a legitimate war measure, was not the ultimate object of the War, which was to protect Germany and the Netherlands[1]. This statesmanlike advice Grenville seems to have disregarded as an unheard-of departure from the traditions of diplomatic reserve endemic at Downing Street.

The ominous tightening of the financial situation, the arrival of serious news as to the daring outrages of the United Irishmen[2], and the popularity of Erskine's pamphlet, *A View of the Causes and Consequences of the present War with France* (January, 1797), concurred to arouse in Pitt once more the resolve to seize the first opportunity for a general pacification. His desire was strengthened by the course of the War. Though Jervis's brilliant victory over a greatly superior Spanish fleet (February 14th) had dealt a heavy blow at that navy, yet the general prospects were gloomy. As usual, Austria was a load about our neck. The surrender of Mantua (February 2nd) and the speedy collapse of her defence of the Carnic Alps portended a final disaster. Naturally enough, the attacks in Parliament on the Government's policy of subsidising Austria became more bitter. On April 4th, Sheridan's motion for an enquiry into this subject gained 87 votes, as compared with 37 for the anti-War motion of December 30th. The numbers would have trebled, if members could have read the reports then being penned by Eden and Colonel Graham at Vienna as to the refusal of Austrian officers and soldiers to fight and the utter confusion at headquarters. The Emperor, it is true, had repelled suggestions for a peace made by General Clarke through the Grand-duke of Tuscany, and Thugut was struggling manfully against a surrender. But they both complained that we were compromising the campaign by withholding adequate pecuniary support and naval assistance in the Adriatic. Thugut demanded a large subsidy and the despatch of Jervis's fleet (then observing Cadiz) to operate on the Venetian coast. The British Government

---

[1] *Dropmore Papers*, III. 258; Sparks, *Life of G. Morris*, III. 93.
[2] Lecky, VII. ch. XXVIII.

declined both requests, but on April 4th decided to send a force of frigates and light craft to that quarter[1].

On the same day, Grenville signed a despatch to Eden, affirming the willingness of Great Britain to treat for peace conjointly with Austria. He again suggested the issue of a joint Declaration stating their wishes for a combined negotiation. If France agrees, then Austria may propose the locality, provided it be not too far from London. Great Britain will sacrifice certain of her Colonial conquests in order to assure the welfare and security of her Ally, "on which His Majesty holds that of Europe essentially to depend[2]." These proposals were prompted, not only by Austria's defeats, but also by news which reached London on March 30th from Lord Elgin, British Ambassador at Berlin, as to the Secret Treaty of that Court with France on August 5th, 1796[3]. Grenville, true to his earlier conviction of the value of a Prussian Alliance, had decided to make one more bid for it. Now, it seemed hopeless; and the need of peace was the more urgent. On April 9th the Cabinet decided to send Hammond to Vienna to arrange a joint negotiation to that end. George III deemed the measure big with evils, but did not actively oppose. He could scarcely do so, in view of Pitt's statement that the Cabinet was unanimous. The following words in his letter of April 9th to the King are noteworthy: "In this opinion he knows that none concur more decidedly than those of Your Majesty's servants who have been most anxious to resist, while they thought it possible, the sacrifices now proposed." Grenville's letter to the King of the same date is equally decisive[4].

The Instructions of April 11th, 1797, to Eden, taken by Hammond, were drawn up with the special purpose of safeguarding Habsburg interests. They aimed at securing a general armistice, so as to allow time for consultation with Vienna and Petrograd, but set forth alternatives in case Austria needed to act at once. If so, Eden and Hammond might advise the cession of the Belgic Provinces, provided that she acquired indemnities in either Germany or Italy sufficient for the maintenance of her position as a Great Power. On other topics, Grenville

---

[1] F.O. Austria, 48. Eden to Grenville, March 8th, 22nd, 25th, 1797. For Thugut's opposition to the French offers of peace sent through General Clarke and with the recommendation of the Grand-duke of Tuscany see *Appendix D*, also Hüffer, *Quellen*, Pt II, vol. 1. pp. 112 *et seq.* Sorel, III. chap. IV.

[2] *Ibid.* Grenville to Eden, April 4, 1797.

[3] *Dropmore Papers*, III. 304.

[4] Stanhope, *Pitt*, III. *App.* p. v. *Dropmore Papers*, III. 310. But see Windham's account (*Diary*, p. 357) of George III's remark to him: "I honour you for your firmness" (probably in opposing the peace proposals).

proposed as a general basis the *status quo ante*, the French recovering all their former Colonies except Martinique: or, if we gave up that island, we claimed, in lieu of it, Trinidad and either Tobago or St Lucia. Similarly, we would restore to the Dutch their Colonies taken in the War, except the Cape and Ceylon, deemed essential to the protection of our East Indies. No British possessions having been lost, we offered these restitutions, in order to assure satisfactory terms to Austria and Portugal[1]. The arrival of news of further defeats of Austria, probably also of the outbreak of the mutiny at Spithead, decided Grenville, by April 18th, to name conditionally further concessions, viz. that, if it were necessary to save her from complete disaster, His Majesty would forego all his recent conquests in the West Indies, except Tobago, where British commercial interests were supreme.

These despatches and others printed in the *Appendix* vindicate the good faith of the Cabinet in regard to this overture. George III disapproved of it; but he had long ago regarded persistence (not to say obstinacy) as the foremost of the political virtues. Statesmen who viewed the whole situation with an open mind must have deemed peace essential. Great Britain, though severely strained by recent events, held strong ground. She could fight on alone, unencumbered by Allies; but at present she was bound to do her best for them. On their behalf, she now prepared to rescind her earlier decision not to surrender her colonial acquisitions, in order to alleviate their peace conditions. Of what use, indeed, was it to continue a conflict in which Austria's military disasters continually cancelled the effects of British naval triumphs? The statesmen of London and Paris must already have seen that affairs were approaching a deadlock. The French fought desperately to secure the "natural frontiers" as a safeguard against Austria and England; while those Powers struggled on from a conviction that the new frontiers would place France in a position of dangerous preponderance. In the process, Austria was losing Northern Italy and her possessions in Suabia and the Rhineland. Great Britain was pouring forth subsidies and making conquests overseas, whose chief use was to serve as barter at some ever receding pacification. The result would be either the destruction, or some artificial reconstruction, of the old Flemish Barrier. If so, as in the Peace of Aix-la-Chapelle (1748), the British navy would have served merely to redress the Balance of Power on the Continent. As Burke truly said respecting the horrible loss of life in our West India campaigns: "If we look for matter of exchange in order to ransom

[1] See *Appendix D.*

Europe, it is easy to show that we have taken a terribly roundabout road[1]."

Grenville feared that the British proposal might arrive too late; and therefore sent after Hammond another, to the effect that, if Austria had made peace, he was to proceed to Berlin and accept an earlier, and rather suspicious, offer of that Court to mediate for peace[2]. On arriving at Vienna at the end of April he found that Bonaparte had imposed on that Court the Preliminaries of Leoben (April 18th). Thugut maintained the utmost reserve and concealed them from him. Hammond, therefore, said nothing about the projected overture at Berlin[3], which was certain to annoy Thugut. Proceeding to Berlin, he acted warily, and again fulfilled Grenville's revised intention, which was that he should state merely Britain's readiness to enter into pacific negotiations, saying nothing meanwhile as to our actual relations to Austria. By this cautious reserve, Grenville and Hammond rendered possible a resumption of close relations with Austria. The wonder is that, after reiterated proofs of the bad faith of Prussia, Grenville should, even in the present desperate straits, have thought of seeking her mediation.

Starhemberg, who believed that Hammond had unguardedly disclosed the secrets at Vienna, reproached Grenville and expressed the hope that Great Britain would never cease to trust Austria and Russia, united as they were by friendly ties. But the mischief of the situation was that we were drifting apart from Austria, who answered our invitation to a joint negotiation with excuses and reserve, or by complete silence. Further, it was clear that neither did she wholly trust the Tsar Paul, nor he her. Grenville had contemplated an application even to that unaccountable potentate for his good offices; but the mere intention illustrates the British statesman's desperation[4]. It would be unfair to blame Francis II and Thugut overmuch for the collapse of 1797, in view of the utter demoralisation of the Austrian army, the craven spirit of nobles and burghers, and the delays in our financial succour[5]. But it soon transpired that the Habsburg Court was contemplating an alluring alternative—an entente with France with a view to the partition of the Venetian Republic[6]. Herein lay the chief reason

---

[1] Burke, *Letters on a Regicide Peace* (No. II).

[2] *Dropmore Papers*, III. 298.

[3] So he declared (*Dropmore Papers*, III. 322) Starhemberg heard the contrary (*Ibid.* p. 325); he thought the secrecy of his Court culpable.

[4] *Ibid.* III. pp. 299, 312; Ballot, chap. IV. Vorontzoff at London was working for a *rapprochement* with England; but the inconstancy of Paul made it very difficult.

[5] Hüffer, *Quellen*, Pt II, vol. I. pp. clv, 178–184.

[6] See *Appendix D*; also, Hüffer, *Quellen*, Pt II, vol. I. p. 153.

for the secretiveness of its policy during the spring and summer of
1797. Frequently did Grenville and Eden ask for the communication
of the Austro-French terms signed at Leoben. Thugut kept them
jealously secret. He, also, refused to ratify a convention for the repayment of sums lent by Great Britain to Austria; and, in spite of reiterated
protests from the British Government that such conduct sapped all
confidence in Austria's integrity, he took no steps to satisfy these just
claims, believing probably that her isolation and need of an Ally would
lead to the cancelling of the debt. Sharp opposition in Parliament compelled the Pitt Administration to hold firm in this matter, the result
being a marked divergence between British and Austrian policy. Thus,
the hope of setting on foot joint negotiations for peace came to naught.

In fact, the Triple Alliance of 1795 was defunct. Paul pirouetted
apart; Francis II was drifting towards a tame but not unprofitable
surrender; and Great Britain, hard pressed by the mutinies in the
fleets at Spithead and the Nore, seemed for a time at the mercy of the
French. The cheery pessimism of George Canning found expression
in the following lines (May 12th, 1797):

> Come, Windham! celebrate with me
> This day of joy and jubilee,
>   This day of *no* disaster.
> Our Government is *not* o'erturned—
> Huzza! Our fleet has *not* been burned,
>   Our army's *not* the master[1].

The intensity of Pitt's desire for peace is at no time more evident
than his venturing, even in the midst of these civil discords, to sound
the disposition of the French Directory on this question. On June 4th
he privately assured Lord Carlisle that overtures were being made at
Paris[2]. To take such steps while the Nore mutineers were blockading
the Thames and Consols were down to 48, was the most questionable
proceeding in Pitt's career; and it was, almost certainly, disapproved
by Grenville. On May 26th he ordered Hammond to leave Berlin,
where nothing could be effected, and on June 2nd he informed Eden
that we were making peace overtures at Paris in consequence of Austria
having come to terms with the French and observing complete silence
on those terms; but he ordered Eden merely to state these facts as a
proof of our desire still to remain in concert with her. As to the method

---

[1] *Windham Papers*, II. 53.
[2] See *Appendix D*, also, for the reasons why Grenville refused Austria's futile,
because belated, proposal of a General Congress.

of our negotiations with the Directory, there arose a sharp division in Downing Street. Grenville, Portland, Spencer and Windham still desired close cooperation with our Allies, Austria and Portugal. Pitt, Loughborough, Dundas, Chatham, Cornwallis and, finally, Liverpool, carried the day in favour of a limited negotiation[1]. George III, very reluctantly, concurred. Grenville, however, in his note of June 17th to Delacroix, declared that Great Britain must look after the interests of her Ally, Portugal, and that those of Spain and Holland might be considered on the representation of France.

We can here consider merely the causes of the failure of the ensuing negotiation at Lille. Malmesbury, our Plenipotentiary, well summarised the influences at work in the concluding sentence of his letter of July 25th to Grenville: "The fate of the negotiation will depend much less on what passes in our conferences here than on what may shortly happen at Paris." This remarkable forecast was prompted by the critical state of affairs at Paris. There, the violent trio that controlled the Directory procured the dismissal of Delacroix and other Ministers, the Foreign Minister's place being taken by Talleyrand as Plenipotentiary at Lille. Not that this diplomat was, either by nature or conviction, a Jacobin; but, since at this juncture his diplomatic talents would be invaluable, he became their man for a time. In his opinion, the British Government was secretly encouraging Austria to resist the French terms, or rather the terms which Bonaparte was thrusting on her. "Force the Austrian peace by hurrying on the British peace"— such was his motto. If left to himself, the young conqueror would probably have humoured the islanders to some extent, in order to crush Austria. That Power was playing a dangerous game. Obstinately, she held her British Ally at arm's length, until Grenville declared that her suspicious reserve and belated proposals for a General Congress left the Court of St James's free to go its own way, cooperation with her being out of the question, unless Gallic haughtiness compelled both States to fight on to the death. Malmesbury, also, affirmed that we had done more than our duty by her, while she forgot what she owed to us[2]. As for Portugal, her Envoy complicated matters on August 10th by hurriedly signing a Separate Peace, which his own Government promptly disavowed.

Thus, in the month of September, the Directory seemed to have

---

[1] *Life of Sir G. Elliot*, II. 408. Windham, *Diary*, pp. 365–8. For Burke's last despairing letter on public affairs, see *The Windham Papers* (1913), vol. II. pp. 53–6. For the British peace proposals of July 8th, 1797, see Ballot, *App.* XIV.

[2] *Malmesbury Diaries*, III. 465.

the ball at its feet. Recent events had puffed up its leading members with intolerable pride. They hoped to arouse a great revolt in Ireland, stir up panic in England by invasions and plots of malcontents, and group the Baltic States in a new Armed Neutrality against her. The Tsar Paul being inclined towards peace, they hoped to refashion the Armed Neutrality of 1780, and to overwhelm both Great Britain and Austria. Their forceful policy having succeeded in the domestic crisis, the *coup d'état* of 18th Fructidor (September 4th, 1797), which led to the triumph of the violent trio and the exile of their moderate opponents, the victorious faction was about to apply similar methods to their foes abroad. Reubell, the most energetic of the three, hated England virulently and believed that she could be revolutionised and ruined[1]. A week later, Talleyrand and Maret were replaced by Treilhard and Bonnier, Talleyrand becoming Foreign Minister. On September 16th, they sent a note, asking Malmesbury whether he had full powers to agree to a complete restitution of all British conquests made from France or her Allies; failing which, he should leave Lille within twenty-four hours. This brusque demand involved the restitution to the Dutch, not only of their settlements in Ceylon (as to which Pitt and Maret were ready for a compromise), but also of the Cape, as to which no British statesman would give way[2]. On other questions, an agreement had been virtually reached during informal discussions between Malmesbury and Maret; but this sudden demand was equivalent to a rupture. In vain did the French Plenipotentiaries declare that it was designed *pour activer la négociation*, and that, if Malmesbury chose to depart, they would await his return. That device was a sop to public opinion in France, which had longed for peace. With more reason, the British Government could urge that France had broken off the negotiation by a sudden and imperious demand. Accordingly, the whole affair tended to accentuate the war spirit on both sides of the Channel.

It is, however, doubtful whether a compromise was practicable. The French Plenipotentiaries might, in private, deride the lofty claims of their Spanish Allies for the recovery of Gibraltar and Nootka Sound, the demand of territory in Newfoundland for their fisheries and of a virtually exclusive possession of the Pacific coasts of America. But, after the revival of Spanish pride consequent on Nelson's repulse at

---

[1] Ballot, chap. XVIII.
[2] *Malmesbury Diaries*, III. 385, 400, 456, 471, 557. Pitt and Grenville differed respecting Ceylon.

Teneriffe, the Directory could not entirely overlook the claims of its chief Ally, nor indeed those of the Dutch, who, while less pretentious, were far more persistent. Maret believed that if Great Britain would forego Ceylon, she might retain the Cape by bribing each Director to the extent of £50,000[1]. On the score of character the suggestion is quite credible; but on that of expediency it is more than questionable. For such a proceeding could not remain secret; and its disclosure would damn for ever the men who resorted to it at the expense of a faithful Ally. There was, apparently, some chance of the Dutch accepting a substantial sum from England for the Cape, in order to discharge their pecuniary obligations to France, that Colony being then regarded as financially burdensome and useful only as the outpost guarding the East Indies[2]. But the spirit prevalent at Paris after Fructidor forbade any chaffering on this head. Probably, Bonaparte's influence prevented the cession of the Cape to "the intriguing and enterprising islanders" who alone stood between him and the conquest of the East. Ostensibly, the question of the Cape was the chief crux at Lille, Ceylon and Trinidad presenting fewer difficulties. But, in reality, it was the domineering spirit of the Directors which occasioned the rupture[3]. Could they have foreseen the events of the next nine months—the Dutch navy crushed by Duncan at Camperdown (October 12th), the revival of British finance and prestige, the miserable failure of French plans for Ireland, the hatred aroused by the French invaders of Switzerland and Rome, and the rapid rise of Bonaparte at the expense of "the lawyers of the Directory," they would have made peace and have figured as the benefactors of Europe, not as the dupes of the Great Corsican.

In view of the evidence now in our possession, the charge that Grenville always desired the breakdown of the negotiation at Lille must be revised. He felt the need of peace, if it could be obtained on terms neither dishonourable nor too disadvantageous[4]. But, clearly, Pitt was more eager than he for a settlement. His desire to end the War appeared in his entertaining some vaguely alluring offer to restore peace on not unfavourable terms, if £2,000,000 were secretly paid to the five Directors. The offer was either a hoax or an attempt to manipulate the Stock Exchange; and Pitt's dallying with so suspicious

[1] Ballot, p. 237.
[2] *Malmesbury Diaries*, III. 439, 454, 464, 470.
[3] Ballot, pp. 474–6, 298–309.
[4] See *Appendix D*; also *Dropmore Papers*, III. 372, 378; Hüffer, *Quellen*, Pt II, vol. I. p. cxx *note*.

a proposal seems to have induced Windham to write the sarcastic letter of October 10th, referring to the constant lowering of our terms, in the hope of some day finding at Paris a Government that would grant conditions of peace "not utterly destructive"; for to that course Pitt's system of "tiding over" was rapidly reducing us[1]. The prestige and credit of Great Britain never sank lower than in the summer of 1797. Thenceforth, under the pressure of French pretensions she began to recover spirit and energy.

In every respect, the *coup d'état* of Fructidor marks the beginning of a new period. In France, it brought about a recrudescence of Jacobinical violence. The rupture at Lille also opened the period of definitely offensive war. Both events were decided largely by the forceful will of Bonaparte, which, with military help, overbore the Moderates and launched France on a career of conquest and plunder. An attempt has been made by Sorel to prove the essential unity of all the Revolutionary and Napoleonic Wars; but that theory is at variance with certain plain facts. Before Fructidor and Lille, the military efforts of Frenchmen had been to a large extent directed to the acquisition of what they deemed secure boundaries. Afterwards, they aimed at foreign conquests. There is a wide difference between the campaigns of Carnot and those of Bonaparte. The former was now an exile, the latter was now the uncrowned king of the French. Up to September, 1797, the hopes of democrats everywhere centred in France. Thenceforth, they turned against her. That month marks the turning point both in the French Revolution and in European History. Brumaire and the Empire were but the natural sequel of Fructidor.

That event also led the Directory and Bonaparte to conclude peace promptly with Austria. "We have war with England (wrote Bonaparte on October 18th), that enemy is formidable enough." Fearing that she was about to frame a new Coalition, he bullied Cobenzl into a surrender of the chief outstanding Austrian demand, the Ionian Isles, then forming part of the Venetian Republic, which the two disputants had resolved to partition. By the resulting Treaty, signed at Campo Formio near Udine on October 17th, 1797, France acquired the Venetian fleet, and for her subordinate Cisalpine Republic the western districts of the Venetian mainland, while Austria obtained the city of Venice, Eastern Venetia, Istria and Dalmatia. She also ceded to the French the Belgic Provinces, recognised the (nominal) independence of the lands now forming the Cisalpine Republic, promised to transfer

[1] *Windham Papers*, II. 61.

her Breisgau to the dispossessed Duke of Modena and agreed to the assembly of a Congress for the settlement of German affairs. The main outlines were marked out in secret articles whereby the Emperor pledged himself to use his good offices to procure from the Empire the cession to France of all German lands west of the Rhine, she in return using her endeavours to secure for him the Archbishopric of Salzburg and part of South-East Bavaria. The signatory Powers further agreed that, if one of them made more acquisitions than these in Germany, the other should gain an equivalent indemnity[1].

Such was this disgraceful compact. The two Powers now extinguished the unoffending Venetian Republic and agreed on a policy of spoliation at the expense of the lesser States of the Holy Roman Empire. The Emperor consented to schemes which involved the breach of his coronation oath; and the French Republic placed itself on the level of the despoilers of Poland. The success which, also, attended the French negotiations at the Congress of Rastatt hastened the dissolution of the Holy Roman Empire and assured the predominance of France in German affairs. Bonaparte, after participating for a few days in the early sessions at Rastatt, repaired to Paris, where he received a rapturous welcome, and was bidden by Barras to proceed to the northern coast and overthrow "the giant corsair that infests the seas." Duncan's victory at Camperdown deprived this verbiage of all significance; but unrest in England and unceasing outrages in Ireland darkened the outlook in the autumn of 1797[2]. If the French Republic had not soon belied its reputation of liberator of oppressed peoples, the democratic ferment in our large towns would have been formidable. For a time British malcontents looked with hope to Bonaparte's forces mustering on the coasts of Picardy and Flanders. It soon appeared that those preparations were, on his part, a blind to hide his real aims which pointed towards Egypt. When his ambitions became manifest and the plunder of the Swiss Cantonal treasuries was known, the sympathy of British democrats with France rapidly cooled; and the War received whole-hearted support. The rise of Bonaparte synchronises closely with the decline of British Republicanism, fear of which had in a measure influenced Grenville's foreign policy.

The truth that the excess of an evil works its own cure likewise became manifest, though slowly, in the international situation. The domi-

---

[1] Garden, v. 415–425. Austria lost 3,604,300 inhabitants, but gained 3,050,000 in Italy, etc.
[2] *Dropmore Papers*, III. 378, 385–9.

neering behaviour of the French Envoys at Rastatt, the rapacity of French officials in the Rhineland, and the spoliation of Rome and central Switzerland alarmed and disgusted all neighbouring Powers. Thugut, while secretly satisfied with the terms signed at Leoben, resented the far more onerous conditions of the Treaty of Campo Formio, and regarded it as a truce, to last until the Triple Alliance could be renewed under more favourable auspices. The conduct of the French convinced the statesmen of Vienna, Petrograd and London that the time was fast approaching[1].

For a brief period, some hope was entertained that Prussia would enter on a different course. In November, 1797, the death of Frederick William II brought to the throne his son of the same name. The new monarch was virtuous; and his accession and that of his beautiful consort Louisa, ended the scandals which had disgraced the Court of Berlin. His national patriotism revolted at the terms of the Treaty of Campo Formio and the intrusion at Rastatt of French influence into Germanic affairs. He, therefore, sought to come to an understanding with the Emperor Francis II. The attempt produced little result, owing to the incurable distrust between the two Courts. Further, there appeared in Frederick William III signs of that narrowness of outlook and paralysing indecision which were destined often to warp or thwart Prussian policy; and the hopes of a change of policy harboured by Lord Elgin, British Ambassador at Berlin, soon faded away. The Duke of Brunswick, who went thither with the purpose of influencing the new monarch in favour of Great Britain and Austria, soon had to lament his timidity and reliance on the old clique, especially on Haugwitz, a man (said Brunswick) "whom no honest man could trust."

Very different was the character of George III. As he once wrote to Pitt, "I never assent till I am convinced what is proposed is right, and then I keep." This excellent quality, together with the quenchless optimism of Pitt, the stern tenacity of Grenville, the valour of her fighting men and the marvellous buoyancy of her finances, made Great Britain the sole hope of European independence. Mallet du Pan, on reaching our shores in the spring of 1798, was astounded at the confidence which prevailed. "The nation (he wrote) had not yet learnt to know its own strength or its resources. The Government has taught it the secret, and inspired it with an unbounded confidence almost amounting to presumption." This dogged determination was certain to reinvigorate our former Allies, so soon as they had full

[1] *Dropmore Papers*, III. 384, 395-7.

experience of the dealings of France with her neighbours. On January 11th, 1798, George III wrote to Pitt, urging the need of an alliance with Austria, Russia and Prussia, and the despatch of Lord Minto to Vienna for the initial negotiations, England acting as a guarantor for an eventual Austro-Prussian settlement. No such steps, however, were taken for the present, but de Luc, George III's agent in Germany, worked hard to safeguard the Princes of the Holy Roman Empire and remove the obstacles to a union of the Powers. For the present, the scramble for "indemnities" at Rastatt left Central Europe a prey to French intrigues; and, by a vote of the Congress on March 9th, 1798, France secured the Rhine boundary, the ecclesiastical domains further east being earmarked for the dispossessed German Princes from beyond that river[1].

These and other high-handed actions on the part of the French induced Thugut to angle warily for support from London; but, on the score of Austria's poverty, he declined to repay her loan of £1,600,000, now overdue at London. Pitt and Grenville insisting on the discharge of this obligation, a diplomatic deadlock ensued, destined to produce serious consequences. True, on April 1st Starhemberg proffered to Grenville proposals, drawn up by Thugut on March 18th, probably owing to the French diplomatic success of March 9th at Rastatt. They aimed at the formation of a league between the four great monarchies in order to oppose France, now "decidedly bent on the subversion of every part of Europe and totally regardless of the faith of treaties." Austria, also, asked for pecuniary aid, the despatch of a British fleet into the Mediterranean, and enquired whether, if necessary, action could be taken in the year 1799. Starhemberg, further, hopefully suggested that the one thing necessary to make the Tsar act was to convince him that peace with anarchic France was impossible, and that, if Prussia were unfriendly, he should at least neutralise her. At best, however, a Quadruple Alliance could be formed with which the Scandinavian and Italian States would probably coalesce. He, also, opposed the notion of the Belgic Provinces ever falling to Prussia, but in any case begged for British financial support[2]. Here he encountered the fixed resolve of Pitt and Grenville, which barred further progress. For a brief space, the question of reparation for an insult to the French flag at Vienna on April 13th promised to lead to a rupture; but the

---

[1] Rose, *Pitt and Napoleon: Essays and Letters*, pp. 240, 243; *Dropmore Papers*, III. 400–7, IV. 43–60; Guyot, pp. 673–684; *Le Congrès de Rastatt*, I. pp. 1–256; H. Hüffer, *Der Rastatter Kongress*, vol. II. *passim*.

[2] *Dropmore Papers*, IV. 153–9.

incident ended in a tame compromise which for a time seemed likely to lead even to an Austro-French entente. The Directory sought to entice both Austria and Russia to a partition of the Turkish Empire, but met with little response. Prussia, likewise, rejected its overtures for an alliance.

In the early summer of 1798, the impasse in European affairs seemed hopeless. Great Britain was for a time distracted by the formidable revolt in Ireland, which the fleets of Brest and Rochefort promised, but failed, to foster. Italy and Switzerland lay at the feet of the French; and the helplessness of the Holy Roman Empire stands revealed in the remark of Bonaparte, that, if that institution did not exist, France would have to create it. But now, as was so often to happen, his masterful ambition launched France into an ocean of adventure, overburdening her with new responsibilities and exasperating all the Powers. Instead of striking at Ireland, where the blow would have been mortal, he purposed to ruin Great Britain by the seizure of Malta and Egypt, as a preliminary to the acquisition of her Indian Empire. Setting sail from Toulon on May 19th, his great armada easily captured Malta (June 12th). The news aroused a profound sensation at Rastatt. "It caused, first stupor" (wrote Debry, the French plenipotentiary on August 6th), "then rage. Not for a week has a single friend of Austria come to my house[1]." Bonaparte's capture of Alexandria produced an equal sensation. It threw light on the French projects for a partition of Turkey, and spurred on that Power to a declaration of war. On August 15th, the Sultan appealed to the Emperor of Morocco and other Moslem Princes for a joint effort against the French, who had without "any declaration of war, as practised by all regular governments, sent a wretch named Bonaparte against Egypt with a view to an attack on the whole Mohammedan world." Though the Sultan failed to stir up a Jehad against France, he found an unexpected Ally in Russia. The seizure of Malta, for whose Knights the Tsar Paul had long cherished a romantic admiration, threw him into transports of rage and ended his hesitations as to a war with France. His zeal for the expulsion of the French from Malta increased, when many of the exiled Knights repaired to Russia and, in October, 1798, elected him Grand-master of their Order. At once, he prepared to help Turkey with a fleet, and Austria with troops subsidised by Great Britain. The news of Nelson's victory at the Nile (which did not reach Paris until September 14th, and London on

[1] *Le Congrès de Rastatt*, I. 270.

October 2nd and 3rd) aroused intense satisfaction in Austria and Russia and ecstasies of joy throughout southern Italy, where a French invasion had seemed imminent. Bonaparte's Eastern expedition was, immediately, seen to be a gigantic blunder. Besides shutting up in Egypt the best Generals and troops of France, it incited Paul to hostility, encouraged Austria, and brought on immediate war with the Turks, on whom France had always counted to immobilise half the armies of the Imperial Courts. Soon, the subjects of the Sultan witnessed the strange spectacle of a Russian fleet sailing down the Bosphorus to help the Porte in the Mediterranean. What British diplomacy had failed to effect, British seamanship accomplished by one mighty blow. Nelson's exploit brought to life all the latent elements of opposition to the domination of France, and threw back that Power on the defensive.

IV

Nevertheless, so discordant were the Gallophobe States that neither the zeal of the Tsar nor the persistence of Grenville could fuse them into lasting union. Now, as ever, the hostility of Austria and Prussia was incurable, and Talleyrand counted on it for paralysing the nascent league. Of late, he had declared that he did not fear Coalitions, and had sent Sieyès to Berlin to keep Prussia quiet. The Envoy so far succeeded in working on the fears or covetousness of the Berlin Court, that neither the efforts of Russia nor those of Great Britain could effect a reconciliation with Austria[1]. Frederick William III professed a strong desire to expel the French from the Netherlands, but would not move until Great Britain paid him a subsidy and the Habsburgs opened the game. They, again, would not stir without money from London.

Similar requests had also arrived from Petrograd. On July 24th, 1798, the Chancellor, Prince Besborodko, officially declared to Whitworth the desire of Paul to become a principal, instead of an auxiliary, in the war, for the purpose of re-establishing peace on safe and honourable terms, not for the restoration of the Bourbons to the throne of France. Russia's cooperation, however, was conditional on the receipt of a British subsidy. Grenville, in his reply of August 27th, pointed out the straightened condition of the finances of Great Britain, her extraordinary exertions in all spheres of the war, and stated that, having been disgracefully abandoned by the Habsburgs, she could not frame a concert with them. She would, however, accept the Tsar's

[1] *Dropmore Papers*, IV. 272, 306–313, 350, 358, 363.

mediation for the re-establishment of such a concert, especially with a view to restoring the cantonal system in Switzerland; and Whitworth was empowered to sign a Subsidy Convention for the support of "a powerful Russian army" to cooperate with Austrian forces in the west. If such action were impossible, Grenville suggested an Anglo-Russian expedition to free the Dutch Republic, "exasperated as it is by the insulting tyranny of the French." If, however, Austria would help the Swiss, equally irritated against the French, we would assist Russia in acting conjointly with Austria for their liberation[1].

In these suggestions appear the first outlines of the campaigns of 1799. They proceeded largely on the lines sketched at Downing Street —a fact which differentiates the Second from the First Coalition. The British programme matured very slowly, owing to distrust of Austria and to the impossibility of satisfying the pecuniary demands of merely potential Allies. Pitt and Grenville agreed that, despite the excellent revenue returns, we could not possibly spare more than £2,000,000 for the three exigent States; and Pitt sagaciously concluded that the best course for the present was to continue "to fight well our own battle; and Europe must probably be left some time longer to its fate[2]." The formation of the new league was, also, hindered by the skill of the French Plenipotentiaries at Rastatt in fomenting German jealousies, and by Austro-Russian disputes concerning Suvóroff's army destined for service under the Habsburgs.

While diplomats bargained at Rastatt and the Tsar showered angry notes on Vienna, Ferdinand IV, King of the Two Sicilies, rushed into the fray. He had reasons for prompt action. By the Defensive Treaty of May 20th, 1798, with Austria, he would, in case of attack by the French, receive help from 60,000 whitecoats, or send 40,000 Neapolitans to succour the Habsburgs if they were assailed. On July 16th, the Court of Vienna ratified this compact, together with two supplementary articles whereby the Emperor promised to defend Naples, if attacked in consequence of opening the ports of the Kingdom to the British fleet. That case soon occurred, Nelson with some initial difficulty procuring at Syracuse the provisions and water which his Instructions from Earl St Vincent entitled him to demand. These resulted finally from the understanding with Austria, which involved the right of procuring provisions from Austrian and Neapolitan ports. As it was Austria which first pressed for the despatch of a

[1] F.O. Russia, 40. Grenville to Whitworth, August 27th, 1798.
[2] *Dropmore Papers*, IV. p. 355.

British fleet to that sea, within which there was no British station, she was bound to succour the Neapolitans in case of a French attack, consequent on their supplying the needed provisions and water; and the aggressiveness of the French (witness their forcible occupation of Turin on July 3rd) warranted the belief that they would attack Naples on the first plausible pretext. In this respect, then, the despatch of Nelson's squadron to the Mediterranean, primarily for the protection of Naples, was almost certain to lead to a new war; and Thugut's assurances to Eden, especially on June 23rd, pointed to the proffer of prompt assistance to that State, if it were assailed in pursuance of actions necessarily resulting from Austria's demand.

Nevertheless, so dependent was she on the Tsar (himself a waving reed) that, on October 3rd, Grenville warned Hamilton as to the danger of Naples breaking with the French Republic, unless it had "the fullest assurances of support from the Court of Vienna." By some mischance, this despatch did not reach Hamilton until November 19th; and, two days earlier, King Ferdinand had rushed into war. Whether he counted on armed help from Austria is doubtful. On September 28th General Acton assured Nelson and Hamilton that "Naples was determined to declare war, not wait for the Emperor; that they well knew the plan of the French against them." His rival, the Marchese di Gallo, inculcated caution and therefore incurred the hot displeasure of Nelson. Succumbing to the fascination of Lady Hamilton (herself the favourite of Queen Maria Carolina) the Admiral urged instant war. When admitted to their councils he roundly scolded Gallo and strengthened the party of action. The arrival of the Austrian General Mack, and his belief in the soldierly qualities of the 30,000 Neapolitan troops who made a fine show at Caserta, clinched the matter. On November 12th, Nelson assisted at a council at which it was decided that he should carry 4600 men to Leghorn, to menace the French rear, and, on the 17th Mack advanced to attack them at Rome, "trusting to the support of the Emperor." The latter plan must, however, have been formed during the absence of Nelson off Valetta (October 24th–31st); for, so early as November 10th, news from Naples reached Thugut to the effect that the kingdom was about to make war; and, on behalf of the Emperor, he angrily declared to Eden that if it acted thus, it would receive no help from Austria. He had sent a similar warning to Naples, which arrived late on the 12th, five days before the Neapolitans were to advance; but the King and Queen, stimulated thereto by Nelson, nevertheless resolved to attack. Evidently, the Admiral had jumped to the conclusion that the Emperor would act, or must be forced to act[1].

The result was disastrous. The Neapolitans broke at every encounter, rushed back in rout to the capital; and, on December 23rd, Nelson in H.M.S. *Vanguard* carried the royal family and the Hamiltons for safety to Palermo. This ignominious collapse exasperated the Emperor; and on December 22nd he hotly asserted to Eden that the precipitate action of his father-in-law, King Ferdinand, in attacking France was due to the British Government, which had sought to drag Austria into war, though it knew her to be unprepared. The charge against the Government is demonstrably false; if it had been levelled at Nelson, it would have contained some measure of truth. In any case, the precipitate action of Ferdinand marred the opening of the War of the Second Coalition and deprived that struggle both of the momentum and the general goodwill which might have assured the overthrow of France. Never was she weaker and more hated; never were her opponents stronger than after the Battle of the Nile; and it is a matter of enduring regret that the rashness of Nelson at Naples compromised the political results of that glorious triumph.

Meanwhile, the whims of Paul, the narrow suspicions of Francis, and the conscientious objections of Frederick William to any forward move, let slip the opportunity. While France was arming systematically in pursuance of her new Law of Conscription (September 23rd, 1798), the three Powers were engaged in futile chaffering. In order to bring the Tsar to a point, Grenville on November 16th despatched to Whitworth proposals for an Anglo-Russian Alliance which should form the basis of a European League. Taking warning from the fate of the First Coalition, he sought to effect a just and stable settlement of Continental problems by means of a firm compact between the two Great Powers that were but slightly concerned in the central tangles. Great Britain and Russia were to lay the foundations of a Quadruple Alliance with Austria and Prussia for the master-aim of reducing France within her ancient limits, the Allies contracting not to lay down their arms until this purpose should be attained. Since, however, its attainment might be hindered by the territorial ambitions and mutual jealousies of the Central Powers, Grenville sought to exorcise them by a preliminary understanding, the Habsburgs being invited to look towards Italy, in order not to exasperate Prussia. Her monarch was to be

[1] Sir H. Nicolas, *Despatches of Nelson*, II. 144, 148, 170, 171. See also *Appendix E.*

invited to indicate his desires for territory—a request not calculated to placate Vienna. For the rest, Grenville assumed that neither of the Central Powers would desire the Belgic lands, and that the best plan was, therefore, to add them to the United Netherlands under the restored Stadholder, the Prince of Orange. The freedom of Switzerland and the restitution by the French of Savoy (Nice was not named) and of the Rhenish lands to their former owners were, also, stipulated[1].

Viewed at large, the document may be called a rough draft of the Treaties of Vienna and Paris of 1814–15; while the almost nervous bid for Prussia's aid for the deliverance of the Netherlands associates this programme with the Anglo-Dutch-Prussian Alliance of 1788. At several points, the outlines are shadowy, notably as relating to the expansion of Prussia and the future of the kingdom of Sardinia. The latter State is not named, doubtless because it had on April 4th, 1797, framed a close Alliance with the French[2], and was now under their control. Nevertheless, the future of Sardinia should have been as much a matter of concern as that of the Dutch Republic, which was equally in the hands of the enemy.

Grenville's Instructions of November 16th led to the formation of the provisional Anglo-Russian Treaty of December 29th, 1798, which stipulated pecuniary support by Great Britain for a subsidised Russian army of 45,000 men, to act in the west together with a Prussian force. At this time, Grenville cherished high hopes of inducing Prussia to take up arms for the liberation of the United Provinces. Cooperation with her almost necessarily involved alienation from Austria. Accordingly, as the Court of Vienna maintained its suspicious reserve, he sharply rebuked Whitworth for allowing himself, at the instance of Paul and in contradiction to Instructions from home, to be drawn into futile *pourparlers* with that inveterate schemer, Count Lewis Cobenzl[3]. These were cut short, and Grenville despatched his brother Thomas on a special mission to Berlin, for the purpose of arranging an Anglo-Prusso-Russian invasion of Dutch territory, if possible with the help of Denmark or Sweden. The family connexion of Frederick William with the House of Orange, and his known desire for the liberation of that land, told in favour of the scheme; but, finally, Francophil influences, added to his innate indecision of character, prevailed. He decided to stand aloof, but considered that his profession of benevolent

---

[1] *Dropmore Papers*, IV. 377–380.
[2] Sorel, V. 154. On December 9th, 1798, Charles Emmanuel IV abdicated and retired to the island of Sardinia.
[3] F.O. Russia, 42, Grenville to Whitworth, January 25th, 1799.

intentions warranted the payment of a British subsidy. Haugwitz, then posing as Anglophil, early in May started a scheme for putting 60,000 Prussians at our disposal on good financial terms; but this proposal, whether sincere or not, was shelved by Frederick William near the end of July, when the adoption of any other extensive plan of operations was almost impracticable[1]. Accordingly, the British programme of a great Coalition with Russia and Prussia (Austria, Naples and the Scandinavian States being accessories) fell through. Nothing, therefore, remained but hastily to adopt more limited schemes for the remainder of 1799—a fact which goes far to explain the very unsatisfactory operations of that year[2]. To these, so far as they resulted from British initiative, we must now turn.

For reasons already stated, no compact was possible with Austria. But the provisional Anglo-Russian Treaty of December 29th, 1798, was prolonged by a Convention of six months later. Compacts of the two Powers with Naples and Turkey added to the scope, though not to the strength, of the Second Coalition. Meanwhile, an Austro-Russian Alliance had led to the despatch of Suvóroff's army (finally about 60,000 strong) with a view to assistance against the French in northern Italy; but disputes between the two Courts delayed, first its departure, then its progress, and not until the end of March, 1799, did that doughty warrior and his vanguard enter Vienna. At once, disputes broke out with the *Hofkriegsrath*, which regarded him as an Austrian Marshal entirely under its control. That any success was ever gained under this insensate arrangement is a supreme tribute to his genius. Scarcely more promising were the Anglo-Russian plans for the campaign. Not until the end of April, 1799, on receipt of the British ratification of the December Treaty, did the Tsar issue orders for the westward march of the subsidised Russian army under Korsakoff— a delay which hindered the successful opening of the campaign on the Upper Rhine. It soon transpired that the effective strength of this force was far below what Great Britain was paying for. Disputes also arose with Austria as to the objective of this army, she pointing to the Palatinate, while we desired the liberation of Switzerland as a preliminary to an Austro-Russian invasion of Franche-Comté. Finally, the British alternative prevailed.

---

[1] *Dropmore Papers*, IV. 464, 479, 492, 514, 519–527; v. 3–8, 14, 46, 68, 195–9. *Wickham Corresp.* II. 86.

[2] H. Hüffer, *Der Krieg des Jahres 1799 und die zweite Koalition* (2 vols. Gotha, 1904), has missed this important consideration.

With the Court of Vienna a close understanding was impossible, owing to the mystery in which Francis II and Thugut shrouded all their proceedings. Eden surmised that they were considering attractive offers from France; and his suspicion was correct. This obscure situation was cleared up by the action of the Directory, which, in March, 1799, issued what amounted to a declaration of war against Austria. Seeing that France then had only 235,000 troops ready for action, her aggressiveness can be explained only by the conviction of her Envoys as to the weakness of the new Coalition. The long-drawn-out farce of the Rastatt Congress now ended in tragedy, when Szekler Hussars assassinated two of the French Plenipotentiaries. Such was the opening, chaotic and barbaric, of the War of the Second Coalition.

Thenceforth, British policy was directed chiefly towards the following objects—the healing of Austro-Russian discords, with a view to a joint invasion of Franche-Comté; the expulsion of the French from Dutch territory, the strengthening of our position in the Mediterranean and the East as a retort to Bonaparte's oriental efforts, and the breaking-up of the Armed Neutrality League. It will be well to treat these topics in the order here indicated.

The triumphs of the Russian and Austrian armies in Italy, under Suvóroff and Melas respectively, soon brought to a head the discords of those Governments. Apart from military disputes, a question of high policy soon sundered the two Courts. On the recapture of Turin from the French (May 20th, 1799), Paul, the self-styled champion of divine right and legitimacy, ordered the reinstatement of the King of Sardinia at his capital. This behest Francis II countermanded[1]; and the diplomatic efforts of Great Britain and Russia at Vienna elicited proofs that he looked to the kingdom of Sardinia as one of his indemnities. Anxious, now that northern Italy was conquered, to be rid of Suvóroff, the Emperor concurred in a British proposal for the transfer of that army to Switzerland, and a joint invasion of Franche-Comté. To humour the Tsar, Grenville first made the proposal at Petrograd; when Paul agreed, Francis II expressed his assent, and forwarded corresponding instructions to Suvóroff. The veteran, who was planning an incursion into Nice, received the news with astonishment and indignation. To force the St Gothard in face of the French defence, to find subsistence in the Central Cantons, already impoverished by strife, and to join Korsakoff near Zurich signified a succession of problems never contemplated by the civilians who drew up the scheme.

[1] R. Gachot, *Suvóroff en Italie*, p. 192; Hüffer, pp. 55 *et seq.*

In fact, the whole story forms an instructive commentary on paper strategy and Coalition campaigns.

In order to pave the way for the liberation of Switzerland, Grenville had despatched Wickham (latterly in close relations with General Pichegru and other French Royalists) to stir up the Swiss, to concert a rising of the malcontents of eastern France, and so far as possible to cooperate with the Russian and Austrian commanders in Switzerland. Arriving at Schaffhausen late in June, Wickham found that the Austrian Government discountenanced the diversion of the Archduke Charles's army into Switzerland, and that he felt unable either to attack the French or to restore the Cantonal system which the majority of the inhabitants desired. It soon appeared that nothing would induce Thugut to act promptly in that quarter[1]; and he alone had influence with the Emperor. In truth, the early successes in Germany and Italy, and the absence of Bonaparte and his army in the East, had conduced at Vienna to a mood of boundless confidence; and, since Great Britain supplied no money and much advice, she counted for nothing.

Yet the importance of her influence ought not to have been ignored. It alone had imparted some consistence to the First Coalition, and was now needed as much as ever. Her squadrons in the Mediterranean not only cut off Bonaparte, but prevented a large Franco-Spanish fleet under Bruix (which entered that sea in May, 1799) from achieving more than the revictualling of the French garrison besieged in Genoa. That single incident should have opened the eyes of Francis II. But they were blind, save to the near and the obvious. Concentrating his efforts on Italy and the Rhineland, he refused to push on with the British plan, which, if properly backed, might have produced great results. The secretiveness of Austrian policy exasperated Grenville. Deeming Eden somewhat slack in his duties and too subservient to the masterful Minister, he recalled him in June, substituting for him Lord Minto (formerly Sir Gilbert Elliot)[2]. But the change was of little avail. On July 16th, Grenville wrote that Thugut, regarding the conquest of Italy as complete, seemed bent on thwarting his friends or Allies, and did so as thoroughly as if he were paid by France[3]. This was no exaggeration. The uncertainty as to the schemes of Francis and the intentions of Paul and Frederick William hampered the

[1] *Wickham Corresp.* II. 194 *et seq.*
[2] *Dropmore Papers*, IV. 515, 523; V. 85. Minto did not arrive until August 2nd.
[3] *Ibid.* V. 147. Cf. 199, 400–6; VI. 254.

British naval and military plans to an unparalleled extent; and the key
to the mistakes committed in both services in that War is to be found
in the halting or perverse diplomacy of Petrograd, Vienna and Berlin.

The transference of Suvóroff's army to Switzerland, far from
ending Austro-Russian disputes, exacerbated them. Jealous of the
Marshal's fame, the Austrian authorities did nothing to further, and
much to clog, his difficult task[1]; and before his heroic Russians could
struggle across the St Gothard and hew their way down the defile
of the Reuss, Masséna had crushed Korsakoff at Zurich (September
25th–26th). The Court of Vienna, having ordered the Arch-duke to
leave Switzerland, only a small Austrian force was left to help that
Russian army, and it was overpowered. Suvóroff thereupon turned
aside, and, brushing away the French, forced a passage into the Grisons,
arriving at Chur on October 8th with an exhausted, but still undaunted,
army. He swore never again to work for Austria, and all cooperation
between her and Russia was thenceforth impossible. As for Paul, he
was beside himself with rage, forthwith declared his Alliance with
Austria at an end, and sought spasmodically to frame a fantastic union
with Great Britain, Prussia, Turkey, Sweden and Denmark, for setting
limits to Habsburg aggrandisement in Italy[2].

Thus ended the British plan for the liberation of Switzerland and
the invasion of Franche-Comté. As a political conception it possessed
certain merits; for the occupation of Switzerland by the French had
given them control over northern Italy, Tyrol and Suabia. To eject them
thence was the alpha and omega of Europe's liberation. But to attempt
that task, especially from Italy, without making sure of wholehearted
support from the valley of the Upper Rhine, bordered on the fantastic.
Even apart from the tenacious French defence, the achievement
demanded the most exact cooperation between the armies of Korsakoff,
Suvóroff and the Archduke Charles. Austrian schemings and jealousies
disarranged a programme which called for the most energetic and
punctual performance. But the underlying conception, when carried
out faithfully and intelligently in 1814, contributed materially to the
overthrow of Napoleon.

The liberation of the Dutch Netherlands bulked large in the Anglo-
Russian schemes for 1799; and, as has been seen, the help of Prussia long
seemed a possibility. Had it come to pass, a great Russo-Prussian army,

[1] Gachot, chaps. VI, XVII; Hüffer, II. chap. II. Minto thought Thugut's aim was
to spare the Austrian army (*Wickham Corresp.* II. 215).
[2] *Dropmore Papers*, VI. 19, 32; *Wickham Corresp.* II. 329; Hüffer, II. chap. II.;
Waliszewski, *Paul I*, chap. XII.

with British and possibly Danish or Swedish contingents, would probably have swept the French out of that land, as a composite Allied force did in 1814. In May, 1799, the prospects were highly favourable; for the French, owing to their defeats by the Austrian arms, had withdrawn most of their troops from the United Provinces[1]. Nevertheless, on July 21st, 1799, Frederick William decided that he would try to arrange by negotiation for a French evacuation of that country. It was now full late for Great Britain and Russia to prepare adequately for the alternative course, a joint landing on the Dutch coast. The preparations were, however, hurried on, the most ardent advocate of the scheme being the usually cautious Grenville. Indeed, his optimism called forth a mild rebuke from Dundas (since held up to scorn as the embodiment of ignorant presumption!), who warned him against endorsing the hopeful estimate of George III, that the Allies ought to occupy the whole of the Netherlands before the advent of winter[2]. Dundas promised to do his best to send enough British regiments; but the calls for them in Ireland (now menaced by French raids) and elsewhere were so exacting as to leave only a sprinkling of good troops among a number of raw battalions. Admiral Duncan's force, indeed, captured 13 Dutch warships at the Helder, thereby completing his previous two years' work and putting an end to all fears of invasion from that quarter. The land operations, however, miscarried. The Batavian troops did not rally to the proclamations of the Prince of Orange, as his supporters had led us to expect. First, the late arrival of the 17,000 Russian troops, and then their precipitate action in the attack at Bergen, marred the whole enterprise, and the Duke of York, by the capitulation of October 18th, withdrew the Allied forces.

This failure, coming soon after the miscarriage of Suvóroff's enterprise, exasperated the Tsar, who in December wrote to Vorontzoff at London, that he intended to abandon the Coalition and recall his troops to Russia. He would, however, during the winter of 1799–1800, leave them in their present quarters, hoping that those in England (really in the Channel Islands) might in the spring be used against the Biscay coast of France. If he remained in the Coalition, it would be on condition of the dismissal of Thugut and the renunciation by Austria of her system of unjust and excessive acquisitions. His effort would be the last chance of saving Europe[3]. With this characteristic explosion

---

[1] F.O. Russia, 42. Grenville to Whitworth, May 3rd, 1799.
[2] *Dropmore Papers*, v. 198, 206–210; *Spencer Papers*, II. 352; Fortescue, IV. Pt II, *passim*.
[3] *Dropmore Papers*, VI. 109, 286.

the Second Coalition collapsed. It is a tribute to the forceful personality of Thugut that the fury of the Tsar, the representations of Minto, and the fixed hostility of Arch-duke Charles alike failed during six months of bewildering change to shake his authority. Hectoring, yet at times insinuating, passionate but adroit, the veteran in his "infernal cavern" now wore himself out for the aggrandisement of the Habsburgs in Italy; and, as Fortune favoured the Habsburgs in 1799 and frowned on their Allies, he could defy all the protests that came from London and Petrograd.

But now there befell an event which placed everything at hazard. On October 9th, 1799 (the day after Suvóroff's veterans had struggled into Chur) Bonaparte landed in Provence. Nelson and Sidney Smith considered that his escape from Egypt was due to the strange in-activity of the Turkish and Russian squadrons, which ought to have helped in patrolling the Eastern Mediterranean[1]. His arrival in France and overthrow of the Directory brought about a bewildering change. France, latterly divided and dispirited, rallied to his call for unity; and Habsburg haughtiness so far abated as to consent to a settlement of the wearisome loan dispute with Great Britain, thus opening a prospect of an Anglo-Austrian Alliance[2]. The old suspicions, however, hindered joint action far into the year 1800, probably because Francis II and Thugut were wavering between alluring arrangements held out by Bonaparte and a treaty with Great Britain, offered by the long-suffering Grenville. In the month of May, Thugut begged for three days to consider some of its provisions; but the three days lengthened out to six weeks. This exasperating delay hindered, *inter alia*, the despatch to the Genoese coast of Sir Ralph Abercrombie's force (finally sent to Egypt), which otherwise might have doubled the effectiveness of the help tendered by the fleet of Lord Keith to the Austrians engaged in besieging Masséna in Genoa[3]. As it was, that General's defence was so prolonged as materially to assist Bonaparte in the re-conquest of Italy. The lightning stroke of Marengo (June 14th) blasted the wide-spreading designs of Vienna, and reduced that Court to the position of a suppliant.

Shortly before the arrival at Vienna of news of that disaster, Minto signed with Thugut a Subsidy Convention for £2,000,000 (June 20th,

[1] Nicolas, IV. 44, 76, 89, 131, 140, 145, 171.
[2] F.O. Austria. Minto to Grenville, December 10th, 1799.
[3] *Dropmore Papers*, VI. 163–7, 174, 186, 243, 250, 256, 262, 300. Plans of Anglo-Russian operations on the Biscay coast also came to naught. See *ibid*. V. 407–9, 434; VI. 53, 60, 85, 89, 146, 151.

1800). As usual, that compact came too late to retrieve the situation, and served merely to pay part of the debts heaped up by Habsburg ambition. Wickham had signed similar compacts with Bavaria, Würtemberg and Mainz, in the hope of filling up the void caused by the departure of the Russians. But these scrambling efforts merely dissipated British treasure, and scarcely even delayed the collapse of this ill-knit confederacy. In September, 1800, Francis on the advice of the Minister Count Lehrbach, accepted an armistice with the French; whereupon Thugut indignantly resigned, and a time of confusion ensued, ending with the Treaty of Lunéville (February 9th, 1801), a replica of the compact of Campo Formio. The dependence of Naples on the Habsburgs was illustrated by her surrender to the French in the Treaty of Florence (March 28th, 1801), whereby she ceded to them her part of Elba, excluded British vessels, and admitted French troops to her south-eastern ports. The chief Land Power now controlled all Italy, and seemed once more about to dominate the Mediterranean.

While the grandiose schemes of Austria on the shores of the Mediterranean made shipwreck, those of Great Britain gained in strength. In 1800 the siege of the French garrison in Valetta went steadily forward. The native Maltese made no impression whatever on its ramparts; but the blockade by sea became increasingly close, until on September 4th, 1800, the gallant Vaubois, hard pressed by famine, surrendered to the British commander, General Pigot. The Russians and Neapolitans did next to nothing in assuring this surrender. Hitherto, the British Government had entertained no thought of retaining the island. The restoration of the Knights of St John was more than once stated by Grenville to be the aim of his policy[1]. Indeed, the touchiness of the Tsar on that subject and his insistence that Russian troops must form part of the future garrison of Valetta were alike notorious; and both British Ministers and Nelson were puzzled that he had not sent his Mediterranean fleet, with troops on board, to assist in the recapture of the island. Nevertheless, in the hope of humouring Paul, Grenville maintained that the island should either revert to the Knights or be assigned to him. On the other hand, Sir Augustus Paget, who had succeeded Hamilton at Naples, insisted on due satisfaction being accorded to that Court, which possessed ancient rights of suzerainty over the island; and he protested against Pigot's conduct in not hoisting the colours of Naples and the Knights by the side of the Union Jack.

[1] E.g. Grenville to Whitworth, October 5th; November 15th, 1798; Grenville to Hamilton, October 3rd, 1798. (F.O. Russia, 40, 41.)

The Home Government, finally, justified Pigot's conduct. These incidents revealed the extraordinary difficulty of finding any durable settlement of the Maltese problem; but there is no sign, before mid-October, 1800, that the British Government desired the retention of the island. Dundas, Wickham, Windham and other correspondents had long sought to bend Grenville to this decision, but without success[1]. It is also noteworthy that the Maltese strongly opposed the rule either of Russia, Naples or of the Knights, and more than once solicited British sovereignty over the island. By October 17th, 1800, Grenville had decided on the retention of Malta, on the ground of the commencement of hostilities against us by Russia[2].

The expulsion of the French from Malta facilitated the despatch of a British expeditionary force against their army still holding Egypt. This measure had long been urged by Dundas, ever preoccupied concerning the security of India; and it is worth noting that on September 7th, 1798, when news reached the East India House in Leadenhall Street of the landing of the French in Egypt, the Directors begged Pitt to regard India as the French objective, so that the crisis concerned the nation, and not merely the Company. Nevertheless, it was ready to advance the sum of £500,000 for the defence of India, trusting, however, to be reimbursed by Government[3]. The news of the battle of the Nile allayed these fears, and, at the close of 1798, the resourceful Dundas advised the despatch of a force from India to aid in the expulsion of the French from Egypt[4]. Nothing, however, was done for the present. Sidney Smith's brilliant success in beating off the French attack on Acre, and his generally successful blockade of their force left in Egypt, induced him to conclude with Kléber, Bonaparte's successor, the Convention of El Arisch (January 24th, 1800), for the peaceable evacuation of Egypt, the condition being exacted that they should not serve again during the War. The British Government having previously instructed Admiral Keith to insist on unconditional surrender, he disavowed the action of his subordinate; and, though the Government finally decided to honour the Convention, the French, after defeating a Turkish army at Heliopolis, resolved on holding Egypt. Bonaparte, as First Consul, made repeated, but fruitless, efforts to succour the French troops, his persistence serving to convince Dundas of the im-

---

[1] *Dropmore Papers*, VI. 75, 187, 199, 207, 385, 400, 421, 430, 449, 452.
[2] See other evidence in Hardman, *History of Malta* (1798–1815), ed. by J. H. Rose, Introd. and chaps. XI, XII; *Paget Papers*, I. 274.
[3] Pitt MSS. (in Pub. Record Office) 353.
[4] *Dropmore Papers*, V. 413.

portance of expelling them from that land. The other Ministers saw grave difficulties in the way; and undoubtedly, the imminence of hostilities in the Baltic, and the presence of French and Spanish squadrons in the Mediterranean, rendered an expedition to Egypt highly perilous. The British Government has been sharply censured for plunging blindly into the Egyptian enterprise[1]. The Addington Administration actually sent a message to recall the expeditionary force[2]. Fortunately, the message arrived too late. Thanks to the skill and devotion of Admiral Keith and General Sir Ralph Abercrombie, the landing was successfully accomplished. After the death of the latter, the enterprise was successfully carried through by General Hutchinson, who received the surrender of the French force at Cairo on June 17th, 1801, their last garrison, that at Alexandria, surrendering on August 30th. In both cases, conveyance to France on British and Turkish vessels was stipulated, no restriction on the use of those troops in the War being imposed[3]. Considering the uncertainty as to the advent of peace, the removal of 25,000 veterans from Egypt, where they were almost harmless, to France, where they might take part in one of Bonaparte's invasion schemes, must be pronounced a singularly lame ending to a brilliant exploit.

Meanwhile, Great Britain had confronted a formidable confederacy in the North. Its soul was the Tsar Paul. His unaccountable whims, unbridled wilfulness and frequent convulsions of rage had long been the despair of his advisers, who from the first noted the dominion of mere trifles and baubles over him. The Order of the Knights of St John shared with a new mistress and an intriguing valet the chief place in his fancies. "The rock of Malta" (wrote Whitworth) "is that on which all the sufferers split[4]." As his wrath at Bonaparte's seizure of Malta largely accounts for Russia's participation in the Second Coalition, so, too, his childish joy at receiving the island as a present from Bonaparte when it was certain to surrender to the British goes far to explain Paul's swing round from friendship to hostility in the summer of 1800. Bonaparte further incited him by tales of English maritime tyranny and hopes of the conquest of India. The Swedes and the Danes, noting his change of front, plied him with complaints of the rigours of British maritime law; and, when his hope of controlling the Mediterranean from Corfu

---

[1] J. W. Fortescue, IV. Pt II, chaps. XXVIII, XXIX.
[2] Parl. Debate of December 8th, 1802.
[3] H. Bunbury, *The Great War with France*, pp. 139–168; *Diary of Sir J. Moore*, II. chaps. XVIII, XIX; R. T. Wilson, *British Expedition to Egypt*, pp. 157 *et seq.*
[4] F.O. Russia, 41; Waliszewski, *Paul I*, chap. XII; *Dropmore Papers*, VI. 279–287.

and Malta vanished, he resolved to be at least the guardian of the
Baltic and liberator of the seas. This new mood chimed in perfectly
with the fixed policy of Bonaparte; and the two potentates began to
plan a Northern League which should complete the isolation and ruin
of the islanders.

Circumstances favoured the renewal of the first Armed Neutrality
League of 1780. The Danes, the chief carriers of the North, now again
had cause of complaint against us, especially concerning the capture
of their frigate *Freya* and her convoy in July, 1800. The British
Government instructed Whitworth (now Lord Whitworth) to proceed
to Copenhagen, with a view to a friendly settlement of this affair. The
desire of Grenville for such a settlement appears in his note of July
30th, 1800, to the Danish Government; and Earl Spencer instructed
our cruisers to refrain from looking for neutral convoys, so that we
might tide over that critical period without further disputes[1]. In order,
however, to back up Whitworth's negotiations, the Admiralty despatched a squadron to the Sound. Thereupon, on August 27th, Paul
invited Sweden, Prussia and Denmark to reestablish the Armed
Neutrality of 1780; and, two days later, he proclaimed an embargo on
British ships in his ports, placing the crews under restraint. This
hostile action led to no countermeasure by Great Britain, probably
from a hope that a change of the moon would alter his mood.
The news of a friendly settlement between England and Denmark
mollified him for a time; but, early in October, the tidings of the
surrender of Valetta to the British threw him into a paroxysm of rage;
he reimposed the embargo, rigorously imprisoned the crews and
expelled the British Embassy. Again, Grenville did not retaliate, and
he counselled a conciliatory demeanour towards the other Baltic
States, which had manifested no desire to join the new League. The
only threatening sign was the occupation of Cuxhaven (a possession
of Hamburg at the mouth of the river Elbe) by Prussian troops.
Against this act Lord Carysfort, British Ambassador at Berlin, was
ordered to make a firm protest.

On December 16th Russia concluded Conventions with Denmark
and Sweden, defining the claims of the Armed Neutrals. They were
in substance the following: (1) All vessels may sail on the coasts of
belligerents. (2) Goods of belligerents, except contraband, are free

---

[1] F. Piggott and G. W. T. Omond, *Documentary History of the Armed Neutralities*,
I. 379–384, 398–439; J. B. Scott, *Armed Neutralities of 1780–1800*, pp. 478–480;
Dropmore Papers, VI. 287.

on board neutral shipping. (3) No port is reckoned as blockaded, unless the blockade be effective. (4) Neutral ships may be stopped only on adequate cause; and procedure as to prizes shall be judicial and uniform. (5) The declaration of a naval officer escorting a convoy, that it carries no contraband, shall guard it against search. In addition to these general principles, severe penalties are imposed on officers allowing contraband on board their ships, and other neutrals are invited to join the League[1]. This programme, but for the addition of the fifth item, follows in general terms that of the First Armed Neutrality. But Catharine then assured Sir James Harris of her friendship for Great Britain and twice termed her league *la Nullité Armée*. The present procedure of Paul was avowedly hostile. Further, in view of the readiness with which, in 1793, Russia and Prussia had accepted the British policy of excluding all neutral commerce from France, those two Powers could not consistently complain of the maintenance of milder measures at the end of the same War. The fact that in 1793 they were Allies, and in 1800 were neutrals, could not justify their change of front if the question at issue were solely one of principle. It proved the question to be one, not of principle, but of expediency.

Here, indeed, was the weak part of the schemes of 1780 and 1800. Excellent in theory, in practice they were always infringed by States that held, or hoped to hold, command of the neighbouring seas. From the time of Philip II of Spain to that of Catharine, such had been the case. Besides, experience proved that the carriage of goods by neutrals to belligerents brought profits so enormous as to tempt to the breach of well recognised rules, and that, in the last resort, these could be upheld only by the maintenance of the right of search. In practice, therefore, the whole problem centred essentially in two questions: (1) Is due consideration shown to neutrals in the method of search? (2) Is the tribunal which adjudicates on doubtful cases a fair one?

British Ministers were resolved to uphold our claims, the stern and unbending nature of Grenville asserting itself the more markedly as the national danger increased. The sudden rally of half Europe to the side of France could not daunt him. He knew the fallaciousness of a mushroom Coalition well enough to expect that she would fare no better, and England would fight far better, for this transference of numbers. Nelson had always deemed the Allies a burden. The British navy and army were now highly efficient; and, while our seamen kept

---

[1] Piggott and Omond, I. 385 *et seq.*; *Camb. Mod. Hist.*, IX. pp. 45–9.

watch over Brest, Cadiz and Toulon, and were reducing the hostile Colonies, it would have been alike weak and foolish to allow neutrals to convey unhindered the timber, hemp and tar of the Baltic lands to our enemies. "If we give way to them" (so wrote Grenville on December 2nd), "we may as well disarm our navy at once and determine to cede without further contest all that we have taken as a counterbalance to the continental acquisitions of France[1]." The argument was sound. Moreover, we had to do with a semi-lunatic whose sudden access of Anglophobia was deplored by most of his subjects. A sharp blow would probably bring his 'system,' if not himself, to the ground. The preparations, therefore, went on apace for a great expedition to the Baltic; and on January 14th, 1801, an order was issued for laying an embargo on all Russian, Danish and Swedish vessels in British ports.

But at this moment, when Pitt and his colleagues were defying half the world in arms, they were overtaken by a crisis which revealed the frail hold on life even of the strongest Cabinet. That Administration had weathered eighteen years of storm. In its infancy it had triumphed over a parliamentary majority. The nation beheld with wonder and delight a mere youth steadily restoring the finances and prestige of an apparently bankrupt and discredited State. His Ministry, frequently changing in *personnel*, yet ever informed by his master spirit, confronted with success both domestic crises and the convulsions of the French Revolution. When dragged reluctantly into war, he and his cousin framed two Coalitions to limit the overgrown power of France. They saw those Coalitions fall asunder, yet they themselves stood firm; and their Government aroused the admiration of friends, the malicious despair of enemies, and the wonder of all.

Nevertheless, as is well known, that Administration fell—a victim to one of its own measures and to the excessive conscientiousness of the King. Early in February, 1801, Pitt and most of his colleagues tendered their resignations, assuring the King of their desire to facilitate, so far as possible, the task of their successors. Thereupon George invited a dull, safe man, the Speaker, Dr Addington, to form a Cabinet which, when completed in March, comprised Lord Hawkesbury at the Foreign Office, Earl of St Vincent at the Admiralty, Lord Hobart at the War Office. The agitation excited by these events produced a return of the King's besetting ailment, lunacy, which induced all patriots to seek by all possible means to end the internal crisis, in order

[1] *Dropmore Papers*, VI. 400.

unitedly to confront the foreign crisis[1]. It is significant that the secret orders issued to Vice-Admiral Sir Hyde Parker, in command of the Baltic fleet, were signed on March 15th, 1801, in pursuance of Instructions issued the previous day by Henry Dundas. Thus, the policy which led to that brief campaign was that of the Pitt Cabinet, though its successors reaped the credit of the success achieved both there and in Egypt.

Parker, with Nelson as nominally the second in command, was ordered to proceed to the Baltic, guiding his proceedings, while off the Danish coast, by the negotiations then pending with that Power. Whether peace or war resulted, he was as soon as possible to attack Reval and then Cronstadt. If Sweden proved to be hostile, he must attack her, or, in the contrary case, protect her from the resentment of Paul. Prussia was not named in these Instructions, which further evinced a desire to avoid a rupture with Denmark and Sweden. Not until late in March did Prussia declare her intention of occupying Hanover and closing the mouths of the Elbe, Weser and Ems to British commerce. As the Russian and Swedish fleets were still ice-bound, the brunt of responsibility fell upon Denmark. With her, efforts at conciliation were made by Parker, but without effect. Nelson's conduct at this crisis was marked by political insight no less than naval daring. Knowing that Russia was the real enemy and the Danes little more than her catspaw, he was far more eager to strike at her than at them, and he used the first moments of decided triumph at Copenhagen for pacific overtures, couched in the friendliest words. They produced a speedy effect, all the more so because the Danish Government had just received news of the assassination of the Tsar Paul.

In the light of modern evidence, it would be superfluous to refute the stupid slander, inserted in the *Moniteur*, which ascribed that tragedy to England. Whitworth, who had long left Russia, was, of course, guiltless. The chief conspirators were Pahlen and Platon Zuboff, Panin and others having suggested the plot, of which the Grand-duke Alexander had but a limited knowledge. But nearly everyone welcomed the event. The *mot* of the occasion was uttered by Talleyrand: "Assassination is the usual method of dismissal in Russia."

---

[1] Evidently, this motive prompted the assurance of Pitt to the king, during his recovery, that he would not bring forward again in his reign the question of Catholic Emancipation. See *Dropmore Papers*, VI. 443, 445–7, 458, 474; G. Rose, *Diaries*, I 305–8; *Castlereagh Corresp.* IV. 10–12, 32, 39–48; *Cornwallis Corresp.* III. 350; Sir G. Cornewall Lewis, *Administrations of Great Britain*, pp. 151–3; J. H. Rose, *Pitt*, II. chap. XX.

Nelson proceeded to Reval, and had a friendly reception, the new Tsar, Alexander, expressing a desire for peace with Great Britain[1]. By the subsequent compromise of June 17th, 1801 (accepted by the other Baltic States) Great Britain and Russia agreed that in wartime the neutral flag should exempt from capture all cargoes except contraband of war and enemy property; and that blockade, to be legal, must be effective; contraband was defined, the right of search limited, and the rules of prize-courts were declared subject to the principles of equity[2]. Finality in such a matter was not to be expected, and the usual disputes soon supervened; but, for the time, this Convention went far towards reconciling Continental peoples to the British maritime code and put an end to Bonaparte's plans of rousing all nations against "the tyrant of the seas."

Indeed, he had no chance now of overcoming Great Britain, who, when rid of embarrassing Allies, displayed her full striking power in the two brilliantly successful expeditions of the year 1801. Apart from these major operations, her arms had prospered. Saumarez retrieved his failure at Algeciras by a signal triumph over a Franco-Spanish squadron in the Gut of Gibraltar (July 12th–13th, 1801); and the capture of several West India Isles crowned the naval triumphs of the year. Other signs were propitious. The national finances had acquired stability since 1798, the temper of the nation was firm, and Ireland under the Union was becoming less unsettled. The supremacy of France on land being as incontestable as that of Great Britain at sea, peace seemed to be the natural outcome of the equipoise reached by eight years of warfare.

But, while some Britons pointed out the hopelessness of reducing the power of Bonaparte, others, noting his high-handed interference with the Dutch Republic whose independence he was pledged to respect, deprecated a surrender that must be the prelude to endless humiliations. Such were the objections of Grenville to any accommodation with Bonaparte. His implacable spirit (the epithet is Cornwallis's) had been shown in the reply to Bonaparte's pacific overture of Christmas, 1799—to the effect that peace would best be assured by the restoration of the French royal House. That reply was evidently designed primarily to satisfy the two Imperial Courts and the French Royalists, with whom we were then concerting extensive plans; but

---

[1] Czartoryski, *Memoirs*, I. chap. XI.; Waliszewski, *Paul I*, chaps. XV, XVI; General Löwenstern, *Memoirs*, I. p. 75; Nicolas, IV. 370–9.
[2] Scott, pp. 595–606. For Grenville's criticisms see *Dropmore Papers*, VII. 30–3.

it, undoubtedly, tended to rally all Frenchmen around the First Consul. Pitt, at that time, probably shared Grenville's animosity; for passion pervaded his speech of February 3rd, 1800, in which he recounted the aggressions and perfidies of Bonaparte. The great work of reconstruction accomplished by the First Consul had now altered the whole situation; and Pitt did not oppose the proposals for peace, which took form in September, 1801. His conduct was not consistent; for the Netherlands, which, alike in 1793, 1796 and 1797, he had declared to be essential to Britain's security, were now virtually at the disposal of France. But his change of front was probably due to war-weariness or hopelessness. He was in honour bound to support the Addington Ministry; yet he knew it to be unequal to the struggle with Bonaparte. Better, then, to end the War while we could do so without discredit. Such seem to have been his views. They clashed with those of Grenville; and the two kinsmen were destined never again to act together.

The Addington Ministry lent a friendly ear to pacific overtures from Paris. They were begun, in March, 1801, by Otto, deputed to this country for the exchange of prisoners; and they continued in London intermittently until the early autumn. Then, negotiations were resumed in earnest. On September 17th, Bonaparte issued Instructions to hurry them on, because he conjectured that Menou and the French garrison could not hold out at Alexandria beyond September 23rd (in point of fact, they had surrendered on August 30th), and, therefore, he desired to finish with England before the arrival of those tidings. The Addington Cabinet, weak in procedure, unlucky in regard to news, and eager for the French evacuation of Egypt, was conceding point after point, in order to secure this illusory advantage. It held out for the retention of that mainly British island, Tobago; but Bonaparte opposed a stiff refusal to this and other contentions, and ordered Otto to present the alternative of signature before October 2nd or war[1]. Hawkesbury signed, on October 1st, the very day before the arrival of news of the French surrender at Alexandria and the forthcoming evacuation of Egypt. In no important British Treaty of modern times have haste and secrecy played so prominent a part; and there is little definite evidence as to the motives which led to so singular a compact. It may be thus summarised. All the British conquests overseas were restored to France, Spain and the United Provinces, except Trinidad (Spanish) and the Dutch settlements in Ceylon. The restitution of the Cape to the Dutch was conditional on its being opened to British and French

---

[1] *Nap. Corresp.* VII. 255.

commerce. Malta was restored to the Knights of St John, subject to various conditions. The French agreed to evacuate the kingdom of Naples and the Roman States, also Egypt, which reverted to Turkey, the British retiring from Elba. The integrity of the Turkish and Portuguese dominions was reaffirmed. The Signatories further recognised the independence of the Republic of the Seven Islands (the "Ionian Islands"), and reasserted the former rules as to the Newfoundland fisheries, leaving room, however, for new arrangements by mutual agreement.

The complacency of Hawkesbury appears in the fact that he at once sent news of this compact to Grenville, who received it with the utmost concern and indignation. "At no period of the greatest difficulty" (so he wrote to Dundas), "did I ever entertain an idea of agreeing to concessions that can be named with these." And he declared that he could not remain silent respecting sacrifices which would bring only a short interval of repose. Thomas Grenville thought the maintenance of a strong navy to be far more important than the details of the compact. Pitt, also, regarded peace as very precarious; but, while regretting the surrender of the Cape and the vagueness of the Maltese settlement, he pronounced the Treaty honourable[1]. This verdict he amplified during the debate of November 3rd. Grenville and several other Pittites having bitterly attacked the Peace, the ex-Prime-Minister declared that the retrocessions of the Cape and Malta were matter for regret; but certain authorities held them to be of secondary value (a statement backed by the vigorous assertions of Nelson in the Upper House), and he believed Ceylon to be far more important than the Cape for the defence of India. As to the Mediterranean, that was a sphere of secondary import, when compared with the East and West Indies. In these last, we had secured Trinidad, more valuable for its wealth and its strategic position than Martinique, Guadaloupe or St Lucia. With respect to our former Allies, Naples, Sardinia and Portugal had made peace with the enemy, and we were not bound to do more for them; also, the claims of the House of Orange were still under consideration. As regards the French Royal House, we had never insisted on its restoration, but merely declared such a settlement to be the best safeguard for peace and security. In conclusion, he predicted that, if Bonaparte wished to establish a military despotism, this nation had proved itself so redoubtable that it would not be the first object of his attack. If the wishes of France corresponded to our own, we might

[1] *Dropmore Papers*, VII. 47–50.

hope for a long term of peace. The motion in favour of the Treaty, in spite of sharp attacks, was carried without a division. Pitt's pronouncement, while unsatisfactory even on the score of consistency, evinced small strategic insight and a lamentable lack of political foresight. At nearly every point, Grenville's sagacious pessimism was destined to be justified, at the expense of Pitt's kindly optimism. Public opinion was sharply divided as to the terms of peace. The *Times*, *Sun*, *Herald* and *True Briton* defended them, while sharp criticisms came from the *Morning Post*, *Morning Chronicle*, *Courier*, *Star*, *St James's Chronicle*, and, most of all, from Cobbett's *Porcupine*. Canning declared that the unreflecting multitude welcomed peace, while, after conversation with "many persons, merchants, planters and gentlemen," he found a universal condemnation of its conditions[1].

But worse was to follow. The Addington Cabinet now added to its mistakes by sending to Amiens, for the redaction of the definitive Treaty, the Marquis Cornwallis, who had lately described himself to a friend as out-of-sorts, low-spirited, and tired of everything[2]. Though well supported by Merry, this weary negotiator utterly failed to hold his own against Joseph Bonaparte and Talleyrand; and the serious rebuffs sustained at Amiens were with reason ascribed to the "drowsiness" and utter want of experience of Cornwallis[3]. It is impossible within our limits even to refer to the negotiations. After numerous surrenders by Cornwallis, the terms of the Treaty of Amiens (March 25th, 1802) repeated those of the Preliminaries of London, except that (1) Portugal now surrendered part of her Guiana territory to France; (2) the Maltese compromise was defined in Article X, consisting of 13 clauses, the purport of which will appear later; (3) the Cape was ceded to the Dutch "in full sovereignty"; (4) the House of Orange was promised an indemnity, not at the expense of the Dutch Republic. It soon transpired that the indemnity would be found in the Germanic body, then in a state of flux owing to the Secularisations.

The omissions from the Treaty were also remarkable. It did not require that Bonaparte should evacuate Dutch territory or recognise the independence either of that Republic or of the Helvetic and Ligurian (Genoese) Republics. In his Treaty of Lunéville with Austria, he had undertaken to respect their independence; but events were to prove that the Addington Government erred in not insisting

---

[1] *The Windham Papers*, II. 174.
[2] *Cornwallis Corresp.* III. 382.
[3] Malmesbury, *Diaries*, IV. 71, 261; *Eng. Hist. Rev.* April, 1900.

on a similar contract. Neither did the Treaty of Amiens stipulate the
renewal of a treaty of commerce with France, Addington declaring on
May 3rd that he opposed such a measure. Therefore British merchants
soon saw their products virtually shut out not only from France, but
from the French Colonies which Great Britain now restored. The
Treaty, also, effected little for the House of Orange, and nothing for
that of Savoy, both of which, in 1793, we had undertaken to uphold.
Above all, in face of the well-marked trend of Bonaparte's oriental
policy, the Peace of Amiens surrendered the keys of India, viz., the
Cape and Malta, to weak authorities over whom he could readily
acquire complete control. It reestablished at Valetta the Order of
the Knights of St John (much enfeebled by recent events), required
the speedy withdrawal of the British garrison and the temporary
admission of 2000 Neapolitan troops, and placed the island under
the guarantee of the Great Powers. Obviously, these arrangements
were precarious; and the events of the next few months proved that,
while extending his power in Europe, Bonaparte was resolved to make
the Mediterranean a French lake and to recommence the plans which
had been shorn asunder by the genius of Nelson.

CHAPTER III

THE CONTEST WITH NAPOLEON
1802–1812

I

A TREATY of peace has small chance of surviving, unless it corresponds to the vital needs of the signatories. If it cramps the expansive energies of great nations, it will prove to be but an uneasy truce. In these fundamentals, as also in lesser details, the Peace of Amiens was radically defective. It concluded a War in which Great Britain and France parted on even terms. The British, triumphant at sea, had taken all the Colonies of France, besides expelling her troops from Egypt. The French had conquered the Belgic Provinces and large parts of Germany and Italy, but had failed to acquire any British territory. Their primacy in western and southern Europe was more than balanced by the world-supremacy achieved by the British Navy. Their commerce and industries had been held as in a vice, while, thanks to the Industrial Revolution and Sea Power, those of the United Kingdom continued steadily to advance. Strategically, the combatants had come to a stalemate. Economically, the advantage lay with the Island Power.

Nevertheless, the Addington Administration had concluded the Peace " in such an unskilful, hasty and conceding way " (the words are those of Pitt[1]), as to lead to the restitution of all the French Colonies, leave Bonaparte almost a free hand in Continental affairs, and fetter British industries and commerce. The Treaty of Amiens repeated and even exaggerated the characteristic defects of that diplomatic deadlock, the Treaty of Aix-la-Chapelle of 1748; for, while sacrificing the conquests achieved by the British Navy overseas, it failed to assure the Balance of Power on the Continent. Consequently, the military and political energies of France, now directed by the untiring brain of Bonaparte, were to have free play on the weak and crumbling States on her borders; whereas the industrial energies of the British people, far from gaining the full advantages expected from a peace, in certain quarters experienced a check; for, owing to the strange dislike of

---

[1] Malmesbury, *Diaries*, IV. 76

commercial treaties entertained by Addington and Hawkesbury, no condition as to the renewal of commercial relations was stipulated at Amiens. Accordingly, Bonaparte was free to exclude British products, not only from France and the States subject to her, but also from the French Colonies, which Great Britain restored at the Peace. On June 30th, 1802, he instructed General Andréossi, about to proceed to London as his Ambassador, that he would accord "if not a Treaty of Commerce, at least a series of private arrangements and compensations"; and to this end he sent over commercial agents, who were to visit the chief British centres. But the Addington Government, regarding them with suspicion, refused to let them proceed in their official capacity, because there was no Treaty of Commerce between the two nations; while Bonaparte declared their investigations a necessary preliminary to any such compact. Accordingly, a deadlock ensued on this important question.

Equally serious was the failure of Addington and his colleagues to require in the Treaty the recognition by Bonaparte of the independence of the Batavian, Helvetic, Cisalpine and Ligurian Republics. They regarded those questions as settled by Article 13 of the recent Austro-French Treaty of Lunéville, which stipulated the independence of those States. He, on the contrary, maintained that those stipulations concerned France and Austria, not Great Britain; and he instructed Andréossi that his "first care" must be "to prevent on every occasion any intervention of the British Government in Continental affairs." In fact, before the signature of the Treaty of Amiens, he had intervened in the affairs of the Batavian and Cisalpine States, retaining his troops in the former, securing his nomination as President of the latter (now entitled the Italian Republic), and largely deciding the character of their Constitutions. The weakness of Addington, in not formally protesting against these actions before the signature of the Peace, deprived him of the technical right of protest against further proceedings consequent upon them. But the affairs of nations are not decided by technicalities; and Bonaparte's claim to exclude Great Britain from all participation in Continental affairs was certain, if persisted in, to lead to war; for such a claim, when emphasised by the continuance of French troops in Dutch territory, implied French control of the ports facing our eastern coast and of the Cape of Good Hope. The Preliminaries of London had stipulated that Cape Town should become a free port belonging to the independent Batavian Republic; but by the Treaty of Amiens it was ceded to the Dutch "in full sovereignty"; and they were, therefore, free to dispose of it as they thought fit. Great concern was expressed on this head by Windham, Grenville and others in the debates of May 3rd–13th, 1802; and the bland optimism of Addington and Hawkesbury failed to restore confidence. Much concern was also felt at the cession by Spain of the vast territory of Louisiana to France.

Passivity or timidity also characterised the policy of the Continental monarchies; and Napoleon (his Christian name was officially used after the assumption of the Consulate for Life in August, 1802) pushed on his designs without hindrance. Supreme in the Ligurian and Italian Republics, he assured his control over that Peninsula by annexing Piedmont, Parma and Elba, in September and October respectively. Against these encroachments the British, Austrian and Neapolitan Governments alike failed to proffer any effective protests. The Tsar Alexander, preoccupied in domestic affairs and annoyed at the Maltese settlement effected at Amiens, treated Great Britain with marked coldness; and Napoleon, for a time, successfully flattered his vanity by arranging with him many of the details respecting the Secularisations of the German Ecclesiastical States. Francis II, cowed by the defeats of 1793–1800, acquiesced in the tame counsels of dull but acquisitive bureaucrats of his own stamp. At Berlin, Frederick William III followed suit. "The King's chief happiness" (wrote the British *Chargé d'affaires*, Sir George Jackson), "consists in the absence of all trouble. ...He is guided by his fears and distrusts his own powers." Furthermore, in view of the Francophil tendencies of President Jefferson, the precarious mental condition of George III, and the subservience of Charles IV of Spain to his consort's paramour, the world seemed to lie prostrate at the feet of Napoleon.

The first sign of a revival of spirit occurred early in October, 1802, when Napoleon intervened in the civil strifes of the Swiss, marched a French column into their land and bade them send delegates to Paris to accept his mediation. On this question, the Addington Cabinet acted with a show of firmness. On October 9th, Hawkesbury drew up a note expressing regret at this infraction of the Treaty of Lunéville, and a hope that France would not "further attempt to control that independent nation in the exercise of their undoubted rights." He also instructed Paget (now at Vienna) to enquire whether that Court would aid the Swiss to resist; and he despatched an agent, Moore, to concert plans with the leaders of the Federals. Both overtures failed.

Vienna, expectant of further favours from Paris, declined to move on behalf of Helvetic Independence; the Tsar was equally inert; and the Swiss Federals, overawed by a large French force, acceded to the demands of Napoleon[1].

That these events caused a marked change in Anglo-French relations, appears in the difference of tone between the Instructions of September 10th and those of November 14th, issued to Lord Whitworth when proceeding as Ambassador to Paris. The former emphasise "our desire to give proof on all occasions of our sincere disposition to cultivate a good understanding between the two countries." The latter authorise Whitworth to "state most distinctly His Majesty's determination never to forego his right of interfering in the affairs of the Continent on every occasion in which the interests of his own dominions or those of Europe in general appear to him to require it." Further, Hawkesbury pointed out that, as Talleyrand had recognised the reasonableness of Great Britain acquiring compensations for the recent extensions of French territory and influence, she might now justly claim the retention of certain of her conquests. In particular, Whitworth was charged to protest against the continued occupation of Dutch territory by French troops, seeing that we had restored important Colonies to that Republic, on consideration of its remaining entirely independent. He was to keep silence respecting the aims of British policy, especially respecting Malta; for, though we should be justified in holding that island as some counterpoise to the immense increase of French power, no decision had yet been reached on that subject. Instructions of this character proved that the Peace of Amiens was hanging by a thread. In part, the dispute resembled that which had brought the two nations to war ten years before: had the French the right to interfere with the independence of the Dutch Republic? On the present occasion, however, the menace to this independence was far more serious than in 1792–3. Then, Pitt and Grenville had resisted the French attempt to abrogate the treaty rights of the Dutch to control the Scheldt estuary. Now Addington and Hawkesbury were protesting against Napoleon's endeavour to control by armed force the policy of that people.

Moreover, the extension of his power over Italy, his keen interest in the recovery of Egypt and the partition of the Turkish empire brought Mediterranean questions to a prominence undreamt of in 1793, and made Malta a storm-centre no less threatening than that of

[1] Cobbett's *Ann. Reg.* (1803), pp. 1018–20; *Dropmore Papers*, VII. 128.

the Dutch Netherlands. Malta was an outpost of Egypt, as Egypt was of India. If the island were held only by the moribund Order of the Knights of St John, then the overland route to India would speedily pass into the hands of Napoleon. If he continued to control the Dutch Republic, then the Cape of Good Hope, and with it the sea route to the East Indies, would be at his disposal. Thus, the increase of French power in the Netherlands and on the shores of the Mediterranean in time of nominal peace was bringing within his grasp the two alternative schemes for the ruin of Great Britain which the events of 1798 seemed to have wrecked, viz. an invasion from the coast whence it can best be attempted, and a resumption of the oriental adventures cut short by the exploit of Nelson.

By the autumn of 1802, so clear were the danger signals that Addington assumed a firm tone; but, by this time, so accustomed was Napoleon to submission or complaisance that he abated not one of his demands. The protests of the Dutch Ambassador against the retention of French troops in his country were disregarded. Delegates from the Swiss Cantons were summoned to Paris to receive eventually at the hands of Napoleon the Act of Mediation, sagaciously designed by him, as Mediator, for healing their schisms and assuring his control. Spain was sinking under his control. The Turks were alarmed by French intrigues in Corfu, the Morea and the Levant, which portended a partition of their empire. Early in the year 1802, Lord Elgin, our Ambassador at Constantinople, wrote as follows: "The Porte considers her interests and tranquillity secure while England possesses Malta, but not so after our abandoning it." Whitworth, also, reported, in December, 1802, that Egypt was the great object of Napoleon's ambition and that he might acquire it by coercing or bargaining with the Turks[1].

So threatening was the outlook that public opinion in these Islands began to harden. Protests against the overbearing conduct of Napoleon multiplied in the Press and called forth angry retorts in the *Moniteur*, often from the First Consul himself. He, also, complained of the deference shown to the Comte d'Artois at Holyrood and the harbouring of French *Émigrés*. Nevertheless, Ministers, while refusing to fetter the Press or expel refugees, endeavoured to humour the First Consul. Even after the Swiss embroglio, Otto, the French agent at London, could write as follows:

[1] F.O. Turkey, 35. Elgin to Hawkesbury, January 5th, 1802; *Paget Papers*, II. 61, 72; O. Browning, *England and Napoleon*, pp. 6–10, 16, 25–9.

I have received the most peaceful assurances from the Cabinet, who mark with the greatest satisfaction anything which is likely to strengthen the control of the First Consul in home affairs, and would even wish to see his family secure the hereditary tenure of his office, a wish that is very generally felt in this country; but anything that tends to the *external* aggrandisement of this power must necessarily claim the attention of the British Minister[1].

Andréossi, who arrived early in November, had a friendly reception from the King and the Prince of Wales, who manifested a keen desire for peace, even while expressing some apprehensions, because Bonaparte was "still greater as a politician than as a warrior." Andréossi reported that the *Émigrés* in England were losing all hope. Another reassuring fact was that, on November 20th, the British Government despatched orders to the Cape of Good Hope for the withdrawal of British troops.

It is clear, then, that the Court and Cabinet were not opposed to Napoleon on personal grounds, and during some time hoped for the resumption of friendly relations with him. The King's Speech, read on November 23rd to the newly-elected Parliament, dwelt on the national prosperity (increased by a bounteous harvest), and the need of watchfulness in European affairs and of measures to guarantee our security. Thereupon, Fox, while deploring the immense aggrandisement of French power, deprecated any increase of armaments; but he, Wilberforce, Whitbread and Burdett stood alone in offering determined opposition to an increase of the army. In the ensuing debates, Lord Hobart, Secretary at War, stated that it had been reduced from 250,000 men at the end of hostilities to 127,000, whereas that of France numbered 427,000 men, and that, in face of her hostile proceedings, it was desirable to raise our total to 200,000 exclusive of the forces in India. The discussion was rendered remarkable by a speech of Sheridan, in which he declaimed vehemently against Bonaparte's encroachments, as aimed at the enslavement of Europe and the destruction of British commerce. Earl Temple and Windham complained of the apathy of Ministers and their belated and clumsy intervention on behalf of the Swiss. Grenville, also, adverted to the increase of the French and Dutch navies and to our exclusion from every port in the Mediterranean except Valetta, which therefore it was an urgent necessity for us to retain. In reply, Addington admitted the gravity of the situation, but stated that, as France, Spain and Holland together could muster only 131 sail of the line, while we possessed 196, there was no serious danger

---

[1] Coquelle, *Napoleon and England* (Eng. edit. p. 5); *Lettres inédites de Talleyrand*, p. 24.

of invasion. Hawkesbury advised the country to "try the experiment of continuing the Peace," because the maintenance even of the proposed large forces would cost £25,000,000 a year less than war. In the main, the debates showed the rising indignation of the people at the overbearing conduct of Napoleon—a feeling that pervades the Sonnets of Wordsworth of the autumn of 1802. It is, indeed, unquestionable that Napoleon's interference in Swiss affairs, now as in 1798, contributed, even more than issues of greatest practical import, such as the subjugation of the Dutch, to inflame popular resentment[1]. It found expression in newspaper articles couched in terms so disrespectful as to elicit formal and bitter complaints. Despite the reply, that the Press of this country was free, and that its alleged insults were no more objectionable than those against England which appeared in Napoleon's own official *Moniteur*, he raised the affair to the level of high policy, until, as will duly appear, the Addington Ministry, in its desire of placating him, prosecuted one of the most conspicuous offenders.

The year 1803 opened gloomily. As Windham phrased it, France was roaming at will all over the world, and the Addington Cabinet said in effect: "Go where you please, so that you keep your hands off us." Our troops were about to evacuate Egypt and the Cape, and arrangements were proceeding for their withdrawal from Malta, when an alarming incident occurred. On January 30th, the *Moniteur* published a menacing Report of Colonel Sebastiani on his mission to the East. Though ostensibly he was merely one of Napoleon's Commercial Commissioners, his Report contained next to nothing about commerce and much that portended a resumption of hostilities. It set forth the utter weakness of Turkey, her deadly feud with the Mamelukes, her discord with General Stuart, commanding the British force still in Egypt, the conclusion being that 6000 French would easily reconquer that land. The official publication of so warlike a document caused a great sensation. It was probably due to Napoleon's desire of glozing over the lamentable failure of his attempt to reconquer Hayti. The ravages wrought by fever in that expeditionary force rendered further efforts in the West Indies impossible; and, in face of the determined opposition of the United States to the French acquisition of Louisiana, he now determined to sell that vast domain to them (as he did soon after) and to concentrate on Oriental schemes that were nearer his heart. The Turco-Mameluke feuds provided an opportunity. He now turned the energies of France Eastwards by publishing Sebastiani's Report. That it would provoke Great Britain, he must have surmised.

[1] *Life of Sir S. Romilly*, 1. 425.

All his proceedings were governed by calculation; and one of his Councillors deemed this provocation intentional[1].

Another of his actions serves to strengthen this inference. In the same month, January, 1803, he issued secret instructions to General Decaen, now appointed Governor of the French East India Colonies, to proceed with a small expeditionary force to Pondicherry, there carefully to investigate Indian affairs and prepare for the future, which (so he informed him) might be such as to invest his name with lasting renown. He, also, referred to the renewal of hostilities with England as probable in September, 1804; and, since they were certain to involve the Dutch in hostilities with her, he instructed Decaen in that case to be ready to occupy the Cape or any other desirable *point d'appui*. The despatch of Decaen's expedition in March, 1803, caused some apprehension at London, which was finally to be justified by his proceedings at the Cape.

For the present, the anxiety of Ministers centred chiefly on French schemes that threatened the security of the overland route to India. From the Mediterranean came news as to movements of French troops to its coasts, especially to Corsica; and their agents were reported to be very active in the Republic of the Ionian Isles and on the coasts of Albania and the Morea. Similar information reached Petrograd. There, the sympathies of the Tsar had been Francophil. Annoyed at the terms of Article X of the Treaty of Amiens respecting Malta, he withheld his guarantee of those arrangements, and in this was followed by Prussia. But the French moves against Turkey caused him grave concern. On January 7th, 1803, Admiral Sir John Borlase Warren, British Ambassador at Petrograd, reported that, according to Russian official advices from Paris, Napoleon was about to notify to Russia his resolve to acquire the Morea. Prince Czartoryski, Foreign Minister, when confirming that information, added that the Emperor Alexander disapproved these projects of partition; and on January 20th he told Warren that the Emperor Alexander "wished the English to keep Malta." On February 27th, he stated that Napoleon "wished to oblige Great Britain to declare war against France." On March 25th, Warren reported that the Russian Government "would even be sorry that the British troops evacuated the island," and favoured the issue of a decisive declaration by us such as would "finish the affair[2]."

Apprehensions concerning the Levant were not confined to

---

[1] Pelet, *Opinions de Napoléon*, ch. III.

[2] F.O. Russia, 174. See, too, Hardman, *History of Malta* (chs. XVII, XXI, XXII); O. Browning, *England and Napoleon*, pp. 70 et seq.; Mollien, *Memoirs*, I. 334.

Ministerial circles in London. In a conversation which Pitt had with George Rose, he at once entered on the topic of Sebastiani's Report, deeming its publication an announcement of the actual designs of France on Egypt. The two friends agreed that her acquisition of Egypt would seriously imperil British India; also, that the intrigues of Sebastiani in the Ionian Islands, with a view to their reoccupation by France, warranted a thorough explanation[1]. So general were these fears that the Addington Administration assumed a firm attitude. On February 9th, Hawkesbury charged Whitworth not to enter into any discussion respecting Malta, until the French Government consented either to restore completely the *status quo* at the time of the Peace of Amiens, or to admit the reasonableness of our receiving some suitable compensation for the recent extensive additions to French territory.

In reply to this request no satisfactory assurance was forthcoming. Talleyrand blandly reasserted that Sebastiani's mission was "strictly commercial," and that Napoleon sincerely desired peace, which moreover was imperiously dictated to him by the penury of his finances. Shortly afterwards, on February 18th, the First Consul sent for Whitworth and treated him, not to soothing falsehoods, but to pugnacious half-truths, complaining that all the provocations came from London, that we had broken the Treaty by not evacuating Egypt and Malta, that we harboured assassins, that every wind which blew from England bore nothing but hatred. He declared that he could easily reconquer Egypt, but would not do so, lest he should seem the aggressor, besides which that land must sooner or later fall to France. Moreover, what had he to gain by a war with England? Why should not the two nations come to an understanding and so govern the world? But nothing (he proceeded) would overcome the hatred of the British Government; and the issue now was—would we fulfil the terms of the Treaty of Amiens or have war? Whitworth, thereupon, temperately set forth the material difference between the present state of things and that when peace was concluded. Napoleon cut him short: "I suppose you mean Piedmont and Switzerland: *ce sont des..., vous n'avez pas le droit d'en parler à cette heure.*" He added that Sebastiani's mission was necessitated on military grounds by our infraction of the Treaty of Amiens; but, soon afterwards, he authorised Talleyrand to state that he was contemplating a guarantee of the integrity of the Turkish empire, which would remove our fears respecting Egypt.

[1] G. Rose, *Diaries*, II, 18–20; *Papers on the Discussions with France* (1802–3), pp. 377–86.

Whitworth believed that this softening of tone was due to Russia's remonstrances against Napoleon's encroachments and his refusal to grant any suitable indemnity to the dispossessed King of Sardinia. But it seems probable that the naval unpreparedness of France, and the desire of Napoleon to assure the safe return of his unfortunate expeditionary force from Hayti, explain his subsequent manoeuvres, which the Addington Cabinet henceforth ascribed to a resolve to gain time. Hawkesbury now stiffened his demands. He pointed out that Russia and Prussia had not guaranteed the Maltese settlement, as was required by the Treaty; also, that the confiscation of the Spanish Priories of the Order of St John, and other pecuniary losses, must incapacitate the Order for the defence of the vast fortifications of Valetta and tempt Napoleon to renew his facile exploit of June, 1798. True, Article X, relating to Malta, stipulated the presence of 2000 Neapolitan troops there for a year. But of what avail was a temporary occupation by the troops of a Power which itself existed on sufferance? And what chance of survival was there for the truncated Order, now that Malta, emerging from happy obscurity, had become the crux of the Eastern Question? Indeed, the Maltese compromise of 1802 was workable only in an era of sincere goodwill, and Napoleon had made peace more dangerous than open war.

Apprehensions were also aroused by the official *View of the State of the Republic*, issued at Paris on February 21st, 1803. After dilating on the prosperity of France, and referring to the continued British occupation of Egypt and Malta, the Report stated that two parties, one of them pacific, the other warlike, struggled for mastery in England. Therefore, by a deplorable necessity, France must possess an army of half a million men, "ready to undertake its defence and avenge its injuries....Whatever success intrigues may experience in London, no other people will be involved in new combinations. The Government asserts with conscious pride that England alone cannot maintain a struggle against France." Even so, the attitude of the British Government was cautious. On February 28th, Hawkesbury instructed Whitworth to point out that Egypt had been evacuated, and all the other conditions of the Amiens Treaty had been fulfilled, except Article X; and Malta had not been evacuated, because of the refusal of Russia and Prussia to act as guarantors, the weakening of the Order of St John, and the threatening moves of France in the East. A guarantee of the integrity of the Turkish empire by France would, indeed, banish our fears regarding Egypt; but we would not withdraw from Malta until she offered some "substantial security." This was an invitation to a compromise, and, on February 28th, Andréossi assured Talleyrand that the British Ministers were peaceably inclined. This appeared in their prosecution at this time of a French *Émigré*, Peltier, who in a journal, *L'Ambigu*, had declaimed against the First Consul. Despite a brilliant defence by Sir James Mackintosh, the accused was condemned, but, when a rupture with France became imminent, punishment was deferred, and he was finally released. The French also released a few British ships that had been unjustly seized[1].

These slight relaxations of tension were nullified by the sight of the armaments proceeding in French and Dutch ports. Though designed, it was said, for Colonial expeditions, they were deemed part of the French programme announced on February 21st. Accordingly, on March 9th, a royal message was read to Parliament, inviting it to adopt further measures for the national defence, and an increase of 10,000 seamen was unanimously voted. By way of retort, the First Consul issued a Memorandum justifying the retention of French troops in Holland and Switzerland and the formation of armed camps near Calais. He also, on March 13th, subjected Whitworth to a violent tirade before the diplomatic circle at the Tuileries. The Ambassador kept his temper, and then privately intimated his resolve to cease attending receptions if he received such treatment. Napoleon seems afterwards to have regretted his outburst; for the Russian Ambassador, Markoff, resented it and forwarded to the Tsar unfavourable comments on the incident. The support of Russia being highly desirable, both disputants sought to impress the Tsar with the justice of their cause. Of late, Alexander had repelled French offers for a partition of Turkey and inclined towards a neutrality not unfavourable to us. Malmesbury, however, shrewdly surmised that now, as in the days of Catharine, Russia would cajole all the Powers, but act with none of them. Addington, more optimistic, cherished some hopes from that quarter. The chief reason, however, of his forbearance towards France was (as he privately stated to Malmesbury) his resolve to wait "till she had heaped wrong upon wrong, and made her arrogant designs so notorious, and her views of unceasing aggrandisement so demonstrable, as to leave no doubt on the public mind, nor a possibility of mistake on the part of the most uninformed pacific men[2]." That

---

[1] Cobbett, *Pol. Register* (1803), pp. 276, 289, 315, 374, 798; Coquelle (chs. IV, v); *Dropmore Papers*, VII. 140.
[2] Malmesbury, IV. 210, 246, 247.

Addington's patience and Napoleon's petulance were disgusting the nation with the peace became abundantly evident. Canning, an enthusiastic admirer of Pitt and a persistent belittler of Addington, pointed the contrast between them in his celebrated song:

> And oh! if again the rude whirlwind should rise,
> The dawning of peace should fresh darkness deform,
> The regrets of the good and the fears of the wise
> Shall turn to the Pilot that weathered the storm.

Much, however, could be urged in favour of Addington's waiting policy. Peace having been concluded, its author had to ensure for it a fair trial. Moreover, so impetuously self-willed an opponent as Napoleon was likely to put himself in the wrong. Addington, Alexander I, Fox, Metternich, Hardenberg, Castlereagh and Talleyrand were, in succession, to find out the advantage of giving him free rein at a crisis; or, as the last named phrased it: *Il n'y a jamais eu de conspirateur dangereux contre lui que lui-même*[1]. The sole hope for the preservation of peace in the spring of 1803 was that he should substitute reason for menace, and, admitting that his annexations and other proceedings had naturally alarmed Great Britain, should offer either to forego one or more of them or to admit the justice of her claim to compensation, conceded in the negotiations at Amiens.

This was the gist of Hawkesbury's note of April 3rd to Andréossi, which pointed out that France had hitherto refused to give the assurances and explanations we had a right to expect; but that a settlement was desired on the following bases: Great Britain to retain Malta in perpetuity, indemnifying the Knights of St John; France to evacuate the Dutch Netherlands and Switzerland, but to retain Elba; Great Britain to acknowledge the kingdom of Etruria and the Italian and Ligurian Republics, provided that the King of Sardinia received a suitable indemnity. These demands were large; but Hawkesbury added that, if they were deemed impracticable, the French Government should suggest "some other *equivalent security* by which His Majesty's object in claiming the permanent possession of the island of Malta may be accomplished, and the independence of the island secured." These terms, then, were merely our first word in a new negotiation[2]. In reply, Talleyrand, while urging complaints, declared that France would accord all possible satisfaction and security, short of

---

[1] Talleyrand, *Mémoires*, II. 135.
[2] Coquelle, p. 54; O. Browning, pp. 54-7.

acquiescing in our possession of Malta. But, after he had seen the First Consul, his statement became more defiant. Napoleon, he declared, would rather be cut to pieces than consent to a British acquisition of Malta, and he took his stand on the inviolability of the Treaty of Amiens. Talleyrand suggested, as alternative plans of solving the Maltese problem, either a mixed garrison of French, British, Italians and Germans in Valetta, or (as Joseph Bonaparte, also, suggested) the British possession of Corfu or Crete in lieu of Malta. Whitworth declared that nothing but the occupation of Malta for a term of years would relieve our apprehensions. Privately, however, he outlined to Hawkesbury a possible compromise, viz. either the retention of Malta for a term of years or the garrisoning merely of the fortifications of Valetta, the rest of the island being left to the Knights.

By this time, a fresh cause for apprehension had arisen. Early in April, Napoleon despatched 7000 more French troops into the Dutch Netherlands, where they occupied commanding positions. Here was an occasion for the British Government to protest against this further violation of the Treaty of Lunéville; but Hawkesbury let slip the opportunity, and allowed the discussion to turn almost entirely upon Malta. On April 13th, he approved Whitworth's proposals and suggested ten years as the minimum term for our occupation of Malta— which would admit of the construction of docks at Lampedusa, with a view to the permanent occupation of that neighbouring islet. Joseph Bonaparte, in the absence of the First Consul at St Cloud, favoured some such solution; and, on April 18th, Whitworth expressed hopes of a peaceful settlement. What, then, was his surprise three days later to hear from Talleyrand that the crux of the problem was, not the reestablishment of the Order of St John, but "the suffering Great Britain to acquire a possession in the Mediterranean!"

This brought the dispute to a climax; and the British Ministers resolved to bring it to a decisive issue. They were moved thereto by news as to the concentration of troops on the Northern coasts of France and in Zealand as if for an invasion. Further, as the French navy comprised only 40 effective sail of the line, a rupture, if it were to come, as seemed inevitable, had better come soon, while we possessed a clear superiority over the French and Dutch fleets. True, our supplies of seamen and naval stores had run dangerously low, owing to the economies of the Earl of St Vincent at the dockyards; but, even so, the advantage at sea lay with us in 1803, while in 1805 it would be precarious owing to Napoleon's control of nearly all the ports of western Europe, from Amsterdam to Spezzia[1]. His policy of coast control and the avowal of a design to exclude us from the Mediterranean threatened the national existence; and no Ministry, however pacific, dared run risks on so vital a point. All the advice that reached Downing Street was in favour of firmness. From the beginning of the crisis, George III, whose influence over the Cabinet was great, had been eager for war. The Grenvilles and Malmesbury had throughout censured Hawkesbury's proceedings as weak, undignified and certain to lead to further humiliations. Pitt, deeming himself privately pledged to support Addington, was more tolerant; but he viewed the European situation with "infinite anxiety," and after Napoleon's official Declaration of February 21st, 1803, held that we must not give up Malta "without fresh and substantial security[2]." Refusing the suggestions of several friends that they should all seek to overthrow the Cabinet, he continued to it a general support, and privately advised Lord Chatham, Master of Ordnance, to act firmly on the Maltese question. This indeed was the general opinion; and Addington, for his own credit, could not now retreat. In common with nearly all our leading politicians, he and Hawkesbury deeply distrusted Napoleon, believing him to be animated by boundless ambition, an inveterate hatred of this country and an utter disregard of principle. Thus, personal considerations, not less than regard for national security, led Ministers to insist on a speedy answer to the alternatives: either the possession of Malta for ten years, or war. To this fundamental condition, Hawkesbury on April 23rd, appended articles requiring the consent of France to the cession of Lampedusa by His Sicilian Majesty[3], the evacuation of the Dutch Netherlands within a month of the signature of a convention on these topics, and the provision of a suitable indemnity for the King of Sardinia, failing which last Great Britain would refuse to acknowledge the Italian and Ligurian Republics. If these conditions were not accepted within seven days, Whitworth was to leave Paris.

The arrival of terms so uncompromising, which in all but name formed an ultimatum, surprised Whitworth, who, in the first instance stated them informally to Talleyrand; but, when that Minister declined to receive them in this way, he repeated them officially, only to meet with a stiff refusal. He then requested an interview with the peacemaker, Joseph Bonaparte, who admitted that, in private conversations

---

[1] *Dropmore Papers*, VII. 148; *Barham Papers*, III. 68, 69; O. Browning, 44, 100, 174, 191; Coquelle, 62–5.
[2] *Dropmore Papers*, VII. 149, 151.
[3] Ferdinand IV was willing (A. Bonnefons, *Marie Caroline*, p. 261).

with the First Consul, three or four years had been named by the latter as the longest possible term for a British occupation of Malta. Joseph Bonaparte, also, now declared that he found in his brother a disposition to avoid a rupture, and that he was perplexed how to act. Whitworth, therefore, considered that negotiation was still possible, but that it was likely to be with the sole purpose of gaining time for French preparations. The First Consul had just sent off General Lauriston to London, with despatches for Andréossi, who would probably be recalled, as too Anglophil in sentiment. Talleyrand, however, also wrote to Andréossi, urging him to see Hawkesbury and try to bring him to a reasonable decision. But the British Cabinet had uttered its last word, and was now as inflexible as it had previously been complaisant. At Paris, Joseph Bonaparte and Talleyrand worked hard for peace; and their efforts can hardly but have been furthered by the arrival of news of the almost complete destruction of the French forces in Hayti. Foreseeing the effects of these tidings on the temper of the First Consul, Whitworth did not attend the Sunday reception at the Tuileries, and thus escaped the tirade prepared for him, which in fractions was vented on those present.

Various expedients were resorted to by the friends of peace for the purpose of delaying Whitworth's departure from Paris, fixed for May 3rd. Joseph Bonaparte sent a belated proposal to hand over Malta to Russia, which Whitworth declined to consider. Talleyrand pointed out, that the final British terms would in any case necessitate a consultation of all the Powers named as guarantors in Article X— a proceeding evidently designed to gain time. The final proposal, that, after Malta had been in British hands for a term of years, it should revert to Russia, met with some support from Whitworth, as calculated to humour Bonaparte, whose violent temper, if crossed at all points, might lead to something desperate. Markoff did not think the Tsar would accede to this plan, and, on May 7th, Hawkesbury brushed aside all these proposals as "loose, indefinite and unsatisfactory," adding that he had authentic information that Russia would not consent to garrison Malta. Nevertheless, he sent to Whitworth Instructions practically identical with those of April 23rd. But Napoleon would not hear of a longer occupation of Malta than a year or two. In a Council of seven persons held at St Cloud on May 11th only two, Joseph Bonaparte and Talleyrand, were for peace. The others followed the First Consul, in approving a course certain to lead to a rupture.

Unfortunately, the war party was now strengthened by the arrival of an offer from the Tsar to intervene in the Maltese affair; and this was taken as a sign of his intention to support France. Afterwards, Napoleon would not listen to any pacific proposal, even from his brother. Accordingly, Whitworth quitted Paris on May 12th, having been delayed (as he phrased it) by "infamous chicanery." On the morrow, Talleyrand sent after him a note, evidently inspired by the First Consul, setting forth with much acerbity the faults of the British Government, dilating on his championship of the sanctity of Treaties, and declaring that, if France gave way now, she would next be required to destroy her harbours, fill up her canals, and ruin her manufactures. He charged Great Britain with insulting the French nation and aiming at the destruction of the Order of St John; and he once more offered to place Malta under the control of either Russia, or Austria, or Prussia. Hawkesbury declined the proposal, as calculated merely to spin out the negotiation. Whitworth embarked at Calais on May 17th, and was received in London somewhat coolly by Ministers as having exceeded his Instructions and listened to dilatory proposals. He, for his part, privately criticised Hawkesbury and stated that France, being unprepared for war, would have given way about Malta, if our terms had not been so specific. Certainly, Joseph Bonaparte, Talleyrand, and a few other leading men, desired peace even at the price of extensive concessions; but the British Ministers had become convinced that Napoleon's sole aim was to gain time until the naval situation became less unfavourable. Talleyrand, finally, declared that, if the British Government had humoured Napoleon to some extent, he would have made them a present of Malta[1]. No words of the First Consul bear out that statement.

In one important matter, however, the Addington Cabinet had offended Russia. If we may trust the statements of Vorontzoff, Russian Ambassador at London, he had, previous to the rupture, handed to Hawkesbury the Tsar's offer of mediation on the Maltese affair. No notice was taken of this offer; and, after the outbreak of war, Vorontzoff was astounded by Addington's statement in the House of Commons that, if such mediation had been offered, due regard would have been paid to it. To his request for an explanation, Hawkesbury replied that he had not had time to bring the matter before the King, but would take an early opportunity of doing so. As will shortly appear, Fox pressed the House to declare in favour of Russia's mediation, and Ministers complied; but, after Hawkesbury's evasion, Alexander, of

[1] O. Browning, 224–69; Malmesbury, IV. 250–4.

course, refused to deal with the Addington Cabinet. Well might Vorontzoff declare that our Foreign Office "spoilt all[1]."

In a question so complex as that of the rupture of the Peace of Amiens it is not easy to adjust the responsibility with any approach to exactitude. That the British Government was, in a technical sense, guilty is obvious; and there is no force in the plea that the terms of that Peace were unworkable; for the men who signed it were also those who infringed Article X. Moreover, in the last stages of the negotiation, their insistence was so rigid as to expose them to the charge of breaking the peace of the world in order to acquire Malta. Further, their procedure was inconsistent. In the month of April, 1803, they assumed an unbending attitude, which was all the more surprising and annoying by contrast with their tame acquiescence throughout nearly the whole of the year 1802. Doubtless, their intention finally was to impress Napoleon with the power of the British Government to make out a good case, and of the nation to support it, if need be, by force of arms. If so, the change was belated and abrupt. Probably, it seemed to him unreal; for it evoked from him further efforts at intimidation, nor did he lower his tone until, to his surprise, he discovered the imminence of hostilities which might cost him an expeditionary force. There seems, therefore, good ground for concluding that Addington and his colleagues never recovered the ground lost by their previous tame acquiescence, and that, by the end of the year 1802, Napoleon had concluded that they were amenable to methods of intimidation which he had found successful in every other instance. A study of history should have revealed to him the error of coercing the Island Power overmuch. But it should, also, have prescribed to the British Government the maxim *Principiis obsta*, in dealing with a man who both in power and ambition dwarfed Lewis XIV. Moreover, they took no steps effectively to explain the British case; and by failing to bring home to the public Napoleon's violations of the Treaties of Lunéville and Amiens, and by letting the whole stress lie on Malta (the weakest part of their case) they appeared before the world as treaty-breakers, while he figured as the champion of international justice. No important negotiations have ever been more signally mismanaged than those of Amiens and their sequel by Addington and Hawkesbury. From this censure however, the impartial critic will except Whitworth, who, throughout, tempered firmness with discretion, manliness with extreme forbearance.

[1] G. Rose, *Diaries*, II. 41–4. Vorontzoff detested Hawkesbury. See Malmesbury, IV. 192, 247, 253.

On the other hand, it must be admitted that for a self-respecting Power to keep at peace with Napoleon was at all times difficult, and in 1803 wellnigh impossible. His military and civic triumphs filled him with boundless confidence and swelled his inordinate pride. The diplomatic success over Great Britain gained at Amiens transcended the fondest hopes of Frenchmen[1]. Yet every month of peace aggrandised his power, and so swift was the transformation as to bewilder all beholders. Great Britain, who both could and ought to have protested at the first infraction of the Treaties of Lunéville and Amiens, was informed by him that the former Treaty did not concern her; and her statesmen, intent on the "experiment of continuing the Peace," failed to insist emphatically on the maintenance of the order of things established by those Treaties. But this technical omission could not bind their hands indefinitely; and, when even the Orient came within the sweep of Napoleon's designs, they could not but intervene. They did so awkwardly, even clumsily. They took no effective steps to concert with Russia measures such as would, probably, have imposed moderation on the First Consul. And when her offer of mediation arrived it received cavalier treatment, which was destined to postpone for a year all hope of an Anglo-Russian alliance.

These shortcomings, however, arose from slackness and incompetence, not from lust of domination. In view of the Eastern projects of Napoleon, it was but reasonable for Great Britain to require the occupation of Malta during a period which would admit of the construction of docks at Lampedusa, which islet would then serve as a Mediterranean base, while Malta reverted to the Maltese. In the circumstances, nothing short of this could safeguard the interests of Great Britain in the Levant. Her retirement from the Mediterranean at the end of 1796 had given free play to the Oriental designs of 1798, which had been directed against India. Her exclusion from that sea and its domination by France were clearly the aims of Napoleon in gaining control over large parts of its coastline in 1802–3. A Peace so fertile in menacing aggressions was no peace; and for its rupture he was in effect responsible. Doubtless, he would in any case have made war, so soon as the French and Dutch navies were ready; and his Instructions to Decaen point to the autumn of 1804 as the probable time[2]. Thus, the Addington Administration, notwithstanding all the futility of its procedure, was right in its final resolve to bring matters to an

---

[1] Pasquier, *Mémoires*, I. 161.
[2] For Decaen's doings at the Cape see *Eng. Hist. Rev.* January, 1900.

immediate issue. News that arrived from Naples justified their decision. Our Ambassador there, à Court, wrote to Hawkesbury, on April 20th, that the French Envoy, Alquier, had required the Government to make common cause with France against Great Britain; for (said Alquier) "the interests of the two countries are the same....It is the intention of France to shut every port to the English from Holland to the Turkish dominions, to prevent the exportation of her merchandise and to give a mortal blow to her commerce, for there she is most vulnerable. Our joint forces may wrest from her hands the island of Malta." Acton, in reply, refused to violate the neutrality of Ferdinand towards his former Ally[1]. These tidings from Naples clinched the evidence that Napoleon was planning a war of annihilation against the Island Power[2].

The British Government declared war on May 18th; and, on that same day, H.M. frigate *Doris*, after a running fight, captured off Ushant an armed French lugger which resisted detention. The conduct of the *Doris* was perhaps a little severe, Admiral Cornwallis, who commanded the squadron off Brest, having on May 16th ordered his cruisers merely to detain French vessels[3]. Infuriated by this event, the First Consul ordered the detention of all British males of military age then in France, a tyrannical act which more than anything else tended to make our people wholehearted in the War. These incidents and the diatribes of Napoleon against *la perfide Albion* tended to popularise a War which the great mass of Frenchmen had previously disliked. On this side of the Channel, the contest was at first taken up somewhat doubtfully. Parliament was kept in the dark as to the merits of the case, and not until May 23rd was it in possession of information sufficient for a debate. Fox, Grey and Whitbread protested against the rupture. The views of Fox were a curious mixture of fatuity and good sense. To his friends he had long been declaring that Bonaparte was really afraid of war, and that the French annexation of Piedmont and treatment of Germany were defensible. As for Malta and Egypt, he belittled their importance, and more than once asserted that the question of Peace or War was bound up with that of turning out the Addington Ministry. On the other hand, he saw clearly that we could not possibly help the Swiss, and that war with France would probably

---

[1] F.O. Sicily and Naples, 54.

[2] French troops soon reoccupied the heel of Italy, an act which the French Foreign Office sought to justify by reference to an alleged secret article of the Treaty of Amiens, which had no existence. See *Eng. Hist. Rev.* April, 1900, pp. 331–5.

[3] J. Leyland, *Blockade of Brest*, I. 14.

tend to aggrandise her power[1]. In his speech of May 23rd, he declared vehemently that the War was all about "bare Malta, unconnected with any great, general, generous interest of Europe"; but he concluded by strongly urging acceptance of the recent proposal of the Emperor of Russia to mediate between us and France on the Maltese question. Hawkesbury made a lame reply, stating that, while he sympathised with the end proposed, yet its realisation must cause hesitation, delay and the enfeebling of the nation's effort. Pitt, also, applauded the motives of Fox, but advised trust in the Government as to the time and manner of giving them effect. Above all, he pleaded for unity in the prosecution of the struggle for national security. Finally, Hawkesbury promised to use all possible means for coming to an understanding with Russia respecting the subject in dispute. On May 28th, he drew up a Note requesting the Tsar to mediate, not merely respecting Malta, but also in the affairs of Europe. The following was suggested as a basis: Great Britain to retain Malta, unless France would either renounce all her Italian possessions and reinstate the King of Sardinia, or retire from the Belgic Provinces, placing them under some powerful sovereign. The Tsar waved aside these proposals, probably from dislike and distrust of the Addington Cabinet.

The tongue-tied *gaucherie* of Ministers, when contrasted with the effective diatribes of Bonaparte, created so general a prejudice against Great Britain as to preclude much hope of her finding an Ally. Consequently, she had to trust to the pressure of maritime warfare; and the course of the War was to reveal the slowness of such methods, when contrasted with the swift action of the Land Power, possessing the central position and nearly all the strategic points, from the Texel to the heel of Italy. The first events of the War, as Fox foretold, at once aggrandised the might of Napoleon. Having already massed a considerable force in the Dutch Netherlands, he launched it against Hanover, despite the Declaration of George III, as Elector and Prince of the Empire, on May 16th, that he would maintain strict neutrality. The Tsar, though guarantor of the Germanic System, offered no effective protest against the invasion of Hanover, and the King of Prussia, guarantor of the neutrality of Northern Germany, likewise maintained a prudent reserve, probably because he had been cajoled or coerced by General Duroc, despatched by Napoleon to Berlin in March, 1803. Hanover, therefore, was occupied without opposition by General Mortier. He concluded with the Duke of Cambridge, at

[1] *Memorials of C. J. Fox*, III. 372, 381, 384, 388, 391.

Suhlingen, a Capitulation, which George III refused to ratify. Mortier therefore, treated the Electorate as a conquered land. Its revenues were controlled by France and her troops were supported by the population. Napoleon, also, excluded British commerce from the north-western coast of Germany, which was, therefore, blockaded by the British fleet[1]. The consequent stagnation of trade in Germany induced the Tsar to undertake a negotiation for a general settlement, on the basis of the evacuation by France of the Dutch Netherlands, Switzerland and all Italy (except Piedmont), Malta also being occupied for a time by Russian troops. To these proposals neither belligerent acceded, Napoleon deeming them excessive, while the British Government feared to place Malta as a pledge in Russian hands. There were some grounds for this mistrust. Alexander had taken the Republic of the Ionian Isles under his suzerainty and was now seeking to gain a foothold in Albania and the Morea. The designs of Napoleon were similar, but far wider, extending to the eventual partition of the Turkish dominions. At present, these schemes clashed. But what guarantee was there that, so soon as Malta was in Alexander's hands, he would not become an accessory to the designed partition?

In the Mediterranean, circumstances favoured Great Britain far more than in the North Sea. True, Napoleon marched a large force to hold the heel of Italy and menace Sicily, Corfu, the Morea and Egypt. But the menace was hollow, so long as a strong British fleet held that Sea. Conscious of the cardinal importance of Levantine interests, the Cabinet despatched to Malta a powerful fleet under Nelson. His Instructions, of date May 18th, 1803, bade him protect Malta, Naples, Sicily, the Ionian Isles and any part of the Turkish dominions that was threatened, while preventing Spanish warships from joining the French[2]. It soon appeared that there was no immediate prospect of a Franco-Spanish Alliance; but Nelson was fully occupied in covering the Levant and watching the French in Toulon and southern Italy. Their designs on Corfu and the Morea caused general anxiety. The Porte, alarmed by French and Russian intrigues in Albania and the Morea, heard with much satisfaction of the arrival of Nelson's fleet at Malta; for its presence at that commanding port sufficed to sterilise the Oriental schemes of the two potentates. Fresh light was thrown on Russian designs by a letter which Pitt received from the young Earl of Aberdeen, dated Patras,

---

[1] Garden, VIII. 193; *Paget Papers*, II. 92; *Dropmore Papers*, VII. 151.
[2] Nicolas, V. 68; also V. 87, 107, 110, 166, 282.

November 10th, 1803. The Earl, after a lengthy tour in the Morea, expressed his sympathy with the downtrodden Greeks, but added: "the Russians are more detested than even the Turks themselves. They have conceived such an idea of the ignorance and barbarity of that nation as renders it perfectly impossible for the Greeks to view their conquests with a favourable eye, notwithstanding their being of the same race, and other circumstances tending to promote a friend-ship[1]."

Seeing that Great Britain regarded the Turkish empire as a bulwark against French or Russian moves towards India, accord with Alexander I was difficult. And, early in the year 1804, another com-plication occurred. The childish behaviour of George III betokened a return of his mental malady. The change caused much apprehension, not only in England but in every Court friendly to us; for, in case of another attack of lunacy, large powers would be wielded by the Prince of Wales, still a patron of Fox and the pacifist group[2]. This consideration, the political nullity of Ministers, and the coy abstention of Pitt from public life, depressed British prestige, and nothing worthy of note occurred until the spring of 1804. Then, the participation of certain subordinate British Ministers in the Pichegru-Cadoudal plot for kidnapping or murdering Napoleon, brought fresh discredit on the Administration—a farcical sequel to the affair being the fooling of Francis Drake, our Envoy at Munich, by an *agent provocateur* of Fouché's, Méhée de la Touche[3]. This affair, and the inefficient preparations of Ministers against a French invasion, helped to pre-cipitate a crisis which had long been imminent; and, near the end of April, Addington advised the King (who had now in some measure recovered) to send for Pitt.

The opportunity now again presented itself of forming a truly national Administration, such as had been proposed in 1794. But now, as then, the bitter prejudices of the King against Fox led him to veto Pitt's proposal to include the Whig leader and his followers. Nothing could bend the royal will. The results were disastrous; for the Gren-villes and Windham had latterly united with Fox to overthrow Addington, and now declined to join a Cabinet formed "on a principle of exclusion." Their abstention, especially that of Grenville, was a national misfortune; for it deprived the country of his great experience

---

[1] Pitt MSS. 104 (Pub. Record Office).
[2] *Dropmore Papers*, VII. 214, 223; G. Rose, *Diaries*, chs. II, III; Malmesbury, IV. 288.   [3] For evidence see Rose, *Life of Napoleon*, I. 450–4.

and stern objectivity, which in time past had so often corrected the
sanguine viewiness of Pitt. The Prime-Minister now assigned the
Foreign Office to the Earl of Harrowby, the Dudley Ryder of Pitt's
happier days at Cambridge and Wimbledon. In 1789–91, Ryder
served as Under-Secretary for Foreign Affairs with the Duke of Leeds,
and afterwards as Paymaster of the Forces and Vice-president of the
Board of Trade. In the House, his knowledge of currency questions
and power of exposition gained him repute. He was raised to the
peerage, as first Earl of Harrowby, in 1803. Uncertain health and
temper limited the circle of his friends, but these recognised his
abilities, and augured for him a distinguished career at the Foreign
Office. Hawkesbury now went to the Home Office, Camden to the
War Office, and Melville (formerly Henry Dundas) to the Admiralty,
from which St Vincent gladly retired. Addington was shelved; but six
of his colleagues were retained by Pitt. Party spirit was by no means
assuaged by these arrangements, completed in May, 1804; but the
genius of Pitt and the recovery of the King's health now encouraged
our former Allies to regard less unfavourably an Alliance with Great
Britain.

Thus, at last, she emerged from the discredit into which the
Addington Cabinet had allowed her to sink; but in regard neither to
home nor to foreign politics was her situation so favourable as it had
been at the beginning of 1801, when Pitt and Grenville resigned office.
The weakness and incapacity of their successors may justly be considered as the fundamental cause of the defective Treaty of Peace, of
its infraction by Napoleon, and of the resumption of hostilities under
conditions far less propitious than those which had marked the close
of the Revolutionary War.

II

The month of May, 1804, which saw the return of Pitt to office,
was marked, also, by the proclamation of the French Empire. That
dramatic event, a sequel to the kidnapping and execution of the Duc
d'Enghien, caused not less satisfaction to the French Jacobins, most
of whom welcomed the advent of a dynasty stained with the blood
of a Bourbon, than abhorrence to other Emperors. But, whereas
Francis II (still German Emperor) resorted to the tame rejoinder
of declaring himself, Francis I, Hereditary Emperor of Austria,
Alexander I evinced great indignation and for a time suspended diplomatic relations with France. There were, however, few signs that he,

still less that Francis, would draw the sword on behalf of the Bourbons or to avenge the Duc d'Enghien, as Gustavus IV of Sweden desired. In the previous winter, that monarch had received from Paris tempting offers for a Franco-Swedish alliance with a view to obtaining the use of the Swedish fleet for the invasion of England. In return for this help, Napoleon offered him Norway at the cost of Denmark, the latter Power to acquire Bremen and Verden. Prussia he tempted by the offer of Swedish Pomerania and part of Hanover[1]. Gustavus, then on a lengthened tour in Germany, rejected these degrading proposals, and made repeated overtures to her leading States for a monarchical crusade. His eccentric behaviour and extravagant profession of faith did little to recommend the scheme.

The first signs of a *rapprochement* between Russia and Great Britain appeared early in 1804 owing to their alarm at the intrigues of Napoleon in Albania and the Morea. On March 9th, the Tsar's Foreign Minister, Prince Czartoryski, wrote to Vorontzoff, Russian Ambassador at London, expressing satisfaction at Great Britain's intention to oppose a French partition of the Ottoman Empire. On March 10th, Warren reported a similar resolve on the part of the Tsar. A Russian force had left Sevastopol for Corfu, and it was hoped that Great Britain would send troops to Malta to cooperate. Thus, out of the revival of the Eastern Question sprang the Anglo-Russian accord of 1804[2]. It was furthered by sympathy with the dispossessed King of Sardinia and anxiety respecting the kingdom of Naples. Here, the royal authority existed on sufferance only. Soon after his rupture with Great Britain, Napoleon ordered French troops into Neapolitan territory in defiance of his Treaty of Florence with Ferdinand IV. Moreover, by occupying the heel of Italy the French threatened the Russians at Corfu and the anarchic western provinces of Turkey. British and Russian policy, therefore, began to converge on the object of expelling the French from southern Italy. Since Russia could do little in the Mediterranean without the protection of the British fleet, which needed Malta as base, Alexander ought to have acquiesced in Britain's occupation of that island, which he alone could not possibly hold against the French fleet. Naval considerations, therefore, should have led him to forego his claim to Malta; but, as will duly appear, he revived it, thereby nearly ruining the Anglo-Russian entente. Moreover, Russia's demands for subsidies were lofty, and on so vast a problem as the future settle-

---

[1] F.O. Austria, 73. C. Stuart to Hawkesbury, March 10th, 1804.
[2] Rose, *Third Coalition*, pp. viii–x.

ment of Europe there arose certain differences of opinion. During the summer of 1804 discussions proceeded satisfactorily, but, on October 10th, Harrowby wrote that Russia and Austria seemed not disinclined to join in schemes for a partition of Turkey which Napoleon was dangling before them[1]. Accordingly, Russian overtures were scrutinised closely, especially when they were followed by a demand for the evacuation of Malta. Apparently, Alexander hoped that the increasing power of Napoleon and the growing difficulties of Great Britain would induce her to surrender that island.

The general situation was complicated by Napoleon's seizure of Sir George Rumbold, British Minister-resident in the Free City of Hamburg; and by the rupture between Great Britain and Spain. The former incident illustrates the methods of the Land Power, the latter those of the Sea Power. On the flimsy pretext that British Envoys on the Continent had conspired against him, Napoleon, on October 7th, ordered Fouché, Minister of Police, to prepare to carry off Rumbold from his residence on the river-front at Hamburg[2]. On the 24th, the seizure was skilfully effected, and Rumbold, with all his papers, was hurried off to Paris. Not even the eagerness of Bonaparte and the guile of Fouché could detect signs of conspiracy in the papers. Moreover, the violation of the territory of a Free City, which was under the protection of the Tsar and the guardianship of Frederick William, constituted a challenge to both those potentates. The Prussian monarch, as Protector of the Circle of Lower Saxony, sent to Paris a pressing request for Rumbold's liberation, with which the French Emperor ungraciously complied[3]. The incident showed that the Corsican vendetta spirit, incarnate in Napoleon, would stoop to any outrage calculated to wreak revenge upon the hated islanders and drive them from the Continent.

The same month, however, witnessed a high-handed infraction of the law of nations by Great Britain at sea. True, she had grave cause of complaint against the Court of Madrid for its breaches of neutrality in the present conflict; but it could plead *force majeure*. By the Convention of October 19th, 1803, Spain had agreed to pay to Napoleon the yearly sum of 72,000,000 francs. Further, the *Aigle*, a French '74, had long been in harbour at Cadiz, and five French warships took refuge at Corunna, remaining in harbour for months, and necessitating the

[1] *Third Coalition*, p. 47.
[2] *Nap. Corr.* No. 8100.
[3] G. Jackson, *Diaries*, I. 242–52; Malmesbury, *Diaries*, IV. 330–5; Hardenberg, *Denkwürdigkeiten*, II. 94 *et seq.*

presence of British ships under Cochrane to observe them. Indeed, Napoleon acted in a way which implied control over those dockyards; and Melville, in a review of the naval situation on July 3rd, stated that we must regard the Spanish fleet as a probable enemy[1]. The repeated protests of Frere, British Ambassador at Madrid, against Spain's infraction of neutrality, were ignored or explained away, until, in September, news arrived that some 1500 French troops were marching from Bayonne to Corunna to reinforce the crews of the five ships; and Cochrane forwarded information as to extensive naval preparations there and at Cadiz. The British Government, thereupon, sent orders to Frere to leave Madrid unless he received satisfactory assurances. But it, also, resolved to seize four Spanish treasure-ships which were reported as soon due at Cadiz. On September 18th, the Admiralty issued orders to Admiral Cornwallis, commanding the British fleet off Brest to detach two frigates, which, with other ships from the Straits or off Cadiz, were to detain the treasure-ships. Unfortunately, Captain Graham Moore of the *Indefatigable* could pick up only two more British frigates before October 5th, when he sighted the four armed Spaniards; and Spanish pride scouted the thought of surrender to a nearly equal force. In the ensuing conflict, one of the Spaniards blew up, and the others were overpowered and captured. The Admiralty Instructions clearly contemplated the muster of enough British ships to banish all thought of resistance. Even in that case, to capture four armed treasure ships before a declaration of war constituted a breach of the Law of Nations. The British Government, therefore, erred, first, in not taking an earlier opportunity to bring matters to a decisive issue; secondly, in deferring action until the Spanish treasure-ships were nearing home; thirdly, in not assuring the despatch of a sufficient force to satisfy the *amour propre* of the Spanish commander. Frere did not leave Madrid until November 10th, and was of opinion that, apart from this unfortunate incident, a rupture must have occurred[2]. But it came about in a way detrimental to British prestige, and made an unfavourable impression on the Tsar, thereby increasing the difficulty of an Anglo-Russian *rapprochement*.

This development was to be furthered by the arrival at Petrograd of a far abler Ambassador than Warren, who begged to be recalled for service afloat[3]. Lord Granville Leveson-Gower, first Lord Gran-

---

[1] *Nap. Corr.* 7007, 7098, 7113, 7742; Nicolas, v. 484; *Barham Papers,* III. 42.
[2] J. Leyland, *Blockade of Brest,* II. 34, 36, 64, 87–9, 126; Nicolas, v. 241; *Parl. Debates,* III. 74, 89, 91. [3] Czartoryski, *Memoirs,* I. 319; Malmesbury, *Diaries,* IV. 254.

ville (1773–1846), was a devoted Pittite, who in 1800 had been appointed a Lord of the Treasury. He arrived at Petrograd early in November, 1804. His Instructions, dated October 10th, bade him assist in the Austro-Russian accord, arrange for a suitable compromise between Austria and Sardinia in North Italy, and set right a mis-understanding that had arisen as to the proposed Anglo-Russian operations in South Italy. Harrowby pointed out that, if the French seized the whole of southern Italy, and perhaps Sicily also, the pro-visioning of Nelson's fleet would become so difficult as greatly to increase the chances of the Toulon fleet capturing the Russian force at Corfu, and gaining a foothold in the Morea. Even these arguments produced little effect at Petrograd; for larger questions now arose to overshadow them.

Alexander had decided to lay the basis of a new European System, and for this purpose despatched to London his confidant and counsellor, Novossiltzoff, who was charged to communicate direct with Pitt and Harrowby. His Instructions, dated September 11th [O.S.] 1804, pre-scribe as guiding principles the liberation of Europe from Napoleonic control and the establishment of institutions "founded on the sacred rights of humanity." France is to be restrained within just limits, Sardinia and other States gaining at her expense. A Federal System is suggested for Germany. Above all, European Peace will be guaranteed by a league of the Great Powers, headed by Russia and Great Britain, a Code of International Law being drawn up for the guidance of all States, binding them to use their united forces against any member guilty of its infraction. A partition of the Turkish empire is hinted at as possible; and the document closes with the suggestion that, if other States gain in territory, the two protagonists should secure equivalent advantages; Great Britain, however, being urged to mitigate her Maritime Code. This ideal programme was corporealised by Czartoryski in a secret Memorandum, which placed Alexander on the throne of a Great Poland comprising the "kingdom of Prussia"; as an equivalent for which Austria was to absorb Bavarian and Suabian lands, Frederick William annexing States in western Germany, and even the Dutch Netherlands, if necessary. Turkey was to be left alone, until she should somehow dissolve into a Federation of States acknow-ledging Alexander as "Protector of the Slavs of the East." Whether this secret Memorandum received the Tsar's authorisation or was merely Czartoryski's pro-Polish gloss on his phrase "equivalent advantages," is far from clear. Alexander, more than once, drew up a lofty programme and left to subordinates its reduction to profitable practice. In any case, Novossiltzoff's mission bristled with difficulties. He had to humour the Anglophil Vorontzoff, and yet lower British maritime claims; to remould the Continent on ideal principles by means of a Coalition likely to prove distressingly worldly; and, if possible, to arrange for the peaceful demise of Turkey and the resurrection of Poland at the expense of the Tsar's expected Ally, Prussia. It is not surprising that Czartoryski finally declared that "Novossiltzoff did not execute the mission to our satisfaction[1]."

His further statement that neither Pitt nor Vorontzoff approved all the Russian proposals is open to question; for there is documentary proof that Pitt acceded to the most important of them. Harrowby having been injured by an accident just after the preliminary interviews, Lord Mulgrave at the close of 1804 came to supervise affairs at the Foreign Office; but the negotiation for the Third Coalition needed the action, not of a *locum tenens*, but of the Prime-Minister. In a long Note of January 19th, 1805, to Novossiltzoff, the British Government declared its fundamental agreement with the generous designs of the Tsar for the deliverance of Europe and its future tranquillity. The basis of Anglo-Russian union should be the restriction of France within her former limits, the adoption in the liberated territories of measures calculated to ensure their peace and wellbeing and to constitute them a barrier against French aggrandisement; also to establish, at the peace, a guarantee for the safety of the different Powers and to reestablish in Europe a general system of Public Law. For the attainment of these great objects a general Coalition must be formed, including if possible Prussia. The Dutch and Swiss Republics, the kingdom of Sardinia, and Tuscany and Modena should be reestablished, while the other lands previously conquered or controlled by France must form part of the new Barrier System. For the same purpose, the Sardinian monarchy should be strengthened, and Austria and Prussia placed in strong positions over against France in Italy and near the Netherlands[2]. The British Note made no reference to the vaguer topics named in Novossiltzoff's Instructions, nor did it mention Malta and the Maritime Code. Probably, he left them unnoticed in these his first interviews, and maintained a discreet silence concerning Czartoryski's favourite scheme for

---

[1] Czartoryski, *Memoirs*, chs. IV, v. The Grand-duke Mikhailovich (*L'Empereur Alexandre* I, I. 38) considers the Novossiltzoff mission the Tsar's first independent effort in diplomacy.

[2] C. K. Webster, *British Diplomacy* (1813–1815), App. I.

absorbing the original kingdom of Prussia and pushing her westwards. Perhaps, Vorontzoff dissuaded him also from naming Austria's acquisition of Bavarian and Suabian territories, a notion always firmly opposed by George III and his Ministers.

Distinguishing the chimerical from the practical portions of the Russian programme, we may conclude that Pitt laid stress on the latter and kept them to the fore in the negotiations; also, that Malta and the Maritime Code were not at first mentioned; for, on or about January 19th, Novossiltzoff reported that the British Government entirely agreed with the proposals he had hitherto made, especially when he characterised them as designed to restore the Balance of Power. Pitt, after promising subsidies amounting to £5,000,000 to the Allies, declared that the aims of the two countries exactly coincided, as indeed will appear from a comparison of the present proposals with those made by Pitt and Grenville to Russia in their Note of November 16th, 1798, outlining the programme for the Second Coalition. Perhaps the more practical portions of the Tsar's programme were inspired by that Note, which, in its turn, focussed Grenville's settlement suggested on December 22nd, 1795. There is a marked similarity between the British proposals of 1795, 1798, 1805 and 1814[1].

Novossiltzoff's caution in holding back some of the more contentious of the Russian demands probably arose from a desire not to complicate further an already tangled situation. As had happened at the close of 1799, when Great Britain was discussing with her Allies the terms of a possible pacification, so again now, early in 1805, Napoleon sent New Year's offers of peace to George III[2]. The King in his Speech from the Throne, of January 15th, referred to them courteously, but declined further discussion "without previous communication with those Powers on the Continent with whom I am engaged in confidential intercourse, and especially with the Emperor of Russia, who has given the strongest proofs of the wise and dignified sentiments with which he is animated, and of the warm interest which he takes in the safety and independence of Europe." This reply, like that of January, 1800, was calculated to reassure our friends that we would not lay down our arms without due consultation with them. Vorontzoff, in further interviews with Pitt, found him ready to concur in

[1] For the British draft treaties of January 21st and March 15th, 1805, see *Third Coalition*, pp. 90, 119.
[2] *Nap. Corr.* No. 8252. On the same day (January 2nd, 1805) he wrote to the King of Spain urging him to make war on England.

the Russian proposals for the settlement of Europe, but "quite decided not to give up Malta," and not to relax the British Maritime Code. In the month of May, a breakdown of the negotiation seemed inevitable, for Pitt, though deeply grieved at such an issue, would not give way, and intimated that Leveson-Gower's hands were tied on those two questions.

Meanwhile, on April 11th, 1805, that Ambassador had signed with Czartoryski a Treaty which, in the main, corresponded closely with a draft sent from London a month earlier. He met with several difficulties; for, though Novossiltzoff, on his return to Petrograd, gave a satisfactory account of British policy, yet Alexander and Czartoryski began to insist on modifications. They required that the King of Sardinia should acquire the Genoese Republic, to which Leveson-Gower demurred as harsh and unjust to its inhabitants. Then, they haggled over the conditions of the British subsidies, and demanded that Novossiltzoff, who was to go to Paris to present the Allied terms, should stipulate the revision of the Maritime Code by a Congress, also the evacuation of Malta by the British troops, and its occupation by Russian troops, in case Napoleon absolutely insisted on such a clause as a *sine qua non* of peace. The British Ambassador fought these two proposals and finally procured the abandonment of the former, the other being made conditional on the consent of the British Government, which of course, would not be forthcoming. Leveson-Gower counted the insertion of this proviso a diplomatic triumph; but he had not reckoned on the pertinacity of Alexander, who finally demanded the inclusion of the original demand. It met with an equally firm refusal at London, Mulgrave declaring, on June 5th, that Great Britain was ready to give up important conquests in the East and West Indies, but could not now surrender Malta, which protected the Levant and the kingdom of Naples. The island in British hands was a purely defensive station, but in those of France would be a constant menace to Sicily, southern Italy and the East[1]. Moreover, in April, 1805, Great Britain had despatched about 7000 troops, under General Sir James Craig, to the Mediterranean over a sea not under her control[2]; while the Tsar was sending from Sevastopol and Corfu a larger force, under General Lacey (Lasci), which depended largely upon British transports. How Great Britain was to support these forces in southern Italy if she gave up Malta, was not explained by Alexander and his advisers.

[1] *Third Coalition*, pp. 127–40, 155.
[2] Gen. H. Bunbury, *The Great War*, pp. 181–97.

In a final effort to placate them, Pitt and Mulgrave consented to the eventual admission of a Russian garrison to Valetta, provided that the States bordering on France should be strengthened sufficiently to form a solid barrier against French aggression, and, also, that arrangements could be made with Spain for the cession of Minorca to Great Britain in place of Malta. This last provision found definite expression in Mulgrave's despatch of June 7th, while Pitt, in a majestic survey of the services of Great Britain to the common cause, set forth cogent reasons why the transfer of Malta to Russia would not strengthen her efforts. Yet, very reluctantly, he consented to accept some other station in the Mediterranean, provided that Sardinia were greatly strengthened, that Switzerland gained entire independence, and that Prussia acquired Luxemburg and the country between the Moselle, Rhine and Meuse, so as to interpose a strong military barrier between France and the Dutch Netherlands[1]. The scheme adumbrates that which came about in 1814.

Long before the British despatches of June 5th and 7th reached Petrograd, Novossiltzoff had left for Berlin, en route for Paris[2]. The situation accordingly was complex and obscure. Ostensibly, he was about to offer to Napoleon, in answer to his New Year's appeal, the Anglo-Russian terms for a general pacification; but the two Powers disagreed on important topics; and their disagreement could hardly escape his eager scrutiny. We now know that Napoleon was resolved not to listen to Russia's mediation[3].

Indeed, during his Italian tour of the early summer of 1805, his deeds and writings betrayed supreme contempt for the other Powers. A prey to megalomania, he expressed complete belief in the success of his schemes for the invasion of England or Ireland, adding that, as a result, "the Indies are ours when we want to take them." He scoffed at the Anglo-Russian negotiations and ridiculed the notion that another Coalition could be formed[4]. Yet he took the steps that were best calculated to provoke it. First, he declared himself King of Italy— a signal infraction of the Treaty of Lunéville—and, soon afterwards, he framed the daring plan of annexing to France the Ligurian or Genoese Republic, which he carried into effect on June 4th[5]. This

---

[1] *Third Coalition*, pp. 165–74; Corbett, *Campaign of Trafalgar*, App. A. The Minorca proposal has been overlooked by Sorel (VI. 417) and most writers.
[2] He left Petrograd on June 11th and reached Berlin on June 23rd (G. Jackson, *Diaries*, I. 300).
[3] *Lettres inédites de Talleyrand*, p. 121.
[4] *Nap. Corr.*, Nos. 8788–92, 8807, 8813.
[5] E. Driault, *Austerlitz*, p. 179.

coup de foudre at once cleared away the murk that hung over the Continent. The timid acquiescence of Francis in threats that came from Paris, and his peevish exaggeration of trifling differences with the Courts of London and Petrograd, gave place to a secret resolve to end the humiliating subservience to France.

Even more marked was the change in the Tsar. Annoyance at the stiff resistance of Pitt was overborne by fierce resentment at the rapacity of Napoleon; and he sent off Instructions to Novossiltzoff at Berlin, to return to the Prussian officials the French passports which they had procured for him and to break off the overture to Napoleon. The Envoy, in doing so on July 10th, informed Hardenberg that the French annexation of Genoa and the manner of its accomplishment ended all hopes of peace. He, also, wrote to Vorontzoff at London, stating that the selfishness and isolation of Prussia precluded all hope of assistance from her, but that Austrian troops would be ready to march westwards by the middle of August. As for the North-Germans, they now saw that Napoleon was "no angel but a devil," ready to swallow Germany if she remained inactive. At Petrograd, also, after a final protest on the Maltese affair, Czartoryski consented to shelve both it and the Malta-Minorca exchange proposal. Accordingly on July 28th, the Anglo-Russian Treaty of April 11th was ratified, the former article respecting Malta being omitted. On August 9th, Stadion, the Austrian Ambassador, signified secretly the accession of Francis II to that Treaty[1]. Thus, within nine weeks the Genoese incident brought about the formation of a Coalition which British diplomacy had failed to effect during twenty-six months.

The Treaty of April 11th, 1805, forms the first official attempt at reestablishing the European System on firm and just foundations. Its main object is to form a General League of European States in order to restrict France within her ancient borders, and restore the Balance of Power on the territorial basis noted above, so as to "guarantee the safety and independence of the different States and oppose a solid barrier to future usurpations." For this purpose, Great Britain will supply her sea and land forces and her transports where necessary, and will aid her Allies throughout the War by subsidies at the yearly rate of £1,250,000 for each body of 100,000 regular troops, also by preliminary subsidies. The Allies agree not to lay down their arms before the conclusion of a General Peace. Ten separate articles provide for

---

[1] *Third Coalition*, pp. 189–97, App. I, II; *Paget Papers*, II. 186; G. Jackson, *Diaries*, I. 458.

the accession of "the Emperor of Germany" and the King of Sweden, if they will act against France within four months; also of Prussia and Denmark; the addition of the Belgic Provinces to the Dutch Republic, and of Geneva (then French) to the Swiss; the furnishing of 250,000 troops by Austria and 115,000 (finally increased to 180,000) by Russia, "besides levies raised by her in Albania, Greece, etc." other contingents raising the total to 500,000 men; also, the accession of Spain and Portugal, Great Britain using Russia's mediation to make peace with, and win over, Spain. By the sixth and seventh separate articles the Allies bind themselves not to interfere with the desire of the French respecting the form of government, or with that of other countries where their armies shall act, not to appropriate to themselves conquests made before the Peace, but on its conclusion to assemble a Congress to discuss and fix the bases of International Law. They also assign to Prussia, in case she joins them, her former lands west of the Rhine, with an addition "more or less great," which will extend her dominions to the French frontier on the side of the Belgic Provinces (Cologne and Juliers are implied). By a separate and secret article they agree to respect the agrarian settlement effected by the French Revolution, and state that, though monarchy will best assure the repose of France and of Europe, they will seek its restoration by spreading that conviction in France, not by a preliminary and formal proclamation. They leave the Dutch and Swiss free to choose their Governments, but will see with pleasure the choice of the House of Orange by the former, and will advise the King of Sardinia to grant to his people suitable institutions. They also express the hope that a System of International Law may be "guaranteed by general assent and by the establishment in Europe of a federal system assuring the independence of weak States and presenting a formidable barrier against the ambition of the stronger."

The proposals for the assembly of a Congress for the redaction of principles of International Law and the foundation of a European Federal System were due to the generous initiative of Alexander; but, according to the testimony of Czartoryski, Mulgrave and Leveson-Gower, they met with complete sympathy and support from the British Government. The statement just quoted respecting the French monarchy also accords with Pitt's earlier declarations; and, but for some trace of resentment in Alexander's mind about Malta and Maritime Law, the agreement between the British and Russian Governments was complete. By insisting on the differences between the British draft treaty of March 15th, 1805, and the elaborate document that we have now summarised, Thiers and other historians have been led to expatiate on the distinction between the generous spirit of Alexander and the narrowly insular aims of Great Britain. That distinction is overdrawn. The early drafts of a compact generally differ greatly from its final form; and the British Foreign Office was not accustomed to insert ideal aspirations in its treaties. Moreover, in this case it sought to provide primarily for the establishment of peace and security. But popular liberties were also to be safeguarded and, as we have seen, Leveson-Gower championed those of Liguria against Czartoryski There is, also, good reason for thinking that, except in regard to Maritime Law, Pitt and his colleagues did not fall short of Alexander in desiring the foundation of an International System. Where they differed was in facility of expression.

To root ideas in actuality is the test of statesmanship. The task was peculiarly difficult in the year 1805. Great Britain could act only through the slow and indirect method of maritime blockade. Russia could act only by means of the territories of Austria or Prussia, the latter of whom clung to a profitable neutrality, while the former was a prey to poverty, nervousness and divided counsels. The Habsburg Power joined the Allies under the impulse of the news from Genoa, which yielded one more proof that peace with Napoleon was more dangerous than war. Towards Paget, the British Ambassador, the Court of Vienna maintained extreme reserve, and, perhaps for the sake of secrecy, it conducted all its negotiations with us at Petrograd, finally, after much insistence, securing the offer of an initial subsidy. The Chancellor, Count Lewis von Cobenzl, entreated that negotiations with France might be kept up to the last so as to avert the danger of an attack from Napoleon before the Russians arrived. Yet Austria's plan of campaign, first sketched in outline on July 19th, erred in two important respects. Believing Napoleon to be absorbed in his scheme of invading England, the *Hofkriegsrath* assigned to the chief army under Arch-duke Charles the operations in North Italy; while General Mack, with whom he was on bad terms, was to advance with a smaller force into Bavaria. Still more serious was the miscalculation as to time, 80 days being reckoned as the minimum within which Napoleon's Grand Army could march from Boulogne to the Upper Danube, and 60 days for the Russian army cantoned near the Galician border to arrive in support of Mack. The latter calculation was nearly correct; the former was too long by three weeks; and in that error lay the chief cause of the disaster of Ulm which struck the Third Coalition to the heart[1].

Other causes, however, contributed to this event. Austria counted on the aid of the Elector of Bavaria, but wrongly; for, after dissembling his intentions, he joined Napoleon so soon as the vanguard of the Grand Army appeared on the River Main. Consequently, the Allies were unexpectedly weak at their centre; and it soon appeared that they had spent too much strength on enveloping moves at their extreme right and left. Russia and Great Britain sent large contingents into northern Germany. After wearisome negotiations with Sweden concerning the choice of Stralsund in Swedish Pomerania as base[2], an Anglo-Russo-Swedish force began to assemble on the lower Elbe, much to the annoyance of Frederick William, who, besides being on the worst of terms with Gustavus, regarded Hanover as his by reversion. Pitt and Mulgrave, hoping to bribe Prussia into active support of this expedition, expected that in the spring of 1806, at the least, 250,000 Allies would sweep the French from the Netherlands and attack France through the northern plain—a dream cherished in 1794 and 1799, but not destined to fulfilment until 1814.

Nor was this all. The Anglo-Russian expedition destined for southern Italy was to assist in driving the French from the Peninsula. As a political move the plan had some merit; but on naval and military grounds it was open to censure. For it was clear that, if (as sound strategy required) Napoleon recalled his troops from the heel of Italy in order to concentrate in her northern plain, the expedition would merely beat the air. This is what happened—and not only in south-eastern Italy, but also in Hanover. Recalling his troops from those extremities, the great captain massed them in central positions where they would act with telling effect. Thus, as happened in the case of all the Coalitions, France opposed swift concentration to the enveloping and ill concerted movements of Allies, who greatly outnumbered her except at the one essential point.

The danger of Austria succumbing before the arrival of Russian succours ought to have stirred Prussia to prompt action. This the British Government sought to assure. So soon as Napoleon's moves towards the Danube were fully ascertained, it despatched Harrowby on a special mission to Berlin, for the purpose of bringing that Court, and if possible those of Denmark, Saxony and Hesse-Cassel, into line

[1] *Third Coalition*, pp. 190, 283.
[2] Koch and Schöll, 11. 366, 370.

against France. Alopeus, Prussian Ambassador in London, had already been sounding the Pitt Administration about pecuniary help; and, on October 27th, Mulgrave instructed Harrowby to offer Prussia £2,500,000 a year in subsidies for the support of 200,000 men in active service, the purpose being to drive the French from the Dutch Republic and to protect Dutch and North German territory during the war. In order to complete the Barrier system, the Belgic Provinces were to be offered to Prussia, intermediate districts between them and her present domains being added, so as to facilitate her communications with this new territory. These offers were subject to the approval of the Tsar and his representative at Berlin, who would also discuss with Harrowby the additions to Austria's territories, if she manifested jealousy at Prussia's proposed acquisitions. Great Britain, for her part, while vetoing all discussion of her Maritime Code, was prepared to forego her colonial gains except Malta and the Cape of Good Hope[1].

The choice of Harrowby for so difficult a mission is unaccountable; for his accident had shaken a constitution naturally infirm; and Jackson, with a spice of jealousy, pronounced him a peevish invalid, often incapacitated by fits and incapable even of ordinary duties[2]. He arrived at Berlin on November 16th, a stranger to its intrigues, and needing constant instruction from Jackson, whom for the time he superseded. The situation at that capital was highly critical. The Tsar had arrived there three weeks earlier, for the purpose of gaining permission (hitherto firmly refused) for his troops to enter Prussian territory. In this he now succeeded, thanks to the effrontery of the French in violating the principality of Ansbach (ceded to Prussia in 1791). Under the sting of this insult, Frederick William seemed inclined to act with vigour against France. He allowed the Russians to enter his territory and entered into friendly discussions with Alexander as to cooperation with the Allies, in case Napoleon should refuse to accept the armed mediation of Prussia. Meanwhile, the French having evacuated Hanover, in order to concentrate against Mack, he ordered a Prussian force to occupy that Electorate. The news followed of the surrender of practically the whole of Mack's army at and near Ulm. It clinched the predominance of Prussia, and enabled her to raise her terms, while the Tsar felt bound to humour her, in order to ensure speedy and vigorous action against Napoleon's flank or rear.

These circumstances explain the conditions which Prussia virtually

---

[1] *Third Coalition*, pp. 207–20.
[2] G. Jackson, *Diaries*, 1. 377; Rose, *Pitt*, p. 545, Pt II.

dictated to the Tsar in the Secret Treaty of Potsdam (November 3rd, 1805). With 180,000 troops, she would join the Allies, if within four weeks Napoleon should refuse her terms for a general settlement on the following lines: for France, the boundaries of the Peace of Lunéville (*i.e.* "the natural frontiers," with the exception of the south of the Dutch Netherlands); an indemnity for the King of Sardinia at the expense of the "kingdom of Italy" (a clause which implied the retention of Piedmont by France); the withdrawal of French troops from Germany, the Dutch and Swiss republics and Naples; the independence of the kingdom of Lombardy; the line of the Mincio, with Mantua, for Austria in northern Italy; and a surer frontier for Prussia. One or two phrases pointed to a more rigid restriction of French power, should Fortune favour the Allies. But the sting of the Treaty lay in the first secret article, which stipulated Prussia's eventual acquisition of Hanover either by exchange or other arrangement. For the attainment of this object the Tsar promised, very reluctantly, to use his good offices. As for the exchange, Prussia's principality of East-Frisia was named; and Hardenberg (who disliked the whole proposal) spoke of the possible acquisition by the House of Brunswick of Upper Gelderland and Juliers—the latter of which Harrowby was about to offer to Prussia[1].

These last proposals were kept secret from Harrowby; but a Russian Special Envoy, d'Oubril, was charged to present the whole Treaty to the British Government. Its disclosure came as a shock to Pitt and Mulgrave. That Prussia should angle after Hanover was not surprising, though their offers to her (if in time) might have caused some sense of shame at her present demand; but that the Tsar should, however reluctantly, support a scheme for despoiling his Ally to benefit a calculating trimmer, passed belief. The proposal was made shortly after the news of Trafalgar had sent a thrill of sorrow but also of exultation through these islands. Well, therefore, might Pitt remark to Vorontzoff that, if England had been beaten at sea and compelled to sign a separate peace, such a proposal would have been out of the question. He refrained from so much as naming it to the King, for fear of killing him or driving him mad. Vorontzoff regarded it "with inexpressible astonishment" and begged that he might be spared the

---

[1] Hansing, *Hardenberg und die dritte Coalition, ad fin.*; H. Ulmann, *Russisch-preussische Politik* (1801–6), pp. 237, 270–2; Hardenberg, *Denkwürdigkeiten* (II, p. 353) stated that Harrowby offered the Dutch Netherlands to Prussia; but he offered "such acquisitions on the side of Holland and the Low Countries" as would strengthen her influence upon them (*Third Coalition*, pp. 226, 227).

humiliation of presenting a formal demand on this head. If he felt the shock, how much more did Pitt! Cut to the quick by Mack's disaster at Ulm, though hereupon cheered by the triumph at Trafalgar, he was once more struck down by Prussia's demand, backed as it was by Alexander. Collecting himself by a visible effort, he declared to Vorontzoff his readiness to make great sacrifices to satisfy Prussia, but never at the expense of the patrimony of George III. He, also, protested against the utter indifference of our Allies to the sentiments and interests of Great Britain[1].

With a last rebound of his sanguine nature, he sought to satisfy Prussia's land-hunger by some other means and thus bring about her armed mediation at Paris, which Napoleon, full-blown with triumph, would certainly reject. Then Prussia and the Allies might liberate the Dutch Netherlands, and a general peace might come to pass, Great Britain restoring all her conquests except Malta and the Cape. Or, at the worst, she could fight on, leaving "our perfidious Allies" to do what they could for themselves. On December 5th, he wrote more fully in the same strain. Criticism of Pitt's plans in 1805 is generally based on the assumption that they were fantastic and unsound. But all the dictates of sound policy should have induced Prussia to take up arms against the French Emperor, whose enormous power and unconcealed contempt for her threatened her overthrow. It was the conduct of Frederick William and his advisers that ran counter to the reasonable expectations on which statesmanship is based. Who could have foreseen the surrender of Frederick William to Napoleon, his mean acceptance of Hanover at the Emperor's hands, and the sequel—Jena, with the countless humiliations that followed?

For a time, Frederick William prepared to draw the sword; Hardenberg (always a friend to England) strove to find some compromise as to Hanover; Harrowby, though now exceedingly ill, made tempting offers to Prussia; and her General Staff not only took under Prussian protection and control the Allied forces in Hanover, but also held in leash a great army of veterans ready to spring at Napoleon's rear, so soon as he should reject the conditions offered by Haugwitz, her Plenipotentiary, at the sword's point. Through this web of schemes the French Emperor struck at Austerlitz. Four days later, Austria concluded with the conqueror an armistice on the basis of the withdrawal of the Russians from her territory. The Tsar now appealed for help to the King of Prussia, who, during a few days, seemed about to grant it. But, mean-

---

[1] Czartoryski, *Memoirs*, II. ch. IX.

while, the Allied cause had been betrayed by Haugwitz. That time-serving politician was only too ready to rise to Napoleon's bait, Hanover, and, bringing with him the attractive offer of peace and the Electorate, he returned to Berlin.

Tidings of these disasters filtered through slowly to the British Government in the closing days of the year. Pitt had gone to Bath to recover from a sharp attack of the gout and to gain strength for the struggle with the Foxites and Addingtonians in the coming session. Their recent attacks on Lord Melville (accused of malversation at the Admiralty), and their arraignment of the Government's lavish expenditure in aid of uncertain Allies, had already been so fierce that Huskisson taunted them with building their hopes of place and power on the ruins of Europe[1]. Now their opposition bade fair both to overthrow Ministers and to reverse their foreign policy. Pitt alone could defend it adequately before the half-doubtful, half-hostile Commons; and even his oratory would pale if Fortune frowned on all his enterprises. The Grenvilles had bitterly censured his sending a large force to Hanover on the chance of Prussia's cooperation, and so did the Army itself[2]. And now there came news of the havoc dealt by a storm to the expeditionary force, then of the defection of Austria and retreat of the Tsar, lastly, of the sinister behaviour of Prussia. Surmising the truth, that Hanover was her overmastering desire, Mulgrave on January 6th, 1806, urged on Pitt the necessity of tempting her to immediate action by the offer of the Dutch Netherlands[3]. This degrading suggestion elicited no reply. A week later, there fell on Pitt the last blow of all, the news that Frederick William had acceded to Napoleon's terms. It was true. That monarch, as usual, had resolved to take the easiest and most profitable course. His decision to accept peace with dishonour was fraught with momentous results. On Prussia, it entailed a loss of *moral* worse than a dozen defeats in the field. For the Allies, it involved the reversal of their plans for the liberation of the Dutch Netherlands and their withdrawal from Hanover at the *fiat* of Berlin. For Pitt himself, it meant death. On January 23rd he sank to rest.

The political causes of the collapse of this imposing Coalition are not far to seek. The inveterate jealousy between Prussia and Austria still defied the utmost efforts of Great Britain and Russia to bring those

---

[1] Horner, *Corr.* I. 347.
[2] *Dropmore Papers*, VII. 316–20.
[3] See *Appendix F*.

Powers to accord. For a short space after the Ansbach incident, a union of the four Great Powers appeared to be near at hand; and if Hardenberg had been sovereign of Prussia, her splendid army, launched against Napoleon's rear, might have altered the course of history. But short-sighted selfishness then dictated her policy; and the Coalition, strong at the wings but weak at the centre, reeled under the home-thrust of a master of war whose expansive policy in time of peace had not yet betrayed him into a diffuse and ineffective strategy. Eight years were to pass before adversity grouped them in a compact phalanx, and prosperity relaxed his grip on both political and military combinations.

III

The Pitt Administration was succeeded by an ill-assorted union of the Grenvilles with Foxites and Addingtonians, soon to be dubbed "the Ministry of all the Talents." Lord Grenville became First Lord of the Treasury, and in September, 1806, his brother Thomas succeeded Grey at the Admiralty; Fox took the Foreign Office; Spencer, Home Affairs, and Windham the War and Colonial Office. Addington (now Lord Sidmouth) became Lord Privy Seal, and, in October, 1806, Lord President. The Grenville Ministry, as it should be called, carried the Abolition of the Slave Trade, and some other useful measures of late postponed by Pitt. But its *raison d'être* was, first, opposition to his policy of European Coalitions, and, second, the conclusion of peace, if it could be secured without too great sacrifices. Accordingly, Ministers sought to withdraw from Continental entanglements and to embark on a more purely British policy. Trafalgar, Austerlitz and the defection of Prussia pointed the moral of the situation. The three Coalitions against France, sapped by mutual distrust and jealousy, had served but to aggrandise her power. Thanks to the First Coalition, she had acquired "the natural frontiers" together with a firm control over the United Netherlands and northern Italy. The Second Coalition yielded to her Piedmont and the hegemony of Switzerland. And now, the pitiful collapse of the Austro-Russian defence enabled her to acquire from the Habsburgs eastern Venetia, Istria, and Dalmatia, to drive them out of Germany and exalt their rivals, Prussia and Bavaria. Well might Napoleon defy Great Britain to attempt to form yet another Coalition[1].

[1] *Nap. Corr.* 9929.

The diffuse efforts of the Allies against southern Italy and Hanover were now speedily reversed. Napoleon's swift centripetal moves from those outlying parts having won decisive triumphs in the valleys of the Danube and the Po, he now prepared to reoccupy southern Italy and to make profitable use of Hanover in the hitherto unratified compact with Prussia. In both cases, as also in the crushing terms imposed on Austria, there appears the new *Leitmotif* of his policy, his "coast-system," soon to be re-named the Continental System. A note of intense eagerness pervades all his references, early in the year 1806, to southern Italy and Sicily. As Ferdinand IV and Maria Carolina had thrown off the mask of neutrality and admitted the Anglo-Russian expedition, he now accused them of perfidy, declared them deposed, and ordered Masséna and Joseph Bonaparte with a large French force to drive the Allies into the sea. "Above all do not lose a moment in trying to capture Sicily[1]." The Crown of the Two Sicilies was held out as the prize for Joseph. On the collapse of the Neapolitan defence, General Craig determined to embark for Sicily, which his original Instructions pointed out as far more important than Naples; and, despite the clamour of Maria Carolina and the representations of our Ambassador, Hugh Elliot, he withdrew the British force to Messina. Lacey also retired with his Russians to Corfu. The King, Queen and H. Elliot sought refuge at Palermo, where General Acton (latterly out of favour) resumed his position as Chief Minister. There can be little doubt that Craig's prompt withdrawal and the measures taken by Collingwood to protect the Bourbons at Palermo saved Sicily from French domination. The Sicilians detested the Bourbons and longed for British rule, a fact which partly explains the tortuous intrigues of Maria Carolina against our officials in Sicily. A British victory at Maida in Calabria (July, 1806) averted all danger of a speedy French conquest of that island[2].

Though Great Britain thus retained in the Mediterranean two islands which prevented Napoleon's domination of that sea—*but principal de ma politique*—yet on the coast of the North Sea he achieved over her a bloodless triumph, the fruit of his masterly bargainings with Prussia. That Power, having occupied Hanover and assured the ignominious retirement of the Anglo-Russian forces, demobilised, as though peace were secure. Never was there a worse blunder. Napoleon,

[1] *Nap. Corr.* 9781, 9788.
[2] Bunbury, *The Great War with France*, pp. 210–56, 415–36; Collingwood, *Memoirs*, 183–96; *Diary of Sir John Moore*, II. ch. XXII.

encouraged by this news and by the appointment of Fox as British Foreign Minister, believed that he had the game in his hands; and, when Haugwitz at Paris in February, 1806, sought to gain his consent to certain changes in the Franco-Prussian compact of December, 1805, he found the Emperor inexorable. Finally, on February 15th, 1806, that luckless statesman had to sign what was in effect a new Treaty, whereby Prussia ceded Ansbach to the Elector (now King) of Bavaria, and was forced to agree to the immediate and definitive acquisition of Hanover, and to close all that coastline to British trade. Frederick William must now have seen the significance of Napoleon's "Greek gift" of Hanover. Eventually, it must involve war with Great Britain. Nevertheless, on March 9th, he ratified the new Treaty, and sought to placate George III by offering him East-Frisia and certain other districts. In reply, King George protested against the spoliation of his ancestral territory, urged the King of Prussia not to "set the dreadful example of indemnifying himself at the expense of a third party," and concluded by appealing to the Head of the Empire, and to the Tsar as guarantor of the Germanic System. Nothing came of this appeal; for the Holy Roman Empire was tottering to its fall. But Great Britain, already indignant at Prussian perfidy, promptly retaliated against exclusion from the most valuable corridor still open to British commerce. On May 16th, Fox ordered the blockade of the estuaries of the Trave, Elbe, Weser and Ems, and this was soon extended to the whole coastline between the Elbe and Brest. This "paper blockade" caused great annoyance to neutrals, especially to the United States; and the blockade of Prussia's new territory led to a state of hostility which was formally recognised on June 11th. Thus did Napoleon extend his coast-system. He had "thrust Prussia into the North" and compelled her to annex Hanover, in order to embroil her with the Island Power[1].

When peace aggrandised the Napoleonic System no less swiftly and surely than war, it might have seemed futile to enter into negotiations for a general settlement. Yet, so sanguine was the nature of Fox that he made the attempt. The warm sympathy that endeared him to all his friends had welled forth to all the manifestations of French democracy; and an admirer noted that his excessive hopes for that movement sprang from his habit of giving free rein to sentiment and too little time to enquiry and reflexion. The same generous failing, probably, accounts for his predilection for Napoleon. After a visit to Paris in

[1] *Nap. Corr.*, 9810, 9811.

1802, the Whig leader expressed the belief that the First Consul, however hostile to this country, desired to reduce the military spirit and to make the French a commercial people[1]. Romilly, who was also in Paris, came to an opposite and far saner conclusion[2]. The belief that Napoleon was wedded to peace and "afraid of war to the last degree" was another of Fox's delusions, worthy of a place beside his conviction that, if war came, Grey was "literally" the only Briton who could conduct it[3]. The situation was therefore *piquant*, when Fox, with his fervid aspirations after peace, sought to compass it under a chief whom he had firmly opposed because of his bellicose and reactionary tendencies. Unfortunately, his letters are rare in these last nine months of his career; but his actions betoken so unruffled a dignity amidst countless disappointments, so firm a resolve to tread the path of honour, as to reveal the loss which the nation sustained through his exclusion from office in 1794 and in 1804 by the *fiat* of George III.

On February 20th, 1806, Fox prepared the way for the negotiations by revealing to Talleyrand the details of an alleged plot for the murder of Napoleon, which had been mooted to him. The Emperor replied in suitable terms and, in his speech of March 2nd to the *Corps Législatif*, offered peace to Great Britain on the basis of the Treaty of Amiens. Conscious, perhaps, that this Treaty was now defunct, he modified the offer in his survey of French affairs to the Senate (March 5th). True, he spoke in terms which implied the continuance of French domination over the Netherlands, the Rhineland and Italy, the annexation of Genoa being also explained as a necessary result of that of Piedmont. He further alluded to the extension of his federative system over the Dutch Netherlands, Istria and Dalmatia as indispensable to French power, and therefore irrevocable; but he proposed a pacification on the general principle of recognising our recent acquisitions in the Indies as an equivalent to the extension of his power in Europe[4]. Here was a conceivable basis for a settlement; and, on March 26th, Fox replied, stating that some of the Amiens terms were vague, but expressing the hope of the British Government for an equitable compromise between the two Powers and their respective Allies. He added, however, that he could not negotiate, still less conclude, a treaty without the participation of Russia. To this statement, Talleyrand, on April 1st, sent the rejoinder, that Napoleon attributed the rupture of

---

[1] F. Horner, *Memoirs*, I. 255, 348.
[2] *Life of Sir S. Romilly*, I. 415–23.
[3] *Corr. of C. J. Fox*, III. 372, 381, 385, 391, 406.
[4] *Nap. Corr.* No. 9929; *Moniteur*, March 6th, 1806.

the Peace of Amiens, not to this or that article, but to his refusal to conclude with Great Britain a treaty of commerce such as would harm French industries; that she must give up all thought of interfering in French arrangements (presumably those relating to commerce); that she was a great Sea Power, while France was a great Land Power; therefore, the participation of another Land Power (Russia) would be unfair, and he would never place himself, as regards Continental affairs, at the discretion of Great Britain and that of Russia operating conjointly.

This reply augured ill for an accommodation. Under the specious plea that Great Britain and France were equal in strength on their respective elements and therefore must meet each other alone, Napoleon was about to eliminate our Ally from the negotiation which Fox had declared must proceed conjointly with her, or not at all. Besides, it was certain that Napoleon would bring in his Spanish, Italian and Dutch Allies; otherwise the peace would be partial. Accordingly, Great Britain must, in honour, include Russia and Sweden in the negotiations. Such was the purport of Fox's answer on April 8th; and he further stated that, while deeming a treaty of commerce advantageous to both countries, he would postpone it as a matter for future arrangement. Napoleon, however, absolutely declined to discuss matters with the Coalition and insisted on treating with Great Britain alone. To this demand Fox, on April 21st, sent a firm refusal, repeating it on June 14th, with the expression of a hope that the negotiation might secure the tranquillity of Europe. Meanwhile, Talleyrand had sent for the Earl of Yarmouth, who was then at the depôt for British prisoners at Verdun, and proposed through him to make secret communications to Fox[1]. With this proposal Fox concurred. Talleyrand, therefore, when pressed by Yarmouth, stated that Napoleon would make no difficulty about the restitution of Hanover by Prussia to George III. As for the Bourbons and Sicily, "vous l'avez; nous ne vous la demandons pas." Asked whether France would guarantee the integrity of the Ottoman empire, he replied in the affirmative; but it must be soon; for "beaucoup se prépare, mais rien n'est fait."

The hint gained in significance from the weekly extensions of Napoleon's authority. After aggrandising his South-German Allies and proclaiming Joseph Bonaparte King of Naples, the Emperor

[1] Francis Seymour, Earl of Yarmouth and second Marquis of Hertford (1743–1822), sat in Parliament from 1766 to 1794, and was Plenipotentiary to Berlin and Vienna in 1794 (see ch. 11). The despatches summarised above are in *Parl. Papers* (December 22nd, 1806). See, too, *Ann. Reg.* (1806), pp. 708–91.

declared his brother Lewis King of Holland, a project dating from March 8th, 1806, and carried into effect on June 5th. On the same day, he appropriated the Papal enclaves of Benevento and Pontecorvo, assigning them as dukedoms to Talleyrand and Bernadotte[1]. Meanwhile, he was pressing on with his German lieges the scheme of the Confederation of the Rhine; and on July 12th he secretly signed with the Kings of Bavaria and Würtemberg, and certain lesser Princes, a Treaty to that effect[2]. For the present, he concealed it, probably in the hope of inducing Great Britain and Russia to sign separate treaties of peace before they heard of this revolutionary change in Central Europe. Thus, partly by intimidation, partly by secret diplomacy, he intended to separate his opponents and compel them to surrender at discretion.

His intentions appear clearly in his Correspondence. On May 31st he writes to Talleyrand, complaining that the extreme weakness of Prussia leaves him little hope that she will assist him in compelling England to make peace. She will not even close the Sound to British ships. Therefore, he must go on with the British negotiation and look about for some other lands to grant to Prussia, in case she has to give back Hanover to George III. Some domain of 300,000 inhabitants, say, Hesse-Cassel, will do for her. Further, he urges King Joseph to prepare to seize Sicily; for peace will be made with the British when that island is secured. By July 4th, he decides never to allow Great Britain to keep Malta and maintain control over Sicily; for this would form an "impassable barrier" to French communications with the Adriatic and the Levant. She must therefore give up either Malta or Sicily; and in either case, he will humour her about Hanover. Similarly, he will grant a separate peace to Russia, reluctantly leaving Corfu to her[3]. These letters explain why neither Great Britain nor Russia could make peace with him, and why Prussia broke with him. For the present, his divulsive plans prospered. The Russian Plenipotentiary, d'Oubril, who arrived at Paris on July 6th, was so dazzled by his splendour, or cowed by his threats, as to sign with Talleyrand a separate Treaty, a secret article of which stipulated the cession of Sicily to King Joseph, Ferdinand IV receiving from Spain the Balearic Isles

---

[1] *Nap. Corr.* 9944, 10314, 10316.

[2] H. A. L. Fisher, *Napoleonic Statesmanship: Germany*, ch. v; E. Driault, *Austerlitz*, pp. 376–88. On August 6th, Francis II abdicated as Head of the Holy Roman Empire; and that venerable organism expired.

[3] *Nap. Corr.* Nos. 10396, 10409, 10416, 10448, 10499. For Gentz's comments on the negotiations of 1806, see Sir R. Adair, *Mission to Vienna, ad fin.*

for his son Francis, the former Prince Royal (July 20th). Believing that he had saved Germany from the projected Napoleonic League and Austria from ruin, d'Oubril hurried back to Petrograd, there to meet with an indignant reception by his master, who repudiated this degrading compact.

Yet Napoleon had won a respite of some weeks, and had for the time separated the Allies. He now turned against Great Britain, resolved to wrest Sicily from her at all costs: witness the last sentence of his letter of August 6th to King Joseph—"Peace or war, you shall have Sicily[1]." Accordingly, his Plenipotentiary, General Clarke, declared to Yarmouth that, since France had gained a signal success by separating the Allies, she must now raise her terms. Yarmouth being so indiscreet as to produce his full powers for treating in regular form, the negotiation promised to be short. But Fox, rebuking Yarmouth for this lapse, sent out to Paris a statesman known for his pacific views, the Earl of Lauderdale, to assist him and finally to take over his duties.

The conferences with Clarke during the month of August revealed the hopelessness of coming to an accord. Napoleon now scornfully rejected the original basis of *uti possidetis*, which implied Great Britain's retention of St Lucia, Tobago, the Cape and Surinam. True, early in September, on hearing that Alexander I refused to ratify the Oubril compact, he seemed inclined to lower his tone. But now, as ever, the crux was Sicily. The principle of good faith to our Neapolitan Ally and the dictates of naval strategy alike forbade the surrender of that island to Joseph Bonaparte. Moreover, Fox is said to have attached great importance to the maintenance of British power in the Mediterranean[2]. Unfortunately, early in August, he fell seriously ill of the dropsy. The symptoms, perhaps, were aggravated by despair at the unfavourable turn of the negotiation. When his nephew, Lord Holland, ventured to suggest that, after all, some indemnity might be found for the Bourbons in lieu of Sicily, he replied: "It is not so much the value of the point in dispute as the manner in which the French fly from their word that disheartens me. It is not Sicily, but the shuffling, insincere way in which they act that shows me they are playing a false game; and in that case it would be very imprudent to make any concessions which by possibility could be thought inconsistent with our honour, or could

[1] *Nap. Corr.* 10657.
[2] Lord Holland, *Memoirs of the Whig Party*, II. 340; also, *Ann. Reg.* (1806), ch. IX, which is by him.

furnish our Allies with a plausible pretence for suspecting, reproaching or deserting us[1]."

Fox died on September 13th. French writers have often represented that event as the chief cause for the breakdown of the negotiation, asserting that Fox's colleagues and Lauderdale were less peaceably inclined than the deceased statesman. Such assertions are at variance with the evidence. Holland, who knew both Fox and his colleagues, believed that no difference of opinion occurred between him and them on this head, and that his death made no difference to the issue of the negotiation. Further, with one immaterial exception, the despatches sent to Lauderdale after that event deviated neither in matter nor in tone from those of March–August 23rd. Moreover, Lauderdale continued to make every possible effort to bring about an honourable peace, for which since the year 1793 he had consistently striven[2]. He remained at Paris until October 6th; but in vain. On September 24th, Napoleon left St Cloud to direct the War to which his insolent treatment of Prussia had now driven her long-suffering monarch[3]. The Instructions left behind for Champagny precluded all hope, either of a joint negotiation with Great Britain and Russia or of the retention of Sicily by the Neapolitan Bourbons. On September 25th, the French Plenipotentiary offered to Great Britain the Cape, Malta, Hanover, Tobago and the French settlements in India; but he insisted on the cession of Sicily, the Bourbons receiving the Balearic Isles and an annuity from the Court of Spain. As these cynical terms were Napoleon's ultimatum, the negotiation lapsed.

Thus, Sicily was the chief cause of the prolongation of the War, as Malta had been of its inception. At this point, as at all important crises since November, 1792, the Franco-British dispute turned essentially on questions of naval strategy. On the surface, there appear in 1793, 1797, 1803, 1806 altercations respecting the Scheldt, Gibraltar, Malta, Sicily. What was really at stake was the French control of the Dutch Netherlands and mastery of the Mediterranean. A sure instinct impelled even peace-loving Ministers to hold out firmly on matters that concerned, first, the safety of the East Coast and, finally, the communications with India. For the present, Great Britain had to

---

[1] *Corr. of C. J. Fox*, IV. 476. Sir Robert Adair, *Mission to Vienna* (Introd.) refutes the assertions of Bignon that Fox had offered to cède Sicily; but the slander has been widely accepted.

[2] Holland, *Memoirs of the Whig Party*, II. 76–81, 346–52.

[3] The chief cause of the rupture was Hanover (Garden, X. 153). See, too, G. Jackson, *Diaries*, II. 12–14, 501–11.

acquiesce in French control of Dutch territory; but she reduced the danger by occupying the Cape; and Napoleon's Levantine schemes now warned her to hold on both to Malta and Sicily.

He revenged himself by overthrowing Prussia. So swift were his moves that neither Russia nor Great Britain could help her. Austria, who could have done so, remembered Prussia's inaction of the year before[1]. Consequently, this second phase of the Third Coalition corresponds closely to the first. Prussia takes the place of Austria. Her main army having been utterly beaten at Jena-Auerstädt (October 14th), the survivors scatter eastwards; not until February, 1807, do the Russo-Prussian forces make a determined stand, at Eylau; and not until April 26th is the revived Coalition placed on a firm basis by the Treaty of Bartenstein between those Powers. To this Treaty Great Britain (who had made peace with Prussia) soon acceded, offering a subsidy of £1,000,000 on June 27th, a fortnight after the Russians were utterly overthrown in the battle of Friedland. So halting had been the moves of the Allies, whereby they threw away the few chances left open to them by the perfervid genius of Napoleon.

The sole interest attaching to Great Britain's policy in these gloomy months belongs, not to her dilatory diplomacy, but to the development of the elemental struggle between her and Napoleon. On November 21st, three weeks after his triumphal entry into Berlin, he issued thence his famous Decree, declaring the British Isles in a state of blockade, and all commerce and communication with them forbidden, all British subjects in French or Allied lands subject to imprisonment and all British property good prize, the half of it being used to indemnify merchants for the losses inflicted by British cruisers. The preamble justifies this measure by a recital of the harsh British customs which enjoined the capture of the crews and cargoes of hostile merchantmen, the blockade of non-fortified harbours, the practice of nominal blockade, even over an entire coast, and, in fine, of all her measures calculated to ruin the trade of the Continent. All Napoleon's Allies are ordered strictly to carry out this Decree, so that a cordon may be drawn against the Islanders, from the Elbe to the south of Italy. The King of Holland is urged to great activity in enforcing this Decree—"the sole means of striking home at England and compelling her to peace"—also, to build 25 sail of the line, so that in four or five years Napoleon and his Allies may challenge her maritime supremacy[2].

---

[1] Adair, *Mission to Vienna*, p. 142.
[2] *Nap. Corr.* 11283, 11377, 11378.

Such, then, was the Emperor's policy—to utilise the resources of all lands under his control, to close them to British commerce, and finally to mass their fleets for the utter overthrow of the Island Power. The construction of warships which he now pressed on in Dutch, French, Spanish and Italian ports furnished a telling commentary on this Decree. Commercial war was to prepare for political destruction. The programme was merely a gigantic development of ideas set forth by the French Jacobins. The Report of January 1st, 1793, to the French Convention insisted on the artificiality of the British Empire and the facility with which it might be attacked in so many quarters as to ensure the ruin of British credit. This notion inspired Bonaparte in his Egyptian Expedition. And now, that avenue being closed by the British occupation of Malta and Sicily, he expanded the alternative scheme, named in his letter of February 23rd, 1798, of seizing the north-western coast of Germany, the probable sequel being the inclusion of Prussia and Austria in his "coast-system."

His plan of commercial warfare against Great Britain having its roots far in the past, we need not take very seriously the diatribes against her maritime tyranny in the preamble to the Berlin Decree. But her proceedings at sea had aroused much discontent among neutrals, especially in the United States. Already, President Jefferson, in his official Message of December 3rd, 1805, had protested against the depredations of privateers on United States and other shipping even close to their ports, declaring that he had armed light squadrons to capture the offenders and have them tried as pirates. He, also, referred to captures made by warships contrary to the Law of Nations, and declared that neutrals had as good a right as belligerents to decide what was legitimate trade for a neutral to carry on with belligerents. Equally obnoxious to him was the custom whereby "a belligerent takes to itself a commerce with its own enemy which it denies to a neutral." Probably, he was referring either to the Licence system then commencing, or to the Rule of 1756, cited above. But his charges were vague, Great Britain not being named. He named her, however, in his Message of January 17th, 1806, as infringing the terms of the Jay Treaty of 1794–5, and as impressing seamen from United States shipping. That practice and the right of search which it involved was certainly productive of infinite friction[1]. In April, 1806, Congress passed a Non-Importation Act, prohibiting the import of many British products. It came into force on November 15th, but, owing to the

[1] See *Camb. Mod. Hist.*, VII. 327–31.

clamour against it, was soon withdrawn. Negotiations were then on foot between Washington and London, and, in December, Jefferson announced that they were "proceeding in a spirit of friendship and accommodation which promises a mutual advantage[1]." The blighting of these hopes resulted from the Berlin Decree and the retaliation to which the British Government resorted.

The first retort to that drastic measure took the form of the British Order in Council of January 7th, 1807, which, while asserting the inherent justice of retaliating by the prohibition of all maritime trade with France, such as she threatened to apply to the British Isles, yet restricted such punitive measures to vessels trading between any two ports whence British ships were excluded. It therefore aimed at stopping all trade, even that of neutrals, from harbour to harbour (except in Portugal) between Hamburg and Venice. Inasmuch as British cruisers now swept the seas, neutral trade probably suffered more from the thorough application of this limited measure than from the Emperor's *brutum fulmen* of a blockade of the British Isles. In truth, he must have resorted to that bombastic declaration chiefly as a means of intimidation and of spurring on his antagonist to reprisals certain to arouse the wrath of neutrals. In this, as will shortly appear, he succeeded.

The month of February, 1807, witnessed the failure of the Sea Power to help Russia. Driven from Warsaw by the pressure of Napoleon's arms, she was now threatened by her secular rivals, the Turks. General Sebastiani, French Ambassador at Constantinople, having induced the Porte to declare war on Russia (December 24th, 1806), the British Government ordered a squadron to force the Straits and compel the Turks to make peace. Vice-Admiral Sir James Duckworth with seven sail arrived at Princes Islands, near Constantinople, on February 20th, 1807. The wind failing, he anchored there and then weakly complied with the request of the British Ambassador, Charles Arbuthnot, now on board, that he should seek to end the Russo-Turkish War by peaceful negotiation. Thereupon, the Turks amused him with specious offers, until their preparations were complete both on the spot and at the Dardanelles. Then they defied him, and he, realising his helplessness, ran for the Straits, passing the repaired forts with considerable loss. Subsequently, the Russian squadron which should have aided him hove in sight. War with Turkey having arisen out of our futile effort to help Russia, the British squadron

[1] *Ann. Reg.* (1807), p. 679.

proceeded to Alexandria, where the operations on land completely miscarried[1]. Altogether, the naval and military policy of the Fox-Grenville Ministry proved a disastrous failure. From Trafalgar to the Dardanelles was a plunge from the sublime to the ridiculous.

The conviction gained ground that "All the Talents" had frittered away the national resources on distant and difficult enterprises, when they should have struck at France. Deprived as she was, for seven or eight months, of the presence of Napoleon and the Grand Army, then in Prussia or Poland, she presented a good target[2]. But the genius of Chatham appealed in vain to Grenville, Fox and Howick; and their dull, unenterprising régime sensibly contributed to the overthrow of the Third Coalition. In March, 1807, Great Britain had, exclusive of artillery, 259,000 men under arms. Of these, 93,000 were serving abroad, while 165,000 Regulars and Militia were in these islands, without reckoning that uncertain factor, the Volunteers. But only 33,000 were deemed ready for foreign service; and, owing to our diverse responsibilities in the Mediterranean, the Cape, and South America, it was deemed hazardous to send abroad more than 12,000 men[3]. Pitt and Barham had always kept transports ready for the immediate des-patch of such a number. But, as their successors discontinued this practice, no force could be sent speedily to the help of our Allies. To this cause may be ascribed the very discreditable failure to aid Russia and Prussia in the spring of 1807, when the scales of war were hovering in the balance.

In March, 1807, the Grenville Cabinet fell, owing to its resolve to carry Catholic Emancipation and the King's invincible repugnance to that measure[4]. The cares of State now fell on the unimpressive Duke of Portland, the equally mediocre Hawkesbury (soon to become Earl of Liverpool) at the Home Office, the Earl of Chatham at the Ordnance, and Perceval at the Exchequer. Far stronger men were Lord Eldon as Lord Chancellor, Lord Castlereagh for War and the Colonies, and Canning for Foreign Affairs. In this Tory and Old-Whig Ministry, George Canning (1770–1827) alone calls for special notice here. His conversational and literary gifts had first shone in the brilliant society of Fox and Sheridan; but the French Revolution, fretting the rich

---

[1] F.O. Turkey, 156, 157; Collingwood, *Memoirs*, pp. 251–67; *Parl. Papers*, March 23rd, 1808; E. Driault, *La Politique orientale de Napoléon*, pp. 85–110; Adair, *Mission to Vienna*, p. 223.

[2] See *Plain Facts, or a Review of the Conduct of the late Ministers* (Stockdale, 2nd edit. June, 1807).

[3] *Castlereagh Memoirs*, VIII. 46–8; Temperley, *G. Canning*, p. 72.

[4] *Castlereagh Memoirs*, IV. 374–92; *Dropmore Papers*, IX. 100–20.

vein of sentiment in his nature, ranged him with Burke and Windham on the side of Pitt. Admiration of Pitt's genius and hatred of French Jacobinism were thenceforth the animating motives of his career. As Under-Secretary for Foreign Affairs in 1796–9, he displayed equal firmness and imagination. Sympathising with his leader on the Catholic claims, he retired with him in 1801, but could not be restrained from contemptuous sallies on Addington as responsible for the detested Peace of Amiens:

> Hail, thou, on whom our State is leaning!
> O Minister of mildest meaning!
> Head of wisdom, soul of candour
> Happy Britain's guardian gander,
> To rescue from th' invading Gaul
> Her 'commerce, credit, capital!'

Returning with Pitt to office in May, 1804, as Treasurer of the Navy, he flung himself with ardour into the struggle against Napoleon, but refused to have a part in the gathering of "All the Talents," with "no Elijah near." Such was the statesman, versatile but resolute, generous but self-willed and intriguing, who, after four months of responsibility, was suddenly called on to solve one of the most complex and momentous problems of that age.

Like his father seven years previously, Alexander delighted Napoleon and exasperated his Allies by throwing the weight of Russia suddenly into the opposite scale. True, he had cause of complaint against us. In the spring and early summer of 1807, we had done little to help him in the Baltic except by the tardy despatch of a small force under General Cathcart to Stralsund. Three British sloops strove hard to harass the French besiegers of Danzig. But of what avail were three sloops? Danzig surrendered on May 27th; and its fall set free a considerable force for service in the field. Exasperation against the British was therefore rife at the Allied headquarters[1], especially after the catastrophe of Friedland (June 14th). Despite the arrival of large Russian reinforcements, Alexander soon decided to sue for an armistice; and, in a letter of June 24th, he stated to his Envoy, Prince Lobanoff, his desire for a Franco-Russian Alliance, which "alone can guarantee the welfare and repose of the world....An entirely new system ought to take the place of that which has existed here, and I flatter myself that we shall easily come to an understanding with the Emperor Napoleon, provided that we treat without intermediaries[2]." Probably,

---

[1] G. Jackson, *Diaries*, II. 148.   [2] Tatischeff, *Nouvelle Revue*, June 1st, 1890.

this avowal of a desire to break with Prussia and Great Britain became known at the Tsar's headquarters at Tilsit. Certain it is that a British agent, Mackenzie, who was there on June 23rd–5th, met with a friendly reception from the Commander-in-Chief, Bennigsen, and heard him exclaim at dinner on the 25th: "The two Emperors have shaken hands. Europe has cause to tremble."

On that day, Napoleon and Alexander met in the friendliest fashion on a raft in the middle of the River Niemen at Tilsit; and the question arises—How did the British Government come to know of Alexander's *volte-face*? A fantastic story states that a British spy was on the raft and heard all their private converse; but it is far more probable that secrets leaked out through Bennigsen or some other malcontent Russian officer. On his way back to London, Mackenzie arrived at Memel on June 26th, and brought news of the Armistice and other threatening symptoms to a group of British officials, including General Sir Robert Wilson, Sir George Jackson, Lord Hutchinson, then on a special mission, and the British Ambassador, Lord G. Leveson-Gower.

Nor was this all. Leveson-Gower's earlier despatches to Canning had contained warnings that Bernadotte's corps, near the southern border of Holstein, might invade that duchy, so as to compel Denmark to close the Sound to British ships; and now, on the 26th, he sent off by Mackenzie news of the Franco-Russian *rapprochement*. It reached Downing Street on July 16th. Already, our Envoy at Copenhagen, Garlike, had reported the Francophil tendencies of that Court. Further, the Earl of Pembroke, on proceeding *via* Copenhagen to take over the British Embassy at Vienna, had reported (incorrectly as afterwards appeared) considerable activity in the Danish dockyards. Official news from Altona also mentioned menacing moves of the French near by. Hence, the arrival, on or before July 16th, of very disquieting information from Memel, Copenhagen and Altona aroused intense anxiety at the Foreign Office. Were France, Russia and Denmark, possibly Prussia also, about to form a League like that of 1800–1 for the closing of the Baltic? On this occasion, the problem confronting the new Portland Cabinet was exceptionally complex; for a Northern League would threaten the communications of the British expeditionary force cooperating with our Swedish Allies at Stralsund. Further, the Portuguese and Danish fleets (the latter consisting of 15 sail of the line) might easily be seized by the French troops in their vicinity; and the combined Napoleonic fleets, backed by some 20 Russian sail, would form an armada equal, at least on paper, to the 103 British sail of the line in commission early in 1807[1].

Such was the problem, as it confronted Canning on July 16th. A dull and unimaginative man would probably have decided to await further developments before making even preliminary preparations. But Canning's was an imaginative mind, keenly patriotic and fired with intense hatred of Napoleon. Aware of the impressionable nature of Alexander, and piecing together the fragments of information from Memel, Copenhagen and Altona, he pictured to himself as imminent a vast conspiracy for the ruin of Great Britain. Evidently, the Danish fleet was the heart of the problem. Very early on the 18th, F. J. Jackson, formerly Ambassador at Berlin, was summoned to Downing Street. He found Canning in a state of great perplexity, but convinced that Napoleon was about to seize that fleet, with a view to the invasion of England. On the same day, he framed his resolve. Mulgrave, First Lord of the Admiralty, at once issued most urgent orders[2] for the immediate preparation for sea of 22 sail of the line, and 29 smaller craft, and this, too, in addition to 13 warships, the commission of which he had ordered on July 15th. Those ordered on the 18th were for a particular service under Admiral Gambier[3]. The purpose of this formidable armament appeared in Canning's Instructions of July 16th to Brooke Taylor, whom he appointed successor to Garlike at Copenhagen. The new Ambassador was to proceed forthwith to that city and declare to the Danish Government that a British fleet was coming to support it in repelling all offers from Napoleon.

On July 21st the arrival of news up to June 25th from Tilsit (probably brought by Mackenzie) clinched Canning's determination; and, on the 22nd, he informed Brooke Taylor that Napoleon had proposed to the Tsar the framing of a Maritime League, in which Denmark would be included. Distinct and satisfactory assurances must therefore be required from her that no such demand had been made, or that, if so, it had been rejected. Above all, Brooke Taylor would demand the deposit of the Danish fleet in British hands, in order to remove the object for which Napoleon was striving. Great Britain offered to Denmark her Alliance and the yearly payment of £100,000 during such time as the fleet was held in pledge. It is clear that

---

[1] See my articles in *Transactions of the R. Historical Society* (New Series, vol. xx) and in *Napoleonic Studies*, pp. 133–65; also, James, *Naval Hist.* IV. 201 and *App.* xv; *The Athenaeum*, September 17th, 1902.

[2] *Journals...of Sir T. Byam Martin*, I. 326, 328.

[3] *Admiralty* (*Orders and Instructions*), 152.

Canning offered the Alliance as a device for gilding the pill; for it was extremely unlikely that so spirited a Power would peaceably accept terms so humiliating from a State with which its relations were unfriendly. Probably, too, he hoped that the arrival of Gambier's overwhelming force, finally numbering 25 of the line and many smaller craft, would save the honour of Denmark and avert a conflict. If so, he was disappointed. The overtures, unskilfully made by Jackson and Brooke Taylor, were indignantly rejected, and hostilities ensued, a landing force finally on September 7th compelling the surrender of Copenhagen and the Danish fleet. The latter, comprising 15 sail of the line (mostly very old), as many frigates, and 31 smaller vessels, was brought away near the end of October.

Such was this discreditable episode. In seeking to reach an impartial judgment upon it, the enquirer is first faced with the question: Was the information as to the designs of Napoleon on Denmark sufficiently cogent to warrant action so drastic as that taken by Canning and his colleagues? Search in the British Archives (which, though abundant on this topic, may not contain all the documents bearing on it) reveals the fact that the evidence before them by July 21st was merely circumstantial, and not so complete as to be conclusive. It warranted no more than an inference that the seizure by Napoleon of the Danish fleet was highly probable. In the ensuing debates on this question, Canning referred to sources of information (doubtless those named above) and to a British Minister—probably, Leveson-Gower—as furnishing the proofs. But his despatches were not decisive on this question; and Lord Hutchinson, who had been at Memel, denied in the House of Lords, on February 8th, 1808, that there had existed proofs sufficient to justify the action taken against Denmark. Castlereagh, also, admitted that, so early as July 19th, 1807, Ministers "took His Majesty's pleasure as to the propriety of the expedition[1]." But not until August 8th were even the public articles of the Treaty of Tilsit known in London; and they contained nothing derogatory to Danish Independence. Further, Canning's despatch of August 4th urged Leveson-Gower to find out whether there were any secret articles[2]. Now, it was the Secret Treaty of Alliance of July 7th which contained the proviso: that, if Great Britain refused the Tsar's offer to mediate for peace between her and France, he would then make common cause with the latter; and Russia and France would summon

[1] Hansard (1808), p. 169 et seq.
[2] F.O. Russia, 70.

Denmark, Sweden and Portugal to declare war against the Island Power[1]. That Canning's keen intuitions divined the beginnings of what might have developed into a formidable plan may be granted; but his imagination soared high, when, on September 25th, he wrote to Paget that the Copenhagen expedition had prevented "a northern confederacy, an invasion of Ireland and the shutting of Russian ports[2]." More probably, it hastened the latter proceeding and its sequel, the Tsar's Declaration of War against Great Britain, which was issued so soon as he believed two of his squadrons to be secure. On the whole, the parliamentary debates of January–March, 1808, on this topic somewhat shook public confidence in the Ministry. Its harsh treatment of Denmark was reprobated by the Duke of Gloucester, Lord Grenville, the Duke of Norfolk, Lords Sidmouth, Darnley, Erskine, Moira, Hutchinson and Grey, as also by Windham, Ponsonby and Whitbread in the House of Commons.

To pass censorious judgments on Canning and his colleagues, as if the problem of July, 1807, had been a simple one, is unjust. The very existence of Great Britain was at stake; and the evidence which reached Downing Street on or before July 21st rendered it very probable that Napoleon would coerce Denmark and compel the surrender of her fleet. Moreover, Canning's intentions towards the Danes were, as his letters and despatches show, friendly. He even hoped for the formation of an Anglo-Scandinavian Alliance, which might save the North from the grasp of the two Emperors[3]. All this must be admitted. Nevertheless, the information on which he founded his inference as to Napoleon's designs on Denmark amounted, not to proof, but only to a high degree of probability; and it is very doubtful whether, on such evidence, he was justified in a course of action which might lead to hostilities with a weak Power. Would it not have been better to run the risk of the addition of 15 Danish sail of the line to the Napoleonic Armada than to incur the odium that must result from the seizure of those ships? This is the question. The conscience of that age, as of our own, has in general answered it in the affirmative.

In November, 1807, British policy exercised a somewhat stringent pressure on Portugal. Since our rupture with the Court of Madrid at the end of 1804, her existence had been precarious; and now the accord of the two Emperors at Tilsit portended ruin. Early in August, 1807, the Portuguese Ministers were aware that France and Spain

[1] Vandal, *Napoléon et Alexandre*, I. 505–7. [2] *Paget Papers*, II. 363.
[3] Rose, *Napoleonic Studies*, pp. 146–50; Lane-Poole, *Life of Stratford Canning*, I. 30.

would force them into war with Great Britain. They therefore begged our Government through its Ambassador, Viscount Strangford, to put up with a nominal state of war; but they failed to convince either Canning or him of the feasibility of their proposal. The British Government, also, urged resistance to Napoleon's demand for the confiscation of British ships and property; and to such a measure the Prince Regent promised never to stoop. By September 27th, however, Napoleon had laid his plans for the complete partition of Portugal, and these led up to the Franco-Spanish Treaty of Fontainebleau (October 27th), which assigned parts of the kingdom to Godoy and the dethroned King of Etruria, reserving the major portion for future disposal. French and Spanish forces now advanced towards Lisbon, the French being instructed to enter as friends, so as to seize the Portuguese fleet. On their near approach, Strangford with some difficulty induced the Prince Regent and his Government to retire from Portugal to Brazil under escort of the British fleet. Canning, also, signed with Portugal a Convention empowering us temporarily to occupy Madeira, as was done late in the year[1].

Thus, in the year 1807 the Sea and Land Powers bore hard upon Denmark and Portugal respectively, our treatment of the former being honourable and straightforward by comparison with the vulpine conduct of Napoleon towards Portugal. Yet his moves, equally skilful and forceful, pushed successively along the inner arcs of the Continent, everywhere prevailed; while Great Britain, acting without any system and with slighter forces at diverse points of the circumference, nearly everywhere failed. In that fatal year, Napoleon riveted the Continental System on Russia, Prussia and Spain, gained the Alliance of Denmark, annexed Etruria and the Ionian Isles, drove the Swedes from their Pomeranian province, and partitioned Portugal. The sole successes of the Islanders were the capture of Curaçoa and St Thomas, the seizure of the Danish fleet and the rescue of the Portuguese fleet from his clutches. It would be superfluous here to describe the Russian offer of mediation for a general peace. Conceived as it was in a spirit friendly to Napoleon, it could not find acceptance at Downing Street. Somewhat similar proposals coming from Vienna met with a friendly response[2]. But the deep-rooted distrust of Napoleon had increased with every year of triumph of his forceful policy; and the pitilessness with which he

[1] F.O. Portugal, 55; Garden, x. 372; *Nap. Corr.* nos. 12839, 13235, 13237, 13243, 13314, and *Lettres inédites*, nos. 171, 188. *Tout discours est bon, pourvu qu'il* (Junot) *s'empare de l'escadre portugaise.*
[2] Coquelle, chs. XXI, XXII.

trampled upon Prussia and other opponents banished all thought of compromise, even in that season of gloom, the winter of 1807-8.

Yet there was no reason for despair; and Canning and his colleagues never despaired. The failures of·the overseas expeditions of the year 1807 were clearly due to the bad management of the Grenville Administration; but the nation was united in the resolve not to surrender, and was uplifted by the belief that the Napoleonic colossus could not long bestride the earth. Meanwhile, Ministers sought to tighten their Maritime, as a retort to his Continental, System. The Order in Council of November 11th, 1807, stated that, whereas the Order of January 7th had not had the desired effect of compelling Napoleon to withdraw his Berlin Decree or of inducing neutrals to intervene for that purpose, Great Britain now considered all French and subject ports to be in a state of blockade, and would be justified in treating ships sailing to and from such ports as good prize. Nevertheless, certain exceptions favourable to neutrals were granted; but vessels carrying "certificates of origin" (viz. that all the goods carried by them were non-British) were to be counted good prize. A second Order, of November 11th, extended the facilities granted in 1803 to neutral importers for storing their goods in bond without payment, with a view to reexportation. This Order was permissive, not, as has often been represented, compulsory. A third Order, of the same date, declared illegal the sale of enemy vessels to neutrals, a clause designed specially to prevent bogus sales which would be cancelled when the said hostile vessels reached port. Orders of a fortnight later accorded facilities to neutrals sailing between British ports and ports in America or the West Indies, or between the Channel Islands, Isle of Man, Gibraltar or Malta, and any hostile port not actually in a state of blockade by H.M.'s ships. The most rigorous of these Orders was that directed against ships carrying "certificates of origin," as ordered by Napoleon for all vessels trading with his ports. As he confiscated ships carrying goods of British origin, so Great Britain now retaliated by similar treatment of ships carrying the products of his or Allied States. Both Decrees were highly oppressive and enabled acquisitive captains, especially those of privateers, to carry off or hold up ships on the suspicion that part of their cargoes consisted of enemy goods. Since nearly all cruisers were British, the burden of neutral complaints fell upon us.

Napoleon's retort to these Orders in Council appeared in the Milan Decrees of mid-December, 1807. Declaring that Great Britain was about to compel neutral ships to resort to her ports and pay duties, he now threatened to confiscate all that should so act or should peace-fully submit to search; and all vessels sailing from any British port were to count as good prize. Each of the two antagonists, then, justified its Decrees as a natural retort to those of its rival; and the system which began early in 1806 with the exclusion of British commerce from north-western Germany now, by the end of 1807, covered all civilised lands and rendered neutral commerce wellnigh impossible. Sharp friction, consequently, resulted with the United States. Our relations with them had long been strained, owing partly to their inability to understand the necessity for Great Britain of maintaining her maritime claims as a counterstroke to Napoleon's Continental System, partly to the inefficient statement of the British case at Washington. Such was the belief of the Anglophil Gouverneur Morris, who strongly urged the despatch of an Ambassador of high rank and great talent[1]. The difficulty was to find such a one; for the days of Malmesbury were past, and those of Stratford Canning had not yet dawned. So exasperating were the restrictions now imposed on neutral commerce by both belligerents, and so much friction resulted from our seizures of deserters from British warships (notably in the *Chesapeake* case of February, 1807) that war seemed imminent. Seeking to find a *via media*, Jefferson, in December, by a general Embargo Act reinforced the Non-Importation Act of the previous year, and legal trade with all foreign countries ceased. North American shippers sought by all possible means to evade this legislation, which proved ruinous. Consequently, in March, 1809, a change was made, prohibiting trade with Great Britain and France and their Allies, until they should revoke their obnoxious Decrees. Unsuccessful attempts were made by the British Govern-ment, in the spring and summer of that year, to effect a compromise with the new President, James Madison; for the first negotiator, David Erskine, exceeded his Instructions, while the second, F. J. Jackson, offended American officials by his haughty demeanour[2]. Consequently, trade went on only through clandestine channels between Great Britain and the United States, to the intense annoyance of manufacturers here and shippers there. The Portland Ministry received many petitions from Lancashire and Yorkshire to cancel the Orders in Council; but for the present it maintained them, doubtless nerved thereto by the masterful will of Canning.

[1] Sparks, *Life of G. Morris*, II. 245. Auckland strongly disapproved our Orders in Council (*Dropmore Papers*, IX. 158).
[2] E. Canning, *The American Nation* (1801–11), ch. XVIII; H. Adams, *Hist. of the United States*, IV. 387 et seq. V. 90–132.

But now, when every month witnessed the diminution of Britain's resources and the aggrandisement of her enemy, there occurred an event destined to call forth her best energies and to alter the character of the struggle. On May 2nd, 1808, Madrid rose in fury against its French oppressors, and in a short space of time all the Spanish provinces threw off the yoke of Napoleon. It is alike impossible and superfluous to describe here the tortuous intrigues whereby he had occupied the Spanish strongholds, compassed the ruin of the Spanish Bourbons and placed Joseph Bonaparte on the Throne of Spain. By the first of May, he seemed to have at his feet the whole of the Peninsula, and to be about to marshal its forces for the two enterprises foremost in his thoughts, the utter isolation of Great Britain and the eventual partition of the Ottoman empire[1]. By the end of the month, the Spaniards were in revolt against his usurped authority and three provinces were sending to London Envoys begging help from the then hostile British Government. The first to arrive were those of Asturias. They received a hearty welcome both from the people and from officials, Canning entertaining them at his house, and inviting Sir Arthur Wellesley to meet them. The honour of first proposing to Parliament the offer of aid to Spain fell to an orator who had generally opposed warlike measures. Sheridan, on June 15th, urged Ministers to seize the opportunity as the greatest that had occurred since the French Revolution for the rescue of a nation's liberty. "Hitherto" (he exclaimed) "Bonaparte has had to contend against princes without dignity and Ministers without wisdom. He has fought against countries in which the people have been indifferent as to his success. He has yet to learn what it is to fight against a country in which the people are animated with one spirit to resist him." Canning, thereupon, declared that Ministers viewed with admiration the rising of the Spaniards and desired to aid them immediately. "Sir" (he exclaimed), "it will never occur to us to consider that a state of war exists between Spain and Great Britain. We shall proceed upon the principle that any nation of Europe that starts up with a determination to oppose a Power which...is the common enemy of all nations, becomes instantly our essential Ally[2]."

This principle, which was confirmed and extended in the King's Speech of July 4th, marked the dawn of a new era in British Foreign Policy. The old policy had been based upon Treaties of the traditional type with monarchical Governments which were out of touch with

---

[1] *Nap. Corr.* February 2nd; April 29th; May 10th, 13th, 17th, 19th, 1808; *Lettres inédites*, no. 275.   [2] Hansard, xi. 886–96.

their peoples. The new policy involved trust in informal, but none the less binding, agreements with the peoples themselves. The old was always formal, frequently hollow, and not seldom secret. The new, springing out of vital sympathies, relied on the fundamental promptings of human nature, and therefore needed no very complicated, still less secret, stipulations. From the universal experience of mankind it was to be expected that the old method would persist long and would often invade and vitiate those of the new order. The new methods were often discarded amidst the complex arrangements of 1814–5 and of a later age; but, when once clearly asserted and shown to be workable, they were certain to gain ground; and their vitality could not but increase with the quickening of national consciousness and the growth of popular education. Thus, the months of May and June, 1808, inaugurate, not merely a novel policy, but, what is more important, a fresh spirit, destined to influence nations as well as Governments. The latter now tend to become the mouthpiece of the former; and it is significant that this development began with two essentially conservative nations. Spain and Great Britain led the way in asserting the claims of national independence as against the overweening pretensions of the "heir to the French Revolution." The wheel had come full circle. France, which, in 1793, had summoned all peoples to a crusade for freedom, now found embattled against her the primeval instincts of two great peoples, whose union was destined to arouse and invigorate other communities and reduce her to her former level.

For the present, Canning and Castlereagh sent help in money and arms to the juntas which forthwith sprang up in all districts of Spain. Canning strongly advised them to form a Central Junta, to which he would at once send a duly accredited Minister. Dreading the deep-rooted provincialism of the Spaniards, he forthwith urged them to a national union; and his despatches to the first British Envoy, Charles Stuart, and afterwards to Hookham Frere, refute the charges of Napier, that he lavished money heedlessly on local juntas[1]. Meanwhile, the success of the Spaniards at Baylen (July 19th) where more than 20,000 of Napoleon's troops surrendered, assured the liberation of the south and centre; and, a month later, Sir Arthur Wellesley's force, sent out by Castlereagh with no very distinct aim in view, overthrew the French Army of Portugal at Vimeira. The arrival of incompetent seniors, Burrard and Dalrymple, before the end of the battle, alone saved that

---

[1] Napier, *Peninsular War*, 1. Bk 2, ch. 1. See my article in *American Hist. Rev.* October, 1906.

army from disaster. Thereupon, at Torres Vedras, the British leaders (Wellesley rather reluctantly acceding) signed with General Junot a Convention, misnamed that of Cintra, whereby they secured control of a Russian fleet sheltering in the Tagus, and allowed the conveyance of the French army back to France on British ships. This compact has been defended on strictly military grounds; but it erred in not preventing the salvage of valuable booty by the French troops, and, still more, in not imposing restrictions on their future use in the Peninsular War. These omissions exasperated both the plundered Portuguese and the Spanish patriots, the latter declaring that, as the French veterans would soon again march through the Pyrenees into Spain, the British Generals had betrayed Spanish interests. The Convention, therefore, aroused the distrust of both Portuguese and Spaniards in British Generals, including Sir Arthur Wellesley. He and the senior officers were summoned home to face the enquiry which public indignation demanded. The King and Canning shared the widespread feeling, which was not dispelled by a generally favourable official verdict. The affair entailed another unfortunate result. Castlereagh, as was his wont, loyally supported Wellesley, and, after the enquiry was over, insisted on his reappointment to the Peninsular command. To this Canning objected; and the quarrels between these two masterful Ministers became acute. Nevertheless, popular depression and the naggings of the Opposition failed to bend the Cabinet's resolve to persevere with the struggle in the Peninsula; and on December 9th, Canning despatched an indignant refusal to the Tsar's offer of mediation (agreed on at Erfurt), couched in terms which implied the recognition of Joseph Bonaparte as King of Spain.

The resolution to support the Spaniards was not shaken by the glorious but lamentable failure of Sir John Moore's campaign in northern Spain. On January 14th, 1809, a Treaty of Alliance was signed with the Central Junta of Seville. Sharp differences with the Spaniards and the reverses that were to be sustained during four years of wearing conflict failed to break that compact, which led up to the Treaty of 1814 with the restored Ferdinand VII. This fact alone emphasises the contrast between the Anglo-Spanish union and the artificial Conventions which built up the first three essentially fragile Coalitions. Well might the prophet of that age say: " In all that regarded the destinies of Spain, and her own as connected with them, the voice of Britain had the unquestionable sound of inspiration[1]."

[1] Wordsworth, *Convention of Cintra* (Oxford edit. 1915, p. 110).

IV

In other quarters than the Iberian Peninsula, British policy for the present worked ineffectively. To the German national movement, which began to make headway early in 1809, Ministers, especially Castlereagh, were irresponsive. Yet, after the interview of Napoleon and Alexander at Erfurt in September to October, 1808, there were clear signs that the French Emperor would fall upon Austria so soon as he had defeated the Spanish patriots; and, at the end of 1808, when success had crowned his arms in the Peninsula, he hurried back to Paris to prepare for the new conflict. At that time, marked by the utter humiliation of Prussia, the hopes of all German patriots centred in Vienna. Reforms, both civil and military, were renovating the energies of the Habsburg States; the Tyrolese longed to return to their allegiance to the Emperor Francis; and his patriarchal sway was regretted by many other South-Germans. For a brief space, there appeared a faint hope that Canning might league Great Britain, Austria, Turkey and Persia together against Napoleon and the Tsar. Such was the scheme which he entrusted to Sir Robert Adair, urging him to effect a reconciliation with the Turks. Perceiving that we had acted against them early in 1807 solely on behalf of Russia, they were by no means loth to make peace; but oriental pride and lethargy spun out the negotiations until January, 1809; and then it was too late to frame so extensive a league in time for the War that speedily ensued[1].

The dictates of sound policy should have led Prussia to act in conjunction with Austria—a course which Hardenberg and Gneisenau secretly, but strongly, urged. Indeed, in the spring of 1809, there appeared the first signs of a widespread union of the peoples from the Tagus to the Niemen. But on their side all was vague, and the advantages of central position and effective organisation remained with Napoleon. He seemed to have mastered the Spaniards, and his union with Alexander was unimpaired. Moreover, Austria's preparations were far from complete, and the German patriots, besides being unorganised, could not receive from Britain the timely and effective help which her fleet could afford to those of Spain and Portugal. These considerations and the notorious indecision of Frederick William told against the acceptance of requests for help either at Stralsund or on the Hanoverian coast. Austria, also, sent lofty demands for pecuniary aid, and suggested diversions by us in Spain, Italy and the mouth of the Weser.

---

[1] Adair, *Mission to Constantinople*, i. *ad fin.*

Thus, the choice open to Ministers was bewilderingly wide, the presence of a French squadron at Flushing also inviting a dash on that important post and Antwerp. It is, therefore, not surprising that sharp divisions of opinion should have arisen in the Cabinet, accentuating the disputes between those temperamental opposites, Castlereagh and Canning. The former, however, in March carried his point for the despatch of Sir Arthur Wellesley to Portugal for the defence of that country and such wider operations as he should judge expedient. The sum of £30,000 was accorded to the German patriots, with the promise of a British squadron in the Baltic. Lastly, after some initial difficulties, Liverpool signed an Alliance with Austria (April 24th)[1].

All these arrangements were belated; for, though the Tsar warned Austria against action, and Frederick William obstinately clung to inaction, she rushed into the fray with the nervous haste that had assured her doom in 1805. Now, again, it fell on her quickly. Archduke Charles invaded Bavaria on April 12th, and, on May 13th, Napoleon entered Vienna in triumph. The patriotic risings of Dörnberg, Schill and the young Duke of Brunswick came to naught in April–May, the British squadron in the Baltic being too fully occupied with the Russians and Danes to render effective help to the brave Schill in his last stand at Stralsund[2]. Signal ill fortune beset all the British plans for 1809. In April, an attack by Admiral Gambier with a powerful squadron on the French fleet in the Aix roads off Rochefort was a failure despite the gallant but unsupported efforts of Cochrane with fireships and small craft. Far more costly and disastrous was the Walcheren expedition, directed against Antwerp. Knowing the importance which Napoleon attached to that dockyard, on which 66,000,000 francs had of late been expended, Castlereagh drew up a plan of attack so early as July, 1808. In March, and again in May, 1809, he revived the scheme, and on the 18th offered the command of the land forces to Lord Chatham[3]. He was therefore responsible for what proved to be a very unfortunate choice. His nominee, far from having adequate experience in war, had displayed, even in civil affairs, a tardiness which won him the nickname of the *late* Lord Chatham. Indeed, so soon as Thomas Grenville heard of this appointment to the command of "35,000 of our best and last troops," he foretold the failure of the expedition. His forecast was but too true. Chatham

[1] Fortescue, *British Army*, Bk 13, ch. xxv.
[2] Sir J. Ross, *Memoirs of Adm. Lord de Saumarez*, ii. ch. ix. *Journals...of Byam Martin*, ii. 67–112.
[3] *Castlereagh Memoirs*, vi. 247, 256.

delayed the sailing of the fleet unnecessarily[1]: it weighed from the Downs on July 28th, three weeks after the overthrow of Austria; and the local difficulties, added to disagreements with Rear-admiral Sir Richard Strachan, marred an enterprise which, if pushed on betimes with forceful energy, might have turned the scales of war on the Danube. By comparison with this costly failure, Wellington's Talavera campaign was successful. He won a decisive victory, and, though compelled by the follies and selfishness of the Spanish commanders to retreat hastily on Portugal, his advance revealed the artificiality of the Napoleonic régime in the Peninsula. Three years full of disaster were however needed, in order to teach the Spaniards the necessity of close and loyal cooperation with him.

Meanwhile, the Walcheren fiasco brought to a climax the long series of disagreements between Canning and Castlereagh. Inheriting the hot temper and self-will of their Anglo-Irish ancestry, they always clashed. Even in affairs of high moment which demanded cooperation, they held aloof from each other with untoward results. Portland, now nearing the end of his ineffective career, utterly failed to maintain harmony. Indeed, his forgetfulness complicated the quarrel between them; and the feud came to an appropriate ending—a duel on Putney Heath, in which Canning was slightly wounded, and a partial reconciliation. The Portland Cabinet now collapsed. Spencer Perceval, its pedestrian but conscientious Chancellor of the Exchequer, sought to refashion it, with the addition of Lords Grenville and Grey; but the King's invincible repugnance to Catholic Emancipation, which they made a test question, deprived the country of their services[2]. The new Perceval Cabinet was, therefore, distinctly Tory: five Ministers, Perceval, Camden, Eldon, Mulgrave and Chatham retaining their former executive functions, while Liverpool became Secretary for War and the Colonies, and Bathurst for Foreign Affairs. The last-named was soon succeeded by Marquis Wellesley, who, after a distinguished viceroyalty in India (1798–1805), had latterly gone to Seville as Envoy to the Central Spanish Junta. A novice in diplomacy, he soon fell into the adversary's traps, and his inexperience was not made good by assiduity; for young Stratford Canning at the Constantinople Embassy complained that he only received scanty despatches from him, and at long intervals[3]. Nevertheless, Wellesley was well fitted by administrative

PM.

---

[1] *Dropmore Papers*, IX. 311, 312.
[2] *Dropmore Papers*, IX. 322 *et seq.* F. Horner, *Memoirs*, II. 499.
[3] Lane-Poole, *Life of Stratford Canning*, I. 91, 129.

experience, and by special knowledge of the peculiar difficulties confronting his brother in Spain, to forward the most important enterprise undertaken by Great Britain since 1792. In the dark years, 1809-11, everything turned on the Peninsular War; and, while some of his colleagues at times shrank from the responsibility of continuing that apparently hopeless struggle, Wellesley never quailed. To him, Perceval and Liverpool is due the credit of persisting in an enterprise which elicited the croakings of the Grenvilles, the gibes of Cobbett, and the nervous remonstrances of the City of London[1].

Meanwhile, difficulties beset us from other quarters. The mad obstinacy of Gustavus IV, having foiled our efforts to help him[2], he was constrained to abdicate. His successor, Charles XIII, though friendly to Great Britain and supported by her fleet, was fain to come to terms with Russia (September, 1809), and, early in the next year, with Napoleon. This capitulation involved the entrance of Sweden into the Continental System, and consequently war between her and Great Britain; but the Admiralty privately instructed Vice-admiral Sir James Saumarez, commander in the Baltic, to avoid hostile action; and the tactful manner in which he carried out this difficult duty rendered possible the resumption of friendly relations in 1811-12[3]. For the present, however, British trade was almost entirely excluded from the Baltic.

Further, the movements of two French army corps on Holland portended the annexation of that kingdom. Napoleon had long complained of the softness of his brother Lewis in tempering the severities of the Continental System; and he now devised the expedient of a threatened annexation, in order to compel Great Britain to make peace on his terms. This device he put into effect, partly through King Lewis, partly through the Dutch Foreign Minister, Roëll. Believing that a general peace could alone stave off annexation, they lent themselves to the plan; and Roëll selected as a go-between Labouchère, a Dutch banker of high repute, son-in-law of Sir Francis Baring of London, who was a Director of the East India Company. Having reason to believe in Wellesley's desire for peace, now that the Spaniards were on the verge of disaster, they hoped to induce him and his colleagues to mitigate the Orders in Council of 1807 in proof of their pacific desires. After the experience of the peace negotiations of 1806, and

---

[1] *Dropmore Papers*, IX. 287, 313-21, 370-2; Cobbett's *Political Reg.* (February 17th, 1810).
[2] *Diary of Sir J. Moore*, II. ch. XXIV.
[3] Sir J. Ross, *Memoirs of Saumarez*, II. ch. XI.

even more of Napoleon's offers in the years following, British Ministers should have distrusted all such proposals. Nevertheless, early in 1810 Wellesley toyed with a peace overture emanating from that arch-intriguer, Fouché, Napoleon's Minister of Police. He, on his own account, sent an *Émigré* named Fagan, of Irish extraction, to sound the Perceval Cabinet as to possible terms. Since Fouché insisted that Spain was now conquered and that France must have Sicily, the overture was soon at an end. Fouché was not daunted. He next sent over Labouchère, accredited from the tottering Dutch Government. On February 7th, 1810, Wellesley gave him a cordial reception, but then, and on the 11th, informed him that the Orders in Council must remain in force, unless Napoleon would withdraw his Decrees, to which they were a reply. Labouchère, hereupon, pressed him to save the Dutch from annexation, an aim with which Wellesley expressed sympathy, adding however that in other matters (Spain and Sicily were meant) Napoleon evinced no desire for a reasonable compromise. Perceiving that he could not bend the British Government, Napoleon ordered the military occupation of Holland, and in March, 1810, annexed her southern provinces.

A third overture, made by Fouché on his own responsibility through Baring and a speculator, Ouvrard, belongs rather to the sphere of Court comedy than of international policy. Purporting to come from Napoleon as a kind of wedding gift to the world (he married Marie-Louise of Austria on April 2nd, 1810), it proposed to assign Spanish America to Ferdinand VII of Spain, and to effect a partition of the United States between Napoleon and George III. On April 6th and 14th Wellesley discussed this fantastic scheme with Baring, even consulting Canning about it, and not until May 8th are there signs that he suspected a hoax. Indeed, it was Napoleon who discovered the secret, whereupon he dismissed and exiled Fouché, and arrested Ouvrard. His rage gave full publicity to the affair, thus arousing much merriment among the *frondeurs* both of the Boulevard St Germain and of St James's. Wellesley was covered with ridicule; and pacific offers from Paris thenceforth seemed mere tricks to weaken and divide the Cabinet. Proposals for an exchange of prisoners went on until the autumn of 1810, but thereupon lapsed, probably owing to Napoleon's confident belief that Masséna's great army would compel Wellington to a capitulation[1].

[1] For a full account of these negotiations, based on new evidence, see Coquelle, chs. xxviii–xxxi; also xxxii–xxxvi for the exchange of prisoners.

Until October 10th, when the British commander began his triumphant defence of the lines of Torres Vedras, the prospects were indeed gloomy. At home, the Government, which nervously, but faithfully, supported him, was barely warding off the attacks of the Opposition leaders, who continued to declaim against the folly and expense of the Peninsular War. The Reform movement, championed by Sir Francis Burdett, was gathering head owing to notorious administrative abuses; and the existing discontent was increased by the decline of the export trade and dearness of corn. When work was scarce and wheat sold at five guineas the quarter, the demand for peace became insistent; and it required all the firmness of Perceval to stave off a national surrender to an antagonist whose power and good fortune seemed boundless. On the whole, it appears that the charges of timidity and time-serving brought against his Administration in regard to the War in Spain are unfounded. True, he and Liverpool, on several occasions, warned Wellington that it might become necessary to withdraw his army; and their private intimations sometimes differed inexcusably from their official communications. But, in view of the weakness of the Cabinet, the strength of the Opposition and the tightness of the money-market, they seem to have done their best; and it was well to apprise Wellington betimes that evacuation might, on other than military grounds, become necessary. He framed his measures accordingly[1]. Later, on mature consideration of the difficulties of the Government, he exonerated Perceval and Liverpool from the savage censures which Napier heaped upon them[2]. His vindication deserves to be quoted:

I have always, in public as in private, declared my obligations to the Government for the encouragement and support which they gave me, and the confidence with which they treated me. I was not the Government, as the Duke of Marlborough was....There was a formidable opposition to the Government in Parliament, which opposed itself particularly to the operations of the war in the Peninsula....It is quite certain that my opinion alone was the cause of the continuance of the war in the Peninsula. My letters show that I encouraged, nay forced, the Government to persevere in it. The successes of the operations of the army supported them in power. But it is not true that they did not, in every way in their power, as individuals, as Ministers and as a Government, support me[3].

Fortunately, Wellington had faced about at the Lines of Torres

[1] *Wellington Despatches*, v. 280–2, 343, 426, 470, 481, 542; VI. 6–10, 51, 147, 320, 370; *Suppl. Despatches*, VI. 547.
[2] Napier, *Peninsular War*, Bk XI. ch. X, Bk XIV. ch. II.
[3] Stanhope, *Conversations with...Wellington*, 82, 83.

Vedras, before home affairs entered upon an acute crisis. In October, 1810, George III became insane, and the Opposition hoped that the accession of the Prince of Wales as Regent would be fatal to the Ministry. Sharp altercations occurred in Parliament as to the Ministerial proposals for restrictions on his authority; but finally they were carried. The Prince made tentative offers to Grenville and Grey for the formation of a Cabinet, but in vain, owing to the stringency of their conditions; otherwise, it is probable that Wellington and his army would have been recalled from the Peninsula. By degrees, the Prince drifted away from his Whig advisers; and in February, 1812, when a permanent Regency Bill was passed, all risk of such an issue was at an end. It is not too much to say that, in the latter half of 1810, the whole burden of the Napoleonic War rested on the shoulders of Wellington; and never was a crushing load borne so prudently, so manfully, so triumphantly.

The same months witnessed the completion of the Continental System by the annexation of Holland in July, and of the north-western districts of Germany in December. Napoleon also tightened the cordon against British commerce by the Trianon and Fontainebleau decrees of August and October. The former was an involuntary tribute to the success of our merchants in importing colonial produce into his lands; for, assuming that all such produce was of British origin, he now subjected it to heavy imposts, averaging 50 per cent. *ad valorem*. Alone among his Allies, Alexander I declined to enforce this oppressive tariff; but he complied with an imperious missive from Paris requiring the confiscation of a very large number of neutral (mostly British) ships then in the Baltic[1]. This was the severest blow yet sustained by our commerce, and the heavy loss of merchantmen (viz. 619) in that year, as well as the sharp decline in exports, doubtless explain the prevalence of discontent and the timidity of our foreign policy[2].

Lack of information or want of enterprise accounts for the neglect in the year 1810, of a favourable opportunity for coming to a friendly understanding with the United States. As has been seen, ineffectual efforts were made in the previous year; but President Madison, though originally Francophil, had not been irresponsive. Moreover, Napoleon in his conduct towards the States had been both harsh and insincere, retorting on their Non-intercourse Act of 1809 by secret measures

---

[1] Probably many were American. See H. Adams, *Hist. of the United States*, v. 408–19.

[2] *Camb. Mod. Hist.* IX. 242, 372–4; *Eng. Hist. Rev.* (Jan. 1903) p. 122.

which, in May, 1810, led to the confiscation of American cargoes valued at $10,000,000. Further trickery ensued, the result being hot indignation against him in the States. Yet, for reasons which it is difficult to explain, Wellesley failed to profit by the Franco-American friction. Madison, therefore, issued a proclamation on November 2nd, stating that, unless Great Britain within three months withdrew her Orders in Council, all intercourse with her would absolutely cease. Why he acted thus harshly towards Great Britain, and did not retaliate against the far severer methods of Napoleon, is far from clear; but it seems that the French Foreign Minister, Champagny, Duc de Cadore, succeeded in humouring him and inducing a belief at Washington that reparation would be offered and facilities for trade opened up. The whole question, however, is obscure[1]. Certain it is that friction with Great Britain continued unabated. But the events which led to the War of 1812 must be detailed in the following Chapter.

Though British Ministers failed to assign due weight to American sentiment and to the personal factor always so important at Washington, yet in Europe they were by degrees feeling their way towards effective measures. Their policy, necessarily based on sea power, was strengthened by the capture of Senegal, Martinique and Cayenne in 1809; of Guadaloupe, Amboyna and the Île de France (Mauritius) in 1810; and of Java in 1811. Thenceforth, the resources of the tropics were wholly at their disposal and cut off from the Napoleonic States, except through British agencies. This fact, added to the manufacturing superiority of the United Kingdom, rendered the Continent dependent on it at the very time when the French Emperor sought to sever all connexion between them. In transferring the contest to the economic sphere he was unconsciously marshalling on the side of the Islanders forces against which the mightiest potentates struggle in vain. The severer his Decrees, the severer was the distress inflicted on the French people and their Allies, until, as will duly appear, his Continental System broke down in the country where it pressed most harshly.

For Great Britain, then, the best course of action was to attack that System from as many sides as possible. This involved ceaseless activity at several points of the circumference; and, since Napoleon enjoyed the advantage of the central position, the contest, in a strictly military sense, seemed hopeless. In an economic sense, it was certain

---

[1] G. Canning in *The American Nation: a History*, vol. XII. 246–50; *Camb. Mod. Hist.* VII. 332–4. See new evidence in F. E. Melvin, *Napoleon's Navigation System* (New York, 1919), chs. VI–VIII.

finally to succeed, provided that the British Government and nation possessed enough patience and determination to carry it through. Those qualities they displayed to a degree which led him in 1814 to declare them "the most powerful, the most constant, and the most generous of my enemies." Constancy was now the characteristic needed for methods of warfare certain to be fruitful in disappointments and therefore ill-adapted to a parliamentary system. That they succeeded, in spite of Ministerial mistakes and Opposition naggings, was a riddle utterly incomprehensible to Napoleon's clear-cut Italian genius, as also to every Continental autocrat.

In this circumferential strategy, by far the most important sector was that of Spain and Portugal. There, the Sea Power acted with the greatest possible advantage from excellent harbours against French armies, whose communications straggled across six or seven hundred miles of difficult and hostile territory. Furthermore, the Spanish and Portuguese Colonies were now opened to British commerce, affording a welcome relief to our overcharged industrial system[1]. But the Iberian Peninsula was not the only sector of importance. Next came Sicily. The urgency of the conquest of that island was a theme inspiring scores of letters from Napoleon to Murat, King of Naples; and, as we have seen, a sense of its value had induced the Grenville-Fox Cabinet to break off the peace negotiations of 1806, which finally turned on its surrender. On March 30th, 1808, Drummond, British Envoy at Palermo, signed with the Bourbon Government a Convention for alliance and mutual support, Great Britain maintaining in Sicily a corps of 10,000 men and paying to King Ferdinand a yearly sum of £300,000, while he in return granted commercial and other privileges[2]. The British occupation was effective in several ways. The possession of Sicily and Malta virtually closed the eastern Mediterranean to a French fleet, was a constant menace to Murat, and strengthened all the Gallophobe elements in Italy. Further, from Sicily British goods were often run in successfully through the close cordon of the Continental System. On the whole, then, the maintenance of this large garrison in Sicily (about which Wellington sometimes complained) was fully justified.

But the effort was considerable. It was greatly enhanced by the haughty temper and frequent intrigues of Queen Maria Carolina. The truth about them will perhaps never be fathomed; for her neurotic

[1] Sir F. d'Ivernois, *Effets du Blocus continental*, p. 12.
[2] Koch and Schöll, III. 86.

nature and furious likes and dislikes complicated even the plainest issues. On the failure of British efforts against Ischia and the Neapolitan coast in 1809, she seems to have entered into secret relations with Murat's underlings. Certainly, she conceived a violent hatred against the British officials in Sicily, as also against its quasi-parliamentary régime. Not even the increase of the British subsidy to £400,000 a year satisfied her extravagance or softened her complaints. Consequently the Sicilians and the British drew more closely together, and many were the demonstrations in which the islanders shouted *Viva il Re Georgio*. Our Envoys, à Court and Lord Amherst, successively failed to assuage the disputes with the Queen; and, when her autocratic proceedings caused a deadlock between her and the Sicilian Constitutionals, the home Government despatched as Envoy a man of commanding gifts. Lord William Bentinck, formerly Governor of Madras, was more than a match for Maria Carolina, who was moved to strong aversion by his somewhat hard and ungracious disposition. After reporting at London, he returned in December, 1811, armed with authority to end the crisis. The stoppage of the British subsidy and threats of a British occupation of Palermo induced Ferdinand early in 1812 to transfer his authority to the Prince Royal; but Bentinck deemed it necessary in March, 1812, to remove Ferdinand and his Queen into the interior. These high-handed proceedings cleared the way for the promulgation by the Sicilian Parliament of a Constitution closely modelled on that of Great Britain (June, 1812). The abolition of feudal privileges and other changes soon produced a slight reaction, of which the Queen sought to take advantage. Further disputes ensued, and Bentinck finally resolved to procure her departure from the island. When about to return, she died in Austria, in September, 1814. The new régime in Sicily soon vanished during the period of reaction which then set in; but, in the gloomy years that followed, it remained the cynosure of all Italian patriots; and the events of 1848 and 1860 made it clear that, of all the influences exerted by Great Britain in these years of strife, none was more fruitful than the "English Constitution" of 1812[1].

The British occupation of Sicily, as we have seen, helped to cover Turkey against Napoleon's schemes of partition, which in 1808 prompted his Spanish enterprise. The resumption, early in 1809, of friendly relations with the Sultan was of great service, inasmuch as, from 1810

[1] Sir H. Bunbury, *The Great War*, 278–80, 329, 442, 462, 464; R. M. Johnston, *The Napoleonic Empire in Southern Italy*, II. ch. VIII; *Castlereagh Memoirs*, VIII. 213–32; Blaquière, *Letters from the Mediterranean* (1813). A. Bonnefons (*Marie-Caroline*, ch. XI) gives a more favourable verdict on her. See too *infra*, p. 455.

to 1812, his empire was the only neutral State in Europe, and his ports opened up trade routes, devious it is true, into its central plain. Austria, southern Germany, even France, received the costly trickles that found their way in, *via* Salonica, Belgrade and up the course of the Danube. The hostilities between Russia and Turkey never stopped this traffic. And so, from the Balkan Peninsula, Sicily, Malta, Gibraltar, the Channel Islands, Heligoland and Anholt, the Continental System received constant punctures which rendered it largely inoperative. The United Kingdom suffered, but on the whole less than the States subject to Napoleon; so that a French Royalist lampoon of the year 1810 thus pictured the result—

> *Votre blocus ne bloque point,*
> *Et, grâce à votre heureuse adresse,*
> *Ceux que vous affamez sans cesse*
> *Ne périront que d'embonpoint.*

The general situation towards the end of 1811 was one of extraordinary interest. The Continental System, stretched to its utmost, showed signs of cracking. Yet Napoleon's power seemed boundless. Central and southern Europe obeyed his behests. Only Portugal and a few outlying parts of Spain defied the Imperial eagles. The Tsar had as yet given no clear sign of political alienation from Napoleon, who swayed Europe from Seville to Tilsit. Moreover, the United Kingdom suffered seriously from the severer measures imposed by Napoleon on his States late in 1810. The value of our exports of manufactures fell from £34,061,901 in 1810 to £22,681,400 in 1811; and that of foreign and colonial merchandise reexported, from £9,357,435 in 1810 to £6,117,720 in 1811[1]. This serious decline, together with the increase in the cost of the Peninsular War, and the outbreak of serious outrages known as the Luddite Riots, gave cause for grave concern. Yet there was little thought of surrender. The Tsar, while remaining outwardly friendly to Napoleon, had, in January, 1811, imposed taxes on certain French products, and so far relaxed the Continental System in Russia and Finland, as to throw open his ports to all vessels sailing under a neutral flag. This sign of economic independence not only annoyed Napoleon, but offered the means of surreptitiously introducing British and colonial produce, of which Russia stood in dire need. Equally pressing was her need of the export trade to the British Isles, which had taken her corn, timber, hemp, tar and similar products. She and Sweden stood in vital relations to

[1] Porter, *Progress of the Nation*, 357.

Great Britain, who, besides being their best customer, could then alone supply the silks, cotton, dyes, fruits, sugar, tobacco and other tropical products, without which life was a long drawn-out discomfort. Subtropical lands such as Italy and the southern parts of France and Austria could furnish some of these products. The northerners sulked, and meditated rebellion against the Continental System. There it was, accordingly, that Napoleon's vast experiment of pitting the land against the sea first showed signs of collapse.

A perception of this economic truth probably influenced Marquis Wellesley in seeking a reconciliation with Sweden. On October 9th, 1811, he issued instructions to Edward Thornton [1766–1852] (previously our representative at Hamburg and then at Stockholm) to proceed to H.M.S. *Victory*, flying the flag of Vice-admiral Saumarez off the coast of Sweden, and seek to enter into relations with that Government. He was to point out that the present state of nominal hostility between the two countries could not continue indefinitely, and Sweden must choose between war and peace. We offered peace, together with naval support and a good commercial treaty, and expressed a hope for Swedish cooperation with any Baltic Power that broke with Napoleon; also, more immediately, for Sweden's help in reducing the Danish island of Bornholm—another sign of the British policy of securing commercial bases opposite hostile coasts. The ardent desire of Prince Bernadotte (lately acknowledged by Charles XIII as heir to the Swedish Crown) to aggrandise his adopted country by wresting Norway from Denmark, was an open secret. Consequently, the Instructions proceeded: "The Prince Regent is aware of the views of Sweden towards Norway; but H.R.H. cannot authorise any encouragement of those views, until the conduct and intentions of Denmark shall be ascertained. If, however, any proposition should be made to you on the subject of Norway you will not reject it....If any proposition should be opened to you for the eventual cession of any West Indian colony or possession to Sweden, you will not reject the proposal, but will receive it amicably for future discussion[1]." Reaching H.M.S. *Victory* in Wingo Sound in mid-October, Thornton soon procured a secret interview on shore with the Swedish Minister, Count Rosen, and found that the Prince Royal and he were resolved to secure Norway; but Thornton suggested as preferable the liberation of Norway from the Danes and her future independence. It soon appeared that Sweden shrank from a rupture with Napoleon until she

[1] F.O. Sweden, 70.

had sounded the Russian Court; and, on November 20th, the British overture was rejected, first, because the Prince Royal regarded it as almost a threat, secondly, because he feared an attack from France, Russia and Denmark. The veiled menace in the Instructions was, indeed, gratuitous and unwise, unless Wellesley made a definite offer of effective protection, which he did not. The overture therefore deserved to fail. Thornton expected success only from a definite offer made directly to the Prince Royal[1]. Proceeding to London for consultation with Wellesley, he remained there until March, 1812, when a far abler man took command at the Foreign Office.

Robert Stewart, better known as Viscount Castlereagh, afterwards second Marquis of Londonderry [1769–1822] had long displayed firmness of will and skill in the management of men and affairs, first in Ireland in 1797–1801, then as President of the India Board of Control under Addington, and afterwards as War Minister in the Pitt, Grenville and Portland Administrations. He must bear his share of responsibility for the errors of judgment then committed; and that costly fiasco, the Walcheren expedition, was peculiarly his own, alike in the original design and in the choice of Chatham as commander. Yet— strange psychological contradiction—the same man who carefully selected that portentous misfit, also placed Wellington in the sphere peculiarly suited to his indomitable will and consummate prudence. To Wellington Castlereagh accorded loyal and wholehearted support, both while in office and afterwards by vindicating the general policy of the Perceval Cabinet. He was not a good speaker. His circumlocutions bored the House, though occasionally a Hibernian pursuit of conflicting metaphors afforded passing relief. But his full powers were revealed only in his Office and in interviews with Generals or Ambassadors. There, he inspired confidence in the Allied cause and in himself as its steadfast champion. A pupil of Pitt, he carried on the traditions of the European settlement set forth in 1795, 1798 and 1805; and to the serene hopefulness of the master he added a physical strength and a capacity for managing men, which, thanks to the belated access of wisdom brought about by two decades of defeats, enabled him to build up and maintain a compact Coalition.

Such was the Minister who now took in hand the negotiation with Sweden. Fortunately, that Power, annoyed by the French invasion of its Pomeranian Province, had sent to London a proposal, first, for peace, and, secondly, for alliance with Great Britain; provided that

[1] F.O. Sweden, 70. Thornton to Wellesley, November 20th, 1811.

we accorded naval, military and financial succour, transferred a West India island to her, and assured her territorial extension, especially on the side of Norway. On March 13th, 1812, Castlereagh wrote to Thornton (then on his way to Sweden *via* Leith), welcoming the proposal of peace and alliance. He stated that we did not require Sweden to declare war on Napoleon, but (subject to the demands of the Peninsular War which was our chief concern) we would defend her by a fleet in case of a Russian invasion or a Franco-Danish attack through Norway. We would consider her request for a West India island, and, while deferring a decision respecting Norway, would endeavour to meet her wishes for compensation for the loss of Finland and Swedish Pomerania. In separate and "secret" letters, he instructed Thornton to see the Prince Royal and sound his intentions; and he added that Mr Liston would at once proceed to Constantinople to seek to promote peace between the Sultan and Russia[1].

These despatches reveal the combination of foresight and prudence characteristic of a statesman. Avoiding the veiled threats that had lately given offence, Castlereagh now displays full consideration for Sweden in her difficulties, promises to help her if she is attacked by France and Denmark, but holds out no unreal hopes either of assistance from us or of aggrandisement for her. Thus, the affair was placed on a sound footing. A fortnight later, he promises that, when Sweden makes peace, the Orders in Council of January, 1807, so far as they concern her, will be revoked (a proof that those Orders were in part designed to exert diplomatic pressure and that Ministers were beginning to consider the question of abrogating them). He also points out that her ports will then become the depôts for British trade in the Baltic, and he adds the significant statement that, on the conclusion of the hoped-for Russo-Swedish peace, a British officer will be sent to discuss the operations to be carried on against the enemy; and he notes Sweden's present proposal "that measures should be adopted to induce Denmark to join the confederacy against France, and [that] in exchange for Norway, to be ceded to Sweden, an extension of territory should be given to Denmark on the side of Germany." As to this, the Prince Regent declares that such extension must not be at the expense of Hanover. It is clear that Castlereagh, remembering the flash of Danish pride in August, 1807, had little hope of inducing that people by threats of coercion and invasion to side against France; for, on April 14th, he writes to Thornton suggesting the offer to Denmark

---

[1] F.O. Sweden, 71. (See *Appendix* for extracts.)

of Swedish Pomerania and some other German land as a friendly exchange for Norway. On April 24th, he charges Thornton to inform the Swedish Government that the Prince Regent had resolutely declined Napoleon's offer of recent peace on the basis of the recognition of Joseph Bonaparte as King of Spain. As this implied the abandonment of the Spanish patriots, the British answer could not be doubtful[1].

Though Napoleon's peace overture to Great Britain implied a desire to dissolve the nascent Coalition, and was so regarded by the negotiators, yet the Anglo-Swedish accord progressed very slowly. Sweden required the restoration of peace with Great Britain to be accompanied by the framing of a joint concert with Russia. Castlereagh demurred to this proviso, especially since Russia was preparing with Sweden a compact, the purport of which she withheld. On the ground of our responsibilities to the Spaniards and Portuguese, he declined as excessive the Swedish requests for a subsidy of £1,200,000; and, as for the acquisition of Norway, he suggested that, preferably, Denmark should join the future League and obtain the compensation for the surrender of Norway, as noted above. While welcoming the news of a Russo-Swedish understanding, Castlereagh was evidently puzzled by the aloofness of Russia, but, on May 8th, expressed his willingness to meet her advances when proffered. It came to this, then: that Sweden expected from us a large subsidy and an assumption of wide and vague responsibilities, she herself offering nothing very tangible in return, but the hitch in the Swedish negotiation was clearly due to Bernadotte's resolve not to move against France unless the Allies guaranteed Norway to him. This fact, and others of curious import, are set forth in the Castlereagh-Thornton despatches[2], which throw light on the schemes of the Prince Royal and Napoleon, proving *inter alia*, that the latter was bidding high for Swedish support. Hence, perhaps, the delay on the Swedish side. At Petrograd, the Tsar seems to have wished for a speedy peace with Great Britain. As will soon appear, she was working at Constantinople on his behalf, and the desire to propitiate him, as well as the United States, explains the sudden (though belated) abrogation of the Orders in Council on June 16th, 1812. Nevertheless, up to the end of June his desire for union with her was thwarted by his Francophil Minister, Romanzoff, who, by various dilatory devices, staved off a decision.

---

[1] F. O. Sweden, 71. Castlereagh to Thornton, March 25th, 27th; April 14th, 1812. *Nap. Corr.* no. 18652. Fain, *Manuscrit de* 1812, I. 98–102, with Castlereagh's reply.
[2] See *Appendix H*.

Meanwhile, as so often happened, Napoleon put an end to these lengthy chafferings by a sudden attack. But he had occupied Vilna during three weeks and was advancing on Vitebsk, before Russia and Sweden signed a Treaty of Peace with Great Britain at Örebrö in Sweden (July 17th). Thornton at once warned Saumarez to do all he could to help our new Allies; but the delays just noticed prevented the timely direction of British naval power against the French heavy transport, which was largely carried on by sea from Danzig to their line of operations in Lithuania. Later, Saumarez and his captains did much to harass that service; but far more would have been done but for the protracted delays in signing the Treaties of Örebrö. The Russian force, designed to cooperate with Sweden in an attack on Copenhagen (now that the Danes remained obdurate) was, also, not ready in time. Consequently, that part of the Allied plans of 1812 was postponed; and not until the end of the year did Thornton announce a definite rupture between Sweden and France[1]. Meanwhile, General Lord Cathcart had been deputed by Liverpool (Prime-Minister since the assassination of Perceval) to proceed as Ambassador to Petrograd. On his arrival early in September, Alexander intimated his resolve to place in deposit with Great Britain the Russian Baltic fleet, lest, when frozen in at Cronstadt, it should fall into the enemy's hands. It is one of the ironies of history that the deposition of the Russian fleet for safe keeping with the British Government should have been arranged by Cathcart, who took over the Danish fleet in 1807, with the Sovereign who had fulminated against that measure as an act of unpardonable perfidy[2].

It is now time to return to our relations with Turkey, which were destined largely to influence the course of events near the close of the Moscow Campaign. The Alliance of Alexander with Napoleon at Tilsit, renewed with some modifications at Erfurt, had involved Russia in hostilities, not only with Sweden but with the Turks; and, early in 1810, she had captured nearly the whole of the Danubian Provinces. The Porte, however, refused to cede them, doubtless relying on the probability that plans for the partition of Turkey would lead to friction between the two potentates as to the apportionment of the spoils. Adair, British Ambassador at Constantinople in 1808–11, proposed various means for restoring peace between Russia and the Turks,

[1] *Castlereagh Memoirs*, VIII. 283.
[2] *Ibid.* Thornton to Castlereagh, July 18th; Cathcart, *War in Russia and Germany*, ch. I; *Letters of Sir T. Byam Martin*, II. 311; *Life of Saumarez*, II. 281–9.

even suggesting to Wellesley, in March, 1810, the cession to her of one of our West India Islands, in order to bring about a conjoint settlement and an eventual Anglo-Russo-Turkish Union. Nothing resulted from his proposals, except that the Porte became convinced of our goodwill[1]. Adair, therefore, recommended the adoption of a vigorous Mediterranean policy, involving the occupation of Corfu, Cattaro and Elba, so as to enclose and throttle the Continental System from the south. With that aim in view, the islands of Zante, Cephalonia, and Cerigo had been captured from the French in 1809; Sta. Maura was taken in 1810; but the French in Corfu held out until after the first abdication of Napoleon. It is clear, then (despite the denial of Sir Henry Bunbury[2]) that the British Government had a definite Mediterranean policy. From the Ionian Islands, it threatened the Napoleonic States on the Adriatic and also screened Turkey from the attacks, which, at and after Tilsit, the French Emperor meditated against her from those islands, from Cattaro and from Dalmatia. His inability to push on the schemes of partition foremost in his thoughts, also, fomented a feeling of annoyance with the Tsar, who, after the conquest of the Danubian provinces, was in a position easily to overrun Serbia (then in a state of ferment) and even to threaten Roumelia and Constantinople. This feeling of jealousy played its part in bringing about the rupture of 1812.

Adair being compelled by illness to return home in June, 1810, the honour of furthering British, Turkish, and eventually Russian, interests in the impending world-crisis devolved upon his young secretary of legation, Stratford Canning, the ambition of whose life it had been to serve England in England. Fate willed that he should serve her at Constantinople. Before he took his degree at Cambridge, he was reluctantly pressed into the diplomatic service, of which he became the most distinguished ornament during the 19th century. Owing to the precarious health of Adair, George Canning in July, 1809, appointed his young cousin, provisionally, Minister-plenipotentiary in case of the collapse of the Ambassador; and this duty devolved upon him at Midsummer, 1810. French influence was then unbounded and the Porte bowed before it. This youth of twenty-three had to fight against it single-handed: for he very rarely received instructions or advice from the next Foreign Minister, Marquis Wellesley. Probably the negligence of the chief developed the resourcefulness and resolu-

---

[1] Sir R. Adair, *The Peace of the Dardanelles*, II. 10–21, 95, 270.
[2] *The Great War with France*, p. 327.

tion of the young Envoy. Confronted by intrigues at the French Embassy and corruption and apathy at the Porte, he did not lose heart. From Consul-general David Morier (father of sons destined to high repute in the public service), he gained good advice as to dealing with orientals: but his native shrewdness and force of character utilised every opportunity. He continued Adair's policy of supporting the Anglophil Ali Pacha, of Jannina (" the Lion of Epirus ") whose masterful and cruel nature inspired terror among the Greeks and apprehension at the Porte. He also seconded the efforts of Sir Gore Ouseley, British Envoy at Teheran, to thwart the efforts for a Franco-Persian alliance which Napoleon had begun in the spring of 1807. In short, it fell to him, without advice or help from Downing Street, to try to foil Napoleon's enterprises from the Adriatic to the borders of Afghanistan[1].

It is difficult to account for Wellesley's neglect of the Constantinople embassy; for, besides being the only important British mission on the Continent, it offered a ready means of influencing Levantine, Austrian and Russian politics. Furthermore, if (as Adair and Stratford Canning urged) a powerful British squadron could have been spared for the Black Sea to join the Turks in an attack on Sevastopol, the Tsar would, probably, have consented to negotiate for peace with both Powers. But, the strain on the British navy being very great, the young Minister had to rely on diplomatic means. Here, circumstances favoured him. By the autumn of 1811, the young Sultan, Mahmoud II, and his Ministers expressed a desire for the good services of Great Britain to end their conflict with Russia, and they declined the mediation of any other Power, although that of France would have been more in accord with custom, she being an Ally of the Tsar, while we were at war with him. After further Russian successes, an Armistice was concluded in November; and at the end of the year the Tsar despatched a Plenipotentiary, Italinski, to negotiate for peace with Turkey—a sign that he expected a rupture with Napoleon and desired to concentrate all his resources upon that struggle. Negotiations, accordingly, began at Bukharest.

Naturally enough, the French sought to thwart them. They pointed out that, with the help of the French, Turkey might hope to reconquer not only the Danubian Provinces, but also part of the Ukraine, and thus renew the glories of Suleiman the Magnificent. Ambition and the promptings of Napoleon spurred her on to this

---

[1] *Nap. Corr.* no. 12563; Gardane, *La Mission du Gén. Gardane en Perse*; S. Lane-Poole, *Life of Stratford Canning*, I. 105, 128–39.

adventurous course. Prudence and the advice of Canning counselled otherwise. The chaotic condition of the Ottoman realms, the penury of their finances, the bad discipline of their troops, the rebellions of their Pachas and the restiveness of the native Christians, called aloud for a speedy peace as the only means of averting disintegration and ruin. On one point, the Divan was irrevocably pledged. "Not an inch of land" was the maxim which it opposed to the land-hunger of the Muscovites. At times, the clash of Turkish pride and Russian persistence seemed irremediable. On February 6th, Canning wrote to Wellesley that the French Embassy deemed the negotiation at an end. Such was the general impression, and it induced in Napoleon, even at the end of March, the confident belief that a renewal of the Russo-Turkish War would embarrass the Tsar and prevent him braving the power of France[1]. Meanwhile, on February 19th, Stratford Canning had taken the unusual step of writing (with the approval of the Sultan) to the Neapolitan Minister at Petrograd, asking him to use his good offices at that Court and to represent the need of moderation in the Russian demands and the danger of exasperating the Turks so highly as to drive them into the arms of France. On the same day, he wrote to the Turkish and Russian negotiators at Bukharest, ending his letter to Italinski with these words: "The conclusion of peace between Russia and the Porte would be one obstacle the less to peace between Russia and England, and consequently to that peace which alone can secure the true repose of the universe." To the Turkish negotiator, he explained the course of French intrigues for the prolongation of the Russo-Turkish War, and in cautious terms he offered the services of Great Britain for its settlement[2]. But this was not all. On hearing that the Divan was strongly inclined to reject Russia's terms, he (to quote his words), "sent to tell the Reis Effendi that I trusted every effort consistent with the dignity, and every concession not incompatible with the safety, of the Empire would be made for the restoration of peace at the present crisis, and that, in order to give a striking proof of H.M.'s sincere regard for the Porte, I was ready to lend every assistance in my power towards the accomplishment of so desirable an object[3]."

How far the actions of Stratford Canning influenced the final issue is uncertain. The belligerents knew that his actions were not authorised

[1] *Nap. Corr.* no. 18622. See Zinkeisen, *Geschichte des Osmanischen Reichs*, VII. 718–29.
[2] Lane-Poole, I. 161–3.
[3] F.O. Turkey (1812). Stratford Canning to Wellesley, February 21st.

from Downing Street. Indeed, on March 11th, he wrote to Wellesley, pointing out the unfortunate results of his long silence on eastern affairs, which contrasted with the activity of the French Embassy. But, six days later, he reported that the Grand Vizier had now received full powers to conclude peace with Russia on the best terms possible— a decision due to fear lest Napoleon and Alexander should come to an understanding and recur to their policy of partitioning Turkey[1]. Moreover, at the end of April, the Tsar, through the medium of the Prince Royal of Sweden, had informed the British Government that he "had given instructions to make peace at all events with the Porte and on any concession of his pretensions, provided only that they [i.e. the Turks] would enter into the alliance with England, Russia and Sweden[2]." The Turks declined an offer of offensive alliance which would involve hostilities with Napoleon. Indeed, they feared that even a peace with Russia might bring on them an attack from his Illyrian and Dalmatian Provinces[3]. Their apprehensions were not unreal; for he was about to send as Special Ambassador General Andréossi, with offers of alliance rich in allurements but not devoid of threats. The attitude of his Ally, Austria, was also menacing[4]. On the other hand, Sweden sent a mission to reassure the Sultan of her support.

Against diverse difficulties, Stratford Canning struggled manfully. Unfortunately, the accession of Castlereagh to the Foreign Secretaryship took place too late to afford official support at Constantinople. Liston [1742–1836] was appointed Ambassador at that court; but he arrived too late to influence the negotiations at Bukharest. Meanwhile, Stratford Canning worked with equal diligence and success to persuade Russia to reduce her claims and the Turks to abate their pride and their suspicion. Finally the Tsar's dread of Napoleon and the Turkish fear of a union of Russia, Austria and France for the partition of the Ottoman Empire, brought about a settlement in the Peace of Bukharest (May 28th, 1812), Turkey thereby ceded Bessarabia to Russia, but retained her former frontier in Asia Minor and her military hold on Serbia. The Treaty was ratified too late to enable the Russian forces in the Danubian Provinces to help in resisting Napoleon's march to Moscow; but that delay contributed to the completion of his mad enterprise, and, at the Beresina, those forces very nearly cut off his retreat.

[1] F.O. Turkey (1812). Stratford Canning to Wellesley, March 11th, 17th, 1812.
[2] F.O. Sweden, 72. Thornton to Castlereagh, May 2nd, 1812.
[3] F.O. Turkey (1812). Stratford Canning's despatch of April 25th.
[4] Zinkeisen, VII. 726; Lane-Poole, I. 165, 166.

Thenceforth, the retreat became a pitiable rout which encouraged the rally of the Prussian army of General Yorck to the Allied cause.

On the surface of these events, the eye beholds a vast efflux and reflux of armies, whose fate is decided less by the puny efforts of man than by the resistless powers of nature. But the trained imagination sees far more. It beholds the westward undertow of the Peninsular War, the weakening effect of the British naval blockade on all parts of Napoleon's empire and the thwarting of his attempts to capture Riga. It notes the efforts of British diplomacy to disengage Russia from the troublesome hostilities on her flanks and to convert Sweden and Turkey into Allies. Further, it recalls the unswerving efforts of Pitt, Grenville, Hawkesbury, Canning, Wellesley and Castlereagh to resist the territorial predominance of the French Revolution and of its heir, Napoleon. Those efforts were often unskilful, diffuse and wasteful. Their plans of European reconstruction were, also, in large measure artificial; for, in general, they were prompted by military considerations, and often erred in neglecting the interests of the peoples concerned. Yet Great Britain's Foreign Policy was honest and disinterested, when compared with that of her great antagonist and of her Allies. Externally imposing, his policy was marred by an unbounded selfishness. The conduct of the Central Powers was impaired by a petty egoism, a paralysing jealousy, and by half-heartedness that faltered at the first great reverse. Hers were at least the virtues of constancy and doggedness. Her work was slow but it was sure. Finally, her efforts, often failing but ever renewed, enabled the Continental monarchs to gain wisdom from bitter experience, and, after Napoleon's ambition had overreached itself, to enter into a close union such as had formerly been impracticable. As they gathered together in the year 1813, they might have ascribed to her the lofty praise with which the shade of Anchises hailed the spirit of him who foiled the fiery genius of Hannibal:

Tu Maximus ille es,
Unus qui nobis cunctando restituis rem.

CHAPTER IV

THE PACIFICATION OF EUROPE, 1813–1815

I. FROM THE TREATY OF KALISCH TO THE END OF THE YEAR 1813

DURING the year 1812, Great Britain had been able to do little to influence the course of the struggle that was taking place on the Continent. What she could do she had, under the guidance of the new Cabinet, on the whole done promptly and well. The unremitting pressure of the Blockade had been continued unrelaxed despite the opening of the American War. The assistance which had been given to Russia in money and material had shown that such aid was always at the command of any Power which would attempt to throw off Napoleon's ascendancy. British diplomacy had been, also, employed to some effect in relieving Russia from the pressure of both Turkey and Sweden, and the latter Power was now ready to become an active foe of Napoleon. At the extremities of Europe, where sea power could give her a footing, Great Britain had maintained her position. The steady improvement in the British and Portuguese armies had given solidity to the national resistance in the Peninsula, where greater success had been obtained than in any previous year. Sicily had, also, been kept free to serve as a base for attacks on Italy. But the main current of events was entirely outside the control of Great Britain; and she remained a mere spectator of the clash of forces on the Continent.

To some extent, this position is further maintained during the year 1813. In the great series of military and diplomatic events which changed Europe from an inert congeries of French vassals into a hostile Alliance whose armies were assembled on the French frontiers, British policy played only a subordinate part. She was, indeed, the paymaster of the Coalition. But a real voice in strategy or diplomacy could not be purchased by money alone. It needed military prestige and diplomatic ability of the first order to make use of the position which finance and sea power gave to her statesmen, and these she was only just beginning to command after long years of fatal blundering. Moreover, for most of the year the centre of operations was too far away for her statesmen to obtain any control over the bewilderingly rapid changes of situation on the Continent. It was not until 1814, when France itself became the scene of action, that the skilful diplomacy of Castlereagh was able to secure the position which her statesmen and people felt to be due to her proved power of resistance. Even in 1813, however, she played a more important and more successful part than in any previous Coalition against Napoleon, and, though she did not fully secure her objects, she prepared the way for the overwhelming success of the next year.

That this was so, was due to the fact that her statesmen had, at last, in some measure learnt by bitter experiences how to fight the Napoleonic Empire. The situation was, indeed, changed by the fact (which her Foreign Minister from the first perceived) that a national resistance was now being offered to Napoleon in the north of Europe. But his position was still far stronger than it had been in 1801 or in 1805, and if the forces arrayed against him were not more skilfully utilised than on previous occasions, it might be once more the fate of Great Britain to see the new Coalition dissolve as others had dissolved before. If British strength was again frittered away in useless expeditions and British diplomacy unable to secure the Coalition against the insidious methods which Napoleon knew so well how to employ, the result might yet be an Austerlitz and a Friedland, followed by a Peace as disastrous as that of Pressburg or Tilsit.

But the new Cabinet which had come into existence in 1810 contained men, mainly the pupils of Pitt, who, while lacking the ability or prestige of their master, had yet learnt much from his mistakes and proved themselves far more capable than their predecessors. Liverpool, who had become Prime-Minister after Perceval's assassination in June 1812, was a man of only moderate ability; but he possessed two great characteristics—a large experience, including nearly every Cabinet office, and an unfailing tact, which kept his Cabinet together and left the Opposition powerless. Castlereagh, the Secretary of State for Foreign Affairs, who had succeeded Wellesley in 1812, not only led the House of Commons with notable skill, but filled the most important office in the Cabinet as a pupil of Pitt, not less courageous than he was cautious and self-restrained. For this position Canning had been designed by Liverpool; and he could have secured it by a very slight exercise of self-subordination. But, though Canning would have brought to the Ministry imagination and brilliance, he would almost certainly have impaired its unity and hence its efficiency. Bathurst, the Secretary of State for War, was completely conversant with his colleague's ideas, and was an experienced and energetic administrator. Both Vansittart, the Chancellor of the Exchequer, and Sidmouth, at the Home Office, were dull and self-opinionated; but they served their turn as strenuous supporters of the policy of their abler colleagues. Almost all the rest of the Cabinet, which included Lords Harrowby as Privy Seal, Eldon as Chancellor and Mulgrave at the Ordnance, were men of experience who, however mediocre in political ability, not merely gave the Ministry weight, but were Ministers who could be trusted to follow loyally where they could not lead. There were, also, in the minor offices several men of high ability, among them Huskisson and Palmerston, and the Earl of Clancarty. Certainly, Pitt had never been fortunate enough to possess a staff so competent and experienced, and, though his commanding genius was lacking, the triumvirate of Liverpool, Bathurst and Castlereagh, who controlled the main lines of foreign and military policy, included among them some gifts which Pitt lacked, while they had learnt from the faults as well as from the good qualities of their master[1]. They were thus able to put Pitt's ideas into force only too successfully, when at last the opportunity came.

Of these three, Castlereagh was by far the ablest and, from 1814 onwards until his death, he obtained over British Foreign Policy a supremacy which he shared only with Wellington, who was to be so much by his side during the settlement of 1814-15. He won it not only by sheer hard work and force of character, but also by a sense of reality and a certain broadness of view which few of his Tory contemporaries possessed. He was, of course, blind to many things—as blind as Pitt. He accepted all the articles of the Tory creed for which the War had secured the active support of three-quarters of the upper classes of Great Britain. But he applied it with caution and self-restraint to Continental affairs. The ideas which he had inherited from Pitt he endeavoured to apply to this new phase of the struggle, and he added to them a few expedients of his own. These we shall see appearing in the course of this year, and carried into some sort of fruition in the settlement that followed in 1814-15.

The influence of the Prince Regent himself was not negligible.

---

[1] All three had held the offices both of Foreign Minister and of Secretary of State for War, and the unity of political and military strategy obtained was doubtless partly due to this fact.

He gradually obtained a considerable knowledge of men and events, and his personal relations with the Sovereigns had some influence on events in 1814 and 1815. On the whole, he was entirely amenable to the advice of his Cabinet at this period; but the personal wishes of himself and some of his royal brothers on minor points were apt to cause inconvenience. The Prince Regent was, also, Sovereign of Hanover, and the interests of that country, which had proved so fatal to Pitt's schemes in 1805, were still an embarrassing charge upon his Ministers. Fortunately, Count Münster, who represented him in Hanoverian affairs, was shrewd and moderate in action, though imbued with the most intense reactionary views. He could always, in the last resort, be controlled by Castlereagh, who, at the same time, left him so far as possible the last word on such matters as the German Constitution, in which British Ministers were only indirectly interested. From Münster and other Hanoverian Ministers, such as Count Hardenberg at Vienna and L. von Ompteda, Castlereagh undoubtedly learnt much about Continental affairs which was of great use to him.

Castlereagh was but imperfectly served by his diplomatic subordinates. The curse of jobbery still lay heavy on all appointments. Castlereagh obeyed the natural instinct of the British aristocracy in putting his relations, friends and the friends of his political associates into all the good jobs that lay in his patronage. Seniority counted for something, good men might possibly be rewarded after many years, and actual incompetence was not tolerated; but far too many of Castlereagh's subordinates were connexions of himself and his colleagues, who had obtained their position for this reason. Further, as always at the close of a great war, military and diplomatic functions were not clearly distinguished. Castlereagh's representatives were sometimes soldiers who combined a dual function—and soldiers, unless they are exceptional men, do not often make good diplomatists. From this cause, also, it resulted that Castlereagh was represented in Italy at a most critical period of our relations, by a fierce Whig like Lord William Bentinck. For years, of course, the profession of English diplomacy in Europe had almost been suspended, since diplomatic relations had practically ceased to exist with the majority of European States. Inferior agents, half-diplomatists, half-spies, like King or Horn, were the only links connecting the British Government with Continental Courts. Castlereagh was lucky enough to find Sir Henry Wellesley at Cadiz, and Stratford Canning temporarily in charge at Constantinople. For the rest, until Clancarty came to help him at Vienna, he had no one but untrained mediocrities in his principal missions. Over these he had, however, so far as time and distance allowed, a complete control. He had moreover their loyal support and complete confidence, and to many of them he could write with great intimacy, though he rarely revealed all he was aiming at. He handled a difficult team, half-amateurs, with great tact. He praised freely and, when he had to censure, he generally knew how to gild the pill. On the whole, he was too kind to them; but they repaid him with a real devotion which made them sometimes better instruments of his policy than abler men would have been. At the outset, Castlereagh lacked, like all British statesmen, any real knowledge of the statesmen of other countries. He and his colleagues had been cut off from the Continent, and the new men that were now rising to power were known to them only by gossip and very imperfect reports. Aberdeen, so late as the autumn of 1813, had to explain to Castlereagh that Metternich was not an old man[1]. It was only because, in 1814 and 1815, Castlereagh went himself to the Continent and became acquainted with all the principal figures in European diplomacy, that he was able to attain to that intimate touch with affairs which he afterwards displayed.

The new situation, brought about by the complete destruction of Napoleon's army in Russia, was only gradually understood in England, and the events that immediately succeeded were not anticipated. British diplomacy, while securing Sweden for an active participation in the War on the Continent, had then concentrated on Austria rather than Prussia, though little had been expected from what Liverpool described as the imperial Government's "abject" policy[2]! Nor had the secret mission of Lord Walpole, Cathcart's Secretary of Embassy at Petrograd, to Vienna (December 1812–January 1813) produced any result but vague assurances from Metternich; and the British Ambassador had to withdraw to the country on Napoleon's discovery of his presence there. The Treaty of Kalisch between Russia and Prussia, which bound them to prosecute the War until the latter Power was restored to a position at least equivalent to that which she had held in 1805, was made without reference to Great Britain; though Prussia, of course, once the die was cast, appealed for pecuniary assistance in

[1] Lord Stanmore, *Life of Lord Aberdeen*, p. 35.
[2] December 22nd, 1812. Liverpool to Wellington, *Supplementary Despatches*, VII. 503.

money and material, in both of which she was sorely lacking. The news of her action, however, at once opened a prospect of an entire change in the European situation; and Castlereagh had, for the first time since his acceptance of office in June, to formulate his principles of action.

The main lines of policy which he was to follow in these years were laid down for him by history and tradition. They comprised, first of all, the maintenance of the colonial and maritime supremacy of Great Britain which, despite the unexpected rebuffs received by her in the American War, was now absolutely established. Not only were all the French Colonies now hers, but also the Dutch and Danish. In fact, the only overseas possessions not under her control were the South-American Colonies of her Allies, Spain and Portugal, and with those of the former now in revolt against the mother-country, she was rapidly establishing commercial relations—a far wiser and more lucrative policy than the schemes, at one time seriously considered, of bringing them under her own rule. She thus had in her hands an immense dominion, which she could keep as pledge for the Continental settlement. It was already clear that those portions of it which were regarded as vital to her maritime strategy she intended to retain; but the rest remained as a means at her disposal for securing such a Continental peace as she desired, and provided her with a diplomatic weapon of great value. Even more sensitive were British statesmen as to the "Maritime Rights" of Great Britain. For these, she was, even now at the height of her struggle with Napoleon, waging war with the United States. The principal champion of Neutral Rights on the Continent had been Russia, now her Ally, and it was not difficult to see that Napoleon would, if he could, try to bring this matter under discussion. It was, therefore, always a cardinal point of British policy to exclude any discussion of British rights on this head from the negotiations as to the European settlement, and this point was easily gained.

Secondly, Great Britain had obligations to Allies on which she must insist if she was to obtain an honourable peace. Most important of these were her promises to restore complete freedom to Spain as well as to Portugal. Sicily had also been guaranteed to the Neapolitan Bourbons, who confidently expected to be restored to Naples by British help, and Sweden had received the promise of Norway in return for active assistance on the Continent. Throughout the negotiations of 1813, these obligations were made a *sine qua non* of peace with France.

Thirdly, Great Britain had to consider the political arrangement of the Continent. It had been her consistent policy to try to erect a barrier to the overwhelming power of France. How far the destruction of the Napoleonic empire would proceed, it was impossible to say. Even at this moment in England, there were some who hoped to reduce France to her ancient limits[1]. But such a result must depend on the resolution and skill of the European Powers, and few hoped that they would succeed so far. On this point, therefore, Great Britain depended on her Allies. She could not force them to go further than they wished. But, throughout, she encouraged them to go as far as possible, hoping to use her Colonial conquests as a means to drive back the power of France from the centre of Europe.

Lastly, when the final settlement came to be made, much of Castlereagh's energy was to be expended in endeavouring to force on the rest of the world the great reform that had been carried in Great Britain by the short-lived Whig Ministry—the Abolition of the Slave-trade, devotion to which public opinion, inspired by the efforts of Wilberforce and Clarkson, now made essential to the popularity, and even to the existence of a British Cabinet.

Bound by these considerations, which were imposed by the necessity of the case on all British Cabinets, Castlereagh drew up his Instructions at the beginning of April 1813, on the news of the Treaty of Kalisch. They were addressed to Earl Cathcart, special British representative at Alexander's headquarters, who had been sent to Russia in 1812. A soldier turned diplomatist, he was entirely unfitted for the important position which he now held. Even in military matters, he was unable to obtain satisfactory intelligence, while he never understood clearly the political and financial affairs which he had to handle. Already over middle age, "*le vieux général diplomate*," as George Jackson called him, lacked energy as well as ability. He fell under Alexander's influence, and no one could have been more unsuited to the task of interpreting the subtle and rapidly shifting diplomacy of 1813 to his distant chief. His rank and courage, and the confidence of his bearing, alone enabled him to maintain his position. In April, Castlereagh sent out in a similar capacity to Prussian headquarters Lord Stewart, his own half-brother. Like Cathcart, he was a soldier and had been Wellington's Adjutant-general. But the Duke, while very friendly to him, was far too shrewd a judge of men to accede to his fervent wish to command a cavalry division. Stewart had some

---

[1] *Bath Archives*, II. 54.

fine qualities. Brave to a fault, he succeeded in being in the thick of most of the great actions of 1813, and was wounded at Kulm. He had plenty of energy and sent home military intelligence of great value. He established close relations with the Prussian military commanders and learnt much from them; while his surveillance of the Swedish army, which was also one of his duties, was of real importance at critical stages in the struggle. But he was pompous, vain and wrong-headed, and as he often confessed, without any knowledge of diplomacy. He had been originally intended to be subordinate to Cathcart; but, though Castlereagh's affection (which was very strong, and was returned with real devotion and respect) secured for him an independent position, he was quite incapable of taking advantage of these favours. Thus, although intimate with the Sovereigns and statesmen, and present on all great diplomatic occasions, his vanity and love of display made him one of the standing jests of the Continent at the Congress of Vienna. His subordinate G. Jackson, who had been attached to his brother in 1807 in a mission to the Prussian Court, was a professional diplomatist of skill and knowledge. But he was not adequate to supplying the defects of his chief. With the two Ambassadors Extraordinary were, also, a number of British officers commissioned to act as intelligence officers. Notable among these was Sir Robert Wilson, who enjoyed a high reputation at Russian, and subsequently at Austrian, headquarters—an astonishingly brave and foolish man. He had a sort of roving commission, which he had made for himself in the War of 1812; and Cathcart's intense distrust and suspicion of him were not unjustified, if it is remembered that he was a violent Whig and in correspondence with Grenville and Grey on the faults of the Tory Government. The diplomatic staff, which gradually increased in numbers as the year went on, was largely composed of young relations and friends of the Tory Ministers, some of whom, as well as some of the Intelligence officers, were not without ability.

To Cathcart and Stewart Castlereagh addressed his Instructions, dated April 9th, 1813[1]. They were empowered to conclude new Treaties with Russia and Prussia, granting to both considerable financial assistance. Subsidies up to $2\frac{1}{2}$ millions were promised, of which sum Russia was to have three-quarters; and, further, Great Britain was also prepared to guarantee half of a common issue of paper-money of

---

[1] Castlereagh to Cathcart, April 9th, 1813; Oncken, *Oest. u. Preussen im Befreiungskriege*, II, 687.

five millions, not to be redeemed before July 1st, 1815, or six months after a treaty of peace had been signed. In return, Russia was to be asked to supply 200,000, and Prussia 100,000, men. Political considerations were only mentioned in so far as the whole scheme was to depend on concessions to Hanover, to which, owing to the pressure from the Prince Regent and Münster, Prussia was now called upon to cede the enclaves of Hildesheim, Minden and Ravensberg, as she had promised in 1802[1]. The connexion between Hanover and Great Britain, which had ruined Pitt's diplomacy in the Third Coalition, was still to cause great inconvenience; but, as will be seen, Castlereagh was successful in relegating it to a subordinate place, and even derived some advantages from it. Far more anxious was he to obtain in the Treaty an Alliance which should be able to withstand the arms and diplomacy of Napoleon. "The official assurances," he wrote in the Instructions, "already interchanged between Great Britain and Russia not to treat for peace except in concert should be reduced into a formal shape, Prussia being included, and the three Powers should engage to unite their arms and their councils with a view to such arrangements as may be best calculated to secure the independency of Europe[2]." Castlereagh did not enter into the details of these arrangements. We are in no doubt, however, as to the principles on which he intended to found his policy for the reconstruction of Europe. In a private letter to Cathcart accompanying the despatch, he referred the Emperor to Pitt's reply to the Instructions of Novossiltsoff on which the Third Coalition was founded. The important paper in which Pitt had then replied to Alexander's grandiose schemes for a new Europe, in which a reestablished Balance of Power should be protected by a specially constructed alliance, was the basis of the policy which Castlereagh was now to endeavour to pursue[3]. But he did not yet wish to commit himself.

"The political arrangement of Europe," he wrote, "in a larger sense is more difficult at this early moment to decide on. So much depends on events, that it is perhaps better not to be too prompt in encountering litigated questions. The main features we are agreed upon—that, to keep France in order, we require great masses—that Prussia, Austria and Russia ought to be as great and powerful as they have ever been—and that the

---

[1] Castlereagh to Cathcart, April 9th, 1813; Oncken, *op. cit.* II. 691; Webster, *British Diplomacy*, 1813-15, p. 2.
[2] Oncken, *op. cit.* II. 690.
[3] Castlereagh to Cathcart, April 8th, 1813. *Castlereagh Correspondence*, VIII. 356. Pitt's despatch is given in the Appendix to *British Diplomacy*. See also *supra*, Chapter III. pp. 335-37.

inferior States must be summoned to assist or pay the forfeit of resistance. I see many inconveniences in premature conclusions, but we ought not to be unprepared."

Castlereagh was right in not expecting too much on these questions. Through the whole of 1813, he was to press for a comprehensive alliance, which should give him such a peace as Pitt had outlined in 1805, and at the same time contain some permanent guarantee as to its continuance. To Castlereagh mere subsidy treaties, negotiated with the Powers separately, were not enough. He wished for a treaty combining all the Powers at war in a bond which Napoleon would be unable to break by a sweeping victory or a subtle piece of diplomacy. But, though the Allied armies and the diplomacy of Metternich secured the triumph of his cause, throughout 1813 the British Ambassadors proved quite unable to secure such a treaty. And, when the Allied forces were assembled on the Rhine, the "federal bond," as Castlereagh conceived it, was still lacking.

These Instructions, with which Lord Stewart reached Allied Head-quarters in April, resulted in the Treaties of Reichenbach, which were not concluded until June 14th, by which time they were already out of date. Only three meetings could be held in the days from May 5th to 24th between the two Ambassadors and the Prussian and Russian statesmen, though Lord Stewart, to his great mortification, missed the battle of Lützen by his endeavour to transact a little business. Prussia was very stiffnecked as to the cessions to Hanover, and it was with great difficulty that Stewart obtained a promise of the cession of Hildesheim. Hardenberg had even the audacity to hint that he would appeal to public opinion in England, always jealous of using British money to promote Hanoverian interests. Prussia, also, insisted on a clause guaranteeing her restoration to a position equivalent to that which she occupied in 1806, such as she had already obtained from Russia in the Treaty of Kalisch. There were great difficulties in arranging the methods of payment, both of the subsidies and the "Federative paper" (specially guaranteed paper money); and the exact quota of men each Power should be required to furnish caused considerable discussion. Thus, though the two Powers were eager to get their money, the Treaties were not signed till June 14th. With the exception of a clause that no separate negotiations should be entered into with the enemy the stipulations as to Prussia and Hanover were the only political points contained in them.

Before this, however, the diplomatic situation had completely changed. Beaten, but not overwhelmingly so, at Lützen and Bautzen, the Allies had accepted Napoleon's offer of an armistice and secured favourable terms at Pläswitz (June 4th, 1813). In concluding this Armistice, no reference had been made to the British Ambassadors, and no stipulation had been added as to the Spanish War. More serious, however, were the negotiations with Austria. Metternich had now completed his plans for the offer of armed mediation, which was accepted by the Allies as soon as the armistice was signed. The tortuous negotiations by which Metternich accomplished the transition from Alliance with Napoleon to Alliance with his enemies still remain difficult to follow, and their various stages have been much a matter of dispute among historians. They were certainly only very imperfectly understood by the British Ambassadors, who were only partially informed as to events. So soon as it was clear that Russia intended to prosecute the War in the centre of Europe, Metternich had perforce to choose his line of action. With wonderful skill, he maintained negotiations both with Napoleon and the Allies for over six months, before he finally declared himself, and so subtly did he ring the changes that Napoleon never completely penetrated his designs, while the Allies were not sure of him until almost at the moment when the Austrian armies joined them. In a sense, Austrian policy remained undecided to the last moment, and, though Metternich himself may, as he afterwards claimed, have seen clearly that his negotiations could have but one end, there is much to be said for the view that he really desired a peace, which, while strengthening Austria and Prussia, would leave neither France nor Russia, whose designs on Poland he soon discovered, in a position to overawe the Austrian dominions.

In any case, it was his policy to elude the proposals of Russia and Prussia by proffering his good offices to effect a peace between them and Napoleon. This offer he also made to Great Britain, whither he despatched Wessenberg in the early months of 1813. The Austrian Envoy was, however, coldly received by the Government, and the Press, in publishing the news of his mission, was vehement in its denunciation of a Power regarded as entirely subservient to Napoleon. The Austrian overture which suggested that the British Ministers might help to make a Continental peace by offering to give up the maritime conquests, though it made no specific proposals as to the main lines of such a peace, was, therefore, naturally rejected by them. The rejection was made even more certain by a passage in Napoleon's speech in the Legislative Assembly, which was intentionally inserted for that purpose. The overture was, accordingly, not merely rejected; it was refused with indignation[1].

This rebuff was however used by Metternich with great adroitness. Instead of, as Napoleon had hoped, forcing him to take the French side, he used it as an excuse to substitute a policy of armed mediation instead of mere peaceful good offices. If Austria was disregarded, it was necessary for her to make herself respected, to increase her armaments and to insist upon peace by a threat of force. It was difficult for Napoleon, when about to enter on a struggle with the joint Prussian and Russian armies, to resent this policy as he would have liked to have done. Metternich was, therefore, free to increase his military preparations without concealment, while, at the same time, he renewed his secret negotiations with Alexander. These went so far, under the influence of Stadion, who was head of the anti-French party, that on May 16th he obtained from Alexander, through that Envoy, his terms for the settlement of Europe, which insisted on French withdrawal, not merely from Germany, but from Italy also.

The battle of Bautzen (May 22nd) and the acceptance of Napoleon's offer of the Armistice (June 4th) made Austria hesitate. The moment had now come when she must declare her terms; but she was not prepared to go so far as Alexander desired. In the early days of June, Metternich and Francis went to Gitschin in Bohemia, to be near the Allied headquarters; and here Nesselrode obtained a statement of Austria's position. She was prepared to go to war against Napoleon, unless he granted four conditions: (1) the dissolution of the Duchy of Warsaw; (2) the enlargement of Prussia, including the restoration to her of Danzig; (3) the return of the Illyrian provinces to Austria, and (4) the freeing of the Hanseatic Towns. Two other points Metternich was prepared to state that he regarded as of high importance, viz. the restoration of Prussia, as far as possible, to her position in 1805, and the dissolution of the Confederation of the Rhine. But he would not promise to make these last two conditions absolute. Nevertheless, Alexander was so convinced that Austria really meant to come in on the Allied side that, on June 14th, he agreed to the Austrian conditions, and Metternich was allowed, if he chose, to propose a Mediation to Napoleon on these terms.

Meanwhile, the British Ambassadors had been almost entirely ignored in these negotiations. Their Subsidy Treaties had been signed

---

[1] Castlereagh to Cathcart, April 9th, 1813. *Castlereagh Correspondence*, VIII. 359.

in draft before they were told of the Armistice, and, though the
Emperor informed them before the formal completion of the Treaty,
it was too late for them to express an opinion. Cathcart accepted this
position easily enough; but Stewart, though he considered the Armistice as justifiable, was soon rendered suspicious and indignant at
the practical exclusion of the British Plenipotentiaries from the important negotiations which were in progress. Hardenberg defended the
negotiation on the ground that, while Prussia had bound herself not
to make peace except in concert with her Ally, yet she remained at
liberty to communicate with a neutral the grounds on which she
would be prepared to sign peace[1]; and he justified the whole transaction on the ground that Prussia and Russia had no option but to
accede to Austria's terms. On June 21st, Hardenberg informed Stewart
that Austria and Prussia had consented to send negotiators to Prague,
who were however not to deal direct with the French Plenipotentiaries, but only through Metternich, and tried to reassure him by
explaining that Metternich's policy was only to lure Napoleon on to
expose himself, and that there was no prospect of peace. But, in all
these transactions, there was no mention of those points to which
Britain attached the greatest importance; while, though information
was given to the British representatives after the transaction, no communication was made in time for any influence on affairs to be exerted
by them[2]. Stewart, however, despite his pessimism, had no love for
so tedious a business as the negotiations. He went off to the north,
to inspect the Swedish troops, leaving Jackson with Cathcart to
survey and report the course of events. None of the British Envoys
were, however, informed that the arrangements between Austria and
the Allies had been put into treaty form by the Treaty of Reichenbach, signed on June 27th after Metternich's departure. This step
was kept secret from them at the express desire of Metternich, probably because he was anxious that no news of it should leak out, until
his negotiations with Napoleon were completed.

[1] Stewart to Castlereagh, June 16th, 1813. F.O. Prussia, 87. *British Diplomacy*,
p. 67. Information was sent to Castlereagh also in a despatch to Jacobi dated June 14th.
[2] Cathcart was, however, informed of Nesselrode's mission to Gitschin, and
he offered to supply the money necessary for any bribes that would help the negotiations. Cathcart to Castlereagh, June 1st, 1813; "Being well assured that no endeavour would be spared by B. P. to draw the councils of Austria to his interest, I
advised H.I.M. to have recourse to every expedient; and knowing the absolute want
of means in the Department of Secret Service, I thought it right in giving this
advice to offer to make good any engagement in that way by which a determination
to act in concert might be obtained and Count Nesselrode is authorised and instructed accordingly." F.O. Supplementary, 343; *British Diplomacy*, p. 4.

Meanwhile, on the news of the attitude of Austria at the end of May reaching England, Castlereagh had, for his part, determined to press her to declare herself. Cathcart was ordered by an Instruction of June 30th to demand an "explicit avowal of her sentiments and determination," and to offer her a credit of £500,000 immediately for her preliminary preparations, if she determined to come in. Before this Instruction reached Cathcart, however, Metternich was hurrying off to Dresden to meet Napoleon, so that it exercised but little influence on the course of events[1]. The news of the Armistice and the basis agreed upon by the Allied Powers produced at first no fresh Instruction from Castlereagh; for, as he confessed, he was powerless to say anything when Spain was deliberately left out of the negotiations. At the beginning of July, however, news came both to London and to the negotiating Powers of the battle of Vittoria and the virtual destruction of Napoleon's power in Spain. The news, as will be seen, had an important effect on the negotiations at Prague and Reichenbach; but it also produced a fresh set of Instructions from Castlereagh, dated July 5th[2]. In these, while promising that Wellington's army would not relax its efforts, he stated that the British Government would leave to the Continental Powers the initiative in arranging the Continental Peace. On Four Points, however, he declared, Great Britain could not compromise because bound by Treaty, viz. the independence of Spain, Portugal and Sicily, and the British engagements to Sweden. Further, Great Britain was ready, "in conjunction with her Allies," to insist "as absolutely necessary to lay the foundation of some counterpoise in the centre of Europe," on "the restoration of the Austrian and Prussian Monarchies to such an extent of power and consequence as may enable them to maintain such a counterpoise"; while the independence of Holland and Hanover was regarded as equally necessary. Lastly, Castlereagh urged as a demand, in his view important, but on which the Allies must decide, "the restoration of the rest of Germany, including Switzerland and Italy, to an order of things more consonant to the common safety." He admitted that the extent to which these matters could be pressed depended on whether Austria joined the Alliance, but promised the full support of Great Britain to Russia and Prussia, "so long as they would stand by each other and the cause of the Continent against France."

---

[1] Castlereagh to Cathcart, June 30, 1813. F.O. Russia, 83; *British Diplomacy*, p. 5.
[2] Oncken, *op. cit.* II. 702.

This statement was followed, eight days later, by two other Instructions[1] which were undoubtedly meant to conciliate Austria. In
the first place, the Armed Mediation was formally accepted, and,
secondly, a statement was made, though in general terms only, of the
principles on which Great Britain was prepared to surrender her
Colonial conquests. Of these, Castlereagh said, some must be kept,
and, while the Dutch Colonies might be restored, if Holland regained
her independence, and the Danish used to facilitate the Swedish
arrangements, the French Colonies would only be returned if a satisfactory Continental peace was secured, on conditions which, it was
indicated quite clearly, must be more consonant with British ideas
than the Four Points which Metternich had consented to make his
test for declaring war. Castlereagh thus still reserved some control
over the negotiations; for he could still refuse to make concessions on
the Colonial conditions, if an unsatisfactory peace was proposed, while
Metternich still lacked one weapon indispensable for his becoming
complete master of the situation, if Napoleon showed himself really
inclined to treat for peace[2].

It is now known that Napoleon had not the slightest intention of
treating for peace on any terms that could be accepted by the Allies;
but, for six weeks longer, the issue appeared to hang in the balance,
and more than once Austrian policy veered towards a pacific settlement. Metternich had set out for the famous interview at Dresden
on June 24th, leaving Stadion to sign, on the 27th, the Treaty of
Reichenbach between Russia and Prussia, which put in treaty form
the arrangements already agreed upon by the three Powers. At
Dresden, Metternich produced no terms of peace, but succeeded,
after two stormy interviews, in inducing Napoleon to accept a meeting
between French and Allied negotiators at Prague under his mediation
(June 30th). At the same time, an extension of the Armistice to
August 10th was agreed upon—an interval which both Metternich
and Napoleon desired, in order to complete their military preparations, and which Russia and Prussia had, therefore, perforce to accept.

No sooner had this been settled than the news of Vittoria reached
Dresden and, in a few days, Reichenbach. It did nothing to shake the
Emperor's resolution; but its effect on Austrian policy was, no doubt,

---

[1] Castlereagh to Cathcart (nos. 45 and 46), July 13th, 1813. F.O. Russia, 83;
British Diplomacy, pp. 12-13.
[2] As a further concession to Russia, Castlereagh was, also, now ready, though still
persisting in refusing Russian mediation, to negotiate for peace directly with the
United States, and Russia was asked to support this offer. See p. 532.

considerable. Jackson had no hesitation in declaring that it was the determining factor in Metternich's decisions, while Stewart wrote from Stralsund: "Wellington will save Europe yet." They exaggerated. Even after the receipt of this news, it is clear that there still existed a large Austrian peace party and that Metternich was not uninfluenced by it. He was, perhaps, more moved by the offers which Cathcart, after the receipt of Castlereagh's Instructions of July 5th, made to him of an immediate sum of money; for the Austrian finances were in a deplorable state. At any rate, by the end of July all reports tended to show that Austria would fight, unless Napoleon made immense concessions. At Trachenberg, as early as July 12th, the Russian and Prussian military leaders had already, with the assistance of Bernadotte, drawn up a plan of campaign, which involved the co-operation of the Austrian army in Bohemia. The so-called Congress of Prague, meanwhile, for which the French Envoys, after serious delay in arriving, were unable to obtain any Instructions at all from their master, gradually revealed the fact that Napoleon had no intention of treating. On August 7th Metternich put an end to the farce by at last producing his peace terms in the form of an ultimatum to Napoleon. The fact that he included all the six points agreed upon, and not merely the Four Points *sine quibus non* of the Reichenbach Treaty, showed that he had now fully determined on war. Napoleon was not prepared to reply in time; and, on August 12th, the news was signalled to the waiting armies on the Bohemian frontier, that Austria had declared war. Yet, even now, Metternich's reply (August 21st) to Maret's insulting Note of August 18th, which repeated the offer of a Congress, was studiously moderate and left him with the opportunity of reopening negotiations with Napoleon at any time that suited his own diplomacy. He avoided any specific refusal by pleading the necessity of referring to his Allies; and a copy of the Note was sent to London.

The fact, therefore, that, in this long series of negotiations, British interests had played an entirely subordinate part, made no difference to the ultimate settlement. How far there was a danger of a "Continental" peace, leaving Great Britain to accept the situation, may be doubted. The suspicion, certainly, occurred to her representatives and was duly reported[1]. Undoubtedly, if Napoleon had possessed any sense of the reality of the situation he might have obtained terms

---

[1] *E.g.* Jackson to Stewart, August 2nd, 1813. F.O. Prussia, 88; *British Diplomacy*, p. 74.

far more favourable than British statesmen, or even Alexander, desired. It is true that Russia and Prussia were bound by Treaties to Great Britain; but Metternich was free, except for the Four Points, and it cannot be gainsaid that the Allies were in no position to withstand the threat of his intervention against them, while even Austrian neutrality left them in a very dangerous position. Castlereagh could indeed fall back upon the Colonial conquests; but he would have found it difficult to resist a peace, if Metternich had declared it to be one which Austria would support. Even now that Austria had joined the Alliance, was it so welded together that it could withstand defeat in one big battle? And what guarantee was there that, if Napoleon was forced to conclude a peace, it would not be, once more, merely a truce until he had recovered his power, and until some incident had divided the Eastern Powers? These were the questions which Castlereagh was asking himself, when he received news, four weeks old, of the negotiations at Reichenbach, Prague and Trachenberg. He hoped that, at least, the points which he had urged in his despatches of July 5th and 13th would have been taken into consideration by the Allies, and he pressed urgently that Spain should not be left out of sight in laying down the preliminary basis[1].

It was, however, now indispensable to come into closer touch with Austria. Whether the negotiations continued or hostilities were resumed, it was obvious that the key to the position lay at Vienna. Accordingly, at the beginning of August, it was determined to send out a special Mission to the Austrian Court; and to this important post Castlereagh nominated the young Earl of Aberdeen, to whom for some time the Tory Ministry had been anxious to give official employment. His Instructions, dated August 6th, show how far Castlereagh was prepared to go to win Austria over. As to his general attitude towards Continental affairs, Aberdeen was to follow the Instructions already sent to Stewart and Cathcart; but Austria's special interests in Italy were dealt with in two separate despatches. In the first of these, the importance of concluding a convention with Murat, whom Castlereagh thought to be still in Italy, was emphasised, and reference was made to the fact that he had already made overtures both to Austria and to Great Britain. In this despatch, it was suggested that Murat should be given compensation in the centre of Italy, so that Ferdinand might be restored to his kingdom. In a separate despatch, however, Castlereagh agreed that Murat might

---

[1] Castlereagh to Cathcart, August 7th, 1813. *Castlereagh Correspondence*, IX. 39.

retain Naples, if he made it a *sine qua non*, compensation being found for Ferdinand, and Aberdeen was authorised to sign a convention to that effect *sub spe rati*. As will be seen, this second Instruction, which Castlereagh only intended to be used in the last resort, was to have important consequences. On the more general question, likewise, Castlereagh made no secret of his anxiety to see Austria "resume its preponderance in the North of Italy" including the territory of Venice[1].

For the rest, Castlereagh let events take their course, until he received definite information early in September, that Austria had joined the Allies. The risks British interests had run during the recent negotiations now determined him to take a step which appears to have been in his mind throughout the year, and for which he now thought the time was ripe. On September 18th he forwarded new Instructions to the Continent, which went deeply into the main issues of the conflict and put forward an entirely new view of the Alliance against Napoleon. They opened with a review of the nature of the Confederacy arrayed against France, which Castlereagh claimed was distinguished from all previous combinations, "by the number and magnitude of the Powers engaged" not less than "by the national character which the war has assumed throughout the respective states. On former occasions it was a contest of Sovereigns in some instances perhaps against the prevailing sentiment of their subjects. It is now a struggle dictated by the feelings of the people of all ranks as well as by the necessity of the case." The Sovereigns of Europe, having at last learnt the dangers of isolation, were now bound together, for the first time, by a consciousness of common danger. Their only chance of safety was not to allow any offer of the enemy to divide them. The War in Spain and the War in Germany were one, and, if the Allies held together and persevered, they must in the long run triumph. But, though the Powers had concluded a number of separate Treaties with one another, there was as yet no common Instrument, and even so essential a point as the independence of Spain had not yet been agreed to by the Allies as a whole, though Russia and Prussia were morally bound to support that claim, and Austria now presumably also, since she had agreed to fight for the objects laid down on May 16th, among which Spanish independence was expressly stipu-

---

[1] Castlereagh to Aberdeen (nos. 2, 3 and separate), August 6th, 1813. F.O. Austria, 101; *British Diplomacy*, pp. 94–97. The "most secret and separate" despatch appears to have been unknown to historians, and has caused much confusion in dealing with the later policy towards Murat.

lated. Castlereagh, also, indicated quite clearly that the Congress of Prague had occasioned great uneasiness to the British Cabinet, and, while professing the fullest confidence that Russia and Prussia had not contemplated signing a separate peace, pointed out that, supposing Napoleon had accepted the Austrian basis, the Armistice must have been prolonged, for the purpose of ascertaining the views of the British Cabinet, with perhaps disastrous results in the Peninsula. Castlereagh therefore pressed for a new Public Treaty, in which the Powers bound themselves not to make peace or to conclude any convention except in common. The Spanish Cortes, Portugal and Sicily, the principal Allies of Great Britain, were to be invited to accede to it. The ideas of the State Paper of 1805 are, however, specially perceptible in two clauses designed to make the Treaty a permanent part of the Public Law of Europe. They stipulate

That, after Peace shall be concluded by common consent, there shall continue between the said High Contracting Parties a perpetual Defensive Alliance for the maintenance of such Peace and for the mutual Protection of their respective States;

and

That in case of attack hereafter by France or any one of the said High Contracting Parties, the several Powers will support the Party so attacked with all their forces if necessary, and see justice done[1].

This was the first statement of the policy which Castlereagh was to carry through, six months later, at Chaumont. He was aware that such a measure necessitated an agreement among the Powers on the general principles of the Peace which it was intended to secure. He suggested, therefore, that Secret Articles should be attached to the Treaty, in which the objects of the Allies should be clearly specified, and a suggested draft of these Articles was also enclosed. They were based on the Russo-Prussian demands of May 16th, which Castlereagh assumed Austria to be now ready to sign; but he made additions to them specially safeguarding the points in which Great Britain had a special interest, but which had hitherto been neglected. Of these, Norway, Naples (or compensation to Sicily) and the restoration of the House of Brunswick were in the zone of the demands. But Castlereagh, also, added the provision of an "adequate Barrier" for Holland, which meant abandoning the Rhine frontier.

---

[1] Castlereagh to Cathcart, September 18th, 1813. F.O. Russia, 83; *British Diplomacy*, p. 19.

Otherwise, the Treaty would have left France with her "natural limits" of the Rhine, the Alps and the Pyrenees[1].

He seems scarcely to have been aware of the difficulty of carrying out these Instructions and of the inadequacy of his subordinates for securing so important an Instrument. In private letters to Cathcart[2], he urged the importance of pressing the matter forward, so that Parliament, which was to meet on November 4th, could be informed and the Cabinet take the Treaty into consideration in planning the campaign of 1814. He anticipated that Austria would be the most likely Power to offer opposition, and he devoted a special letter to arguments likely to convince Metternich that no adequate peace could be made, unless his policy was accepted. Before the Instructions arrived, however—and it was two days after the battle of Leipzig that Cathcart received them—further negotiations had taken place among the Allied Powers. At the headquarters of the main Allied army in Bohemia, the two Emperors and the Prussian King, with their Ministers, were now assembled, and in the intervals of discussing the Allied strategy they drew up new Treaties to regulate their political conduct. They were accompanied by Cathcart and Stewart. When the latter returned from his northern journey, he discovered the existence of the Treaty of Reichenbach of June 27th, and wrote off furious protests to his Court. Hardenberg made a great favour of even showing it him, and justified the breach of faith by the absolute necessity of agreeing to Metternich's conditions at this stage. Jackson was not slow to point out that he had suspected the Treaty, but that Hardenberg had positively denied it. Stewart drew from the whole transaction confirmation of the suspicions he had repeatedly expressed of Austria's conduct during the course of the Armistice, and maintained his conviction that, had Napoleon accepted the Four Points, Austria would have brought about a peace substantially on those terms[3].

Metternich, who was now the arbiter of the Allied diplomacy, nevertheless took pains to put himself on the best terms with the British Envoys. In interviews with Stewart and Cathcart, he said that he knew himself to be distrusted by the British Cabinet; but that throughout the period of his subserviency to France he had always

[1] Castlereagh to Cathcart, September 18th, 1813. F.O. Russia, 83; *British Diplomacy*, p. 25.

[2] Castlereagh to Cathcart, September 18th and 21st, 1813. F.O. Supplementary, 343; *British Diplomacy*, pp. 27, 29.

[3] Stewart to Castlereagh, August 12th and August 20th, 1813; Jackson to Stewart, August 12th; Hardenberg to Stewart, August 20th. F.O. Prussia, 89; *British Diplomacy*, pp. 76–78.

had in view the situation in which he now found himself. These efforts still left Stewart suspicious, though Cathcart (as ever) was fully satisfied. It was for Lord Aberdeen, however, that Metternich reserved his greatest efforts, and in a short time he had established a commanding influence over the British Plenipotentiary. Aberdeen, then only twenty-nine years of age, had been the ward of Dundas and of Pitt, in whose house he had often lived. He was a far more able and cultured man than either of his colleagues, and the favour that Pitt had shown him, as well as his own good qualities and high rank, had caused him at a very early age to be marked out by the Tory Ministry for office. He had, more than once, refused high diplomatic appointments. At last, doubtless partly owing to the death of his wife in 1812, he acceded to the urgent requests of Castlereagh and other Ministers to undertake the mission to the Austrian Court. His shy and reserved character, his moderation and breadth of view and the Liberal principles and peace-loving disposition which distinguished him always from his partisan colleagues and made him at a later stage the valued confidant of Peel, might have exercised considerable influence on the course of events, had he known more of the pitfalls of diplomatic intercourse. But he was absolutely without experience, and, though not without knowledge of European politics, he was far too academic and unskilled to penetrate the complicated situation presented to him. Castlereagh treated him with studied courtesy, and kept him by his side till Peace was made. But Aberdeen was ill at ease with men like Cathcart and Stewart, and never gave them his full confidence. In a very short space of time, admitted daily to the Imperial table, and treated with infinite tact by the Austrian Minister, he saw only with the eyes of Metternich. Another disturbing factor was, that he also fell under the influence of Sir Robert Wilson, who was aiming at establishing himself as Military Representative at Austrian headquarters, and saw in Aberdeen a means of overthrowing the determined hostility of Cathcart. Wilson was, also, flattered by the Austrians, and, as he upheld views of a speedy peace which, whatever their ultimate intention, were in direct opposition to those of the British Cabinet, the result was to make Aberdeen's arrival a source of weakness rather than strength to British diplomacy, and to increase the ascendancy of Metternich over the whole course of the negotiations. At the same time, it is to be remembered that Aberdeen was specially instructed to pursue a line of close confidence in Metternich.

"I am inclined to think," wrote Castlereagh, "it is best to make a Hero of him and by giving him a reputation to excite him to sustain it....If you deem it useful you may tell him from me, I am perfectly ready to adopt him upon his own avowal, and to meet vigorous exertion on his part with perfect goodwill and confidence on mine—and that, as long as he will wield the great Machine in his hands with determination and spirit, I will support him as zealously as I have done the Prince Royal against all his calumniators, and I hope not less successfully[1]."

One of Aberdeen's first tasks was to communicate to Metternich the fact that, during the course of the Armistice, Great Britain had accepted Austrian mediation. This had hitherto been studiously concealed from Austria at the urgent request of Alexander, and the disclosure was now made with sufficient tact to relegate the incident to oblivion. Aberdeen's communication of the points of interest to Great Britain, in which besides making Spain an absolute condition of policy, he urged the independence of Holland and Hanover as absolutely necessary, and the freeing of Germany and Italy as very desirable, came too late to produce any effect on the Treaty of Töplitz between Austria, Russia and Prussia, which was signed four days after his arrival at headquarters.

As to Murat, Aberdeen was surprised to find that he was at Dresden in an important command. After Bautzen and Lützen, Murat had, indeed, felt himself no longer able to resist Napoleon's summons. But his troops remained in his kingdom and gave no assistance to the Viceroy, while neither he nor his Queen ever broke off relations with the Austrian Court. In these circumstances, Metternich had little difficulty in inducing Aberdeen, not only to inform him immediately of the whole of his Instructions, but also to furnish him in writing with a statement that he was authorised to treat with Murat on the basis of Naples being retained by its *de facto* ruler.

In the Treaties of Töplitz, which were only communicated to the British Envoys a week after they were signed, no mention was made either of Spain, Holland, Italy or Norway. The British Ambassadors, however, professed themselves as satisfied with explanations that no peace would be made without Great Britain's claims being taken into account. Metternich went no further in his Subsidy Treaty with Great Britain, signed on October 9th, which was confined merely to a promise not to make peace except in common. Meanwhile, though

[1] Castlereagh to Aberdeen, September 21st, 1813. F.O. Austria, 101; *British Diplomacy*, p. 97.

it was apparent that negotiations would only be resumed when the issue of the autumn campaign was known, Metternich was building up a diplomatic basis by which his own ascendancy over events could be preserved. If, indeed, Murat had for the moment returned to his old allegiance, Metternich was now tempting Bavaria to desert. This "spirit of negotiation," as Castlereagh termed it, on which Aberdeen's colleagues were not slow in commenting, caused great uneasiness in London. The communication of Maret's note proposing a Congress had already provoked a despatch from Castlereagh to Aberdeen on September 28th[1], deprecating the conclusion of any armistice, or the entering into any prolonged discussion, with Napoleon, before the substance of the Allies' terms had been granted. "When Buonaparte proposes a Congress," he wrote, "let him state the principles on which he is ready to negotiate, and it will then be in the power of the Allies, comparing them with the acknowledged principles which bind them together, to judge whether discussion can be advisable on such a basis." And, while asserting that Great Britain would always be ready to enter into negotiations in conjunction with her Allies, he "deprecates illusory discussions which must damp the ardour of the Confederacy, and conceives that no steps ought to be taken to assemble a Congress, till some satisfactory basis is previously understood." And such a basis was, surely, to be found in the Russian proposals of May 16th, with Castlereagh's additions.

Aberdeen was, a little later, instructed in a private letter to urge Austria to put more faith in the sword and less in diplomacy. His rather hasty step as regards Murat was, indeed, immediately approved by Castlereagh, though he was cautioned against committing his Court to any formal guarantee of Naples to its ruler. It was, moreover, to be clearly understood that any engagement to Murat must be contingent on his active participation in the struggle against France; and it was assumed that Austria would find an indemnity for Ferdinand[2]. In the private letter[3] accompanying the despatch, Castlereagh showed that he scarcely hoped much from these negotiations, though he admitted that the military advantages to be obtained were worth the sacrifice.

"I lose no time," he wrote, "in relieving you from all anxiety upon the point of Murat. It is a strong measure, but warranted by the state of Italy,

[1] F.O. Austria, 101; *British Diplomacy*, p. 98.
[2] Castlereagh to Aberdeen, October 15th (no. 21) (Most Secret). F.O. Austria, 101.
[3] Castlereagh to Aberdeen, October 15th (Private and Confidential). F.O. Austria, 101; *British Diplomacy*, p. 102.

of which important portion of Europe, in a military sense, I consider the *soi-disant* King of Naples to be completely Master, for with his army he can at once march uninterruptedly to the Tagliamento, and, unless the Viceroy evacuates the whole of what is called the Illyrian Provinces, his communications and his kingdom of Italy are in equal jeopardy. I own, however, I am not sanguine as to the result of the negotiation, because I assume Murat to be a mere calculator, and there is a spirit of negotiation about Metternich upon which such adventurers will always so far speculate as to endeavour to gain time."

Perhaps it was this distrust of the whole matter that prevented Castlereagh from informing Bentinck of the change in British policy—an omission which was to cause much confusion in the ensuing months.

Castlereagh was, indeed, far from satisfied with Metternich's general attitude and the spirit in which he was conducting the War. The reply to Maret was termed a "milk-and-water" answer to an insulting letter. Let Austria "imitate Prussia," wrote Castlereagh, "and make the Austrians an armed people," if she was desirous of obtaining peace from Napoleon.

"If you ever mention to Mr de Metternich my individual sentiments upon these subjects," he continued, "you can from your own knowledge assure him, that I am not one of those who cannot reconcile themselves to contemplate the possibility of peace even with Bonaparte, but I am satisfied it must be a peace founded upon a principle of authority and not of submission. That to obtain and still more to preserve it, we must rouse and arm the people we have to conduct, and it is in the earnest desire of peace that I wish to see him employed, rather in preparing the nation for sacrifices and exertions than in idly flattering them with the notion that peace is at hand."

And the rôle he designed for Austria in Italy is clearly indicated in the phrase "Until a solid organisation of the mass of the population is secured, we shall always find them timid as to acquisitions to the southwards and avaricious of extensions on their eastern frontier." In a postscript, written after perusal of Napoleon's appeals in the *Moniteur* after the breaking of the Armistice, he added one of those passionate if uncouth entreaties which moments of emergency sometimes drew from him.

I cannot, I own, but consider [them] as a serious and awful summons to us all for renewed vigilance concert and exertion. It convinces me that Bonaparte has determined to be numerically powerful on all points. This, I think, he has the means of doing for a limited period, and upon the confines of France. Having men under arms in abundance, he can make this gigantick array but he cannot sustain it. If confined even for a time to the sphere within which he now moves, it must dissolve; but the whole military history of the Revolution has taught us to dread that the monster once engendered on French ground may break loose to seek its sustenance elsewhere. This is the true danger against which the Continent and especially Austria has to provide, and she ought not to lose an hour in appealing forcibly to the nation. The people are now the only barrier. They are against France, and this is the shield above all others that a State should determine to interpose for its protection which is so wholly destitute as Austria of a defensible frontier.

But while Castlereagh was penning these lines the Allies had triumphed. The insistence of the German Generals, and the impetus that Stewart and others had given to the lagging steps of Bernadotte, had at last united the three armies in overwhelming force against Napoleon at Leipzig, and the issue of the three days' fighting had barely left enough troops to win their way to the Rhine past Wrede's Bavarians at Hanau. All Germany, except a few northern fortresses, including Hamburg was now at the mercy of the Allied armies; and the petty States of the Confederation of the Rhine hastened to make their peace with Metternich. To the King of Saxony alone was it denied, and his country remained in military occupation of the Allies. The others, by a series of Treaties, bought their recognition by transferring their military resources to swell the armies of the Alliance.

Castlereagh's despatches of September 18th, instructing his Ambassadors to form the common Alliance, reached Cathcart on October 20th amid the ruins of Napoleon's army. The energetic Stewart and Jackson wished to press the negotiation at once; but Cathcart was put off by the Emperor, and, as headquarters split up while the Allied armies were marching to Frankfort, no opportunity was given to broach the matter until the 26th. Nor would Cathcart allow the other Ambassadors to approach their respective Sovereigns until Alexander's views were known[1]. But, before the Tsar's views could be ascertained on this subject, another negotiation of considerable importance had taken place with the enemy—the offer known as the "Frankfort Proposals." During the course of the battle of Leipzig, Napoleon, having taken the Austrian General Count Merfeldt prisoner, had seized the opportunity to attempt to use him as an intermediary between himself and the Allies. He had indicated to him, in vague

---

[1] Stewart to Castlereagh, October 21st, 1813. F.O. Prussia, 90; *British Diplomacy*, p. 80; Cathcart to Castlereagh, October 21st. F.O. Supplementary, 343. "I think there is nothing proposed which will occasion much difficulty or delay, and if it had arrived a day sooner it might perhaps have been signed here. It will be sent home as soon as possible."

terms, it is true, and without committing himself in writing, that he was now prepared to make great concessions for the sake of peace. He was ready to abandon Germany and, in reply to the skilful insinuations of Merfeldt, offered some concessions as to Italy also. Only England, he said, who wished to reduce the French fleet to thirty ships, was the obstacle to negotiation. This overture was faithfully reported to Metternich, while the battle was still in progress; and after the great victory he determined to make an answer by a similar method, choosing for that purpose St Aignan, Napoleon's representative at Weimar, who had been taken prisoner by the Allies in the course of their advance. The idea was Metternich's own. The Prussians disapproved of it; Alexander acquiesced half-heartedly. It was in Aberdeen that Metternich was to find his most eager collaborator. On October 29th the English Ambassador had been informed, that "in consequence of the British answer having been received" (*i.e.* Castlereagh's despatch on Maret's note) "it has been determined to open a communication with Bonaparte, but in such a manner as to give rise to as little speculation as possible, and indeed the whole affair is to be kept a profound secret." All written communications were to be avoided. Aberdeen's colleagues were not informed of the transaction. The excuse was the extreme secrecy of the proceedings; but Metternich could not but know that Stewart at least was likely to adopt a very different tone to Aberdeen's.

The Austrian Minister was anxious at the situation which the overwhelming victory of Leipzig had created. He had long been doubtful of Russia's designs on Poland. Now, Prussia's claims were disturbing him. "Nothing," reported Aberdeen, "would induce Austria to agree to the incorporation of Saxony in Prussia[1]." Metternich was, indeed, very doubtful whether Austrian interest would be served by a prolongation of the War. It might now be hoped that a peace could be obtained on the basis of the Treaties signed at Töplitz. The Allies were ready to offer Napoleon the "natural limits" of France—the Pyrenees, the Alps and the Rhine. If he refused them, an instrument would be in the hands of the Allies for undermining the national resistance of the French. If he accepted, on the Throne of France the Emperor's son-in-law might then help Austria to save Poland from Russia and Saxony from Prussia. But Austria was also bound to Great

---

[1] Aberdeen to Castlereagh, October 29th, October 30th, 1813. F.O. Austria, 102. Oncken, "Aus den letzten Monaten des Jahres 1813," *Historisches Taschenbuch,* VI. 2.

Britain, and, further, without some countenance from Great Britain the offer would be open to the same innuendoes that Napoleon had made to Merfeldt. Hence, the necessity of including among the negotiators Aberdeen, who, like Metternich but for different reasons, was anxious to bring about a peace.

The *mise-en-scène* was skilfully laid. Metternich saw St Aignan alone on the morning of November 8th, and prepared him for a further interview. Then, in conjunction with Nesselrode, whom the Tsar had with some diffidence allowed to act, and Aberdeen, he planned what should be said to him. In this interview, it was Aberdeen who combatted Nesselrode's desire to place the terms of peace as high as possible at the outset, and reduce them later in negotiation. The protest he made did credit to his honesty.

I told him that, if the propositions were made with the hope of being accepted, common-sense dictated that they should be as palatable to Bonaparte as was consistent with the fixed views of the Allies. If the propositions were made without any such hope, I deprecated the whole proceeding as being most erroneous in principle, and calculated to produce the greatest injury to the common cause. I observed that it would be much better to defer making any overture at all, if it was not thought that we were in a sufficiently commanding situation to make that which we were determined to press.

Metternich acquiesced. It was his own policy, and the "natural limits" were offered without restriction, though it was understood by Aberdeen that the frontiers of Holland and Piedmont should not be considered as irrevocably fixed. He urged the necessity of secrecy in the strongest possible manner, and made Metternich promise that St Aignan should not see the two Emperors, as had been originally intended. In deference, also, to his wishes, the proclamation to the French people which Metternich had intended to issue simultaneously with the opening of the negotiation was deferred till its result should be known. The preparations for war were to go on with undiminished activity[1].

Next morning, when St Aignan again saw Metternich and Nesselrode, Aberdeen joined them "as if by accident." But they had to deal with a diplomatist. St Aignan immediately, before Aberdeen's entry[2], reduced to writing the terms that were indicated. The terms

---

[1] Aberdeen to Castlereagh, November 9th, 1813. F.O. Austria, 102; *British Diplomacy*, p. 107.

[2] According to St Aignan's account; Aberdeen's despatch reads as if the writing had been done in his presence.

of the Continental Powers were sufficiently explicit—the frontiers of the Rhine, the Pyrenees and the Alps, and the absolute independence of all countries outside of them, except that in Holland the form of government and the frontiers were to be left open to discussion. But Aberdeen went on to report:

M. de St Aignan noted also that England was ready to make great sacrifices in order to obtain peace for Europe, that she did not interfere with the freedom of commerce or with those maritime rights to which France could with justice pretend. I particularly cautioned him against supposing that any possible consideration could induce Great Britain to abandon a particle of what she felt to belong to her maritime code, from which in no case could she ever recede, but that with this understanding she had no wish to interfere with the reasonable pretensions of France. I took this opportunity to contradict the assertion which Bonaparte had made to General Merfeldt, of the intention of the British Government to limit him to thirty ships of the line, and declared that so far as I knew it was a prejudice without any foundation.

All this was sincerely meant by Aberdeen as a way towards peace. But, in the Note which St Aignan subsequently drew up of the interview, the British Ambassador found himself committed to the proposition, "*que l'Angleterre était prête à faire les plus grands sacrifices pour la paix fondée sur ces bases, et à reconnaître la liberté du commerce et de la navigation, à laquelle la France a droit de prétendre.*" This Note he had not received when he drew up the despatch for his Court, which, however, shows his anxiety to excuse the step which he had taken[1]. In this despatch, he emphasised again his object that "the transaction should be conducted with the utmost secrecy and expedition." In order to secure this secrecy, Cathcart was not taken into confidence until after Aberdeen's courier had gone, and Jackson, who was acting for Stewart, was not informed officially of the transaction until the 11th. Cathcart, who was rapidly sinking to a very subordinate position, acquiesced. Jackson had, however, learnt, so early as the 8th, what was going on; and he agreed with Hardenberg's view, which was openly expressed to him, that the offer was a mistake. He warned Stewart, in letters which were sent to London, that Austria and Russia were anxious for peace. Stewart shared his apprehensions, and Berna-

---

[1] "I trust your Lordship will not disapprove of the part which I have taken in this affair. My great object, if any propositions were made, was to frame them so as to afford the greatest probability of success, consistent with the fixed policy of the Allies. I hope the communication which has been made will be found to embrace the most essential points and to demand as much as our actual situation entitles us to expect." Aberdeen to Castlereagh, Nov. 9th, 1813. F.O Austria, 103; *British Diplomacy*, p. 110.

dotte was irritated at having been kept in the dark. It was not, however, till Stewart returned to Frankfort that he learnt the contents of the note.

By that time, Napoleon's answer—the last penned by Maret, before Caulaincourt superseded him as Foreign Minister—had arrived. As Metternich predicted, it contained no acceptance of the basis, but merely declared a readiness to treat. St Aignan's minute was, however, skilfully used to insinuate that maritime questions would be discussed at the Congress. The unofficial and secret conversation had thus been made the basis of bringing into the European settlement the question of the Freedom of the Seas, which it was a cardinal point in British policy to refuse to discuss. Aberdeen had no alternative but to send in a minute of protest to Metternich, who returned an acceptable answer, which, now that Napoleon had rejected his terms, he had no difficulty in sending. His reply to Maret reiterated the necessity of accepting the terms before any discussion could take place. Aberdeen was satisfied with these proceedings. He explained to Castlereagh in a despatch of November 28th that the basis was merely meant to indicate the boundaries of France. Thus, no mention had been made of Poland, Sicily, Norway and other objects, some of which were of vital interest to Great Britain, and he assured him that "both the imperial Courts have framed their conduct on their belief of what would be most approved of by the British Government[1]." Stewart, however, was now alarmed and indignant. It was only from Maret's answer that he learnt the contents of the note, and both he and Jackson were naturally angry at being kept in the dark. A despatch was sent to London which criticised in the warmest language Aberdeen's conduct[2]. This did not make Stewart any more popular with the Courts of Austria and Prussia, and it was soon obvious that he and Aberdeen had no confidence in one another, and the latter at Metternich's request concealed from his fellow Envoy everything concerning the important negotiations. Cathcart in vain tried to make peace between them; but the quarrel broke out openly on the receipt of another reply from Napoleon, this time signed by Caulaincourt, whose nomination to the Foreign Ministry in place of Maret was a concession to the growing peace party at Paris. The arrival of this Note was concealed even from Aberdeen, until Pozzo di Borgo, who, as will be seen, was

[1] Aberdeen to Castlereagh, November 28th, 1813. F.O. Austria, 103; *British Diplomacy*, p. 113.
[2] Stewart to Castlereagh, November 28th, 1813. F.O. Prussia, 91; *British Diplomacy*, p. 88.

despatched on a special mission to England, could take with him a copy. But Stewart was not so easily put off. He succeeded in obtaining a copy of this note through a subordinate in Metternich's office, and his messenger was able to leave at the same time as the Russian General with a letter of protest against the way in which the British Envoys were being treated. Pozzo's mission he regarded as an insult to himself and his colleagues and hoped that Castlereagh would give it no countenance. Neither Cathcart nor, of course, Aberdeen supported him. The Note that caused so much distress was an acceptance of the Frankfort basis and of the suggestion that a Congress should meet at Mannheim as soon as possible. But it was now too late. Stein's arrival at Frankfort had made Alexander far less inclined than before to stay his armies at the frontier. The Declaration of the Allies, drafted by Metternich, had been issued, which, while promising the French people the natural frontiers, had announced an invasion, of France. Reply was made that the answer of Great Britain must be awaited before the negotiation could go forward, and meanwhile all preparations were made for the invasion.

Under such conditions it was not likely that Castlereagh's project of a Grand Alliance would make much progress. No answer was given to Cathcart, until the St Aignan negotiation had taken place. Then, to Cathcart's surprise, it came in the form of a despatch to Lieven which suggested that Castlereagh's project was now out of date. Alexander proposed that the new Treaty should be connected with the British Subsidy engagements for the ensuing year, and he further pressed that Great Britain should state in it the cessions of Colonial conquests which she was prepared to make in the interests of peace. When Cathcart protested, Alexander proposed, instead, merely a renewal of the Subsidy Treaty with an engagement as regards Spain; but, when urged to add the independence of Holland, with a "Barrier," Switzerland, and Sardinia, he showed great disinclination to anything of the kind, stating that "perhaps it was better to avoid binding more than was necessary by Treaty, lest in striving to do too much we should lose the opportunity of doing anything[1]." Stewart won the full assent of the Prussian Court[2]; but further negotiations on the 17th only revealed the fact that neither Russia nor Austria had any intention of going so far as Castlereagh wished. Aberdeen had hopes that Metter-

[1] Cathcart to Castlereagh, December 5th, 1813. F.O. Russia, 87; *British Diplomacy*, p. 48.

[2] Stewart to Castlereagh, November 24th, 1813. F.O. Prussia, 91; *British Diplomacy*, p. 88.

nich would carry the matter through, and Cathcart left the negotiations mainly to him—a device all the more congenial to Austria and
Russia, as it left Stewart out of the game. But, though Metternich
was much more encouraging than Alexander, he, in a conference
with Aberdeen and Nesselrode, backed the Russians in demanding
that Great Britain should furnish a declaration as to her conquests.
Aberdeen offered to make a general declaration in vague terms; but
Metternich used the Tsar's wishes as an excuse for insisting.

"I see clearly," wrote Aberdeen, "that Prince Metternich, although
perfectly ready to sign the Treaty himself, is unwilling to follow the example
of Prussia in separating herself from the Allies, for fear of giving umbrage
to Russia. He therefore will endeavour if possible to draw Russia with
him. This may be all very right, but I could not help observing to them
that they appeared by their conduct almost as anxious to make common
cause against us as against France[1]."

The result was that the negotiation failed. Nothing whatever
was signed; and, instead, Pozzo di Borgo was sent to London
with special Instructions for himself and Lieven to conclude a
treaty with the British Government, in which both next year's Subsidies and the cession of the Colonial conquests were to be specified.
In spite of Metternich's apparent goodwill, there can be no doubt
that the insistence on this latter point was mainly due to him;
for it reiterated the demand he had made at the beginning of the year.
Without it, indeed, he could not have that complete mastery over the
issue of peace or war, which it was his settled purpose to obtain
before the Congress, now agreed upon, met. Meanwhile, during the
month of December, the disunion of the British Ambassadors was
reflected in the disputes that were appearing amongst the Allies on
all sides. Bernadotte, now that Leipzig had rendered him far
less indispensable to his Allies, was being treated with much less
attention and respect than before, even on military questions. He was
clearly loath to invade French soil, preferring to attack Denmark, and,
though Stewart visited his headquarters in December to urge the
importance of an attack on Holland, whither the British Ministry were
now despatching an expeditionary force and the Prince of Orange,
he remained sullenly occupied with his own projects of Swedish
aggrandisement and the ambitious design on which he had long
meditated of replacing Napoleon on the Throne of France.

[1] Aberdeen to Castlereagh, December 5th, December 9th, 1813. F.O. Austria,
103.

Far more serious was the rivalry that began to appear between Austria and Russia. The main reason, ostensibly, was a dispute between Alexander and the Austrian Generals as to the necessity of passing through Switzerland on the march to France. Under the influence of La Harpe and Jomini, Alexander refused to violate the neutrality of Switzerland, which Napoleon, who could not but win strategic advantage from it, had promised to respect. The dispute was only settled by Metternich's skill in arranging for a mild revolution in Switzerland, which ensured a welcome for the Allied armies; yet the incident did much to embitter his relations with Alexander. But there were far graver causes for the prevailing discontent among the Allied diplomatists. The Powers were now deeply preoccupied with the future settlement of the territories which had come into their possession as a result of the break-up of the Napoleonic empire. Metternich had resumed negotiations with Murat who had left the remnants of the Grand Army and returned to his kingdom, vowing to avenge himself on the Emperor. Aberdeen, hereupon, tried to restrain Metternich from offering too much; but he had already committed himself, and Metternich had a free hand to offer him his kingdom in return for military assistance, if Austrian armies found themselves unable to deal with the French under Eugene, as was soon seen to be the case. By his Treaties with Bavaria and other members of the German Confederation, Metternich had already done much to undermine Stein's plan of a consolidated Germany. But he was even more closely concerned with the questions of Poland and Saxony. Austria was indeed looking for her own compensation in Italy; but she felt that a revived national Poland under Russian control would be a terrible menace to her Eastern frontier. Even the entire absorption of Saxony by Prussia would be preferable to this. The eyes of the Sovereigns and statesmen were accordingly directed towards the Vistula as much as to the Rhine, which their armies were preparing to cross. It was only natural, therefore, that they should wish to commit themselves as little as possible, and they were in no mood to fall in with Castlereagh's comprehensive schemes of Alliance.

Upon these difficult negotiations Castlereagh could exercise little influence from London. The advance of the Allied Armies had brought headquarters a week nearer to him; but contrary winds delayed the packets, and it sometimes took six or seven weeks for a message to go and return. Before the news of Leipzig reached him, he continued to press the Allies to raise their demands as high as possible, and to make the exertions necessary to enforce them; above all he pointed out again and again the necessity of uniting their counsels in a common bond. He dwelt persistently on the magnitude of French preparations and the certainty that Bonaparte would accept no possible peace, unless resisted with perseverance as well as energy —facts which, also, furnished "unanswerable arguments in support of the system of unqualified union amongst the Powers contending against France." He was dissatisfied with the limited extent of the Treaties of Töplitz, and especially with the fact that they made no mention of Spain; and he gave Cathcart a tolerably strong hint that the absence of any recognition of this essential point might affect the Subsidy arrangements for the next year[1]. His formal approval of Aberdeen's Subsidy Treaty with Austria at Töplitz was couched in a similar strain.

The question of Holland and the Low Countries now began to form one of the principal preoccupations of the British Government. The result of the battle of Leipzig had been to bring about an insurrection in Holland, and, on December 2nd, the Prince of Orange was received at Amsterdam and placed himself at the head of the national movement. This step had been concerted by the British Government, and troops were despatched under Sir Thomas Graham. But it was not merely Holland that it was now hoped to free from French control. So early as November 5th, Castlereagh informed Aberdeen that at this point the Rhine could not be a suitable frontier for France, and every argument was brought forward that might induce the Powers to see their own interests in the complete freedom of Holland and the necessity of a 'Barrier' (a term inherited from the struggle with Lewis XIV) between Holland proper and France. The British Cabinet had come to close agreement with William of Orange, and the project of establishing that Prince as ruler not only of Holland, but of a considerable portion at least of Belgium and possibly of northern Germany, was being actively pursued. Such a kingdom, in conjunction with a restored and consolidated Hanover, was regarded as the best means to keep French power in check on the north-eastern frontier[2].

---

[1] Castlereagh to Cathcart, October 14th, 1813. F.O. Supplementary, 343; *British Diplomacy*, p. 34. Castlereagh to Cathcart, October 15th. F.O. Russia, 87.

[2] Castlereagh to Aberdeen, November 5th, 1813. F.O. Austria, 101; *British Diplomacy*, p. 106. One argument for Holland's independence is noticeable. "If in no other point of view than as the natural centre of the money transactions of Europe, all interested nations are interested in its being again raised to the rank of a free and independent state." Castlereagh to Aberdeen, Nov. 5th, 1813. F.O. Austria, 101.

On November 30th, after the receipt of the news of the success of the
insurrection, this point was again urged by him in words which have
been often quoted. "The destruction of that arsenal is essential to
our safety. To leave it in the hands of France is little short of imposing
upon Great Britain the charge of a perpetual war establishment[1]";
and he directed Aberdeen in the strongest possible terms to remedy
the Frankfort proposals on this point. To Cathcart he wrote "I must
beg of you never to lose sight of Antwerp and its noxious contents,—
recommend also the Orange cause to the Emperor's warmest protection. The popular spirit which has shown itself there I look upon
as amongst the most fortunate events of the war." Aberdeen sent
agents and money to the Low Countries. But Metternich was not
yet ready to agree that the Low Countries should be taken from
France, and he had, moreover, not completely abandoned the idea
of creating an independent kingdom there under the Arch-duke Charles,
if the French were removed. Stewart did his utmost to bring Bernadotte's force into action upon Holland; but, in spite of letters from the
King of Prussia and Alexander, the Prince-Royal was not anxious
to use his Swedes at a point where his own interests would scarcely
be much served, and preferred instead to move against Holstein, so
that Denmark would be compelled by this threat to her German
dominions to cede Norway to him.

Meanwhile, Castlereagh had to consider the greater questions
which were raised by the news of the Frankfort proposals and the
failure of his Ambassadors to obtain the Treaty of Alliance. The
freeing of Germany, and especially the recovery of Holland, had acted
like wine on the spirits of the Cabinet and the nation. "It has operated
here as magical," wrote Castlereagh of this latter event; "there is
nothing beyond the tone of this country at this moment[2]." But,
though he was urgent to obtain the best possible peace, he remained
true to his policy of not pressing Great Britain's Allies too far. He
approved Aberdeen's action at Frankfort on receipt of his first despatches, and accepted the basis, merely trying to interpret the term
"natural frontiers" so as to secure "protection" for Holland, whose
cause he again warmly commended. But he indicated, once more, that
Great Britain's attitude towards her Colonial conquests would depend
on a satisfactory result on this point. He, also, urged that, if the basis

[1] Castlereagh to Aberdeen, November 30th, 1813. *Castlereagh Correspondence*,
IX. 35. The date there given is 13th, but it seems clear that 30th is more correct.
[2] Castlereagh to Cathcart, November 30th, 1813. F.O. Russia, 83.

was not at once accepted, the negotiation should be forthwith terminated. When, however, the British Cabinet had received the text of St Aignan's memorandum, they were much alarmed at the form which the negotiation on "Maritime Rights" had now assumed. Peremptory orders were sent to Aberdeen to make a written protest against the assumption that Great Britain could allow any discussion of this question in the Peace Congress. The document was also subjected to further criticisms. Exception was taken to the word "natural" in the phrase "natural limits"; and it was asserted that, if the enemy rejected this basis, he could have no claim to receive the offer again at a later date. It was, also, held that the reference in St Aignan's minute to the "natural influence" of France over the secondary States of Germany was liable to misinterpretation, and might be used to prevent the German States from forming "a Federal connexion under a constitutional head" to the exclusion of foreign influence. Castlereagh did not, however, agree with Stewart's criticism that Norway should have been included in the basis, accepting Aberdeen's explanation that only the frontiers of France were relevant; and his brother received a snub for the line which he had taken[1].

But on the question of the Grand Alliance, Stewart found his views more readily accepted, and Castlereagh expressed himself in strong terms to Cathcart, when he received the first news of Alexander's objections. He peremptorily refused to buy the Alliance at the price of subsidies and Colonial conquests. "If this species of negotiation is persisted in, better at once decline the measure altogether," he wrote, "and I am yet to learn why Great Britain is more interested in cementing the Confederacy than Russia." He noted that the principal point of his proposal had obviously been missed in these attempts of the Allies to utilise it for their own ends. "The main question is," he insisted, "shall the Confederates by a common treaty now identify their cause, and lay the Foundation of a defensive alliance against France?" He still hoped, therefore, that the Alliance would be carried through.

When, therefore, he learnt from Lieven the counter-proposals of Alexander, emphasising and expanding these demands, he showed himself extremely indignant. He refused even to enter into an official discussion with Lieven of such terms, but took pains to impress

---

[1] Castlereagh to Aberdeen, December 7th, 1813. F.O. Austria, 101; *British Diplomacy*, p. 116. Castlereagh to Stewart, December 17th. F.O. Prussia, 86; *British Diplomacy*, p. 92.

on him, in an informal conversation, the feelings of his Government. He was indignant at Alexander's suggestion that the British proposal seemed to indicate a distrust towards the Allies. It was not because the particular interests of Great Britain stood most in need of the Alliance that it had been put forward. Great Britain, he intimated, could look after herself better than any Continental Power, and she had approached Russia first, as being all but equally invulnerable. The Confederacy, he pointed out, was designed to restrain France—the France of Napoleon or the Revolution—in the future as well as up to the termination of the War—"not only to procure but to preserve peace."

"The terms of peace," he said to Lieven, "are no doubt of essential moment, and the arrangement of limits indispensable to the common safety. Nothing, however, but a defensive League is likely to deter France from returning to the old system of progressive encroachment. The proposition for such a League, it was conceived, would come with most propriety from Great Britain and from Russia, as the Powers least exposed in the first instance to French encroachments. It appeared that the example of two such leading Powers, ready to lend themselves to a system of common protection, would give confidence to the more exposed States, and encourage them to lean on such alliance for security, rather than attempt to fall back within the circle of French influence. That, whatever might be the hazards of a system of this nature, upon every enlarged view of policy it became Great Britain and Russia, even with a view to their own separate interests, not to shrink from bearing their share in it[1]."

He was prepared to make some modifications in his first proposals, to restrict the Treaty in the first instance to the Great Powers—Spain, however, being included—and to stipulate precisely the amount of force each should contribute to the Alliance. But he made the position quite clear as regards the Colonial conquests of Great Britain. She was ready to make, as she had already made, a general promise to restore conquests, if a satisfactory Continental peace was assured. But she was not ready to bind herself to details and simply hand over all the negotiations to her Allies. "The British Government never once conceived," he wrote, "that it could be expected that Great Britain would by treaty pass this discretion into other hands, and confide to its Allies the trust of negotiating for her at a general peace." He pointed out that the Allies had not said what they intended to do with their conquests, and Great Britain meant to preserve the same liberty of action. Finally, he added an appeal which showed how far he was removed from the insular position traditional to

[1] Castlereagh to Cathcart, December 18th, 1813. F.O. Russia, 83; *British Diplomacy*, p. 59.

British statesmen, and how deeply he had been impressed by the necessity of her maintaining her rôle of the protector of the Continent against France.

"Amongst the fluctuating policy of States," he wrote, "which too frequently varied with the predominance of particular statesmen, it appeared to me not less an act of wisdom than of duty to the world, that Great Britain and Russia should take this occasion of solemnly binding themselves in conjunction with the more exposed States of the Continent to oppose a Barrier hereafter to the oppression of France. The determination to take upon themselves this generous and provident task could afford to Europe the best, perhaps the only prospect of a durable peace; and when the experience of latter times was examined with respect to the policy of indifference to the fate of neighbouring States, the most anxious and interested politicians would find little to give countenance to an abstracted and selfish line of policy."

While Castlereagh held these views, it was not likely that Pozzo di Borgo could add much to Lieven's arguments; and Castlereagh refused to carry the negotiation further. It was, at first, his intention to request the Allies to send full powers to their Ambassadors at London for signing a Treaty of Alliance on the terms he had indicated. But the news from the Continent finally decided the Cabinet to take a more important step. The dissensions between the Allies were growing, and the British Ambassadors, so far from being able to prevent them, were themselves at issue and concealing their proceedings from one another. Jackson, who had been sent home for the purpose by Stewart after the Frankfort proposals, brought news, on the 15th, of Stewart's growing alarms and suspicions. Austria and Russia were now reported as on the verge of a rupture, and Bernadotte's conduct was arousing the gravest doubts. In spite of the favourable military situation, there appeared to be a real danger that a Treaty might be made without obtaining those securities which British statesmen thought necessary to the peace of the Continent. In these circumstances, it was decided that a member of the Cabinet should proceed to the Continent, furnished with specific and comprehensive Instructions, so that he could make decisions on the spot. Castlereagh at first thought of sending Harrowby, who had been Pitt's agent in the unfortunate negotiations of 1805. But it was clear to his colleagues that the Foreign Minister must go himself. If he remained in London, as had been proved, affairs changed so rapidly that he could obtain no control over events, and he was too far away to judge accurately between his rival Ambassadors.

"You have passed from operations so rapidly to negociations," he wrote to Cathcart, "that my arrangements have not kept pace with you. Had I foreseen that you were likely to open an intercourse at Paris, I should have deemed some central authority indispensable and should have at least required the three Ministers at Head Quarters to deliberate and decide on matters of general interest collectively. As it is, I hope no real mischief has occurred and I rely upon finding you all drawing cordially together[1]."

II. THE FALL OF NAPOLEON AND THE FIRST PEACE OF PARIS

The Instructions which Castlereagh took with him to the Continent were drawn up in the form of a Cabinet Memorandum[2]. This important document was prepared by his own hand and approved at a full Cabinet meeting, from which Camden was the only Minister absent. Before submitting his views to his colleagues, Castlereagh had obtained from the Ambassadors of the three Allied Powers Memoranda on the wishes of their Governments, and this information had been supplemented by unofficial discussions with Lieven and Pozzo di Borgo. Jackson, on his return from Frankfort, must also have furnished him with a good deal of that kind of information which cannot be conveyed in writing. He was thus fairly well acquainted with even the less obvious aspects of the situation. The effect of the recent discussions at Frankfort can, therefore, be clearly discerned in the Cabinet Memorandum; but the document is singularly moderate in tone, and evades some of the most controversial points. It was intended to deal in detail with only those questions in which Great Britain was specially interested, and the general Continental settlement is only very briefly considered. Designed as it was to enable Castlereagh to make decisions on the spot and so avoid the delay and consequent lack of influence which frequent reference to his Cabinet would entail, a very great deal was left to his discretion, revealing the fact that his colleagues had already great confidence in his ability and judgment, though he had not yet completed his second year as Minister for Foreign Affairs.

Castlereagh had already received from the three Ambassadors satisfactory assurances on the question of Maritime Rights, which the Frankfort proposals had brought under discussion. There could be no question of compromise on this point, and one of his first tasks

---

[1] Castlereagh to Cathcart, December 22nd, 1813. F.O. Supplementary, 343; *British Diplomacy*, p. 62.

[2] Dated December 26th, 1813. F.O. Continent. Archives, 1; *British Diplomacy*, p. 123.

when he arrived at headquarters was to secure a further declaration from the principal Ministers to the same effect. But the question of the restoration of the Colonial conquests still remained an open one, and how much importance was attached by the Allies to an explicit declaration on the subject had been seen in the course of the recent negotiations concerning the Alliance. This question, therefore, occupied the principal place in his instructions. Once more it was laid down that British concessions were to depend upon the nature of the Continental Peace. So far as this fell short· of what was considered necessary to the security of Holland, Italy and the Peninsula, a greater share of the conquests must be retained by Great Britain. Since it was now known that the Allies would be prepared to insist at least on the "natural limits" of the Alps, the Rhine and the Pyrenees, it was really the protection of Holland with which the Cabinet was mainly concerned; and to this point the Instructions recur more than once. Antwerp itself and "the absolute exclusion of France from any naval establishment on the Scheldt" were made conditions *sine qua non* of any material concessions by Great Britain. But it was hoped that more than this would be obtained, and that the whole of the Low Countries would be made into a "Barrier" against France. Only in that case would the majority of the Dutch and French Colonies be returned to Holland and France. It should be noticed that the actual union of the Low Countries and Holland was not yet finally decided. Metternich's hint that he might, after all, desire to set up an Austrian prince there was taken into account, and was to be accepted if pressed. It was also understood that part of Belgium might have to be left in French hands, if the Allies were not sufficiently successful, and the extension of the Prince of Orange's dominions into Germany was to depend on their consent. But the negotiations that Castlereagh had been carrying on with the Prince show that he had a clear policy, though he did not wish to bind himself too strictly in his Instructions; and, since the marriage of the Prince of Orange with the Princess Charlotte was expressly suggested, there could be no doubt as to the intention at this moment to make Holland as large as possible, though Castlereagh modified his views on this head after his first interviews with the Allied Ministers.

If Holland were restored in this way, the conquests, except for those which were to be considered as absolutely necessary to her maritime strategy, were to be regarded as objects of negotiation. But, since it was not possible to lay down express conditions as to how many

Colonies would be returned, the number was to depend on the kind of peace secured, and was therefore susceptible to many variations. In Castlereagh's[1] "Memorandum on a Maritime Peace" (an unsigned and unfinished document which accompanies the Instructions, and may be considered as part of them), the principle on which Britain was acting is clearly laid down:

> Her object is to see a maritime as well as a military Balance of Power established among the Powers of Europe, and as the basis of this arrangement she desires to see the independence of Spain and Holland as maritime Powers effectually provided for. Upon the supposition that these two objects shall be obtained in the proposed arrangements, that the limits of France shall be reduced within proper bounds, and that the peace of the Continent shall be secured by an amicable understanding between the Allies, Great Britain will then be prepared also to return within corresponding limits and to throw her acquisitions into the scale of the general interests. As nothing is yet defined with precision either as to the state of the enemy's limits or as to that of the Allies, it is impossible to do more than state on the part of Great Britain the nature and extent of concession she would be prepared to make upon given data as to the continental arrangements. The object will best be effected by stating what the maximum of concession might be on the part of Great Britain upon assuming the reduction of France within her ancient limits, and the Allies having amicably arranged their own state of possession.... (the British Government) do not desire to retain any of these Colonies for their mere commercial value—too happy if by their restoration they can give other states an additional motive to cultivate the arts of peace. The only objects to which they desire to adhere are those which effect essentially the engagement and security of their own dominion.

It was thus left to Castlereagh's discretion to restore all or none of the Colonies placed at his disposal, according as he was satisfied or not with the proposals of the Allies; and it will be seen that this power was of great importance to him at moments of crisis. The conquests which were to be retained on the plea of strategical necessity were few in number. Malta, of course, and the Cape of Good Hope, were included, Holland being compensated with £2,000,000 for the latter possession, which were to be spent in fortifying the Barrier. Mauritius, the Isle of Bourbon and Les Saintes were also considered necessary to the protection of the route to India. Guadeloupe was considered as in pledge to Sweden; but, if France insisted on its return, Bourbon could be assigned to Sweden (or some Dutch Colony for which Bourbon could be exchanged) in its place. All the

---

[1] F.O. Continent. Archives, 1 (undated); *British Diplomacy*, p. 126.

remaining West and East Indian Islands that had belonged to France or Holland Great Britain was prepared to surrender.

The Cabinet's views on the Continental settlement, apart from Holland, were only briefly indicated. Spain and Portugal were to be free, and, it was hoped, guaranteed against attack by the Continental Powers. In Italy, it was suggested that the King of Sardinia should receive Genoa in exchange for Savoy, as well as the control of the new routes over the Alps which the War had opened up. The Pope was to be restored; the centre of Italy left open for discussion. Lastly, if Austria made peace with Murat, the Sicilian Bourbons were to receive as a compensation Tuscany or Elba. All that was said as to Germany was that Great Britain was to offer her mediation. Any concession to Denmark was to be discussed with Sweden. Castlereagh had thus almost complete freedom of action in all the great questions that were dividing his Allies.

He was empowered to offer £5,000,000 in subsidies for the coming year to the Continental Powers, if they signed satisfactory engagements as to the Peninsula and Holland. Only a single short clause was inserted on the project of the Treaty of Alliance, which "was not to terminate with the War, but to comprise defensive arrangements with mutual obligations to support the Powers attacked by France with a certain amount of stipulated succours." The *casus foederis* was to be an attack by France on the European dominions of any of the Contracting Parties. Castlereagh had thus slightly modified his scheme in view of the criticisms of the Allies. The obligations to the Alliance were to be definite, instead of the vague phrase in the Instructions of September 18th, and the scope of the Alliance was to be restricted to Europe. Further, though Spain and Holland were to be contracting parties, it was now suggested, in view of the objections raised by Alexander and the dubious conduct of Bernadotte himself, that Sweden should not be an original signatory of the Treaty.

Doubtless, this short document was merely a *résumé* of a long discussion in the Cabinet, and Castlereagh had verbally gone into matters with his colleagues more fully than the Instructions record. The omissions cannot be accidental. Already, public opinion in England was discussing the policy of "no peace with Bonaparte" and the Bourbon Princes were making ready to act. There is nothing in the Instructions on this head. Castlereagh's own views, however, were clearly revealed in his discussions at headquarters. He was prepared to make peace with Napoleon, if a peace such as was implied in the

Instructions could be obtained. Like all the British Ministers, he wished the Bourbons to be restored if possible. But to avow such a policy was impossible for a Minister of the House of Hanover, and Castlereagh was convinced of the folly of attempting to impose the Bourbons on France by force of arms. To this policy he adhered, in spite of public clamour and opposition in the Cabinet, until the last chance of signing peace with Napoleon had vanished.

Even more significant is the absence in the Memorandum of any direction as to the disposition of the conquered territories of Poland and Germany. Castlereagh was well aware of the jealousies which had already arisen among the Allies on these points. That he considered an amicable termination of them of the highest importance is seen in the clause quoted above, which makes the Colonial concessions depend on "the Allies having amicably arranged their own state of possession." But he was apparently desirous of having a completely free hand on this point, so that he could make his decisions only after personal examination of the situation at headquarters. This was an important omission, for it is doubtful whether Castlereagh could have taken with him Instructions to pursue the line of policy which he followed during the next few months.

Castlereagh had no illusions as to the difficulty of the task before him, and he had already conceived the rôle he was to play in the great problem of the reconstruction of Europe. To F. J. Robinson (later Viscount Goderich and Earl of Ripon) whom he took with him as assistant, he stated in the course of the journey some of his ideas as to the situation he was about to meet, and the methods he meant to apply to it.

"In the course of our journey from Frankfort to Basle," wrote Ripon in a letter to Castlereagh's brother in 1839, "he stated to me that one of the great difficulties which he expected to encounter in the approaching negotiations would arise from the want of an habitual, confidential and free intercourse between the ministers of the great Powers *as a body*; and that many pretensions might be modified, asperities removed, and causes of irritation anticipated and met, by bringing the respective parties into unrestricted communications common to them all, and embracing in confidential and united discussions, all the great points in which they were severally interested[1]."

He had thus already taken upon himself something more than the duties of a British Minister anxious to defend British interests. He

---

[1] The Earl of Ripon to the Marquess of Londonderry, July 6th, 1839. *Castlereagh Correspondence*, 1, 128.

was prepared to play the part of Mediator between the statesmen and Sovereigns of the Allies whose decisions already threatened to break up the Alliance and to wreck the European settlement. It is this wide conception of his activities that marks out Castlereagh as the most European and the least insular of all British Foreign Ministers and, despite his limitations and his failures to appreciate the growing strength of the new forces of Liberalism and Nationality on the Continent, he had many of the qualities necessary for the task which he had set himself. Lord Ripon's comments, though designed to be read by an affectionate brother engaged in defending Castlereagh's reputation, have been justified by the researches of historians.

No man was ever better calculated so to transact business himself, and to bring others to act with him in such a manner, than Lord Londonderry. The suavity and dignity of his manners, his habitual patience and self-command, his considerate tolerance of difference of opinion in others, all fitted him for such a task: whilst his firmness, when he knew he was right, in no degree detracted from the influence of his conciliatory demeanour[1].

Thanks to these qualities, he was able to give to the Alliance a unity of view and a firmness of purpose which it sorely lacked, and ultimately to effect a European settlement which at least brought peace for a generation. In so doing he also laid the foundations for a new experiment in International Government, which, though it failed for the moment, was not the least of the stepping-stones in Europe's progress towards International Peace.

Castlereagh left England on the evening of the New Year, and arrived at Bâle on January 18th. He passed through the Hague and there opened to the Prince of Orange his views on the "Barrier," the Dutch Colonies and the marriage with the Princess Charlotte, and pressed him to expedite the siege of Antwerp, which Carnot was defending with all his old skill. At Bâle he found Metternich, Stadion and Hardenberg, but not Alexander, who had departed for the headquarters of the Allied armies at Langres. He was impatiently expected by all. Alexander had left a message with Cathcart, entreating Castlereagh to see him first before any of the statesmen, so much did he dread the impression that Metternich might produce in his absence. Metternich, as his intimate letters to Hudelist show, built many hopes on the effect Castlereagh's arrival would produce both on Napoleon and on his own colleagues. It was indeed time that some new factor

---

[1] The Earl of Ripon to the Marquess of Londonderry, July 6th, 1839. *Castlereagh Correspondence*, I, 128.

was introduced into the Allied Councils. For, as Metternich complained, though the armies had marched beyond the Rhine to the confines of the Vosges the Alliance had now no definite object. All the agreements that had been made in 1813 had been by this time fulfilled. Napoleon had accepted the proposals put forward at Frankfort, and Caulaincourt was impatiently waiting to begin discussions with the Allies, who had, however, spent the interval in mutual recrimination instead of preparing terms with which to meet him. The difficulty with regard to Switzerland had caused the first rupture between the Tsar and the Austrians. But a more important difference had now added to the prevailing dissensions. Alexander had openly announced his intention of dethroning Bonaparte, and it was Bernadotte he was suspected of wishing to put in his place. This was the first news which Castlereagh heard, not merely from Metternich but from his own Ambassadors and many other channels. It was thus necessary to deal at the outset with this question rather than the terms of Peace, for Metternich threatened to withdraw the Austrian forces unless the project was abandoned. Castlereagh found little difficulty in coming to an agreement with Metternich. By warmly supporting his objections to Bernadotte, Castlereagh obtained from the Austrian minister an admission that a Regency under the Empress (which Austria was suspected of favouring) was equally undesirable. He pressed on him the view that, if Bonaparte fell, the Bourbons were the only alternative, but that the issue must depend upon the French themselves.

"I left the question there," he reported on the 22nd, "having I thought done enough when I brought him to admit that there were only two alternatives in fact, Bonaparte or the Bourbons, and that the latter was the most desirable, if France took that tone upon it which could alone lead to its successful accomplishment accompanied with the good will and favourable sentiments of the nation[1]."

Thus early was the issue stated which had as yet occurred to few on the Continent—though among these were Talleyrand and Napoleon himself.

Once agreement had been reached on this question, Castlereagh and Metternich could discuss the question of peace terms. They went over the whole field of settlement. Castlereagh found Metternich still inclined to offer the Frankfort basis, but was able to report that "his geographical notions are improved," and that on the northern frontier he was ready to make concessions to the British point of view.

---

[1] Wellington, *Supplementary Despatches*, VIII. 535.

Metternich had now finally determined to abandon the Austrian claims on the Netherlands, and he was, also, prepared to insist on depriving France of a portion of the left bank of the Rhine. Castlereagh suggested that the Prussian dominions might be made to include territory to the left bank, remembering that "it was a favourite scheme of Mr Pitt," and doubting the expediency of extending the frontier of Holland too far—a policy in which he was to some extent influenced by Münster, who had no wish to see Holland overshadow Hanover and also absorb those compensations by which he hoped to improve the Hanoverian frontiers.

It was, also, necessary to enter into the questions of Poland and Saxony and "other questions of delicacy." For Castlereagh was strongly opposed to the policy which he found prevailing and which Alexander especially was urging, of excluding France from all knowledge of these plans of the Allies, and simply informing Caulaincourt of the frontier which the Allies offered to France. Castlereagh saw clearly, that France had interests in the disposition of the rest of Europe and therefore a right to be informed, at least in outline, of the plans of the Allies before Peace was signed. Moreover, he could not but be aware that the former course would postpone the Continental settlement, which he was anxious to arrange as soon as possible, and in which he thought the interests of his own country were involved as well as those of France. He had hopes that the Polish and Saxon questions were susceptible of an immediate solution. Metternich had already given Hardenberg a verbal promise to support his Saxon plans, and Cathcart had reported that Alexander was prepared to make the Vistula his frontier[1]. In this Cathcart was completely mistaken; but Castlereagh's first impression was so favourable that he hoped to be able to draw up a complete outline of the new Europe to submit to Caulaincourt. His knowledge and moderation made a great impression on Metternich. He had expected to find Castlereagh far more *intransigeant*, and he flattered himself he had made a good impression. Herein he was not mistaken, for, though Castlereagh was not blind to Metternich's faults, he found his Austrian colleague by far the most congenial personality at headquarters, and alone possessed of that spirit of compromise and readiness to face the facts which animated himself. He objected to Metternich's timidity and procrastination; but his other merits stood out in contrast to the impetuous and

[1] Cathcart to Castlereagh, January 16th, 1814. *Castlereagh Correspondence*, IX. 169.

emotional character of the Tsar, with whom Castlereagh was soon to have some stormy interviews.

The Ministers joined the Tsar at Langres on January 25th, and by February 1st the Alliance had compassed its object, and the Instructions were drafted for the Conference at Châtillon. Agreement was only reached, however, after prolonged discussions. The Austrians, both soldiers and diplomatists, were anxious to obtain peace as quickly as possible. Alexander, on the other hand, was determined to march on Paris and to refuse to treat with Napoleon. He denied, indeed, that he favoured Bernadotte; but he would not listen to any idea of the Bourbons, and talked vaguely of allowing the French nation to choose a ruler for themselves after Paris had been taken. Castlereagh, hereupon, suggested that the Ministers of the Four Powers had better discuss all the questions in dispute, and thus a Council was formally set up, in which during three days the whole policy of the Alliance was reviewed. Castlereagh, from the first, took a leading part in the discussions, and was eventually able to harmonise the conflicting views of Metternich and the Tsar. The Austrians he persuaded that military operations must go on unchecked, while the negotiations proceeded; the Tsar, or at least his Ministers, that terms must be offered to Napoleon and peace made with him, if he accepted them. As to the terms themselves, he succeeded in persuading Metternich to abandon formally the Frankfort basis, which, as he claimed, the military successes of the Allies and the Peace recently concluded with Murat had now rendered obsolete, and to substitute for them a project which practically reduced France to her ancient limits, with some concessions in Savoy and possibly on the left bank of the Rhine. All the Powers further agreed to his demand that Caulaincourt should be informed at the outset that the "Maritime Rights" must be left entirely out of the discussion. Less satisfactory were the consultations as to the outlines of the new Europe to be communicated to Caulaincourt. Here, only the vaguest formulae could be drawn up, and no mention was made of Saxony or Poland. On these points, Castlereagh found the Powers full of suspicion and the hopes he had formed at Bâle quite illusory. Nevertheless, he insisted that France must be given some information on this head, and that, Great Britain having declared her readiness to conclude peace with Napoleon, the offer must be made in such a shape as to render its acceptance possible[1].

[1] Castlereagh to Liverpool, January 29th, 1814. F.O. Continent. 2; *British Diplomacy*, p. 141. See Oncken, "Lord Castlereagh und die Ministerconferenz zu Langres," *Historisches Taschenbuch*, VI. 4. p. 5.

These conclusions were drawn up in the form of a Protocol, and embodied in Instructions to the Allied Plenipotentiaries at Châtillon. Here, Russia, Austria and Prussia were represented merely by one subordinate each, the principal Ministers remaining at Schwarzenberg's headquarters with their Sovereigns. Castlereagh sent, not only Aberdeen, but also Cathcart and Stewart, apparently in order not to offend any one of them or the Powers to which they were severally accredited; but he also appeared in person, to keep watch over the proceedings. That he should leave headquarters at this period, showed how much importance he attached to the way in which the negotiations were conducted. It was not that he expected Napoleon to accept the terms offered; but he felt that the cause of the Allies, and even more the restoration of the Bourbons, depended on the impression which the transaction was to make on the public opinion of France and Europe; and, with some reason, he distrusted the capacity of the diplomatists sent to Châtillon to carry out their Instructions in the spirit in which he at least had drawn them up.

Events were soon to show how well founded these doubts were. At Châtillon, Caulaincourt revealed himself as a sincere patriot and eager to obtain peace, for he had no illusions as to the situation. But, when confronted with the offer of the "ancient limits," he quite naturally pressed for information as to the intentions of the Powers with regard to such territories as Saxony and Italy. This was precisely the information which the Allied Plenipotentiaries could not give him; for they had not settled the matter among themselves. Moreover, it was soon apparent that Razumoffski, the Russian Plenipotentiary, was anxious to stop the discussions altogether. He had indeed, almost immediately, received orders from Alexander to do so, for the successes of the Allies in the early days of February had convinced the Tsar that the War was practically over, and that he could march straight to Paris. Castlereagh appears to have shared this view to some extent, but he was anxious that there should be no sudden rupture on the part of the Allies, and he wished to use Caulaincourt's interrogatories as a means to settle the points of the Continental settlement on which the Allies were at variance. He told the Plenipotentiaries frankly at the outset that he would only be prepared to sign away the Conquests, after three preliminary conditions had been satisfied.

"The first was," he said, "that France should submit to retire, if not literally, substantially within her ancient limits. Secondly—that Great Britain should have an assurance by an amicable arrangement of limits between the three Great Powers, that, having reduced France by their union they were not likely to re-establish her authority by differences amongst themselves. And thirdly—that we should be satisfied that the arrangements in favour of the Powers of whose interests we were especially the guardian, were likely to be attended to, and especially those of Holland and Sicily—the point of Spain being abandoned by France herself[1]."

But at Troyes, now the Allied headquarters, reached after Napoleon's defeat at La Rothière (February 21st) by Blücher, Metternich found that he could no longer control Alexander. The Tsar was urgent that Schwarzenberg should support Blücher's army and a direct march be made on Paris. The Austrians, both soldiers and diplomatists, were much alarmed, and Metternich especially so, since he feared, with reason, that Alexander had returned to the views he had held at Langres. The Tsar, at last, sent a formal order to Razumoffski to suspend negotiations[2]. Castlereagh, therefore, left for Troyes on February 10th. There, he found that the Tsar's order had been issued on his own authority, so as to prevent any further discussions till the Allies should have reached Paris, where he intended to summon a Representative Assembly to decide the future Sovereignty of France, Napoleon himself not being excluded from candidature. The Austrians were indignant and alarmed, especially as it was rumoured that Bernadotte was about to place himself at the head of the Allied corps nearest Paris. It was Castlereagh's task to convince Alexander of the danger of these intentions; and this he accomplished in two stormy interviews. The Tsar was still hostile to the return of the Bourbons, particularly of Lewis XVIII himself, and talked of satisfying his Allies by setting up the Duke of Orleans or another member of the younger branches of the Family. Castlereagh, in his efforts to convince the Tsar, went to the extreme limit of free speech permitted from a statesman to a Sovereign. It was the first of many such interviews in the ensuing twelve months. He asked the Tsar how long he would keep his troops in France to support a new Sovereign on the Throne, after the Allies had refused to make a peace on their own terms with Bonaparte. Alexander remained obdurate. He attempted to refute Castlereagh by producing a despatch from Lieven of January 26th, which declared that the Prince Regent and Liverpool wished Napoleon to be dethroned and the Bourbons substituted. Castlereagh replied that he was bound by his Instructions, and denied the

---

[1] Castlereagh to Liverpool, February 6th, 1814. F.O. Continent. 2; *British Diplomacy*, p. 147.
[2] Fournier, *Congress von Chatillon*, pp. 313, 372.

Tsar's right to question them[1]. He was very indignant at this attempt to undermine his authority, and the incident was perhaps a turning-point in his relations with the Tsar. For several days, the issue hung in the balance. But, in the Council of Ministers, where each Power replied in turn to a series of queries drawn up by Metternich, both Hardenberg and Castlereagh supported, in the main, the Austrian point of view, and Nesselrode was at heart of their opinion. A compromise was at last effected, in which Metternich obtained most of what he wanted, though not before he had secretly threatened to make a separate peace with Napoleon. He had to submit to a refusal of the armistice which Caulaincourt had offered, for on this point Castlereagh was strongly against him; but Alexander had to consent that the negotiations at Châtillon should be renewed, and circumstances soon made it clear that the march to Paris was out of the question. The Tsar's design had, however, caused a Convention to be drawn up by the three Continental Powers, as to the mode of occupation of the city. Castlereagh refused to sign this document, though he approved its contents, since he thought it advisable not to associate himself unnecessarily "in delicate questions relating to the interior of France[2]."

A new and more detailed document was, also, drawn up to be submitted to Caulaincourt. To effect this, Castlereagh had to make concessions. He now, for the first time, named the Colonies which he was prepared to give back to France, subsequently explaining to his Cabinet that, "as this is a document upon which, if the negotiation breaks off, the appeal [*i.e.* to public opinion] will be made, I thought it expedient to put the British terms forward in a liberal shape." The only French Colonies reserved, therefore, were Les Saintes, Tobago, Mauritius and Bourbon, and the French were to be allowed to have commercial settlements on the coast of India. In return, the limits of France were now expressly laid down as those of 1792, and, further, Castlereagh was allowed to add a clause stipulating that the Slave-trade should be abolished in all the Colonies so restored. But he had entirely failed to obtain his second point—an amicable arrangement among the Allies themselves, which he stipulated as necessary before he signed away the Colonies. On the contrary, Austria and Russia were more openly at variance than ever, and, in these circumstances, Castlereagh

---

[1] Castlereagh to Liverpool, February 16th, 1814. F.O. Continent. 2; *British Diplomacy*, p. 147.

[2] *Ibid.*

could do little either to bring his Allies to an agreement or to complete his project of a permanent Alliance.

But it was the question of the dynasty that had caused the greatest alarm, and Castlereagh took immediate steps to deal with it. He sent Robinson home to prevent any repetition of Lieven's intrigues, and naturally obtained Liverpool's full support. In spite of the opposition of one or two members of the Cabinet, a definite Instruction was sent to Castlereagh, that peace might be concluded with Napoleon if he accepted the Allied terms. At the same time, the Cabinet could not be deaf to the growing insistence of public opinion in England on the dethronement of Bonaparte. *The Times* and other papers were now vehement against him, and it was obvious that a peace with him, however satisfactory the terms, would be very unpopular. The Cabinet, therefore, urged that, if the terms were not at once accepted, an appeal should be made to the French nation to get rid of their ruler, and that, without attempting to prescribe to them their new sovereign, it should be suggested to them that only the Bourbons could bring them peace[1].

Castlereagh returned to Châtillon on February 16th, and the new *projet* was handed to Caulaincourt on the 17th. But, while these discussions had been in progress, the military situation had entirely changed; and, indeed, this had been one of the factors which had at last produced agreement. Napoleon had thoroughly beaten Blücher's troops in a series of battles in February, and then, turning on Schwarzenberg's army, had forced it to retreat in disorder. Thus it was now Caulaincourt and not the Allies who delayed; for Napoleon had withdrawn the permission to accept the terms previously given to his Envoy, who could now do nothing but refer to his master for new Instructions. Meanwhile, at the Allied headquarters, something like panic reigned, and the decision was taken to ask for an armistice. When this news reached Châtillon in a letter from Metternich, urging the necessity of expediting peace, Castlereagh immediately replied in an indignant letter, and entreated the Allies in passionate words not "to descend from the substance of your peace[2]." The letter betrays the emotion he felt; and, full of anxiety, he returned to headquarters, which had now retired to Bar-sur-Aube, so soon as the negotiations at Châtillon had been suspended. There, he found the greatest des-

---

[1] Bathurst to Castlereagh, February 27th, 1814. F.O. Continent. Archives, 2; *British Diplomacy*, p. 161.

[2] Castlereagh to Metternich, February 18th, 1814. F.O. Continent. Archives, 2; *British Diplomacy*, p. 158.

pondency. It was Alexander who had given the orders as to the
armistice offer, and he was now almost as urgent for peace as Austria.
The soldiers and diplomatists of both Powers were full of bitter recriminations. Each suspected the other of saving its army, while the
threatened appearance of Czartoryski and Radziwill at Alexander's
side renewed all Metternich's apprehensions about Poland. Castlereagh's patience was almost worn out. The Allies, by their previous
hesitation, had let slip the opportunity of signing a peace on the basis
of the old limits, and now they appeared to be ready to grant any concessions. "Nothing keeps either Power firm," he wrote, "but the
consciousness that without Great Britain the peace cannot be made[1]."
His own position, however, he made quite clear. He would refuse to
conclude any peace except that which had been agreed on at Troyes,
and, since it was unlikely that Napoleon would sign without assurances
from Great Britain as to the Colonies, without Castlereagh peace
could not be made. By this means, with some assistance from the
Prussians, he succeeded in reestablishing confidence. At the same
time, he played an important part in the military councils of the
Allies, where some timid spirits were already pressing for a retreat
to the Rhine. It was urgent to reinforce Blücher's beaten army,
against which Napoleon had once more turned after driving back
Schwarzenberg. The only means of obtaining these troops was to
detach from Bernadotte's command the corps of Bülow and Wintzingerode, which were now advancing from the Belgian frontier. When
the Allies hesitated lest such a step should offend Bernadotte, Castlereagh insisted that the order should be sent, and took upon himself
the responsibility of soothing the Crown-prince. These troops reached
Blücher just in time to save him at the battle of Laon, and Napoleon's
failure in that battle marked the beginning of the end[2].

For the moment, the situation was saved. Instructions were sent
to Châtillon to demand a definite answer within a reasonable time
from Caulaincourt to the *projet* previously given him, and, urged by
Castlereagh, Metternich sent a sufficiently warlike reply from the
Emperor of Austria to a letter recently addressed to his father-in-law by
Napoleon. Castlereagh did not return to Châtillon. The negotiations
there now depended more on the firmness of headquarters and their

---

[1] Castlereagh to Liverpool, February 26th, 1814. F.O. Continent. 3; *British
Diplomacy*, p. 160.
[2] Cf. the Earl of Ripon's account, *Castlereagh Correspondence*, I. 129. Bernadotte
was conciliated by being given nominal command of all the troops besieging the
French fortresses.

military and political energy than on what was said to Caulaincourt, and, above all, Castlereagh was anxious to use the financial necessities of his Allies to construct the Treaty of Alliance which recent events showed to be so urgently needed. He had kept this project in view, ever since he had joined the Allied Ministers. But the successive crises prevented him from doing more than discuss the question informally with his colleagues, as opportunity offered. So early as the middle of February, he had prepared a project of a Treaty based on his Instructions, and had secured the general approval of the Ministers of the three Powers. Even Alexander now gave his consent to the Treaty, stating that the restriction of the *casus foederis* to the European dominions of the Powers had removed his principal objection. The real motive of the Allies was, however, their anxiety to obtain Subsidies for the campaign; for Castlereagh refused to sign any Treaty on this subject, unless the larger question of the Alliance was likewise included. He had thus been forced to abandon the position which he had taken up in December, when approached by Lieven. This was, however, only a minor matter. Far more serious was it, that he had, also, to abandon his plan of making the Treaty contribute to the settlement of the outstanding questions between the Allies. His first weapon, the Colonial conquests, he was obliged to abandon, in order to obtain a suitable offer to Caulaincourt. Now, he had to promise the Subsidies without achieving his purpose. The truth was gradually becoming manifest, that the Allies were so divided as to render any result hopeless until after a long series of discussions. Castlereagh had, therefore, to be content with merely including in the Treaty the Articles already delivered to Caulaincourt at Châtillon, which, although they provided specifically for Holland, contained only vague references to the future of Germany, and made no mention of Poland or Saxony.

The Treaty of Alliance had a double object. First, to provide the means for ending the War then in progress. For this purpose, each Power agreed to keep 150,000 men in the field. The share of Great Britain was, however, a double one. For she not only bound herself to subsidise the armies of the other three Powers with five millions per annum, but she, also, agreed to provide 150,000 men herself. She was allowed, indeed, to employ the troops of the smaller Powers in the army for which she was responsible, and, as Castlereagh pointed out, the three other Powers had to raise considerably more than 150,000 men, for the Subsidies were based on the active strength of the troops. Still, even Castlereagh felt it was a bold offer on the part of Great Britain, which had scarcely been considered a great military Power. But since the Allies pressed him, he felt that Wellington's successes had justified him in accepting the challenge, and he was convinced that, if his country wished to have real influence on the Continent, she must be ready to assume military as well as naval responsibilities. "There can be no reason," he wrote, "why Great Britain should not assume that station in Europe as one of the great military powers which the exploits of her armies and the scale of her resources have so justly entitled her to claim[1]"; and, in a private letter, "My modesty would have prevented me from offering it; but, as they choose to make us a military power, I was determined not to play second fiddle[2]."

This agreement, which contained the usual clauses not to make peace except in common, was, however, only a continuation of the usual Subsidy engagements. The novel part of the Treaty, which was entirely due to Castlereagh, was to provide for the continuance of the Alliance in peacetime. In order that the Peace, when won, might be guaranteed, the Four Powers bound themselves to protect one another against France for a period of twenty years—but, in this case, the stipulated force was to be only 60,000 men. This is the origin of the Quadruple Alliance, which after some vicissitudes was to be revived again at Vienna and at Paris. It was Castlereagh's great scheme for preserving Europe from a repetition of the evils of the last twenty years. There can be no doubt that, if he had been able, he would have phrased it differently, and made it an Alliance, not merely against France, but against whatever Power broke the Peace. But, after all, it was France which, in the eyes of British statesmen, was most likely to cause a war in the future, and the equilibrium which the Treaty was to ensure was mainly to be obtained by balancing the rest of Europe against France. At least, so Castlereagh thought at the moment. He reserved the wider guarantee foreshadowed in Pitt's despatch of 1805, until the Allies should have settled their disputes. For it was not possible to broaden the scope of the Treaty, so long as it was uncertain what shape the New Europe would assume.

The Treaty was signed only by the Four Great Powers. Even Sweden was only asked to accede, and it marks the beginning of that

[1] Castlereagh to Liverpool, March 10th, 1814. F.O. Continent. Archives, 3; *British Diplomacy*, p. 165.
[2] Castlereagh to Hamilton, March 10th, 1814. *Castlereagh Correspondence*, IX. 335.

formal ascendancy of the Great Powers which was to be the characteristic of the nineteenth century. Spain, Portugal and Holland were also to be invited to place themselves under the protection of the Treaty, the minor German Powers not being included, because it was possible that they would shortly be welded together in a Federation which would be able to act for them all.

Castlereagh had thus accomplished only a part of the task which he had set himself, when he took his departure for the Continent. The Powers had shown themselves so undecided in their attitude towards the enemy, and so jealous of each other's claims, that no other course was possible. The European settlement had perforce to be left in a condition of uncertainty. But security against France, at least, had been won, and, with Napoleon still in the field, this had to override all other considerations. Even as it is, the Treaty, which was accepted by the Cabinet without alteration, and greeted with a chorus of praise by Castlereagh's subordinates, who knew how difficult the task had been, remains as, perhaps, his greatest achievement. At any rate, it symbolised the fact that, but for his intervention in 1814, the Coalition against France would almost certainly have been forced by its own dissensions to make a peace which, sooner or later, would have left Europe again at the mercy of Napoleon.

The Treaty of Chaumont, though dated March 1st, was not signed till March 9th, by which date the time limit for Caulaincourt's reply to the ultimatum of February 28th, had expired. During that period, Napoleon almost crushed Blücher's armies, but was foiled at Laon (March 9th) in a repulse which was equivalent to a heavy defeat; for Blücher, now reinforced by Bülow's and Wintzingerode's corps, was quite able to resume the offensive. But, in the meantime, Napoleon had entertained high hopes, and, up to March 9th, had sent no answer to Caulaincourt. The interval at Châtillon was passed in disputes as to the phrasing of the Protocol; but the information that reached the Plenipotentiaries made Caulaincourt even more anxious for peace—if this had been possible. Schwarzenberg's army won some minor successes, and from the south came the news (by way of London), that Wellington had resumed the offensive, defeated Soult at Orthez (February 27th) and was marching on Toulouse. On March 10th Caulaincourt sent an answer on his own initiative which evaded the direct question. Still, the Allied Plenipotentiaries did not break off negotiations, but referred the answer to headquarters; so that, as Stadion pointed out to Metternich, it was still possible to prolong the discussion almost indefinitely if he wished. Caulaincourt explored every possible channel, especially in the direction of Austria, by which he might obtain concessions, and thus perhaps secure a peace which his master would sign. But the Chaumont Treaty had been concluded, and the reply that came back from headquarters was an order to enforce the ultimatum. Even then, so anxious was each side to throw on the other the odium of refusing peace, that the rupture did not ensue till March 19th. The Declaration to the People of France, which made Napoleon responsible for the miseries the War was inflicting upon them, had been drawn up long before at head-quarters, not without considerable discussion; but it was not issued till March 25th, owing to the necessity of obtaining the Tsar's express approval before it was published.

By this time, however, the last act of the drama had begun. The Emperor, after the bloody battles of Craonne and Laon, which at least gave him a few days breathing space, turned once more against Schwarzenberg's army. Even now, he had no intention of sending to Caulaincourt the word that could alone bring peace. Checked at Arcis-sur-Aube, he formed the idea, which had long been in his mind, of throwing himself on the Allied line of communications, relieving his besieged fortresses in the east, joining forces with Augereau and com-pelling his enemies to retreat, in order to escape destruction. But, before this audacious plan could be put into operation, the Allied armies had reached his capital and made it certain that he would lose, not only the campaign, but his Throne.

The series of events that led to the Restoration of the Bourbons are intricate and obscure. As has been seen, Castlereagh had through-out the negotiations with Napoleon insisted that the Allies were bound to conclude peace with him, if he would agree to it. But he made it clear that, if another dynasty was to take the place of Napoleon, it could only be the Bourbons. The British Cabinet was, from the first, by no means united as to the possibility of making peace with Napo-leon. Harrowby and Eldon, and even Bathurst, were, as early as January, against such a conclusion. Sidmouth and Vansittart supported Liverpool in backing up Castlereagh's policy; but the Prime Minister found increasing difficulty in making head against the strong pre-dilection of the Prince Regent, which Münster's despatches must have intensified, and the ever increasing clamour of the Press. The Marquis Wellesley had also expressed himself strongly on the Bourbon-side, and was reported to be gaining in favour with the Prince; and, deprived of Castlereagh's assistance, the Ministry was losing ground everywhere[1].

On March 19th, the news of the prolongation of the Châtillon Conference caused the Cabinet to send a strong protest to Castlereagh, who was ordered to inform the Allies that, unless the negotiations were brought to a speedy close, the British offers as to the Colonial conquests would be withdrawn[2]. At last, when the news came that Bordeaux had declared for the Bourbons, the firmness of the Cabinet broke down. On March 22nd, Instructions were sent to Castlereagh that no peace must be signed with Bonaparte[3]; he was also told that, if one had already been signed, it would not be ratified until the Cabinet were convinced that the Emperor still possessed the allegiance of the French people. Neither of these Instructions, however, had any influence on the course of events. Before they reached their destination, the wishes of the Cabinet had already been fulfilled.

Throughout the campaign in the north, no signs had been given by the French people that they wished for the return of the Bourbons. Monsieur (Charles X) had taken up residence at Vesoul; but his emissaries had exercised no effect. On the contrary, the exasperation of the French peasants at the brutality of the Allied troops had, as Castlereagh noted, made them look to Bonaparte once more as a protector. In the south, however, where Wellington's army paid for all it took, and where plundering was repressed by an iron discipline, the people showed a very different spirit. To the south the Duc d'Angoulême had been allowed to proceed; but Wellington, though he was desirous of his success, gave him no open countenance. The Bourbon Prince was, however, able to get in touch with his supporters, much more numerous in the south, and, on March 12th, Bordeaux raised the white flag. Though an intrigue of an emissary of Bernadotte's confused the issue for a moment, this example was soon followed by other towns.

The real intrigue, however, took place in the north. Throughout the negotiations with Napoleon, the conduct of the Allies was studiously correct. Alexander indeed, as has been seen, had no desire to help the Bourbons, and Metternich, to the last possible moment, pre-

---

[1] See C. K. Webster, *The Congress of Vienna*, p. 28.
[2] Bathurst to Castlereagh, March 19th, 1814. F.O. Continent. 1; *British Diplomacy*, p. 166.
[3] Bathurst to Castlereagh, March 22nd, 1814. F.O. Continent. 1; *British Diplomacy*, p. 171.

ferred a peace with his Emperor's son-in-law. But, once the Châtillon Conference was broken up, events moved quickly. Metternich had now to guard against what action Alexander might take if he found himself at Paris with a free hand. The Bourbon cause had there been slowly winning adherents, and Talleyrand, with Dalberg and others, were preparing the ground. No communication, however, as Castlereagh reported with surprise to the Cabinet, had been entered into with the Allies until the middle of March. Yet Baron Vitrolles, who then appeared at headquarters, was not received by the Allied Ministers, until the rupture with Napoleon was announced. Then, under Metternich's presidency, a formal meeting was held, and it was determined to support the Bourbon cause. The Bourbons were promised by the Continental Powers the immediate administration of any districts that declared in their favour. Castlereagh, for his part, offered funds, which, however, he wished to furnish through his Allies, "as not only the most prudential in a financial point of view, as rendering the expense definite on our part, but as relieving the question of much of the political difficulty, which must always attend, in a Government like ours, the voting a sum of money for effectuating a change in the Government of France." In fact, Castlereagh, while now determined to bring the Bourbons back, was anxious to take no step which would enable the Opposition to accuse the Government of not allowing the French to choose their own Sovereign. In the same way, he hoped that events at Paris, towards which the Allied armies were now making progress, would be regulated by the Convention drawn up at Troyes, to which he had refused his signature, so as to effect "the object I have in view, which is, to bring Great Britain forward, in whatever may regard the interior of France, rather as the Ally and auxiliary of the continental powers than as charging herself in chief[1]."

Alexander's consent was assumed, but not obtained, to these negotiations; for the Tsar was marching with the King of Prussia on Paris. Napoleon, on discovering their intentions, hesitated, and, before he could strike a blow, Marmont and Mortier had been defeated, and Paris capitulated. Castlereagh and Metternich, meanwhile, remained at Dijon with the Emperor of Austria, who, like Castlereagh, was anxious to avoid the final scene. There, on March 25th, the cause of the Bourbons was publicly toasted, Castlereagh joining in with the

---

[1] Castlereagh to Liverpool, March 22nd, 1814. F.O. Continent. 3; *British Diplomacy*, p. 168.

rest, and an Austrian agent was despatched to Monsieur, to urge him to raise the country, when the Allies would support him. Metternich's messenger to Paris was captured; but Castlereagh established communication by a letter to a friend in that city which brought a new agent to Dijon. When, therefore, on April 4th, Castlereagh and Metternich learnt that the Allies were in Paris, they knew that Talleyrand was assured of their support and that the Bourbon cause was in safe hands. Thus, though they were somewhat perturbed at the Tsar's pledge to guarantee a Constitution[1], yet they were quite easy in their minds on the question of the dynasty, in spite of the fact that Alexander's declaration merely excluded Napoleon himself from the Throne. Bernadotte's intrigues with Joseph and others, which were known through intercepted letters, had quite put him out of court, and Nesselrode had secretly reassured his colleagues on this head. Alexander at Paris had thus no real alternative to the Bourbons. He was easily persuaded, therefore, by the ingenious Talleyrand to take the necessary steps for their recall in a manner which ensured some show of popular approval, and the entreaties of the Marshals and Caulaincourt for a Regency were of no avail. That the Tsar had found it necessary to support Lewis XVIII, whom he regarded as absolutely unfit for the Throne, was due to causes over which no statesman had any control. But the steps that Castlereagh and Metternich took in the last days of March certainly contributed much to the course of events, and, but for the British statesman's intervention, the differences between Austria and Russia might have led to serious results. Alexander, however, was able by his solitary action to secure a Constitution for the French people—a step of sound wisdom, on which he would certainly have found it difficult to insist, if Castlereagh and Metternich had been on the spot. For, as will appear, with all his desire for a peaceful and contented Europe, Castlereagh had no wish to help the cause of Constitutional liberty on the Continent. Nor was he, when he arrived on April 10th, satisfied with the Treaty of Fontainebleau, which Alexander was on the point of signing with the dethroned Emperor. To this Treaty, which guaranteed the Emperor the full sovereignty of Elba, recognised his titles, assigned the duchies of Parma, Piacenza, and Guastalla to the Empress, with succession to her son, and made ample financial provision for Napoleon and all his family, Castlereagh raised many objections; but he was persuaded by Talleyrand that the situation made its acceptance inevitable. He

---

[1] "Without knowing what it is," reported Castlereagh.

refused, however, to sign it, and only acceded to it so far as the territorial arrangements were concerned. Thus, Great Britain persisted to the end in refusing to recognise the Imperial title, and Napoleon remained, for her, "General Bonaparte" to the end of the chapter.

Like some others, Castlereagh was not happy at the choice of Elba; but no other less objectionable alternative could be found. "I did not feel," he wrote to his Cabinet, "that I could encourage the alternative which Caulaincourt assured me Bonaparte repeatedly mentioned, namely, an asylum in England[1]."

The Treaty of Peace had now to be made with a Bourbon Government, and it was nearly two months before it was concluded. The necessity of consolidating the power of the new monarchy and arranging for the withdrawal of the Allied armies and the surrender of the French fortresses, occupied most of the month of April. The Treaty was, moreover, delayed by the attempt of Talleyrand to obtain for the Bourbons an extension of the frontiers of 1792, while the disposition of the conquered territories had still to be determined. These discussions kept Castlereagh in Paris till the end of May, in spite of the desire of his Government that he should return to their assistance. He was occupied there, not merely with the Peace with France, but also with attempting to compose the differences between the Allies; while the War had left problems of importance all over Europe, in some of which, notably in those concerning Norway, Sicily, Spain and Holland, British interests were especially concerned. One of Castlereagh's first actions on arriving at Paris was to offer the post of Ambassador to Wellington, who accepted it with the same cheerful readiness to undertake any duty which he displayed throughout all these years. But Wellington could not come to Paris at this time; and, meanwhile, Castlereagh, with no one of high calibre to assist him, was unable to expedite matters, though he claimed to work as hard as it was possible for a man to do in a city like Paris.

In the Peace with France, Castlereagh was prepared to make concessions to the new monarchy, provided that they did not interfere with his plans for the Netherlands. He urged his Cabinet to be as liberal on Colonial questions as possible. France, he pointed out, was weak, and any Colonies returned to her could be easily reduced if a new war broke out. He was prepared, therefore, to limit his

---

[1] Castlereagh to Liverpool, Apri 13th, 1814. F.O. Continent. Archives, 4; *British Diplomacy*, p. 176.

demands to Mauritius and Tobago, retaining also, of course, Malta and the Cape, and confining the French in India to commercial occupation. He thus abandoned Les Saintes, but after pressure from the Admiralty added St Lucia in its place. He was even more anxious not to annex Dutch Colonies. "I am sure our reputation on the Continent," he wrote to Liverpool, "as a feature of strength, power and confidence, is of more real moment to us than an acquisition thus made[1]." Castlereagh was, therefore, all the more indignant when he found that in his Counter-project delivered in the middle of May (which was shown to him unofficially before presentation), Talleyrand had refused to cede St Lucia and Tobago, demanded compensation for Mauritius and, worst of all, said nothing about the Slave-trade. His protests recalled Talleyrand to a sense of reality. But the most difficult question was the Slave-trade. Both Castlereagh and his Cabinet knew that it was necessary to satisfy public opinion in England on this point. The Abolitionists were well organised, and had captured the imagination of the nation. From this time onwards, not merely the British Ministers, but the Allied Sovereigns, were importuned by letters, memoranda and appeals of all kinds, in order to carry through universal abolition. The French, perhaps naturally, suspected this zeal on the part of a nation that had only recently been converted to the Abolitionists' views. They hinted that the British statesmen were utilising public opinion to prevent the French Colonies from rivalling the British in prosperity. In this they erred, for there is not the slightest doubt that both the nation and Ministers were perfectly sincere on this question—a fact of which the sacrifices which they were prepared to make during the succeeding years are sufficient evidence. But Castlereagh recognised the difficulties of the case. "My feeling is," he wrote, "that on grounds of general policy we ought not to attempt to tie France too tight on this question. If we do, it will make the Abolition odious in France, and we shall be considered as influenced by a secret view to prevent the revival of her colonial interests." He pressed, therefore, the advantage of conciliating French public opinion, rather than imposing by force concessions which France would do her best to defeat in practice[2].

Talleyrand, also, tried to obtain substantial concessions on the Netherlands frontier. This, again, Castlereagh peremptorily refused

[1] Castlereagh to Liverpool, April 19th, 1814. *Castlereagh Correspondence*, IX. 474.
[2] Castlereagh to Liverpool, May 19th, 1814. F.O. Continent. 4; *British Diplomacy*, p. 183.

to allow, telling Talleyrand that, if he wished for a lasting peace, he must extinguish "in the minds of the army, this false notion of Flanders being necessary to France." It was only a threat to transfer the negotiations to London that produced a settlement by May 30th, thus saving a month's Subsidies to the Exchequer.

In its final form, the Treaty gave Castlereagh almost everything that was essential to British interests. Her maritime position in the Mediterranean was secured by Malta and the protection of the long route to India by the Cape, Mauritius, St Lucia and Tobago. Holland was compensated for the cession of the Cape with two millions of money, which, however, she was to expend on constructing a "Barrier" against France. Holland's extension in the Netherlands was, also, especially mentioned in one of the Secret Articles of the Treaty; for Castlereagh felt it of the first importance not to leave this point open until the Congress. The mouth of the Scheldt was thus placed in the hands of a Power which it was hoped would be sufficiently strong to protect Antwerp, and, moreover, would be closely united to Great Britain by the marriage between the Prince of Orange and Princess Charlotte, to which all the Powers had agreed. France had been reduced to the frontiers of 1792, with some small concessions at Landau and Saarlouis, and in Savoy. No indemnities had, however, been imposed; for Castlereagh, like the Russian and Austrian statesmen, had declined to agree to Prussian demands on this point. This liberal concession, as well as the refusal to insist on the return of the art treasures accumulated at Paris, which had been either extorted by Treaty or frankly carried off as plunder, was due to the desire on the part of the Allies to be as lenient to the new Bourbon dynasty as possible. When the brutal exactions of France during the Napoleonic Wars are remembered, this decision deserves to rank as one of the most notable examples of political moderation in modern history. Alexander and Castlereagh were the main instruments in bringing it about, but the final word lay with the British, who saw France left without a National Debt, while their own had mounted to over seven hundred millions in the effort to overthrow her domination of Europe. It must be remembered also that the Subsidies had been given, not lent, and, save for a small loan to Austria which dated from 1796 and one or two other small sums, Great Britain had nothing to recover from her Allies in mitigation of her huge debt, which was causing her the most serious anxiety.

From Castlereagh's point of view, the settlement was, however,

marred by the failure once again to determine the reconstruction of
Europe. At the opening of the negotiations, he had the idea of settling
with France quickly and then completing the European arrangements
in London. But, as he reported on May 5th, "the desire felt by
Prussia and Austria to bring both Russia and France to some understanding upon the main principles of the Continental arrangements,
in a secret article or otherwise, previously to our stipulating away
our conquests, had led to a very tedious and elaborate examination
of this very complicated question[1]." Of the precise part played by
Castlereagh in these discussions there is no complete record, for he
wrote very little to his Cabinet about it. But Münster's despatches
and other evidence leave no doubt that he took a strong line on the
Polish question, even at Paris. His support was given wholly to
Austria in refusing Alexander's demands, which included Cracow
and Thorn, and he began the policy, which he was to follow at the
Congress of Vienna, of trying to unite Austria and Prussia against the
Tsar by securing Austria's consent to the annexation of the whole
of Saxony to Prussia. In other German questions, and especially in
the form to be taken by the Federation, he showed less interest,
leaving them to Münster, unless some vital point arose. Though great
efforts were made to settle all these questions, they were without
avail, and the only express stipulations which the Treaty with France
contained, besides the settlement of the Netherlands frontier, were
the extension of the Austrian possessions to the Mincio, and the
incorporation of Genoa in Sardinia. As to the rest, they were to be
settled at a Congress to be held at Vienna in August, to which all
the Powers of Europe, great or small, who had taken part in the War
were to be invited. The Allied Powers, however, by a Secret Clause,
reserved to themselves the right to determine the disposition of the
conquered territories, and bound France to agree to their decisions.
The Tsar and the King of Prussia, with Metternich and the other
principal statesmen, had accepted the Prince Regent's invitation
to London. Castlereagh and Metternich, therefore, hoped that all
matters could be settled there, where the Poles would have less
influence than at Paris. No one, at this time, regarded the coming
Congress as anything more than an opportunity for communicating
the decisions of the Great Powers to the rest of Europe and for adjusting minor points. They could not foresee that their discussions

---

[1] Castlereagh to Liverpool, May 5th, 1814. F.O. Continent Archives, 4;
British Diplomacy, p. 180.

would bring Europe to the verge of war, and that over twelve months would be required before a final settlement could be effected.

These difficulties, in any case, did not loom large in the eyes of the British people, who cared little for the rest of the Continental settlement, if France was rendered impotent. The absence of vindictive conditions in the Treaty, such as France had inflicted so often on other countries, indeed, caused a great deal of discontent. "No Murders, No Torture, No Conflagration,—how ill the pretty Women of London bear it?"[1] wrote Whitbread; but he was himself delighted with the Treaty and honestly said so.

Castlereagh's return was something of a triumph, and the House of Commons rose to receive him when he entered it. The Treaty was approved without a division. Castlereagh's most serious difficulties, indeed, were in connexion with the events subsidiary to the settlement, some of which met with considerable criticism both in the House and at the Court. In the first place, the Norwegians, though their country had been ceded to Bernadotte by Denmark in the Treaty of Kiel in January, refused to submit and organised a national resistance. Disgusted as the Allies were with Bernadotte's conduct in 1814, they could not see their way to breaking with him completely. Thus Great Britain, in compliance with her Treaty engagements, was forced to assist in the subjection of Norway by a naval blockade—an odious necessity which Ministers had to defend against hot attacks from the Opposition. Spanish questions, also, caused great difficulty. Ferdinand, on his restoration, had straightway abolished the Spanish Cortes and returned to the ideals of the Middle Ages. The British had to see patriots with whom they had fought against Napoleon subjected to imprisonment and persecution. The abolition of the impracticable Constitution of 1812 caused little uneasiness to Castlereagh; but he protested vigorously, though without avail, against Ferdinand's increasing tyranny. The question of the Spanish Colonies was also a difficult one, in which we had a great interest, for our trade with them was growing by leaps and bounds. Nevertheless, the Treaty signed with Spain contained a clause binding Great Britain to strict neutrality in the struggle between Spain and her over-seas possessions. In the same Instrument, however, there was secured a stipulation which, like the "Barrier," went back to the 18th century; for, by a Secret Article, Ferdinand engaged not to renew the "Family Compact."

Most difficult of all the questions with which Castlereagh had to

---

[1] *Creevy Papers*, I. 191.

deal was the situation in Italy, where an extraordinary situation had arisen during the spring campaign, which had already caused him much uneasiness, and was to lead to much equivocal diplomacy before it was finally settled. Fortified by Aberdeen's consent, Metternich had hastened to conclude a treaty with Murat so early as January 3rd, 1814. It was urgently needed, if Austrian arms were to be immediately successful in Italy. For the Viceroy, with his small army of conscripts, successfully withstood all the attacks of Bellegarde's much larger forces. Murat was, therefore, not only recognised as King of Naples, but was promised some increase of territory and Austria's good offices to obtain his recognition by Great Britain and Austria's other Allies, as well as by the Sicilian Bourbons, who were to be given compensation elsewhere. But Murat was threatened from the south by the Anglo-Sicilian army of Bentinck, who was virtual Governor of the island, where he professed to cherish, as an instrument for the regeneration of the Italian people, the remarkable Constitution established by him in 1812.

Lord William Bentinck[1] is one of the most curious figures of this time. A military career of considerable success had made this *intransigeant* Whig a Lieutenant-General at the age of 38 and the representative of a Tory Ministry in one of the most important posts in Europe. From Sicily, aided by sea power, Bentinck could strike at will at Spain or Naples, or further afield, if events proved propitious. To a man of his unmeasured ambition, masterful character and ultra-Whig views the temptations were immense. During the earlier part of the year 1813, he carried on in person tentative negotiations with Murat at Ponza, soon put aside to engage in a campaign in Catalonia which (at least not wholly by his fault) ended in failure. The close of the year found him back in Sicily, evolving great schemes for the liberation of the Italians by appealing to their sense of nationality, and endowing them with the institutions he had set up in Sicily. To these views, which, of course, were in direct opposition to those of his Government, he perhaps added others, even more extravagant, for the retention of Sicily as a British possession, and a model of Constitutional liberty to the oppressed Mediterranean peoples. Castlereagh appears to have left him completely in the dark as to the Instructions which he had given to Aberdeen. He perhaps distrusted Bentinck's discretion. When, therefore, the latter received from Aberdeen Instructions to support Neipperg and Mier, the Austrian Envoys at Naples, and to conclude a treaty with Murat

[1] See *supra*, p. 380.

similar to that of Austria, he flatly refused. In spite of the vehement entreaties of the Austrians, he refused all cooperation with Murat, and it was only on February 3rd that he concluded an Armistice, which entirely ignored political considerations and merely suspended hostilities between the two forces. In this, he was only acting prudently, for he could not accept Instructions from Aberdeen on so vital a point[1]. For his later conduct there can, however, be no excuse. He had his own plans for the Italian campaign, and absolutely refused to subordinate them to the necessities of the situation. On March 8th, he landed at Leghorn, but, instead of cooperating with Murat, he began an embittered controversy as to the control of Tuscany, which provided the King of Naples with an excellent pretext for not attacking the Viceroy and carrying out his obligations under the Austrian Treaty. The Hereditary Prince was allowed to address a proclamation to the Anglo-Sicilian army, which denounced Murat as a usurper. Even Sir Robert Wilson, Bentinck's fellow Whig, could find no excuses for this strange conduct, which is only to be explained by Bentinck's personal dislike of Murat and his rage at the complete overthrow of the plans that had long been fermenting in his own brain.

Meanwhile, Castlereagh and Metternich, engaged in the final struggle against Napoleon, had had scant leisure to deal with the Italian deadlock. Complaints against Bentinck, however, began to pour in at headquarters, and Castlereagh at last awoke to the situation. He approved Bentinck's conduct in merely signing an armistice; for, as has been seen, the offer to Murat had never been really to his liking, and Aberdeen had committed himself far too rashly. Metternich himself was dissatisfied with the Treaty, and made some alterations in its language. Castlereagh, however, had no alternative but to accept the situation, and he admitted that, at the moment when the Treaty was made, "it was both wise and necessary," while at the same time he urged a full indemnity for Ferdinand. On February 21st, he wrote to Bentinck that "The British Government are perfectly ready to act up to the spirit of the Austrian Treaty and to acknowledge Murat upon a peace upon two conditions: 1st That he exerts himself honourably in the war; and 2nd that a reasonable indemnity (it cannot be an equivalent) is found for the King of Sicily." When it gradually became clear that no headway was being made in Italy, Castlereagh

---

[1] See R. M. Johnston's article "Lord William Bentinck and Murat," in *The English Historical Review*, April 1904. But while Mr Johnston successfully establishes this point against M. Weil, he is in error in thinking that Aberdeen had no authority to sign. See above, p. 409.

grew all the more indignant. It was some time before he credited all
the reports against Bentinck, and his just indignation was levied more
against Murat himself and the Austrian Commander-in-Chief[1]. But,
by the end of March, the situation had become clear, and Bentinck
was severely reproved in letters which Castlereagh wrote to him on
April 2nd, which he made all the more incisive, inasmuch as the
Sicilian Court had communicated direct to London the insinuations
which, they asserted, Bentinck had allowed himself as to Great
Britain becoming Sovereign of Sicily—a subject on which he was
ordered at once to enlighten them as to the true views of the
British Government. Castlereagh had, in fact, now determined to get
rid of Bentinck as soon as possible, and William A'Court, a shrewd
and moderate diplomatist of the true Tory creed, was nominated as
his substitute at Palermo, while Bentinck was told that he might take
leave of absence as soon as convenient. Before he departed, however,
Bentinck was to involve Castlereagh in further embarrassments. On
April 26th he issued a proclamation which promised the Genoese
their independence. Castlereagh had already agreed, as has been
seen, to assign Genoa to Sardinia. He at once repudiated Bentinck's
action, and to a deputation from Genoa and Lombardy who came to
Paris to plead for independence he was inflexible. He listened patiently,
but could only advise them to make the best of their new Sovereigns[2].
Bentinck's attempts to encourage Italian independence were all the
more distasteful to Castlereagh, since it was associated with the idea
of setting up new Constitutions in Italy on the model of that in Sicily,
which in his opinion—and the facts bore him out—had been a complete failure. The experience of these doctrinaire Instruments, set up
in Spain and Sicily, had, indeed, not been encouraging. That Castlereagh had judged accurately the main cause of their impotence is seen
by a letter to Henry Wellesley (afterwards Lord Cowley) on May 10th.

I hope, if we are to encounter the hazards of a new constitutional
experiment in Spain in addition to the many others now in progress in
Europe, that the persons charged with the work will not fall into the
inconceivable absurdity of banishing from the legislature the Ministers of
the Crown; to which error, more perhaps than any other, may be attributed
the incapacity which has distinguished the march of every one of these
systems which has placed the main authorities of the Constitution in
hostility instead of alliance with each other[3].

[1] Castlereagh to Bentinck, February 4th, 15th, 21st, 1814. *Castlereagh Correspondence*, IX. 235, 237, 286, 362.
[2] Hansard, XXX. 391.
[3] *Castlereagh Correspondence*, X. 26.

To Bentinck he wrote even more strongly—perhaps more strongly than he felt, since it was necessary to put a stop to the policy which might ruin Castlereagh's schemes at Paris.

"It is impossible not to perceive," he wrote on May 7th, "a great moral change coming on in Europe, and that the principles of freedom are in full operation. The danger is that the transition may be too sudden to ripen into anything likely to make the world better or happier. We have new Constitutions launched in France, Spain, Holland, and Sicily. Let us see the result before we encourage further attempts. The attempts may be made and we must abide the consequences, but I am sure it is better to retard than accelerate the operation of this most hazardous principle which is abroad.

"In Italy it is now the more necessary to abstain if we wish to act in concert with Austria and Sardinia. Whilst we had to drive the French out of Italy we were justified in running all risks; and with a view to general peace and tranquillity, I should prefer seeing the Italians await the insensible influence of what is going on elsewhere, than hazard their own internal quiet by an effort at this moment[1]."

In this there is much truth, and the same common-sense is shown in Castlereagh's conversation with the Italians in Paris. But his hostility to Constitutional liberty was not merely one of form. On no single occasion in these years is Castlereagh found giving it any encouragement or sacrificing to it the cardinal point of his policy; union with Austria against Russia. His deliberate plan for perpetuating Austrian influence in the Peninsula he had inherited from Pitt, and he applied the prescription only too well when the opportunity came[2]. It was a fundamental part of his policy to the end of his career; and, indeed, it was, in a sense, part of the Tory creed until Italy won her independence. At the same time, it must be remembered that Castlereagh's policy was itself a necessary element in the struggle against Napoleon, and that Bentinck's wild-cat schemes, which had little real support among the Italians themselves, would have only produced chaos and civil war—whereby ultimately the Coalition's main objects might have been lost.

Bentinck had, however, saved Castlereagh from the recognition of Murat as King of Naples. It might, indeed, be claimed that Great

[1] *Castlereagh Correspondence*, x. 18.
[2] There is, of course, no truth whatever in the story first put forward by Bianchi, that as early as July, 1813, Castlereagh had concluded a Secret Treaty with Metternich concerning Italy, the existence of which is based on a supposed letter from Metternich to Castlereagh, dated May 26th, 1814. Fournier and others have proved the impossibility of the document, which would refute itself, even if examination of the British and Austrian Archives had not shown it to be a forgery.

Britain was morally bound to support him; but, meanwhile, his relations to her were only defined by the Armistice. Castlereagh had thus, to some extent, a free hand, and already there were signs that the interests of the Sicilian Bourbons had not been forgotten by the British Government. In June, the Duke of Orleans pleaded Ferdinand's cause at Paris and London, and the Prince Regent did not hesitate to promise him his support, while Liverpool did not conceal his hostility to Murat, and even Castlereagh, though cautiously, gave the Bourbons some hope[1]. This interview was, of course, a profound secret, but even publicly in the House Castlereagh had spoken of the Neapolitan Question as not yet decided[2]. The greatest obstacle was indeed the folly of Ferdinand himself. In July, Bentinck's last act had been to allow the King to resume power in Sicily, though he had carefully safeguarded the Constitution on which he had built such extravagant hopes. But it was not long before A'Court reported that King Ferdinand was breaking his promises, and, however hostile to the Constitutional régime, the British Government could not immediately betray those whom they had put in power, and protected for so long. It remained to be seen whether Murat could utilise these difficulties, so as to win his recognition from the British Government at the coming Congress. Meanwhile, in the north of Italy Austrian influence was dominant and Lord Burghersh, who had been appointed British Minister to the Grand-duke of Tuscany, was well-fitted for cooperating with the Austrians, and for removing the ideas which Bentinck and Sir Robert Wilson had spread of Great Britain's interest in Constitutional liberty.

III. THE CONGRESS OF VIENNA

The numerous negotiations made imperative by the close of the War had not prevented the questions reserved for settlement at the coming Congress from being attentively considered. Castlereagh was, however, disappointed in his hope that affairs could be brought nearer to a solution during the visit of the Sovereigns and statesmen to England. On the main questions, indeed, no progress at all was made. The lavish and warm, if not very refined, hospitality offered to the Tsar and the King of Prussia took up most of their time. The four Ministers managed to meet for business; the stubbornness of the Russians, however, prevented anything being done, though a good deal of dis-

---

[1] Weil, *Murat*, I. 127 ff.

[2] Hansard, xxviii. 464. (In response to a remark of Canning's in favour of the Bourbons. Cf. Weil, *op. cit.* I. 167.)

cussion took place. Of the actual details of these discussions, little is known, except that a serious attempt was made to come to some agreement. It would appear that Castlereagh was anxious to avoid a rupture with the Tsar in London; for Metternich complained of his lack of support to Austrian policy. Alexander, indeed, seemed to look beyond the Prince Regent and his Ministers for support. He had long been in touch with the Whigs through Sir Robert Wilson and others. Now, like his strange and unconventional sister Catharine, who had preceded him to England, the Tsar seemed to go out of his way to show marked attention to the Ministry's opponents. More than this, the Grand-duchess was with difficulty prevented from recognising the unhappy wife of the Prince Regent, whose rupture with her husband was now complete. The Grand-duchess saw much of the Princess Charlotte, and to her influence and that of Princess Lieven was attributed the uncompromising refusal given to the suit of the Prince of Orange. The result was that Alexander mortally offended the Prince Regent, and made a very bad impression on his Ministers. The Cabinet as a whole, and particularly Liverpool, had been scarcely content with Castlereagh's policy of support to Austria. A more diplomatic behaviour on the part of Alexander might have done much to smooth his path to his Polish Kingdom. But when Czartoryski and Radziwill were seen in close conference with the Whigs, the Tory Ministry naturally became suspicious. Alexander attributed his failure to the intrigues of Metternich and Count von Merveldt, the Austrian Ambassador, who doubtless let slip no opportunity of increasing these suspicions. But the Tsar had only himself to blame for conduct apparently dictated, partly by a personal dislike to the Prince Regent, which may perhaps be pardoned, and partly by a conviction that the unpopularity of the Prince and some of his Ministers with the London mob indicated that a change of Government would soon take place. The result was a capital blunder, which rendered of no avail later efforts on the part of Russia to influence the British Cabinet against Castlereagh.

In these circumstances, the only decisions of importance to be recorded were the approval by the Allies of the Constitution of the new Netherlands kingdom, to which the Belgian Provinces were now provisionally assigned (though the frontiers of the new State with Germany still waited on other arrangements) and the signing of a Protocol, by which the Four Powers agreed to keep at least 75,000 troops on a war footing until the Congress closed. It was, also, soon found that the Congress could not meet in August, as had been intended. Castlereagh could not finish his parliamentary business in time, and the Tsar therefore insisted on a postponement to a still later date, in order that he might return to Russia. The opening was accordingly arranged for the beginning of October; but the four Ministers agreed to meet at an earlier date before the arrival of the Sovereigns, so that the procedure of the Congress might be arranged among themselves. For, although they had made no progress in their disputes, yet they were still firmly resolved not to allow the settlement to go out of their hands.

The interval of July and August was spent by Castlereagh in winding up parliamentary affairs and in the transactions narrated at the close of our last section. But correspondence was also carried on between Castlereagh, Metternich and Hardenberg on the Polish-Saxon question. The former two Ministers endeavoured to convince Hardenberg, now that he was away from Russian influence, of the dangers of Alexander's Polish plans. Hardenberg's reply to Castlereagh, which entered at length into all his plans for Germany, showed little sign of breaking with the Tsar, and displayed considerable jealousy and suspicion of both Austria and Bavaria. It was evident how difficult it would prove to persuade the German Powers to resist Alexander's Polish plans, which every intelligence from Petrograd and Warsaw showed to be more intently pursued than ever[1].

Castlereagh had also, throughout this period, been in close touch with Talleyrand. That experienced diplomatist, who was already engaged in planning the disruption of the Chaumont Alliance, was at the same time the Minister of a Bourbon King. The old French connexion with Poland did, indeed, pledge him to some exertion on her behalf; but his real interests, and those of Lewis XVIII, which he was forced to consider equally with those of France, lay elsewhere. To save Saxony from Prussia and drive Murat from Naples were the main objects for which he invented the doctrine of legitimacy, on which his famous Instructions were founded. Both Alexander and Metternich had made overtures at Paris, but it was to Great Britain that Talleyrand looked for support. When, therefore, Castlereagh gave him an opportunity by communicating the Convention of June 29th with some courteous explanations, he made every endeavour to establish a connexion with him. Throughout July and August, he

---

[1] Castlereagh to Hardenberg, August 8th, 1814; Hardenberg to Castlereagh, May 27th, 1814. F.O. Continent. Archives, 20; *British Diplomacy*, p. 190.

emphasised to Sir Charles Stuart, and later to Wellington, the coincidence of French and British interests and the necessity of the two "Constitutional" Powers of Europe acting together. To these overtures Castlereagh replied by a cautious but unmistakable response. He made it clear that he had no intention of separating from his Allies; but he encouraged Talleyrand to develop his views and promised to visit Paris on his way to Vienna. His main object was to secure the support of Lewis XVIII and Talleyrand to his policy of resisting Alexander's Polish plans. This support was actually offered with an embarrassing readiness, and Castlereagh had to point out that "the Four" still intended to settle matters in accordance with the Secret Article of the Treaty of Paris. But he promised to do his best to harmonise the views of the Allies with those of the French Government, and, with this understanding, preceded Talleyrand to Vienna, where the Ministers of the Four Powers proposed by a preliminary discussion to settle the procedure and constitution of the Congress, before the representatives of the other States assembled[1].

Castlereagh arrived in Vienna on September 13th. Stewart and Cathcart accompanied him as Plenipotentiaries, and the former (now made a Baron in his own right) was Ambassador to the Austrian Court. Aberdeen had declined further employment, and it may be imagined that Castlereagh did not press him. In his stead, he brought the Earl of Clancarty, a member of the Ministry and recently, since the return of the Prince of Orange, British representative at the Hague, where he had already obtained a very commanding position. Stewart owed his position entirely to his brother's affection, and scarcely anyone approved of his appointment. He played a subordinate part, though his relations with the Prussian military chiefs were not without importance. His egregious vanity and love of display, which obtained for him the nickname of "Lord Pumpernickel," made him one of the standing jests of the Congress. Cathcart was far less in evidence, and was only nominated lest Alexander should be offended. It was on Clancarty alone that Castlereagh could rely for really hard work and business capacity. The stiffest of Tories, and not too subtle or quick-minded, he was a conscientious and consistent subordinate, who could be trusted to carry out his chief's ideas. Throughout, he did much valuable work, and, after Wellington left, he handled the complicated diplomacy connected with the closing of the Congress

---

[1] Castlereagh to Liverpool, September 3rd, 1814. F.O. Continent. 7; *British Diplomacy*, p. 191.

with considerable skill. Edward Cooke, a permanent official of great experience, was the principal member of Castlereagh's staff. He stood in the most confidential relations not only to Castlereagh but also to the Prime-Minister, with whom he corresponded in private letters which retailed much cynical gossip. The rest of the staff, besides Castlereagh's discreet Private Secretary, Planta, was composed of four young sprigs of the nobility and five commoners from the Foreign Office. Six of these remained during the whole period. Wellington brought over three more of them during his stay, and Clancarty two, and one other at the close. This small staff, which was overworked throughout the whole period, was one of the most zealous and discreet of those at Vienna. Lady Castlereagh accompanied her husband, and the conjugal bliss of the British Ambassador caused much amusement to Vienna society. The fourteen rooms taken in the Auge-Gottes were not sufficiently imposing for this establishment, which was removed to the Minoritenplatz. There, a grave and decorous hospitality was dispensed by Lady Castlereagh, which the Viennese found extraordinarily dull. Many wits were inspired by the fact that she wore her husband's Garter as a hair ornament. Divine service was held every Sunday at Lord Stewart's residence for all the English in Vienna, and, in deference to their susceptibilities, the first performance of Beethoven's new concerto was postponed to a weekday. But, however deficient in some of the arts which characterised the Congress in general, Castlereagh's establishment was one of the most zealous and discreet, and the Secret Police entirely failed to penetrate its secrets[1].

From his Government at home Castlereagh only received a single definite official Instruction during the whole of his stay at Vienna; and this he deliberately ignored. He reported to his colleagues, however, at fairly frequent intervals, and maintained with Liverpool a private correspondence of considerable length. The Prime-Minister conveyed to him the sense of the Cabinet on the large general questions which arose at Vienna, as well as the state of public opinion in England, and thus undoubtedly influenced him on certain points. But Vienna was too far away for much to be accomplished in this way. The despatches often took a fortnight to reach their destination, and, before they could be answered, events had changed. The Cabinet, in truth, displayed only a moderate interest in the settlement since the main points of British policy were already secured. It was essential, for the sake of

[1] See C. K. Webster, *The Congress of Vienna.*

public opinion at home, that every effort should be made to secure the Abolition of the Slave-trade; but in other matters it was not thought that Great Britain ought to play a very decided part. Events, however, forced Castlereagh's colleagues to pay more attention to questions of foreign policy than they wished. The Opposition, which under Whitbread's influence had been studiously moderate during the crisis of 1814, saw in the embarrassing prolongation of the Congress a means of harassing the Ministry. The propaganda of Talleyrand and others had some effect in London. Thus Bragge, Bathurst, Robinson and Vansittart found themselves persistently attacked by Whitbread, Ponsonby and others, especially on the questions of Genoa, Saxony and Naples; and they found it exceedingly difficult to return convincing replies. They took refuge, for the most part, in an obstinate refusal to furnish any information whatever about the course of the negotiations, while Liverpool pressed Castlereagh to return as soon as possible to their assistance. Neither this nor the alarm produced by various developments of the Saxon Question had, however, very much influence on the course of events at Vienna, where, from the first, Castlereagh took a prominent part in all the leading Questions, and whence he refused to return until all danger of a rupture was at an end.

For Castlereagh had gone to the Congress, not only with fixed principles, but with a plan for carrying them out, and a conviction that upon his own efforts, more than upon anything else, depended the reconstruction of Europe. Unlike his colleagues, he regarded Great Britain as part of the Continent, and he saw clearly how difficult it would be for her to keep clear of any conflict, if a peaceful settlement was not obtainable. Thus, he was prepared to play his part in the forefront of the battle, not merely on such questions as the Netherlands, in which all recognised that his country had a special interest, but in the more difficult and even more important, if more remote, disputes as to Poland and Saxony, on the solution of which the whole reconstruction of Central Europe depended. More clearly than any of his colleagues, he looked on the problem as a whole, and, continuing the ideas put forward in Pitt's paper in 1805[1], he wished to establish a Balance of Power in Europe, which should prevent any one State from threatening the rest. The First Peace of Paris had allayed for the moment the fear of France, to whose Government Castlereagh was already looking for assistance in the prosecution of his plans, and this fear was partly replaced by that of Russia, whose

[1] See above, p. 400.

expansion had caused Pitt so much anxiety in the period immediately preceding the Revolution. It must also be allowed that, blind as he was to the importance of recognising national and Liberal forces, which he regarded as mere survivals of the dangerous influence of the French Revolution, yet he had ideals of a new system of government for Europe which might perchance prevent the recurrence of a period of warfare such as had been lately experienced.

To produce a Balance of Power—the "just equilibrium," as it is so often called in despatches and documents of this period—Castlereagh endeavoured to strengthen by all the means at his disposal the two principal States of the Centre. During the Napoleonic period, Austria, and even more completely Prussia, had been reduced in extent, while not only France but also Russia had secured great acquisitions of territory. France had now been driven back to her old frontiers, though it was thought that she might again become dangerous to the liberties of the small States which fringed them. Russia had obtained Finland, a large portion of Polish territory and acquisitions in the south, particularly Bessarabia, and she was now aiming at absorbing (though under a separate Constitution) almost the whole of Poland. To protect Europe against both French and Russian preponderance, it was imperative that the Centre should be made sufficiently strong to resist them. Castlereagh perceived that this object could not be obtained merely by a territorial redistribution, but necessitated the establishment of cordial relations between Prussia and Austria, and an amicable settlement of the disputes still dividing them. By helping forward such an agreement, he hoped to produce a combination which would prevent the Tsar from carrying out his Polish plans. A strong Federal Germany would also be the natural result of the union of the two Powers, and an impenetrable barrier might thus be erected both on the Rhine and the Vistula. As for Italy, he had long regarded that peninsula as the natural sphere of Austrian influence. The domination of Austria would prevent that of France, which might threaten British sea-power in the Mediterranean, and it has been seen that, so early as August 1813, he found it necessary to encourage Austrian expansion in this direction, with a view to preventing her from looking for compensation at the expense of the Turkish Empire.

Such principles were, no doubt, laid down in the Instructions which he, apparently, took with him, but which unfortunately have not been preserved. At any rate, they were the principles on which he founded his reports to his timid and reluctant Cabinet in the course of his stay at Vienna. No doubt, also, there were added covering phrases as to the advantages of the restoration of a completely independent Poland, if circumstances permitted. But Castlereagh had no illusions on this subject. He knew that the three Eastern Powers would never consent to give up their spoils, and, though he was careful to make, at the outset, and subsequently as the occasion required, official representations as to the desire of his Cabinet for the reestablishment of Polish Independence, such declarations were merely intended to safeguard his Government against possible attacks in Parliament. For, from so early a date as February 1814, Castlereagh had announced to the Austrian statesmen that he would not tolerate any separate Polish Kingdom, whether openly declared or created in some indirect manner, and since then all his efforts had been directed to combining Prussia and Austria in a refusal to give up any part of their shares of the Polish Partitions to Russia. In order to detach Prussia from the influence of the Tsar, it had been necessary to promise her the bribe which Alexander had already offered her at Kalisch—the whole of the kingdom of Saxony. Metternich had, very reluctantly, made a verbal promise to this effect so long ago as January 1814, and Castlereagh had accepted this arrangement as the basis of the agreement between the two Powers. In the discussions at Paris and London, and subsequently, though other points of difference had arisen, particularly as regards Mainz, which Austria wished Bavaria to acquire, so as to facilitate her own acquisition of Salzburg from that Power, this arrangement had been maintained by Metternich, without any written agreement having been exchanged. There was, however, in Austria a strong party opposed to it. This feeling was naturally shared by the smaller German Powers, who were in effect guilty of all the offences of which Saxony was accused, while the preservation of Saxony was the principal point in the Instructions which Talleyrand had drawn up for himself, and even took precedence of his desire to dethrone Murat. Nevertheless, Castlereagh founded his whole plan of campaign on Austria's consent to the absorption of all Saxony by Prussia.

It was with issues of such magnitude impending that Metternich, Castlereagh, Hardenberg and Nesselrode began their preliminary discussions, on September 15th. Their first task was to make a plan for the deliberations of the Congress; and none of them appear at the outset to have quite understood how difficult this task was. In these discussions, Castlereagh took up a slightly different attitude to that of his colleagues. He agreed that "the Four" must preserve the "initiative" granted to them by the Secret Article of the Treaty of Paris, and arrange all matters between themselves before they were discussed with other Powers. But he carried out his promise to Talleyrand to do his best to make the position of France as little derogatory as was possible under the circumstances. He acquiesced in the strongly expressed wish of his colleagues to exclude her from the preliminary discussions, but entered a protest in the Protocol of September 22nd, against this decision being too bluntly laid down. Similarly, he was anxious that the decision of the Great Powers to keep matters in their own hands should be made as palatable as possible to the smaller Powers, and that they should maintain their control "without openly assuming authority[1]." He failed, however, to convince his colleagues, and, when Talleyrand appeared at Vienna, he found no difficulty in preventing the acceptance of the schemes of "the Four," with the result that the opening of the Congress was postponed, while the points at issue began to be discussed amongst the Plenipotentiaries of the Four in an informal way, but with the fixed intention of producing some settlement, before either France or the smaller Powers were allowed any opportunity to put forward their views in any formal manner.

In the discussions on the Polish and Saxon questions thus opened, Castlereagh played a prominent and, in some respects, a dominant rôle. The formal agreement between Austria and Prussia as to Saxony still hung fire, and, until this was reached, neither Hardenberg nor Metternich could assume too bold an attitude towards the Tsar. It was on Castlereagh, therefore, that the main burden fell of arguing the case, and endeavouring to make the Tsar understand that his plans for a kingdom of Poland under the Russian Crown were opposed by all his three Allies. A diplomatic duel thus began of extreme bitterness, which very nearly indeed produced a European war. If Castlereagh suffered some heavy defeats, he managed at last to produce a settlement which he could conscientiously defend, and the courage and address with which he managed his attack have rarely been excelled by a British statesman.

Though Nesselrode retained his position of principal Minister, Alexander kept the control of affairs in his own hands, and was

---

[1] For details on these points of organisation see C. K. Webster, *The Congress of Vienna*, Part II.

advised by a group of foreigners of whom Czartoryski, Capodistrias,
Stein and Anstett had the most influence. Castlereagh's negotiations
during this first period were, therefore, conducted with the Tsar
himself, and it was only when Alexander had completely failed to
overcome the stubborn resistance offered to his plans that he asked
for the employment of the regular diplomatic channels. The discussions began with two interviews at the end of September; and, from
the outset, it was apparent that there was little hope of agreement.
Alexander, doubtless with much sincerity, defended his policy as one
dictated by a wish to help Poland, and not merely by Russian interests
or personal ambition. He hinted, however, that he was prepared to
modify his views as to the erection of a Polish kingdom, and he had
already, in deference to the loudly expressed wishes of his Russian
advisers, abandoned the idea of including in it Lithuania and White
Russia. Castlereagh, with great frankness, insisted that the Tsar's
plans ran counter to the wishes of all his Allies as well as of his own
Russian subjects. He said that, so far as England was concerned,
the creation of an independent Poland would be welcomed, and he
secured an admission at the outset that this course was rendered impossible by the attitude of all the Three Eastern Powers. He refused
to admit, therefore, Alexander's plea of a moral duty towards the
Poles. So long as Russia denied them full independence, she could
only rely on the Treaties concluded between the three Powers to
justify herself, and these precluded the granting of a Constitution
(which, as Castlereagh held, would cause grave discontent among
those Poles who were left under Prussian and Austrian rule), and bound
Russia to an equitable Partition with her Allies. At the end of a second
interview, the discussion grew warm, and Alexander hinted, though
in a less menacing tone than he was employing towards Metternich
and Talleyrand, that he was in possession, and meant to remain so.
To this threat Castlereagh returned an answer which he was to make
on more than one occasion during the course of the Congress; that
only the recognition by Europe could enable a Power to enjoy new
possessions with tranquillity[1].

Meanwhile, Castlereagh was working hard to cement the tentative Alliance already formed between Austria and Prussia. Both
Metternich and Hardenberg were anxious to come to an agreement,
but both had, throughout the Congress, to reckon with forces in

---

[1] Castlereagh to Liverpool, October 2nd, October 9th, 1814. F.O. Continent. 7;
British Diplomacy, pp. 197, 201.

their own country which made a decided course of action difficult. Hardenberg's principal obstacle was his King, who, in his heartfelt gratitude to the Tsar, found it almost impossible to oppose his wishes. There was, also, a strong military party to reckon with in Prussia, who were not only determined to secure all Saxony, but were passionately opposed to allowing Mainz, which they regarded as the key to southern Germany, to remain in Bavarian hands. Metternich was himself ready to yield Saxony to Prussia. But Stadion, Starhemberg and others were urgent against such a course, and, if he was to satisfy them, it was necessary that the loss of Saxony should be compensated by large concessions to Austrian interests, not only in Poland, but on the whole of the German Questions, including not only Mainz but the form of the Confederation, which was now being tentatively discussed in a Special Committee.

Castlereagh could do little to strengthen the infirm will of the King of Prussia, though he early made the attempt; but he succeeded in bringing the two Ministers to an arrangement, which, though it did not completely satisfy either of them, would, he hoped, prove a stable Alliance. The initiative came from him, and without his intervention the experiment could hardly have been tried. It was he who drew up a Memorandum as to the method by which the negotiation should be handled, for it was imperative that his Allies should not use arguments which, as a Constitutional Minister, he could not defend. He wished the offer of an entirely independent Poland to be put forward at the outset by the two Powers, being convinced that Alexander could not accept it: so that the arguments for Partition might be more strongly supported by Great Britain and France. He was anxious, also, that the negotiations should be begun as soon as possible, for Alexander was every day committing himself more deeply in private conversations to the plan which he had laid down for himself. Hardenberg, however, told his Allies that he would take no step in the Polish question until he was fully assured of the possession of Saxony. On October 9th, he addressed letters to Castlereagh and Metternich categorically demanding an answer in writing to his demand. Castlereagh's answer of October 11th was explicit. He gave formal consent to the total absorption of Saxony by Prussia and, provided she loyally supported his Polish plans, offered no objections to her immediately taking over the provisional administration of the country from Prince Repnin, the Russian governor. He also denied the King of Saxony's right to any indemnity, for he had no desire to complicate the rest of the settlement by the necessity of finding another realm for Frederick Augustus. Metternich's answer was more difficult to obtain; but he at last yielded to Hardenberg's pressure. His answer, on October 22nd, gave a reluctant consent to the annexation of Saxony, but only on the express condition that Prussia should, in her turn, consent to arrangements satisfactory to Austria in the rest of Germany. This was scarcely an Alliance, and Castlereagh only secured the consent of both Hardenberg and Metternich to joint action after a long and stormy interview. Even then, some of the points in dispute between them were merely waived for the moment. They, however, agreed to follow the plan of action drawn up by Castlereagh himself, and thus the formal offer of an independent Poland was made. But the real intention was to confine Russia to the eastern bank of the Vistula[1].

Meanwhile, the original controversy between Alexander and Castlereagh had been continued by an exchange of formal notes. Castlereagh had sent the Emperor, for his information, the Memorandum which he had drawn up as a basis of joint action between the Powers. He was embarrassed at receiving from the Emperor a vigorous reply, of which Czartoryski was the author, though Alexander assumed personal responsibility for it. Nevertheless, Castlereagh felt compelled to return an answer in which he adroitly ascribed the Russian Memorandum to Alexander's advisers, and thus was able to re-state his case with the utmost possible firmness[2]. Even then, this rather futile method of negotiation was not brought to a close, for a final answer was returned by Alexander, together with a cold note asking that the negotiations should henceforth be carried on by the regular channels of communication. Neither party to the dispute had yielded in the slightest degree, and Castlereagh was confirmed in his opinion that it was not by this method that the Tsar would be made to give way. Only a united demand by the Three Powers could, he thought, force the Tsar to a compromise[3].

But the Alliance, the making of which had occupied all the month of October, fell to pieces almost before it was put into force. Advantage was taken of a visit of the three Sovereigns to Buda-Pesth to make

---

[1] Castlereagh to Liverpool, October 24th, 1814. F.O. Continent. 7; *British Diplomacy*, p. 212.

[2] Cooke was suspected of having drawn up this and some others of Castlereagh's notes; but it was not Castlereagh's habit to entrust such important work to subordinates, however competent and trustworthy.

[3] Castlereagh to Liverpool, November 5th, 1814. F.O. Continent. 8; *British Diplomacy*, p. 222.

the onset on the Tsar, Castlereagh purposely leaving the affair in the hands of Metternich and Hardenberg. Alexander was furious and heaped bitter reproaches on the two Ministers in the presence of their masters. Frederick William was not proof against the charge of ingratitude, and withdrew his support from Hardenberg. Castlereagh's scheme thus completely failed. Hardenberg refused to follow up the first attempt, and suggested compromises which Metternich could not accept. Nor could he give any guarantee that he would join with Austria in enforcing these conditions, if the Tsar refused to accept them, as he surely would. The situation which Castlereagh had been dreading and which it had been his object to avoid, even more than the increase in Russian power, had now been brought about. If Austria could not obtain a Polish frontier, she refused to consent to the incorporation of Saxony in Prussia; which meant that the two German Powers would become completely estranged. This Castlereagh had foreseen, as he explained to his Cabinet in narrating his failure, and he clearly perceived the consequences that might ensue.

"I deemed it," he reported on November 11th[1], "of great importance to contribute as far as depended upon me to this concert; considering the establishment of Russia in the heart of Germany not only as constituting a great danger in itself, but as calculated to establish a most pernicious influence both in the Austrian and Prussian Cabinets; and I also foresaw, that if these two Powers, from distrust of each other, gave up the Polish point as desperate, the contest in negotiation would then turn upon Saxony, Mayence and other German points, and through the contention of Austria and Prussia, the supremacy of Russia would be established in all directions, and upon every question: whereas an understanding previously established on German affairs gave some chance of ameliorating the Polish arrangement, and, in case of its failure, afforded the best if not the only means of counteracting the Russian influence in the other European arrangements...."

This was his defence for agreeing to the annexation of Saxony by Prussia, which he knew could not be palatable to his colleagues, and at the same time he explained somewhat anxiously how he came to assume so prominent a part in the negotiations. Though the Polish question was remote, he contended that all British interests, even her interests in the Netherlands, were ultimately bound up in securing a pacific settlement.

"I have certainly been led from circumstances," he continued, "to take a more active share in the discussions on this question than I should have permitted myself to do if it had been any part of my policy to push the

[1] Castlereagh to Liverpool, November 11th, 1814. F.O. Continent. 8; *British Diplomacy*, p. 229.

Polish point to a hostile issue. In preparing for so serious an alternative, I should have felt the propriety, as a British Minister, of preserving a greater degree of reserve: it being the province of Great Britain to support rather than lead, on such occasions. But in proportion as I felt that an effort ought to be made successively, by conciliation, by moderation, by persuasion, by pressure of argument, and ultimately if necessary by an imposing negotiation, uniting the general sentiments of Europe upon sound and popular grounds, and not by armies, I felt the less precluded from taking a forward part. Some advantages have perhaps resulted from my being the person to do so, as the same arguments, had they been urged by the parties most interested, might have rendered accommodation more difficult...."

In requesting approval of this line of conduct he laid down for the benefit of the Cabinet the principles on which he conceived it was founded.

In the first place, so to conduct the arrangements to be framed for the Congress, as to make the establishment of a just equilibrium in Europe the first object of my attention, and to consider the assertion of minor points of interest as subordinate to this great end. Secondly, to use my best endeavours to support the Powers who had contributed to save Europe by their exertions, in their just pretensions to be liberally re-established upon the scale to which their treaties entitled them to lay claim, and not to be deterred from doing so by the necessity of adopting, for this end, measures which, although not unjust, are nevertheless painful and unpopular in themselves. And, thirdly, to endeavour to combine this latter duty to our friends and Allies with as much mildness and indulgence even to the offending states, as circumstances would permit.

It was for these objects, he said, that he had combatted Russia's plans so warmly. But he was convinced that a milder policy would have produced worse results, and he was not hopeful of the future.

"Your Lordship may rest assured," he concluded, "that no effort on my part shall be omitted to prevent disunion and still more war; but I am confident I speak the universal sentiment, when I declare my perfect conviction, that, unless the Emperor of Russia can be brought to a more moderate and sound course of public conduct, the peace, which we have dearly purchased, will be but of short duration."

The Cabinet had need of these explanations and admonitions; for the proceedings at the Congress were now beginning to be the cause of public alarm throughout all Europe. Talleyrand's opposition had prevented any plan being accepted for the formal opening of the Congress, and he had skilfully fomented the jealousy of all the small Powers at their exclusion from any important business. While all the energies of the Four Powers were directed to the Polish-Saxon question, but little progress could be made on any of the other points of dispute. So long as Austria and Prussia were at enmity, the German Committee could come to no conclusion, and its meetings soon ceased altogether. Of Italian Questions, only the incorporation of Genoa in Piedmont, which had already been settled by the Treaty of Paris, could be formally considered. Though public opinion in England was not seriously interested in the main Questions in dispute at Vienna, yet the attitude of the Opposition in the House of Commons was very different from what it had been during Castlereagh's absence in the early part of the year. The conclusion of peace had liberated them from all such restraints as they had at that time felt, and, as the rumours of dissensions at Vienna grew more and more prevalent, they began a vigorous and concerted attack. Talleyrand and others made it their business to convey to the public as much information as possible, and it was not long before tolerably authentic news of Castlereagh's note on Saxony reached London. Whitbread took the first opportunity to uphold the cause of the Saxon King, while the Whigs also defended Alexander, declaring that he wished to restore the independence of Poland. The Ministers, in the face of Castlereagh's pessimistic despatches, found great difficulty in coping with these attacks; and their task was all the more uncongenial, since none of them were sincerely convinced of the necessity or wisdom of Castlereagh's conduct. They cared little about the Continent, except to keep out of trouble; and the prominent part that their Plenipotentiary was playing in the thorny questions of Saxony and Poland gradually began to create a real feeling of alarm. This was expressed in Liverpool's private letters to Vienna, which, without giving any specific Instructions, dwelt continually on the difficulties of the Ministry in Parliament, and urged a cautious line of policy. At the end of October, Vansittart (who was much embarrassed by the financial questions which had arisen on the conclusion of peace) attacked Castlereagh's Polish policy in a Memorandum which was duly forwarded to Vienna; and these warnings were repeated in November[1].

Yet at the Congress, after a short interval, Castlereagh continued his policy of active mediation. He was far too much involved in the negotiations to play a passive rôle there, and he never wavered in his belief that it was only by his own active participation in the negotiations

---

[1] Liverpool to Castlereagh, October 28th, 1814, November 2nd, November 18th. Wellington, *Supplementary Despatches*, IX. 382, 401, 438.

that a rupture could be averted, which, if it took place, must involve all
Europe and ultimately, therefore, Great Britain, in war. Throughout
November, the relations between the three Powers grew steadily
worse. Hardenberg made some pretence of endeavouring to induce
Alexander to yield, and after his failure still insisted on the retention
of Saxony. Since he could no longer obtain it from Metternich, he
went over completely to the Russian side, and it was not long before
the chances of war were openly discussed at Vienna. On November
8th, Prince Repnin, the Russian Governor of Saxony, handed over
the administration to the Prussians, with, as he declared in his proclamation, the consent of Austria and Great Britain. This act, designed
by Alexander to foment the differences between Austria and Prussia,
produced exactly the effect which he had anticipated, and caused,
moreover, great discussion throughout Europe and a special debate
in the British Parliament. For some time, Castlereagh kept away from
these discussions, which were prolonged by an illness of Alexander;
but, by the beginning of December, affairs had assumed so alarming
an aspect that he was approached on all sides for help in order to
arrive at a settlement, and he took up once more his rôle of Mediator.
He had now, however, to pursue a different plan. A Polish settlement such as he had desired, he felt to be now impossible, since
Prussia had refused to combine with Austria to extort it from Alexander. The great question now was that of Saxony, and as to this Castlereagh threw his whole weight on the side of Austria. His change of
attitude was attributed by public gossip at the Congress, which later
found expression in the House of Commons, to a change of Instructions from home. This was, however, not a true statement of
the case. Liverpool did, indeed, suggest to Castlereagh in his letters,
that the total extinction of Saxony was not popular in England.

"I ought to apprise you," he wrote on November 18th, "that there is a
strong feeling in this country respecting Saxony. The case against the King
appears to me, I confess, to be complete, if it is expedient to act upon it;
but the objection is to the annihilation of the whole of Saxony as an independent Power, particularly considering the part which the Saxon troops
took in the operations on the Elbe. Considering the prominent part which
Saxony has always taken in the affairs of Germany, it would certainly be
very desirable that a *noyau* of it at least should be preserved, even if it were
under some other branch of the Saxon family; and I am fully convinced that
the King of Prussia would gain more in character and influence by agreeing
to such an arrangement than he would lose by any reasonable sacrifice[1]."

---

[1] Wellington, *Supplementary Despatches*, IX. 438.

There was, however, no vehement feeling in Great Britain on this subject, in spite of the efforts of various diplomatic agents to foment it, and *The Times*, which attached far more importance to the establishment of Polish independence than to the preservation of the Saxon monarchy, probably represented the views of those sufficiently interested in the affairs of the Congress to have any opinion at all.

Castlereagh's change of front, in fact, though approved and commended by the Cabinet, was the natural result of his own actions, and not dictated from home. He sought, indeed, not the preservation of the whole of Saxony, but a compromise which would enable Austria and Prussia to come together once more and free the latter from Russian influence; and, as will be seen, after a two months' struggle he was successful in bringing his plan to fruition.

Until the beginning of December, Castlereagh made no attempt to reopen the negotiations. When, however, Alexander had peremptorily rejected the suggestions which Hardenberg had hesitatingly put forward as a means of "saving his face," and Metternich had intimated that, in such circumstances, Austria withdrew her consent to the Prussian annexation of Saxony, it was imperative that he should declare his attitude, before an open rupture of relations between the two German Powers took place. Hardenberg's Notes had begun to assume a menacing tone, and Castlereagh was thus induced to seek an interview with him in the first days of December, in order to make it clear that, in the new aspect of affairs which had arisen as a consequence of the failure to oppose Alexander, he supported the Austrian case. He took with him the extract from Liverpool's private letter of November 18th, quoted above, in order to show that his change of view was in accordance with the wishes of his Government. Hardenberg met him with menacing words, declaring that he "would run all risks rather than return home under such an humiliation." Castlereagh's answer was the same as he had given to Alexander when he used similar language with regard to Poland.

"I represented," he reported, "that this was not a case of war, that he was in occupation of Saxony, and that I apprehended no one would think of removing him hostilely from thence; but that he could not regard an unacknowledged claim as constituting a good title, and that he never could, in conscience or honour, advise his sovereign to make the mere refusal of a recognition cause of war against other states: That Prussia would then remain in a state of disquietude and doubt, compelled to remain armed, and that his return to Berlin would, under such circumstances, be more painful than if he brought back the accession of all the Powers of Europe to an equal extent of dominion, though differently constituted[1]."

Such language was not without effect. Hardenberg promised at least to consider any proposal which Austria might make, and Castlereagh hastened to Metternich to endeavour to make this as conciliatory as possible. But the omens were not favourable, and in a private letter Castlereagh directed the attention of his Cabinet to the chances of war and to the necessity of his interference, if it was to be prevented. It was impossible, he pointed out, for Great Britain to keep out of such a war for any length of time; her engagements to the Netherlands, if nothing else, would bring her in. He suggested, therefore, that the only chance of peace was an Armed Mediation between the three Eastern Powers, and that, in order to make this effective, France should be asked to join Great Britain in such action. By this means, she would be prevented from fishing in troubled waters, while the united force of the two Powers might be sufficient to prevent the threatened explosion[2].

The course of the negotiations showed how wellfounded Castlereagh's fears were. Austria's Memorandum was far from conciliatory. There was an open quarrel between Hardenberg and Metternich, in which all their private correspondence concerning Poland was betrayed to the Tsar. Alexander himself, after vainly attempting to obtain Metternich's dismissal, showed some signs of willingness to compromise, and offered the Tarnopol district to Austria; but there appeared to be no possibility of agreement on the Saxon point.

Meanwhile, the Cabinet had been growing more and more alarmed. On November 25th an attack had been made by the Opposition in the House of Commons, pressing for information on the rumours of dissensions concerning Naples, Saxony and Poland, to which Ministers found the greatest difficulty in returning an effective reply. A meeting of the Cabinet was held and an official Instruction was sent to Castlereagh—the only important one received by him during the whole course of the Congress—which, while approving of his attitude as regards Poland, expressed the greatest alarm at the general state of Europe, and concluded: "It is unnecessary for me to point out to you the impossibility of His Royal Highness consenting to involve this country in hostilities at this time for any of the objects which have hitherto been

---

[1] Castlereagh to Liverpool. December 7th, 1814. F.O. Continent. 8; *British Diplomacy*, p. 255.

[2] Castlereagh to Liverpool, December 5th, 1814. Wellington, *Supplementary Despatches*, IX. 463.

under discussion at Vienna[1]." How little attention Castlereagh was to pay to this communication will be seen. The Cabinet, on receipt of his despatches of December 5th and 7th, moved further in his direction. Liverpool agreed that an Alliance with France was desirable, and that, to obtain it, some concession to her on the question of Murat was expedient. Any settlement of Poland, Germany and Italy was, he said, to be preferred to war, of which, however, he admitted Great Britain could not indefinitely remain a mere spectator. He renewed, at the same time, his warning against committing this country to hostilities, and intimated that the Cabinet could not sanction such a course, until they were in possession of all the circumstances of the rupture[2]. But these warnings had little effect on the negotiations at Vienna. Castlereagh had made up his mind as to the course to be taken, and, during three weeks of ever-increasing strain, he persisted steadily in a line of action which, if it had not been successful in its object, must have resulted in an immediate outbreak of hostilities. The boldness of his action was justified by the result: peace was preserved, and it is difficult to see how it could have been preserved in any other way. But no Foreign Minister has ever taken upon himself a greater responsibility than Castlereagh assumed in the negotiations at Vienna, and, however his action may be criticised in its final results, due recognition must always be given to the courage and energy with which he acted at this all-important moment in the history of Europe.

He had, first, to make sure of Talleyrand; and this task proved far less difficult than might have been expected. Talleyrand had been successful in preventing the formal opening of the Congress; but, until the Powers came to almost open rupture, he had exercised little influence on their discussions. As a result of the interview in Paris, his relations with Castlereagh had been closer than with the other Ministers. His insistence on the interests of Saxony, rather than of Poland, had indeed, caused some discontent; but Castlereagh's influence had held back any direct step on his part, and through Wellington he had impressed his views on the French Court. At one time, there had been a suspicion that Talleyrand might make a bargain with Alexander; but his Instructions and the wishes of Lewis XVIII really left him no alternative. When, therefore, Castlereagh, and subsequently Metternich, began to make overtures to him, he showed every

---

[1] Bathurst to Castlereagh, November 27th, 1814. F.O. Continent. 6; *British Diplomacy*, p. 247.

[2] Liverpool to Castlereagh, December 23rd, 1814. Wellington, *Supplementary Despatches*, IX. 497.

disposition to meet them. Castlereagh throughout treated him with regard, though he never gave him his full confidence until the moment of crisis came. Through Castlereagh's influence, the issue of the French Note on Saxony was postponed until the first plan had been shown to be impossible, and, when the Prussian demands grew more menacing, Castlereagh, as has been seen, began to look forward to a French Alliance. Talleyrand's only condition was the expulsion of Murat, which Lewis XVIII regarded as of equal importance to the preservation of the King of Saxony. As will be seen, Castlereagh had himself long desired the same end, if it could be obtained without an actual breach of faith. Though he could not give Talleyrand definite assurances on this point, he put forward a plan by which Murat was to be offered a pecuniary indemnity as a preliminary to his expulsion, and urged Talleyrand to have the French archives searched for proofs of Murat's treachery in 1814, so that public opinion in England and Europe might be satisfied. With these assurances, though Metternich was far less explicit, Talleyrand was content, and pressed eagerly for a treaty, from which, however, Castlereagh held back until the very last minute. For, though he desired the French Alliance, if a rupture seemed inevitable, he was anxious not to force it prematurely, lest it should give an excuse for the outbreak which it was meant to prevent[1].

In the latter half of December, Castlereagh made a final effort to settle the matters in dispute. The Three Powers all pressed him to accept the office of Mediator, and with this end in view he consented to fresh interviews with the Prussians. They now brought forward a new plan by which the King of Saxony was to receive, as compensation for his kingdom, a large part of the left bank of the Rhine; but Castlereagh peremptorily refused to have anything to do with this scheme. Such a State would, he thought, fall entirely under the influence of France, and the safety of the Netherlands would be compromised. It was now impossible, he said, for Prussia to obtain the whole of Saxony. She must look for compensation elsewhere; and, in order that the whole matter might be discussed without the constant disputes as to the figures of population of the various territories concerned, he proposed that a Statistical Commission should be set up, composed of representatives of the Four Powers, to ascertain from the best information at hand the numbers of "souls" which the

---

[1] Castlereagh to Liverpool, December 18th, 1814. Wellington, *Supplementary Despatches*, IX. 485.

Powers had severally at their disposal. Though Prussia as yet showed no signs of compromise on the Saxon Question, she assented to this proposition, and the Committee, which proved of great service in settling the disputed points, was set up on December 24th. It contained a French representative, for Talleyrand had threatened to leave the Congress, if admission were refused him. Castlereagh, therefore, though he had not intended to expose his hand so soon, pressed for his inclusion, and Prussia and Russia gave way. On December 25th he went further, and in a letter to Talleyrand assured him, though in vague terms, that British policy, with regard not only to Saxony, but also to Naples, was aiming at the same ends as that of France[1].

The final crisis was now at hand. The Tsar, now that he felt assured of obtaining almost all his Polish demands, was anxious for peace. But Hardenberg, urged on by the Prussian military leaders, refused all compromise, and Metternich, who was supported by almost all the small States, showed himself equally unyielding. Matters were brought to a head by the Tsar's demand for a formal Conference to settle the Polish question. When this met, on December 29th, it was inevitable that Saxony must be discussed as well as Poland. Castlereagh and Metternich, therefore, refused all formal discussion until a French Plenipotentiary should have been admitted. Hardenberg vehemently objected, for such a course, in view of Talleyrand's zeal for Saxony, was equivalent to accepting defeat. The Prussians endeavoured to carry their point by a show of force before it was too late, and Hardenberg, in unguarded words, threatened war, unless the Prussian claims on Saxony were immediately recognised. His language rid Castlereagh of his last hesitations, and he went straight from the Conference to Talleyrand and Metternich, with the project of a Secret Treaty, which he had himself drafted. The Treaty was an application of the provisions of Chaumont to the new situation. France, Austria and Great Britain were each to contribute 150,000 men, if attacked by Prussia. Bavaria, Hanover and the Netherlands were to be asked to accede so soon as it was signed. Metternich, of course, accepted it, while Talleyrand was no less ready, and made no objection to a Clause which bound France to respect in any event the stipulations of the Treaty of Paris. He was content that "the Coalition was dissolved," and the French redaction which he drew up at Castlereagh's request only made one or two insignificant alterations

---

[1] Castlereagh to Liverpool, December 18th, December 24th, 1914. F.O. Continent. 9; *British Diplomacy*, pp. 260, 268.

in the original draft. Even in the matter of Saxony, he showed himself accommodating, for Castlereagh informed both him and Metternich, before they signed, that he did not intend to refuse Prussia some increase of territory in that quarter[1].

The Treaty meant war, if Prussia persisted in her demands; and Castlereagh's decision, which was made in direct opposition to the Instructions of his Cabinet, was, therefore, of the greatest possible moment. But, as he told Liverpool, Great Britain was bound to be drawn into the war in any case, and it was far better to enter into it with such a Treaty than to let events take their course. By safeguarding the Treaty of Paris, British interests in the Netherlands were protected and no temptation was offered to France to try to win back her conquests. The decision was at once accepted by the Prime-Minister, as Castlereagh had anticipated. In fact, before information of it had arrived, Liverpool had already indicated, in a letter of December 23rd[2], that the Cabinet were prepared for the French Alliance. But this despatch had not reached Castlereagh when he signed the Treaty; nor can it be said that the news of the signature of the Treaty of Ghent with the United States, which reached him on the morning of January 1st, was a deciding factor in the decision. His policy had long been leading up to such an event. The occasion was provided by the threats of Prussia, which gave sufficient excuse. Castlereagh perceived that the psychological moment had come when the final battle must be fought over Saxony, and the Treaty was therefore only a precautionary measure and was justified by its success.

In a few days, however, all danger of war was over. In the second and third meetings of "the Four," Metternich and Castlereagh, emboldened by their Treaty, persisted in their demand for the inclusion of France, and Hardenberg, after a vain struggle, yielded. Another attempt was made by the Prussians to press the scheme of compensating the King of Saxony by a territory on the left bank of the Rhine. Castlereagh countered this by a special interview with Razumoffski, the Russian representative, which was followed by one with the Tsar himself. There could be no doubt of Alexander's desire for peace. He had heard something of the Secret Treaty, and challenged Castlereagh pointblank on the subject. The reply which he received must have left him in no doubt that some formal bond existed, and he

---

[1] Castlereagh to Liverpool, January 1st, 1815 (nos. 43, 44, 45). F.O. Continent. 10; *British Diplomacy*, pp. 276-279.

[2] See *supra*, p. 477.

showed great alacrity in accepting the scheme for the reconstruction of Prussia which Castlereagh had drawn up[1].

Thus, when the Council of Five met on January 10th, the main issue on the Saxon question had already been decided. Prussia knew that she must give way, and it only remained to settle how much of Saxony was to be given her, and how her other losses in Poland were to be compensated. But the settlement occupied another five weeks of arduous discussions, before it was finally concluded. In these discussions, Castlereagh throughout acted as a real Mediator, and fully redeemed his promise to Hardenberg, that he intended to make a large and powerful Prussia. From the first, he had great difficulties with his Allies. Both Metternich and Talleyrand were anxious to exploit their victory to the utmost, and to exclude Prussia from obtaining any considerable portion of Saxony. In these circumstances, Castlereagh had himself to take the initiative and to force concessions on Prussia's behalf, speaking to the Emperor Francis in person, when Metternich confessed himself unable to cope with the demands of the Austrian military party. He did not, indeed, obtain anything like enough to satisfy the pretensions of the Prussians, who insisted for a long time on the retention of Leipzig. A complete deadlock arose on this head, which threatened to wreck the negotiations completely, and, after long and painful interviews with Hardenberg and the King of Prussia, Castlereagh was unable to bring them to accept the last Austrian offer. It was only by inducing Alexander to cede the fortress of Thorn to Prussia that he was at last able to wring a reluctant consent from Hardenberg to relinquishing Leipzig. Finally, after repeated interviews with the Ministers and their Sovereigns, he secured a scheme to which all parties consented[2].

In this rearrangement, the whole German and Polish settlement was concluded; and, except on one or two minor points, all the boundaries of Europe north of the Alps were thus settled before Castlereagh left Vienna. In order to satisfy the Allies and to obtain more territory for the purpose of Prussian reconstruction, he cut down to the lowest possible limit the claims of the Netherlands and Hanover. In the last resort, both these States depended on Great Britain's goodwill, and Castlereagh was able to use his influence with them for

[1] Castlereagh to Liverpool, January 8th, 1815. F.O. Continent. 10; *British Diplomacy*, p. 283.
[2] Castlereagh to Liverpool, January 11th, 22nd, 29th, 1815. F.O. Continent. 11; *British Diplomacy*, pp. 287, 292, 294.

the advantage of the general settlement. The final result satisfied his expectations, so far as the centre of Europe was concerned. The Prince of Orange, now King of the Netherlands, was master of what was thought to be a solid and compact State, and Luxemburg was also under his sovereignty, though it remained part of the German Confederation. Prussia received the left bank of the Rhine and was thus at hand to protect the Netherlands, as Pitt had planned in 1805. Hanover, strengthened by the absorption of East Frisia in its territory, reached the mouth of the Ems, and thus, as Castlereagh hoped, a solid *bloc* was made on the north-eastern frontier of France, where she had always gained such signal successes. Prussia received nearly two-fifths of Saxony in which Castlereagh had insisted on including, much to Austria's annoyance, the Elbe fortresses of Torgau and Erfurt. Even more important, however, than the actual details of the Saxon compromise was that it again made possible good relations between Austria and Prussia, and prepared the way for a renewal of the negotiations on the subject of a German Confederation, to which, as a means to solidify and strengthen central Europe, Castlereagh attached the highest importance.

In the Polish matter, Castlereagh had to be content with such concessions as Alexander would grant. Almost the whole of the duchy of Warsaw remained in Russian hands, and out of this Alexander created a separate kingdom of Poland. The cession of Thorn to Prussia and the establishment of Cracow as a Free Town implied a certain concession to the Central Powers, but the whole result was regarded as a menace to their peace. Before the settlement was completed, Castlereagh made a special declaration of the wish of Great Britain for an independent Poland, had such a result been possible. In this he was quite consistent, for he had at the outset of the negotiations declared himself in the same sense. But, as has been seen, he had never intended it seriously, and the declaration now made was merely to satisfy public opinion in England, which had throughout consistently advocated Polish independence, and had even accused Castlereagh of thwarting Alexander's good intentions on the subject. In this point, he only anticipated the wishes of his Cabinet, for Liverpool wrote specially a few days later to urge its importance[1]. More sincere, perhaps, were his solemn injunctions to the three Eastern Powers to grant the Poles special privileges.

---

[1] Liverpool to Castlereagh, January 16th, 1815. Wellington, *Supplementary Despatches*, IX. 539.

"Experience has proved," wrote Castlereagh, "that it is not by counteracting all their habits and usages as a people, that either the happiness of the Poles or the peace of that important portion of Europe can be preserved. A fruitless attempt so long persevered in by institutions foreign to their manners and sentiments, to make them forget their existence and even language as a people, has been sufficiently tried and failed. It has only tended to excite a sentiment of discontent and self-degradation, and can never operate otherwise than to provoke commotion and to awaken them to a recollection of past misfortunes.

"The Undersigned, for these reasons, and in cordial concurrence with the suggestions which have been thrown out, and which appear to have been favourably received by the respective Cabinets in the course of the present Conferences, ardently desires that the illustrious Monarchs, to whom the destinies of the Polish nation are confided, may be induced, before they depart from Vienna, to take an engagement with each other, to treat as Poles, under whatever form of political institution they may think fit to govern them, the portion of that nation that may be placed under their respective sovereignties[1]."

It may be doubted if Castlereagh, who had from the first aimed at a partition of the duchy of Warsaw between the Three Powers, had any right to make such a protest, at any rate to Alexander, who, among all the statesmen at Vienna, was alone really desirous of making any concession to Polish nationality. But the Tsar did not resent it, and, as a result of it, the Treaty of Vienna contained a guarantee to the Poles of a separate administration and institutions which at least served as a legal basis for the protests which were to be made on their behalf by Great Britain and France during the nineteenth century[2].

The main territorial settlement north of the Alps had thus been settled before Castlereagh left Vienna. Such was, however, not the case with Italy, where some problems had been postponed until the great dispute was settled. Nevertheless, Italian Questions, and particularly the position of Murat, played a by no means inconsiderable part in the diplomacy that led to the Treaty of January 3rd; and, throughout, the Powers were fully aware that this difficulty had to be dealt with before the peace of Europe could be assured. Metternich had succeeded in preventing any formal discussion on Italian problems, except that of Genoa, which was already decided by the Peace of Paris, until he should have settled matters with the Tsar. He had naturally no wish to raise difficulties in Italy which would weaken

[1] *British and Foreign State Papers*, II. 642.
[2] The Poles approached Wellington after Castlereagh's departure for further action in their favour, which he declined to take. Wellington to Castlereagh, February 18th, 25th, 1815. Wellington, *Supplementary Despatches*, IX. 571, 579.

his position in his negotiations concerning Poland and Saxony. Thus, neither Talleyrand nor Labrador was able to open formally the Question of Naples during the period of crisis. It was, however, often referred to in the negotiations, and Alexander no less than Metternich and Castlereagh endeavoured to use it as a means to influence Talleyrand's policy, which was, however, as has been seen, determined by other considerations. Nevertheless, Talleyrand had to be satisfied on the head of Naples, and, before the final crisis, he had received assurances, from Castlereagh at least, that the Bourbon claim to overthrow Murat would be met in some way or other. The means by which this promise was carried out led to one of the most obscure and intricate diplomatic incidents of the period[1]. None of the parties to the discussion dare act openly, and the exact processes by which the final result was brought about are still to some extent unknown.

As has been seen, Castlereagh, in spite of his acquiescence in the Treaty between Austria and Murat, had attempted to keep his hands free. Of his personal desire to restore the Bourbons there can be no doubt, though he in no way committed himself towards the Duke of Orleans before he set out for Vienna. From the first, he showed himself cold and reserved towards Murat's able representatives at Vienna, the Duc de Campochiaro and Prince Cariati. These Envoys, from the opening of the Congress onwards, never ceased to press for the formal recognition of Murat, which, they claimed, had been promised at the time of the Armistice. Castlereagh eluded all these attempts, and gradually felt his way towards a solution. The task was not an easy one. Unless Murat could be shown to have broken his engagements, Great Britain, if not so deeply committed as Austria, had yet virtually agreed to his retention of his kingdom. It remained to be seen whether a way could be found to break this agreement without too open a breach of faith. Castlereagh and Metternich proved equal to the problem, but they were immensely assisted by Murat's own lack of judgment and control, while the return of Napoleon made the final *dénouement* very different from what had been anticipated, and obscured the fact that Murat's deposition had already been decided when Castlereagh left Vienna. The first act of Campochiaro was to present to Castlereagh and other statesmen a *Mémoire Historique*, defending Murat's conduct during the period between the

---

[1] The most complete account is given in Commandant M. H. Weil's *Joachim Murat* (1909–10) which is based on extensive researches in Italian, Austrian, French and British archives, and furnishes an immense collection of documents.

Battle of Leipzig and the conclusion of the First Peace of Paris. Murat had become alarmed, and justly so, at the hostility displayed against him in so many quarters. France and Spain were openly and fiercely supporting the claims which Ferdinand IV had never abandoned. The Papacy, though under the distinguished influence of Consalvi, it was, at this time, by no means disposed to acquiesce in Austrian domination of the peninsula, yet was disputing with Murat the control of the Marches and refused him recognition. From the Northern Powers he could expect nothing. He had therefore to rely on his Treaty with Austria and the self-commitments of Great Britain. The support of this latter Power was, indeed, most vital of all, for she still virtually controlled Sicily, which her troops still occupied and her subsidies furnished with revenue, while her sea power prevented such an attack as France and Spain might be disposed to contemplate. The *Mémoire Historique* was intended to force Castlereagh's hand. It merely, however, gave an opportunity to Bentinck and Nugent, the Austrian General, to whom it was referred for observations when the right moment came, to repeat all their accusations against Murat, and left matters exactly as they were. In his interviews with Campochiaro, Castlereagh replied coldly and cautiously to all attempts to ascertain his views. He told the Envoy, frankly, that he considered the Question an open one while at the same time he tried to prevent Murat from taking any action by pointing out that the Armistice could only be denounced with three months' notice. Meanwhile, he asked A'Court to find out how far the Bourbons could look for support in Naples itself[1].

The death of Maria Carolina, Bentinck's constant foe, on September 7th, removed one possible obstacle to a Bourbon Restoration, which events at Vienna made more and more necessary, and Murat's relations with the Tory Government were not made easier by the visit of the Princess of Wales to Naples and her openly expressed admiration for the King, while such English friends as Lord Oxford, who was arrested at Paris when on a secret mission from Murat, did him more harm than good.

Meanwhile, at Vienna, Talleyrand and Labrador had been pressing not only the dethronement of Murat, but also the restoration to the Spanish Bourbons of the Parma duchies, assigned to Marie-Louise and her son by the Treaty of Fontainebleau. These overtures had no immediate result, and it was only the incorporation of Genoa in Piedmont which was formally agreed to at this time. This cession

---

[1] Castlereagh to A'Court, October 2nd, 1814. *Castlereagh Correspondence*, X. 145.

provoked considerable criticism in the British Parliament; for the Whigs, instructed by Bentinck, seized on this point as a means of embarrassing the Ministry. Nor was it long before the attention of the Opposition was turned to Naples. They were well informed by Murat's agents of the actual situation and, in a debate on November 25th, Castlereagh was accused of bad faith by Whitbread and Horner. These attacks had, however, little influence on Castlereagh, though they may have contributed to Murat's fall by making him imagine that his cause had powerful supporters in England. On the contrary, as the dispute over Saxony grew hotter, Castlereagh drew closer to Talleyrand, and this necessarily meant some agreement on the Neapolitan Question. He was, perhaps, influenced to some extent by Wellington's opinion, freely communicated from Paris, that the Peace of Europe could not be considered secure while Murat was on the Throne of Naples. Gradually, therefore, Castlereagh came to a decision; and when, on December 13th, Talleyrand in a formal Note proposed that all the Powers should recognise Ferdinand as King of Naples and that Murat should be deposed by a maritime expedition, so as to avoid the sending of French troops through Italy, he promised to seek Instructions from London. This he did in a long letter to Liverpool on December 18th, in which he went further than he had indicated to Talleyrand[1]. It was clear, he wrote, that Murat had not fulfilled his engagements, and that, therefore, Great Britain was free to act in favour of the Sicilian Bourbons. He proposed, accordingly, that a definite offer should be made of a pecuniary compensation to Murat himself and his heirs, together with a solemn guarantee to the Neapolitans of an amnesty and "such rights and privileges...as may be just and reasonable." If Murat refused this offer, then the future course must be decided according to events; but it was obvious that Castlereagh did not anticipate much difficulty in overthrowing him by force, and that Austria would not offer much objection. Metternich had, indeed, as yet not committed himself; but, so early as the middle of November, direct negotiations had been opened between him and Blacas at Paris without the knowledge of Talleyrand, which were to play an important part in the solution of the whole question. By the end of December, these had developed into a proposition to settle the Neapolitan question at Paris, and, by the middle of January, these *pourparlers* had carried the matter considerably further. Meanwhile, how-

---

[1] Castlereagh to Liverpool, December 18th, 1814. Wellington, *Supplementary Despatches*, IX. 485.

ever, Castlereagh's letter, backed by the strong support of Wellington[1], who made out the military problem to be one easily solved, had won over Liverpool. In a letter of January 11th, the Prime-Minister agreed to Castlereagh's scheme, provided Great Britain took no active part, and Castlereagh was therefore able to give Talleyrand a definite promise that action would be taken against Murat, and thus win his French colleague's consent to all the compromises necessary to settle the German Questions[2].

The final stages by which the deposition was to be carried out were, however, arranged between Castlereagh and Metternich without Talleyrand's knowledge. Metternich appears to have made up his mind by the middle of January, that Murat must be abandoned. He wished, however, to ensure that Bourbon influence should not disturb the Habsburg control of Italy, and he accordingly determined to make his consent depend on the French acceptance of Austrian plans for the centre of the peninsula, and in particular of the establishment of Marie-Louise and her son in the Parma duchies, in accordance with the Treaty of Fontainebleau. He took Castlereagh fully into his confidence, and a project was drawn up for the final settlement of Italy, which Castlereagh was to present at Paris on his way home from the Congress. In this paper the whole outline of the proposed settlement was sketched out and the hope was expressed that, in return for the overthrow of Murat, Lewis XVIII would agree to all the rest. Castlereagh made some reservations of his own as to this plan, especially as regards the Duchies, but in substance he was prepared to back Metternich. At Paris on February 27th he had a long interview with Lewis XVIII, followed by one with Vincent, Metternich's Envoy, and when he left on March 1st he had won Lewis' consent to the whole scheme, except the succession in the Duchies of the young Napoleon, a change which Castlereagh himself had recommended as desirable[3]. At the same time, he took back with him to England a number of documents which Blacas, in response to requests from Vienna, had collected as proofs of Murat's "treachery"

---

[1] Sorel's observation (*L'Europe et la Révolution française*, VIII. 412) on Wellington "*qui poursuivait dans Murat le dernier lieutenant de Napoléon*," is altogether beside the mark. No one was less susceptible to such a motive. Wellington was, undoubtedly, genuinely convinced that Murat was a menace to the Peace of Europe.

[2] On January 18th, Murat addressed a letter to the Prince Regent, professing his devotion to Great Britain; but Liverpool merely referred Gallo to Vienna, where he knew the case would be already decided against Murat.

[3] Castlereagh to Wellington, Paris, February 28th. Wellington, *Supplementary Despatches*, IX. 583.

in 1814. Meanwhile, at Vienna, Metternich had prepared the way for
a rupture by responding to yet another demand for recognition on
the part of Campochiaro in a Note which was almost an ultimatum;
and the Austrian forces were steadily growing stronger in northern
Italy. The stage was thus set for the final scene, when the whole
situation was altered by the return of Napoleon from Elba.

For the moment the return of Napoleon made no difference to
Castlereagh's policy. The fear of cooperation between Murat and
Napoleon, and the reports that a correspondence existed between
them, had indeed been one of the motives which induced Castlereagh
to desire Murat's removal. The papers sent from Paris and the reports
of Murat's recent conduct sent by Wellington from Vienna appear to
have overcome all hesitation on the part of the Cabinet, and, on
March 12th, an Instruction was sent to Wellington authorising him
to enter into engagements for the removal of Murat from the Throne
of Naples.

"As there will be some nicety," wrote Castlereagh, "in giving to our
line on this question the form most likely to prove satisfactory to Parliament,
it might be desirable that we should accede, according to our own form,
to the Treaty previously agreed to by Austria and France, in the negotiation
of which you will assist with a view of rendering the details as little objectionable as possible[1]."

When this Instruction was sent, the full extent of Napoleon's success
was not understood. But when it was seen that a new struggle had to
be entered upon, the issue of which was doubtful, Castlereagh became
less certain of the expediency of attacking Murat, who was indeed in
no sense an ally of Napoleon's, and had offered to place his forces on
the side of the Allies. The Chevalier Toco, Murat's representative in
London, though he had no official character, presented a Memorandum to the British Government on the part of his master, which
asserted in the strongest possible terms his desire to act with the
Allies against Napoleon. In referring this communication to Vienna
on March 24th, Castlereagh authorised Wellington to conclude a
Treaty with Murat, so as to liberate the Austrian forces to fight
against France[2]. But in Italy events were moving too quickly towards
a rupture for this Instruction to have any effect. Though, so late as
March 23rd, Wellington had been doubtful whether it was expedient for

---

[1] Castlereagh to Wellington, March 12th, 1815. Wellington, *Supplementary
Despatches*, IX. 592. Memorandum enclosed. F.O. Continent. Archives, 7.
[2] Castlereagh to Wellington, March 24th, 1815. Wellington, *Supplementary
Despatches*, IX. 609.

Austria to attack, the hasty conduct of Murat, who, perhaps judiciously, in the end decided that his one chance for security lay in summoning all Italy to arms while the Allies were still occupied with Napoleon, brought matters to a head, and by the beginning of April he had virtually begun hostilities[1]. Bentinck, who had returned to Genoa during the winter, was authorised by Wellington to attack Murat, if he moved against the Austrians, and Great Britain was thus at once brought into the War. In any case, it may be doubted whether the issue could long have been postponed; for Wellington assured Castlereagh that, if Murat had not been attacked, the plan for his deposition originally agreed upon would have been put into force before the Congress dispersed. When, therefore, Clancarty, who had been fully instructed by Wellington as to the plan of operations, on April 8th received Castlereagh's suggestion of March 24th, he took no action on it, and did not even communicate it to Metternich, allowing events to run their course[2]. On April 10th, Austria, in spite of the continued protests of Campochiaro and Cariati, declared war. Though Bentinck again quarrelled with his Allies, the issue was not long in doubt, and before the orders for Bentinck's recall could be issued, Murat had been defeated and driven out of his kingdom.

Castlereagh had, of course, to defend his actions against vehement attacks in the House of Commons. Much of the correspondence of the spring had become public property, and the Opposition were able to support a charge of breach of faith with quotations from the documents which had passed between Castlereagh and Bentinck. But, in such circumstances, when only part of the facts are known, the position of a Minister of the Crown is a strong one. Castlereagh was able to make a convincing and effective reply which he supported by laying before the House numerous despatches to prove his case. These were carefully chosen, and included the documents supplied by Blacas as well as the comments of Bentinck and Nugent on the *Mémoire Historique*. Though Wellington admitted that Blacas' documents failed to convict Murat of a breach of faith, the evidence of Bentinck and Nugent did to a certain extent show him to have failed to carry out the promise on which the Treaty with Austria had been made, and in which Castlereagh had consented to recognise the Armistice. Castlereagh made skilful use of this evidence, while the

---

[1] Wellington to Burghersh, March 23rd, 1815. Wellington, *Supplementary Despatches*, IX. 604.
[2] Clancarty to Castlereagh, April 8th, 1815. F.O. Continent. 17; *British Diplomacy*, p. 321.

French documents were employed to prejudice Murat's character. Of the secret negotiations of January and February, no mention was, of course, made, and Castlereagh, though he mentioned Murat's offer transmitted by Chevalier Toco, carefully concealed the fact that he had been quite ready to accede to it at the time[1]. The case against the Government, therefore, completely collapsed; nor did Bentinck, though he protested hotly against his dismissal, care to raise Neapolitan matters at a later stage, for on the question of Murat he had gone even further than his Government. Murat's second expedition, which resulted in his capture and execution, finally disposed of the question of dynasty. Castlereagh was thus free to lend his support to all Metternich's measures for establishing Austrian control over Italy. In Sicily, thanks to Bentinck, Ferdinand was a Constitutional monarch, and Metternich was not prepared to risk Parliamentary institutions being set up in the peninsula itself. As the price of his restoration, Ferdinand signed, on June 12th, a Treaty with Austria, by which, in a Secret Article, he pledged himself not to allow a Constitution to be set up in Naples. The Treaty was communicated to A'Court, who, though he considered formal approval almost unnecessary since "the unfortunate experiment which has been made in Sicily has sufficiently disgusted His Majesty with innovations of every description," yet had no hesitation in saying that anything which contributed to consolidate the good understanding now prevailing between Austria and Naples could not but prove extremely satisfactory to the British Government[2]. Castlereagh quite approved of this attitude; but of this dubious transaction, naturally, the Opposition knew nothing.

Castlereagh, before he left Vienna, had thus established, as he thought, a new arrangement of the European States which he hoped would safeguard the peace of Europe. He had, also, however, another expedient by which the Peace so hardly won might be specially preserved from attack. Immediately before his departure, he produced a scheme by which the new order of things was to be specially guaranteed by all the Powers of Europe. The idea of some special machinery for the preservation of peace was in the air. Castlereagh's scheme, however, undoubtedly dates back to the discussions between Pitt and Alexander in 1804 and 1805. In the letter to the Russian Ambassador, Pitt, after laying down the plan of the New Europe (a plan which

[1] Hansard, xxx. cols. 3–154, where the 19 documents placed before the House are printed.
[2] A'Court to Castlereagh, July 18th, 1815. F.O. Sicily, 70.

Castlereagh might now claim to have brought into being, almost to the smallest details), had dealt with Alexander's proposal to "form at the restoration of peace a general agreement and guarantee for the mutual protection and security of different Powers, and for reestablishing a general system of public law in Europe." On this point, Pitt (with, it will be remembered, Castlereagh's assistance), had replied:

It seems necessary at the period of a general pacification, to form a Treaty to which all the principal Powers of Europe should be parties, by which their respective rights and possessions, as they shall then have been established, shall be fixed and recognised. And they should all bind themselves mutually to protect and support each other, against any attempt to infringe them:—It should re-establish a general and comprehensive system of public law in Europe, and provide, as far as possible, for repressing future attempts to disturb the general tranquillity; and above all, for restraining any projects of aggrandizement and ambition similar to those which have produced all the calamities inflicted on Europe since the disastrous aera of the French Revolution.

It was this scheme which Castlereagh now endeavoured to put into operation[1]. He was the more anxious to do so since he was being pressed by Alexander to renew the Quadruple Alliance, while Talleyrand and Metternich were hinting that further secret engagements on the model of that of January 3rd would be to their liking. Castlereagh, of course, considered the Treaty of Chaumont as one of the safeguards of the European Peace. But he was naturally not anxious at this moment to emphasise that Instrument, while he was also unwilling to increase his secret engagements with other Powers, now that the settlement had been peacefully arranged. Accordingly, he avoided these special engagements by producing a proposal that the Powers should publicly declare "their determination to uphold and support the arrangements agreed upon; and, further, their determination to unite their influence, and if necessary their arms, against the power that should attempt to disturb it." Alexander welcomed the idea with enthusiasm, and Gentz drew up a declaration which in elaborate and highflown language expressed Pitt's idea. It might, perhaps, have been signed immediately; but Castlereagh, going further than Pitt, wished to include the Turkish dominions among the territories thus guaranteed. Even to this proposal Alexander agreed, on condition

[1] Castlereagh to Liverpool, February 13th, 1815; *British Diplomacy*, p. 303. For the details see also C. K. Webster, *The Congress of Vienna*, pp. 83 and 85, and also an article in *Transactions of the Royal Historical Society*, 3rd Series, vol. VI. November 16th, 1911.

that his disputes with the Porte should be first arranged. The Sultan, however, refused to take advantage of this offer, and, meanwhile, the return of Napoleon had caused the original scheme to be dropped. The project had thus no immediate result; but it marks the direction of Castlereagh's thoughts, while it was this scheme which suggested to Alexander the idea of the Holy Alliance.

After Castlereagh's departure, British influence at Vienna was never a determining factor in affairs. Though Wellington's prestige stood even now extraordinarily high, and he was treated with the greatest respect by the Congress, yet his energies were soon almost entirely absorbed in organising Europe to resist Napoleon. Moreover, almost all affairs of firstclass importance had been settled before Castlereagh left; so that neither Wellington nor Clancarty, who succeeded him, had more to do than fill in the details of the arrangements their predecessor had concluded. The disposal of Murat has been narrated above. In one other part of the Italian settlement, however, British diplomacy exerted considerable influence. The arrangement which Castlereagh concluded with Lewis XVIII as to the exclusion of the young Napoleon from the succession to the Parma duchies was never finally accepted by Metternich[1]. The return of Napoleon reduced the French influence to a negligible quantity, and Metternich was not anxious to see another Bourbon family established in the peninsula. When therefore, Alexander, with his usual chivalry, pressed for the enforcement of the Treaty of Fontainebleau, even though Napoleon had freed the Powers from all obligations under it, Metternich refused to insist on the arrangement to which he had previously agreed. Had it not been for the vigorous opposition of Clancarty, who was now in charge, the young Napoleon would have been recognised as the heir to the duchies in the Vienna Final Act. The spirit in which Clancarty approached the subject is illustrated by a phrase in one of his private letters to Castlereagh: "Will you set a precedent of placing Bonaparte's bastard on the Throne[2]?" His fierce opposition was sufficient to prevent any recognition of the young Napoleon's rights in the Treaty,

[1] Castlereagh himself, however, admitted, so late as April 12th, that he had been wrong in agreeing at his Paris interview that the young Napoleon should be excluded from the Succession. He pointed out that his rights under the Treaty of Fontainebleau were explicitly guarded, and Marie-Louise had no power to deprive him of them. If they were taken away, therefore, it must be on the plea that Napoleon's return had abrogated the Treaty of Fontainebleau. If Napoleon had remained at Elba, his son would almost certainly have been recognised as heir to the Duchies. *Castlereagh Correspondence*, x. 306.

[2] Clancarty to Castlereagh, May 19th, 1815. *Castlereagh Correspondence*, x. 355.

where the succession was left open. Unknown to him, however, a
Secret Protocol was signed between Austria, Prussia and Russia recognising these claims, which was to cause Metternich much embarrassment when Castlereagh discovered it in 1817.

Another subject bound up in the fate of Italy was the settlement
of the Ionian Islands. Castlereagh had been much exercised as to how
to dispose of them in such a way as to exclude both French and
Russian influence. At one time, they had been considered as a possible
indemnity for Ferdinand IV; but, when he recovered Naples, Castlereagh recognised that Austria could not allow both sides of the Adriatic
Gulf to be held by the same Power. He would himself have been
ready to hand them over to Austria; but this was vetoed by Russia,
Capodistrias taking a special interest in the fate of his native country,
and having been entrusted by Alexander with all his authority on this
question. It was eventually owing to him that Great Britain retained
control of the Islands as Protector, by the Treaty concluded between
the Four Powers at Paris on November 5th, 1815[1].

In other minor arrangements, the British influence was exerted
almost always on the side of Austria. In these, as in the more important questions of the reconstruction of the German and Swiss
Confederations, her diplomatists played only a subordinate part.
From the first, Castlereagh had determined to have as little to do as
possible with the details of the thorny and intricate problem of the
new Constitution of Germany. He was, indeed, anxious that the
German States should be combined in an effective Constitution, so
that they should be able to hold their own against Russia and France.
His own wishes would probably have led him to support Stein's proposals for a strong central government, with real control over the
several States. He was especially anxious for the creation of a Federal
army, and these ideas he supported in the period subsequent to the
Congress. But he was aware of the difficulties of the situation, and
does not appear to have attempted to exert any direct influence on the
tortuous negotiations which eventually resulted in the eleven articles
which formed part of the Final Act. In the Commission set up to
consider this question, Great Britain was not directly represented
and Münster was allowed an almost entirely free hand. While more
"Austrian" than "Prussian," he was yet sufficiently moderate in

---

[1] *British and Foreign State Papers*, III. 250. The suggestion made by Bavaria
that the islands should be given to Prince Eugène de Beauharnais in compensation
for his claims under the Treaty of Fontainebleau was immediately rejected by
Wellington. *Supplementary Despatches*, IX. 570.

his views to act as a mediator between rival parties, which was all that Castlereagh could desire. However, therefore, he may be blamed for supporting Metternich in later years in the equivocal proceedings which resulted in the Carlsbad Decrees and the Vienna Final Act, Castlereagh was in no way responsible for the halting solution reached at the Congress of Vienna itself.

As to the Swiss Confederation, he laid down for his subordinates a similar policy. Nevertheless, the young Stratford Canning, who assisted Lord Stewart in this matter, was too able and energetic a diplomatist to be content with a passive rôle, and he played a considerable part in the series of negotiations which eventually adapted the Constitution of 1803 to the altered circumstances of the time, and finally succeeded in composing the differences among both the Swiss and the Allies. He was, for example, not satisfied with Capodistrias' drafting of the Protocols, and was tactfully allowed to draw them up himself. He supported the policy of allowing the wishes of the Diet to prevail, and successfully opposed Capodistrias' rather sweeping proposals. He, also, tried to save the Valtelline from Austria without success. None of the Powers seem to have understood the importance of their Declaration guaranteeing the neutrality of Switzerland, which was not finally executed until the Second Peace of Paris, and there is no sign that British statesmen took a special interest in this question. They were, indeed, more concerned in bringing Switzerland into the Coalition against Napoleon and inducing her to allow the Allied troops to move across her territory, than in arranging the details of the new policy, which was to form a precedent of great value, and prove of enormous advantage to Switzerland in the coming century.

The Abolition of the Slave-trade was made one of the principal questions of the Congress, solely through the agency of the British Ministers. They had indeed no alternative. On this Question, public opinion in England was stirred to the uttermost, and was, moreover, concentrated and organised so that it could exert its full force on the Legislature and the Executive. The Additional Article of the Treaty of Paris had by no means satisfied the recognised spokesmen of this subject in the country. The concession to France, that she might continue to bring slaves for five years to the Colonies, was considered a betrayal of the cause. It was in vain that Castlereagh pleaded that France must be treated as an independent nation, and that the cause would ultimately be better served by her agreement than by her submission. He was held to have thrown away a unique opportunity for abolishing the detested traffic. "What could be done when your own Ambassador gave way?" Alexander asked Wilberforce, doubtless not unwilling to make things difficult for the Tories. But Wilberforce was himself a good Tory, and, though he would have sacrificed his party if any advantage could be secured for the cause, he saw clearly that it was useless to press the Ministry too far. The motion, therefore, which he moved on June 27th, in a speech that was a severe rebuke, was one which could be accepted by Castlereagh, whose defence was "that France could not be taught morality at the point of the bayonet." Motions by Grenville in the Upper House and Horner in the Commons calling for papers the Ministry were able to meet; but it was obvious that they had disappointed the country.

The efforts of the Government as well as those of the leaders of the agitation were immediately redoubled in view of the possibilities of the approaching Congress. Eight hundred petitions, containing nearly a million signatures, were presented to the House of Commons. Wilberforce prepared a mass of pamphlets, including an open letter to Talleyrand, in order to convert the Continental Sovereigns and statesmen. The Government, meanwhile, made the cause of Abolition a first charge in their endeavours. Orders were sent to Wellington at Paris and to Wellesley at Madrid to prepare the way for the efforts to be made at the Congress itself. In neither country, however, could much headway be made. All that Wellesley had been able to obtain in the Treaty of Alliance, signed on July 14th, was a promise by Spain to limit the traffic to ships of her own subjects. He was now authorised by Castlereagh to offer considerable subsidies, amounting to two million pounds, if Spain would limit the trade to the south of the line and promise to abolish it in five years, to which offer that of a loan on British credit for ten million dollars was added, if the Abolition was made immediate. But both these offers were rejected, and nothing had been accomplished by the time the Congress opened.

In France, the Abolitionists exerted their utmost efforts, and sent over Clarkson on a special mission. But French public opinion was vehement against concessions, and the support of the notorious Abbé Grégoire did not assist their cause. Extensive slaving expeditions were being prepared in French ports, and it was suggested that here, as in Spain, British capital was finding employment. Talleyrand, however, hinted to Lord Holland that France might grant immediate abolition in return for a Colony; and, on the conversation being reported, Wellington was permitted by Liverpool to sound the French as to whether a money compensation would suffice, though both Ambassador and Prime-Minister were agreed as to the impolicy of barter. When Wilberforce and the Whigs heard of the proposal from Clarkson, they took it up so warmly as to render it obvious that some such offer must be made, if only to avoid disastrous criticism at home. By this time, however, the Congress had assembled, and the negotiation was, by Wellington's wish, transferred to Vienna. On October 8th, therefore, Castlereagh addressed an official Note to Talleyrand, making the definite offer to France of a West Indian island or a sum of money as compensation, if immediate Abolition were granted. This action was admittedly forced on the Government by fear of public opinion, and neither Liverpool, Wellington nor Castlereagh himself believed it to be a wise step. Castlereagh, indeed, considered that the whole agitation in England was doing more harm than good.

"The more I have occasion to observe the temper of foreign Powers on the question of Abolition," he wrote to Liverpool, "the more strongly impressed I am with the sense of prejudice that results, not only to the interests of the question itself but of our foreign relations generally, from the display of popular impatience which has been excited and is kept up in England on this subject. It is impossible to persuade foreign nations that this sentiment is unmixed with views of Colonial policy, and their Cabinets, who can better estimate the real and virtuous motives which guide us on this question, see in the very impatience of the nation a powerful instrument through which they expect to force at a convenient moment the British Government upon some favourite object of policy.

"I am conscious that we have done an act of indispensable duty, under the circumstances in which we have been placed, in making to the French and Spanish Governments the propositions we have done, but I am still more firmly persuaded that we should be at this moment in fact nearer our object, if the Government had been permitted to pursue this object with its ordinary means of influence and persuasion, instead of being expected to purchase concessions on this point almost at any sacrifice[1]."

Talleyrand delayed his answer till November 5th, and when it came it was a refusal, as Castlereagh and Wellington had anticipated. Nevertheless, the Note was by no means uncompromising, partly, as Castlereagh thought, because the recovery of San Domingo by the French was now abandoned. In these circumstances, he avoided bringing the subject officially before the Congress, merely circulating documents and memoranda, and adding to the circulars of the Abolitionists others prepared by his own Office, which appealed to the

---

[1] Castlereagh to Liverpool, October 25th, 1814. F.O. Continent. 7; *British Diplomacy*, p. 215.

commercial and financial interests of the Powers concerned. Wellesley had, at last, induced the Spanish Government to offer to abolish the Trade in eight years, and immediately up to 10° on either side of the line; and the Portuguese Plenipotentiaries at Vienna were prepared to go rather further. It was Castlereagh's opinion, therefore, that, instead of concentration on attempts to obtain immediate Abolition, France should be induced to reduce her period to three years, after which coercive measures should be employed against Spain and Portugal by a refusal to admit their Colonial commerce to the markets of other countries, until the Trade was completely abolished. He, also, proposed to set up a permanent Commission in London and Paris to watch over the effectual execution of the regulations; for he was well aware, as events proved to be the case, how difficult in practice it would be to enforce worldwide Abolition. He hinted that exercise of the right of search and the treatment of offenders as pirates might be necessary to put a stop to the traffic—questions which were to occupy the attention of the British Government throughout the nineteenth century. These ideas were submitted to the Government in a special Memorandum on November 21st[1]. Liverpool's reply, on December 9th[2], approved of the plan and urged that five years should be the extreme limit allowed to Spain and Portugal. By the beginning of December, however, when Castlereagh endeavoured to have the matter formally taken up, he was met with the determined opposition of these two Powers to the establishment of a special Commission of the Eight Powers for consideration of the subject, though Talleyrand, who was anxious at this time to win Castlereagh's favour for other reasons, supported him loyally. For the moment, therefore, Castlereagh dropped the formal negotiations, which the extreme tension then existing in the Congress made it difficult to pursue[3]. He succeeded, during the interval, by the offer of money and many other concessions, including the abrogation of some of the more onerous Clauses of the Treaty of Alliance between Portugal and Great Britain, in inducing the Portuguese Plenipotentiaries to sign a Treaty abolishing the traffic north of the line. Similar efforts with Spain were however of no avail.

At last, early in the new year, the formal consideration of the subject was again taken up. By personal interviews with the three Allied

---

[1] Castlereagh to Liverpool, November 21st. F.O. Continent. 8; *British Diplomacy*, p. 233.

[2] Wellington, *Supplementary Despatches*, IX. 469.

[3] Castlereagh to Liverpool, December 18th, 1814. F.O. Continent. 9.

Sovereigns, Castlereagh procured the full support of their Ministers[1] for all his proposals, Alexander showing himself especially zealous. He knew, also, that Talleyrand would go as far as he dared. On January 16th, therefore, he was able to obtain the establishment of a "Conference" of the Eight Powers to consider the subject, which was distinguished in name only from a formal Commission. This Committee held four meetings between January 20th and February 8th, in which all Castlereagh's proposals were formally considered. He was able to confront the Spanish and Portuguese Plenipotentiaries with the united efforts of all the Great Powers, and to place the former in an exceedingly difficult position. Though Labrador and Palmella maintained a determined front, a record was thus obtained of the public feeling of all Governments which bore some immediate fruit, and certainly made easier the task of completing and making effective the work of Abolition in the succeeding years. A formal Declaration that the Slave-trade was against the laws of humanity was easily obtained, since it committed no Power to any express measure, and this Declaration subsequently became part of the Final Act signed in Vienna. An effort to induce Talleyrand to reduce the French term to three years having failed, as Castlereagh knew must be the case, he concentrated his efforts on obtaining Abolition north of the line and complete Abolition in five years. From Portugal, he obtained the former concession, and the latter from all the Powers except Portugal and Spain. Castlereagh then opened his plans for setting up special machinery in the form of Ambassadorial Conferences at London and Paris, to supervise the regulations as to Abolition. Spain and Portugal protested against this, wishing the Colonial Powers to be alone admitted; but Castlereagh refused to give way, since the whole essence of his plan lay in associating with Great Britain the Continental nations, who had no direct interests in the maintenance of the Trade, in order to put pressure on the other Maritime Powers. He, also, adumbrated plans for mutual right of search, and sketched his idea of excluding from the ports of all civilised nations the Colonial produce of any Power who refused to agree to complete Abolition after a lapse of time. This last proposition much alarmed Palmella, who placed a special protest on the Protocol, but Castlereagh was able to obtain a general approval of it[2].

---

[1] Castlereagh to Liverpool, January 1st, 1815; *British Diplomacy*, p. 274.
[2] It was turned against him, in 1817, by Alexander in the question of the Spanish Colonies.

On the whole, Castlereagh thought that Parliament and public opinion ought to be satisfied with the result of his efforts.

"I hope," he wrote on January 26th, "that essential progress has been made at least upon one branch of the question, I mean the liberation of the Northern parts of Africa from the miseries of this Trade; the foundation has also been laid for an entire cessation of the evil at a definite period, with the prospect that the auspicious epoch may be accelerated by future exertion; and what I consider of great importance is that the attention of the Ministers here has been awakened to this important subject in a degree much beyond what I could have hoped for, considering the multiplicity of their avocations and their former ignorance of the question[1]."

The claim was justified. By obtaining a general Declaration against the Trade in the Treaty, by awakening public opinion among the statesmen by the discussions of the final Conference, and by initiating practical measures to ensure that Abolition, once obtained, should be faithfully carried out, Castlereagh had done an immense amount to bring this odious practice to an end. He was to add further services to the cause in the next two or three years. Nevertheless, in spite of his strictures on the vehement manifestations of public opinion in England, it is obvious that, without the unceasing efforts of Wilberforce and his friends, Castlereagh and his Government would have accomplished but little. Their goodwill cannot of course be doubted; but they needed a spur to make them sufficiently active when other matters were pressing on their attention. By forcing Ministers to initiate a policy of sacrifice, Wilberforce may sometimes have caused the Continental Powers to raise their price for acquiescence in a measure which their interests as well as their conscience should have forced them to adopt immediately. But, though a cynical construction was put upon the agitation by statesmen at the time and by many foreign historians since, it cannot be doubted that it was as sincere as it was ultimately effectual, and that, without the sustained and eager insistence of an organised public opinion in this country, the responsible statesmen would have allowed the iniquitous traffic to continue under the pretext that it was impossible to do otherwise.

Even as it was, the Government found it hard to convince the country that they had done all that was possible. Fortunately for the Ministry, the return of Napoleon, as will be seen, led to immediate Abolition by France, so that they were able thenceforth to concentrate their efforts on the Peninsular Powers.

With regard to another important Question at the Congress,

---

[1] Castlereagh to Liverpool, January 26th, 1815. F.O. Continent. 10.

Clancarty represented Great Britain on the Commission which was established to regulate International Rivers. Great Britain does not seem to have exerted much influence on these discussions, in which, naturally, the Continental Powers were much more nearly interested. This Commission was, however, used by Castlereagh to draw up the regulations on one question in which his country had a special interest—the destruction of the fortifications of Antwerp, which by the Treaty of Paris of 1814 it had been agreed to make a commercial port.

In the regulations drawn up by the Commission on the rank of diplomatic representatives Castlereagh took little interest, declaring that they would raise as many problems as they solved, though he acquiesced in the wishes of the majority. An attempt was made to raise the question of naval salutes at this Commission—a sly hit at some extravagant British pretensions—but the objections of the Admiralty prevailed and the matter was not formally considered.

IV. THE RETURN OF NAPOLEON AND THE SECOND PEACE OF PARIS

As has been seen above, Castlereagh was by no means satisfied with the Treaty of Fontainebleau, by which Napoleon was made Imperial Sovereign of Elba. But though he (and still more strongly, Lord Stewart) saw much reason for alarm in the establishment of Napoleon at Elba, yet he could, at the moment, suggest no other suitable destination for him, and consequently accepted the Treaty so far as the territorial arrangements for Napoleon and his family were concerned. Naturally, the surveillance of Napoleon was a considerable anxiety to the British Government during his stay on Elba. The British Commissary, Sir Neil Campbell, was provided with a naval force expressly for the supervision of the Emperor, and Lord Burghersh at Florence was specially ordered to supervise from Tuscany any attempts to enter into correspondence with him. But Napoleon was still a Sovereign Prince, and his actions could not be controlled, unless they amounted to an infringement of the Treaty; and though the archives of all the Powers are full of reports on his activities, nothing definite was known as to his designs. Metternich's secret police watched all the channels into Italy, and Talleyrand had his own spies. But, though some of the reports were alarmist, they came from discreditable sources. Castlereagh appears to have been chiefly disturbed by the possibility of collusion between Murat and Napoleon; but their intercourse was carried on through confidential agents, and there was no definite proof of any plot. Thus, short of instituting a complete naval blockade of the Mediterranean, the British Government had no alternative but to trust to Campbell's watchfulness to prevent an escape.

There was, indeed, some talk at Vienna of removing Napoleon to a more remote and more easily guarded situation. The point is mentioned in one of the first papers laid by Prussia before the other three Allies[1]. But such a plan was never seriously considered, and there can be no doubt that Alexander, and almost certainly Castlereagh and Metternich as well, would have vetoed any such proposition. Talleyrand was reduced to dally with designs for the kidnapping of Napoleon, and, as some think, even assassination was contemplated by the Bourbons, if no seriously planned scheme was ever set on foot. Lewis XVIII, however, refused to carry out the financial terms of the Treaty of Fontainebleau, by which two million francs were to have been paid to Napoleon. Castlereagh, more than once, warned Talleyrand of the danger of this infringement of the Treaty, and spoke strongly to Lewis XVIII about it on his passage through Paris. His words were not heeded; but Talleyrand may have remembered them when he was reduced to begging for money from Wellington, after his own supplies from Paris had been cut off by the return of the Emperor[2].

During his stay at Elba, Napoleon concealed with supreme skill his intention of returning, which he must have contemplated almost from the beginning of his exile. He professed, indeed, alarm at the rumours that he was to be deported to St Helena or elsewhere, as well as at the danger of an attack by Barbary pirates; he, also, complained bitterly of being deprived of his wife and son, and of the financial straits to which he was reduced. But Campbell, no less than all Napoleon's visitors, many of whom were English, was completely deceived by the resigned attitude which he affected. The resolution at which he arrived to take advantage of Campbell's absence in Tuscany for a few days appears to have been the result of intuition rather than of calculation, but it was welltimed so far as France was concerned. So easily was the escape made that for long it was widely believed in Europe to have been effected with the connivance of the British Government. Though Castlereagh generously took the responsibility, and demonstrated to the House of Commons the impossibility of blockading

[1] See *The Congress of Vienna*, p. 160.
[2] No credence should be attached to Talleyrand's assertion that Castlereagh listened with approval to a suggestion that Napoleon should be removed to the Azores.

effectively the island of Elba, it may be questioned whether Campbell was sufficiently alive to the risks of his position.

However, the mischief was done, and Europe was soon faced with the fact that France had accepted Napoleon's return almost without opposition. At Vienna, the first step taken was the memorable Declaration of March 13th, which delivered Napoleon to the vengeance of the nations. No mention was made in this document of supporting the Bourbons, for it was drawn up before the full extent of Napoleon's success was known. When the extent of the disaster was clear, there was but one voice among the Allies. The Treaty of Chaumont had been concluded expressly to guard against this danger. By March 25th, with hardly any alterations in the original text, the Four Powers had renewed their agreement, and six hundred thousand men were, on paper at least, in arms against France. Nor, so far as Napoleon was concerned, was this anything less than the expression of the Sovereigns' deep emotions and those of their peoples against the man who had so often triumphed over them. There was never at any time any sign of defection. When Napoleon found the Secret Treaty of January 3rd in his archives and sent it to Alexander, it told the latter little more than he already knew, and, though Castlereagh had a moment of anxiety, the revelation produced no effect. The Tsar indeed, aware of his own responsibility for the catastrophe, was almost too zealous, and it needed the blunt opposition of Wellington to make him understand that he could not be the generalissimo of the new Coalition[1]. Wellington himself approached nearer to that rôle, and with the Allied military authorities at Vienna produced a plan of campaign which would ultimately bring a million soldiers into the field against the French. At the end of March, he set out for Brussels to take command of the army which England was assembling in the Netherlands, of which, however, only 30,000 were British troops.

But, though united against Napoleon, the Powers were no more agreed as to who should take his place than they had been in 1814. Metternich's intrigues with Fouché were doubtless, as he said, a mere *ruse de guerre*. But his attitude was at least doubtful, while Alexander spoke even more bitterly against the Bourbons than he had in 1814; for they had now added to their other faults ingratitude to himself. Talleyrand himself kept a free hand so far as possible, and refused to leave Vienna for the King's Court at Ghent. Indeed, at Vienna

---

[1] Wellington to Castlereagh, March 12th, 1815. F.O. Continent. 14; *British Diplomacy*, p. 312.

Clancarty was by far the best friend of the Bourbons, and, when it was proposed to issue another Declaration, now that Napoleon had assumed the Crown once more, it was his insistence that obtained the insertion in it of some words of a friendly nature towards Lewis XVIII, while, in a long interview with Alexander, he discouraged the Tsar's predilections for Orleans or even a Republic[1]. So difficult was it to obtain agreement on the question at Vienna, that the Declaration originally drawn up on April 11th, was not formally inserted on the Protocol until May 12th.

Meanwhile, though the British Government were entirely at one with the Allies as regards Napoleon, there was a period of uncertainty before the War with France became irrevocable. Nearly all the "Mountain" and many of the Whigs were against the War, and almost until the outbreak of hostilities in Belgium protested against it. Castlereagh had to defend against hot attacks in the Commons not only the Vienna Settlement, so far as it was already known, but also the policy of the Allied Powers with regard to the Treaty of Fontainebleau. In the Lords, Wellesley as well as Grey protested against the War, though the Grenville party held coldly aloof. In these circumstances, the Ministry, though determined on war, in which they were supported by the mass of the nation, could do nothing openly for the Bourbons. Their sentiments were, indeed, unanimous in desiring Lewis' return, and throughout they were faithful to the confession which Liverpool had made on February 20th, "The keystone of all my external policy is the preservation of the Bourbons on the Throne[2]." But, though on March 12th, when the news of Napoleon's flight first reached him, Castlereagh wrote to Wellington urging the Powers to support Lewis XVIII, by the 14th he had to supplement this despatch by another urging caution. "We can often do more than we can say[3]," he wrote; and this sums up the policy of his Government. Thus, though the Declaration of the 13th was defended against the attacks of the Opposition, who described it as an incentive to assassination, the Treaty of March 25th was only accepted subject to a declaration that it was not intended to impose any particular dynasty on France, and Clancarty was cautioned against committing his Government in any way to the cause of the Bourbons.

[1] Clancarty to Castlereagh, April 15th, 1815. F.O. Continent. 17; *British Diplomacy*, p. 325.
[2] Liverpool to Castlereagh, February 20th, 1815. Wellington, *Supplementary Despatches*, IX. 573.
[3] Castlereagh to Wellington, March 12th, 14th, 16th. Wellington, *Supplementary Despatches*, IX. 592, 595, 597.

And, though Napoleon's letter to the Prince Regent was returned unopened, the Address moved in the House of Commons on April 17th[1], while urging preparation for war and concert with the Allies, did not, as Castlereagh expressly allowed, mean immediate war. But the temper of the nation gradually showed that Ministers had the whole country behind them. Whitbread could only muster 37 votes against 220 for his amendment to the Address, and of the London Press only *The Morning Chronicle* supported a peace policy. Napoleon's bid for British public opinion by decreeing the complete Abolition of the Slave-trade produced no effect. When the Treaty of March 25th became known and had to be avowed, another furious attack was made by the Opposition, who taunted Castlereagh with the futility of the Treaty of Fontainebleau, as well as with the bad faith shown in carrying it out. But this attack was almost as easily repulsed as the other, though the wisdom of the British reservation was made clear. Meanwhile, the blockade had been established and French merchantmen seized; preparations were made to foment insurrection in the Vendée, and the army was being rapidly organised in Belgium. The Duke of Wellington was entrusted with the task of making Subsidy Treaties with the smaller Powers, so that Great Britain could supply her quota as laid down by the Treaty, and through his agency gradually all the petty States were summoned to join in the fray. Sir Charles Stuart was instructed to represent the British Government at the stately, if penurious, Court which Lewis kept up at Ghent, where also all the other Great Powers were represented. Money, munitions and clothing were sent to the King.

After Waterloo, the Duke became the arbiter of the destinies of France. Blücher was no politician, and was too fully occupied with revenge and spoliation to play any important part in the series of events that ensued on Napoleon's abdication in favour of his son. Lewis was, therefore, able to take Wellington's advice and follow closely the victorious Allied armies, and all northern France declared for him before Paris fell. It scarcely needed, therefore, the dexterous intrigues of Fouché to smooth the way for the Second Restoration, which was accomplished before the Sovereigns and their Ministers had time to intervene, even if they had wished. Alexander had thus, for a second time, to accept the despised Bourbons, and soon accommodated himself to the position. So swiftly and easily did all this

---

[1] A very accurate summary of the Debate is given in *The Dynasts*, Part III. Act v, Scene v.

take place, that the wish of the British Government was accomplished without either Castlereagh or Wellington being compromised.

Napoleon fled to the coast; but British ships prevented the accomplishment of his plan of escaping to America. Had he succeeded, Alexander wished the Allies to address a Note to the President to surrender him; but Castlereagh himself had no expectation that much advantage would be derived from such a measure. However, Napoleon had really no alternative but to surrender to Captain Maitland, and, in any case, he could not, and probably did not, expect much mercy, in spite of his famous appeal to the generosity of the British nation. Wellington protested against Blücher's resolve to shoot Napoleon if he caught him; but our Ministers would have welcomed such an escape from an intolerable responsibility. The Allies were only too ready to leave to the British the ignominy of guarding the Emperor, though, since Castlereagh from the first insisted on it against the wishes of the Cabinet, they, by means of Commissaries at St Helena, shared the responsibility of his detention. Castlereagh, who, while still ignorant of Napoleon's surrender, had lamented that the King of France had not the will or the power to execute him as a traitor, wrote to Liverpool on hearing of his capture, "After fighting him for 20 years, as a trophy he seems to belong to us[1]." Since measures were soon on foot by his friends in England to use the machinery of English law to embarrass the Government, he was quickly hurried off to St Helena—a captive, and denied, now as ever, by the British Government the Imperial title and the attributes of royalty.

Their Emperor captive and the Bourbons restored, the French nation had now to be dealt with. So early as March 26th, Castlereagh had written to Wellington that though "France must pay the price of her own deliverance," yet it was imperative that war should not degenerate into "an indiscriminate and destructive pillage," as it had in 1814[2]. Wellington himself was most anxious to avoid measures which, in the previous campaign, had impaired the efficiency of every army but his own and rallied the French nation against the invaders. Accordingly he arranged with Lewis XVIII that Commissaries should be appointed to accompany the Allied armies to regulate their relations with the inhabitants and arrange for their subsistence. But,

[1] Castlereagh to Liverpool, July 17th, 1815. F.O. Continent. 21; *British Diplomacy*, p. 350.
[2] Castlereagh to Wellington, March 26th, 1815. Wellington, *Supplementary Despatches*, IX. 623. See also Sir Charles Stuart's Despatches in Malet's *Louis XVIII à Gand*, vol. II.

though he was able to carry out this measure effectively with his own army, he could not control the others. The Prussians paid scant attention to the royal nominees. Nor did the annihilation of Napoleon's army arrest the march of the Allied troops. On the contrary, so soon as all danger was over, every country was anxious to feed its troops at the French expense, while it continued to earn the British subsidies; and, before long, nearly a million soldiers had entered France. The Prussians who were only prevented by Wellington's influence from the destruction of the Pont de Jéna at Paris levied vast contributions. Castlereagh had foreseen this danger, and took instant steps to mitigate it and regularise the exactions of the Allies so far as possible; while Wellington declared that "the Allies will in a short time find themselves circumstanced in France as the French were in Spain, if the system pursued by the Prussians and now imitated by the Bavarians shall not be effectively checked[1]."

Castlereagh had, also, to formulate the views of his Government on the Question of the treatment to be meted out to those who had abandoned Lewis's service for that of Napoleon in 1815. On this subject the British Cabinet was vehement. In an Instruction dated June 30th, Liverpool urged that a severe example should be made, not only of commanding officers of garrisons and corps who had deserted to Bonaparte, but also of civil functionaries who had gone over. He called for the penalties of High Treason to be inflicted and a severe example to be made[2]. This opinion was reiterated, in letter after letter, in the early days of July, and there can be no doubt that Liverpool was expressing not merely his own views but those of nearly the whole nation. Castlereagh and Wellington to some extent shared these views. Wellington, it is true, in the Convention which he drew up with Fouché, granted a general amnesty; yet he was careful to point out in the later discussions that arose as to Ney's position, that he had no authority to speak for the French King, but only for the Allied Commanders. He does not, however, appear to have taken much part in these early discussions. It was Castlereagh who urged on Talleyrand on July 13th "the importance of adequately vindicating the King's authority," and who, on the 17th, brought the matter before the Allied Ministers. Talleyrand agreed with the principle, or said he did; but how was a Government which contained Fouché

[1] Castlereagh to Liverpool, July 14th, 1815. F.O. Continent. 21; *British Diplomacy*, p. 343.
[2] Yonge, *Life of Liverpool*, ii. 184.

to condemn traitors? Castlereagh reported that "there is a great repugnance to shed blood, the result in a great measure of fear and
party compromise." In another interview, on the 17th, he pressed
the matter on Talleyrand and Fouché[1]. The Minister of Police saw
that some concession must be made to popular vengeance; but the
Decree in which the punishment was announced contained the names
of those against whom it was to be applied, and their arrest was delayed
after this judicious advertisement. Unfortunately, Ney and one or two
others omitted to escape in time, with the result that they alone
suffered. Many efforts were made to save Ney, especially by Lord
Holland. But Liverpool and the Prince Regent were naturally appealed to in vain. Wellington also refused to interfere—an act for
which he has been much criticised, inasmuch as he signed the Convention with Fouché. But his defence holds true, and while Wellington, to whom duty was the watchword of life, had not a spark of
revengeful spirit in him, he was the last man in the world to palliate
what he could not but consider as a betrayal. On the Civil Ministers
and Sovereigns of all the Allied Powers must rest the responsibility
for an act as impolitic as it was unjust, since the worst traitors, if they
were to be considered such, escaped; while Castlereagh must bear
his share of it, though there are signs that he would never have pressed
the question so strongly if he had not been hounded on by his Cabinet
and his country.

Of far greater importance, however, than the fate of Ney or even
that of Napoleon himself, was the punishment that France herself was
to suffer. She could not expect the moderate treatment that she had,
on the whole, received in 1814. It is true that the Allies had proclaimed war on Napoleon, and not on the French people. But the
Emperor had received the support of practically the whole of the
nation, and France herself was, in the eyes of all Europe, responsible
for the contest which had once more called all Europe to arms. On
this Question, the British Cabinet and to a large extent the British
nation were influenced by the passions of the moment. They were
quite ready to join those Continental Powers who wished, not merely
to bleed France white, but to deprive her of large portions of territory,
so as to render her defenceless and impotent for the future. From the
first, however, Castlereagh (and he had throughout the sincere support of Wellington) took an entirely opposite view. He did not deny

---

[1] Castlereagh to Liverpool, July 14th, 17th, 1815. F.O. Continent. 21; *British
Diplomacy*, pp. 344, 347.

that the Allies were entitled to exact an indemnity from France, and he was concerned to establish some means of security for the immediate future. But, from the first, he saw clearly the folly of depriving France of the conquests of the eighteenth century, and of placing her in such a situation as to make her despair of her future. For six weeks, supported only by Alexander, he fought a hard battle with his Cabinet and the Allies, till, in the end, his commonsense and irresistible logic triumphed, and the terms actually offered to France were almost exactly what he had proposed in the first instance. Nor, in the concessions finally made to the French when Richelieu succeeded Talleyrand, did he play a backward part. His despatches at this period are among the best papers which he ever wrote, and scarcely ever has a statesman better served his country and Europe. He stood entirely unmoved by the outburst of emotion which swayed his colleagues and most of his countrymen, and with rare statesmanship carried out coolly, and with infinite tact as well as unbending resolution, a policy which events completely justified. He risked much, for he had nothing to gain as a party leader (as St John had in 1713). He was immensely helped by Wellington, whose papers are models of sound reasoning; but only a Foreign Minister who had obtained a complete ascendancy over his Cabinet and was utterly indifferent to the passing storms of popular passion could have carried such a policy to a triumphant conclusion. Throughout, he made no appeal to sentiment. His despatches are based entirely on an enlightened view of British interests; and their overwhelming commonsense made it impossible to his colleagues ultimately to resist his conclusions.

The opinion of the Cabinet and the country on this point was conveyed to him by Liverpool in a series of letters, which, if less imperatively phrased than those on the French "traitors," were yet clear and strong enough.

"The more I consider the present internal state of France," wrote Liverpool on July 10th, "and the little chance there is of security to Europe from the character and strength of the French Government, the more I am satisfied that we must look for security on the frontier, and in really weakening the power of France. This opinion is rapidly gaining ground in this country, and I think, even if Bonaparte was dead, there would now be considerable disappointment at any peace which left France as she was left by the Treaty of Paris, or even as she was before the Revolution[1]."

On the 15th, when some news arrived of how things stood at Paris, Liverpool wrote, after a long sitting of the Cabinet, that the prevalent

---

[1] Yonge, *Life of Liverpool*, II. 190.

idea in the country was that "we are fairly entitled to avail our-selves of the present moment to take back from France the principal conquests of Lewis XIV[1]." Castlereagh was ordered to sound the Allies on this point; but at the same time he was authorised, if the Allies objected to such strong measures, to agree to a temporary occu-pation of the northern barrier of France until a line of fortresses had been built in the Netherlands at the French expense. Nothing would have better pleased the majority of Castlereagh's colleagues at Paris than to have had placed before them the extreme view of the Cabinet. Of the Allies the Emperor of Russia was alone disposed to adopt a lenient policy—more lenient indeed than what Castlereagh himself advocated, for he would have been content to waive even a temporary occupation. Austria was inclined to go considerably further than Castlereagh in depriving France of territory, while Prussia and the smaller German Powers were demanding extensive acquisitions, including Alsace and Lorraine and the northern French fortresses. Both the Tsar and Castle-reagh admitted that France must pay an indemnity. They wished this, however, to be a reasonable sum, to be settled in accordance with the ability of France to pay it within a fairly short time. Austria, Prussia and the minor German States were simply determined to bleed France, and they had already begun the process by inordinate extortions while they were in occupation. Talleyrand, meanwhile, let it be known that the King and his Ministers would not consent to sacrifice the slightest portion of French territory. In these circum-stances, Castlereagh determined to come to an agreement with the Tsar. In an interview with him, he persuaded him to accept the British proposal for temporary occupation; and so close an agreement was established that the Tsar was induced to press on Austria and Prussia a paper that had been drawn up by Castlereagh and Welling-ton in conjunction with the Russian Ministers[2]. Four days later, Castlereagh was able to forward home a plan of temporary occupa-tion, drawn up by Wellington, which paid due heed to the suscepti-bilities of France, exempting Lille and Strassburg[3]. Neither the Cabinet nor the Allies were pleased with these suggestions. Castlereagh appears to have kept back from the former for two days the Austrian and Prussian answers, in order that his own arguments might have

---

[1] Liverpool to Castlereagh, July 15th, 1815. *Castlereagh Correspondence*, x. 431.
[2] But the paper was in reality almost entirely inspired by the British Ministers. *Sbornik of the Imperial Russian Historical Society*, CXII. 297.
[3] Castlereagh to Liverpool, August 3rd, 1815. Wellington, *Supplementary Despatches*, XI. 123.

time to sink in, and, though his colleagues offered a good many
criticisms, it was not easy for them to argue against Wellington on
specific points. Their opinion, however, is clearly seen in a final para-
graph of Liverpool's letter of August 11th:

As we have not yet seen the Austrian and Prussian projects, we do not
know the extent of the views of these Governments, but we are informed
that they propose to a certain degree the principle of permanent cessions
by France, at least as far as regards the external line of fortresses. We ought
not to forget that these Governments have more of common interest with
us in the whole of this question than the Government of Russia; and, though
we must all have deeply at heart the consolidation of the legitimate Government in France, we should consider that our success in this object must
necessarily be very uncertain, and that the security of the neighbouring
countries against France may be much more easily attained than the
rendering France orderly and pacific[1].

The Austrian and Prussian replies put forward schemes founded
on the same ideas as those of the British Cabinet. The Austrian paper
was indeed fairly moderate, merely asking for a strip of French
Flanders and smaller cessions on the eastern frontier. The Prussian
paper, which was prepared by their Army leaders (for Hardenberg, who
secretly agreed with Castlereagh and told him so, was no longer able
to control the Prussian policy), would have deprived France of every
first-class fortress which she possessed. Such demands it was impossible, in Castlereagh's opinion, for the French Government to
accept. In forwarding these Memoranda on August 12th, Castlereagh
also sent one by Wellington which he had already given to the Allies
at Paris and which was a conclusive exposure of the injustice as well
as the inexpediency of these propositions. Wellington, though he
admitted that France was still too strong for the security of Europe,
asserted, in direct opposition to the opinion of the Cabinet, that the
Declarations of the Allies to the French people prevented them from
making any material alteration of the French frontier. At the same
time, he showed that justice coincided with the true interests of the
Allies, because a policy of dismemberment would necessarily make
France think only of revenge, and result in a state of affairs in Europe
little less harmful than actual war, and he defended the policy of
temporary occupation with great skill. These ideas were pressed home
by Castlereagh in a series of letters to which the ruthless behaviour
of Prussia and the smaller German Powers added force and fire. He,
also, claimed that, by his policy, he had prevented the Emperor of

---

[1] Wellington, *Supplementary Despatches*, XI. 126.

Russia from taking a line of his own and becoming the "exclusive protector of France."

As to Austria and Prussia, he said, both these Courts require to be narrowly watched...in order that we may not be involved in a course of policy in which Great Britain has no interest but rather the reverse.... No doubt the prevailing sentiment in Germany is in favour of territorially reducing France. After all the people have suffered and with the ordinary inducements of some fresh acquisitions, it is not wonderful it should be so, but it is one thing to wish the thing done and another to maintain it when done[1].

Further, he pointed out that France might be a necessary and valuable factor in the Balance of Power, if the Cabinet's views of Russia were justified. Castlereagh was especially impressed by the outrageous nature of the demands of the Prussian military faction, who, he declared, were as bad Jacobins as the French, and he pressed this point on the Cabinet in order to awaken them to the character of the party with which they wished him to associate his country. But the main argument on which he relied was that there was no alternative between absolutely destroying France or leaving her substantially intact.

"We must make up our minds," he wrote, "whether to play a game with any portion of France or against France collectively; if the former, as much security need only be demanded as is compatible with that object; on the contrary, if the other, in order to gratify what I have no doubt is the prevailing temper in England as well as in Germany, the Cabinet ought to instruct the Duke of Wellington and myself not to secure a fortified town the more or the less, but to confer with the other Allies how France may be effectually disqualified for any future attempt to assault Europe. I have no doubt that the middle line would be attended with the most *éclat*; but it is not our business to collect trophies but to bring back the world to peaceful habits.

"The more I reflect upon it the more I deprecate this system of scratching such a Power. We may hold her down and pare her nails so that many years shall pass away before she can again wound us...but this system of being pledged to a continental war for objects that France may any day reclaim from the particular states that hold them, without pushing her demands beyond what she would contend was due to her own honour, is, I am sure, a bad British policy."

His words finally carried conviction or at least assent, though it was not till the end of August that he won over the Cabinet. In order to effect this and to make some concessions to the Continental Powers, he put forward the scheme of reducing the limits of France to those

[1] Castlereagh to Liverpool, August 17th, 1815. *Castlereagh Correspondence*, x. 485.

of the year 1790. This meant taking away from her Landau, the Saar valley, and part of Savoy, while leaving to her Avignon and other small territories, which had in 1789 been *enclaves* in her dominions. By the middle of August, Castlereagh was able to announce that Alexander was ready to support this scheme. On the 24th, he sent what was almost an ultimatum to his Cabinet, together with a long memorandum which reiterated all the arguments previously employed, and Lord Stewart was sent over with the documents to support by word of mouth the arguments of his brother[1]. But the Cabinet had already given way. On the 23rd, Liverpool had already sent a reluctant consent. He and his colleagues now professed themselves entirely convinced, and Castlereagh was assured that he would be "most cordially and zealously supported and upheld by all your colleagues in this country[2]." He was thus able to turn his artillery without reserve on the recalcitrant Allies. On August 31st, he sent an impressive memorandum in reply to the Austrian and Prussian notes, supported by a paper drawn up by Wellington, which contained a vigorous and indeed unanswerable defence of the principle of temporary occupation, and which also put forward a practical scheme for carrying it out. Metternich was easily won over. In fact, he had from the beginning been in sympathy with Castlereagh's policy, but had found it necessary to put forward stronger views in deference to German public opinion. The Prussians put up a more determined fight, but they could not succeed when thus isolated. As for the smaller Powers, Castlereagh did not mince matters with them. To Gagern, who was carrying on an intrigue to transfer Luxemburg to Prussia and compensate the Netherlands with a large slice of French territory, he announced that such a course would mean the loss of the British guarantee. "This view of the question," reported Castlereagh, "appeared altogether to damp His Excellency's appetite for such acquisitions[3]." By this means, and by raising the indemnity from six to eight hundred millions, he at last succeeded in producing agreement among the Allies.

The terms were presented to the Talleyrand Ministry on September 16th. Talleyrand refused to consent to the losses of territory, and sent in an answer couched in very strong terms; but the discussions

---

[1] Wellington, *Supplementary Despatches*, XI. 137.
[2] Liverpool to Castlereagh, August 28th, 1815. *Castlereagh Correspondence*, X. 506.
[3] Castlereagh to Liverpool, September 4th, 1815. F.O. Continent. 26; *British Diplomacy*, p. 376.

were suspended by the dismissal of his Ministry. The Ministers had, indeed, been subjected to ever increasing attacks from the Ultras during their whole period of office. Reaction was now everywhere dominant in France, and the White Terror reigned in some parts, Monsieur and the Duc d'Angoulême placing themselves at the head of the Opposition. Castlereagh regarded the Ultra party with the greatest distrust. "At present it is," he wrote, "a mere rope of sand, without leaders habituated to office, without any fixed system, but with an inordinate infusion of passion, resentment and spirit of inversion[1]." He preferred even Fouché to such a Government. The dismissal of Talleyrand by the King at this moment he considered as especially impolitic, since it threw on the new Ministry the odium of accepting terms which their predecessors had rejected. Fortunately for France, at this grave crisis she found in the Duc de Richelieu one of the most admirable Ministers who ever represented her. He was singularly free from the baser elements of statesmanship, while his friendship for Alexander ensured the support of the Tsar. Castlereagh was, indeed, somewhat alarmed at the increase of Russian influence over the French Government, but he loyally accepted the situation. He told the king bluntly, however, that he must abandon the line which Talleyrand had taken up, and in the course of a long interview succeeded in convincing him of the necessities of the case[2].

With Richelieu, therefore, the negotiations proceeded swiftly. The Allies reduced their indemnity to seven hundred millions of francs, the temporary occupation was reduced to five or possibly three years, and the dismantling of some of the fortresses was waived. The result was to impose a heavy punishment on France, but one not out of proportion to her situation, and which need not, and in fact did not, drive her to a policy of revenge and despair. She lost the territories of Landau, Saarlouis, Mariembourg, Philippeville and certain parts of Savoy, and had to rase the fortifications of Huningen. Out of the sum fixed for her indemnity, 200 millions of francs, including the whole of Great Britain's share, were to be spent in the erection of fortresses on the north-eastern frontier. Moreover, a separate Convention laid on her the duty of compensating private claims against France, the exact amount of which was not specified. The Prussians were, at a later stage, to found enormous claims on this Article, but

---

[1] Castlereagh to Liverpool, September 11th, 1815. F.O. Continent. 27; *British Diplomacy*, p. 377.
[2] Castlereagh to Liverpool, September 25th, 1815. F.O. Continent. 28; *British Diplomacy*, p. 379.

were prevented by Great Britain and Russia from insisting on them, and the total amount was only 240 millions of francs. France had already been forced to allow a large number of the works of art, of which she had plundered Europe during the Revolution and Napoleonic Wars, to be returned to their previous owners. Castlereagh had strongly supported the measure. He had, however, refused to accede to the monstrous suggestion, which the Prime Minister made at the express order of the Prince Regent, that some of these works of art should be brought to London. They were removed, not as a punishment, but as a tardy measure of justice to their original owners, and, as a matter of fact, the British Government helped some of the poorer claimants, including the Pope, to defray the heavy charges of their transference to their old homes. Lastly, Castlereagh obtained from Lewis XVIII, though even now only after much hesitation, the complete Abolition of the Slave-trade which Napoleon had already granted, and his consent to the establishment of a Commission at London, such as had been proposed at Vienna. He might, therefore, fairly claim that he had brought home a Peace which meant security for at least a period, and the infliction of a considerable punishment on France for her acquiescence in the return of Napoleon. It was, however, far from fully expressing the sentiments of the nation, and met with severe criticism when it was discussed in Parliament.

Though the outlines of the Treaty had been laid down by October 1st, the details of the Conventions on the occupation and the financial questions, which accompanied it, necessitated a series of detailed negotiations, and it was not signed until November 20th.

On this date too was signed another Treaty between the Four Great Powers—a renewal of that concluded at Chaumont, which, however, now contained new stipulations of great importance. Castlereagh had, from the first, intended to make the exclusion of Napoleon and his family from the Throne of France "part of the permanent law of Europe."

"There can be no doubt," he wrote so early as July 17th, "that, before we retire, the nation will have felt deeply what it is to be invaded by all Europe. If we make a European invasion the inevitable and immediate consequence of Bonaparte's succession or that of any of his race to power in France, I am confident after the experience they have had of his impotence against such a confederacy and their own sufferings, that there is not a class in France, not excepting even the army, that will venture to adhere to him at the hazard of being again over-run by the armies of Europe, with the certainty of being dismembered and loaded with contributions. We committed a great error when last at Paris in not opposing the barrier of such a stipulation against his return, for there is no doubt he had address enough to make both the nation and the army believe that he might be restored and peace nevertheless preserved[1]."

Such a policy was in his mind throughout all the negotiations of the Treaty of Peace, and his belief that security against a revival of French aggression would be better provided by its means was one of the reasons why he rejected all the plans of spoliation and dismemberment brought forward by the Allies. Before, however, this idea could be worked out in formal discussions, Alexander startled the Sovereigns and statesmen by the proposal which is known as the Holy Alliance. The idea of this extraordinary document had been suggested to him by Castlereagh's abortive proposal for a general guarantee made at the Congress of Vienna. But, in the Tsar's emotional mind, which was now passing through an acute religious crisis, it had assumed an entirely different shape. The document, which was to be personal to the Monarchs concerned, contained no express obligations, except that they would regulate their conduct according to the doctrines of the Christian religion. Both Castlereagh and Metternich regarded the proposal as a ludicrous one; but they could not afford to offend the Tsar. Castlereagh told Liverpool very frankly, that Alexander was not quite right in his head and must be humoured[2]. Thus, though the forms of the British Constitution did not allow the Prince Regent to append his signature to the Treaty, he sent a personal letter expressing his agreement with its principles, which satisfied the expectations of the Tsar. All the other Sovereigns of Europe signed it, except the Sultan and the Pope, who were not invited; and the fact that the terms of the Treaty made it impossible for the former to add his name was by many regarded as a sinister design on the part of the Tsar. He had, indeed, significantly avoided raising the issue of Turkey on which Castlereagh's proposal had foundered; but there is little doubt of his sincerity. Nevertheless, this Treaty, which Castlereagh was soon forced to produce in the British Parliament, caused infinite embarrassment in later years, and, despite the fact that it was in design one of the most innocent documents ever issued, became the symbol of Reaction in the mouths

---

[1] Castlereagh to Liverpool, July 17th. F.O. Continent. 21; *British Diplomacy*, p. 349.
[2] Castlereagh to Liverpool, September 28th, 1815. Wellington, *Supplementary Despatches*, XI. 175.

of the Liberals of all countries, and a specially powerful weapon in the hands of the Opposition in England.

The Treaty of November 20th—the Treaty of the Quadruple Alliance—which expressed Castlereagh's own views, was of a very different nature. He had already indicated its scope in the Memorandum sent home by Lord Stewart, which had finally won the approval of the Cabinet to his policy. Alexander had immediately expressed his particular approbation of the proposal. He had, indeed, hastened to anticipate Castlereagh by producing a draft of such a Treaty, before the British Minister had himself prepared one. To this draft Castlereagh took immediate exception. It was drawn up, he said, in too vague and indefinite shape. It bore on the face of it "too strong and undisguised a complexion of interference on the part of the Allied Sovereigns in the internal affairs of France, without sufficiently connecting such interference with the policy which a due attention to the immediate security of their own dominions prescribed[1]"; for Alexander had proposed that the Allies should guarantee both Lewis XVIII and the *Charte*. Castlereagh's project endeavoured to avoid these pitfalls. With the exception of the Sixth Article, it confined itself to a promise to observe the Treaty quite recently concluded with France, and to a renewal of the Treaty of Chaumont in terms which more expressly excluded the return of Bonaparte or any of his family to the throne of France. The only reference to Lewis XVIII was a promise to adopt this necessary measure "in concert amongst themselves and with his Most Christian Majesty[2]." Except for a few verbal alterations, the draft, as Castlereagh presented it, was accepted by the Cabinet and by his Allies, and it was this Treaty to which he refers whenever he speaks of the Alliance. It was simply a more explicit statement, in the light of the experience of the Hundred Days, of the policy for which he had been contending ever since 1813—the protection of Europe by special treaty against any renewal of aggressive war by France, the return of the Bonaparte family being accepted as implying the immediate renewal of such aggression.

But the Sixth Article actually introduced into the Treaty a new element of great importance, and its presence there appears to have been due to Castlereagh's own express desire. It reveals the fact that

---

[1] Castlereagh to Liverpool, October 15th, 1815. F.O. Continent. 29; *British Diplomacy*, p. 386.

[2] Castlereagh had written in his draft "*roi légitime*," but this phrase was abandoned in deference to Liverpool's criticism that it would cause discussions in Parliament.

Castlereagh proposed to institute a new system of diplomacy by Conference, which he considered as essential to the preservation of the peace of Europe. Article VI in its final shape runs as follows:

To facilitate and to secure the execution of the present Treaty, and to consolidate the connexions which at the present so closely unite the Four Sovereigns for the happiness of the World, the High Contracting Parties have agreed to renew their Meetings at fixed periods, either under the immediate auspices of the Sovereigns themselves, or by their respective Ministers, for the purpose of consulting upon their common interests, and for the consideration of the measures which at each of these periods shall be considered the most salutary for the repose and prosperity of Nations, and for the maintenance of the Peace of Europe.

This Article stands exactly as it was drawn up by Castlereagh in his draft. In Alexander's original proposal, the meetings had been merely intended to supervise the execution of the provisions in the Treaty dealing with France. It was Castlereagh who added the words which founded the so-called "Congress System"—periodic meetings of the statesmen to discuss the affairs of Europe round a table rather than by the old medium of notes and documents interchanged between the Courts through the medium of Ambassadors. The application, therefore, to a period of peace of the idea of diplomacy by Conference, gradually brought into being in the closing stages of the War, was due to Castlereagh more than to anyone else. There can be no doubt that he attached the highest importance to it, and regarded it as a piece of machinery highly essential for the maintenance of the peace of Europe. The Alliance constructed to protect Europe against French domination was clearly thought by him capable of extension into a system of informal Conferences, which, while leaving the Great Powers absolutely free to decide every case on its own merits, would enable them to continue the intimate relations established by these among themselves during the War. The time was indeed not yet ripe for the institution of a formal system of European Conferences, which alone could have rendered permanent so great a conception. The institutions of the various nations and the ideals of their rulers were too dissimilar for such a system to maintain itself, especially since no attempt was made to support it by the public opinion of the nations concerned. Yet, in devising it and stedfastly supporting it throughout his career, in spite of the opposition of his colleagues, Castlereagh showed himself, in a sense, the most enlightened statesman of his time. Blind as he was to the great movements which were to dominate the nineteenth century, he was yet far in advance of all his own countrymen in his recognition of the fact that new methods of diplomacy were necessary, if Europe was to be preserved from the scourge of war. Nor was "the Concert of Europe," the main result of the system which he advocated, without its successes in the century that followed[1].

The reputation of Castlereagh as a Foreign Minister has changed a great deal in recent years. The attitude which Lord Salisbury took up in 1862 and Lord Morley and Mr Balfour were inclined to follow in 1891, has on the whole been justified by the researches of historians since the diplomatic papers of the time have been more closely studied. There is some danger perhaps of the reaction going too far in an age painfully conscious of the difficulty of such work as Castlereagh tried to accomplish. Yet the courage and common-sense of his diplomacy during the Pacification of Europe are such as to compel admiration even from those who detest many of the principles for which he stood. Rarely has a statesman been able to carry out his policy with such consistency and success. If we compare the legacy, which Pitt left to his pupil, with the results actually obtained, we see that, throughout these critical years, Castlereagh was aiming at a definite and complete scheme of reorganisation—nine-tenths of which he successfully accomplished. Much of this was of course in the nature of things, and Castlereagh happened to take office just as the tide of fortune turned. He reaped where other men had sown—Pitt, of course, and Canning in his earliest and possibly most brilliant period. Nevertheless, his own share in bringing about the new order of things was no small one, and the persistence with which he followed a definite line of policy to its logical conclusion is almost without parallel among diplomatists, who are, speaking generally, opportunists.

Castlereagh was, in fact, successful because his policy was dictated by principles which he thoroughly understood and believed in. Of his complete success in obtaining all the main objects for which his countrymen had fought for twenty years there can be no doubt. The maritime and colonial supremacy of Great Britain was completely established. That the Peace of Paris, no less than the Peace of Utrecht, might have been used to amass a few more possessions than were actually obtained is of course obvious. But who will deny that

[1] See C. K. Webster, "Castlereagh et le Système des Congrès?" *Revue des Études Napoléoniennes*, Jan.-Feb. 1919.

Castlereagh's moderation in dealing with the French and Dutch Colonies was anything but wise statesmanship? By the acquisition of the Cape, Malta, and the Mauritius Great Britain completed her strategic control of the trade routes of her Empire; while sane policy forbade her to aim at a monopoly of colonial possession. Moreover, Antwerp, Genoa, and the Ionian Islands were all rendered innocuous for the future; and, so far as human knowledge and foresight could be expected to reach, the strategic supremacy of Great Britain was made complete in every sea.

How mistaken some of Castlereagh's European plans were, the history of the nineteenth century has revealed! But it may be doubted whether any others would have served the needs of the moment so well. If the idea of the Balance of Power was merely the application of an outworn theory to an entirely fresh set of circumstances, yet it still had much in it which was necessary to the stability of Europe. When Castlereagh insisted that the centre of Europe must, at all costs, be strengthened against the dangers which threaten it from France and Russia, he was merely asserting a truth which experience has abundantly confirmed. That he sacrificed to it completely the national claims of Poland, Italy and Belgium was regrettable, but in the circumstances of the time, inevitable. Nor were any of these three peoples prepared to take advantage of national independence if it had been then offered to them. Of German unity, so far as his influence extended, Castlereagh was, of course, a consistent supporter.

Castlereagh's cardinal error, indeed, was, not that he ignored the principle of Nationality, which was not ready for recognition, but that he placed no faith in popular institutions. Had he made any attempt to help the new States to retain or establish some form of Constitutional government, there would have been some prospect of the gradual adaptation of the old system to the new forces. But Castlereagh's influence was everywhere on the side of autocracy. He seems sincerely to have believed that there was no alternative to such democracy as the French Revolution had taught the aristocrats of his generation to dread. He was indisputably in the right when he distrusted the absurd Constitutions which had been erected in the south of Europe. But Bentinck, with all his crudities and extravagances, was in closer touch with reality when he attempted to associate the people in the work of making the new Europe.

Yet Castlereagh was not without his own schemes for the maintenance of his work. Against the greatest danger of all—Revolutionary and Napoleonic France—he hoped that the Chaumont Treaty would prove an adequate safeguard; and he proved right in the issue. This was his special contribution to the problem, and how much preferable to the wild schemes of plunder and spoliation which France's victims would have liked to put into force! French historians have of recent years acknowledged their debt to the magnanimity of Alexander; but they have scarcely given due credit to the services rendered to France by the commonsense and diplomatic skill of Castlereagh. Had he followed the popular line, France would undoubtedly have been deprived of ancient provinces and laden with crushing indemnities, and might easily have been driven to a policy of despair. For in these matters, and especially in the financial question, it was the voice of Great Britain, her most consistent and dangerous enemy, that counted for most—and it was only Castlereagh's commanding influence in the counsels of his countrymen which ensured that Great Britain should speak for justice and even mercy, rather than for revenge and national greed. If France was left with the frontier of the *Ancien Régime*, a fleet, some Colonies and a debt incomparably lighter than that of Britain herself, it was Castlereagh's wisdom and strength of character that was largely responsible for the result.

Castlereagh's larger schemes for the maintenance of the European Peace will be considered further in the second volume of this work. As has been pointed out, the Congress system was due more to him than to any other man. That it was devised mainly to give permanence to the new condition of affairs is probably true. The ideas of statesmen had not yet reached beyond a static Europe. Yet Castlereagh, more than any other statesman of his time, had learnt the lesson that the old system of diplomacy had proved to be hopelessly inadequate. His substitute of diplomacy by Conference was an application of his experiences of 1814-15, and revealed the weakness as well as the strength of his intelligence. He was a diplomatist *par excellence*. The informal Conferences, by which he had helped to solve the appallingly difficult problems of the settlement, he regarded as a new device of immense value. What he failed to see was that such inventions must prove to be unstable and unsuccessful, if they depended merely on the personal relations which two years of close intercourse with Continental statesmen had enabled him to establish. He failed, therefore (and the task was indeed at that time an impossible one), to give to the new ideas either the stability of formal interpretation or the driving force of public opinion. For the latter task, indeed, no one could have been less suitable than he; for he despised and ignored, so far as possible, the public opinion of his countrymen. He was bound to fail, therefore, in the attempt which he made to conquer their insularity and show them that their own peace and happiness was bound up with that of Europe. Nevertheless, he made an experiment of the greatest value to posterity which, also, redeemed the statesmanship of the Pacifications of something of the reproach that it had learnt none of the lessons of its times.

Like all successful men of action, however, Castlereagh was apt to place too much trust in his own contribution to human progress. He was acutely aware that he stood almost alone in England in possessing a knowledge of Continental affairs. It was thus natural that he should exaggerate the importance of the Foreign Office and distrust the share which Parliament or public opinion might play in International policy. He was not above intrigue, as the affair of Murat and one or two later passages in his life reveal, and he had the natural predilection of an expert for methods, which he had been able to employ with success and credit to himself. The weakness of the Opposition which he had to face in the House of Commons doubtless helped to exaggerate these defects. Had Canning gone over to the other side, instead of weakly accepting a place under the Government during these critical years, Castlereagh might have been forced to take a different line. As it was, he was never able to make any impression on the best minds of his generation.

By the end of 1815, in fact, the greatest period of his career was closed. He had controlled the policy of his country at an all-important moment in her history with a firmness of purpose and consistency of aim almost without parallel. He had seen to it that her vital interests had everywhere been protected and maintained. He had by new and ingenious expedients attempted to associate her permanently with the European System. He had established his own position among European statesmen and was a power in their Councils which could not be ignored. But he was the last man to cope intelligently with the new forces which had grown up in his own country during the years of war; indeed, few statesmen are, who conduct a great struggle to its conclusion. Though he was something more than a skilled diplomatist—namely, a Foreign Minister with principles of action—he could do nothing to teach these principles to others. Thus, he died a few years later, the most lonely and friendless of all the great Ministers of England—so hated and contemned that it has been reserved for a later generation to do justice to the great qualities which he undoubtedly possessed.

CHAPTER V

THE AMERICAN WAR AND THE TREATY
OF GHENT, 1814

I

THROUGHOUT the period subsequent to the Peace of Amiens the relations between the United States and Great Britain were strained almost to breaking-point. This condition of affairs was due, very largely, to the attitude which Great Britain assumed as a belligerent Power, though there were also other causes of dispute between the two peoples of a serious nature which would have arisen even if Europe had remained at peace. Two reasons alone had prevented the War which at last broke out in June 1812 from beginning at a far earlier date—the wrongs which France had inflicted on America, and the weakness of the United States against the overwhelming maritime power of Great Britain. Indeed, had British statesmen shown themselves but a little more prescient in the years 1809–1812, they could almost certainly have delayed the outbreak, until the course of events in Europe would of itself have prevented it. As it was, the successes of the later stages of the Napoleonic Wars were embittered by the course of a futile and inconclusive struggle between Great Britain and America, which in itself settled none of the points at issue. Rarely has there been in history a war fought with such bitterness and determination, if with singular incapacity on both sides, which has terminated without a single one of the original causes of the war appearing in the Treaty of Peace. This result was of course due to the fact that the War was a by-product of the European War, and the causes that produced it ceased at the European Peace. Nevertheless, men do not easily give up principles for which they have been ready to shed their blood. Fortunately, in this case Great Britain, the stronger Power, had never insisted on a formal recognition of her rights. She was content if she was able to refuse to surrender them formally. Moreover, though public opinion vehemently supported the War while it was being waged and there was a far greater bitterness displayed in its course than during the Revolution, yet for Great Britain the War was after all a minor affair. Her main energies had been concentrated on Europe, where she had won a more complete triumph than her people had ever hoped to attain. She could accept, not, indeed, without some considerable sacrifice of pride, the humiliations and failures of the American War; and the consciousness that they had been able to inflict these on the British Empire, flushed with victory, compensated the Americans for the failure to establish the principles for which they had fought.

The two main causes of the War were the impressment of American sailors by British ships of War, and the losses imposed upon American trade by the British regulations as to neutral commerce. Both were considered by the British people absolutely necessary to their success against Napoleon; and, in actual fact, their view was to a large extent a correct one. So long as the methods then in vogue for maintaining the naval power of Great Britain continued, it was essential that no easy refuge should be found from the dangers and trials of that service. By 1812, indeed, the main danger of the maritime war had disappeared, and great concessions could undoubtedly have been made to America without endangering British sea power. Nevertheless the extent of the War and the future demands on the fleet could not be foreseen, and one concession might lead to another. Interference with neutral commerce was, also, in some form essential to the winning of the war. Had Napoleon been able to use a neutral fleet, he could almost certainly have successfully defied the maritime power of Great Britain, while irreparable injury would have been inflicted on British commerce. Yet Great Britain was able, in June 1812, to relax to some extent restrictions, which had grown more severe with every year of war, though too late to avert the struggle with the United States.

The long diplomatic struggle that had been carried on between the two Powers has been narrated in the previous Chapter of this Volume. It dated in a sense, as Mahan points out, from before the War and, in one aspect, was a continuation of the War of Independence. But, from the outbreak of the War, the effort which the United States was making to obtain a due share of the carrying trade and colonial commerce of the world took upon itself a new significance. A competition, which in peace time was indeed resented by Britain and France alike, became a vital factor in the decision of the struggle in Europe. Since 1794, when the Senate refused to accept the few concessions which Jay had secured as in any way adequate to satisfy the pretensions of the United States, dispute had succeeded dispute, and incident incident. The Americans gradually found that their position as a neutral was almost as difficult as if they had been a belligerent. Every expedient was tried, even the practical abandonment of their over-seas commerce, to find an issue from the position in which they were placed. But the European War still went on, and, as it broadened and grew yearly more intense, the restrictions to which the Americans had to submit grew more and more irksome.

Most insulting of all to national pride was the exercise of the British right of search. The British navy was recruited by impressment, and it was only natural that many British sailors should seek a freer and more lucrative career in American ships. But Great Britain peremptorily refused to allow any such transference of allegiance, and, alike in British and Colonial ports and on the high seas, they exerted their right to force their sailors to return to British ships. No period of naturalisation was regarded as sufficient to relieve a British sailor from his obligations to his country; and, since the distinction between Britishers and Americans was not great, and many British sailors posed as Americans in order to escape impressment, it was inevitable that many Americans should be forcibly taken from ships of their own country and made to serve in British vessels. The right was exerted with the greatest brutality by the British fleet, and in 1807 the attack on the American frigate 'Chesapeake' appeared to denote that not even American men-of-war were to be exempt and all but led to an immediate outbreak of hostilities. The British Government did not, indeed, defend the action of its subordinates in this case; but it refused, then as always, to discuss the general question of impressment. The right of search, it was claimed, had been exercised from earliest times by Great Britain. No expedient could be devised to distinguish accurately between Americans and British. It must be, therefore, left to the British naval officers to exercise their discretion as to how and when they applied the undoubted maritime rights of their country. The claim to search American vessels of war was, indeed, abandoned, and offers of compensation for the 'Chesapeake' affair were made. But these were not such as to satisfy the American Government. Erskine's conciliatory policy was rejected by the British Cabinet. F. J. Jackson, who succeeded him, carried out his Instructions in so uncompromising a fashion that the American Government refused to negotiate further with him, and from the beginning of 1810 to June 1811 Great Britain was only represented by a *Chargé d'affaires* at Washington. A. J. Foster was then sent by the British Government, and the 'Chesapeake' affair was closed by an offer of reparation which was accepted. The main question still remained open. The British Government increased American bitterness by attempting to prove that British seamen were detained against their will on American warships. At last, the humiliation could no longer be borne by the people of the United States; and perhaps the main cause of the War which was declared on June 18th was the hopelessness of obtaining any relief on this question except by declaring it. At any rate, even when the news of the abandonment of the Orders in Council reached America after the Declaration of War, the United States was prepared to continue hostilities because of this question alone.

More serious, however, to the national interests of the United States was the second cause of the War—the interference by the Belligerent Powers in Europe with her commerce. The destruction of French maritime commerce by the British fleet had thrown open to the United States the carrying trade between France and her Colonies, which had hitherto been as jealously guarded as that of the British Empire. But, by the exercise of a right which had first been applied in the Seven Years' War and hence was called the "Rule of 1756," Britain forbade the United States from taking advantage of the opportunity thus offered to her. Such trade was regarded not as a neutral service but as active assistance to the enemy, and was, therefore, met with the full exercise of the belligerent right of capture. When Spain and Holland became part of the French system, the rule was extended to their Colonies likewise. The Americans, at first, endeavoured to get over the restriction by breaking their journey to Europe at ports of the United States; but the application by the British Government in 1799 of the doctrine of "continuous voyage" defeated this expedient.

If great loss was inflicted on their commerce by this rule, yet it was true that the Americans had not, for the most part, enjoyed the privileges of this trade in peace time. But it was not long before they began, also, to be prevented from carrying on the trade between their own country and Europe, which they had maintained before the War. By the practice of "blockade" Great Britain, so early as 1799, forbade all trading with ports controlled by France, and rendered all ships sailing to them subject to capture. After the peace of Amiens, as Napoleon obtained control over all Europe the area of such "blockade" was extended. That such measures, in part at least, were merely retaliatory to the paper "blockades" established by Napoleon himself, made no difference to the extent of the injuries inflicted on the United States. The Berlin and Milan Decrees and the Orders in Council of 1807 and 1809, which followed them, all but excluded American ships from European ports, and since Great Britain commanded the sea, it was Great Britain who appeared to be mainly responsible for the injuries inflicted upon them. The expedients of the Non-Intercourse and Embargo Acts, devised by the Jefferson and Madison Cabinets in 1806 and 1808 to meet this situation, injured the United States far more than any other country. Gradually, therefore, all classes of the nation were drawn into a common hostility. Nevertheless, the measures of the British Government were just as strongly approved by public opinion in England. Canning was but expressing the feelings of most of his countrymen when he said that Great Britain could not consent to "buy off that hostility which America ought not to have extended to her[1]." Various expedients were suggested for mitigating the rigour of the Orders but almost all were rejected by the British Government. The situation was made more serious by Napoleon's pretence to suspend the Milan and Berlin Decrees in 1810. The British Government with truth held that no such repeal had really been made, and Foster offered to repeal the Orders in Council, if the French Decrees could be shown to be wholly removed. But this could not be done, as the President himself was very well aware. Nevertheless, on June 23rd, 1812, the Orders in Council were annulled so far as American vessels were concerned. The cessation of the American trade had inflicted great injury on British commerce, and it was this motive that induced the Government to give way rather than any fear of hostilities. The repeal, however, came too late to influence the decision of the American Government, who had declared war on June 18th.

The outbreak of the War was due, almost entirely, to the two causes which have been discussed. There were, however, other causes operating to produce friction between the countries, though not of such a nature as to rank with the other two. The purchase by the United States of Louisiana, which Napoleon had forced Spain to transfer to him, had caused much resentment in England, and, in the dispute which subsequently broke out between the United States and Spain

---

[1] Canning to Pinkney, September 23rd, 1808; F. A. Updyke, *The Diplomacy of the War of 1812*, Baltimore, 1915, p. 99. This work is founded on a very complete survey of both the American and British State Papers, as well as on researches in the diplomatic documents preserved at Washington and the Record Office, and the writer is very largely indebted to it in this portion of his work.

as to the Floridas British sympathies were entirely on the side of the latter country. It was becoming clear that the United States was aiming at extending her power to the Pacific, and in such a case British possessions in Canada and the West Indies might be endangered. To some minds, a war appeared necessary to check the growth of the new nation whose future could not be foreseen. These were, however, a very small minority, and, though the boundaries between Canada and the United States were ill-defined and the fishing rights granted to the Americans by the Treaty of 1783 exceedingly unpopular among their Newfoundland competitors, yet these were not in any way acute grievances. On the American side, there was a party which both hated and feared the power of Great Britain and was only too ready to take advantage of her embarrassments. But this antipathy was kept in check by the still more powerful interests which had commercial ties with Britain.

The final stages of the diplomatic struggle were much influenced by the fact that the United States had no Minister at London. Jonathan Russell, the *Chargé d'affaires*, was quite incapable of appreciating all the issues involved, or of keeping his own Government accurately informed of the course of events. That war had been delayed so long, was due, not to the diplomacy of either side, which was almost always as stiff and uncompromising as possible, but to two other causes. In the first place, the United States had almost as great a grievance against France as against Great Britain, and to declare war against Great Britain was, in effect, to support Napoleon. There were indeed in the United States a considerable number of people who remembered the indebtedness of their country to France. But, if the French Republic had only succeeded in alienating almost completely American sympathy, it was not likely that an Emperor, who expressed in himself the antithesis of the ideals of the United States, would secure their support. War with England had therefore to be carefully distinguished from even the semblance of an alliance with Napoleon, and, as a matter of fact, throughout the struggle this attitude was maintained with scrupulous care. The question of war or peace was, also, to a certain extent a party issue in the United States. The Democrats advocated the war while the Federalists opposed it. The division was largely a geographical one. The commercial States, who had most to lose from the War, were mainly Federalist, and were, moreover, bound to England by greater ties of affection and community of outlook than the other portions of the United States.

But the Democrats rightly thought that the events of 1811 had made it impossible for their opponents to resist the strong feeling which was manifest everywhere in the United States. They were proved right by the issue. The case that was presented to Congress was an overwhelming one to American eyes; and, though in States like Massachusetts and Connecticut, opposition went as far as passive resistance to the measures of the Central Administration, yet, on the whole, the mass of the nation was behind the Government in their struggle, however tardily they came to understand the responsibilities which it threw on them.

In England also the War was popular. The commercial interests were, indeed, dismayed, but the governing classes were united in regarding the American Declaration of War as a treacherous attack on a country that was contending for the liberties of the world. The Whigs, naturally, endeavoured to throw as much blame on the Government as possible; but they dared not deny the necessity of the exercise of the British rights which were the cause of the War. Among the mass of the people there was an intense bitterness, and they demanded, not merely the maintenance of British rights, but the punishment of the Americans for their attack on Great Britain at the crisis of her struggle with Napoleon. The confiscation of all American ships in British ports, immediately the news of the American Declaration of War was received, was an index of the manner in which the struggle would be carried on.

Nevertheless, an attempt was made on both sides to put an end to the War almost as soon as it was begun. Neither side had accurately gauged the stubbornness and passion with which their opponents would hold to their own view of the case. Castlereagh, however, who had just come into office when the War broke out, while rigorously maintaining the British case, was from the first as conciliatory in manner as possible in all American questions. The British Government were under the impression that the United States would not continue the War for impressment alone, now that the Orders in Council were removed. Accordingly, Admiral Warren, who was sent out in command of the naval operations against America, was ordered to offer an armistice with a view to a termination of hostilities. No concessions were, however, offered—merely a threat that the Orders in Council would be reinforced if peace were not made. Monroe, Madison's Secretary of State, however, insisted on the right of impressment being given up even before an armistice could be concluded, and refused to treat on any other terms than that this practice should be open to negotiation[1].

Previously to this, Russell had made an offer in London by order of his Government. The Americans had hoped that Great Britain would shrink from a new war while they were so deeply involved in the European struggle. Russell was instructed to offer a law against employing British seamen in American vessels, in return for the cessation of impressment. But the inability of the Government of the United States to enforce any such measure had been all along asserted, and with truth, by the British Government. Castlereagh therefore rejected this overture, though he was careful to add that, if any practical expedient could be found to prevent British sailors being employed on American ships, he would be glad to discuss it. Further negotiations for an armistice by Russell were also without any result, except that the issues, which divided the two countries, were restated in their most uncompromising form[2].

The War was thus continued; but it bore a very different aspect in the two countries concerned. For America, it became the one vital question on which all others must depend. Her party issues, the relations of the States to the Central Government, the ambitions of her politicians, the whole future and prosperity of the country, depended on the result. For Great Britain, dangerous and detrimental to her interests as the War was, it was yet completely subordinate to the far vaster struggle with Napoleon, and the reconstruction of Europe that followed. Not until the middle of 1814 was she able to direct her full military and naval strength towards it, and, even then, her statesmen were more preoccupied with European problems than with America. Nevertheless, she was able to inflict far more damage on the United States than she received. Her defeats at sea and on the Lakes, and the depredations of American privateers on British commerce, were, in themselves, serious additions to the exhaustion and strain of a long war. But they were injuries that could be easily borne by an empire that held the carrying trade of the world in its hands. The United States on the contrary was practically cut off from commerce with the rest of the world. Indeed, as time went on, communications between the several States which largely depended on the sea were seriously impaired. The injuries went so far that, towards the end of the struggle, there was at least a possibility that some of the States

---

[1] *British and Foreign State Papers*, I. 1492.
[2] *British and Foreign State Papers*, I. 1473.

would break away from the Federation and conclude a separate peace. Nor, without allies, could the United States hope ultimately to force her adversary to give in, if events in Europe did not bring about her submission. But, in Europe, the situation grew daily more favourable to Great Britain almost from the moment that the War broke out. It was not long therefore before the statesmen of the United States were more ready for peace than those of Britain.

The first attempt to secure peace came through the mediation of Russia. In 1812 Russia had become the Ally of England, and had therefore an interest in endeavouring to put an end to a conflict which lessened the ability of Great Britain to help her against Napoleon. By British influence, Russia had been able to negotiate agreements with Turkey and Sweden at the critical moment of her struggle with Napoleon. She might now hope to render similar services in return. Moreover, it was but likely that the United States would be disposed to view favourably an offer of mediation from Russia, since the latter Power had been a devoted champion of Neutral Rights. There was, indeed, in Russia a party which viewed the alliance with Great Britain with great dislike, and Count Romantzoff, who was chief of it, held the office of Chancellor until the end of 1813, though he remained at Petrograd deprived of all real power. At the Russian capital, the United States was represented by one of the most brilliant of her statesmen, John Quincy Adams, later the author of the Monroe doctrine and President of the United States. Though he deplored the war, yet he hated and distrusted Great Britain. "The English talk," he noted in his diary in 1812, "much about their honor and national morality—sometimes without meaning, but generally with a mixture of hypocrisy and self delusion in about equal proportions. Dr Johnson, in one of his poems, honestly avows that in his lifetime English honor had become a standing jest; and it has assuredly not since then improved[1]." Adams was also fond of comparing impressment, which Britain was so determined to maintain, with the Slave Trade, which she was anxious to abolish. Count Romantzoff thus found him a congenial companion, and Adams was easily able to convince the Chancellor that the United States had no desire for any connexion with France. The result was an offer, in September, of the mediation of Russia to settle the dispute. This offer did not reach Washington till the beginning of March 1813, when the American Government showed the greatest eagerness to accept it[2]. Despite some notable

[1] *Memoirs of John Quincy Adams*, II. 400.
[2] *British and Foreign State Papers*, I. 1533.

victories at sea, the Americans had failed lamentably in Canada, and events in Europe were not propitious. The offer was therefore immediately accepted and Albert Gallatin, the Secretary of the Treasury, and Bayard, a Senator of experience, were dispatched forthwith to Petrograd to join Adams in negotiating a peace through the mediation of Russia. Bayard was a man of but moderate parts and moreover disliked Adams, but Gallatin was an especially suitable appointment. Of Swiss origin, he was able to combine a devotion to America with an understanding of the European point of view. He had great charm of manner as well as great abilities and he possessed many friends in England. Ultimately it was more due to his wisdom and ingenuity than to any other cause that peace was concluded. The Instructions which the Plenipotentiaries received, however, insisted on the American view of impressment, blockade and other matters in dispute, and showed little signs of concession. But the mediation had already been rejected by Great Britain before the American Envoys arrived in Europe.

It was, indeed, impossible on many grounds for such an offer to be accepted. A dispute with America was still regarded as an almost domestic question in which Foreign Powers could have no concern. To begin negotiations for peace under Russian mediation might perhaps provide an opportunity to bring British maritime rights into the general discussions—and, as has been seen, British statesmen were determined to exclude them completely. Nor could Russia be regarded as a suitable mediator, since she had herself previously shown that she agreed with the position which the United States had taken up. The mediation was therefore rejected, and Instructions to that effect were sent to Cathcart. Since, however, Alexander had ceased to correspond with Romantzoff on public affairs and was anxious to force him to resign, no official notification was sent to Petrograd. The American Commissioners were thus placed in a peculiarly perplexing and humiliating position, though Romantzoff endeavoured to conceal his own impotence by an attempt to make a second offer through Lieven, which that Ambassador refused to deliver. Gallatin's position was made still more difficult by the fact that the Senate refused to ratify his appointment, because he still retained his post as Secretary of the Treasury. Gallatin had, however, not been idle. He got in touch with friends in Europe to whom he wrote conciliatory letters, and, in particular, with Alexander Baring of the famous banking house in London. Baring, in a very frank letter, explained the views of the British Government on mediation[1]. At the same time he suggested that a direct negotiation at London might be substituted with success, provided that the American view of impressment was not finally insisted upon. These were, in substance, Gallatin's own opinions and he hastened to urge them on his Government at the same time making preparations for a journey to London.

Meanwhile, Castlereagh had been taking steps to bring forward a similar proposal. He pressed on Cathcart the necessity of excluding the American War and all maritime questions from Continental affairs. But he was anxious for direct negotiations at London or elsewhere; and he asked the Emperor to press this view on the Americans[2]. In September, as a result of conversations with Lieven, he returned to the question even more warmly. There had been rumours, which had seriously alarmed the British Government, that Napoleon intended to press for the introduction of American Commissioners to the Prague Conferences. The subject might well be used to sow dissensions between Great Britain and her Allies; and Castlereagh was determined to rule the matter out of discussion at once.

"The whole question with America...," he wrote to Cathcart on September 27th[3], "is one not of principle but of practice, the oppressions alleged to be committed in impressing Americans as British subjects [arise] from the impossibility of discrimination. To this the British Government has always professed their willingness to apply a remedy so far as they could do so without essential prejudice to their naval service and to the Right itself—but this cannot by any possibility be a point of difficulty with other nations, and it is one which Great Britain and America are alone competent to settle.

I have been induced to say thus much on this point, as there prevails much misconception and prejudice on this subject, from which I think the Count de Lieven is himself not altogether exempt. I am confident that he has no wish to revive any of those questions which have been happily settled with the Northern Powers. It is only an impatience of the war going on with America to the inconvenience of general commerce which weighs with him; but if this should be the case let America who chooses to stir these questions answer for the consequences. We stand on our long established practice from which we never deviated till the decrees of France led to the adoption of the retaliating Orders in Council, and by which ancient practice we propose to consider ourselves at all times implicitly bound, except towards a Power that renounces all principles of law for the purpose of attempting our destruction."

---

[1] *A Great Peace Maker. The Diary of James Gallatin*, ed. by Count Gallatin, 1914, Appendix I.

[2] Castlereagh to Cathcart, July 5th, 1813. F.O. Russia, 83. *British Diplomacy*, p. 6.

[3] F.O. Supplementary, 343. *British Diplomacy*, p. 33.

It was the wish to avoid embarrassment in the Continental diplomacy that led Castlereagh to make a direct offer to the United States. Gallatin's letters to Baring had, however, revealed the fact that the American Commissioners were unable to open direct negotiations without new Instructions from their Government. In order, therefore, to allow a negotiation to begin as soon as possible and thus prevent any attempt to associate it with the European Peace, Castlereagh himself on November 4th, 1813, made an offer to the American Government to enter into direct negotiations[1]. Though the Note showed no sign of yielding on the points of issue, the offer was accepted by Madison and new Instructions were despatched. To the two Commissioners already in Europe were added Henry Clay, a young and brilliant representative of Kentucky, and Russell, who had been *Chargé d'affaires* at London on the outbreak of the war. Gallatin was subsequently added to the Commission, when it was found that he had remained in Europe—no objection being now offered to his nomination, as he had resigned his post on the Administration. His presence was extremely fortunate; for, though two at least of the four Americans were men of the highest capacity, none of them possessed the knowledge of European habits of mind or the faculty for compromise which Gallatin had in the highest measure. They were, moreover, all jealous and suspicious of one another, as well as of their enemy. The Commissioners were not allowed to conduct the negotiations in London as the British Government had desired. Gothenburg was accordingly designated as the place of meeting. But a long delay ensued before the Commissioners could come together; and, meanwhile, the aspect of affairs on the Continent had completely changed.

It was April before Clay and Russell arrived from America, and Adams did not reach Stockholm until May 25th. Meanwhile, Gallatin and Bayard had proceeded by way of Amsterdam to London. There they found the War with France concluded and the British Government occupied with the European negotiations. The omens for peace were not favourable. It was thought that, now the Continental War was over, Britain might direct all her efforts against America and inflict a severe punishment upon her. The naval forces were increased and preparations immediately made to ship Wellington's veterans to America. Nevertheless, the commercial classes were beginning to be tired of the War, and the affairs of the Continent were not yet decided. But the Government showed no anxiety for the negotiations to begin. They

[1] *British and Foreign State Papers*, 1. 1543.

considered that the reinforcements despatched to America must improve their position there and thus exercise a favourable effect on the discussions. Gallatin was pressed to consent to a removal of the place of meeting to Ghent, as being nearer London; and he succeeded in obtaining Clay's consent to this proposal before Adams arrived. The American Commissioners, therefore, gradually assembled at Ghent in June and the early days of July. Even then the British Commissioners, who were not appointed until May 27th, were slow to put in an appearance. The Government was, indeed, occupied with the visits of the Continental Sovereigns and statesmen and the preparations for the coming Congress; but the delay was not altogether accidental. Gallatin stayed at London long enough to obtain an interview with Alexander, who, however, told him he could give no help. "England will not admit a third party to interfere in her disputes with you," and he intimated that this was on account of "the former Colonial relations." Gallatin, therefore, set off for Ghent without very high hopes of success[1].

The personnel of the British Commissioners was so inferior to that of the American, that it appeared as if the British Government did not attach much importance to the negotiations and wished them to fail. The first Plenipotentiary was Lord Gambier, a sailor of no great capacity and entirely ignorant of the matter which he had now to discuss. The real head of the mission was Henry Goulburn, the Undersecretary of State for War and Colonies, who was later to be Chancellor of the Exchequer in two Administrations. He was, however, a man of but small reputation at this time, and, though not without a certain capacity, was pedantic and narrow minded and entirely incapable of appreciating the great issues which were about to be discussed. The third member of the Commission was William Adams, a lawyer who had a deep knowledge of maritime law, but was in no sense a diplomatist. Such men could not compare with Gallatin and Adams, or even with Clay and Bayard. They had not, of course, to bear the same responsibility as the Americans, since they could easily be furnished with the Instructions of the Government. They became, indeed, for the most part little more than messengers, through whom the Cabinet's decisions could be conveyed to the American Commissioners. They did not arrive at Ghent until August 6th, having kept the Americans waiting a month. The interval had not improved the temper of men like Adams and Clay, and neither side appeared to expect a successful issue of the discussion.

[1] *Diary of James Gallatin*, p. 25.

II

As has been stated in the previous section the negotiations which began at Ghent on August 6th were not viewed hopefully by either side. The Americans were dismayed at the long delay in opening the Conferences, and the personnel of the British Mission appeared so inferior to their own that they could scarcely believe the British Government to intend serious discussion. Goulburn, on the other hand, immediately detected in the American Commissioners an obstinate adherence to their own point of view, which ill became the representatives of a weaker nation in its transactions with the British Empire. The negotiations were also, from the outset, rendered difficult by the fact that the Instructions with which the two Missions were severally furnished for the most part dealt with quite different subjects.

The British Instructions, dated July 28th, 1814[1], were drawn up under the influence of the great successes in Europe. They show that the British Government considered itself now so much stronger than the Americans that it could dictate terms. These went far beyond the causes of the War, and seized the opportunity to place British power in North America in a far stronger position than in 1812. The Instructions were divided into four main heads. In the first place, no concessions whatever were to be made on the questions of British maritime rights—whether impressment, or the "Rule of 1756." Secondly, under the pretence of protecting our Indian allies a large Indian zone was to be removed from the sovereignty of the United States and made into a sort of "buffer" State. Thirdly, extensive rectifications of frontier were demanded, which were urged as necessary on the grounds of the acquisition of Louisiana and part of the Floridas by the United States and their intention, made manifest during the war, of conquering Canada. Last, the special rights given to the United States in the Newfoundland Fisheries by the Treaty of 1783 were declared to be abrogated by the war. Nevertheless, the strategy of the British Government was not ill-conceived, however unskilful were its tactics. They were in fact determined to exploit the military advantages which they considered the European Peace had given them. They were disappointed in their hopes; but the Peace which they eventually secured was no worse than what they could have obtained at the outset, though it was only secured at the expense of a diplomatic defeat.

[1] *Castlereagh Correspondence*, x. 67. An earlier draft, as well as some correspondence between the Commissioners and Castlereagh, was published by Mr Ford in the *Transactions of the Massachusetts Historical Society*, December 1914—January 1915, pp. 138–164.

The British could of course refer to their Court and, as a matter of fact, did so on every occasion before they committed themselves; but the Americans could only obtain further Instructions after a long lapse of time. This inability was not altogether a disadvantage in the manoeuvring for position which formed the first part of the negotiations. Throughout the negotiations, the case of the Americans was handled with far greater skill than that of the British. The stiff and pedantic Goulburn was no match for men like Gallatin and Adams, and was betrayed into admissions which were used with great effect in America. The Government were indeed responsible for large claims made by Britain at the outset of the negotiations; but Goulburn throughout let slip no opportunity of stating his case in as harsh and uncompromising a manner as possible, and his inept diplomacy was to have considerable effect on the public opinion of both countries, when Madison published the first series of Notes exchanged. Neither he nor his Government grasped the difficulty of negotiating with a country like the United States, where the Executive Power was to so great an extent controlled in its conduct of foreign relations, not only by public opinion but by the Constitution itself. The British Commissioners were, also, less well informed as to the legal and historical aspects of their case than the American, with results sometimes unfortunate for our side.

The original American Instructions had been drawn up for the negotiation under the mediation of Russia, and were dated April 15th, 1813. They, naturally, dwelt mainly upon the subject of impressment and made satisfaction on that point a *sine qua non* of the Peace. The American view of other neutral rights, such as a definition of Blockade and the "Rule of 1756," was also urged, but these were treated as subordinate points, which could be waived, if necessary. To all other matters the principle of *status quo antea* was to be applied. These Instructions were supplemented by various letters to the Commissioners, in which the same high tone was maintained until June 25th and 27th, when, the news of the European Peace having reached America, Instructions were addressed to the Commissioners which allowed them, as a last resource, to allow the subject of impressment to be entirely omitted from the Treaty[1].

The Americans, on the whole, handled their case exceedingly well. They drew from the British Commissioners their extremest demands and then proceeded to reply to them in Notes, which were written for

[1] *British and Foreign State Papers*, I. 1552.

publication at home, and produced exactly the impression which was desired. By this means, the negotiation was made to serve important political ends. The chief weakness of the American Delegation lay in their distrust and dislike of one another. But Gallatin gradually obtained something like an ascendancy over his colleagues, and Adams was too patriotic and high-minded not to submit to him. In the end, Gallatin, by judicious conciliation at critical moments, was always able to prevent the negotiations from being broken off; and the Peace must be considered as largely due to his unremitting efforts.

The first meeting at the house of the British Mission—(a circumstance which caused the Americans, always more sensitive as to their dignity than representatives of monarchical States, much searching of heart)—resulted in the British opening their demands[1]. The Americans were dismayed at their extent, and replied at a second meeting that their Instructions did not permit them to discuss the questions of the Indians or the Fisheries, while asking for more explicit information as to the British intentions. These were given them in a third meeting on August 19th. The British then demanded that the Americans should be entirely excluded from maintaining any naval force on the Lakes, the natural frontier between Canada and the United States, and that they should grant to the British a direct route from Halifax to Quebec, which meant extensive cessions of territory, and also access to the Mississippi from Lake Superior. The Indian stipulations had already been made a *sine qua non* of peace by the British Commissioners, in accordance with their Instructions, and they supplied such phrasing to their territorial demands as to make them seem "equally necessary" to the conclusion of peace. In this, they went much further than the Cabinet, or at any rate Liverpool and Castlereagh, had intended. Castlereagh visited Ghent on his way to the Vienna Congress. He did not interfere in the negotiations; but, though Goulburn assured him that the Americans were disposed both to treat and sign the proposed frontier and Indian arrangements, he disapproved of the peremptory tone adopted in the British Notes[2]. Stated, however, as they were, they gave a fine opportunity to the American Commissioners. Even Gallatin now despaired of peace. "Great Britain wants war in order to cripple us," he wrote to Monroe, "she wants

[1] *British and Foreign State Papers*, I. 1578.
[2] Castlereagh to Liverpool, August 28th, 1814; Wellington, *Supplementary Despatches*, IX. 192.

aggrandisement at our expense. I do not expect to be longer than
three months in Europe[1]." Gallatin, indeed, softened the answer of
the Commission somewhat, for he had no wish to break off relations
until the British had thoroughly exposed their hand. But the American
Note, despatched on August 25th, was sufficiently explicit to awaken
Goulburn to the real state of affairs and to impress Castlereagh and
Liverpool. Goulburn now wrote that "the rupture has in effect
taken place." Castlereagh saw, however, that the American Note was
"evidently intended to rouse their people upon the question of their
independence," and pressed for an effective answer, while Liverpool
admitted that the British Commissioners "had taken a very erroneous
view of our policy," and that it was imperative to avoid breaking off
negotiations at this stage[2]. He was anxious, on the contrary, to throw
the responsibility for the rupture on the Americans. Nevertheless,
the British Government still had high hopes of military success, and
the answer, which was despatched on September 4th, therefore still
insisted on acquisition of territory. It endeavoured to compare the
United States to Revolutionary France, in its character of a Power
which was prepared to advance its own frontiers—as the expansion
in the South and the attack on Canada had shown—but in whose
eyes its own territory was inviolable. The Americans were, however,
far too wary to break off negotiations at this stage. Their reply, of
September 9th, pointed out that the Indians would be restored to the
same condition as before the War, and that boundary lines which
could be shown to be undefined might be discussed. Further discussion was thus necessary. The Cabinet, when faced with the position
of continuing the war for the creation of an Indian "Barrier"
recoiled. In further Notes of September 19th, the *sine qua non* as
regards the Indians was restated in a form which really amounted
to little more than the *status quo*, and the Americans, influenced
perhaps by the news of the capture of Washington, which reached
England on September 27th, were able to accept an article of this
nature.

On the other points, however, both parties were as uncompromising
as ever. Goulburn had done everything in his power to bring matters
to a head; but the Cabinet kept a firm check on him, and all the British
Notes were drafted in London. Such alterations as the Commis-

---

[1] *Diary of James Gallatin*, p. 29.
[2] Liverpool to Castlereagh, September 2nd, 1814; Wellington, *Supplementary Despatches*, IX. 214.

sioners were allowed to make were invariably in the direction of stiffening the terms. Even Goulburn, however, succumbed to the fascination of Gallatin, who, he said, was not in the least like an American. The Prime-Minister, moreover, was anxious for peace. The discussions at the Congress of Vienna were now beginning to cause the Cabinet anxiety and henceforward exercised an increasing influence in the direction of peace. Nevertheless, the Cabinet could not ignore the fact of the British successes. Accordingly, on October 21st a new turn was given to the negotiations by an attempt to make the principle of *uti possidetis* the basis of the territorial settlement[1]. The Cabinet hoped thus to profit largely from the expected British advance on the Northern frontier. The British view of the Fisheries question was also insisted upon. The American answer (October 24th) which refused the acceptance of this basis as beyond their powers, made Liverpool abandon hope of concluding peace, though he was still anxious for the discussions to proceed[2]. To this decision he was urged by the first news of the defeat of the British on the Lakes which arrived about this time. Accordingly, the Americans were asked to put forward a *contreprojet* (October 31st).

The Americans took ten days to prepare their answer, which was delayed by lengthy discussions and recriminations among themselves; and, meanwhile, the opinion of the Cabinet underwent a very important change. Preparations were being made for the despatch of further reinforcements to America. It also occurred to the Cabinet that, if Wellington were sent out in command, not only would there be more chance of military success, but any peace that might be made would be protected by his prestige and authority. They, accordingly, offered Wellington the command as an alternative to his relieving Castlereagh at Vienna; for rumours of plots to assassinate him increased their wish to move him away from Paris. Wellington's sense of duty never allowed him to refuse to serve his country in any position, however unwelcome. But his letters left no doubt as to how distasteful the command would be to him, and he seized the opportunity to review the strategic position for the benefit of the Cabinet. His opinion, stated without reservation, that the military position was by no means sufficient to justify the claims that had been put forward at Ghent awakened the Cabinet to a sense of reality, and they were thus ready

---

[1] *British and Foreign State Papers*, I. 1633.
[2] Liverpool to Wellington, October 28th, 1814; Wellington, *Supplementary Despatches*, IX. 384.

to consider the American counter-project in a far more yielding spirit than had seemed possible[1]

The American *Projet* (November 10th) was the result of a violent discussion; but it was, in the main, the work of Gallatin and, therefore, while it stated the American case strongly, avoided needless offence and made one or two suggestions towards compromise. The basis of *uti possidetis* was again refused and that of the *status quo* offered; but boundary commissions were suggested as a means to settle the main territorial points in dispute. Access to the Mississipi was, also, offered in exchange for British acquiescence in the new Louisiana boundaries. The American attitude on the Fisheries question was maintained. Articles were also suggested on impressment and blockade. Indemnities were demanded for the irregular captures of American ships before the outbreak of War, and for the acts contrary to International Law committed during its course. This last article was an attempt to obtain damages for the destruction of the Government buildings at Washington.

Goulburn's comments on the *Projet* amounted to a refusal of almost the whole of it; but the Cabinet viewed the matter in a different light. The unsatisfactory state of the negotiations at Vienna and Wellington's letter had determined them to abandon all claims for increase of territory[2]. The publication of the first part of the negotiations by Madison was, also, a diplomatic stroke of great value. It roused the spirit of the American nation, Federalists and Democrats alike indignantly rejecting the idea of cession of territory, while it also caused strong criticism in Great Britain. Alexander Baring gave expression to these sentiments in a debate in the House on November 21st, and the Government were forced to declare that they had never meant to make territorial cessions a *sine qua non* of peace. The reply, therefore, which the Cabinet sent to Ghent on November 22nd was meant, if possible, to obtain agreement. The basis of *uti possidetis* and the control of the Lakes were completely abandoned and the way to peace thus opened, much to the dismay of Goulburn. That most of the other American demands were refused was of small consequence, since on none of these were the Americans prepared to break off negotiations. The proposals as to boundary commissions was accepted, while access to the Courts of either country was suggested

---

[1] Liverpool to Castlereagh, November 4th, 1814; Liverpool to Wellington, November 4th, 1814; Wellington to Liverpool, November 7th, 9th, 18th, 1814; Wellington, *Supplementary Despatches*, IX. 405, 406, 422, 424, 436.

[2] Liverpool to Castlereagh, November 18th, 1814; Wellington, *Supplementary Despatches*, IX. 438.

instead of indemnities for damages. An article for the payment of the expenses of prisoners of war was also added, and it was further suggested that the hostilities should cease only on the ratification of the Treaty. Possibly, this last stipulation was made in order to give time for the expedition preparing against New Orleans to obtain its objective, but, considering the part played by the Senate in Foreign Affairs, it was not one to which the American Commissioners could object. On the receipt of this Note, Gallatin felt that peace was really in sight and did his utmost to get his colleagues to meet the British demands as far as possible. The Americans, therefore, now withdrew their demands as to impressment, leaving the matter open. Gallatin even succeeded in obtaining the consent of the majority of his colleagues to granting access to the Mississipi on condition of the American view of the Fishery rights being accepted. At the same time, the Americans asked for a conference and the Commissioners thus met again officially after an interval of almost three months. Now that verbal discussions could be substituted for written communications, affairs went on much more quickly and smoothly. Where deadlocks occurred, the matter could generally be solved by omitting altogether the question in dispute. In this way, eventually, both the Mississipi Claims and the Fisheries question were removed from the Treaty and reserved for future discussions. The possession of some insignificant islands in Passamaquoddy Bay was adjusted by a judicious compromise by which neither side gave up any substantial claim. The Americans accepted an article condemning the Slave Trade.

These discussions occupied another three weeks. They were conducted with the utmost secrecy; for, when the Americans saw that peace was really to be obtained they were anxious that nothing should interrupt the harmony of the proceedings. At last, on December 24th, the Treaty was signed with more expressions of mutual goodwill than had at one time seemed possible. The document is a curious commentary on the four months' discussions. Scarcely any of the subjects about which there had been such violent controversy were mentioned in it. Since these include the points for which the United States had gone to war, the Treaty was, in a sense, a victory for Great Britain, who never demanded that other countries should recognise her maritime rights in theory but only insisted on them in practice. But, since the War was now over, the Americans could claim that it was no longer necessary to continue to fight against abuses which had ceased to exist. All that was now left of the British demands brought forward in August was an innocuous clause restoring peace to the Indians. In the same way, the Americans had had to abandon their claims for damages. Apart from the clause on the Abolition of the Slave Trade, which was put in the most general way, the rest of the Treaty merely consisted of clauses referring all the disputed boundary questions to special commissioners.

The British Commissioners had added at the last moment a clause that the Ratifications must be made without any change or reservation, if peace was to result. For this they were criticised by the Government; but the result showed that they were right. In the United States the ratification was hastened so that Peace might ensue. It did not, however, take place in time to prevent the Americans from defeating the British expedition to New Orleans. On the whole, the Treaty was very well received in the United States, and the American Commissioners were welcomed home as men who had conducted a difficult negotiation to the credit of their country. Despite the fact that they had obtained no satisfaction for any of the grievances to avenge which they had fought the War, the American people instinctively felt that they had escaped a great danger by successfully resisting without Allies the might of the British Empire at the height of its power and prestige.

In England opinions were less favourable. The old Tory school was incensed that no castigation had been inflicted for the treacherous attack which, they considered, had been made on them at the crisis of the Great War. But the feeling did not go very deep. The commercial interests were delighted, and other critics might reflect that the maritime principles which had produced the defeat of France had been preserved. The return of Napoleon diverted the thoughts of the nation to other dangers in the midst of which it could not but be thankful that peace had been concluded with America. On the whole, while the jealousy and bitterness roused by the War lasted for generations, there was immediately a very powerful body of opinion in both countries which was determined that it should not recur. A high Tory like Alison could indeed write even as late as 1842: "Little doubt remains that out of premature and uncomplete pacification the germs of a future and calamitous war between the two countries will spring[1]." Yet, before a century had elapsed, every subject in dispute at Ghent had either been relegated to oblivion or amicably settled by mutual concessions.

[1] Alison, *History of Europe*, x. 749.

Appendixes to Chapters II—III

APPENDIX A

THE CAUSES OF THE RUPTURE WITH FRANCE

F.O. Holland, 41.   GRENVILLE *to* AUCKLAND.

Whitehall, Nov. 23, 1792.

H.M.'s satisfaction at the effect of the British Declaration to the Estates of Holland. Auckland is to keep up their resolution. "I am strongly inclined to believe that it is the present intention of the prevailing party in France to respect the rights of this country and of the [Dutch] Republic; but it will undoubtedly be necessary that the strictest attention should be given to any circumstances which may seem to indicate a change in this respect[1]."

Ibid.   NAGEL *to* GRENVILLE.

Londres, Nov. 29, 1792.

"La situation critique où se trouve la République des Provinces Unies, non seulement depuis l'invasion et la conquête que M. Dumourier vient de faire des Pays Bas Autrichiens, mais aussi par la Résolution que le Conseil Exécutif de France vient de prendre le 16 du courant relative à la navigation libre de l'Escaut et de la Meuse, m'impose le devoir de rappeller sans cesse la sollicitude de Votre Excellence sur le danger pressant qui ménace un Allié fidèle; et sans vouloir anticiper sur les ordres que je pourrai recevoir de mes Maîtres, je croirois n'avoir point satisfait à la fidélité que je Leur dois, ni à la confiance dont Ils m'ont honoré, si je ne priois pas Votre Excellence d'observer:

"1. Que le Général Dumourier, en voulant ouvrir le passage de l'Escaut, veut violer le territoire de la République, intention que Leurs Hautes Puissances étoient parfaitement d'accord avec S.M.B. de nullement attribuer à aucune des Puissances Belligérentes, comme il (constate?) par leur réponse à la Déclaration faite le 16 du courant par Son Excellence My Lord Auckland.

"2. Que le Conseil Exécutif de France par sa Déclaration du 16 du courant a manifesté ouvertement ses desseins contre les Intérêts de la République, tout en brisant les obligations les plus sacrées que la France avoit contractées par le Traité de Fontainebleau en date du 8 Novembre 1785.... Ces observations, My Lord, je n'en doute pas, ont déjà été faites par les Ministres de S.M. et je ne saurais non plus envisager comme

---

[1] Grenville had not then heard of the French Decrees of November 16th, 19th. For other letters between Auckland and Grenville see *Dropmore Papers*, vol. II. and *Journal...of Lord Auckland*, vol. II.

problématiques les bonnes intentions de la Grande Bretagne, vis-à-vis de son plus ancien Allié, pour lequel Elle a non seulement fait les efforts les plus généreux, mais encore à qui Elle a garanti sa tranquillité intérieure et extérieure. Ainsi je ne puis craindre qu'il puisse paroître indiscret de ma Part de renouveller les instances, faites et Jeudi et Dimanche passés, auprès de Votre Excellence pour qu'il plaise à S.M.B. de faire veiller très-exactement sur ce qui se passe dans les Ports d'Ostende et de Dunkerque; et si à cette Bonté Elle vouloit ajouter le rassemblement d'une escadre aux Dunes ou à Gravesend, qui pût se porter directement vers la Hollande, en cas de besoin, les Etats Généraux en seroient justement reconnoissants, ceux qui veulent Leur nuire seroient peut-être contenus, et la tranquillité publique ainsi heureusement conservée...."

Ibid. • AUCKLAND *to* GRENVILLE.

Hague, Nov. 30, 1792.

"...The Dutch Ministers are anxious to learn the sentiments of the King and of his Ministers. It is their object in the meantime to temporize as far as may be practicable without essential disgrace or detriment; and the Grand Pensionary assures me that great activity continues to be used in preparing two or three frigates, with gun-boats and floating batteries."

Ibid. SAME *to* SAME.

Hague, Dec. 25, 1792.

He advises the issue of a British Declaration stating our love of peace and order, and our resolve both to support Holland (if attacked) and to aid other peoples to maintain "their religion, constitution, property and independence."

Brit. Mus. Add. MSS. 34,446.

GRENVILLE *to* AUCKLAND.

Whitehall, Dec. 29, 1792.

He sends his despatches for Whitworth and Stratton under flying seal, so that Auckland may peruse them and inform the Dutch Ministers of their contents. "H.M.'s Ministers are sensible that much doubt may be entertained respecting the real views of the Court of Petersburg in the overture they have made. But it has been felt that these could in no manner so well be ascertained as by acceding to the proposal in the manner now adopted. If either the original intention or the effect of this step on our part induces the Empress to take an active share in a war which seems so little likely to be avoided, a great advantage will be derived from it to the common cause. If she withdraws the sort of overture she has made, no inconvenience can result from the measure taken by the King at all to be put in comparison with the benefit of success. It appears probable that, either on the result of my answer to M. Chauvelin or of the answer to be given in Holland to the French agent there, or perhaps by actual aggression against the [Dutch] Republic, the present situation will be brought to its crisis before the answer from the different Courts can be received. In that event it would be of the utmost importance that we should be enabled to bring forward to the public view without delay the papers alluded to in Your Excellency's last despatch[1], so as to prove to this country that, at the very moment when M. Chauvelin was giving here fresh assurances respecting the neutrality of the Republic, and was endeavouring to represent the Scheldt as the only cause of war, the French agents in Holland, and even the ostensible Minister of the *soi-disant* Republic of France, were forming plans of attack and urging the French general to execute them without delay."

F.O. Prussia, 27. EDEN *to* GRENVILLE.

Berlin, Jan. 1, 1793.

General Möllendorf will soon proceed to the East to take command of the Prussian expedition against Poland. "This business is no longer a mystery here, and it is publicly said that the four bailiwicks of which he is to take possession in Great Poland were the promised price of H.P.M.'s interference in the affairs of France, and that he has now exacted the discharge of the promise with threats of otherwise making a separate peace with France. Russia, it is added, consents with reluctance, induced principally by fear of the Turks. I mention this as the public report. Having more than once represented to the Prussian Ministers the extreme injustice of this measure, and even impolicy at this awful crisis, and having been answered only by miserable elusions, it appears unnecessary to say anything further on the subject."

Brit. Mus. Add. MSS. 34,446.

GRENVILLE *to* AUCKLAND.

Whitehall, Jan. 4, 1793.

"...There is still the strongest reason to apprehend a disposition in France to proceed to every extremity rather than to give to this country and to Holland the satisfaction which we have a right to expect on the different points in question between us. No account has yet been received here of the light in which my answer to M. Chauvelin has been considered or of the effect it has produced." He believes that Dumouriez's journey to Paris has been "to pursue his plan against the Dutch Republic, about which the Executive Council had expressed hesitation."

Ibid. SAME *to* SAME.

Whitehall, Jan. 5, 1793.

"Having this day received the enclosed extract of a communication made to the National Convention by M. Le Brun, I lose no time in transmitting it to Your Excellency in order that the Dutch Government may be informed without delay (supposing they have not received this account directly from Paris) of the great probability which this circumstance affords of an immediate rupture with France." In no case must the Dutch supply naval stores to the French.

[1] See *Dropmore Papers*, II. 360.

F.O. Prussia, 27.

EDEN *to* GRENVILLE.

[Cypher.]   Berlin, Jan. 5, 1793.

"The Allies mean to continue the war and persevere in the Resolution
set forth in the Duke of Brunswick's manifesto, of restoring the monarchical
form of government in France under such limitations as may be prescribed
by a free Assembly of the States, and re-instating the German Princes in
their rights, and, what has not hitherto been openly avowed, declaring
that they mean to require a compensation for the expences of the war.
A firm hope is expressed that H.M. will become a party in the war."

F.O. Sardinia, 11.

GRENVILLE *to* TREVOR (at Turin).

Whitehall, Jan. 10, 1793.

"...H.M.'s conduct in abstaining from all interference in the internal
affairs of France, and the neutrality which H.M. had observed in the
present War, have not had the effect which the King was so justly entitled
to expect. The present rulers in France have, notwithstanding those circumstances, adopted measures likely to excite in H.M.'s mind the strongest
jealousy and uneasiness. Their conduct has been such as to indicate a
fixed design of hostility against H.M. and his Allies, and views of aggression
and aggrandisement utterly inconsistent with the general tranquillity and
security of Europe. Under these circumstances H.M. feels himself called
upon by the most important interests of his subjects to adopt such measures
as may be necessary for the security of his own dominions and those of
his Allies and for the general interests of Europe. And H.M. is desirous,
as far as possible, to adopt a system of concert with the different Powers
who have a common interest with H.M. on this subject or who are still
more strongly concerned in opposing a barrier to the progress of French
arms and French principles.

"At the time when the conduct of France had already been judged by
H.M. to be such as to call for vigorous preparations on his part, H.M.
received from the Court of Petersburg an overture expressive of the sense
which the Empress entertained of the danger with which all Europe was
threatened from the designs openly avowed by France and from the recent
progress of the French arms, and conveying to H.M. the wish of H.I.M.
that a concert might be established on this subject between the Courts of
London and Petersburg with a view to provide for the general security of
Europe. H.M. was pleased to direct that in answer to this overture I should
assure the Minister of H.I.M. that the sentiments and wishes of the King
were conformable to those of the Empress, and that H.M. was disposed
to enter into such a concert, confining it to the object of opposing the views
of aggression and aggrandisement entertained by France, without any
view to an interference in the internal affairs of that country. And I expressed H.M.'s wish that some person here might be fully instructed and
authorized by the Empress to arrange the detail both of the objects to be
pursued and of the measures to be adopted for their attainment. Com-

munications of a similar tendency have been made to the two Courts of Vienna and Berlin; and it is H.M.'s pleasure that you should state to the Sardinian Ministers the purport of what I have already mentioned and express H.M.'s wish that the fullest instructions and powers may be given to such person here as H.S.M. shall be pleased to chuse for that purpose, in order that, if occasion should arise, the King may be enabled to concert with H.S.M. either with respect to terms of pacification or as to operations of war, if the continuance and extension of hostilities should become unavoidable. H.M. wishes in the present moment not to make to H.S.M. any specific proposal with respect to either of these two points, because he is sensible that the determination of H.S.M. with respect to them must in a great degree depend on a concert with those Powers with whom he is joined in the war....

"The general outline of such a plan would be that the Powers now at war with France should enable the neutral Powers engaged in this concert to propose to France terms of accommodation and peace. That the basis of such pacification should be, that France should withdraw her troops within the limits of her own territory, should annul all acts injurious to the rights or governments of other countries, and should give some unequivocal pledge and security of her determination to abstain from fomenting troubles in any other country or from intermeddling in any manner in the internal affairs of other Governments. In return for this, the Powers at war with France might consent on their part to disavow expressly and unequivocally any interference in the internal government of France, and might even consent to establish in the usual mode a correspondence and intercourse with such Power in France with whom they might conclude such an agreement...."

F.O. France, 41.   CHAUVELIN *to* GRENVILLE.

Londres, Jan. 11, 1793.

"...La République Française ne peut considérer la conduite du Gouvernement Anglais [on the Aliens Bill] que comme une infraction manifeste au Traité de Commerce conclu; qu'en conséquence elle cesse de se croire elle-même obligée par ce Traité, et qu'elle le regarde dès à présent comme rompu et annullé."

F.O. Prussia, 27.

UNSIGNED DRAFT IN GRENVILLE'S WRITING.

[Whitehall], Jan. 12, 1793.

"In the conversations which I had this day with Count Stadion and Baron Jacobi, they both, after delivering the written answers of their two Courts, informed me that they had a further communication to make, but that they had agreed to do it verbally only, and in such a manner that my reply to it (if I made any) might not form part of the official answer to be given to their written communications. They then explained that they had received information from their respective Courts that, with a view to indemnifying them for the expenses of the war, a project had been brought forward by which Prussia was to obtain an *arrondissement* on the side of Poland, and in return was to withdraw any opposition to the exchange formerly proposed of the Low Countries and Bavaria. Count Stadion read me a paper which contained only reasonings on this subject to prove that the acquisition was beneficial to Austria only as an *arrondissement*, and that it would be a sacrifice in point of revenue, while such an arrangement would on the other hand better answer the views of the Maritime Powers with respect to a barrier against France. Baron Jacobi read out a despatch to him in which this plan was stated, but as a project which still required discussing (particularly with Russia) to ripen it, and on which therefore H.P.M. trusted the King and his Ministers would observe the most profound secrecy.

"I told them both that I was glad they had mentioned this project in the form they had chosen; that I was much better satisfied not to be obliged to enter into any formal or official discussion on the subject of Poland. But that I thought it due to that open communication which I wished to be established between our respective Courts not to omit saying at once and distinctly that the King would never be a party in any concert or plan, one part of which was the gaining a compensation for the expenses of the war from a neutral and unoffending nation. That the King was bound by no engagement of any sort with Poland, but that neither would H.M.'s sentiments suffer him to participate in measures directed to such an object, nor could he hope for the concurrence or support of his people in such a system.

"With respect to indemnification I explained to them the outlines of the plan which Mr Whitworth, Mr Stratton and Sir Jas. Murray are instructed to propose, and added that, if such an offer were made to France and refused by her, it did not seem unreasonable that, in the further prosecution of the war, which would then avowedly be ascribeable only to views of aggrandisement on the part of France, some compensation should be looked to by the Powers engaged in it...."

Brit. Mus. Add. MSS. 34,447.

GRENVILLE *to* SIR JAMES MURRAY.

Whitehall, Jan. 20, 1793.

Expects that rupture will come with France as the French Government insists on terms entirely inconsistent with the Government of this country and H.M.'s dignity and honour. H.M. is making strenuous preparations and hopes to concert plans with Prussia and Austria.

F.O. France, 41.   LEBRUN *to* GRENVILLE.

Paris, Jan. 25, 1793.

"Le citoyen Chauvelin, Ministre Plénipotentiaire de la République Française, ayant reçu l'ordre de se rendre à Paris[1], j'ai l'honneur de pré-

---

[1] This proves that Lebrun recalled Chauvelin before he heard of the British order for his withdrawal; also, that Maret in his so-called mission had no official authorisation to touch on *la haute politique*.

venir Votre Excellence que le citoyen Maret, qui aura celui de lui remettre cette Lettre, se rend à Londres pour veiller aux papiers de la Légation et de les mettre en ordre. Je prie Votre Excellence de vouloir bien lui accorder son appui et sa bienveillance dans les circonstances où il croira nécessaire de les réclamer."

APPENDIX B

BRITISH WAR POLICY

(*February* 1793 to *April* 1795)

Brit. Mus. Add. MSS. 34,447.

MINUTE OF THE EAST INDIA COMPANY.

Jan. 28, 1793.

The French islands in the Indian Ocean depend almost entirely on the Cape for provisions. Fear that the Cape may be taken by the French owing to dissensions there. Some means must be taken for its security and that of St Helena. Mauritius and Bourbon should be taken, as the best means of safeguarding India.

Ibid. 34,448.   AUCKLAND *to* GRENVILLE.

Hague, Feb. 8, 1793.

The Dutch army equalled nearly 50,000 men, but was wholly inexperienced. The chief ruler is lethargic.

F.O. Prussia, 27.   GRENVILLE *to* EDEN (at Berlin).

Whitehall, Feb. 5, 1793.

"...Since M. Chauvelin's departure, an overture has been received by Lord Auckland from M. Dumouriez, with a proposal for an interview between them as likely to afford the means of maintaining peace. Many difficulties were felt in the way of this proposal, especially as an embargo has now actually taken place on our vessels in the French ports. It was however on the whole thought right to consent to the proposed interview, as it might afford the means of knowing the utmost extent to which France is disposed to go in facilitating an accommodation, and as the delay would at all events be in many respects advantageous to us, and particularly with reference to the defence of the Dutch territory."

An objection to the plan was that it might cause jealousy to those with whom we wished to frame a concert (which perhaps might be the cause of the proposal). Eden will explain at Vienna that H.M. will not be led "to depart from the views and principles stated in the correspondence with M. Chauvelin": and will seek to restore a general peace "on such terms as the Emperor may justly expect." H.M. is ready to frame a formal engagement with Austria and Prussia on the principles which have been opened to those Powers. He will not conclude peace unless France abandons all her conquests, and renounces "all views of interference on her part in the interior of other countries and all measures of aggression or hostility against them; provided that the Emperor shall on his part engage that, if France shall within the space of two months from this time agree to make peace on the terms above stated, adding to them stipulations for the personal security of Her Most Christian Majesty and her family, the Emperor will consent to such a peace."

Also that if the war continues, both Sovereigns will not make peace save by common consent, "on any terms short of the abandonment of all conquests which France has made or shall hereafter make," and of renunciation of all policy of interference in affairs of other States. A similar proposal will be made to Prussia. H.B.M. objects strongly to the proposals concerning Poland, but will not oppose them by force.

Brit. Mus. Add. MSS. 34,448.

GRENVILLE *to* AUCKLAND.

Whitehall, Feb. 13, 1793.

As war had been declared by France, H.M. orders that "you should confine yourself to the hearing any proposal which M. Dumouriez may have to make, without expressing in any manner an opinion what terms of conciliation would now be deemed satisfactory under circumstances which have so materially varied. And you will expressly state that you are now only authorized to hear his proposals, to ascertain under what authority they are made, and to transmit them home for H.M.'s consideration."

Ibid.   AUCKLAND *to* GRENVILLE.

Hague, Feb. 15, 1793.

Joubert arrived with a passport from Dumouriez and stated that "de Maulde on arriving at Antwerp found Commissioners of the French Convention who brought a requisition for Dumouriez to recall de Maulde and to march against those [the Dutch] Provinces; that Dumouriez was preparing to obey and that de Maulde had set out for Paris on the 13th."

F.O. France, 41.

PETITION FROM FRENCH PLANTERS OF SAN DOMINGO
(through the medium of M. Malouet)[1].

Londres, Feb. 25, 1793.

"Les Propriétaires de S. Domingue soussignés, considérant l'oppression et l'anarchie qui dévorent la colonie et leurs propriétés, autorisent Monsieur Malouet, l'un d'eux, de solliciter auprès du Gouvernement anglais la protection et les secours nécessaires pour les en délivrer, s'en rapportant à ses lumières sur les détails et adoptant d'avance les moyens qu'il prendra pour parvenir au succès de leur vœu." [About 70 signatures.]

[1] These letters etc. are not printed in the *Mémoires de Malouet* (Paris, 2 vols. 1874) which contain scarcely a reference to this episode.

F.O. France, 42.   GRENVILLE *to* MALOUET.

Whitehall, April 3, 1793.

"Je vous envoye, Monsieur, conformément à ce que vous avez desiré, la Minute ci-incluse de ce qui a été convenu dans les conversations que nous avons eu l'honneur, M. Pitt et moi, d'avoir avec vous par rapport à la position de Ste. Domingue, et au vœu manifesté par les propriétaires de la partie Française de cette Isle de recourir à la protection du Roi."

Ibid.   MALOUET *to* GRENVILLE.

Londres, 78 Titchfield St., April 4, 1793.

"La Minute de l'acte que vous avez la bónté de me communiquer et les additions qui y ont été faites sont parfaitement conformes aux sentimens que je vous ai exprimés, aux propositions que j'ai eu l'honneur de vous faire et me laissent dans la ligne dont je n'ai pas dû m'écarter. Agréez donc, My Lord, mes remercimens et la prière que je vous fais de vouloir bien me renvoyer l'acte signé avant le départ de M. de Charmilli qui doit avoir lieu Samedi...."

Ibid.   MINUTE SIGNED BY GRENVILLE.

April 5, [1793].

After stating that Malouet was deputed to the British Government by the planters of St Domingo he continues—"Les Colons sollicitent très humblement de S.M.B. protection et secours à l'effet de chasser de Ste Domingue les usurpateurs de la puissance publique, d'y rétablir un gouvernement légal sous ses auspices, et de conserver la Colonie, jusqu'à ce que son sort futur soit réglé à la conclusion de la paix entre l'Angleterre et la France, époque à laquelle les Colons Français selon les conditions de cette paix rentreront sous la domination d'une autorité légitime en France ou continueront d'obéir à S.M.B. comme à leur souverain, et deviendront sujets de l'Empire Britannique. Les dites propositions ayant été mises sous les yeux de S.M.B., S.M. a bien voulu y accéder et donner aux dits Colons l'assurance de son Intention d'employer ses forces à l'effet ci-dessus mentionné au premier moment que les circonstances le lui permettront."

Ibid.   GRENVILLE *to* LEBRUN.
[Draft.]   Whitehall, May 18, 1793.

He received on the 26th his letter and declined to give passports to any person until convinced by the most satisfactory proofs—"qu'elles (les Autorités) ont entièrement changé de Principes et de conduite à l'égard des autres Nations. S.M. ne juge pas apropos de se départir en ce moment de sa détermination de ne pas reconnoître dans les circonstances actuelles une nouvelle forme de gouvernement en France. Mais si on y est réellement disposé à terminer la Guerre qu'on a injustement déclarée à S.M. et à ses Alliés, et à leur donner une juste satisfaction, sûreté, indemnisation, on pourra transmettre par écrit aux Généraux des Armées sur la Frontière les propositions que l'on aura à faire à cet effet; ce moyen de communication éviteroit les difficultés de forme, et l'on pourroit alors juger de la nature de ces propositions et de l'esprit qui les dirige."

Brit. Mus. Add. MSS. 34,448.

GRENVILLE to STARHEMBERG.

Whitehall, June 26, 1793.

Lord Beauchamp will go to the Headquarters of H.P.M. for an intimate concert on the war, so as to pursue it with vigour. Hopes for an alliance with Prussia on the same terms as with Austria and the Dutch Republic. The promise of the restoration of the conquests formerly made by France on Austria may entail heavy exertions; but H.M. gladly makes them for H.I.M. and hopes for a new barrier for his Belgic lands, but will not bind himself to secure this.

Ibid.　　　　GRENVILLE to EDEN (at Vienna).

Whitehall, July 26, 1793.

Signature of Convention with Prussia between Lord Yarmouth and Lucchesini on same basis as that with Russia. Lucchesini said that, after taking Mainz, the combined armies would separate—64,000 Austrians and nearly 20,000 Germans being under the Emperor and a *limited* co-operation only would take place.

F.O. Spain, 27.　　　　GRENVILLE to ST HELENS.

[Secret.]　　　　Whitehall, July 19, 1793.

The chief bar to Anglo-Spanish friendship is the jealousy at Madrid about the West Indies. England will seek indemnities for the expenses of this war, and they will probably come in part from the West Indies. Spain must surmise that. St Helens will avoid entering into details, but state the general *principle* of indemnity. If this be well received, "Your Excellency may then try the ground of pointing the views of that Court to acquisitions on its own frontiers as preferable to distant conquests, especially in the West Indies, where Spain is already possessed of territory far beyond what the capital or industry of its subjects will enable them to cultivate." No details to be discussed until the Allies have further succeeded.

French politics are so confused that no views can be stated with profit. "Under these circumstances any declaration on the part of the Allied Powers in favour of a particular party or of a particular form of Government in the interior would tend only to unite all those who were opposed to that system, but could not be looked to as affording a reasonable prospect for the establishment of solid peace and permanent security.

"The acknowledgment of the authority claimed by Monsieur as Regent is evidently a measure of the nature which I have described, and as such has been avoided here...."

St Helens is to point Spain towards French territory in preference to the West Indies, or even to Corsica, and to keep out of discussion our views in the West Indies unless there should be a certainty that Spain may

be brought to concur in them, which seems little probable; and to prevent
the Court of Madrid from committing itself with any description of *émigrés*
or any party in the interior [of France].

Ibid.   SAME *to* SAME.

Whitehall, Aug. 1, 1793.

The Nootka differences ought to be adjusted without difficulty[1].

"H.M. has no intention of making a settlement at Nootka, nor is there
any peculiar advantage in that port which should render Spain desirous
of establishing herself there. It appears from the reports of Lieutenants
Broughton and Mudge that the port of Nootka is clearly situated on an
island, and gives therefore no access to the Continent; that it is by no
means a better port for shipping or trade than many others on the same
coast, and that the furs are neither better in quality nor so abundant in
quantity as on other parts of that coast and of the islands adjacent. The
national honour of Great Britain will be satisfied and the rights (as first
disputed by Spain) of the King's subjects to settle on those coasts [will]
be sufficiently established by the actual restitution of any tract however
small, provided it is understood that the intention of the Court of Spain
in making such restitution is to restore thereby all that was actually possessed
by the British subjects, and that the restitution itself is not accompanied
by unjustifiable reserves, or by claims of exclusive possession in the lands
immediately adjacent, which render it nugatory." Nootka shall be considered as a port "where it shall be free for the subjects of both nations
occasionally to resort and to make temporary buildings for their accommodation, during the time of their being there, but where neither [Power]
is to make any permanent settlement or to establish any claim of territorial
sovereignty or dominion to the exclusion of the other, but mutually to
assist each other in maintaining such free resort and liberty of commerce
and residence against any other nation that shall attempt to establish there
any claim of sovereignty or dominion."

F.O. Austria, 34.   EDEN *to* GRENVILLE.

Vienna, Aug. 31, 1793.

The Austrian Minister, Lehrbach, in a first interview with Lucchesini,
suggested the Belgic-Bavarian exchange as an equivalent to the Prussian
gains in Poland, and as indemnifying Austria for the expenses of the war.
Lucchesini expressed great surprise, as Austria had promised to give up
that project. If it were pressed, H.P.M. would object to any serious
diminution of the power of France as upsetting the balance of Europe.

F.O. Genoa, 6.   PAOLI *to* DRAKE (at Genoa).

Murato di Nebbio, Oct. 7, 1793.

"...Si S.M.B. veut accepter la Corse sous sa domination directe, alors
la forme du Gouvernement pourra être réglée, autant qu'il sera possible,
d'une manière analogue à celle de la Grande Bretagne, dont les lois

---

[1] For the dispute about Nootka Sound, in Vancouver Island, see Rose, *Pitt*, i.
ch. xxv.

garantissent aux citoyens la liberté la plus assurée et la plus tranquille." The Government of Ireland, or that of some of the British colonies, might serve as model.

F.O. Austria, 36. GRENVILLE *to* EDEN.

Whitehall, Jan. 3, 1794.

Grenville acknowledges Eden's despatch stating that Austria would now fulfil her original promise of sending 5000 men to Toulon. Doubtless "if the first promise had been fulfilled, agreeable to the expectation which H.M. was justified in forming, the assistance of such a body of disciplined troops would have sufficed to ensure the defence of that important post; and the injury which the common cause has sustained on this occasion can be ascribed only to the tardiness and indecision which so strongly characterise the Austrian government." Eden is not to expostulate but to try to infuse more vigour, and to get *at last* some definite plan about the Flemish campaign. Only by *renewed* efforts will he succeed in getting this settled. H.I.M.'s journey to Flanders should be *expedited*, as negotiations depend on that. The return of Mack would inspire confidence which at present is not felt here. But something must be settled and at once. Hopes that Malmesbury's mission at Berlin may be helped "by the part which the Empress of Russia appears to have taken."

Ibid. EDEN *to* GRENVILLE.

Vienna, Jan. 4, 1794.

News of Toulon causes consternation, especially owing to weakness of Piedmontese army and the defencelessness of Italy. Austrian troops and engineers were now being sent to examine and fortify the passes of Alps. Delay in Emperor's departure for Flanders. Austria will now limit her offensive plans to Flanders and la Vendée. The retreat of Wurmser's and Brunswick's armies on the Rhine is alarming. Lucchesini behaves pettily, also at times imperiously and with intrigue. Prussia ought now to cooperate honestly. Thugut has ability and experience but he has no family influence, and nobles scorn and often thwart him.

Ibid. SAME *to* SAME.

Vienna, Jan. 18, 1794.

Prussia's demand for financial support from Austria will probably be declined. Prussian Ministers say that, as French principles are no longer dangerous, peace need not be delayed. Thugut declares that, if the Prussian King is at head of a great army and gains successes, he will urge terms of peace hurtful to Austria. The Prussians ought to be split up in *corps and be included in the Austrian armies*.

Ibid. GRENVILLE *to* EDEN.

Downing Street[1], Feb. 18, 1794.

Mack has conferred with Ministers on next campaign, the plan of which had been sent by Coburg after the conference at Brussels. That

---

[1] After mid-January 1794, the F.O. despatches are dated from Downing Street.

plan is generally approved. But Flanders must not be defended solely
by troops in British pay. Part of these *must* take part in the advancing
army of 25,000 men on the right of the Austrian main army, the rest, with
Austrians, being left for defence of Flanders. British objections to the
command of Arch-duke Charles are waived, as tending to delay the campaign. If Coburg retires (as is desirable) then Mack may really direct
under the Emperor. Clerfait, and next to him Cornwallis, might possibly
command the Flanders army.

F.O. Prussia, 32.

GRENVILLE *to* MALMESBURY (at Berlin)[1].

Downing St., March 7, 1794.

Rebuts Prussia's financial demands for her army. Austria and the
Empire will also decline. "By treaty with Great Britain, Russia and Austria
H.P.M. is bound to consider the present war as one of common cause and
to prosecute it with vigour as a principal. Instead of this he proposes to
charge the other confederates with the whole expense of his efforts, which
he is to make only as an auxiliary. By his defensive alliances with Great
Britain, Holland and Austria he is bound to furnish as an auxiliary 52,000
men besides his contingent to the Empire, which cannot be less than 7000
men, which he is to maintain at his own charge, the requiring parties
finding bread and forage except for the contingent to the Empire." But
he now asks Allies to supply bread and forage for all his 100,000 men
besides £2,000,000 towards the pay. This must be refused. Fear that
H.P.M. is protracting this dispute so as to prevent the Allies preparing
their defence. We will raise his subsidy to £1,000,000; but Malmesbury
will resist further demands. Means may be taken to fill the gap caused by
the withdrawal of the Prussians, though the time is very late; but this
"would be infinitely preferable to a disunion of the other confederates."

Ibid.   ### EDEN *to* GRENVILLE.

Vienna, March 11, 1794.

H.I.M. will set out for Pays Bas early in April, and be nominally in
command. England must therefore not press the question of the commands.
Mack was now found to have departed from his instructions, (1) to wage
a defensive war from Basle to Luxemburg, and (2) not to reckon on
Prussian succours beyond the number stipulated to Austria.

F.O. Prussia, 33.   ### GRENVILLE *to* MALMESBURY

Downing St., March 28, 1794.

Austria's refusal to Prussia's demands breaks up the extended plan of
co-operation. We object to the plan of employing the Prussian army
(subsidized by the Maritime Powers) between the Moselle and Rhine,
and H.P.M. also objects to it after what had passed between him and
Austria. She should not dictate to the Maritime Powers where that army

---

[1] See Malmesbury's other despatches in his *Diaries*, III. pp. 70 *et seq.*

should be employed. Her other proposals are equally unreasonable. If she persists, these Powers must defend themselves in their own way. This will bring her to reason and she will then admit the Dutch demand for indemnity and make some contribution towards bringing forward the Prussian force. In that case the Allied conquests in Flanders might go to her in return for a contribution towards the expense of the war. He approves Malmesbury's plan of securing the more limited co-operation of Prussia. Much caution is needed.

Ibid.   SAME *to* SAME.
[Private.]   Downing St., April 4, 1794.

Approves his plan of making the treaty for the duration of the war. Hopes of a happy issue; chief difficulty will be to arrange with Austria any general distribution of force: as she wants to "keep the Prussians back from any effective share in military operations which can lead to acquisitions."

Ibid.   SAME *to* SAME.
[Draft.]   Downing St., April 21, 1794.

Directs him, after signing Conventions, to return from the Hague to London to inform Ministers on many points which he may learn at Brussels, and to advise how the Prussian co-operation may take place with the least friction, "in the most efficient manner but on separate plans of attack." Hope that the weakness and slowness of Austria's policy may end with the arrival of the Emperor, which will at least shorten the time of framing plans. Whoever commands her forces, should be impressed with the gravity of the crisis and "the necessity of a solid and substantial union of the Principal Powers." The Duke of York will inform Malmesbury of the inconsistent way in which Austria has acted with respect to the plan framed by Colonel Mack and agreed to in London. Her gains in the Low Countries must be discussed, also the Dutch demands for indemnity which she has so unjustly resisted. All bears on "the main object of H.M.— the keeping together by influence and weight that great Confederation by which alone the designs of France can be resisted, and which, if left to itself, would be too likely to fall to pieces from the jarring interests of the Powers engaged in it." No opinion yet quite formed here as to the best line of operation for the Prussian army: but Ministers favour the line of the Meuse if the line Mosel-Rhine can be fitly defended.

Ibid.   MALMESBURY *to* GRENVILLE.
         London, May 7, 1794.

He reached Brussels on April 26, and saw Thugut and Mercy. He read to them the treaty of the Maritime Powers with Prussia but (as it was not ratified) did not give them a copy. Mercy spoke sensibly of the need of vigour and union and declared this treaty to be one of the best ever signed. ·Its use would depend on the good faith of H.P.M. and of his advisers, whom he suspected. If the Prussians acted along with the

Austrians "they would inevitably palsy each other." He thought the Belgic provinces a heavy charge to Austria and so would any conquests be on that side.

Thugut was complimentary, but full of jealousy of Prussia and of so many Prussians acting *together* near them. Malmesbury tried to show that H.P.M. was less dangerous employed than unemployed. If not with us, he might be against us.

At Cateau, Malmesbury dined with the Duke of York, and then saw H.I.M. at Catillon, who highly approved the treaty and hoped the Prussian army would be placed on the borders of Luxemburg with its left on Trèves and its right stretching to the Meuse. H.I.M. then said, "We want nothing here but a few more men to put an end to this war; and (with the most spirited animation he said) we must spare neither force nor money in the prosecution of it. We saw the day before yesterday (turning to the Duke of York) to what the British cavalry is equal, and their intrepidity and example will be followed by us all[1]. The resources of my monarchy are great. I trust I may rely on the love and fidelity of my subjects, and I cannot call upon them for a proof of that allegiance and affection more...than to come forth on this occasion. I have already made great efforts. I am ready to make more and shall never consider any as too great in this cause."...

F.O. Austria, 37.   GRENVILLE *to* STARHEMBERG.

Dropmore, June 24, 1794.

Ministers have always wished to have the Prussian subsidized army in Flanders where it is much needed: hopes it will soon move there: "Je suppose que l'idée de ne pas séparer les troupes Prussiennes et d'employer avec les 62,000 hommes les 20,000 que S.M.P. doit fournir à S.M.I. par leur traité d'Alliance, sera très-acceptable à S.M.P., mais c'est à la cour de Berlin à en juger. Nous ne pouvons avoir aucune raison de nous y opposer."

The placing of the Prussian army must be decided on the spot by military reasoning. England can do no more to help the Austrian loan. If there are any difficulties they only arise from the rumours occasioned by the departure of H.I.M. from the army.

Ibid.   SAME *to* SAME.

Dropmore, June 28, 1794.

Good news from army. Moira's force has arrived at Ostend. All is being done to hasten the march of the Prussians to the Low Countries, but many difficulties arise, and (in part) from the Austrian Generals themselves. England can spare no more troops for that part.

F.O. Austria, 38.

GRENVILLE *to* SPENCER AND T. GRENVILLE.

Downing St., July 19, 1794.

Need of an explanation at once with the Austrian Court so as to frame a close concert for stopping the French advance and resume offensive

---

[1] Battle of le Cateau (April 26, 1794).

operations this year or next spring, on an effective scale. Prince of Coburg
is unequal to the command, and real command has rested on Mack,
Hohenlohe or Waldeck. The last has not the confidence of the Austrian
army, or the British H.Q., owing to constant retreats. Suspicion even
of disloyalty to the plan arranged with England for defence of Pays Bas.
Complete change is needed. Would Arch-duke Charles (with Mack) do
well? General Browne also is trusted.

Ibid.   SAME *to* SAME.
                                           Downing St., Sept. 14, 1794.

News had arrived of the disgraceful surrender of Valenciennes and
Condé. This event will not greatly alter the plans formed by the Duke of
York and Clerfait for rest of campaign: but a forward move is still thought
desirable so as to regain part of the Pays Bas and improve the Allied position for winter. Poor prospects for next campaign. There is little inducement to help Austria in the Netherlands. It is therefore desirable to limit
the operations there (as Thugut often hinted) and leave Austria freer to
act more in Italy and on the Rhine. "Instead therefore of proposing a
great addition of Austrian force to serve in the Low Countries under an
English General, in return for the transfer of the Prussian subsidy to
Austria, it will be desirable that you should confine your proposals to the
continuance of the present force in the Netherlands, only stipulating for
its being completed to its full establishment. This may be stated roughly
at 100,000 Austrians, 50,000 British etc., and about 10,000 Dutch."

This force of 160,000 men could recover and hold the Netherlands in
next campaign and attack the barrier where suitable. The guarantee of
Austria's loan entitles H.B.M. to require that her force be kept up to
100,000 men. "In this situation of things above all others, it is evident
that no propositions of peace can hold out the smallest prospect of security."
The Allies would now get bad terms; but when circumstances at Paris
render peace a matter open to question, England will forego her plan of
acquiring French land for Austria in Flanders, and will only guarantee
the restitution of the conquests made by the French, if she will vigorously
proceed with the war. England's separate conquests will not be used so
as to procure better terms for Austria.

F.O. Prussia, 35.   MALMESBURY *to* GRENVILLE.
                                           Frankfort, Sept. 26, 1794.

"Part of the Prussian army had actually put itself in march on the
19th in order to support the intended attack on Trèves...when on the
preceding day intelligence arrived of the success of the French on the
Ourthe and letters from General de la Tour to Generals Nauendorf and
Melas, directing them to give up all thoughts of moving towards Trèves.
These letters...expressed great apprehensions for the consequences of
this defeat and doubts as to the position which was next to be taken.
Marshal Möllendorf, finding he was not to be supported by the Austrians,
did not hold himself obliged to make the attack alone, although there is,

I believe, very little doubt but his force was fully equal to it, and that if he had undertaken it cordially and with spirit, it would have been attended with compleat and easy success. Fortunately Prince Hohenlohe had carried into effect that part of the plan which fell to his share...his conduct on this occasion deserves great praise.

"The day after...I got accounts that the army under Pichegru had made a forward movement...it was also confidently reported that the enemy had actually passed the Meuse...I did not lose a moment in representing through Baron de Hardenberg to Marshal Möllendorf, the critical situation of the United Provinces and the urgent necessity of the army under his command taking some immediate steps to preserve them....

"Baron Hardenberg joined with us in lamenting the complexion and principles of the Prussian H.Q. He is extremely anxious to counteract this and endeavours to persuade himself and me also that on the King of Prussia's return (which is to be to-day) all will go right....

"As the moment draws nigh for the subsidy ending, the Court of Berlin grows apparently more tractable. To this consideration, which from what I know of its general character I am sure is the governing one, may be added the disgraceful termination of the siege of Warsaw, the increasing insurrection in South Prussia and above all an extreme jealousy from Lord Spencer's mission to Vienna that we are drawing towards Austria. This...is the clue of their whole conduct and it will serve to explain as well what Count Haugwitz may say to Mr Paget as what Baron Hardenberg says to me...."

Ibid.   SAME *to* SAME.
                                         Frankfort, Oct. 13, 1794.

"...Three days previous to the arrival of Hertslet with Your Lordship's letter of the 30th inst. Marshal Möllendorf had received an estafette from Baron Jacobi acquainting him with a conference he had had with Mr Pitt and in which he had been told...that the subsidy for the month of October would be suspended. I found therefore Baron Hardenberg fully prepared on this point (although he had not mentioned his being so to me) and I need not say that Baron Jacobi, in his reports, had not softened the conversation he had with Mr Pitt. Thus circumstanced it was impossible for me to suppress any part of my instructions....

I called to Baron Hardenberg's recollection the state of supineness in which the Prussian army had remained from the moment of my arrival near it to this day and the harsh inattention Marshal Möllendorf had thought proper to show to the repeated representations my colleague and myself had made on this subject."...

F.O. Prussia, 37   SPENCER *to* GRENVILLE.
                                         Berlin, Jan. 20, 1795.

"...The greatest variety of opinion prevails here among the different advisers of H.P.M. relative to the present negotiations with the French. General Bischoffswerder openly differs with Prince Henry on the probability of success, and Count Haugwitz said the other day that if the present overtures, which he heartily condemns, should not meet with a completely favourable reception, H.P.M. would be beyond measure anxious to enter into a concert for prosecuting the war with the utmost vigour...

Ibid.　　　　　SAME *to* SAME.

Berlin, Feb. 28, 1795.

"Though I have no reason to suppose that this Court is less deeply committed with the French than I stated...yet so great is H.P.M.'s personal eagerness to make another campaign that I believe it would be still possible to carry that point in opposition to Prince Henry of Prussia and all the ministers if I were to receive immediate instructions for that purpose....I have found means to insinuate to H.M....that it was of the highest importance to wait...before any completely decisive step should be taken at Basel. The news...of the spirited exertions of our government and above all the vote for 150,000 seamen produced a very great effect here both on the public in general and on the king in particular. Ever since the receipt of this intelligence H.M.'s manner with me has been unusually gracious and in his private society he constantly expresses his determination to wait as long as possible for our proposal. This he has indeed done in so marked a manner that I am convinced he wishes it should be repeated to me. Prince Henry of Prussia, who probably wishes to destroy every degree of connection between our two Courts, took an opportunity the other day of entering with me into a long discussion on the war, in the course of which he vented his spleen against our ministers, our officers, our soldiers and our whole conduct, and concluded by telling me that England had forced the French to make war and could not now make peace if she were inclined to it; that the continental powers had not an interest to continue the war, that their resources were exhausted and that though by new subsidy treaties it might enable them to keep their troops in the field, it would not make the country amends for the losses it occasioned. This unfriendly language...is totally inconsistent with the daily professions of H.P.M...."

Ibid.　　　　　SAME *to* SAME.

Berlin, April 21, 1795.

"Colonel Calvert arrived here last night and brought me the three despatches from Mr Dundas. Had I received them a few days sooner I may venture to assert that England would have had at her disposal the best appointed army in Europe....At present this is out of the question, but as I have not yet officially learned the conclusion of the treaty with France, as I know that the king is at heart extremely vexed at the success of the negotiation, and as the Duke of Brunswick gave his opinion that a partial communication of my instructions would certainly produce a good effect, I have determined to endeavour to obtain a private interview with H.P.M. for that purpose. Should this be granted I shall mention in general terms the wish entertained by my Court to renew its connection with Prussia and shall proportion my further communications to the encouragement

I may receive from H.M. At all events the overture will make a very favourable impression on his mind. It will relieve him from the suspicions he has long entertained of H.M. being entirely abandoned by England and sacrificed to the two Imperial Courts, and it will delay if not wholly prevent the alliance which he feels himself under the necessity of contracting with France...."

APPENDIX C

THE SPANISH CRISIS

(*April* 1795—*September* 1796)

Those from Grenville are all from Downing Street; those from Bute are from Madrid.

F.O. Spain, 37-42.

GRENVILLE *to* BUTE.

April 13, 1795.

In spite of the ill humour and despondency of Spain, he hopes that she will persevere to the end of the war. Bute must seek to infuse vigour, especially after the recent Spanish successes in Catalonia. Spain should renew her claims to indemnity from France, which we favour in proportion to the exertions and successes of Spain in war. Bute will protest amicably against any negotiations with France. It is not probable that Spain will propose the renewal of the English alliance in an active form.

"The nature and limits of the respective acquisitions of the two countries in S. Domingo are not sufficiently ascertained to enable me to authorize Your Excellency in the present moment to propose any specific agreement to the Spanish Court with respect to the boundaries to be established to our respective possessions in that island."

JACKSON *to* GRENVILLE.

Aranjuez, April 15, 1795.

The Spanish Government inclines to reciprocate the wishes for peace recently expressed at Paris. Overtures made in Switzerland, also between opposing Generals in Catalonia. Owing to distress in Spain, Alcudia favours them. Recently he said to Jackson "that H.B.M. ought to have abstained from any interference in S. Domingo, upon the whole of which H.C.M. had a well-founded claim; or that if any enterprize was undertaken there by Great Britain, it should have been in the way of auxiliary to Spain, in order to restore to her her ancient possessions in the West Indies."

GRENVILLE *to* BUTE.

June 12, 1795.

Encloses instructions for Malouet, who has been appointed British Commissary in S. Domingo, to arrange the claims of the inhabitants in the British part. Desire to satisfy the claims of Spain there.

GRENVILLE *to* BUTE.

June 15, 1795.

Death of Lewis XVII does not alter their conviction that "the restoration of monarchy in France, if it can be effected, would afford the best prospects of tranquillity both to that country and to the rest of Europe"; but Monsieur will not be recognized as Regent until a sufficient party in his favour is formed in France.

SAME *to* SAME.

Dec. 25, 1795.

Wish to avoid, if possible, a rupture with Spain despite her arming and her evident partiality to the French. We will not make peace through her. She now complains of our plan to attack them in S. Domingo, as if it were Spanish and not French. Whose is it? She should not complain of our balancing French successes on the Continent by our successes in the French colonies.

BUTE *to* GRENVILLE.

May 10, 1796.

He protested against French squadron continuing at Cadiz. A Spanish fleet will soon sail for West Indies. Spain is urging Sweden to revive the Armed Neutrality. Denmark seems to agree.

SAME *to* SAME.

May 18, 1796.

Godoy (Prince of the Peace) says Spanish preparations due to rumours of British schemes against Buenos Ayres and Mexico. Bute denies these, and asks about the reported Franco-Spanish alliance. Godoy says it "is perhaps not far distant." Spain must seek help from France. Bute reports plan of the French squadron to leave Cadiz with a Spanish fleet.

GRENVILLE *to* BUTE.

June 3, 1796.

Alarm at Godoy's words. England desires friendly relations with Spain. Denmark and Sweden now reluctant to join an Armed Neutrality though French victories in Italy assist that scheme.

SAME *to* SAME.

June 18, 1796.

We have no designs on Mexico or Buenos Ayres. When S. Domingo becomes French, we may attack it. We must stamp out French principles in the West Indies because they sap the foundation of all European colonies.

BUTE *to* GRENVILLE.

June 22, 1796.

Godoy spoke to him of the necessary connexion of Spain with France. Bute said that implied war. He expects a rupture, as the French control Godoy.

GRENVILLE to BUTE.

July 15, 1796.

We wish still to conciliate Spain, but her conduct points to a rupture.

BUTE to GRENVILLE.

July 22, 1796.

He thinks that "Spain is actuated by her fears. Those fears engage her, much against her inclination, to go to war with England. She will postpone it as long as the perpetual threats of the French will admit, and even then, unless we force it, [will] not absolutely engage until the several preparations are completed, which will be carried on in the same slow negligent manner." He encloses Godoy's private appeal that the late treaty [of S. Ildefonso] with France may not lead to war.

GRENVILLE to BUTE.

Aug. 26, 1796.

Though Spain has let out the French squadron under the protection of a Spanish force, we will await the result of the overtures at Madrid which give Spain a chance of reconsidering her resolve which can only benefit France. Bute must not leave Madrid without fresh instructions from London or orders from Court of Madrid.

H. DUNDAS to MAJOR-GENERAL FORBES (at S. Domingo).

Aug. 28, 1796.

"Intelligence has been received of the departure of a squadron consisting of 7 French and 19 Spanish ships-of-the-line from Cadiz on the 4th of this month, of which number 9 at present and 2 more after touching at Carthagena are supposed to be destined for S. Domingo. The prevailing influence of French Councils at Madrid, the unfriendly disposition manifested on several late occasions by that Court towards this country and particularly the departure of their fleet in company with that of H.M.'s enemies afford the strongest grounds to apprehend an approaching rupture with Spain." The commander is to be on his guard against Spain; but he is to avoid all hostilities (unless attacked), until authentic news arrives of hostilities.

BUTE to GRENVILLE.

Sept. 10, 1796.

Godoy stated that "Should Spain be obliged to draw her sword against England, one comfort remained—it could not be for any length of time; he hoped soon to see revive the most intimate union." He would never wish Bute to leave Spain. Bute asked "Was it impossible to make matters up? Why not at once form some agreement?" Godoy said Spain had many insults that might justify war, but the war (if it came) could not last, for they ought to be friends.

APPENDIX D

ANGLO-AUSTRIAN RELATIONS

(November 1795—November 1797)

Grenville's despatches are from Downing Street; those from Eden are from Vienna.

EDEN *to* GRENVILLE.

Nov. 10, 1795.

Thugut says Austria cannot wage an active war unless (1) Great Britain support her with a loan of £3,000,000, (2) Russia help on the Rhine, (3) the Empire form an army on the Lower Rhine. Otherwise she will act defensively, "waiting the effect which the distresses and distractions of France may produce."

SAME *to* SAME.

Dec. 5, 1795[1].

News of Allied defeat at Loano. He will help Trevor at Turin reassure that Court of Austria's desire to regain its lost territories. Else it may make peace with France in hope of securing part of Milanese.

SAME *to* SAME.

Jan. 28, 1796.

"A jealousy of the views and sentiments of the Sardinian Government has long existed here, and M. Thugut now expressed his conviction that, if the plan of concluding a separate peace be pursued at Turin, it is with the view of obtaining some compensation on the side of the Milanese for the loss of at least Savoy, the recovery of which he considers as unattainable.... And he expressed the wish that, if the King of Sardinia persisted in his negotiation, the arrears of the subsidy due to him from England should be withheld, on the principle that he has not on his part fulfilled the conditions engaged for, and to prevent his having the means increased of acting against this country."

SAME *to* SAME.

Feb. 27, 1796.

Thugut thought that the proposed Anglo-Austrian Declaration might produce favourable effects on the French nation, but did not, from the principles of the present rulers in France, expect that it would be met by any conciliatory step on their part.

GRENVILLE *to* EDEN[2].

March 1, 1796.

Much concerned that the mission of M. de Castel Alfer from Turin to Vienna had aroused "distrust and resentment in the minds of the

---

[1] For Grenville's important despatch of Dec. 22, 1795 to Eden see Rose, *Napoleonic Studies*, pp. 47–9.
[2] See also documents in *Eng. Hist. Rev.*, April, 1903.

Austrian Ministry." The defection of Sardinia would be a serious blow. She had striven loyally, and Eden was to represent this.

EDEN to GRENVILLE.

[Most secret.]   March 2, 1796.

Though H.I.M. declined making at this moment the declaration proposed by H.M., yet it was H.I.M.'s intention, at the same time he put an end to the Armistice, to issue a similar paper, stating that H.I.M. took that step in consequence of being actuated by the same sentiments as the King.

SAME to SAME.

March 5, 1796.

H.I.M. was gratified by the frankness of the British Government. "No reliance whatever could be placed on the most solemn assurances of the Prussian Government," and it behoved the two Governments to guard against its bad faith. The assembly of a Prussian army in Westphalia was merely that Prussia might act as arbiter in case of peace. H.I.M. would strive to regain his Netherlands along with Liége; but failing that he must seek another indemnity. "He (Thugut) intimated for this purpose the exchange of the Belgic provinces for part of Bavaria, or even for the Duchy of Würtemberg; in which case these should be guaranteed to the prince put in possession of them." Eden dissented.

SAME to SAME.

March 12, 1796.   ·

"Wretched evasion" shown by Russia in her offers of help. She was absorbed in preparations for a Persian war—a probable prelude to an attack on Turkey.

GRENVILLE to EDEN.

April 12, 1796.

Eden is urged to press on cordial co-operation with the Court of Turin as any "relaxation in the efforts of either Court might lead to consequences the most fatal to the future peace and safety of Europe."

SAME to SAME.

April 29, 1796.

An advance of £100,000 may be made to Austria at once, to relieve the "immediate and pressing distress" of that army.

EDEN to GRENVILLE.

July 21, 1796.

The late unexpected disasters have produced no panic at Vienna. Resolve that Belgium must not remain in French hands. Austria grateful for our help and promise of its continuance. England need not fear an armistice by Austria, unless it became absolutely inevitable.

SAME to SAME.

[Most secret.] July 27, 1796.

After a conference with the Emperor, Thugut was very dejected; said the disasters had shaken the alliance; rumours current that Austria was the dupe and tool of England. The Emperor however speaks with dignity and firmness. Financial distress of Austria.

GRENVILLE to EDEN.

Aug. 2, 1796.

Hammond's mission to Berlin to be explained fully to Thugut, as arising solely from the urgent need of bringing in Prussia so as to stop the French. Hammond will open this subject at once to H.P.M. without waiting for Austria's consent, but any arrangement will depend entirely on her consent.

Hammond is directed to find out whether H.P.M. wishes for indemnities in Germany or in the Netherlands. Eden must seek to reconcile Thugut to one of these alternatives; for no advantageous peace can be made, either jointly or separately, without the aid of Prussia.

SAME to SAME.

Sept. 7, 1796.

Failure of our negotiation at Berlin; but it ought to convince Austria of our wish to help. Dark military outlook; the only hope is from union, firmness and vigour. As Eden had failed to convert Thugut to British views, H.M. will seek to influence the Empire through the King of Denmark. In view of the advanced season H.M. must make an effort for a general peace; and if the French Government sends passports, Jackson will be sent to Paris with Instructions; he is authorized to discuss terms of general pacification at some neutral place, where the Emperor's representative would be invited. This has been found to be the only effectual means of restoring peace to Europe. If France accepts, she will probably bring in Holland. If she refuses, Jackson will try to bring this also to a clear issue, and in writing.

With a view to facilitating peace, H.M. is ready to restore as many of his overseas conquests, "as may be judged reasonable in consideration of advantages to be procured to his Allies and particularly to Austria." The principle *uti possidetis* to be taken as a general basis, so as to regulate reciprocal cessions and to maintain the influence of Austria and oppose French efforts at further conquests on the Continent. The Pays Bas must be restored to Austria, "an arrangement which the King would be willing to purchase at the price of very considerable sacrifices on his part of the nature above stated."

SAME to SAME.

Sept. 20, 1796.

Proposal (through Vorontzoff) of Catharine to offer 60,000 troops against France for next campaign, if England pays them by a subsidy. No answer yet given to this last condition, as our finance is heavily drained by Austria.

Same *to* Same.

Oct. 7, 1796.

Russia expects nearly £8,000,000,—an impossible sum; the utmost would be about £3,000,000; even that depends on consent of Parliament, which will not be granted unless objects of war are deemed to warrant it.

Though Great Britain and Austria desire to see the restoration of monarchy in France, it is believed that they do not "mean to bind themselves to continue the war for that object, supposing that terms of peace in other respects reasonable and acceptable can be established on a secure and solid foundation." If this negotiation with Russia fails, Thugut will probably claim the full amount for Austria. This must be resisted.

On Wednesday a resolution of the Directory arrived from Paris. Therefore Lord Malmesbury would be sent in about a week; but he will reject at once "all idea of separating H.M.'s interest from that of Austria or of treating for any other than a general peace." This last is very doubtful; but a failure would give new spirit both to Great Britain and Austria.

Same *to* Same.

Oct. 14, 1796.

Long delay in Eden's despatches. Nevertheless Malmesbury would set out this evening for Paris. His Instructions enclosed. The substance of them may be told to Thugut; but no copy be given or allowed. It is known that France longs for peace. Hope for close union with Austria.

Same *to* Same.

Oct. 18, 1796.

Glad at Austrian successes. Thugut seems to fear our overture will encourage France and that Catharine may find in it an excuse for withdrawing her help. But we know that it greatly embarrasses the Directory, which tries to elude the King's demand, while pretending to consider it. If French ambition and obstinacy continue the war, both Great Britain and Austria will make greater efforts than before. We are seeking to prepare for them on a great scale, as she ought to recognize. But before making them, we want to know as to possibility of peace. If war continues, then Russia's help will certainly be of high value.

Same *to* Same.

Oct. 28, 1796.

Malmesbury will soon see Delacroix. Malmesbury had said that we would act in close concert with Austria for a general peace. Austria should decide on her terms. Naples has made peace with France at Paris. Spain is said to have declared war on us, and this is probable.

Same *to* Same.

Nov. 7, 1796.

Delacroix's note leaves small chance of peace. It demands the production of full powers from H.I.M. before any negotiation begins in which Austria is concerned. Great Britain and Austria must obviously not place difficulties in the way of such a negotiation for which France seems rather more disposed than before. But if France is disposed to break off the negotiation, we must still try to bring it to a clear issue. She may cavil as to place, time and mode of the negotiation. Austria must be informed that, if she declines the negotiation, "it might eventually become necessary for H.M. to go even one step further and conclude peace with France, securing only to his Ally the offer at the same time of such terms as the faith of treaties and the King's regard to the general interests of Europe would in such case induce him to require from France. This extreme case would not be resorted to by H.M. without the utmost reluctance and concern." But it may become necessary, and good faith compels us to state the fact.

SAME *to* SAME.

Nov. 7, 1796.

There ought to be the closest confidence between Great Britain and Austria; but Starhemberg has shown much reluctance to enter into any explanation, and this may arise from Austria entertaining plans unfavourable to us, *e.g.* perhaps on the Belgic-Bavarian exchange. On this Eden will say that H.M. wants Belgium back in Austria's hands, *if solidly held*; for this too is a link of union between Great Britain and Austria. But even that exchange would be duly considered by H.M. as an item in the negotiation if desired by Austria; and the Pays Bas should be in hands able to defend them against France. This is essential to the balance of Europe. Prussia is the only Power except Austria that could hold them: and, if Austria objects to this she should remember that Prussia will oppose the exchange unless she gets a good indemnity; and her interests must be considered in a general settlement. "Any overture to Prussia formed on such grounds, explained with frankness and supported by the joint weight of the Imperial Courts, might possibly be attended with success. Much explanation would be necessary with respect to the various arrangements affecting other parts of the Empire, which might be connected with this idea." In any case Austria must form her decision and formulate her plans without delay.

EDEN *to* GRENVILLE.

Nov. 16, 1796.

Thugut insists on the need of great caution lest we offend Catharine; but "if it were ascertained that the French would treat with the Emperor on the basis of the *status quo ante bellum* for his dominions, and if the King, in order to fulfil his engagements to the Emperor by the Convention of 1793, should press upon him the acceptance of a negotiation on that basis, H.I.M. must acquiesce in it, and the necessity under which he would then act would be sufficient to justify his conduct in the eyes of the Empress of Russia; but that otherwise it would not be prudent for H.I.M. to take any active or public share in the business without previously concerting it with the Empress."

Thugut feared that Russia was already cooling in her offers of help. Therefore it was impossible "that the Emperor could either send a Plenipotentiary to Paris or full powers to Lord Malmesbury to treat in his name or take any positive share in the negotiation until it be ascertained that the Directory has ceased to consider the union to France of the countries conquered from the Emperor as irrevocable, and consented to restore them to H.I.M."

In reply Eden said H.M. had made a long and most honourable series of efforts in the common cause, and the present negotiation must lead either to an honourable peace or fresh energy in conducting the war.

GRENVILLE *to* EDEN.

[Draft. Most secret.]   Nov. 26, 1796.

French conduct seems to denote a wish to break off; but the state of opinion at Paris compels the Directory to appear to continue. Public opinion there favours the restitution of Pays Bas to Austria if Great Britain will grant to France a sufficient compensation. On these lines the enclosed memoir is drawn up, presuming that the principle of compensations is ultimately agreed to by the Directory.

EDEN *to* GRENVILLE.

Nov. 26, 1796.

On Eden naming to Thugut the possible alternative of the Pays Bas going to Prussia, he expressed great astonishment and some degree of passion, and said the Emperor would oppose it by force of arms. Austria had rejected French offer of armistice on Rhine, but Austrian Generals insisted on it owing to fatigue of troops.

SAME *to* SAME.

Dec. 14, 1796.

Death of Catharine a great calamity. Paul offers to fulfil her engagements to Austria; but his first acts arouse distrust. Thugut hopes the British subsidy to Russia will be transferred to Austria.

SAME *to* SAME.

Dec. 31, 1796.

'H.I.M. thanks Great Britain for her care of his interests. If the British proposals are accepted by the Directory, he will send to Paris a plenipotentiary, or will vest Lord Malmesbury with sufficient powers to treat in his name. (This last will be resorted to only if the Directory requires from Austria the recognition of the French Republic.) Thugut insists that Prussia be kept out of the negotiation and be prevented from making any further gain of territory, which (as it must be at expense of the Germanic Body) must cause the dissolution of the Empire. All hope of acquiring Liége is at an end, since the death of Catharine it is no longer attainable without Prussia gaining some equally valuable acquisition.

GRENVILLE *to* EDEN.

[Most secret.]   Jan. 3, 1797.

Probable that Paul will not help us. But if so, H.M. will advance to Austria a subsidy of £200,000 per month; but the first two months shall be at the rate of £300,000. These payments shall be terminable at two months' notice; H.I.M. shall open a loan in England which shall go to the discharge of these advances. Renewal of the 1793 Convention would be censured here, because it was then fully understood "that Austria was bound by former treaties towards Great Britain not to alienate without the consent of the latter any part of the Low Countries."

These are still binding. But in recent discussions with France she has proposed so many projects of exchange and equivalent, all tending to alienate the Netherlands from Austria and this has weakened those treaties. We would prefer by an article of the new Convention to renew "the engagements by which the King is bound not to make peace (but by the consent of Austria) without the restoration to H.I.M. of all his dominions as before the war, and that by which Austria is bound not to alienate the Low Countries without the consent of Great Britain." Believes that another vigorous effort in 1797 will make France sue for peace—such is the exhausted state of her finances. Desire to sign a Convention with Austria on these terms. H.M. will immediately advance £300,000 for January.

EDEN to GRENVILLE.

March 8, 1797.

Thugut agrees that the recent favourable terms offered to Austria by the French through General Clarke are a trick to separate the Allies, or indicate the weakening of French resources. H.I.M. will reject them, especially as his acceptance of an indemnity west of the Rhine would involve the dissolution of the Empire, which he is resolved to preserve "in its present form." He will direct the Grand Duke [of Tuscany] not to interfere further in the business but refer General Clarke to Vienna through official channels. H.I.M. has directed Arch-duke Charles not to listen to any overtures from Bonaparte nor to grant him any interview. H.I.M. will (if further pressed by these offers of France) intimate that only a Congress of all the Powers can initiate negotiations for peace. Thugut then set forth Austria's great difficulties, her steadfastness to the alliance, but also the urgent need of a corps of auxiliaries and the co-operation of a naval force.

GRENVILLE to EDEN.

[Most secret.]   March 17, 1797.

Austria's requests for British naval support in the Adriatic are being carefully considered; but no promise can yet be given. "The fleet under Sir John Jervis which is destined to oppose itself to the forces which the enemy may be able to draw from their southern ports, must of necessity be directed in some degree by the motions of the enemy; and while the principal Spanish force is collected at Cadiz it can hardly be expected or even desired by the Austrian Government that Sir John Jervis's fleet should proceed up the Mediterranean; but I am not without considerable hopes of being shortly able to announce to you that such arrangements of a more limited nature have been adopted as may be sufficient amply to provide for the safety of the navigation of the Adriatic, which appears to be the principal object of M. Thugut's solicitude in the present moment."

EDEN *to* GRENVILLE.

March 25, 1797.

French advance to Tarvis. Arch-duke Charles's journey to Vienna had delayed his arrival on that front, and his plans for ending the *confusion* there. Colonel Graham reported grave abuses there. Clamour for peace renewed at Vienna. Complaints of want of our financial succour; but Thugut still hopes if we grant naval co-operation.

SAME *to* SAME[1].

April 1, 1797.

The Directory has signified to Prussia its desire for peace with Austria, restoring to H.I.M. such conquests as have not been annexed to the French Republic and requesting H.P.M.'s good offices. H.P.M. has announced this at Vienna but (as a member of the Germanic Body) can announce the fact only on the ground of integrity of the Empire and a general pacification being made.

Thugut thinks it a Prussian trick to increase clamour for peace at Vienna and will inform M. de César that H.I.M. cannot entertain the offer until he has consulted his Allies. Thugut dwelt on the uniform bad faith of Prussia, and suggested that the Tsar become a joint mediator so as to hold Prussia in check.

GRENVILLE *to* EDEN.

April 4, 1797.

Glad at Austria's repulsing the French offer of peace through Grand Duke of Tuscany. Such a peace would give free play to Prussia's ambition. Hope that the new elections in France will send up more moderate men. But the Allies might declare that they will not refuse to enter into joint negotiations for peace, "carried on by their Ministers at one and the same place, and with one person authorized by France to treat with those Ministers conjointly." If France agrees, then Great Britain leaves it to Austria to fix the place, if not too far from London. "The King's wishes would be to direct and employ any restitutions of conquests to which he might be induced to agree in such way and to such objects only as may be best calculated, according to the present state of affairs in Europe, to promote the interests, welfare and future security of his Ally, on which H.M. holds that of Europe essentially to depend."

SAME *to* SAME.

[Secret.] April 4, 1797.

Orders now have been sent to Jervis to send to the Adriatic such force of frigates as shall suffice for the service required. But we cannot send a fleet into Mediterranean as that would mean dividing Jervis's fleet now doing splendid service off Cadiz: neither have France nor Spain any squadrons capable of service in the Mediterranean. The sending the frigates shows our regard for Austrian interests.

[1] For Eden's second note of April 1 see Hüffer, *Quellen*, Pt II. vol. I. p. 153.

Grenville *to* Eden.

April 11, 1797.

Prussia's strange proposal to the Czar will probably incline him towards Austria and Great Britain, unless France persuades him that the Allies are against peace. But we urgently desire it, on the terms and in the way now proposed to H.I.M. He therefore encloses a Note Verbale for Austria and Great Britain to be presented jointly to the Emperor of Russia (in case Austria agrees); also a Note for Whitworth authorizing him to present that Note or a similar one as approved at Vienna.

He then discusses the cession of the Austrian Netherlands to France and fears that the disastrous opening of the campaign makes it inevitable...

Same *to* Same.

[Most secret.]   April 11, 1797.

Mr Hammond is sent with this despatch to assist Eden with his thorough knowledge of the situation. "The King confidently relies on the assurances he has received from Vienna that no separate negotiation will have been entered into with the enemy in the interval." But if at the time of Mr Hammond's arrival the Court at Vienna thinks that the delay of a reference to Russia involves too great a risk, the following are the best lines of conduct which seem to be open for them to pursue, and Eden has authority to accede to them:

"The first measure might be to endeavour to conclude a general armistice, avowedly for the purpose of allowing time for the intervention of the Courts of Petersburg and Berlin (as the French would, in such a case, certainly require the adjunction of the latter) extending such armistice to all the belligerent Powers and stipulating respecting the naval war that proper time should be allowed for notices in the distant parts of the world and that no change should be made in the stations of the respective naval forces after the receipt of such notices and until the expiration of the armistice." Eden has full authority to accept such an arrangement....

But H.M. is sensible that the situation may demand immediate negotiation with France, and to avoid unnecessary delay which might seriously prejudice the common interests, he is ready to refer the decision as to the necessity to the Austrian government, which can alone pronounce on the exigency of its own situation....

If the Court of Vienna wishes to proceed to direct negotiations, Eden and Mr Hammond will act as follows:

"You will enter with the Austrian Minister into the fullest and most unreserved discussion of the different points which may come in question respecting the terms of peace both for Great Britain and Austria. With respect to the latter you will remark that from the moment that the resolution is taken by this government to consent to and even to advise the cession of the Netherlands to France, if absolutely necessary as the price of general peace, the most important and pressing interest which this country can possibly have with a view to the affairs of the Continent is that the House of Austria may by some just and adequate compensation be continued in a situation capable of opposing, as it has hitherto done, a powerful barrier to the ambition of France. But the mode of providing for this must naturally be left to the decision of the Austrian government, and you will therefore explain that your instructions are to co-operate with the views of the Emperor in this respect....

The terms which H.M. would propose are:

(1) Restitution of all conquests except Martinique, which is not nearly the equivalent for the great accession of maritime, commercial and colonial power which France would derive from the possession of the Netherlands and San Domingo. (2) Restitution to Spain of Trinidad, unless it is settled that H.M. retains this with Tobago or St Lucia or some other conquest in the West Indies, in lieu of Martinique. (3) Restitution to Holland of all conquests in the East and West Indies except the Cape and Ceylon, the possession of both which points is of the greatest importance to the defence of the East Indies under the new state of things which would arise in Europe from the possession of the Netherlands by France. (4) Peace for Portugal...."

GRENVILLE to EDEN.

April 11, 1797.

"I hoped before this to have advised you of the Convention with the Emperor, but the question of pecuniary aid can only be brought forward as a part of the general financial arrangements and the loan about to be negotiated. But the loan is delayed and it is not proper that the Convention should be signed before this is settled. To remove disappointment and obviate despondency at the delay you are authorised to give M. Thugut most positive assurances that 3½ millions of the loan are for H.I.M., subject to the consent of Parliament, destined in part for the repayment of advances made by H.M. to the Emperor, and the rest for aid to H.I.M. for the current year. The terms will be made as favourable as possible to the Emperor, though in the great financial distress of this country they must unquestionably be very disadvantageous. The whole will be submitted to Parliament as expeditiously as possible."

GRENVILLE to EDEN AND HAMMOND.

[Most secret.]   April 18, 1797.

"As it is possible that the cession of Trinidad may be repugnant to engagements between France and Spain, you are authorised to accept instead Tobago with either St Lucia or Demerara or the part of S. Domingo held by H.M. when the preliminaries were signed. This is the utmost H.M. thinks proper to concede. But if Vienna is in actual peril the King would consent to confine his demands to Tobago only, which he desires to retain as it is settled wholly by British planters. But in case of extreme necessity, rather than this peace of Austria should be concluded separately, the King will ultimately abandon all claim to West Indian acquisitions, provided the fullest liberty is given to individuals to remove their property. In such case there would be left of the acquisitions only the Cape and Ceylon...."

GRENVILLE *to* EDEN.

May 2, 1797.

Uneasiness about the issue of the negotiations with Buonaparte. "From your silence about the terms which Merafeldt is instructed to propose or accept, we conclude a reserve has been observed towards you on this subject very different from the open and ample communications which were made from hence during the whole course of Lord Malmesbury's negotiations. It is impossible not to feel that this reserve is incompatible both with the faith of existing engagements and with the conduct which is on every account due to H.M., and it has accordingly given occasion to much remark, and that of the most unpleasant nature.... If a precipitate and separate Peace has been concluded without any previous communication to this Government as to the terms to be agreed to, this can only be lamented as a striking addition to the instances, already much too frequent in this war, in which our enemies have been allowed to triumph not only over the rights and interests but over the honour, good faith and probity of the old and established governments with which they have had to contend...." The House of Commons voted the subsidy [to Austria] last night by a majority of nearly four to one....

HAMMOND *to* GRENVILLE.

[Private.]   May 3, 1797.

" I cannot avoid expressing to Your Lordship the concern and mortification with which I have learnt *from every quarter* the present helpless condition of the Austrian army from the total want of discipline and subordination and the lassitude of the war which universally pervades it."

GRENVILLE *to* HAMMOND.

May 26, 1797.

Order to return home. "The late conduct of the Prussian Government is such as to afford very little prospect of any measure being adopted there consistent with the general interests of Europe or in any manner favourable to those of this country."

GRENVILLE *to* EDEN.

May 28, 1797.

Extreme disappointment at the conduct of the Austrian Government, equally contrary to the faith of treaties and to those sentiments of friendship which have been professed. That Mr Hammond was allowed to leave without being charged with any communication must be considered a strong indication of a change of sentiment and system towards this country.

SAME *to* SAME.

June 2, 1797.

Overtures for peace are being made at Paris. The natural consequence of the treaty (*sic*) between Austria and France and the silence of the former about the stipulations. Eden will communicate this to the Austrian

Minister with no other reminder than that the communication itself, at such a moment, is the best proof of H.M.'s anxious desire still to maintain harmony with the Court of Vienna.

Pitt MSS. Pub. Record Office.

PITT *to* LORD CARLISLE.

[Private.]   June 4, 1797.

"...I can also venture to assure you that I feel not less strongly than yourself the expediency of taking every step towards peace, that can be likely to effect the object consistent with the safety and honor of the country; and I have no difficulty in adding (for your *private* satisfaction) that steps are taken of the most direct sort, and of which we must soon know the result, to ascertain whether the disposition of the enemy will admit of negotiation. On this point the last accounts from Paris seem to promise favourably. You will have the goodness to consider the fact of a step having been actually taken as confidentially communicated to yourself."

GRENVILLE *to* EDEN.

June 30, 1797.

Notification of pourparlers with the Directory for peace, to include Portugal, Spain and Holland. Malmesbury appointed plenipotentiary. Remains to be seen if French are sincere. If so, little doubt remains of speedy and favourable termination.

SAME *to* SAME.

July 7, 1797.

Difficulties made by Thugut as to ratification of the Convention signed by Starhemberg re the Austrian Loan. Such a breach of faith in satisfaction of our financial claims on Austria is incredible. We insist on completion of the affair.

GRENVILLE *to* STARHEMBERG.

Juillet 21, 1797.

In treating for peace separately we might each get better terms, but without being nearer its accomplishment in fact. "On nous propose donc de renouveler le concert et de ne traiter notre paix définitive qu'au Congrès futur. Nous répondons que, pour ce qui est du concert, nous rendrons bien volontiers confidence pour confidence, mais que pour attendre le Congrès, il est déjà trop tard. Nous avons attendu (comme vous le savez bien) des nouvelles de ce Congrès autant qu'il étoit possible d'attendre. On ne nous a pas voulu communiquer un mot, ni sur les conditions de la Paix, ni sur la tenure du Congrès jusqu'à ce qu'il n'étoit plus possible de garder un secret que tous les papiers de Paris auroient annoncé aux cafés de Londres et de Paris. La communication qu'on nous a fait enfin étoit aussi bornée et aussi peu amicale qu'il étoit possible de l'être.

"Voilà notre justification...pour avoir consenti d'ouvrir des négociations avec l'ennemi pour une Paix définitive sans attendre pour cela un Congrès qui très probablement ne s'assemblera jamais. Que cette démarche soit bonne ou mauvaise, elle est faite: l'engagement est pris de traiter de bonne foi pour une paix définitive, et S.M. le remplira comme Elle remplit tous ses autres engagements. Cependant le résultat de cette négociation n'est rien moins que certain. Il se peut que l'ennemi, qui par la désunion qu'il a jeté entre nous se flatte de nous jouer tous les deux, insistera avec nous sur des conditions inadmissibles et continuera à enfreindre, comme il le fait journellement, les stipulations des Préliminaires qu'il a signé[s] avec vous. Dans ce cas nous pourrions encore nous entendre et renouveler sous de plus heureux auspices un concert, qui, s'il avoit été observé de bonne foi de votre part, comme il l'a été de notre part, aurait indubitablement sauvé l'Europe. *Dixi*—et c'est à vous de broder ce cannevas et donner à cette vérité *toute nue* les habits et les ornemens dont elle auroit besoin pour se présenter à des étrangers. Tout à vous."

GRENVILLE *to* EDEN.

July 23, 1797.

"The long perseverance of the Court of Vienna in its refusal to make to H.M.'s Government any communication of the terms of the separate peace between Austria and France and the unfriendly manner in which that communication was at last made, unaccompanied as it was by any overture or measure which indicated any desire of further co-operation or concert, were among the leading motives which induced H.M.'s servants to advise H.M. to accede to the proposals of France in this respect. The King, having upon this ground entered into that engagement, no longer considers himself at liberty to depart from it, but will observe it with the same good faith with which he has executed on his part all his treaties with his Allies."

EDEN *to* GRENVILLE.

Aug. 16, 1797.

H.I.M. has professed a desire for union with Great Britain but made no definite offer. As Great Britain had opened negotiations, and the Czar was indifferent as to a Congress, H.I.M. abandoned the idea.

SAME *to* SAME.

Sept. 16, 1797.

News arrived through Basel of the *coup d'état* of Fructidor. Thugut said this would break up the negotiations at Lille and Udine, and he inveighed bitterly against French perfidy and aggressiveness. He said he was not guilty of signing the Austro-French Preliminaries, "and repeated his opinion that Europe can be saved only by a thorough concert between the King and the Emperor and by the overthrow of the present ruling party in France." He lamented the prospect of an Anglo-French peace, as it must prejudice the chances of Austria obtaining reasonable terms at Udine. The seizure of Corfu by the French harmed both countries, and in case of war a joint expedition should be made by them to recover it.

EDEN *to* GRENVILLE.

Sept. 18, 1797.

General Meerveldt, who left Udine on Sept. 14, reported that before he left, Bonaparte had been dejected, but on receiving news of the *coup* of Sept. 4 at Paris, was much elated and then declared to the Imperial Ministers that France could not cede what she had promised to Austria in the Preliminaries, and demanded that the Emperor should treat at Udine for peace for the Empire, "evidently aiming to extort by this means the cession of the territory on the left bank of the Rhine as the price of the promised indemnification to H.I.M. in Italy. Bonaparte further declared that the Directory meant to retain Corfu and to annex Venice to the new formed Republic." He urged Austria to make peace on these terms, as France was about to conclude peace with Great Britain.

Thugut said H.I.M. would not treat for the Empire, but would await the news from Lille and the opportunity of a further concert with Great Britain. He also asked whether Spain had offered to conclude separately with Great Britain; and if so, could a British fleet be sent to the Adriatic to secure the transport of supplies to the Austrian army and cover the vulnerable coast of Istria? Cobenzl looks upon Bonaparte "as more than mortal," and combats him feebly.

GRENVILLE *to* EDEN.

Sept. 22, 1797.

"I have to inform you that the negotiation which was carrying on at Lille has been abruptly terminated by a demand made to Lord Malmesbury by the new French plenipotentiaries, Treilhard and Bonnier...that he should either declare whether or no he had full powers to agree to a complete restitution of all the conquests made by H.M. on France and her Allies, as a preliminary to the negotiation, or should quit Lille in 24 hours. A demand so unreasonable and unexpected undid at once whatever progress had been made in the negotiation and threw the business back to the point from which it had started two months before, and in such a manner as to leave little hope that it can be further pursued with any prospect of success.

"The French plenipotentiaries indeed continued to the conclusion of the very last conference to repeat and enforce in the strongest manner the most distinct assurances that nothing was further from the views of the Directory than an abrupt and unfavourable termination of the negotiation; that they were desirous of pursuing it with the greatest rapidity and to a happy issue; and that the very step which they were now taking was that which appeared to them the best calculated to lead to such an end; that so far from considering the business as completely terminated even by Lord Malmesbury's departure, they still conceived it to be capable of being resumed and prosecuted with success. It is not necessary for me to say that these assurances, however strongly urged, appear wholly incompatible with the conduct which has been pursued by the Directory on the present occasion, and that but faint hopes can be entertained here, under such circumstances of any other issue than a continuation of the war."

EDEN *to* GRENVILLE.

Nov. 1, 1797.

Thugut told him confidentially that he considered the Austro-French peace so unfavourable to Austria and so vague in its terms that it could not be concluded: that therefore H.I.M. wished to enquire from the British Government as to an eventual compact for the prosecution of the war, Great Britain sending a sufficient naval force to the Mediterranean and furnishing a loan to Austria. H.I.M. would confine "his views of acquisition to the side of Italy, from a wish of preserving the German Empire in its present shape." Eden in reply requested Thugut to state what were Austria's engagements to France. This Thugut refused to do, but he gave a vague outline of the terms. He said H.I.M. would ratify them but would keep his forces up to full strength, as the French troops would probably not evacuate E. Venetia. Eden replied that the fulfilment of Austria's financial responsibilities to Great Britain was a *sine quâ non* to any agreement.

GRENVILLE *to* EDEN.

[Most secret.] Nov. 24, 1797.

With reference to Starhemberg's proposal at London, Austria must state her obligations to France, etc., without which no proposal can be discussed. Great Britain and Russia have been kept out of the Austro-French discussions and agreements, probably because H.M. will disapprove them. Repayment of the loan is again insisted on; otherwise Parliament will not agree to any further efforts for Austria.

APPENDIX E

ATTEMPTS TO FORM THE SECOND COALITION (1798)

Grenville's despatches are from Downing Street; those from Eden are from Vienna.

EDEN *to* GRENVILLE.

Jan. 3, 1798.

H.I.M. orders the repayment of the Austrian loan to Great Britain in certain products (quicksilver, iron, corn, etc.), specie not being available. Eden pointed out that, as France controlled the Adriatic, the export of these was impossible; and long delays would result from this method of barter.

GRENVILLE *to* EDEN.

Jan. 16, 1798.

Insists on the loan being repaid. The Austro-French peace creates universal disgust. "Europe can be saved only by the union of the four Great Powers." H.M. labours to effect it, but is hindered by the acts of Austria which create distrust.

EDEN *to* GRENVILLE.

March 10, 1798.

Prussia's subversive proposals *re* Empire at Rastatt. H.I.M. requests her to unite with him to preserve the Empire as far as possible. Reports of the French at Rome. Great alarm at Naples, whose King begs help from Austria. Thugut says if the French attack Naples or Tuscany, H.I.M. will defend them.

GRENVILLE *to* SIR W. HAMILTON (at Naples).

April 20, 1798.

Hamilton will at once see the Neapolitan Ministers and "convince them in the strongest manner of the zeal and sincerity with which H.M. enters into the interests and feels for the present situation of their Sicilian Majesties."

It would have been impossible for H.M. to witness the plain and undisguised declaration of the French Government of their intention to overwhelm the dominions of H.S.M. without feeling the most lively desire to interfere so far as he might have the means and opportunity to rescue from destruction a Power with whom he has always been anxious to maintain the most friendly intercourse. The discussions which have lately taken place between H.M. and the Court of Vienna respecting the common interests of the two Governments and of Europe lead H.M. to hope that he may find occasion to interfere with effect, provided the period to which his assistance can be afforded be not too remote to prevent the difficulties which appear to be impending over Naples, and he has only to lament that the other Powers of Europe have so tardily awaked to the true sense of their general danger as to leave any doubt upon this point, and to have made it impracticable for him to be either more early in his offers of assistance or more certain of their success. H.M. has come to the determination of sending a fleet into the Mediterranean for the protection of Naples so soon as it is possible for it to be brought forward without detriment to the indispensable objects of his naval service or imminent hazard to the safety of his dominions.

GRENVILLE *to* EDEN.

April 20, 1798.

Refuses to consider Starhemberg's recent Mémoire[1] for an alliance until the loan is repaid. When it is, we will consider a union either with her alone or with Naples. But success will more result from a Quadruple Alliance, including Russia and Prussia. Austria and Prussia must lay aside their jealousies. Great Britain strives to prepare for a Quadruple Alliance. He has explained to Starhemberg the British proposal to be made at Berlin by Elgin so framed as not to betray the confidence of Austria, also for the friendly intervention of Russia. The Quadruple Alliance would guarantee the respective dominions of the four Powers, and possibly also

---

[1] See *Dropmore Papers*, IV. 154–9.

of the smaller Powers. Meanwhile "the great object appears to be that the plan of pacification for the Empire should be arranged by Austria and Prussia and presented at once as an ultimatum to France." If she refuses, the four Powers should make common cause against her. Our quota would then be partly in the British fleet to be sent into the Mediterranean, partly in pecuniary succours. If Prussia refuses to join, H.M. will make a concert with H.I.M. Austria's pecuniary demands are inadmissible, but H.M. would eventually send a commissioner to Austrian H.Q. to supply her commander with monthly bills on H.M.'s treasury at the rate of £1,000,000 for 12 months, for her armies in Italy and Germany. The general aim must be "that of reducing France within her ancient limits, particularly on the side of the Netherlands and of delivering Holland and Italy from the uncontrolled dominion which she now exerts over them." Fear that Austria may in the future make a separate peace. French attack on England would have the directly opposite effect. H.I.M. is invited to specify a plan of co-operation through Starhemberg.

SAME *to* SAME.

April 20, 1798.

In view of a possible French invasion, H.M. cannot much weaken his fleet in home waters; for if Earl of St Vincent's fleet were sent into Mediterranean the Spanish fleet might join that at Brest, which would involve the recall of his fleet from the Mediterranean. And to detach only a part of it to that sea would expose it to the Spanish and Toulon fleets. A great increase to the British fleet is therefore necessary: and H.M. will incur that expense so as to be able to send thither an adequate force. Reinforcements to St Vincent's fleet will sail early in June. It must be admitted to any of the Austrian or Neapolitan ports, also into those of Leghorn and Genoa. It is expected that Austria will supply 3000 seamen from her Adriatic ports: also Naples the same number or even more. We cannot guarantee the continuance of that fleet in the Mediterranean indefinitely. Will not Naples seek to induce Spain to come to terms with us and then remain neutral or even join "the general defensive alliance now in agitation"? For this purpose Great Britain was and is ready to sacrifice her recent conquests from Spain. If the latter agrees, H.M. could safely engage to keep an adequate fleet in the Mediterranean during the war.

EDEN *to* GRENVILLE.

April 28, 1798.

Continued friction between Austria and Prussia on German affairs. Prussia's aims subversive. The Czar's influence on her will be *nil* unless he places an army on her frontier. Thugut fears for the safety of Naples, and thinks the French armament at Genoa [*sic*] is destined for Malta, Sicily or Sardinia[1].

---

[1] These despatches prove that Bonaparte's Oriental plans had not been surmised at London or Vienna.

Grenville *to* Eden.

April 28, 1798.

Bernadotte having left Vienna, and hostilities being imminent, H.M. is ordering St Vincent to send at once to the Mediterranean a force sufficient to hold in check the enemy's force there. Hopes that Austria will appreciate the magnanimity of this step which involves some danger to England. British finances prove the stability and power of the country. Eden must urge the necessity of obtaining for H.M.'s ships free admission to Naples and other Italian ports. St Vincent is at liberty "to treat as hostile all ports and countries in Italy by which these demands shall be refused." Eden to forward a copy of this despatch to Hamilton at Naples.

Same *to* Same.

[Most secret.]   May 15, 1798.

"...In consequence of the publication of the despatches of the American Commissioners at Paris and of the scandalous scene of corruption and insolence there displayed, Congress has resolved on measures of hostility against France." If the Baltic Powers would concur, "there would then remain no neutral flag to protect the commerce or supplies of France."

Eden *to* Grenville.

May 23, 1798.

Russia will promote an armed mediation, and will send an army to the Austrian frontier and despatch a fleet to help British fleet in North Sea. Thugut makes little of all this and says Czar is for peace, influenced thereto by Prince Repnin, who believes France irresistible; also by jealousy of Suvoroff whom he does not want to employ. Eden contested these statements but fears them correct. Thugut apprehensive for Germany in case of a war. Eden said Naples must be helped. Italy and Switzerland would probably rise against the French. This would derange their schemes, especially that of the Toulon armada, which Thugut thought might be against the Mediterranean Islands or Egypt, where there is plenty of ready money. H.I.M. urgently desired an entente with Prussia, and for it would see her acquire much land in Germany if it were under the mediation of Russia. Eden again urged the necessity of the Quadruple Alliance, and of the loan being settled. Thugut said this was impossible at present. The Austro-Neapolitan Treaty is a highly gratifying event. If followed up, it must bring a rupture with France, which Thugut expected.

Same *to* Same.

June 23, 1798.

After the arrival of Hamilton's messenger, Eden informed Thugut of "the disposition of the Court of Naples to acquiesce in H.M.'s demands relative to the Mediterranean fleet." Thugut was gratified, and said that "H.I.M. would decidedly support the King of Naples against any consequences that might result, as H.S.M. was already assured of, by the defensive Treaty signed here on the 20th ult. which had arrived at Naples on the 1st inst. But, on my asking if he would enable me by this opportunity to transmit an answer to my note of Monday last, he requested that it might be deferred till positive accounts arrived of the determination of the Court of Naples, and of the measures adopted there, which, he said, must now be received in a very few days."

SAME to SAME.

July 4, 1798.

After a letter from Hamilton, he regrets the timidity of the Neapolitan Government with regard to the "free and unqualified admission of H.M.'s fleet" into any Neapolitan port. The Austro-Neapolitan Treaty is of the usual defensive character. Gallo objects to it and says H.S.M. cannot ratify it in its present form; and presents a slightly different treaty for consideration, confining the *casus foederis* to a French aggression in Italy. Thugut objects to this as onesided seeing that Austria is *strong* in Italy.

HAMILTON to EDEN.

[Enclosure.]   Naples, June 13, 1798.

Had pointed out that the British fleet could not remain in Mediterranean unless it could enter the Neapolitan ports. Gallo always deferred an answer, and clings to half measures. He (Hamilton) anxiously awaits news from Sicily respecting the French and British fleets.

EDEN to GRENVILLE.

July 10, 1798.

News of seizure of Malta by the French came from Rastatt, where it arrived by telegraph from Paris. Cobenzl made no progress at Rastatt. Naples has not ratified the Treaty with Austria. Eden begs Thugut to conclude some treaty now that Naples is in such danger. Thugut said H.I.M. would not abandon Naples.

SAME to SAME.

July 14, 1798.

A messenger arrived from Naples bringing ratification of the Treaty of May 20. Thugut said both H.I.M. and H.M. should induce Naples to enter into the war eventually. A letter from Hamilton of June 20 stated that Nelson with 14 sail on June 17 appeared off Isle of Caprea (*sic*). Troubridge landed to inquire if Neapolitan ports were open to H.M.'s ships, and "attended Sir W. Hamilton to General Acton, who at length gave him an order in H.S.M.'s name to all the governors of the ports of Sicily to allow the British sick and wounded to be put on shore and taken care of in any of the ports of that island, and also that they might be allowed to get provisions for the fleet from any of these ports."

HAMILTON to GRENVILLE.

Naples, Aug. 4, 1798.

Nelson had missed the French; seven British frigates and a cutter had been for more than a fortnight looking for Nelson, who was very angry that any difficulty was made by the Government of Syracuse in admitting all the fleet[1]. But "the Court of Naples could not without great risk throw off the mask until it had received the ratified Treaty with the Emperor of Germany and with the two supplementary articles by which the Emperor is bound to defend H.S.M. in case of an attack from any enemy, in consequence of his having opened his ports to the King's ships without any limitation; and that Treaty arrived here in the night of the 30th of July and was officially communicated to me the next day by the Marquis di Gallo, the Treaty having been finally concluded at Vienna the 16th of July. As soon as I had received Admiral Nelson's last letters, I shewed them, abuse and all, to General Acton, as His Excellency mentions in his answer to that communication; but I flatter myself, having sent to Sir Horatio Nelson the original letter of General Acton of 1st Aug. that he will be perfectly satisfied, as I am, with this Ministry on this head." He hears that full powers are now given to M. de Circello to conclude a new treaty of alliance with Great Britain. "We already here look upon us as united, and there can be no doubt that the French will resent the King's fleet having been admitted into the port of Syracuse. Why then should the King of Naples hesitate one moment to take advantage of the present discontent and rising of the Roman peasantry, and march on Rome where there are not more than 3000 Poles and French?"

EDEN *to* GRENVILLE.

Aug. 29, 1798.

Prince Repnin and the Russian ambassador showed a letter from Sandoz-Rollin to his Court [Berlin] stating that France intends war against Austria. Thugut doubts its authenticity and says it is a plot between Prussia and France to feel the pulse of Austria.

GRENVILLE *to* EDEN.

Sept. 4, 1798.

Russia is ready to aid H.I.M. with troops if war breaks out, if we can help her with funds. Thinks war more remote than is believed at Petersburg. Our measures must depend on the ultimate decision of Austria. We deem it best now not to help Austria by Russian troops rather than by a direct subsidy, and have suggested to Paul I to intervene so as to establish a concert between the three Powers. But the ratification and execution by Austria of her financial engagements is an indispensable preliminary.

EDEN *to* GRENVILLE.

Sept. 5, 1798.

Prince Repnin before his departure assured Morton Eden that he [Eden] must give way on the financial dispute as Austria was desperately low in credit, and must be helped. Eden replied that the former convention must first be fulfilled. He conjured Repnin to persuade Paul I to encourage and stir up Austria; else Naples would be ruined.

[1] Nicolas, Sir N. H., *Dispatches...of Nelson*, III. 25-48; Rose, *Napoleonic Studies,* pp. 350-3.

SAME *to* SAME.

Sept. 20, 1798.

News of Turkish declaration of war against France. Thugut asked whether the proposed Anglo-Russian convention would depend on the ratification of the Anglo-Austrian convention. Eden said it would be. Thugut said in that case Austria could not accept British proffered aid as her finances utterly forbade her fulfilling the loan. Eden showed how favourable was the time to attack France and save Europe.

GRENVILLE *to* HAMILTON.

Oct. 3, 1798[1].

M. Circello has received full powers to conclude a defensive alliance with England. The British Government glad to do so, on the basis of the Convention of 1793 whenever the King of Naples is ready to go to war with France. Grenville warns him that "H.M. was not insensible of the danger which must attend such a resolution, if taken without the fullest assurances of support from the Court of Vienna, though on the other hand it could not be denied that the other alternative, that of remaining a patient spectator of the intrigues, insults and aggressions of France, was also full of danger to H.S.M.'s interests and security." In this situation it appeared that the decision both in point of substance and of time must be left to H.S.M.'s own determination, and that the most friendly conduct which H.M. could pursue on this subject was to refer the negotiation to Naples and thus to leave it to H.S.M. to act in this respect as circumstances may require and particularly as may be found most expedient from a view of the final resolutions (whatever they may be) of the Court of Vienna. "In pursuance of this idea I herewith transmit to you by the King's command H.M.'s full powers for negotiating and signing a treaty of defensive alliance with the Court of Naples; such treaty to be either in the form of a general defensive treaty or in that of a special Convention applicable to the particular case of the present war with France...."

P.S. "Since the above was written, the intelligence has been received here of the glorious results of the attack on the French fleet at Abukir. This happy event makes no change in H.M.'s disposition to consult the views and interests of H.S.M. respecting the conclusion of an alliance in the manner stated in the above despatch, and it evidently affords still greater facility for fulfilling the stipulations of it at present on both sides."

SAME *to* SAME.

Oct. 3, 1798.

Need of attacking France at Malta. Numerous small armed vessels should be furnished by Naples: this would be a "*sine quâ non* of future concert." A declaration should be made that all neutrals approaching Malta will be sunk. As to the future of Malta, "The communications made to H.M. on this subject from the Court of Naples are in the highest degree liberal and friendly. But H.M. does not entertain any idea of acquiring

[1] Received by Hamilton about November 19.

the sovereignty of Malta to himself, or of any of the Venetian Islands. He is ignorant how far any such wish is entertained by the Emperor of Russia or by H.S.M., though it does not appear to H.M. that such an acquisition would be advantageous to either of those Sovereigns. He has however directed the Court of Petersburg to be sounded on the subject, and in the meantime I have H.M.'s orders to transmit to you the copy of a suggestion which has been made here on the subject of the restoration of the Order as the best means of placing the Island in the most beneficial situation for the interests of all the Allies."

Hamilton *to* Grenville.

Naples, Oct. 9, 1798.

State dinner to Nelson and the captains of the ten British men-of-war, on the 'Samnite,' commanded by Captain Carracciolo. General Mack expected at Caserta, whither the Royal Family had removed. "As there can be no doubt of the intention of the French army to plunder the rest of Italy as soon as they shall be in sufficient force, it is a mystery to us all why the Emperor and King of Naples, who have a sufficient force, do not profit of this most precious moment to drive these cruel robbers out of Italy. We hope the arrival of General Mack may clear up this mystery."

Same *to* Same.

Naples, Oct. 16, 1798.

Nelson has sailed for Malta; will return early in November. General Mack will march northward with 30,000 men before Oct. 31, "the Emperor having consented and even promised his powerful support. The glorious victory of August 1 seems to have inspired all with courage and confidence, and we now hope that this fine country may be saved. It is certain that the French Government has ordered an army of 60,000 men to act against this country. Their Sicilian Majesties have the utmost confidence in the brave Admiral; and the conferences we have had with General Acton have certainly decided this Government to the salutary determination of attacking rather than waiting to be attacked."

Eden *to* Grenville.

Oct. 27, 1798.

Report that four Russian columns would cross the Russian frontier *en route* for Constance, to enter Switzerland by the plain, while the Austrians entered by the mountains; they would together invade France.

Hamilton *to* Grenville.

Caserta, Nov. 6, 1798.

Mack now heads 30,000 troops ready to march. The French have only 26,000, including Poles, etc. "According to the late treaty between the Courts of Vienna and Naples, when Naples furnishes 30,000, the Emperor is to furnish 60,000."

EDEN *to* GRENVILLE.

Nov. 10, 1798.

News that Naples would occupy the Roman States, and (as this might lead to war with France) he had called on Austria to help in pursuance of the offensive and defensive treaty. "Thugut then said with much agitation that he had been ordered by the Emperor to declare that if Naples acted thus, she would be left to her own means, but would receive help if France attacked her." Eden earnestly deprecated abandoning Naples. As to Thugut's statement that France must be made to appear the aggressor, why not issue a declaration that it was her ambition and aggression that called the Powers to action? If Austria would do this, he [Eden] believed England would aid her. Thugut thought it a good plan but said he doubted Russia's constancy; he did not know now whether the Czar would let the Russians enter Switzerland.

[For Grenville's important despatch of Nov. 16, 1798, to Whitworth at Petersburg see Rose, *Napoleonic Studies*, pp. 54–61.]

SAME *to* SAME.

Nov. 28, 1798.

Thugut fears Prussia's conduct might hinder the despatch of Austrian troops into Switzerland. The Emperor will try to conciliate her. Eden said how easy it would be to arouse Italy, Switzerland, West Germany and Holland against their French oppressors. Thugut silent as to this, but deprecated the Czar's assumption of title of Grand Master of Malta [*sic*], as the Knights now in Russia could not legally depose the Grand Master, Hompesch, who had acted weakly but not treacherously and now wanted to head the Maltese rising. The Order should be re-established.

SAME *to* SAME.

Dec. 19, 1798.

Has urged Thugut to help Naples and Tuscany; but Thugut blames Naples for beginning the war and compromising fate of Sardinia; Austria not ready for war. Eden said France plotted to ruin Sardinia, conquer all Italy and finally Austria. H.I.M. might save Naples and all Europe: let Austria act with the energy of England, and success was almost certain.

SAME *to* SAME.

[Most secret.]   Dec. 22, 1798.

H.I.M. will not help Naples, having no confidence in her Government, which might make a separate peace. He said warmly that Naples "had allowed itself to be drawn into the measures it had adopted by England, who expected in this manner to force him into a war, in which the English Government, as they knew that he was without the means of carrying it on without them, would become in a certain degree the directors of his operations and of the conditions of peace." The Empress (by the Emperor's express injunction) refrained from speaking. Thugut afterwards said the same, setting aside the promises so often made. Eden ascribes to Thugut the distrust of England to which this change of front is due.

SAME *to* SAME.

Dec. 29, 1798.

Confusion of Austria's finances. She dare not trust England because "conscious of her own offensive and faithless conduct towards H.M." An Anglo-Austrian union is therefore very difficult. Jealousy of Prussia acute. Austria hides her weakness "under the veil of mystery and cunning." She may come to terms with France. She maintains in her territory 20,000 Russian troops sent at her earnest request to co-operate against France; yet refuses a union with England.

APPENDIX F

LETTERS OF LORD MULGRAVE TO PITT

From Pitt MSS. no. 152, P.R.O.

Speenhill, Jan. 5, 1806.

"I think I may congratulate you upon something like hopes of Prussia. The information from the Hague of the 17th of December has probably decided the engagement of Prussia for the security of the British troops, as Kalkreuth with the right of the Prussian army would not be in security against the French force assembling without the assistance of the British and Swedish troops, in addition to the Russians under Tolstoy[1]. Nothing seems more likely to decide the hostility of France against Prussia than a junction of British troops with those of Prussia. The only objection seems to be the locking up those troops for so long a period, if peace should be patched up between Prussia and France, but that inconvenience is nothing compared to the chance of stirring up something. I suppose you will make no difficulty about the additional subsidies desired by Russia or even the loan of the million. Lord G. Levison's [*sic*] despatches are satisfactory except with respect to the determination of Czartoriski and Novossiltzoff not to go to Berlin. You will decide whether Lord G. Levison will be most useful at Berlin or St Petersburg, probably at the latter if Harrowby comes away. You will observe that Czartoriski has already opened the subject of Greece and Egypt."

Fulham, Monday, Jan. 6, 1806.

"...However unwilling I am to press upon your time and attention at this moment I cannot avoid saying a few words to you on a subject which has occupied much of my thought since I received the despatches at Speenhill last night. I have so sincere and long-rooted a deference to your opinions that I am not disposed to press any ideas of mine very far, when you make any objection to them in the first instance; nor do I ever recur again to my own suggestions when they are unconnected with the depart-

---

[1] For an explanation of these circumstances see *ante*, pp. 345–7, also Rose, *Life of Pitt*, Part II. pp. 551–3. Mulgrave was then acting as Foreign Minister.

ment which you have assigned to me; but I confess that so much seems to me to hang upon the half disposition to action which Prussia is manifesting that I cannot refrain from again calling your attention to the subject of Holland. It is not now possible to look back to the old system of European politicks or to the former state of Europe itself, as to objects which can be restored or even approached by any new arrangements, after the state of things which has now arisen. A Republic of Holland, supported by its own resources, making head against the power, or even successfully evading the influence, of France, can never again exist without a second Revolution in the state of Europe, which the time of life and character of the existing Sovereigns, and the nature of the political maxims of their Cabinets, does not place within the reach of any period of rational political speculation. A strong sense of obvious and impending danger is not alone sufficient to determine the Prussian Government. The powerful means of a general Coalition has not been sufficient; an increase of territory has been its leading, and indeed only influencing object. Even for an exchange of Hanover the Court of Berlin would have been bound not to make peace without common consent. Holland, therefore, under present circumstances seems to me alone likely to purchase vigorous and immediate exertions on the part of Prussia, even for its own preservation. The Stadholder (besides his despicable character) is further disqualified by a voluntary compromise for his executive office in Holland, and by the ready acceptance of the sovereignty of Fulda, which might supply his enjoyments and supply his tranquillity. An honourable prejudice in favour of the House of Nassau being thus set aside, the question about Holland appears to rest on these broad grounds, which may be avowed without danger, and may be argued without the possibility of being disproved. Holland must become a province of France or of some other Power. Can it be placed in any other hands capable of defending it except Prussia? Is there any other acquisition which can by its value tempt Prussia to come into contact with France, and which by its frontier will enable that kingdom to keep the French force at bay, except Holland? As long as Prussia shall hold its connection with this country, the United Provinces in her hands will secure all the northern and eastern parts of Great Britain against the danger of invasion.... We must look to large objects and to extensive innovations if we are to meet the gigantick measures of Bonaparte (who will give Tyrol and East Austria and North Italy to his vassals)....No bribe seems to me too high for Prussia at this moment. With that Power it now remains to determine whether Bonaparte is to be Emperor of the Continent of Europe or not. The well-earned exception of Russia from that description of the state of the Continent will alone operate but little for the general peace of the world, or for the ultimate terms for this country, which sooner or later must come to be considered."

APPENDIX G

NEGOTIATIONS WITH SWEDEN AND RUSSIA
IN 1811–1812

F.O. Sweden, 70.

A. Despatches from Thornton *to* The Foreign Office.

H.M.S. Victory, Wingo Sound, Nov. 5, 1811.

Rendezvous at Amal is secretly arranged by the Swedish Minister, Count Rosen. Rosen "entered at once and with great earnestness into the favourite topic of the incorporation of Norway with Sweden." For this our naval co-operation was essential; but Sweden would also need money to help her maintain from 60,000 to 70,000 troops and 17,000 seamen (figures which Thornton doubts). Thornton asked him not to mention the proposal about Norway, on which Rosen had clearly been told to sound him. We must defer this topic until later, and we might test the sincerity of Sweden by proposing, first, the independence of Norway, which would guarantee Sweden's safety as much as its annexation.

Amal, Nov. 11, 1811.

At Amal Thornton saw M. Netzel (formerly Swedish *chargé d'affaires* at Hamburg) who acknowledged the noble conduct of Great Britain in this overture. The Prince Royal wished to preserve the present relations with Great Britain and France; *i.e.* to *appear* to be the Ally of France but undertake no hostility against England (though France might press for it) and to join England rather than yield to the French demand. Sweden had resisted Napoleon's demand last summer to allow French troops in small numbers to pass through Sweden into Norway for the invasion of Scotland. Denmark had allowed this (through Zealand). Sweden would rather fight France than accede to this demand.

The Prince Royal would not take up the annexation of Norway now because it would expose him to hostilities both from France and Denmark and possibly from Russia too.

Thornton then opened the main topic of his mission and pointed out that a change of system was now needed, not as a threat to Sweden but because of "the intolerable burden which the System itself imposed upon Great Britain." He also referred to the probability of a League of the North, which Great Britain would help.

[Private.]   Amal, Nov. 11, 1811.

He thinks Sweden will not take up this proposal seriously till she has sounded Russia, as she may do by a private overture to Romanzoff. Sweden would be in a difficult position if a Treaty with England exposed her to attacks both from Russia and Denmark. Russia resists some of

Bonaparte's demands. He suggests sending a British envoy to St Petersburg as it may be that Russia only needs encouraging in order to resist Britain more firmly.

Amal, Nov. 20, 1811.

Sudden ending by Sweden of this negotiation, which had opened well. Netzel would not state in writing the reasons. Thornton thinks his own conduct has been quite correct. The Swedish Government stated that he was not furnished with clear and precise enough instruction as to terms of peace.

[Secret and confidential.]   Amal, Nov. 20, 1811.

The Prince Royal had been mortified by the announcement of a change of system by Great Britain which he took as a threat (needlessly, as Thornton thinks). France had threatened Sweden and the Prince would resist threats from both sides. Thornton pointed out that this end to the negotiation would cause a bad impression in England and said no threats had been suggested or intended.

[Private.]   H.M.S. Victory, Wingo Sound, Nov. 25, 1811.

He believes the failure due to Engeström alone, and to his misrepresentations: he is under French influence. Nothing can be done now, or in future, except by direct communication with the Crown Prince himself[1].

From F.O. Sweden, 71.

B. Despatches from Castlereagh to Thornton in 1812.

March 13.

He refers to a Swedish overture for peace and a request that a negotiator be sent to Sweden. This change is due to the French invasion of Swedish Pomerania. Sweden does not consider herself yet at war with France; but negotiations with England must be secret. Sweden proposes (1) peace, (2) alliance with us. To (1) we agree, especially as the war with Sweden has been nominal rather than real. We do not wish her to declare war on Napoleon if she desires to avoid it. But if he attacks her, we will defend her by sea. Thornton is to go to Stockholm if possible. If Sweden should decline all further negotiation, he is to return at once to England and declare that no further negotiation can take place except in London by a duly accredited Swedish Minister.

If Sweden wants merely a treaty restoring peace and amity, he [Thornton] may sign such a treaty (draft of which is enclosed); but a system of *concert* may be framed thereafter. Sweden now proposes (1) Protection by our fleet. (2) Transfer of a West India isle to her. (3) Military and financial succour. (4) Territorial extension, especially on the side of Norway.

---

[1] An unsigned letter, dated Stockholm, Jan. 19, 1812, expresses regret that the British Government had not understood the absolute necessity of giving Norway to Sweden, which may otherwise become a Russian or pseudo-French province: 65 Swedish officers and some 3000 seamen had gone to equip and man Napoleon's Scheldt and Brest fleets. The Danes assisted in this owing to their hate of England.

(1) We agree to, and will agree to prevent any invasion of Sweden either directly or through Norway. But she must understand the burden this imposes. (2) is reserved for discussion as to details: but such an island must not be alienated by Sweden without our consent. (3) Great Britain cannot at once accede to, as she throws all her weight into the Peninsular War, which greatly assists the efforts of North Europe for independence. As we must give all our resources to Spain, we cannot subsidize Sweden. But we will send military clothing as far as possible. (4) As Sweden is not yet at war either with France or Denmark, she cannot expect us to frame precise engagements on this head. But if she will act vigorously against France, we will seek to strengthen her. It is natural that she seek an indemnity for loss of Finland and Swedish Pomerania; but not while she is at peace with Denmark and France. Let Sweden therefore open herself clearly on this question. We will at least seek to prevent Danish or French troops being sent into Norway. There shall also be mutual restitution of ships seized.

[Secret and separate.]   March 13.

Thornton will at once see at Stockholm M. Nicolai, Russian *chargé d'affaires*, and state that Mr Liston will go as ambassador to Constantinople to seek to arrange peace between Russia and Turkey, and he will receive suggestions from Russia to this end. England can never see with indifference Russian interests threatened by France.

[Secret and separate.]   March 13.

Thornton will seek a personal interview with the Prince Royal, whose influence is so great in the Swedish Government: but a certain reserve must be maintained by us towards him, until his position is entirely established. His views are to be found out and transmitted minutely to H.M.'s Government.

                                                                      March 25.

Our fleet will prevent landing of French and Danish troops in Norway: also despatch of Danish flotilla.

When Sweden and Russia have more fully concerted their arrangements, we will send an officer to discuss the operations to be carried on against the enemy.

                                                                      March 27.

So soon as peace is restored with Sweden the Orders in Council of January 1807 will be revoked (for Sweden), and our blockade under the Orders of April 1809 will not extend to the Baltic ports. Thus Sweden will become the depôt of British trade with other Baltic ports, and we will encourage this.

                                                                      March 27.

"In the *Projet d'opérations* suggested in M. d'Engeström's letter of 12th inst. it is proposed that measures should be adopted to induce Denmark to join the confederation against France and that in exchange for Norway (to be ceded to Sweden) an extension of territory should be granted to Denmark on the side of Germany." The Prince Regent wishes it understood that no thought must be entertained of indemnifying Denmark from his Electoral dominions.

April 14.

Nicolai has been charged to sound Denmark as to a concert against France on the plan of ceding Norway to Sweden and undertaking a diversion against the rear of the French army in North Germany. This may offend Denmark and may imply conquest of Norway and Zealand, which will require all the year, besides attaching Denmark to France. Why not offer to Denmark Swedish Pomerania and German land in exchange for Norway? If she rejects really good offers it is clear she is welded closely to France. Thornton is to suggest this plan to Sweden.

April 24.

Proposal from Paris of an offer of peace to Great Britain if she will recognize Joseph as King of Spain. The Prince Regent resolutely declined an offer incompatible with his honour. This to be communicated to the Prince Royal.

May 7.

Regrets that Sweden makes the restoration of peace depend on a Treaty of Concert to be framed between Great Britain, Sweden and Russia. This would look as if we were obliged to purchase peace from Sweden. We declined and still decline to mix the question of Concert with that of Peace, especially since Russia has "become a party to discussions which opens [sic] a much more extensive view of the interests to be provided for than whilst the deliberations were confined to Great Britain and Sweden." We know nothing about Russia's views except through the confidential communication made to you by the Swedish Minister as to the Russo-Swedish treaty signed on the (blank) at Stockholm. We must first know more about the views of Russia, and what will happen if she compromises with France, and how that would affect Sweden.

The Swedish request for a subsidy of £1,200,000 is inadmissible, owing to our efforts elsewhere. Respecting Sweden's claims to Norway our first wish is to see Denmark leave France and join us on the plan proposed on April 14. But if Denmark adheres to France then we will aid Sweden against Danish territory and will dispose of the conquests as may be reasonable, especially respecting Norway. The Norwegian deputation now expected in England may furnish an opportunity of pointing out the advantages of a union with Sweden than (sic) by a Swedish conquest.

[Secret.]   May 8.   .

His despatches (Nos. 13–16)[1] just received. The Treaty signed at St Petersburg has been delivered by M. Rehausen. Yet these facts do not influence greatly the considerations stated yesterday; for Russia has not yet shown any disposition to treat for peace with Great Britain. But the Tsar's firmness and his treaty with Sweden are hailed with satisfaction.

[1] Thornton's first despatches from Carlslund. For the Russo-Swedish treaties of April 5, 8, 1812, see Koch and Schöll, III. 234.

We will at the proper moment be cordially disposed to unite with the Powers of the North for the general safety.

May 22.

Has received Nos. 17-24 from Thornton and commends his industry and zeal; also his offer to General van Suchtelen[1] to acquire and produce full powers from both States for a Peace between Great Britain and Russia. These are sent to Thornton consonant with the *Projet* he has forwarded home, which was agreed on with the General.

A British ambassador will be sent to St Petersburg. If the General signs such a treaty of peace with us, will not Sweden do the same? Perhaps the General will use his good offices to this effect.

June 7.

Regrets that Sweden still declines to sign a Peace with Great Britain "without clogging that pledge of returning amity with ulterior conditions which would change the character of the measure." But Thornton's letters of May 20 and 21 open up the prospect of Sweden being ready to join us independently of her connexions with Russia, "considering herself strong enough with the assistance of Great Britain and the acquisition of Norway, to resist the continental Powers, Russia included."

This proposal, if persevered in, will deserve serious consideration.

July 3.

"From the delays which are still interposed both by Sweden and Russia I much fear no peace between Great Britain and either of those Courts will be signed till hostilities shall have actually commenced between them and France. Sweden obviously shapes her conduct to the policy of Russia with whom she has recently connected herself; the latter has shewn so much indecision as to make the result as yet uncertain.... You hint that the Prince Royal feels some apprehension of not being fully supported by Great Britain in case of Russia yielding to France." Thornton may assure Sweden that, if she makes peace with Great Britain and adheres to her engagements, she may securely rely upon the utmost exertions of this country...."You will explain to him in the strongest terms the irresistible force of an appeal to British feelings when Great Britain is called upon to succour an Ally for adhering firmly to her cause against the efforts of a powerful and vindictive enemy, of which her conduct to Portugal and Spain are such conspicuous examples. You may further acquaint both the Swedish and Russian Ministers that Lord Cathcart hold himself in readiness to proceed to his destination so soon as the policy of the Northern Courts shall be decisively disclosed."

July 18.

Has received his notes 43-50. Sweden's request for a subsidy of £1,000,000 is declined. He regrets the delays to sign peace: unless she does Thornton must return. The claims of Spain are pressing and must be preferred to those of Sweden, which concern measures of aggrandisement. Until Sweden brings her troops into contact with the French, she

---

[1] Russian plenipotentiary, recently arrived at Stockholm.

cannot claim the same support as those of Spain. But if she will sign the peace, we will, in case of a proper military concert being made, offer her stores equal in value to £500,000. He approves the reported move of Sweden against Zealand rather than Norway; for it will act as a diversion for Russia and commit Sweden to continental operations: but better still would be a Russo-Swedish expedition to the south of the Baltic in the French rear. If this is impossible, then attack Zealand. Admiral Saumarez will be instructed to help.

July 18.

Cathcart will set out to St Petersburg at end of next week and will touch at Sweden [*sic*] so as to learn the situation there. Hopes that Russia will by then have made peace with us.

Aug. 4.

On July 31 received the treaties of peace signed by Thornton at Örebrö on July 18 with Russia and Sweden[1].

[Most secret.]   Oct. 10.

Great Britain wishes to give Sweden an island that will encourage her and induce her to resist the anti-commercial system of France. Sweden's desire for St Lucia has been changed to Guadeloupe, an isle of much greater wealth. "Naval considerations alone induce a reluctance with respect to St Lucia. These can be but of secondary importance to Sweden, whilst the great produce of Guadeloupe may be expected materially to improve the Swedish resources." It must not be alienated without our consent, nor shall it be used by enemy privateers.

Oct. 10.

Regret that Sweden will not make a treaty with Spain, which hinders formation of a confederacy against France.

Oct. 10.

(As Sweden no longer claims the stipulated services of 18,000 Russian troops, assembled in Finland, who are now gone to Riga to strengthen the Russian right) we will sanction the grant of £500,000 to her, but the additional aid offered by Cathcart cannot now be granted. Sweden wants us to acquiesce in her attack on Norway. We acquiesce reluctantly. But first an application must be made to Denmark according to Art. 8 of Treaty of Wilna. We will also accede to the Russo-Swedish Treaty (with a few reservations) so as to frame a confederacy for the continent.

Oct. 10.

Thornton will press that the Swedish annexation of Norway "will be conducted upon principles of the utmost indulgence and liberality to the feelings, interests, and privileges of those whom it is desired, with a view of securing Sweden against the common enemy, to bring under allegiance of H.S.M. The sentiments recently expressed by the Prince Royal in his letter to the Prince Regent on this subject, afforded H.R.H. the utmost satisfaction. You will represent that it is in a confident reliance upon these

[1] See Koch and Schöll. III. 235.

assurances, and under an expectation that the conciliatory system of Sweden will be announced at the very outset of operations to the Norwegians, that H.R.H. has been induced to consent to be a party to this attempt which Sweden has urged with such earnestness as essential to her national security. You will press this object with the utmost solicitude."

(From F.O. Sweden, 72)

C. Despatches from Thornton *to* Castlereagh in 1812.

[Most secret.]   Carlslund, near Örebrö, April 16.

On the day after his arrival he submitted draft of his treaty to the Swedish plenipotentiaries Baron d'Engeström and Baron de Wotterstedt in two distinct conferences. Engeström said that Russia only waited to see Sweden conclude peace with us, to conclude likewise. Thornton replied that he believed Russia would gladly see the Anglo-Swedish Peace. The three met again yesterday when Engeström showed a draft of the Swedish Russian treaty of April 8 from which Thornton (notes are enclosed) made notes. Sweden now demands of us double the subsidy offered by us in 1808,—viz. £1,200,000.

[Separate. Secret and confidential.]   *Ibid.* May 3. Received May 17.

After describing the means by which he obtained an interview with the Prince Royal, he continues: "He [the Prince Royal] immediately turned the conversation to politics....He began with France. He said that they had just received new overtures from the [French] Emperor, [verbal overtures] and that the Swedish Government would reply to them verbally. They had always, he said, observed the precaution to reply to such propositions in the way in which they were made; that it was a common stratagem of Napoleon to throw out verbally different propositions and to reduce the Governments to whom they were made to give replies in writing, which engaged *them*, while *he* in fact was left free by the disavowal of his verbal overtures. France, he said, was now willing to acquiesce in the perfect neutrality of Sweden, provided she would engage not to take part in the approaching war with Russia; she would in that case oblige Russia to restore Finland to Sweden, although (said the Prince) if I would agree, to behave well, *si je veux me bien conduire*, Napoleon would do much more. He would transfer the Royal Family of Sweden to St Petersburg making for them a Kingdom out of Finland, Petersburg, Esthonia, Livonia and Courland, in fact the two entire shores of the Gulph of Finland, and he would have no objection to extend it to the North so as to include Archangel. And then, said the Prince, I should be the vassal of France; and he is the man soon to avenge himself of the affront which he thinks he has sustained from me.

"I asked the Prince what was the intention, then, of France with regard to Sweden. He said it was certainly the intention of Bonaparte to put an end to it as a monarchy; that his system was, and always had been, by division, by exchanges and cessions, to obliterate every trace of the ancient system of Europe, and particularly of the independence of every

38—2

State; and, as Sweden had tried to assert her independence, and was in fact by her position and by a connection with England more capable of maintaining it than almost any other Power in Europe, he was determined that this example should not be given by Sweden. He [Napoleon] intended to make a Grand Duchy, perhaps by the title of Sweden, or rather by that of Gothland (*Grand Duché de la Gothie*), the seat of which should be at Stockholm, and which should be composed of five or six provinces: other provinces might compose a second Grand Duchy, or, being annexed to Norway, might form an establishment for the House of Denmark, whom it was unquestionably the intention of Bonaparte to dispossess of the German Provinces to the Skaw, and of the Islands nearest to that coast of the Baltic.

"With regard to the projects of Bonaparte for the present campaign, the Prince said that he had unquestionably good information from his personal friends (of whom he possessed many even near the person of Bonaparte) that Napoleon's intention and his expectation were to force the Emperor Alexander by one or two battles to a new peace and to a cession of several provinces, among others for the purpose of re-establishing the King of Poland (which, I understood the Prince, was designed for Jerome Bonaparte) and for making up that kingdom of which St Petersburg was to be the capital. The seat of the Russian Government was to be again fixed at Moscow; and that then, carrying 100,000 Russians along with him as auxiliary troops, he would proceed towards Turkey and establish the French Empire at Constantinople. The Prince Royal observed that he might not push his projects farther than this point for a year or two after he had attained it; but that he had assuredly not in the least degree abandoned the idea of possessing Egypt and of conquering India."

The Prince added that the French were requisitioning for this campaign vast numbers of artisans and quantities of seeds as if for founding colonies or acquiring new countries. He then referred to the signs of vacillation at St Petersburg, due largely to the timid counsels of Romanzoff. Thornton thereupon stated that the last proposal from that quarter did not seem to promise an amicable arrangement with Great Britain; and he begged the Prince, who had great influence with the Emperor, to correspond directly with him. The Prince had urged him to make peace with the Turks; and he [the Prince] requested me to inform Your Lordship that the Emperor had given "instructions to make peace at all events with the Porte, and on any concession of his pretensions, provided only that they would enter into the alliance with England, Russia and Sweden."

Respecting the British proposal to Denmark on the subject of Norway, the Prince said that it "had given him a good deal of pain; for that, circumstanced as he was with regard to this country, and circumstanced as the country was with relation to Norway, it was impossible for him to move for the common Cause, or to induce the country to move without the preliminary possession of that Kingdom. It would at once redeem the debt he had contracted towards Sweden by insisting upon the eternal abandonment of Finland, and it would furnish an inducement to enter into the Continental War, not less than a security against surprise on that side, while they were so engaged. On this topic the Prince entered a good deal into the arguments for this measure, such as I have stated them to Your Lordship on another occasion." The Prince then said that his disappointment at the British refusal of necessary succours would not cause him to relax his efforts for the common cause. With respect to the projected operations against the Island of Zealand, the Prince said "that if H.M.'s Government chose to keep possession of it with a garrison at Copenhagen, and in fact to become the Suzerain, Sweden would not have the smallest difficulty in acknowledging and consenting to it. If, however, the expense of keeping it were thought too great, and if the idea were adopted of razing the fortifications and leaving the island as a *Place ouverte*, it was of no great moment who possessed it; he did not, however, see any necessity for putting it into the hands of Russia. In this I ventured most decidedly to acquiesce in opinion with the Prince, observing that I saw no occasion for bringing Russia in any manner to this end of the Baltic...."

Ibid. May 6.

He reports the arrival of a Russian despatch brought to Stockholm by Baron de Nicolai, who had just returned. In it Romanzoff (doubtless at the suggestion of the Emperor), urged the sending of the Marquis Wellesley as ambassador to St Petersburg, for which the Emperor had stated in writing his great desire.

[Secret and confidential.]   *Ibid.* May 15.

M. Signeul had come from Paris with verbal offers to the Swedish Government. If it will join in the war against Russia it shall receive Finland (to be acquired by Swedish troops), recover Swedish Pomerania together with Stettin and the district as far as Wolgast, also Mecklenburgh, also 6,000,000 livres as *mise en campagne* and 1,000,000 livres per month during the war. Also the Prince Royal shall receive back his appanage (Ponte Corvo). H.S.M. repelled these offers as dishonourable; and the Prince Royal replied that whatever he had done he had done for France, not for Bonaparte; and it was out of Bonaparte's power to offer him a proper recompense; that from the moment of being called to succeed to the Swedish throne he relinquished everything which depended on the will of a foreign Power.

Ibid. May 20.

The Prince Royal seemed to wish to conclude peace with England when Russia did. Thornton asked him to request the Russian Government to send full powers for that purpose. The Prince said that Russia, having been the aggressor, owed it to England to make a simple peace, preliminary to any other arrangement.

Ibid. May 30.

Thornton describes the alleged negotiations at Paris up to May 11 between Kurakin and Duc de Bassano *before* the former left Paris on May 9. He thinks they do not impeach the good faith of the Emperor Alexander;

but Romanzoff had culpably suppressed news of them towards Sweden, with whom Russia had just framed a close alliance, and towards England "to whom the Court of Russia had made an overture of alliance six days before orders were despatched to M. de Kurakin to deliver the Note which is the subject of this despatch." On May 6, Kurakin presented a memorial so as to elicit a precise answer from the French Government and stated that the departure of M. Lauriston from St Petersburg would be regarded as a declaration of war, in which case he [Kurakin] would also demand his passports. Nevertheless Bonaparte gave no answer and left for Dresden, leaving Kurakin in uncertainty.

[Separate. Secret and confidential.] *Ibid.* May 31.

The Prince Royal confidentially urged him to warn Admiral Saumarez that a Swedish squadron of eight sail-of-line and five frigates would leave Carlscrona and cruise off Rügen and Pomerania and begs him to warn Saumarez so that there may be no collision. Thornton views this act as implying great confidence in Great Britain, with whom Sweden is still nominally at war.

[Private and separate.] *Ibid.* June 6.

In pursuance of Castlereagh's despatch of May 22 he requested a private interview with Prince Royal, who was very pleased with it. But he distrusted the Russian Minister exceedingly, especially Romanzoff's recent offer to France to continue all the measures of the Continental System (which were annulled by the recent Russo-Swedish alliance). Prince Royal thought that Bonaparte would attack the Russian centre, occupy Vilna, and then fall on the Russian coast. He hopes to begin the war in July.

[Secret.] *Ibid.* June 24.

A Russian messenger had just arrived with dispatches for General van Suchtelen, with full powers to conclude peace with England. But instead of signing a peace *pur et simple*, as agreed, Romanzoff now sent a treaty burdened with conditions, *e.g.* that Great Britain assume the Dutch debt, and shall have previously signed a treaty with Sweden both of peace *and for subsidies* (a condition which Sweden had waived!). Thornton was indignant and said such a treaty would never be agreed to: thus a fresh delay, of three weeks, is incurred, which is according to Romanzoff's desire to postpone action.

Ibid. June 24.

Engeström assured Thornton that he had never urged the Russian Government to annex those conditions to a peace with England and Sweden. Thornton begged an interview with the Prince Royal and had to-day seen him; *for affairs now depend on him.* He pressed him to urge the Russian Government to give up those conditions: and the Prince proved by letters that he had done all he could in that direction. The Emperor of Russia had said he expected war with France almost at once for the *French were on his frontier*. The Prince Royal then urged the extreme importance of receiving some help from England, *e.g.* £1,000 000 for one year, paid monthly. Thornton said this would never be entertained as part of the Treaty of Peace with England, but might possibly be afterwards. The Prince assented to this form. Sweden could not go on arming if a Treaty of Peace with England were made, without further stipulations which would satisfy the Diet respecting Norway.

Ibid. July 4.

News that the French crossed the Niemen and so began the war without cause alleged. The *casus foederis* now arises for Sweden and Russia and Suchtelen is ordered to place himself under the orders of the Prince Royal so as to arrange the "attack on Island of Zealand and the consequent annexation of Norway to the Swedish Crown, the preliminary measure to the active co-operation of Sweden on the Continent." Thornton asks for guidance, especially as to the action of the British fleet in Baltic. The Archangel squadron will probably come to the Baltic and should be treated by Saumarez with the utmost forbearance.

Ibid. July 18.

He has now signed the two treaties of peace with Sweden and Russia, and will at once inform Saumarez. The Swedish and Russian plenipotentiaries then communicated the Russo-Swedish Treaty of Alliance, offensive and defensive, of April 1812, with the separate and secret articles, and (on the wish of the Prince Royal) urged Thornton to send it to England to invite the British Government to accede to it. He agreed, suggesting a change of procedure. One of the articles of the Russo-Swedish Treaty ran: In case of war taking place, H.M. the Emperor of all the Russias, and H.M. the King of Sweden will invite by common consent the King of the United Kingdom to accede as a *partie intégrante* to this Treaty of Alliance, offensive and defensive, and to guarantee its different stipulations.

Ibid. July 30.

Sweden and Russia had decided that, when matters were duly arranged, joint invitations should be sent to Denmark for her accession to the Alliance, in which case she should acquire an indemnity.

[For further despatches of Thornton to Castlereagh see *Castlereagh Mems.*, vol. VIII. pp. 283 *et seq.*]

APPENDIX H

EXTRACTS FROM STRATFORD CANNING'S DESPATCHES FROM CONSTANTINOPLE, 1812[1]

Feb. 21.

"...As soon as the deliberations of the Grand Council [at Constantinople] were closed I sent...to tell the Reis Effendi that I trusted every effort consistent with the dignity, and every concession not incompatible

---

[1] These are supplementary to those printed in S. Lane-Poole's *Life of Stratford Canning*, vol. I. ch. 4. For affairs at Constantinople see *ante*, pp. 386–90.

with the safety, of the Empire would be made for the restoration of peace at the present crisis, and that in order to give a striking proof of H.M.'s sincere regard for the Porte I was ready to lend every assistance in my power towards the accomplishment of so desirable an object; in short that I would write to Russia in compliance with the wishes of the Porte. The Reis Effendi expressed the highest satisfaction at this and requested that I would do so without loss of time."

March 11.

French efforts to court the Turks. Ill effects of the long silence of H.M.'s Government to the Porte.

March 17.

Full powers given to the Grand Vizier to make peace with Russia on the best terms that can be obtained. Probably due to fear of reconciliation between France and Russia.

April 12.

Constant but fruitless intrigues of French; but at last a conference is arranged. Their disclosure of treaty between Austria and France shows lengths they are prepared to go. Mission from Sweden has a good effect. He has used the disclosure of Austrian plan against Turkey with effect.

April 21.

Communication of the treaty between Austria and France, with offer of help against Russia. Fear of peace not being made before the war in the North begins. The French are making every possible exertion.

April 25.

Strictures on the shameful part played by Austria. The Turks fear that peace with Russia may involve them in war with France.

May 5.

General Andréossi on the way as ambassador of France to Porte. His departure concealed even from the Turkish *chargé d'affaires* at Paris.

CANNING *to* ITALINSKY [at Bukharest].

June 5.

About Persia. Importance of peace between Russia and Porte. Two difficulties, (1) the alliance proposed with Russia, (2) the demand for certain establishments at the mouth of the Phase, with communication with the Russian army in Georgia. Repugnance of Porte to the first. Trusts this may not prove a reason for refusing to sign the treaty. (3) The system of the Cabinet of Russia since four years has sown the greatest mistrust everywhere, and nowhere more than here.' "Cette méfiance diminue à mesure qu'on s'écarte de la connection sinistre qui a servi de base au système auquel je fais allusion. Pour la déraciner entièrement, la Russie doit d'abord prouver par sa conduite que ce système a déjà cessé d'exister. Elle a fait vers cet objet un pas très considérable par la modification généreuse de ses premières prétensions. Mais pour y atteindre tout à fait il faut porter encore plus loin la générosité.... Jamais la Porte ne se fiera cordialement à la loyauté de la Russie tant que celle-ci insiste sur une condition dont le but, dans son opinion, ne peut être que de faire du mal à la Perse."

SAME *to* SAME.

June 7.

Thanks for receiving Gordon[1].

· ITALINSKY *to* CANNING.

May 19, N.S.

On his arrival and state of the negotiations. Ready to correspond with him. Need for swift action to counteract the seductions of France.

GORDON *to* CANNING.

[Bukharest], June 12.

Journey to Bukharest. Arrived 9 May and was conducted to Italinsky. Gave him the two letters. "His first observation was that the information with respect to the measures of the Court of Vienna was very important, as he believed that at the moment the Austrian Cabinet held with that of Russia a quite different language. This information, I have good reason to believe, he had already received from another quarter, to which, however, he did not perhaps attach much credit.

"He remarked that he believed the Emperor of Austria to be personally averse to such measures, but that his Minister[2] was very much a Frenchman.... I endeavoured to impress him with an idea that the Turks were making formidable preparations, but he cut me short by answering that, let them make what preparations they would, this could not be formidable to the Russians, and that the only disadvantageous circumstance attending the war with them was that a body of troops was kept in the provinces which might undoubtedly be of much more use elsewhere. Nothing more took place at the time except that he expressed his gratitude to you for the information.

"On the same day I had audience of the Commander-in-Chief, General Kutusoff. He only asked one question: Whether I thought the Porte was more disposed to connect itself with France than to be on terms of friendship with England and Russia. I replied that I thought the true interest of the Turks was to preserve a strict neutrality; but I did not think they were disposed to purchase peace by any considerable concessions.... The General apologised for not seeing me more at his table, but the French consul was very suspicious and had remonstrated on my arrival. I saw Italinsky almost every one of the seven days of my stay. At first he said Russia was very moderate and could not become more so. Her present demands were lower by one half than those she had at first insisted on, and the Court was surprised at having moderation still recommended to it. He showed me a letter of Count Romanzoff expressing the hope for

---

[1] S. Canning despatched to Bukharest a Scottish traveller, Mr Gordon, to warn the Russian plenipotentiary, Italinsky, of a proposal for a joint Austro-Franco-Turkish attack on Russia (S. Lane-Poole, 1. 169).

[2] Metternich.

cordial relations with the Court of St James, and approving of the correspondence with you, charging him to cultivate and continue it. At first he said that the articles most obnoxious to the Porte had been dropped. Later he expressed chagrin at the negotiations being so much protracted, but he hoped for a favourable conclusion. He complained of the obstruction of the Turks. In the end they would pay very dear for the delay. By this I understood him to mean they would become the victims of French success."

On the eve of my departure he communicated to me, for your information, the state of the negotiations. In Europe the line of the Pruth as boundary. Difficulties about the fort of Ismail, but this rather a point of honour; not essential. Russians abandon all claim for contribution in money. Russians concede all conquests in Asia. Commissioners to decide about province of Imeritia. Desire for connection with Georgia from Black Sea, to avoid Caucasus. He said it would be impolitic of the Turks to drive the Servians to despair, as they were a warlike nation and, if reduced to extremity, would certainly throw themselves into the arms of Austria. Not Russian intrigues but Turkish oppression caused revolts. The Russians could not make concessions about Moldavia and Wallachia without loss of honour. The Russian Government will not connect the affairs of the Turks and Persians or include the latter in this treaty.

"Italinsky concluded by pressing me, as he had frequently done before, earnestly to entreat you to accelerate by your good offices the successful issue of the Congress; in particular to mollify the Porte on the disputed point of Ismail, which seemed to be the principal difficulty; and it was plain from his conversation that he considered you as united in a common cause. He at the same time gave me positive assurances that the Russians, so far from having the design to destroy the Ottoman Empire, were rather anxious for its preservation, being well assured that it was impossible for them to have more quiet or less formidable neighbours. He commended Ghalib Effendi, but said the Grand Vizier was obstructing, from enmity to Ghalib.

"He appeared anxious to impress on my mind that the principal reason for the Russians wishing for peace was that they might be enabled to turn the services of their army in the Provinces (consisting of at least 22,000 good troops) to a quarter where they would be of great utility. He added that the Austrians had given an intimation that, were the peace once concluded, they might perhaps be enabled to preserve their neutrality. Some conversation also about Persia. Italinsky asked me if I thought peace with Persia could be easily brought about. I said, No. War had advantages for the Persians and the Russian's demands were high. He answered that his Court wished sincerely for peace in that quarter.

"I tried to elicit information about the relations between France and Russia, but he did not seem desirous of explaining himself fully. Russia would not consent to observe Bonaparte's Continental System, as war with England was not only ruinous to its finances, but also, when carried on at the command of France, degrading to its dignity."

BIBLIOGRAPHIES

I. INTRODUCTION

UNDER this head, no attempt has been made to accompany the Introductory Sketch of British Foreign Policy before 1783 with a consecutive list of historical works illustrating its course. For these, including both contemporary and secondary authorities, the reader is referred to the bibliographies of Chapters dealing with the Foreign Policy of England or Great Britain in the *Cambridge Medieval* and *Modern History* and in Lavisse and Rambaud's *Histoire Générale*. The present Bibliography contains only the names of works which have been used in the composition of the Introductory Chapter to this work, or which bear directly upon events and transactions specially noticed in it, or on their connexion with general features or points to which it refers in summarising the earlier course of our foreign policy. For a list designed to include references to all important bodies of material for the diplomatic history of England, from 1509 to 1783, referred to in the *Reports of the Historical Manuscripts Commission,* and in the *Catalogue of the Manuscripts at the British Museum,* see *Appendix II* to *Eighteenth Report of the Royal Commission on Historical Manuscripts,* by Miss Frances Davenport, presented to Parliament 1917.

Annual Register, the, 1758–83. Index, 1758–1819.

Armstrong, Edward. Elizabeth Farnese, 'The Termagant of Spain.' 1892.

—— The Emperor Charles V. 2 vols. 1902.

Arneth, Alfred Ritter von. Geschichte Maria-Theresias. 10 vols. Vienna, 1863–1879. [Vols. IV to VI: 1748–1763.]

Ballantyne, A. Lord Carteret, a political biography, 1690–1763. 1887.

Bedford, John, Fourth Duke of, Correspondence of. With an Introduction by Lord John Russell. 3 vols. 1842–1846.

Blok, P. J. History of the People of the Netherlands. Tr. by O. A. Bierstadt and R. Putnam. 5 vols. New York, 1898–1912. [Vols. I–II, to 1559; III, to 1621; IV, to William III; V, 18th and 19th centuries.]

Bourgeois, Émile. La Diplomatie Secrète au 18me Siècle. Paris, n.d. [The Regent Orleans, Alberoni, and Dubois: 1716–1723.]

—— Manuel Historique de Politique Étrangère. 2nd edn. Vol. I. Paris, 1897. Les Origines. [From Richelieu to 1789; esp. Chap. V: L'Angleterre au dix-septième siècle, and Chap. XI: La fondation de l'empire Anglais au dix-huitième siècle.]

Brewer, John Sherren. The Reign of Henry VIII to the death of Wolsey. Ed. J. Gairdner. 2 vols. 1884.

Broglie, J. V. Albert, Duc de. La Paix d'Aix-la-Chapelle. Paris, 1895.

—— L'Alliance Autrichienne. Paris, 1895. These two works form part of Histoire de la politique extérieure de Louis XV, 1741–1756. 10 vols. Paris, 1883–1889.

Brosch, M. Geschichte von England. Vols. vi-x. (Gesch. der europ. Staaten.) Gotha, 1892-1897. [From 1509.]

Burrows, Montagu. History of the Foreign Policy of Great Britain. Edinburgh, 1895.

Busch, W. Drei Jahre englischer Vermittlungspolitik, 1518-1521. Bonn, 1884.

—— Wolsey und die englisch-kaiserliche Allianz, 1522-1525. Bonn, 1886.

Cecil, Algernon. The Life of Robert Cecil, First Earl of Salisbury. 1915.

Chance, J. F. George I and the Northern War. A Study of British-Hanoverian Policy in the North of Europe in the years 1709 to 1721. 1909. [Indispensable for this subject.]

Clément, P. Histoire de la Vie et de l'Administration de Colbert. Paris, 1846. [Esp. Chap. xv: Commercial relations with England, 1655-1677.]

Corbett, Sir Julian Stafford. Drake and the Tudor Navy; with History of the Rise of England as a Maritime Power. 2 vols. 1898.

—— England in the Mediterranean: British power within the Straits, 1603-1713. 2 vols. 1904.

—— England in the Seven Years' War. 2 vols. 1907.

Coxe, William. Memoirs of the Life of Sir Robert Walpole (Earl of Orford). New edn. 4 vols. 1816.

Diplomatic Relations of England with France and Germany. Edited by C. H. Firth. Lists of Ambassadors from England to France, and from France to England, 1603-1688. Compiled by C. H. Firth and S. C. Lomas. Oxford, 1906. List of Diplomatic Representatives and Agents, England and North Germany, 1689-1727. Contributed by J. F. Chance. Oxford, 1907. List of Diplomatic Representatives and Agents, 1689-1763. Contributed by L. G. Wickham Legg. Oxford, 1909.

Droysen, J. G. Geschichte der preussischen Politik. 5 parts in 14 vols. Part v, Friedrich der Grosse. Berlin, 1855-1886. 2nd edn. Vols. i-iv. Berlin, 1868-1872.

Dupuis, Charles. Le Principe d'Équilibre et le Concert Européen de la Paix de Westphalie à l'Acte d'Algéciras. Paris, 1909.

Egerton, Hugh Edward. A Short History of British Colonial Policy, 1569-1713. 1897.

—— British Foreign Policy in Europe to the end of the 19th century. 1917. [Of this outline Chaps. ii and iii deal with the period 1570-1789.]

England, History of. Vols. iv-vi. Edited by C. W. C. Oman. 1905-1911.
    Vol. iv. England under the Tudors. By A. D. Innes.
    Vol. v. England under the Stuarts. By G. M. Trevelyan.
    Vol. vi. England under the Hanoverians. By C. Grant Robertson.
    [Contain useful bibliographies.]

Firth, Charles Harding. The Last Years of the Protectorate, 1656-1658. 2 vols. 1909.

—— The Study of British Foreign Policy. Quarterly Review, October 1916. [England's traditional foreign policy.]

Gaedeke, A. Die Politik Oesterreichs in der Spanischen Erbfolgefrage. 2 vols. Leipzig, 1877.

Gardiner, Samuel Rawson. History of England from the Accession of James I to the outbreak of the Civil War. 10 vols. 1885-1900.

—— History of the Great Civil War. 4 vols. 1901.

—— History of the Commonwealth and Protectorate, 1649-1656. New edn. 4 vols. 1903.

Hanotaux, Gabriel. Études historiques sur le xvime et le xviime siècle en France. 1886.

—— Histoire du Cardinal de Richelieu. Vols. i and ii (-1617). Paris, 1893-1896.

Heatley, D. P. Diplomacy and the Study of International Relations. Oxford, 1919. [Bibliographically serviceable as to particular subjects: The Sovereignty of the Sea; the Literature of Recent British Diplomacy.]

Hill, D. J. A History of Diplomacy in the International Development of Europe. 3 vols. 1905-1914.
    Vol. i. The Struggle for Universal Empire.
    Vol. ii. The Establishment of Territorial Sovereignty.
    Vol. iii. The Diplomacy of the Age of Absolutism.

Hotblack, K. Chatham's Colonial Policy. 1917.

Hunt, W. The History of England from the accession of George III to the close of Pitt's first administration. (The Political History of England, vol. x.) 1905.

Immich, M. Geschichte des Europäischen Staatensystems von 1660–1789. Munich, 1905.

Jones, Guernsey. The Beginnings of the Oldest European Alliance. Washington, 1919. [England and Portugal.]

Klopp, Onno. Der Fall des Hauses Stuart und die Succession des Hauses Hannover in Gross-Britannien u. Irland. 14 vols. Vienna, 1875–1888. [1660–1714.]

Lange, C. L. Histoire de l'Internationalisme. Vol. I. Christiania, 1919. [IV. 2: La Paix universelle du 2 Oct. 1518.]

Lavisse, Ernest. Histoire de France, jusqu'à la Révolution. 9 vols. [Each in 2 parts; esp. from vol. VII onwards.] Paris, 1901–[1911].

Leadam, I. S. The History of England, 1702–1760. (The Political History of England, vol. IX.) 1909.

Lecky, W. E. H. History of England in the Eighteenth Century. 8 vols. 1878–1890. [Vols. I–VI.]

Legg, L. G. Wickham. Matthew Prior: A Study of his Public Career and Correspondence. Cambridge, 1922.

Legrelle, A. La Diplomatie Française et la Succession d'Espagne. 2nd edn. [1659–1725.] 6 vols. Braine-le-Compte, 1895–1899.

Lord, W. F. England and France in the Mediterranean, 1660–1830. 1901.

Mahan, A. T. Influence of Sea-Power upon History. 9th edn. [1890.]

Malmesbury, James Harris, first Earl of. Diaries and Correspondence, containing account of his missions to Madrid, Frederick the Great, Catharine II and the Hague, etc. Ed. by the third Earl. 4 vols. 1844.

Marcks, Erich. Deutschland und England in den grossen Europäischen Krisen seit der Reformation. Stuttgart, 1900.

—— Die Einheitlichkeit der Englischen Auslandspolitik von 1500 bis zur Gegenwart. Stuttgart, 1910.

Michael, Wolfgang. Englische Geschichte im achtzehnten Jahrhundert. Vols. I and II, Part I [to 1720]. Hamburg u. Leipzig, 1896–1920. [The retrospective are not the least valuable portions of this important work.]

Pollard, A. F. History of England, 1547–1603. (Political History of England, vol. VI.) 1910.

Preuss, G. T. Wilhelm von England und das Haus Wittelsbach im Zeitalter der Spanischen Erbfolgefrage. Vol. I, Part I. Breslau, 1904. [General survey of relations between England and France in 17th century.]

Ranke, L. von. History of England, principally in the Seventeenth Century. [English Translation.] 6 vols. Oxford, 1875.

—— Der Ursprung des siebenjährigen Krieges. Leipzig, 1871.

Reynald, H. La Succession d'Espagne, Louis XIV et Guillaume III. 2 vols. Paris, 1883.

Rosebery, Earl of. Chatham: his Early Life and Connexions. 1910.

—— Pitt. (Twelve English Statesmen.) 1891.

Rousset, Camille F. M. Histoire de Louvois et de son Administration. 4 vols. Paris, 1862–1863.

Russell, Earl. The Foreign Policy of England, 1570–1870. An historical essay. 1871.

Ruville, A. von. William Pitt, Earl of Chatham. Tr. by H. J. Chaytor and M. Morison, with Introd. by H. E. Egerton. 3 vols. 1907.

Satow, Sir E. A Guide to Diplomatic Practice. 2 vols. 1917.

Seeley, Sir J. R. The Expansion of England. 1883 and later editions.

—— The Growth of British Policy. 2 vols. Cambridge, 1895. [From Elizabeth to William III.]

Sorel, Albert. L'Europe et la Révolution française. Vol. I. 2nd edn. Paris, 1907.

—— La Question de l'Orient au 18me siècle. 2nd edn. Paris, 1889.

Stanhope, Earl of. History of England; comprising the reign of Anne until the Peace of Utrecht, 1701–1713. 4th edn. 2 vols. 1872.

Stanhope, Earl of. History of England from the Peace of Utrecht to the Peace of
    Versailles, 1713–1783. 5th edn. 7 vols. 1858.
Temperley, Gladys. Henry VII. (Kings and Queens of England.) 1914.
Teulet, J. B. A. T. Relations politiques de la France et de l'Espagne avec l'Écosse
    au 16ᵐᵉ siècle. New edn. 5 vols. Paris, 1862.
Torrens, M'Cullagh. The Industrial History of Free Nations, considered in rela-
    tion to their domestic institutions and external policy. 2 vols. 1896. [Esp.
    vol. II: The Dutch.]
Waddington, Richard. Louis XV et le Renversement des Alliances. Paris, 1896.
—— La Guerre de Sept Ans. Histoire Diplomatique et Militaire. 5 vols. Paris,
    n. d. [To 1762.]
Waliszewski, K. Le Roman d'une Impératrice: Catherine II de Russie. Chap. III:
    Politique Extérieure. Paris, 1893.
Ward, Sir A. W. Great Britain and Hanover. Some Aspects of the Personal Union.
    (Ford Lectures.) Oxford, 1899.
Weber, O. Der Friede von Utrecht. Verhandlungen zw. England, Frankreich,
    dem Kaiser u. d. Generalstaaten, 1710–1713. Gotha, 1891.
Williams, A. F. Basil. The Life of William Pitt, Earl of Chatham. 2 vols. 1913.
Winstanley, D. A. Lord Chatham and the Whig Opposition. Cambridge, 1912.

II. CHAPTERS I—V

In the following Bibliographies a general reference is in each case
made to the Bibliographies of Chapters dealing with Britain in the
Cambridge Modern History; but the titles of the works mentioned in
these are not repeated. Titles of works mentioned in Sections A or B
of the following Bibliographies are not repeated in later Sections. Col-
lections of State Papers and Manuscript Sources are referred to in the
notes to the text.

CHAPTER I
PITT'S FIRST DECADE

See Bibliography to Chap. X of vol. VIII of The Cambridge Modern History (1904).

A. GENERAL

Diplomatic Correspondence of the United States of America from...September 1783
    to March 1789. 7 vols. Washington, 1833–1834.
Heigel, K. T. Deutsche Geschichte vom Tode Friedrichs des Grossen. Vol. I.
    Stuttgart, 1899.
Lecky, W. E. H. History of England in the Eighteenth Century. Vols. IV–VI.
    (2nd edn.) 1887.
Sagnac, P. La Révolution française, 1789–1792. (Vol. II of Lavisse, E., Histoire
    de France contemporaine.) Paris.
Sorel, A. L'Europe et la Révolution Française. Vol. I. (1st edn.) Paris, 1885.
    (Revised edn., 6 vols. Paris, 1897.)

B. SPECIAL

Bloch, C. Le Traité de Commerce de 1786, in Études sur l'histoire économique
    de la France. Paris, 1900.
Burke, E. Correspondence. Ed. by Earl Fitzwilliam and Sir R. Bourke. 4 vols.
    1884.
Butenval. Précis...du traité de commerce...signé...le 26 septembre 1786. Paris, 1869.
Clapham, J. H. The causes of the war of 1792. Cambridge, 1898.

Clausewitz. Der Feldzug des Herzogs von Braunschweig von 1787. In Hinterlassene Werke. Leipzig, 1837.

Doniol, H. Politiques d'autrefois. Le comte de Vergennes et P. M. Hennin. Paris, 1898.

Franklin, B. Memoirs of the life and writings of B. F. written by himself and continued by his grandson W. F. Franklin. London, 1818.

Geffroy, G. Gustave III et la Cour de France. Paris, 1878.

Pallain, E. La mission de Talleyrand à Londres en 1792. Paris, 1889.

Rose, J. Holland. The Franco-British Commercial Treaty of 1786. English Historical Review, 1908.

—— The Mission of William Grenville to the Hague and Versailles in 1787. Eng. Hist. Review, 1909.

—— Pitt and the Triple Alliance. Edinburgh Review, 1910.

—— William Pitt and National Revival. William Pitt and the Great War. 1911.

—— The Comte d'Artois and Pitt in December 1789. Eng. Hist. Review, 1915.

Salomon, Felix. William Pitt der jüngere. Erster Band, bis zum Ausgang der Friedensperiode. Leipzig and Berlin, 1906.

Wolf, A. Leopold II und Marie Christine. Ihr Briefwechsel, 1781–1792. Vienna, 1867.

CHAPTERS II and III

The Struggle with Revolutionary France and the Contest with Napoleon

See Bibliographies in vols. VIII and IX of The Cambridge Modern History (1904 and 1907).

Adams, E. D. The Influence of Grenville on Pitt's Foreign Policy (1787–1798). Washington, 1904.

Aulard, A. Études et Leçons sur la Révolution française. 7 vols. Paris, 1893–1913.

Ballot, C. Le Coup d'État de Fructidor: Documents. Paris, 1906.

—— Les Négociations de Lille (1797). Paris, 1910.

Basham (Lord), Letters of. 3 vols. London, Navy Records Society, 1906–1910.

Blease, W. L. Suvórof. London, 1920.

Brodrick, G. C. Political History of England. Vol. XI (1801–1837). London, 1906.

Caudrillier. La Trahison de Pichegru. Paris, 1908.

Channing, E. The American Nation. A History (ed. by A. B. Hart); vol. XII. The Jeffersonian System (1801–1811). New York and London, 1906.

Chuquet, A. La Guerre de Russie. Notes et Documents. 3 vols. Paris, 1912.

Colenbrander, H. T. Ed. Gedenkstukken der algemeene Geschiednis von Nederland 1795–1840. The Hague, 1905.

Cunningham, A. British Credit in the last Napoleonic War. Cambridge, 1910.

Driault, E. La Politique extérieure du Premier Consul (1800–1803). Paris, 1910.

—— Austerlitz (La Fin du Saint-Empire), 1804–1806. Paris, 1912.

—— Tilsit (La Question de Pologne, 1806–1809). Paris, 1917.

—— Les dernières Thèses d'Histoire sur la Politique extérieure de Napoléon. Paris, 1919.

Dropmore Papers, The. The MSS. of J. B. Fortescue of Dropmore (Hist. MSS. Commiss.). 7 vols. Vols. II–VII (1894–1910).

Duboscq, A. Louis Bonaparte en Hollande d'après ses Lettres, 1806–1810. Paris, 1911.

Fortescue, J. W. A History of the British Army. Vols. I–X. 1899–1920.

—— British Statesmen of the Great War (1793–1814). Oxford, 1911.

Fortescue, J. B. See Dropmore Papers.

Guyot, R. Le Directoire et la Paix de l'Europe (1795–1799). Paris, 1911.

Handelsman, M. Napoléon et la Pologne (1806–1807). Paris, 1909.

Hart, A. B. See Channing.

Holland (Lady), Journal of (1791–1811); ed. by Lord Ilchester. 2 vols. 1909.

—— The Spanish Journal of; ed. by Lord Ilchester. 1910.

Hüffer, H. Quellen zur Geschichte des Zeitalters der französischen Revolution. Pt. II. Vol. I. Ed. by F. Luckwaldt. Innsbruck, 1907.
Hunt, W. Political History of England. Vol. x (1760–1801). 1905.
La Forrest, Comte de, Correspondance de. 7 vols. Paris, 1905–1913.
Luckwaldt, F. See Hüffer.
Mathiez, A. Études Robespierristes. Paris, 1917.
Melvin, F. E. Napoleon's Navigation System. New York, 1919.
Oman, C. A History of the Peninsular War. 5 vols. Oxford. 1902–1914.
Pariset, G. La Révolution française (1792–1799 and 1799–1815). (Vols. II and III of Lavisse, E., Histoire de la France contemporaine.) Paris, 1920 and 1921.
Peez, A. and Dehn, P. England's Vorherrschaft, aus der Zeit der Kontinental-sperre. Leipzig, 1912.
Piggott, F. and Omond, G. W. T. Documentary History of the Armed Neutralities of 1780 and 1800. London, 1919.
Robertson, C. Grant. England under the Hanoverians. (Vol. VI of History of England, ed. by C. W. C. Oman.) 1911.
Rose, J. Holland. Life of William Pitt. Pts. I and II. 1911.
—— Pitt and Napoleon: Essays and Letters. 1912.
—— Nationality as a Factor in Modern History. 1916.
Scott, J. B.? The Armed Neutrality of 1780 and 1810 (Carnegie Series). New York, 1918.
Sichel, W. Life of Sheridan. 2 vols. 1909.
Spencer Papers, The (1794–1801). (Private Papers of the second Earl Spencer.) 2 vols. Edited by J. S. Corbett. Navy Records Society, 1913.
Temperley, H. W. V. George Canning. 1905.
Trevelyan, G. M. Life of Lord Grey. 1920.
Vogel, W. Die Hansestädte und die Kontinentalsperre. Munich and Leipzig, 1913.
Wellesley Papers, The. (Papers of Marquis Wellesley.) 2 vols. 1914.
Windham Papers, The. (Introd. by the Earl of Rosebery.) 2 vols. 1913.

CHAPTER IV

THE PACIFICATIONS OF EUROPE, 1813–1815

See Bibliographies in vol. IX of The Cambridge Modern History (1907).

Antioche, Comte de. Chateaubriand, Ambassadeur à Londres. (Correspondence of Comte de la Chastre, 1814–1815). Paris, 1912.
Colenbrander, H. T. De Belgische Ontwentelung. The Hague. 1905.
Confalonieri, F., Carteggio del. Part I. [Conversations with Castlereagh at Paris, 1814.] Milan, 1910.
Edgcumbe, R. Diary of Frances Lady Shelley, 1787–1817. 1912.
Fisher, H. A. L. Bonapartism. Oxford, 1908.
—— Napoleon. 1913.
Fournier, A. Die Geheim-Polizei auf dem Wiener Kongress. Vienna and Leipzig, 1913.
Halévy, E. Histoire du Peuple Anglais. Vol. I. Paris, 1912.
MacCunn, F. J. The Contemporary English view of Napoleon. 1914.
Masson, F. Napoléon à St Hélène. Paris, 1912.
Maycock. The invasion of France, 1814. 1814.
Mikhailowitch, Grand Duke Nicholas. Correspondance de l'Empereur Alexandre Ier avec sa sœur, la Grande Duchesse Catharine. Petrograd, 1912. (Diary of Princess Lieven in 1912.)
Phillips, W. A. The Confederation of Europe. 2nd edn. 1920.
Rain, P. L'Europe et la Restauration des Bourbons, 1814–1818. Paris, 1908.
Runciman, Sir Walter. The tragedy of St Helena. 1911.
Ward, Sir A. The Period of the Congresses. Vols. I and II. 1919.
Webster, C. K. The Congress of Vienna, 1814–1815. 1919.
—— British Diplomacy, 1813–1815. 1921.

Weigal, Rachel. Correspondence of Lord Burghersh, 1808–1840. 1912.
Weil, M. H. Joachim Murat, Roi de Naples. 5 vols. Paris, 1909–1910.
—— Les Dessous du Congrès de Vienne. 2 vols. Paris, 1917.
Articles:

> Escoffier, M. La Restauration, l'Angleterre et les Colonies. Revue d'histoire diplomatique. 1907.
> Omond, G. W. T. Our War Aims in 1814—and to-day. Nineteenth Century and After. March, 1918.
> Webster, C. K. Some Aspects of Castlereagh's Foreign Policy. Transactions of the Royal Historical Society, III, VI. 1912.
> —— England and the Polish-Saxon Problem at the Congress of Vienna. Transactions of the Royal Historical Society, III, VII. 1913.

CHAPTER V

THE AMERICAN WAR AND THE PEACE OF GHENT

See Bibliographies in vol. VII of The Cambridge Modern History (1907).

Gallatin, Count (Ed.). A Great Peace Maker. The Diary of James Gallatin. 1914.
Perris, H. S. A short History of Anglo-American Relations and of the Hundred Years' Peace. 1914.
Smith, T. C. The Wars between England and America. 1915.
Updyke, F. A. The Diplomacy of the War of 1812. Baltimore, 1915.
Wood, W. (Ed.). Select British Documents of the Canadian War of 1812. Vol. I. (In progress.) Toronto, 1920.

Article:

> Ford, W. The British Ghent Commission. Transactions of the Massachusetts Historical Society. December 1914—January 1915.

INDEX

END OF VOL. I

PRINTED IN ENGLAND BY J. B. PEACE, M.A., AT THE CAMBRIDGE UNIVERSITY PRESS